# CANADIAN SELECTION
## BOOKS AND PERIODICALS FOR LIBRARIES

1977-1979 Supplement

1977-1979 SUPPLEMENT

# Canadian Selection

## BOOKS AND PERIODICALS FOR LIBRARIES

Compiled by
ISABEL McLEAN
with the assistance of
EDITH JARVI

University of Toronto Press
TORONTO BUFFALO LONDON

Faculty of Library Science, University of Toronto
Printed in Canada
Reprinted in 2018

---

**Canadian Cataloguing in Publication Data**

McLean, Isabel K., 1910–
Canadian Selection: Books and Periodicals for Libraries 1977–1979 Supplement

Includes Index
ISBN 0-8020-4593-6
ISBN 978-1-4875-7707-0 (paper)
1. Canada – Imprints – Catalogs
2. Canada – Bibliography – Catalogs
I. Jarvi, Edith T.
II. Metropolitan Toronto Library Board
III. Title

Z1365.J37 015'.71

---

Publication of this book has been made possible by a grant from the Ontario Ministry of Culture and Recreation to the Metropolitan Toronto Library Board.

# Contents

# Introduction

## PURPOSE

The *Supplement*, like its predecessor, *Canadian Selection: Books and Periodicals for Libraries*, is designed to meet the need for a selective guide to significant English language books and periodicals for adults, published in Canada, about Canada, or written by Canadians at home and abroad. The choice has been made with small and medium-sized public libraries in mind, but school and college libraries may find some sections useful. Some of the more expensive bibliographies and reference works included in the list are more suitable for purchase by the resource centre of a regional library system. The compilers recommend that, like other selection guides, *Canadian Selection: Books and Periodicals for Libraries: 1977-1979 Supplement* be used with discretion to meet the particular requirements of the library for which materials are being selected.

## SCOPE

The catalogue includes some 1856 books which were published between January 1, 1977 and December 31, 1979, and some 35 periodicals. A few titles bearing 1976 imprints which were inadvertently omitted from the basic volume have been included. If a significant book has become available in another format it has been included in the *Supplement* with a reference to the original entry (listed *CS* no. 425). A new annotation is not provided for the new format. If one paperback edition was listed in *Canadian Selection: Books and Periodicals for Libraries*, a second paperback edition has not been added. Recently published volumes of a continuing series of volumes have been included with a reference to the entry for the earlier titles. A new edition or a reprint of a work previously out of print has been included. The emphasis is on in-print materials representing as wide a range of subjects as possible. Although most of the materials have been selected for general reading, the guide contains some indispensable reference works and government publications.

Recognizing the need for strong collections of legal materials in public libraries an extensive collection of significant new titles and revisions of standard works has been assembled by Gail Dykstra, Editor of *CLIC's Legal Materials Letter*. Some of the materials are too specialized for the small library, but might be made available in a regional library collection. Statutes, gazettes, bills and citators have been omitted, but a complete listing can be found in Gail Dykstra's *A Bibliography of Canadian Legal Materials* (*CS*, p. 9). *CLIC's Legal Materials Letter*, which is described in the Part III list of Canadian Periodicals, is an invaluable current guide to new legal literature. Many topics in Canadian law involve provincial legislation and regulation. In order to keep the law section of this catalogue to a reasonable size the policy has been to exclude those works which apply to only one province. The areas most affected are commercial law, consumer law, family law, labour relations law, landlord and tenant law, motor vehicle law, municipal law, real estate law, small claims court regulations, wills and estates. Publications on these subjects are found in the Dykstra bibliography and in the *Newsletter*.

Also excluded from the *Supplement* are music scores, maps, county atlases, unpublished theses, materials of interest to one locality or region of the country, works in other languages, and highly specialized publications. Publications which have been issued in limited editions, or for limited distribution have not been included. Unless other material on the subject was not available, the following have also been excluded: textbooks, society publications, proceedings of conferences and symposia, addresses and speeches, and pamphlets of fewer than fifty pages. If the subject matter of a book has no obvious relevance for Canadian readers the book has not been included even though the author may be resident in Canada, or the work bears a Canadian agent's imprint.

A separate list of selection aids has not been included in the *Supplement*, but useful new titles and new editions of important tools have been incorporated into the text. For a selection of basic materials useful in developing library collections librarians may wish to refer to Part I of *Canadian Selection: Books and Periodicals for Libraries*.

## CRITERIA FOR THE SELECTION OF TITLES

The compilers have attempted to assemble a collection of Canadian titles which is balanced in subject matter and in treatment of the subject, and which illustrates the range of Canadian writing and publishing. The fact that some fields – literature, history and biography, the social sciences – are heavily represented reflects the nature of popular and non-specialized publishing in Canada today. A special effort has been made to include publications from the small presses, and regional writing which has a country-wide appeal. The needs of various interest groups have been considered, as well as differences in education and age within the adult range. The catalogue cannot be called a bibliography of 'best books', but works which fall below a modest standard in quality of writing or in presentation of the subject have not been listed.

## ARRANGEMENT

The *Supplement* consists of four parts. Part I is a classified catalogue, arranged by Dewey Decimal Classification number. Works of fiction are to be found in the C813 classification number.

Part II is a selective annotated list of Canadian periodicals, most of which have begun publication since January 1, 1977. The arrangement is alphabetical by title.

Part III is an author, title and subject index without cross references. Titles beginning with numerals could not be computer-filed alphabetically and appear at the end of the index. Translators and illustrators are not listed in the index.

Part IV is a list of publishers whose publications are included in the catalogue.

## FORM OF ENTRY

This bibliography has not been compiled as an aid in the cataloguing of the titles contained therein and therefore a bibliographic form of entry rather than a cataloguing form has been chosen. Publications have been entered under an author or editor where possible, in order to conform with the practice in *Canadian Selection: Books and Periodicals for Libraries*. For the convenience of users of the catalogue, when an earlier edition of a publication, or the same publication in another format were listed in the basic volume the third paragraph of the new entry in the *Supplement* contains a reference to the original entry.

Annotations have been contributed by some sixty librarians, subject specialists, and students in the University of Toronto Faculty of Library Science. The name of the contributor is shown. Annotations which do not carry a name have been written by one of the compilers. Full bibliographic information has been provided for monographs, and in addition, a Dewey Decimal Classification number, suggested subject headings, the

International Standard Book Number, and the most recent price which could be ascertained. Contents have been shown where appropriate and most of the titles have been annotated. The original title of a translated work and the first publication date of an early work have been indicated. Award-winning titles have been noted. For works published outside of Canada, the Canadian agent's name has been inserted in curves following the name of the foreign publisher.

Data for periodicals include title and subtitle, date of first publication, publication frequency, price, the name and address of the publisher, International Standard Serial Number, the average number of books reviewed in the periodical, the indexes in which it is included, and an annotation.

## CLASSIFICATION

The 18th edition of the Dewey Decimal Classification was used but with some modification in certain subjects. The most obvious modifications have been in the literature section, where very few time signatures have been included. All fiction, plays and volumes of poetry by one author have been placed in one alphabet regardless of the period in which the author was active; that is, in C813, C812, and C811 respectively. Anthologies of fiction which include excerpts from novels are in C813.008; collections of short stories by more than one author are classed in C813.01; history and criticism of fiction in C813.009; and criticism and interpretation of the work of individual writers in C813.4 for 19th century and C813.5 for 20th century. In this way critical works have been separated from creative works. The same scheme was followed in poetry and drama.

Translations of literary works from the French language have been placed in one alphabet with English titles, but critical works on French authors and the history of French Canadian literature have been classed in C840. General bibliographies are listed in 010 and subject bibliographies in the appropriate subject part of the catalogue. For the most part biographies are classed in 920, but those in the fields of sports, music and art have been classified with the subject. This division of biography and bibliography has been somewhat arbitrary and not always as clear-cut as one would wish.

## SUBJECT HEADINGS

Subject headings are based on those used in *Canadiana* entries. Except in a few instances, no subject headings have been suggested for volumes of poetry, for plays, novels, or short stories when these are the work of one author.

## COMPILATION OF THE CATALOGUE

The catalogue has been compiled by a careful examination of general, subject and regional bibliographies and the catalogues of academic and commercial publishing firms, including those of the small and regional presses. General periodicals which review books and a number of periodicals in special fields were perused, as were the book review sections of the major newspapers. Bibliographies compiled by libraries, library associations, government agencies, galleries and museums were studied. Librarians and subject specialists recommended titles for inclusion. Many of the university, special and public library collections in Metropolitan Toronto were examined in the course of assembling the list and evaluating titles for inclusion.

## CONTINUATION OF THE CATALOGUE

It is hoped that the compilation of a selective, annotated list of new Canadian print materials can be continued with publication at regular intervals. The complete revision of the original work, *Canadian Selection: Books and Periodicals for Libraries*, and its supplements, should be planned to incorporate the most important titles in an up-to-date selection guide for libraries. The compilers invite suggestions for policy changes and methodology which would improve future publications in the series. Errors and omissions which occur in this three-year supplement are the sole responsibility of the compilers; that there are not more is due to the careful and accurate work of the many persons who have given their time and shared their knowledge so generously.

# Acknowledgements

The compilers and users of this three-year Supplement are indebted to the generosity of the Ontario Ministry of Culture and Recreation for the special grants which have made possible this publication, and its predecessor, *Canadian Selection: Books and Periodicals for Libraries*. Bringing the two publications to fruition has been achieved largely through the continuing interest and active encouragement of the personnel of the Libraries and Information Branch, its Director, Mr W.A. Roedde, and the Co-ordinator, Public Library Services, Mrs N. Grace Buller.

The compilers are appreciative of the interest and support of the Metropolitan Toronto Library Board and its Director, Mr John Parkhill, under whose aegis the two bibliographic works have been prepared.

The months of intensive work entailed in a bibliographic project of this nature were made easier by the courtesy of Dean Katherine H. Packer, Faculty of Library Science, who provided office space and facilities in the Library Science building. A debt of gratitude is owed also to members of the faculty and to the support staff of the Faculty of Library Science who in many unobtrusive but important ways contributed to the advancement of the work.

The programme for the machine storage and manipulation of the data for the two publications was designed by Professor W.J. Kurmey, University of Toronto, Faculty of Library Science, now Dean, University of Alberta, Faculty of Library Science. As data processing consultant for the two bibliographic compilations Dean Kurmey has contributed significantly to their success.

The exacting work of inputting the bibliographic data for the three-year *Supplement* within a restricted period of time was accomplished by a competent corps of Master of Library Science students: Elizabeth Chan, Cathy Macdonald, Linda Nakamura, Bruce Shaw, and Mai-Ling Shek. Another graduating student, Toby Eines, assumed the prodigious responsibility for the successful running of the programmes and preparing the data for computer type-setting.

The selection and evaluation of books and periodicals for the *Supplement* was a co-operative effort of some sixty librarians and subject specialists in college, public, school, special and university libraries, and a number of students at the University of Toronto Faculty of Library Science. The contributions of the persons listed below in reading and annotating, recommending and rejecting print materials published within the last three years is gratefully acknowledged. Very special appreciation is due to those contributors who cheerfully assumed responsibility for assessing large numbers of publications in one or two discrete subject fields: Sherrill Cheda, Jean Dodd, Gail Dykstra, Hilary Elliott, Ille-Mai Gerdels, Sheila Latham, Catharine MacKenzie and Don Sedgwick. Mary Armstrong, University of Toronto, Map Library; Ethel Auster, Ontario Institute for Studies in Education; Judy Bialkowski, Scarborough Public Library; Fay Blostein, University of Toronto, Faculty of Education; Marilyn Carr, Dataline Systems; Sherrill Cheda, Executive Director, Canadian Periodical Publishers' Association; Caroline Christie, North York Public Library, Technical Services Department; Frances Clutton, Burlington Public Library; Nancy Cohen, North Bay Public Library; Margaret Covshoff, Metropolitan Toronto Library, Business Department; Theresa Crosgrey, M.L.S. II Student; Barbara Dance, University of Toronto, Faculty of Management Studies Library; Paula DeRonde, Toronto Public Library, George H. Locke Branch; Jean Dodd, Seneca College of Applied Arts and Technology, Faculty; Gail Dykstra, Dykstra Research Associates; Hilary Elliott, Georgian College of Applied Arts and Technology, Faculty; Claire England, University of Toronto, Faculty of Library Science; Janet Fraser, M.L.S. II Student; Janet Frost, M.L.S. II Student; Bob Gardner, Metropolitan Toronto Library, Social Sciences Department; Pat George, Toronto Public Library, Jones Avenue Branch; Ille-Mai Gerdels, Etobicoke Public Library; Beth Goble, M.L.S. II Student; Vicki Gill, M.L.S. I Student; Jan Greenwood, M.L.S. II Student; Andrew Gregorovich, University of Toronto, Head, Technical Services Department, Scarborough and Erindale College Libraries; Diane Hart, William A. Porter Secondary School Library; Diane Henderson, University of Toronto, Faculty of Library Science, Chief Librarian; Lucia Herwig, Toronto Public Library, Community Information Services; Margot Hewings, Metropolitan Toronto Library, Head, Municipal Reference; Brenda Hughes, East York Public Library, Leaside Branch; Ethel Kellen, Toronto Public Library, Jones Avenue Branch; Marilyn Koch, Freelance Librarian; Merike Koger, M.L.S. II Student; Brian Land, Director, Ontario Legislative Library Research and Information Service; Sheila Latham, Toronto Public Library, Northern District Library, Literature Specialist; Nikki Lawrence, Freelance Librarian; Frieda Ling, Toronto Public Library, Riverdale Branch; Gwen Liu, Toronto Public Library, Co-ordinator Adult/Young People's Resources; Catharine G. MacKenzie, Midland Public Library, Reference Librarian; Beth Marcilio, Toronto Public Library, Main Street Branch; Beth Martin, Metropolitan Toronto Library, Science and Technology Department; Peter Moffet, Etobicoke Public Library, Albion Branch; Ann Morrison, M.L.S. II Student; Patricia O'Sullivan, M.L.S. II Student; Linda Pulver, M.L.S. II Student; Carole Rhodes, Metropolitan Toronto Library, Science and Technology Department; Barbara Schon, Newcastle Public Library, Chief Librarian; Don Sedgwick, Contributing Editor, Quill & Quire; Peggy Sinclair, Toronto Public Library, Beaches Branch; Carl Spadoni, McMaster University, Library, The Bertrand Russell Collection; Glenna Stevens, M.L.S. II Student; Arch Stewart, Ontario Hydro, Central Safety Services Library; Barbara Stewart, Metropolitan Toronto Library, Business Department; Annemarie Toth, M.L.S. II Student; Andrea Trudel, Environment Canada, Reference Librarian; Gartley Wagner, M.L.S. II Student; Kathryn Walker, M.L.S. II Student; Annette Wengle, Metropolitan Toronto Library, Theatre Department; Jay Wolofsky, Freelance Librarian; Janice Zlatarits, Freelance Librarian.

The compilers and contributors are indebted to many libraries within Metropolitan Toronto and on its periphery who have been unfailingly gracious in making books available. The staffs of the Canadian Book Information Centre and the Canadian Periodical Publishers' Association have been supportive of the undertaking and generous in providing access to new publications.

The compilers would like to express their gratitude to all the individuals, the libraries and the organizations which have contributed their time and knowledge to assist in the compilation of the first Supplement to *Canadian Selection: Books and Periodicals for Libraries*.

Isabel K. McLean
Edith T. Jarvi

# Part One
# The Classified Catalogue

## 000 Generalities

4300 001.4'4
**Arlett, Alan,** ed.
The Canadian Directory to Foundations and Granting Agencies. 4th ed. Ottawa: Association of Universities and Colleges of Canada, 1978- 1v Indexes. ISBN 0-88876-056-6 In binder: $20

1. Endowments – Canada – Directories.
2. Research grants – Canada – Directories.
3. Endowments – United States – Directories.
4. Research grants – United States – Directories.

Third edition listed *CS* no. 1.

A change to a loose-leaf format is made in this new edition. Information about Canadian and foreign foundations is listed separately from information about non-profit agencies and federal and provincial government grant programmes. Simultaneous English and French publication.

4301 001.9'42
**Haisell, David.**
The Missing Seven Hours. Markham, Ont.: PaperJacks, 1978. 162p. Bibliography: p. 159. Index. ISBN 0-7701-0079-1 pa.: $2.50

1. Flying saucers.

Seven hours of a boy's life in England have supposedly disappeared. The author maintains that the most plausible explanation points to a UFO experience. An attempt is made to tie this ostensibly strange occurrence to other UFO phenomena encountered by the same man, his family and other people in Canada some twenty years later. Carl Spadoni

4302 001.9'42
**Magor, John.**
Our UFO Visitors. Saanichton, B.C.: Hancock House, 1977. 264p. ill. Bibliography: p. 256-259. Index. ISBN 0-919654-70-3 $9.95

1. Flying saucers.

Close encounters and other forms of UFO activity are the subject of this book by the publisher and editor of *Canadian UFO Report*. Although corroborative evidence is cited from other countries, the emphasis is on Canadian occurrences since 1967. Reports of cases usually consist of each individual's own account of the UFO experience. Carl Spadoni

4303 001.9'44

**Green, John.**

Sasquatch: The Ape among Us. Saanichton, B.C.: Hancock House, c1978. 492p. Bibliography: p. 469-473. Index. ISBN 0-88839-018-1 $14.95

1. Sasquatch.

This is Green's fourth book on the subject, a lengthier, more definitive treatment than previous efforts, based on twenty years of research and a file of some two thousand reports. Evidence from sightings, footprints, photographs and films is offered as tentative proof of the legendary creature's existence. Carl Spadoni

4304 001.9'44

**Moon, Mary.**

Ogopogo. Vancouver: J. J. Douglas, 1977. 195p. ill. ISBN 0-88894-108-0 pa.: $4.95

1. Ogopogo.

The Loch Ness monster has found its counterpart in British Columbia's Okanagan Lake. The author, a freelance journalist, attempts to corroborate the cumulative evidence, primarily from newspapers, of sightings and folklore with the gloss of scientific authority. Various artistic sketches of Ogopogo are included. Carl Spadoni

## **010** Bibliography

4305 010.

**Public Archives of Canada.**

Guide to Canadian Photographic Archives. Guide des archives photographiques canadiennes. Coordinated by Alain Clavet. Provisional ed. Ottawa: Public Archives of Canada, 1979. 222p. ill. Index. ISBN 0-662-50346-5 pa.: $14.95 DSS cat. no. SA2-108/1979

1. Photograph collections – Canada – Union lists. 2. Archives – Canada – Union lists. 3. Catalogs, Union – Canada.

"A catalogue describing the holdings and collections of photographic archives in over 110 Canadian institutions. These institutions include repositories of federal, provincial and municipal governments, universities, historical societies, libraries, museums, research centres, private companies and photographic studios." -Introduction. Some 2,800 entries, in English and French are arranged alphabetically.

4306 013'.375

**Mills, Judy.**

University of Toronto Doctoral Theses, 1968-1975: A Bibliography. Toronto: Published for the School of Graduate Studies, University of Toronto by University of Toronto Press, 1977. 166p. Index. ISBN 0-8020-3342-3 $10

1. University of Toronto – Dissertations. 2. Dissertations, Academic – Ontario – Bibliography.

Continues *University of Toronto Doctoral Theses, 1897-1967*. Arranged by subject with an author index. Diane Henderson

4307 013'.9'71

**Stratford, Philip.**

Bibliography of Canadian Books in Translation: French to English and English to French. Bibliographie de livres canadiens traduits de l'anglais au français et du français à l'anglais. Ottawa: Humanities Research Council, 1977. 78p. Indexes. pa.: $1

1. Translations – Bibliography. 2. Canadian literature (French) – Translations into English – Bibliography. 3. Canadian literature (English) – Translations into French – Bibliography. 4. Canada – Imprints.

First edition listed in *CS* no. 2321.

"This revised edition lists 130 additional titles of works translated from French to English and 70 more from English to French; it also lists 80 new projects for translation". -Foreword.

4308 015'.71

**Canadian Books in Print.**

Edited by Martha Pluscauskas and Marian Butler. Toronto: University of Toronto Press, 1967- 2v Annual. ISBN 0-8020-4577-4 $40 vol. 1.

1. Canada – Imprints.

vol. 1. *Author and Title Index*. 1979. 1976 edition listed *CS* no. 15.

The hardcover edition of *CBIP Author and Title Index* will be issued annually. Microfiche editions will be published quarterly, at extra cost. *CBIP Subject Guide* will continue to be published annually in a hardcover edition. -Publisher's note.

4309 015'.71

**Jarvi, Edith T.,** comp.

Canadian Selection: Books and Periodicals for Libraries. Compiled by Edith T. Jarvi, Isabel McLean, and Catharine MacKenzie. Toronto: Published by University of Toronto Press for the Centre for Research in Librarianship, Faculty of Library Science, University of Toronto, c1978. 1060p. Index. ISBN 0-8020-4554-5 $35

1. Canada – Imprints. 2. Canada – Bibliography.

Designed as a collection building guide for libraries, a selection of 4,300 Canadian books and 275 periodicals in the English language has been annotated. Monographs are in classified arrangement, periodicals alphabetically by title. Has an index to authors, titles and subjects.

4310 015.71

**Manitoba. Dept. of Education.**

In Search of Canadian Materials. Rev. ed. Winnipeg: Department of Education, 1978. 336p. $3.50

1. Canada – Bibliography. 2. Manitoba – Bibliography.

Previous edition listed in *CS* p. 12.

The 1978 edition of this useful selection tool contains 2,100 print and non-print items on a broad range of subjects. A separate section on Women's Studies is a new feature.

4311 015'.719

**Thomas, Heather L.,** comp.

Yukon Bibliography: Update to 1977. Edited by Geraldine A. Cooke and Geraldine Perry. Edmonton: Boreal Institute for Northern Studies, University of Alberta, 1978. 476p. Indexes. (Occasional Publication – Boreal Institute for Northern Studies) ISBN 0-919058-15-9 pa. Processed: $15

1. Yukon Territory – Bibliography.

Supplements earlier bibliographies of the Yukon listed in *CS*, numbers 51 and 52, and *Yukon Bibliography: Update to 1975* edited by Geraldine A. Cooke.

Primarily covers the years 1976 and 1977 in its 756 entries, although many are for earlier publications missed in the previous 4 volumes. Broad subject arrangement and good index. Glenna Stevens

4312 016.013

**Bruchet, Susan Jacques,** comp.

Theses in Canada: A Guide to Sources of Information about Theses Completed or in Preparation. Thèses au Canada: Guide sur les sources documentaires relatives aux thèses complétées ou en cours de rédaction. Compiled by Susan Jacques Bruchet and Gwynneth Evans. Ottawa: National Library of Canada, c1978. 25p. ISBN 0-662-01620-3 pa. DSS cat. no. SN-87/1978

1. Bibliography – Bibliography – Dissertations, Academic. 2. Dissertations, Academic – Canada – Bibliography.

A listing of sources for the location of theses, in three parts general bibliographies, university theses lists, and special bibliographies. Includes citations for listings in journals as well as separately published lists for international sources which include Canadian theses and general bibliographies which include theses. Diane Henderson

4313 016.015

**Wertheimer, Leonard.**

Books in Other Languages: 1979: A Guide to Selection Aids and Suppliers. 4th ed. Ottawa: Canadian Library Association, c1979. 144p. ISBN 0-88802-125-9 pa.: $12

1. Bibliography – Bibliography. 2. Acquisition of foreign publications. 3. Books – Reviews – Bibliography. 4. Book industries and trade – Directories.

Third edition listed *CS* p. 8.

The fourth edition of this useful guide to selecting and acquiring books in languages other than English has added sections on some eight languages. The lists of selection aids and suppliers which have been provided for each language have been revised. An important guide for developing a multilingual library collection.

4314 016.0275

**Larouche, Irma.**

National Library of Canada: A Bibliography. Bibliothèque nationale du Canada: Une bibliographie. Ottawa: Reference and Bibliography Section, National Library of Canada, 1979. 179p. Index. ISBN 0-660-50210-0 pa.: $9.95 DSS cat. no. SN3-11/1979

1. National Library of Canada – Bibliography.

Publications in the French and English languages, of briefs, monographs, papers, reports, articles in periodicals and newspapers, debates and laws, are arranged in three parts to form a chronological view of the development of the National Library of Canada from 1882 to 1978. Contains a bibliography and an integrated index.

4315 016.071'1

**Canadian Newspaper Index.**

Toronto: Information Access, 1977- vol. 1. Jan. 1977. ISSN 0384-983X $195 per annum (monthly issues); $150 per annum (annual cumulation); $395 per annum (monthly issues plus cumulation)

1. Canadian newspapers (English) – Indexes.

A current and comprehensive subject and name index to news and events as reported in seven major Canadian dailies: the Calgary Herald, Halifax Chronicle-Herald, Montreal Star, Toronto Globe and Mail, Toronto Star, Vancouver Sun and the Winnipeg Free Press. Numerous cross references. Eliminates the need for clipping these newspapers.

4316 016.30142

**Canada. Dept. of National Health and Welfare. Library.**

Divorce: A Bibliographical Look at the World. Le divorce: Bibliographie internationale. Ottawa: Health and Welfare Canada, 1977. 183p. pa.: Free

1. Divorce – Bibliography.

Monographs, parts of books, journal articles and government publications are arranged in three groups: general references, writing related to divorce and the individual, and those relating to divorce in various countries. Both recent and older, standard publications are included, but they are neither annotated nor indexed. A useful reference tool for librarians and library users.

4317 016.3231

**Canada. Indian Rights Commission. Research Resource Centre.**

Indian Claims in Canada: Supplementary Bibliography. Revendications des Indiens au Canada: Bibliographie supplémentaire. Ottawa: Published for the Canadian Indian Rights Commission by the National Library of Canada, 1979. 116p. ISBN 0-660-50177-5 pa.: $3.95 DSS cat. no. SN3-109/1979

1. Canada. Indian Rights Commission. Research Resource Centre. 2. National Library of Canada. 3. Indians of North America – Canada – Claims – Bibliography – Catalogs. 4. Canada – Native Races – Bibliography – Catalogs.

Entries are organized in twenty-three chapters according to the source, and, within each chapter the arrangement is alphabetical by author or issuing body. Appendices include Canadian legal decisions relating to Native Peoples and documents respecting the James Bay and Northern Quebec Native Land Claims Settlement Act. College and larger public libraries.

4318 016.3314

**Canadian Research Institute for the Advancement of Women.**

Women and Work: An Inventory of Research. La femme et le travail: Un inventaire de recherches. Ottawa: Canadian Research Institute for the Advancement of Women, c1978. 85p. Index. pa.: $4

1. Women – Employment – Canada – Bibliography.

A well-organized bibliography of English and French research publications (books, theses, articles, studies, working papers, etc.) listed under broad headings such as paid work, unpaid work, unemployment, education for work, and images, myths, and stereotypes. Includes introductory editorials by well-known writers in the field, and an index. Janice Zlatarits

4319 016.370

**Auster, Ethel,** comp.

Reference Sources on Canadian Education: An Annotated Bibliography. Toronto: Ontario Institute for Studies in Education, 1978. 114p. Indexes. (OISE Bibliography Series) ISBN 0-7744-0163-X pa.: $5.95

1. Education – Canada – Bibliography. 2. Reference Books – Education – Bibliography.

This selective guide to educational information contains 318 annotated entries to specialized dictionaries, almanacs, yearbooks, bibliographies, indexes and abstracts, dissertations, projects and studies, directories, and sources for financial aid and instructional materials. Each of the 13 chapters has an introduction. Subject and author-title indexes conclude the volume. -Author.

4320 016.370

**Directory of Education Studies in Canada.**

Annuaire d'études en education au Canada 1977-1978. Edited by Deborah C. Sawyer. Toronto: Canadian Education Association, 1969- Annual. 10th ed. ISBN 0-919078-55-9 pa.: $6

1. Educational research – Canada. 2. Dissertations, Academic – Canada – Bibliography.

This tenth edition of the directory is an annotated list of eight hundred published and unpublished studies in English and French completed by students and staff in faculties of education, school boards, provincial departments of education, professional education associations across Canada. Access is by means of Canadian Education Subject Headings and an author index. Ethel Auster

4321 016.42797

**Avis, Walter S.**

Writings on Canadian English: An Annotated Bibliography 1729-1975, by Walter S. Avis and Murray Kinloch. Toronto: Fitzhenry & Whiteside, c1978. 153p. ISBN 0-88902-121-X bd.: $10 ISBN 0-88902-120-1 pa.: $5.95

1. English language in Canada – Bibliogaraphy.

First edition published in 1965 under title: *A Bibliography of Writings on Canadian English 1857-1965.*

The compilers' objective is complete coverage of relevant items to 1975 (material as late as June 1977 is included), but excluding works strictly in onomastics, technical glossaries and manuals of style. A listing of 723 titles, arranged by author, with generally brief annotations. No index. Diane Henderson

4322 016.9171

**Ryder, Dorothy E.**

Checklist of Canadian Directories, 1790-1950. Répertoire des annuaires canadiens, 1790-1950. Ottawa: National Library of Canada, 1979. Bibliography: p. 288. ISBN 0-660-50409-X $10.95 DSS cat. no. SN3-118/1979

1. Canada – Directories – Bibliography.

Most reference librarians have experienced the challenges and frustrations of sleuthing for clues about non-famous Canadians. This tool will assist librarians and other historical researchers in locating leads in directories held in Canadian libraries. A model of its kind, it is arranged by province, and then by municipality.

4323 016.971

**Robinson, Paul.**

After Survival. Toronto: Peter Martin, c1977. 329p. ISBN 0-88778-147-0 bd.: $15 ISBN 0-88778-150-0 pa.: $8.95

1. Canadian studies. 2. Canada – Bibliogaphy. 3. Canada – Imprints.

This book is a valuable guide to the teacher or librarian developing a collection of Canadian material at the elementary and secondary school level. Its chapters are arranged alphabetically by subject; both French and English print and non-print items are listed. Selection guidelines for material included are discussed. Appendix of publishers' addresses. Glenna Stevens

## 020 Library science

4324 020'.1'48

**Tayyeb, R.,** comp.

A Dictionary of Acronyms and Abbreviations in Library and Information Science. Compiled by R. Tayyeb and K. Chandna. Ottawa: Canadian Library Association, c1979. 146p. ISBN 0-88802-129-1 $7

1. Library science – Acronyms. 2. Library science – Abbreviations. 3. Information science – Acronyms. 4. Information science – Abbreviations.

Definitions of approximately twenty-eight hundred English language terms are arranged alphabetically with necessary cross-references. Some French language terminology is also included. The authors, librarians at the University of Windsor, have compiled a useful, up-to-date list of the proliferating number of abbreviations in these related fields.

4325 020.6

**National Library of Canada. Library Documentation Centre.**

Directory of Library Associations in Canada. 5th ed. Ottawa: Ministry of Supply and Services, 1979. Unpaged. ISBN 0-660-50150-3 $8

1. Library associations.

Third edition listed *CS* no. 65.

4326 020'.711

**Bassam, Bertha.**

The Faculty of Library Science, University of Toronto and Its Predecessors, 1911-1972. Toronto: Faculty of Library Science: Library Science Alumni Association, c1978. 141p. ill., plates, ports. Bibliography: p. 121-126. Index. pa.: $6

1. University of Toronto. Faculty of Library Science – History.

A history of the development of the Faculty and library education in Ontario, from first courses sponsored by the Department of Education, the diploma, BLS and MLS programs, to the present two-year MLS and Ph.D. programs. The author was associated with the Faculty for thirty-six years as professor and director. Includes bibliography and detailed index. Diane Henderson

4327 025.04

**Guide to Canadian Machine-readable Data Bases.**

Guide de bases de données canadiennes ordinolingues. Ottawa: National Library of Canada, 1979. 108p.

1. Data libraries – Canada – Directories.
2. Information storage and retrieval systems – Directories.

A selection from the full *Guide* (available on-line) to be published later, it includes "some of the better-known data bases". Each entry provides: basic information, producer/distributor/generator, availability and charges for tapes, subject matter and scope, indexing data, data-base services and user aids. Diane Henderson

4328 025.2

**Pross, Catherine A.**

A Guide to the Identification and Acquisition of Canadian Provincial Government Publications, by Catherine A. Pross and A. Paul Pross. Halifax, N.S.: Dalhousie University, University Libraries, School of Library Service, 1977. 69 leaves. Bibliographies. (Occasional Paper – Dalhousie University Libraries and Dalhousie School of Library Service) ISBN 0-7703-0153-3 pa. Processed. Spiral binding: $3

1. Acquisition of government publications.
2. Canada – Government publications (Provincial governments).

The authors of *Government Publishing in the Canadian Provinces* (*CS* no. 139) identify the basic tools for acquiring most of the published documents of the provinces. In addition they include useful comments on the status of production of publications and on government structure. All libraries which provide government publication service need this basic document despite the fact that changes are frequent.

4329 025.33

**Canada. Ministry of State for Urban Affairs.**

Canadian Urban Thesaurus: CDN. UT. 1st ed. Ottawa: Ministry of State for Urban Affairs, 1979. 200p.

1. Subject headings – City planning.

Developed to satisfy "the need for a common vocabulary covering the broad domain of urban affairs". In two parts: a main, alpha-hierarchical listing of descriptors with full reference structure, and an alpha-permuted listing which forms an index to the main listing, especially for composite terms. Diane Henderson

4330 025.3'3

**Haycock, Ken,** comp.

Sears List of Subject Headings: Canadian Companion. Compiled by Ken Haycock and Lynne Isberg. New York: H. W. Wilson, 1978. 50p. ISBN 0-8242-0629-0 $5.50

1. Subject headings.

Designed to be used as a companion volume to *Sears List of Subject Headings*, 1977 to provide more adequate representation of Canadian topics. American spelling has been used. The province of Manitoba and the city of Vancouver serve as keys to illustrate the formation of subdivisions of headings. A useful supplement for Canadian libraries.

4331 025.3'3

**National Library of Canada.**

Canadian Subject Headings. Ottawa: National Library of Canada, 1978. 395p. Indexes in English and French. ISBN 0-660-10148-3 pa.: $9.95 (Canada); $11.95 (Foreign) DSS cat. no. SN3-106/1978

1. Subject headings.

Supersedes Canadian Library Association's *A List of Canadian Subject Headings*, 1968.

"Is intended to serve as the English language standard for the subject control of Canadian topics". -Preface. Headings are printed in boldface type, cross references and notes in lightface. Introductions in English and French explain the use of capitalization, sub-divisions, symbols, filing, and plans for updating of the list. The index is English-to-French and French-to-English.

4332 025.3'4

**Weihs, Jean.**

Nonbook Materials: The Organization of Integrated Collections, by Jean Weihs, Shirley Lewis, and Janet Macdonald, in consultation with the CLA/ALA/AECT/AMTEC Advisory Committee on the Cataloguing of Nonbook Materials. 2d ed. Ottawa: Canadian Library Association, 1979. 134p. Bibliography. ISBN 0-88802-130-5

1. Cataloging of non-book materials – Handbooks, manuals, etc.

First edition listed *CS* no. 76.

Parts I and II dealing with policies and cataloguing rules for nonbook materials have been expanded and revised. Three new categories of nonbook materials have been added and some minor changes made in terminology. This authoritative guide is invaluable for every library developing a multi-media collection.

4333 026.3'00971

**Research Collections in Canadian Libraries: Fine Arts Library Resources in Canada.**

Prepared in the Resources Survey Division. Ottawa: National Library of Canada, 1978. 2v Index. ISBN 0-660-10132-7 vol. 1. ISBN 0-660-10133-7 vol. 2. $26 (set)

2. Humanities – Library resources – Canada – Statistics.

Produced with the advice and support of members of the Art Libraries Committee of the Canadian Association of Special Libraries and Information Services, this state-of-the-art report on Canadian library collections in the fine arts in 1978, provides not only a catalogue of collection emphases, but also includes information on collection policies, exhibition and auction sale catalogues, slide collections, pictures and photographs, personnel and users. Useful for interlibrary cooperation in all Canadian libraries which deal with the humanities.

4334 026.33

**Directory of Economic Libraries in Canada.**

Edited by Irene Lackner and Gerald Prodrick. London, Ont.: University of Western Ontario, School of Library and Information Science, 1977. 200p. Index. ISBN 0-7714-0007-1 pa.: $5

1. Economic libraries – Canada – Directories.
2. Business libraries – Canada – Directories.

Lists 367 public and private institutions with significant collections or information services in economics. Names, addresses, telephone and telex numbers, union catalogue symbols, staff, hours, size and scope, special collections, library publications, automation, and cooperative projects are included. Indexed by place, personal name, subject, and type of library. A new edition will be available in the summer of 1980. Beth Goble

4335 026'.3624

**Levy, Steven S.**

Directory of Canadian Information Services for the Physically Disabled. Toronto: Canadian Rehabilitation Council for the Disabled, 1978. 387p. pa. Processed: $15

1. Physically handicapped – Information services – Canada – Directories.

A first step toward the establishment of a National Information Service listing agencies on all levels concerned with the provision of information. Information was compiled from questionnaires, directories, reports. Conveniently arranged by province with each section indexed separately. Comprehensive, straightforward, readily usable resource tool. Linda Pulver

4336 027.071

**Canadian Library Handbook.**

Guide des bibliothèques canadiennes, 1979-1980. Edited by James Quantrell. Toronto: Micromedia, c1979. 256p. Index. ISBN 0-88892-600-2 pa.: $16.95

1. Libraries – Canada – Directories.

In five parts: a review of the year in various areas – e.g., associations, publishing, children's literature; recent literature and research; a directory of libraries, by location, name and subject; general statistics of academic and public librares; calendar of the year. Bilingual text. Index. Diane Henderson

4337 027.4'71

**Amey, L. J.,** ed.

The Canadian School-housed Public Library. Halifax, N.S.: Dalhousie University, 1979. 488p. ill. Bibliographies. (Occasional Paper – Dalhousie University Libraries and Dalhousie School of Library Service) ISBN 0-7703-159-2 pa.: $8

1. Libraries, Community-school – Canada.

The contentious issue of public library service based in schools is examined in a series of articles and reports representative of the thinking in various parts of Canada. A province-by-province directory, English and French language bibliographies, and samples of agreements are included. A useful reference for any community considering school-housed public library service. Public and school libraries.

4338 027.4'718

**Mifflin, Jessie.**

The Development of Public Library Services in Newfoundland, 1934-1972: A Report Prepared for the Newfoundland Public Library Board. London, Eng.: The Vine Press, 1978. 86p. (Occasional Paper – Dalhousie University Libraries and Dalhousie School of Library Service) ISBN 0-7703-0154-1 Processed.

1. Public libraries – Newfoundland – History.
2. Libraries, Regional – Newfoundland – History.

A highly respected Newfoundland librarian offers a well-organized and authoritative summary of the growth and development of city and regional library services in her native province. An important addition to Canadian library history. Spiral binding.

4339 027.5'025

**National Library of Canada. Library Documentation Centre.**

Guide to Legislative Libraries and Public and School Library Agencies in Canada. Guide des bibliothèques législatives et des organismes chargés des bibliothèques publiques et scolaires au Canada. 3d ed. Ottawa: Library Documentation Centre, National Library of Canada, 1978. 30p. ISBN 0-662-50139-X pa. DSS cat. no. SN3-102/1978

1. Libraries, Governmental, administrative, etc. – Canada – Directories. 2. Public libraries – Canada. 3. School libraries – Canada. 4. Libraries and state – Canada.

A listing by province, including for each library or agency, its address, head, department or body to which it is responsible, relevant legislation, and mandate. Separate English and French language listings. Diane Henderson

4340 027.571

**Binks, Kenneth.**

Library of Parliament Canada. Photography by W. J. L. Gibbons. Ottawa: KCB Publications, 1979? 64p. photos., ports.

1. Canada. Parliament. Library.

Delightful coloured illustrations of the library and useful explanatory text of both its history and architecture.

4341 027.5'71

**National Library of Canada.**

The Future of the National Library of Canada. L'avenir de la Bibliothèque nationale du Canada. Ottawa: National Library of Canada, 1979. 88p. ill. Bibliography: p. 85-88. ISBN 0-662-50628-6 Free

1. National Library of Canada.

Recommendations stemming from a three-year review of the objectives, role and services of Canada's National Library are presented. An appendix includes the National Library Act and the Organizational Chart of the National Library. Text is in English and French, separately paged, the French text on inverted pages.

4342 027.5'71

**Wees, Ian.**

The National Library of Canada: Twenty-five Years After: A Retrospective Overview. Ottawa: National Library of Canada, 1978. 60p. ill., ports. Bibliography: p. 59-60. ISBN 0-660-01784-9 pa.: $3 (Canada); $3.60 (Foreign) DSS cat. no. SN3-90/1978

1. National Library of Canada – History.

"Published on the occasion of the Silver Anniversary of the National Library of Canada".

"The emphasis is on the evolution, problems, shortcomings and achievements of the National Library and the major changes that have taken place during its first twenty-five years". -Foreword. Includes a chronology of historical highlights 1883-1978.

4343 028.52

**Amtmann, Bernard.**

A Bibliography of Canadian Children's Books and Books for Young People, 1841-1867. Livres de l'enfance & livres de la jeunesse au Canada, 1841-1867. Montreal: Johanna Lamberger, 1977. 124p. Index. pa.

1. Children's literature, Canadian – Bibliography.

Continues his *Early Canadian Children's Books, 1763-1840.*

A listing of 643 books, with references to major bibliographies in which they are included. Listing is alphabetical by author, with an index to anonymous or pseudonymous works. Diane Henderson

4344 028.52

**Blostein, Fay.**

New Paperbacks for Young Adults: A Thematic Guide. Toronto: Ontario Library Association, c1979. 127p. Indexes. ISBN 0-88969-022-7 pa.

1. Children's literature – Bibliography.

A useful and interesting guide to paperbacks for twelve to eighteen year olds. There are three themes: "right now", dealing with problems, pressures and values; "not right now", for adventure and imaginative literature; "now and then", the past, future, fantasy. Entries are annotated and listed under three age groups. Diane Henderson

4345 028.52
**Kogon, Marilyn H.**
Selected Ontario Government Publications for Schools and Libraries 3d ed. Toronto: Ontario Library Association; Ministry of Government Services, 1979. 22p. ill. ISBN 0-7743-4216-1 pa.: Free

1. Children's literature, Canadian (English) – Bibliography. 2. Ontario – Government publications – Bibliography.

First edition listed *CS* p. 13.

"This booklet updates and replaces the second edition of *Selected Free Government Publications for Children and Young Adults*. Priced items have been added, and subject headings and grade level indicators have been omitted". -Preface.

4346 028.52
**McDonough, Irma,** ed.
Canadian Books for Young People. Livres canadiens pour la jeunesse. Toronto: University of Toronto Press, c1978. 148p. ill. Index. ISBN 0-8020-4547-2 pa.: $8.50

1. Children's literature, Canadian – Bibliography.

An essential tool for public and school libraries building quality collections of Canadian children's books. More than fifteen hundred titles, in English and in French, are arranged by subject and indexed by author and title. A list of publishers' series and award-winning children's books are useful for the selector. A new edition is in preparation.

## 050 Periodicals

4347 051.
**McKenzie, Karen.**
The Art and Pictorial Press in Canada: Two Centuries of Art Magazines, by Karen McKenzie and Mary F. Williamson. Toronto: Art Gallery of Ontario, 1979. 71p. ill. Bibliographies and Index. ISBN 0-919876-47-1 pa.: $7.50

1. Illustrated magazines – Canada – History. 2. Art – Periodicals – History. 3. Magazine illustration – Canada – History. 4. Canadian periodicals – Bibliography.

A collection of 8 essays by Canadian librarians with checklists of 263 periodical titles from 1792 to the present. Each author examines within the historical context the role of Canadian periodicals concerned with art, architecture and photography, of those published by galleries and museums, and of magazines illustrated by artists or produced by artists.

## 060 Organizations and museums

4348 061'.1
**Land, Brian.**
Directory of Associations in Canada. Répertoire des associations du Canada. 3d ed. Toronto: University of Toronto Press, c1978. 675p. Index. ISBN 0-8020-4531-6 $45

1. Associations, institutions, etc. – Canada – Directories.

Second edition listed *CS* no. 121.

The third edition of this essential reference tool provides information about more than eleven thousand associations in Canada, including the year in which each was founded, and a telephone number. The alphabetical arrangement is supplemented by a subject index to the associations.

4349 069.
**Directory of Canadian Museums and Related Institutions, 1978.**
Répertoire des musées canadiens et institutions connexes, 1978. Ottawa: Canadian Museums Association, 1978. 248p. ISBN 0-919106-07-2 pa.

1. Museums – Canada – Directories.

The 1976 edition is listed in *CS* no. 122.

Information on the collections in museums and related institutions has been up-dated. A name and category index is provided.

## 070 Journalism and publishing

4350 070.4'092
**Cash, Gwen.**
Off the Record: The Personal Reminiscences of Canada's First Woman Reporter. Langley, B.C.: Stagecoach, 1977. 170p. ill., ports. ISBN 0-88983-016-9 $9.95

1. Women journalists – British Columbia – Biography.

Sixty-five years of freelance journalism in British Columbia are recalled by one of the province's pioneer newspaperwomen. Chatty, anecdotal reminiscences for popular reading. Public libraries.

4351 070.4'092

**Hambleton, Ronald.**

How I Earned $250,000 as a Free Lance Writer: Even if It Did Take 30 Years. Toronto: B. Green, c1977. 192p. ill., plates, ports. Index. $8.95

1. Journalists – Biography.

The vicissitudes of thirty years as a freelance writer are recalled with wit and occasional acerbity. Replete with anecdotes about writers, media personalities and publishers, the reminiscences cast some light on the problems of the creative writer on his own.

4352 070.5

**The Book Trade in Canada Directory.**

L'Industrie du livre au Canada. Toronto: Ampersand Publishing Services, 1979. 314p. ISBN 0-920262-06-6 $18

1. Publishers and publishing – Canada – Directories.

The 1976 edition listed in *CS* no. 127.

A useful, regularly revised source of information on Canadian book publishing.

4353 070.5

**Humanities Research Council of Canada.**

A Guide to Scholarly Publishing in Canada: For All Canadian Scholars. 3d ed., revised. Ottawa: Humanities Research Council of Canada; Social Science Federation of Canada, 1979. 117, 79p. pa.: Free

The second edition listed *CS* no. 132.

All sections of the text have been revised and brought up to date. The format has been changed so that English and French versions are separately paged and the paging is inverted. College and public libraries.

4354 071.

**National Library of Canada. Newspaper Section.**

Union List of Canadian Newspapers Held by Canadian Libraries. Liste collective des journaux canadiens disponibles dans les bibliothèques canadiennes. Ottawa: Ministry of Supply and Services, 1977. 483p. ill. Free DSS cat. no. SN3-84/1977

1. Canadian newspapers – Bibliography – Union lists. 2. Catalogs, Union – Canada.

This first edition includes almost five thousand titles, original and microfilm holdings, to December 31, 1976. Arrangement is alphabetical under city within each province, with a title index and ample cross referencing. An important acquisition for all libraries for the use of librarians, bibliographers, scholars and researchers.

4355 081.

**Ferguson, Ted.**

Kit Coleman: Queen of Hearts. Markham, Ont: PaperJacks, 1978. 182p. ill., plates, ports. ISBN 0-385-13447-9 $9.95

1. Coleman, Kit, 1864-1915.

The heady era of highly competitive, flamboyant journalism is glimpsed in the writing of Canada's first female newspaper columnist. Coleman interviewed the famous and commented on morals, politics and war with equal aplomb. Brief introductions relate the articles to the milieu of the turn of the century. An entertaining but fragmentary sketch of a colourful personality.

## 090 Manuscripts and book rarities

4356 091'.025

**Directory of Canadian Records and Manuscript Repositories.**

Ottawa: Association of Canadian Archivists, 1977- vol. 1. 1977. ISSN 0700-4850

1. Archives – Canada – Directories.

Based on earlier regional and subject directories and supplemented by membership lists of the regional archivists' associations in Canada, this directory provides address, name of archivist, telephone number, hours and brief description of the records held. It is designed to be used in conjunction with the *Union List of Manuscripts* (*CS* no. 145). Arrangement is alphabetical under each province and indexing is by name of institution.

## 100 Philosophy

4357 128.

**Wilkes, James.**

The Gift of Courage. Toronto: Anglican Book Centre, c1979. 74p. Bibliographical references. ISBN 0-919030-36-X pa.: $3.95

1. Courage. 2. Ontology.

A psychiatrist explores a combined approach of religion and psychiatry to confronting life's realities with courage. He applies Biblical examples to today's problems, and criticizes current popular evangelism which seeks magical solutions. For clergy, counsellors and laity.

4358 128'.2
**Jaynes, Julian.**
The Origin of Consciousness in the Breakdown of the Bicameral Mind. Toronto: University of Toronto Press, 1968, c1976. 467p. ill. Bibliographical references and Indexes. ISBN 0-8020-2306-1 $15

1. Consciousness. 2. Consciousness – History.

This book is perhaps the most intellectually provocative work published in the field of psychology in the last decade. Jaynes argues that in prehistoric times, the human mind was schizophrenically divided into two separate hemispheres. With the invention of writing, both parts interacted, thereby invoking the metaphors of consciousness and the self. Carl Spadoni

## 130 Parapsychology and occultism

4359 133.
**Eisenberg, Howard.**
Inner Spaces: Parapsychological Explorations of the Mind. Don Mills, Ont.: Musson, 1977. 184p. Bibliography: p. 163-177. Index. ISBN 0-7737-0035-8 bd.: $11.95
ISBN 0-7737-1018-3 pa.: $6.95

1. Psychical research.

A straightforward introduction to parapsychology for the layman that briefly covers such phenomena as apparitions, poltergeists, reincarnation, mediums and astral projection. A seven-page glossary and a bibliography of 279 items help compensate for the brevity of much of the material. Barbara Schon

4360 133.4'8
**Skelton, Robin.**
Spellcraft: A Handbook of Invocations, Blessings, Protections, Healing Spells, Binding and Bidding. Toronto: McClelland and Stewart, c1978. 206p. ill. Bibliographical references. ISBN 0-7710-8177-4 pa.: $6.95

1. Incantations.

An unusual book, *Spellcraft* is a handbook of "invocations, blessings, protections, healing spells, love spells, binding and bidding." Skelton is a west coast author, teacher, critic and artist, and he claims to have had many years of success with these incantations. A worthy addition to any collection, if only for the sake of curiosity. Don Sedgwick

4361 133.8'092
**Spraggett, Allen.**
Ross Peterson: The New Edgar Cayce. Foreword by Logan Stanfield. Toronto: Doubleday, 1977. 182p. ill., plates.
ISBN 0-385-12298-5 $7.95

1. Peterson, Ross. 2. Psychical research – Biography.

This biography charts the odyssey of a former spiritual vagrant – an alcoholic, married six times, with a jail record – into the world's alleged greatest psychic. Much of the book is given to testing and evidence of Peterson's paranormal powers, vision of the afterlife and the future. Carl Spadoni

4362 133.9'013
**Currie, Ian.**
You Cannot Die: The Incredible Findings of a Century of Research on Death. Agincourt, Ont.: Methuen, 1978. 288p. ill. Bibliographical references.
ISBN 0-485-93750-9 $9.95

1. Spiritualism. 2. Death. 3. Future life.

The author, a sociologist from the University of Guelph, argues the case of man's immortality, and, more precisely that mental states are but a manifestation of the soul's transmigration. Besides evidence cited from eminent researchers, the reader is presented with numerous personal accounts of supernatural experiences. The work is reminiscent of the style of Erik Von Daniken. Carl Spadoni

## 140 Specific philosophies

4363 149'.7
**Simpson, Evan.**
Reason Over Passion: The Social Basis of Evaluation and Approval. Waterloo, Ont.: Wilfrid Laurier University Press, c1979. 162p. Bibliography: p. 153-157. Index.
ISBN 0-88920-073-4 $7.50

1. Reason. 2. Rationalism.

A common belief among philosophers is that reason is the slave of passion. The author, a philosophy professor at McMaster University, challenges this traditional view by arguing that reason appraises the social appropriateness of our goals and thereby, directs our behaviour accordingly. Carl Spadoni

## 150 Psychology

4364 152.4

**Birnbaum, Jack.**

Discovering the Pleasure Principle: Feeling Up Naturally. Don Mills, Ont.: General Publishing, 1979. 187p. Bibliography: p. 183-185. ISBN 0-7736-0076-0 $12.95

1. Pleasure.

If you don't know how to be happy and joyful this book may help. The advice is reasonable and general enough to have some relevance for many. The thesis that pleasure in self and others rather than material wealth is a desirable goal makes common sense. Popular psychology for the general public. Barbara Schon

4365 155.5

**Cotter, Graham,** ed.

Youth Hot Line: Answers to Questions Kids Are Afraid to Ask, by Graham Cotter, Marion Powell and Bruce Vichert. Don Mills, Ont.: Musson, 1979. 192p. ISBN 0-7737-1032-9 pa.: $4.95

1. Adolescent psychology. 2. Youth – Conduct of life.

In July 1973, 'The Toronto Star' began a syndicated column in which teenagers received factual and realistic advice from three experts – a minister, a social worker and a doctor. This informative manual is a selection from that column. Two appendices list information and referral agencies and crises centres in Canada. Carl Spadoni

4366 155.5

**Mitchell, John J.**

Adolescent Psychology. Toronto: Holt, Rinehart and Winston, 1978. 247p. ill. Bibliography: p. 235-241. Index. ISBN 0-03-920018-3 pa.: $6.95

1. Adolescent psychology.

In this informal but documented study, the author describes adolescence in terms of three stages of psychological and physiologial growth. Adolescent sexual needs and related problems are candidly discussed, and a concluding section attempts to dispel certain cultural myths. Excellent summaries are appended to each chapter. Carl Spadoni

4367 155.6'33

**Washbourn, Penelope.**

Becoming Woman: The Quest for Wholeness in Female Experience. 1st ed. New York: Harper & Row (Fitzhenry & Whiteside), c1977. 174p. Bibliographical references and Index. ISBN 0-06069-259-6 $9.40

1. Women. 2. Women – Psychology. 3. Women – Social behaviour.

Washbourn is a theologian, wife, mother, and assistant professor of religion and women's studies at the University of Manitoba. Her book is an in-depth analysis of ten crisis points in a woman's life as opportunities for growth and development. A fascinating blend of personal experience, psychology, and theology. Janice Zlatarits

4368 165.

**Johnson, Ralph Henry.**

Logical Self-defence, by Ralph Henry Johnson and J. Anthony Blair. Toronto: McGraw-Hill Ryerson, 1977. 236p. Bibliographical references and Index. ISBN 0-07-082348-0 pa.: $7.95

1. Fallacies (Logic). 2. Reasoning.

As a working text on informal logic, this book consists of three major sections: an explanation of the basic concepts of argumentation; an examination of specific kinds of fallacy; a perusal of more extended arguments, and guidelines against the persuasive techniques of the media. The authors employ a chatty style with numerous Canadian examples. Carl Spadoni

## 170 Ethics

4369 174'.2

**Thomas, John E.,** ed.

Matters of Life and Death: Crises in Bio-medical Ethics. Toronto: Samuel Stevens, 1978. 378p. Bibliographical references. ISBN 0-88866-594-6 bd.: $15.95 ISBN 0-88866-595-4 pa.: $7.95

1. Medical ethics. 2. Bioethics.

This anthology of critical essays is an interdisciplinary selection from scholars and practitioners addressing the most controversial issues in bio-medical ethics. Topics discussed include the following: abortion, fetal research, euthanasia, eugenics, human experimentation, psychosurgery, patients' rights, medical care, organ transplants, and professional codes. Carl Spadoni

4370 174'.24
**Walton, Douglas N.**
On Defining Death: An Analytical Study of the Concept of Death in Philosophy and Medical Ethics. Montreal: McGill-Queen's University Press, c1979. 189p. Bibliography: p. 167-186. Index. ISBN 0-7735-0331-5 $15

1. Death and dying. 2. Terminal care – Moral and religious aspects.

Walton, a professor of philosophy at the University of Winnipeg, discusses the problems of defining death and examines the differences between active and passive euthanasia. A thoughtful exposition of a problem which is engaging the attention of professionals and laymen.

4371 176.
**Creighton, Phyllis.**
Artificial Insemination by Donor: A Study of Ethics, Medicine, and Law in Our Technological Society. Toronto: Anglican Book Centre, c1977. 84p. Bibliographical references. ISBN 0-919030-21-1 pa.: $2.95

1. Artificial insemination, Human.

This thought-provoking report written by a fifteen-member task force states the official position of the Anglican Church of Canada on this controversial topic. In arriving at its twenty recommendations, the committee examines and comments on various facets of the problem – religious, ethical, medical, legal and social. Carl Spadoni

4372 179.3
**Clark, Stephen R. L.**
The Moral Status of Animals. Toronto: Oxford University Press, 1977. 221p. Bibliography: p. 200-212. Index. ISBN 0-19824-578-5 $17.50

1. Ethics.

This book's underlying premise is that whenever possible, human action should avoid unnecessary pain. An impassioned, philosophical plea is made on behalf of vegetarianism and against most forms of bio-medical research on animals. The author contends that animals are not mere things but are part of man's environment. Carl Spadoni

## 190 Modern Western philosophy

4373 191.
**Schmidt, Larry,** ed.
George Grant in Process: Essays and Conversations. Toronto: House of Anansi Press, 1978. 223p. Bibliography: p. 200-203. Index. ISBN 0-88784-065-5 bd.: $15.95
ISBN 0-88784-064-7 pa.: $7.95

1. Grant, George P., 1918- 2. Philosophy, Canadian – 20th century.

This collection of essays, the proceedings of a conference in 1977, is a tribute to George Grant, author of several influential Canadian works on social and moral issues concerning our technological society. Also included are a bibliography of Grant's writings and conversations with him recording his views on politics, religion and philosophy. Carl Spadoni

4374 192.
**Greenspan, Louis I.**
The Incompatible Prophecies: An Essay on Science and Liberty in the Political Writings of Bertrand Russell. Oakville, Ont.: Mosaic Press/Valley Editions, 1978. 80p.
ISBN 0-88962-076-8 bd.: $8.50
ISBN 0-88962-075-X pa.: $3.95

1. Russell, Bertrand, 3d Earl Russell, 1872-1970.

In his political philosophy, Bertrand Russell advocated the beneficial use of science for the organization of society, although he acknowledged that governments often abuse technology for repressive purposes. This book's examination of this conflict is based on archival material at McMaster University where the author is professor of religion. Carl Spadoni

## 200 Religion

4376 200'.971

**Slater, Peter,** ed.

Religion and Culture in Canada: Essays by Members of the Canadian Society for the Study of Religion. Religion et culture au Canada: Recueil d'articles par des membres de la Société canadienne pour l'étude de la religion. Toronto: Canadian Corporation for Studies in Religion; Waterloo, Ont.: Distributed by Wilfrid Laurier University Press, c1977. 566p. Bibliographies and Index. ISBN 0-919812-06-6 pa.: $7.50

1. Religion and culture. 2. Canada – Religion.

A series of articles on various aspects of religion in Canada ranging from the place of traditional religion to hockey as a form of religion in our society. The religious orientation of education in Newfoundland, Buddhism in Alberta, Norman Bethune's story, and punishment versus reconciliation in Canada are only some of the subjects discussed in this book. Barbara Schon

4377 220.1'5

**Armerding, Carl Edwin,** ed.

Dreams, Visions, and Oracles: The Layman's Guide to Biblical Prophecy. Edited by Carl Edwin Armerding and W. Ward Gasque. Grand Rapids, Mich.: Baker Book House, c1977. 262p. Bibliography: p. 249-254. Index. ISBN 0-8010-0088-2 $9.95 (U.S.)

1. Bible – Prophecies.

A good introduction to the understanding of Biblical prophecies for the concerned adult reader. This collection of essays is interpretive rather than didactic and with a full bibliography indexed to scripture readings and copious notes, an excellent reference tool for clergy and laymen alike. Ann Morrison

4378 223'.2'06

**Griffith, A. Leonard.**

Reactions to God: Man's Response to God's Activity in the Psalms. Toronto: Anglican Book Centre, 1979. 159p. Bibliographical references. ISBN 0-919030-32-7 pa.: $6.95

1. Bible. O.T. Psalms – Criticism, interpretation, etc.

A sequel to *God in Man's Experience: The Acting of God in the Psalms.*

This thoughtful and eloquent discussion of the emotions expressed in the psalms dealing with God's presence suggests that there is a parallel in the emotions familiar to modern man attempting to understand God's presence in the twentieth century. The ecumenical viewpoint of the author makes this inspirational book suitable for a wide audience. Ann Morrison

4379 228'.07

**Kent, Herbert Harold.**

The Unveiling of Jesus Christ: A Companion to the Apocalypse. Edited by Grace Irwin. Toronto: G. R. Welch, c1978. 252p. ISBN 0-919532-45-4 pa.: $5.95

1. Bible. N.T. Revelation – Commentaries.

Mr. Kent's exposition in layman's terms, of God's message for the individual Christian contained in the book of Revelation, is a useful addition to any collection. The text is the result of judicious editing of lectures given to weekly Bible classes and is suitable for self study or use in groups. Unfortunately, there is no bibliography or index. Ann Morrison

## 230 Christian doctrinal theology

4380 232.9'62

**McRuer, James C.**

This Man Was Innocent: The Trial of Jesus. Toronto: Clarke, Irwin, 1978. 94p. Index. ISBN 0-7720-1173-7 pa.: $2.95

1. Jesus Christ – Trial.

First edition published in 1964 under the title: *The Trial of Jesus.*

Why was the trial of Jesus such a travesty of justice? What political and religious affairs resulted in the crucifixion? The former Chief of Justice of the High Court of Ontario uses his legal expertise to answer these questions and present to the layman a unique perspective on pivotal events in the history of the Christian religion. Ann Morrison

## 240 Moral theology

4381 241.
**Evans, Donald.**
Struggle and Fulfillment: The Inner Dynamics of Religion and Morality. Don Mills, Ont.: William Collins, 1979. 238p. Bibliography: p. 217-224. Index.
ISBN 0-529-05669-0 pa.: $7.95

1. Ethics. 2. Religion.

A professor of philosophy at the University of Toronto sees the individual's success in attaining personal fulfillment hinging upon his readiness to accept moral and religious attitudes and values. A book which merits careful reading.

4382 241.5'2
**MacQueen, Angus J.**
The Ten Commandments: New Light from Old Lamps. Hantsport, N.S.: Lancelot Press, 1978. 95p. ISBN 0-88999-080-8 pa.: $2.95

1. United Church of Canada – Sermons.
2. Commandments, Ten – Sermons.

An educator and United Church Minister offers an interpretation of the Ten Commandments for the adult reading public. The sermons, expressed in clear, thoughtful prose, and presented in book form, will be valuable to Christian workers in the community and parents wishing to teach the tenets of their faith. Ann Morrison

4383 242'.4
**Schaeffer, Edith.**
Affliction. Toronto: G. R. Welch, c1978. 253p. ISBN 0-8007-0926-8 $9.15

1. Suffering. 2. Consolation.

Suffering affects all people at different times in their lives, in different forms, and in varying degrees. Edith Schaeffer examines suffering and makes an honest attempt to answer the "why" of suffering. Offering comfort and practical advice on issues which affect the Christian life, the book will have wide appeal. Ann Morrison

4384 248'.2
**MacDougall, Bruce.**
Rejoice in the Lord. Nashville, Tenn.: Abingdon (G. R. Welch), c1979. 128p.
ISBN 0-0687-35933-3 $8.35

1. Christian life – United Church of Canada authors.

Bruce MacDougall who established the first telephone distress centre in Canada, discusses his own Christian growth experience to help others attain a mature and balanced life encompassing the Christian faith. The changes and stress of Canadian society are viewed positively as opportunities for personal growth. Of interest to adults of all faiths. Ann Morrison

4385 248'.4
**Bolton, Kenneth.**
Wake Up, My People. Toronto: Anglican Book Centre, c1978. 87p. Bibliographical references. ISBN 0-919030-24-6 pa.: $2.75

1. Christian life – 1960-

An eloquent appeal to Christians to assume the social responsibilities which are theirs by reason of their faith, the duty to meet the needs of the world's hungry and poor. Persuasively written.

4386 248'.4
**Hunter, Gordon C.**
Grace Abounding. Toronto: G. R. Welch, 1978. 110p. ISBN 0-687-15679-3 pa.: $4.35

1. Christian life – 1960-

This upbeat, well-written book addresses itself to the difficult task of the definition and understanding of the concept of grace in the Christian life. It will appeal to a wide audience of Christian educators and lay people. Ann Morrison

4387 248.4'2
**Tucker, Graham.**
It's Your Life: Create a Christian Lifestyle. Toronto: Anglican Book Centre, c1977. Bibliographical references.
ISBN 0-919030-22-X pa.: $4.95

1. Christian life – 1960-

Graham Tucker, Chaplain of the Toronto Dominion Centre, has written a "how to" book of above average insight and honesty. The excellent notes and selected bibliography make this book useful as a resource not only for personal growth but also for those counselling and guiding young adults today. Ann Morrison

4388 248'.48'2
**Vanier, Jean.**
Community & Growth: Our Pilgrimage Together. Toronto: Griffin House, 1979. 214p. Bibliographical references.
ISBN 0-88760-100-6 pa.: $6.95

1. Christian life – Catholic authors.
2. Christian communities.

Based upon his fourteen years of community living at "l'Arche", and in founding similar communities around the world, Vanier defines the conditions necessary for successful group living. His suggestions are equally applicable to the family, and to modern forms of the extended family. A thoughtful book which invites reflection. College and public libraries.

4389 248.86

**Leach, George.**

Hope for Healing: An Invitation to Hope and Healing Through Personal and Social Relationships. Toronto: Daniel Books, c1978. 147p. ill. ISBN 0-920724-00-0 $6.95

1. Human relations.

In our impersonal twentieth century society the author sees a need for caring and concern in our relationships with other people. He pleads for attitudes of openness, gentleness, compassion and tenderness. A pleasingly conceived book which invites reading for personal reflection and recommends itself to group discussion. Public libraries.

4390 248'.9'3

**Clough, Jack C.**

It Is There – For Those Who Want It. Brampton, Ont.: Charters Publishing, c1977. 120p. Bibliographical references. pa.: $3.50

1. Christian life – Anglican authors.
2. Faith.

Contents: pt. 1. There is a power. pt. 2. There is principle.

Archdeacon Clough demonstrates through examples from his Ministry that evangelical Christianity can help people experience grace. His approach, by his own definition, is non-intellectual and is designed to appeal to and to help those who retain their belief in Christianity but have drifted away from the church. Barbara Schon

## 250 Pastoral theology

4391 252'.6

**Perkin, J. R. C.**

In Season: Sermons Reflecting Some Seasons of the Christian Year. Foreword by Alex Colville. Hantsport, N.S.: Lancelot Press, 1977. 104p. ill. ISBN 0-88999-075-1 pa.: $2.95

1. Church year sermons. 2. Baptists – Sermons.

This collection of sermons, written and delivered by Canadian preacher and educator J. R. Perkin, spans all seasons in the church and touches on a wide range of subjects and contemporary topics. Of interest to the general reader and students, and a good example of the writing of first-class sermons. Ann Morrison

## 260 Social theology

4392 261.

**Baum, Gregory.**

The Social Imperative. New York: Paulist Press, c1979. 254p. Bibliographical references. (An Exploration Book) ISBN 0-8091-2187-5 pa.: $6.95

1. Sociology, Christian.

On cover: *The Social Imperative: Essays on the Critical Issues That Confront the Christian Churches.*

How can religion help modern man cope with the rapid change in social attitudes in North American society? A noted theologian considers the question in this collection of articles. The sociological perspective gives new insight into religion as a socializing force. Will appeal to a wide audience. Ann Morrison

4393 264.

**Schmeiser, James,** ed.

Initiation Theology: Ecumenical Insights. Toronto: Anglican Book Centre, 1978. 96p. ISBN 0-919030-34-3 pa.: $3.50

1. Rites and ceremonies. 2. Initiations (in religion).

This collection of essays by Canadian scholars, examines the rituals which mark important transition periods in the Christian life. Baptism, marriage etc., are analysed in the context of the Western and Eastern Orthodox Christian traditions. Extensive bibliography and detailed notes make this an excellent book for clergy and the general reader. Ann Morrison

4394 265.3

**Baker, Alfred Gordon.**

Do This: An Analysis of the Basic Structure of the Eucharist and How It Relates to Our Culture. Toronto: Anglican Book Centre, c1978. 96p. "Musical settings": p. 93-94. Bibliography: p. 95-96. ISBN 0-919030-35-1 $3.50

1. Lord's Supper – Anglican Church, Canada.
2. Lord's Supper (Liturgy).

The first part of this concise, lucid study comments on the meaning and place of the Holy Eucharist in the contemporary church and the liturgical forms for its celebration. The second part examines *An Alternative to Canadian Use*, which was authorized by the General Synod as an alternative rite to that in the *Book of Common Prayer*.

4395 266'.025
**Ashwin, James.**
God's Mountain. Toronto: G. R. Welch, 1978. 105p. ill., map, ports.
ISBN 0-919532-52-7 pa.: $3.50

1. Missionaries, Medical – Canada – Biography. 2. Missionaries, Medical – India – Biography. 3. Poliomyelitis – Canada – Biography.

As a missionary to India in the 1950's, Canadian Dr. Ashwin was stricken with polio and spent the remainder of his very productive life confined to a wheelchair. This book is an account of his struggles and the consequent deepening of his faith. An inspiring book for all readers. Ann Morrison

4396 266'.2
**Lillard, Charles,** ed.
Mission to Nootka, 1874-1900: Reminiscences of the West Coast of Vancouver Island. Sidney, B.C.: Gray's Publishing, 1977. 119p. ill., map, ports. Bibliography: p. 119. Index.
ISBN 0-88826-072-5 pa.: $5.95

1. Brabant, Auguste-Joseph, 1845-1912. 2. Catholic Church – Missions – British Columbia – Vancouver Island. 3. Missionaries – British Columbia – Vancouver Island – Biography.

The writings of Father Augustin Joseph Brabant, missionary on the west coast of British Columbia, provide an eyewitness report of the lifestyle of west coast natives and a biased European perspective on the civilization process that resulted in the collapse of their culture. A historical document of interest to both scholar and browser. Kathryn Walker

4397 266'.2
**Loogman, Pia.**
Footsteps of a Giant: The Story of Father M. J. Hawkins, S.J. Belleville, Ont.: Mika Publishing, 1977. 323p. ill., map, ports.
ISBN 0-919303-22-6 $20

1. Hawkins, Michael Joseph, 1901-1969. 2. Jesuits – Ontario – Biography. 3. Indians of North America – Ontario – Missions.

A warm-hearted look at a dedicated and selfless man who cared for those less fortunate than himself. To the Indians of northern Ontario Father Hawkins was more than a priest; he was their friend, leader, helper and confidant. Paula de Ronde

4398 267'.15
**Wiseman, Clarence D.**
A Burning in My Bones: An Anecdotal Autobiography. Toronto: McGraw-Hill Ryerson, 1979. 279p. ill., ports. Index.
ISBN 0-07-077820-5 bd.: $12.95
ISBN 0-07-077821-3 pa.: $6.95

1. Salvationists – Canada – Biography.

An autobiography by the man who held the highest post in the Salvation Army, that of General of the International Salvation Army from 1974 until his retirement in 1977. A personal account of his life with his family and of his work that is told with humour and energy. His story is also the story of the Salvation Army and covers the Depression years, the war years in Britain and Europe and latterly the service that took him to the Third World. Barbara Schon

4399 267'.15'0971
**Moyles, Robert G.**
The Blood and Fire in Canada: A History of the Salvation Army in the Dominion, 1882-1976. Toronto: Peter Martin, c1977. 312p. ill., plates, ports. Index. Bibliography: p. 305-308. ISBN 0-88778-169-1 bd.: $15
ISBN 0-88778-170-5 pa.: $5.95

1. Salvation Army (Canada) – History.

An account of the Salvation Army in Canada from its beginning as a group of enthusiastic members who penetrated cities, towns and outposts with evangelistic fervour, to a respectable, middle-class organization. Covers the exciting drum-thumping days and describes their work with those elements of society ignored by traditional social agencies. Barbara Schon

4400 268.
**Kranendonk, D. L.**
Christian Day Schools: Why and How. St. Catharines, Ont.: Paideia Press, c1978. 118p. ill. Index. ISBN 0-88815-016-4 pa.: $3.95

1. International Union of Christian Schools. 2. Christian education. 3. Church and education.

Canadian parents and educators of strong fundamental Christian convictions will find this book an informative guide to, and explanation of, an educational system which emphasizes Christian ideals. The International Union of Christian Schools is based in St. Catharines Ontario. Ann Morrison

## 270 Christian church history

4401 270.82

**Reimers, Al.**

God's Country: Charismatic Renewal. Toronto: G. R. Welch, 1979. 192p. Bibliography: p. 190-191. ISBN 0-919537-29-2 pa.: $5.95

1. Charismatic Movement.

An Anglican priest interprets the charismatic Christian renewal movement which is currently sweeping all denominations in Canada. Most of the book consists of evidence from individuals interviewed in a cross-country survey. Included are official and semi-official church statements on the topic. Recommended as a thoughtful presentation for both clergy and laymen.

## 280 Christian denominations and sects

4402 283'.092'4

**Swanson, Cecil.**

The Days of My Sojourning: A Reminiscence. Calgary: Glenbow-Alberta Institute, c1977. 141p. ill., ports. Index. $7.95

1. Anglican Church of Canada – Clergy – Biography.

From Victorian England to present day Canada, Dr. Swanson has met the great and the not so great and in his reminiscences provides the reader with a unique view of Canadian history. This book in its wisdom and understanding of human nature, reflects the author's credo "To love people is to discover the meaning of life". An excellent addition to any library. Ann Morrison

4403 283'.71

**Stuchbery, Ian.**

Growing in Christ: New Patterns of Initiation and Education in the Parish Community. Toronto: Anglican Book Centre, c1978. 109p. Bibliography: p. 105-107. ISBN 0-919030-23-8 pa.: $3.25

1. Church renewal – Anglican Church of Canada.

Directed to members of the Anglican Church, this book is meant to be read and discussed in parish groups. Questions raised include the meaning of baptism, how to bring people into an environment conducive to effective Christian education, the valid use of laying on of hands, and how to encourage lay involvement within the parish community. Barbara Schon

4404 288'.71

**Hewett, Phillip.**

Unitarians in Canada. Toronto: Fitzhenry & Whiteside, c1978. 390p. ill., plates, ports. Index. Bibliography: p. 373-377. ISBN 0-88902-446-4 pa.: $8.95

1. Unitarianism – Canada – History.

Hewett has been the minister of the Unitarian Church of Vancouver since 1956. Through a scholarly and readable history of the Church in Canada since its beginnings in 1810, he describes how Unitarians have exerted an influence on Canadian life far in excess of their small numbers. Barbara Schon

4405 289.7

**Epp, Frank H.**

Mennonite Peoplehood: A Plea for New Initiatives. Waterloo, Ont.: Conrad Press, 1977. 120p. ISBN 0-9690458-4-0 pa.: $4.50

1. Mennonites.

Addressed primarily to those within the church the book voices the concern that the Mennonite heritage is in danger of assimilation. Written for the Mennonite World Conference in 1978, Epp opens up questions of the future direction of the church, its place in the international community and its relationship with various governments. Barbara Schon

4406 289.7'7127

**Klippenstein, Lawrence,** ed.

Mennonite Memories: Settling in Western Canada. Edited by Lawrence Klippenstein and Julius G. Toews. Layout and design by Gerald Loewen. 2d ed. Winnipeg: Centennial, 1977. 330p. ill., maps, plans, ports. Bibliography: p. 316-325. ISBN 0-919213-51-0 $15

1. Mennonites in Manitoba – History.
2. Mennonites in Manitoba – Biography.

First published in 1974 under the title: *Manitoba Mennonite Memories.*

These early memories of emigration and settling in Canada abound with detail about daily life for the Mennonites who arrived from Russia to settle in western Canada. The highly readable style, good bibliography, and the many photographs and maps make this book a good addition to any library. Barbara Schon

4407 289.7'713

**Hunsberger, David L.**

People Apart: Portrait of a Mennonite World in Waterloo County, Ontario, by David L. Hunsberger, James Hertel and Koni Lattner, photographers. Text by J. Winfield Fretz. Foreword by Paul Tiessen. St. Jacobs, Ont.: Sands Hills Books, c1977. 111p. ill. ISBN 0-920446-01-9 bd.: $24 ISBN 0-920446-00-0 pa.: $13.50

1. Mennonites in Waterloo, Ont. (County).

A glimpse of the life of "Old Order" Mennonites, with sparse text enlivened by many excellent black and white photographs taken many years ago. For all libraries.

4408 289.9

**Woodcock, George.**

The Doukhobors, by George Woodcock and Ivan Avakumovic. Toronto: McClelland and Stewart; Ottawa: Institute of Canadian Studies, Carleton University, c1977. 382p. Bibliography: p. 370-375. Index. (The Carleton Library) ISBN 0-7710-9807-3 pa.: $4.95

1. Doukhobors.

Clothbound listed in *CS* no. 247. First published Toronto: Oxford University Press, 1968.

## 294 Other religions

4409 294.5'43

**Truch, Stephen.**

TM and the Art of Learning. Toronto: Lester and Orpen, 1976. Bibliographical references. Index. ISBN 0-919630-70-7 bd.: $11.95 ISBN 0-919630-83-9 pa.: $6.95

1. Transcendental Meditation.

An enthusiastic account of TM which outlines the structure and organization of the movement. Emphasis lies in the educative aspect of Transcendental Meditation and the accrued benefits to the individual who is a practitioner. Barbara Schon

## 301 Sociology

4410 301.

**Himelfarb, Alexander.**

People, Power and Process: Sociology for Canadians, by Alexander Himelfarb and C. James Richardson. Toronto: McGraw-Hill Ryerson, cl979. 353p. ill. Bibliography: p. 312-337. Indexes. ISBN 0-07-082865-2 $12.95

1. Sociology. 2. Canada – Social conditions.

This is a good introductory textbook designed for sociology and Canadian society courses. It presents and uses traditional sociological theory to analyze and explain Canadian social conditions. Bob Gardner

4411 301.

**Potts, Malcolm.**

Abortion, by Malcolm Potts, Peter Diggory and John Peel. Cambridge, N.Y.: Cambridge University Press, 1977. 575p. Bibliographical references and Index. ISBN 0-52129150-X bd.: $37.50

1. Abortion. 2. Abortion – Great Britain.

A very well-written survey of abortion, covering legal issues, medical procedures, historical and demographic data, and cross-cultural comparisons. Extensive bibliographic references and an objective treatment make this a valuable reference tool. Bob Gardner

4412 301.15'43

**Aitken, John.**

Conversations: The Diary of a Worried Journalist's Trek Across a Divided & Threatened Canada. Scarborough, Ont.: Prentice-Hall, 1978. 179p. ISBN 0-13-172056-2 pa.: $7.95

1. Public opinion – Canada. 2. Canada – Politics and government – 1963- – Public opinion. 3. Canada – English-French relations – Public opinion. 4. Quebec (Province) – History – Autonomy and independence movements – Public opinion.

Records the coast-to-coast bus trip of a journalist seeking grass-roots opinions about Canada's problems. The pessimistic conclusion that the country is approaching self-destruction is rendered questionable by unrepresentative sampling, but the diary is still a revealing, readable and significant comment on the issue of national unity. Ille-Mai Gerdels

4413 301.15'43

**Butler, Rick,** comp.

Quebec: The People Speak. Toronto: Doubleday, 1978. 335p. maps, ports. Bibliography: p. 332-333. Index. ISBN 0-385-13496-7 $12.95

1. Public opinion – Quebec (Province). 2. Quebec (Province) – Politics and government – 1960- – Public opinion. 3. Quebec (Province) – History – Autonomy and independence movements – Public opinion.

Transcriptions and translations of taped interviews with one hundred people from all levels of society in many parts of Quebec, recorded six months after the November 15, 1976 election, provide useful information on how Quebeckers see the political situation. Some of the views expressed are myths which should be exploded. The concluding chapter attempts to draw the comments together and suggests how the remainder of Canada should respond. Readable and interesting but not profound.

## 301.16 Mass communication

4414 301.16'1

**Brown, Gerald R.,** comp.

Communications Directory. Toronto: Association for Media and Technology in Education, 1978. 128p. pa.: $6

1. Mass media – Canada – Societies, etc. – Directories.

A listing of 128 organizations "in the broad field of communications". For most organizations, information given includes: address, telephone, telex, officers, background, purposes, research activity, membership, organizational structure, publications, and conferences. First edition. Diane Henderson

4415 301.16'1

**Chapin, Henry.**

Who Calls the Tune?: Using the Media to Promote Social Change in Canada, by Henry Chapin and Alison Stirling. Ottawa: Canadian Council on Social Development, 1977. 133p. Bibliography: p. 129-133. ISBN 0-88810-266-6 pa. Processed: $2

1. Mass media – Social aspects – Canada.

This report discusses the findings of a survey done in the summer of 1976 which asked community groups to describe their experiences dealing with the commercial and community media. Complaints of smaller groups are studied, in particular the lack of access to production facilities and little programming control of the commercial media. Bob Gardner

4416 301.16'1

**Hindley, M. Patricia.**

The Tangled Net: Basic Issues in Canadian Communications, by M. Patricia Hindley, Gail M. Martin and Jean McNulty. Foreword by George Woodcock. Vancouver: J. J. Douglas, c1977. 183p. diagrs. Bibliography: p. 177-183. ISBN 0-88894-123-4 $12.95

1. Mass media – Canada. 2. Communication – Canada.

Three telecommunication researchers from Simon Fraser University paint a gloomy picture of the communications media in Canada, especially the newer media: broadcasting, cable and telephone. They deplore both American domination and centralization in Toronto and Ottawa. Useful as a summary of a contentious issue despite its regional bias. Of interest to a broad range of readers.

4417 301.161

**Ontario. Royal Commission on Violence in the Communications Industry.**

Report of the Royal Commission on Violence in the Communications Industry. Toronto: The Commission; available from The Publications Centre, Ministry of Government Services, 1977. 7v ill. $50.00 (set); $3 vol. 1.; $8 ea. vols. 2-7.

1. Violence in mass media. 2. Mass media – Social aspects – Ontario.

An extremely important and valuable examination of the effects on society of violence in films, radio, and television. Judy LaMarsh chaired this Commission, producing an interim report in January 1976 as well as this seven volume final report. Includes recommendations and a very extensive bibliography. Bob Gardner

4418 301.16'1

**Rutherford, Paul.**

The Making of the Canadian Media. Toronto: McGraw-Hill Ryerson, 1978. 141p. Bibliography: p. 128-135. Index. (McGraw-Hill Ryerson Series in Canadian Sociology) ISBN 0-07-082653-6 bd.: $12.95 ISBN 0-07-082559-9 pa.: $5.95

1. Mass media – Canada – History.

A short but valuable study of the

development of newspaper, radio and television media in Canada. Historical in emphasis, but also briefly examines the contemporary social impact of these media. Offers interesting ideas and a good bibliography. Bob Gardner

## 301.18 Groups

4419 301.18'5

**Parr, Jim.**

Any Other Business?: How to be a Good Committee Person. 77p. ISBN 0-7720-1162-1 pa.: $5.95

1. Committees. 2. Meetings.

Written by a senior civil servant in Ontario, this book offers useful suggestions for the best use of committees and committee members. The approach is general and chatty, with brief advice on preparing briefs, minutes and reports. Bob Gardner

## 301.2 Culture and social change

4420 301.29'71

**Donnelly, Daniel K.**

CanAmerican Union Now! Toronto: Griffin House, 1978. 208p. ill., maps. Bibliography: p. 199-201. Index. ISBN 0-88760-096-4 pa.: $5.95

1. Canada – Relations (general) with the United States. 2. United States – Relations (general) with Canada. 3. Canada – Politics and government – 1963- 4. Canada – Economic conditions – 1965- 5. Quebec (Province) – History – Autonomy and independence movements.

To avoid the possibility of Canada's separating into many regions, an Anglophone Quebecker now living in Toronto urges political and economic union with the United States. A solution which many may wish to discuss, this interpretation lacks depth of analysis. Interesting, but not essential.

4421 301.2'971

**Groenewold, H. J.**

Multiculturalism: Can Trudeau's Liberalism Tolerate It? St. Catharines, Ont.: Paideia Press, 1978. 56p. Bibliographical references. ISBN 0-88815-033-4 pa.: $1.95

1. Minorities – Canada. 2. Canada – English-French relations. 3. Canada – Politics and government – 1945-

A brief but provocative study of liberalism and the Liberal Party in Canada from Confederation to the present. It critically examines the extent to which the central government has fostered cultural pluralism in Canada. Bob Gardner

4422 301.29'71

**Hutcheson, John.**

Dominance and Dependency: Liberalism and National Policies in the North Atlantic Triangle. Toronto: McClelland and Stewart, c1978. 182p. ISBN 0-7710-4301-5 pa.: $5.95

1. Canada – Relations (general) with the United States. 2. United States – Relations (general) with Canada. 3. Canada – Economic policy. 4. Canada – Social conditions.

From a nationalistic point of view, a York University professor interprets earlier writing on Canada's economic development as it was affected by its economic relationship with Britain and the United States. The interpretation is overly simplified for the expert, but it is a useful summary for students and lay people to whom it is directed. For purchase by libraries which already have Rotstein's *Precarious Homestead.*

4423 301.29'71

**Lamorie, Andrew.**

How They Sold Our Canada to the U.S.A.. New rev. enl. ed. 133p. ISBN 0-919600-47-6 bd.: $9.95 ISBN 0-919600-46-8 pa.: $3.95

1. Canada – Relations (general) with the United States. 2. United States – Relations (general) with Canada. 3. Canada – Economic conditions – 1945-

An emotional and provocative description of the history of Canadian-American economic relations. The author presents a gloomy but thought-provoking argument for his claim of the economic takeover of Canada by the United States. Bob Gardner

## 301.3 Human ecology

4424 301.31

**Hutchison, George.**

Grassy Narrows, by George Hutchison and Dick Wallace. Scarborough, Ont.: Van Nostrand Reinhold, 1977. 178p. ill., maps, ports. ISBN 0-442-29876-5 pa.: $8.95

1. Water – Pollution – Economic aspects – Ontario. 2. Water – Pollution – Environmental aspects – Ontario. 3. Mercury – Toxicology. 4. Grassy Narrows, Ont. (Indian Reserve).

In relating the social and political effects of

mercury on a community, the author serves a timely warning of the possible consequences of modern technology. This amply illustrated and clearly written book relates the similarity of circumstances in Japan and Ontario, providing interesting reading for the general reader and a factual report of the development of this tragedy for the more seriously concerned. Linda Pulver

4425 301.31

**Leiss, William,** ed.

Ecology Versus Politics in Canada. Edited by William Leiss for the University League for Social Reform. Toronto: University of Toronto Press, c1979. 282p. Bibliographical references. ISBN 0-8020-2298-7 bd.: $20
ISBN 0-8020-6332-2 pa.: $7.50

1. Environmental policy – Canada.

Twelve critical essays examine the Canadian government's response to social, political and health controversies raised by environmental problems. Focuses on problems of industrial pollution, occupational health and safety, nuclear power and the search for energy. Bob Gardner

4426 301.31

**Solomon, Lawrence.**

The Conserver Solution. Toronto: Doubleday, 1978. 220p. Index.
ISBN 0-385-14533-0 bd.: $12.50
ISBN 0-385-14534-9 pa.: $5.95

1. Environmental policy – Canada.
2. Conservation of natural resources – Canada.

A well-written report of the Pollution Probe Foundation. It analyzes the problems of our consumer society and describes in detail an ideal Canadian conserver society. Suggests workable remedies to social, economic, and conservation problems. Bob Gardner

4427 301.32

**Fagan, Margaret.**

Challenge for Change: Geographical Approaches to Selected World Issues, by Margaret Fagan and Marilyn Andrews. Scarborough, Ont.: McGraw-Hill Ryerson, 1977. 336p. ill., diagrs., maps. Bibliographies and Index. ISBN 0-07-082463-0 $10.95

1. Population. 2. Food supply. 3. Geography, Economic.

A secondary school text book designed to provide a framework within which to discuss world issues. It covers topics such as world population growth, population and food supply, economic growth, industrialization and urbanization.

4428 301.32'4

**Avery, Donald.**

"Dangerous Foreigners": European Immigrant Workers and Labour Radicalism in Canada, 1896-1932. Toronto: McClelland and Stewart, c1979. 204p. Bibliographical references and Index. (The Canadian Social History Series) ISBN 0-7710-0826-0 pa.: $6.95

1. Labor and laboring classes – Canada – History. 2. Radicalism – Canada – History. 3. East Europeans in Canada. 4. Canada – Emigration and immigration – History. 5. Canada – Social conditions.

Avery discusses the impact of immigrant workers on the developing labour movement in Canada and the coincident impact of their harsh lives in a new land which further impelled them to radicalism. Although his treatment of the material is brief, it is unusually detailed. An appendix of demographic data and extensive bibliographic references are notable features of the book. Barbara Stewart

4429 301.32'4

**Montero, Gloria.**

The Immigrants. Toronto: James Lorimer, 1977. 222p. ISBN 0-88862-146-9 bd.: $12.95
ISBN 0-88862-147-7 pa.: $8.95

1. Canada – Foreign population. 2. Canada – Emigration and immigration.

A fascinating collection of personal histories of immigrants to Canada and passages of conversation with them. Vignettes are not tied together, and no commentary is given, but this would be of interest to students of sociology as well as the general public because of its unique viewpoint. Marilyn Carr

4430 301.32'6

**Mannion, John J.,** ed.

The Peopling of Newfoundland: Essays in Historical Geography. St. John's, Nfld.: Institute of Social and Economic Research, Memorial University of Newfoundland, 1978, c1977. 289p. ill., diagrs., graphs, maps. Bibliography: p. 276-278. Index. (Social and Economic Papers) ISBN 0-919666-17-5 $10

1. Migration, Internal – Newfoundland.
2. Newfoundland – Emigration and immigration. 3. Newfoundland – Population.

Meticulous field and archival research by nine geographers associated with Memorial University has produced a scholarly study of the settlement of Newfoundland in the nineteenth century. Each essay concentrates on a specific geographic area, and is buttressed by legible maps, figures and tables. Significant because of the lack of comparable studies. Academic and large public libraries.

4431 301.32'9

**Kalbach, Warren E.**

The Demographic Bases of Canadian Society, by Warren E. Kalbach and Wayne W. McVey. 2d ed. Toronto: McGraw-Hill Ryerson, c1979. 402p. graphs. Bibliographies and Index. (McGraw-Hill Ryerson Series in Canadian Sociology) ISBN 0-07-082667-6 $9.95

1. Canada – Population. 2. Canada – Statistics, Vital.

First edition listed in *CS* no. 291.

As in the first edition, this revised edition provides a general overview of Canadian population and social conditions. More recent census data is included. This is a well-written text designed as supplementary reading for Canadian society courses. Bob Gardner

4432 301.32'9

**Stone, Leroy O.**

Canadian Population Trends and Public Policy Through the 1980s, by Leroy O. Stone, Claude Marceau, and others. Montreal: Published for Institute for Research on Public Policy by McGill-Queen's University Press, 1977. 109p. graphs. Bibliography: p. 77-104. Index. ISBN 0-7735-0287-4 bd.: $8.50 ISBN 0-7735-0288-2 pa.: $4

1. Population forecasting – Canada. 2. Canada – Population. 3. Canada – Social policy. 4. Canada – Economic policy.

The trends are broken down by aspects such as age, language, labour force, and are well supported by demographic charts. Projected problems are discussed in a manner suitable for students of sociology. Good bibliography. Marilyn Carr

## 301.36 Urban sociology

4433 301.36

**Porteous, John Douglas.**

Environment and Behaviour: Planning and Everyday Urban Life. Reading, Mass.: Addison-Wesley Publishing, c1977. 446p. ill. Bibliography: p. 369-425. Index. ISBN 0-20105-867-7 $13.75

1. Sociology, Urban. 2. Environmental psychology. 3. City planning. 4. Man – Influence of environment. 5. Architecture – Human aspects.

An interdisciplinary approach has been taken with the aim of integrating the wide-ranging urban Man-Environment Relations field and creating a new discipline called Human Ethology. The author is an academic geographer. The work is indexed, includes an extensive bibliography, and each chapter has a section on further readings. It is more suitable for large urban libraries and as an introductory text for undergraduate students. Margot Hewings

4434 301.36

**Stelter, Gilbert Al.,** ed.

The Canadian City: Essays in Urban History. Edited, with introductions by Gilbert Al Stelter and Alan F. J. Artibise. Toronto: McClelland and Stewart; Ottawa: Institute of Canadian Studies, Carleton University, c1977. 455p. ill., graphs, maps. Bibliography: p. 442-452. (The Carleton Library) ISBN 0-7710-9809-X pa.: $5.95

1. Cities and towns – Canada – History.

Seventeen carefully researched articles, a number of them previously published, examine the various facets of Canadian urban history in the period from 1815 to 1920. An editorial introduction precedes each of the thematically grouped sections. The contributors are urban historians and academics. A scholarly work, with an excellent bibliography, of interest to students of urban history.

4435 301.36'0971

**Gertler, L. O.**

Changing Canadian Cities: The Next 25 Years, by L. O. Gertler, Ronald W. Crowley, and Wayne K. Bond. Toronto: McClelland and Stewart; Ottawa: Ministry of State for Urban Affairs; Publishing Centre, Supply and Services Canada, c1977. 474p. ill., graphs, maps, plans. Bibliographical references. ISBN 0-7710-3279-X pa.: $9.95

1. Cities and towns – Canada.

This authoritative work analyzes past and future growth patterns, the structure of cities, and their effect on behaviour. Well supported by tables, maps and graphs. University-level interest. Marilyn Carr

## 301.4 Social structure and women

4436 301.41
**Schlesinger, Benjamin,** ed.
Sexual Behaviour in Canada: Patterns and Problems. Toronto: University of Toronto Press, c1977. 326p. Bibliography: p. 300-316.
ISBN 0-8020-2262-6 bd.: $15
ISBN 0-8020-6314-4 pa.: $6.95

1. Sex customs – Canada. 2. Sex.

The first collection of Canadian articles on human sexuality, designed as a companion volume to *Family Planning in Canada* (CS no. 336) by a professor of social work. It discusses sexual attitudes and sex research, sexuality and the law, and education for sexuality. Especially useful for professionals in medicine, psychiatry, sociology, law and social work. The general public will find it interesting.

4437 301.41
**Shain, Merle.**
When Lovers Are Friends. Toronto: McClelland and Stewart, cl978. 106p.
ISBN 0-7710-8134-0 $8.95

1. Interpersonal relations. 2. Love.
3. Friendship.

A publisher's note that this book "explores the great emotional preoccupation of our time – fearing intimacy and dreading solitude" overpraises light reading and light philosophy. More "trusting", "connecting", and "touching" is urged by journalist Shain as she repeats the casual, personal approach and chatty style of her first book, *Some Men Are More Perfect Than Others.* Claire England

4438 301.41'2
**Atwood, Margaret.**
Women on Women. Edited with an introductory essay by Ann B. Shteir. Toronto: York University, 1978. (Gerstein Lecture Series) ISBN 0-919604-35-8 bd.: $6
ISBN 0-919604-37-4 pa.: $4.50

1. Women.

Four lectures: Margaret Atwood skillfully analyzes the problems of creating women characters in fiction and of being a woman writer; Laura Sabia talks of women achieving equality by gaining representation on decision-making bodies; Linda Nochlin analyzes women artists; and Patricia Graham examines the role of women in higher education. Janice Zlatarits

4439 301.41'2
**Backhouse, Constance.**
The Secret Oppression: Sexual Harassment of Working Women, by Constance Backhouse and Leah Cohen. Toronto: Macmillan, c1978. 208p. Bibliographical references.
ISBN 0-7705-1789-7 $9.75

1. Sexual harassment. 2. Sex in business.

Sexual coercion in the work place, the bête noire of the working woman, is examined in case studies and interviews with employees, personnel and union officials, and management representatives. Its history, causes, manifestations and possible corrective measures are discussed by a lawyer and a journalist. Lacks a biblography and an index. Written in a smoothly flowing, journalistic style. A must for women's studies collections.

4440 301.41'2
**Clark, Lorenne M. G.,** ed.
The Sexism of Political Theory: Women and Reproduction from Plato to Nietzsche. Edited by Lorenne M. G. Clark and Lynda Lange. Toronto: University of Toronto Press, 1979. 141p. Bibliography: p. 135-141.
ISBN 0-8020-5459-5 bd.: $15
ISBN 0-8020-6376-6 pa.: $5

1. Sex discrimination against women – History. 2. Women – History.

"Each essay deals directly with one or more of the issues which we believe to be central to an understanding of why traditional political theory is deficient from a feminist point of view" -Introduction.

4441 301.41'2
**Fremes, Ruth.**
The Canadian Woman's Almanac. Toronto: Methuen, 1978. 272p. ill. Bibliographies and Index. ISBN 0-458-93740-1 $12.95

1. Women – Canada.

A good, although not exhaustive guide gives information on raising children, gardening, financial planning, coping with family crises, buying a house. Additional sources of assistance for dealing with difficult situations are listed. Janice Zlatarits

4442 301.41'2
**Hauck, Philomena.**
Sourcebook on Canadian Women. Ottawa: Canadian Library Association, c1979. 111p. ill. Index. ISBN 0-88802-126-7 pa.: $10

1. Women – Canada – Bibliography.

An attractively designed, annotated bibliography of books, periodicals, pamphlets and audio-visual materials about Canadian women. Organized under broad subject headings such as women's rights, women and the law, work and day care, health and fitness, literature by and about women, and biography. A useful reading list for women's studies courses and a good basic reference source. Janice Zlatarits

4443 301.41'2
**Kealey, Linda,** ed.
A Not Unreasonable Claim: Women and Reform in Canada, 1880s-1920s. Toronto: Canadian Women's Educational Press, 1979. ISBN 0-88961-052-5 bd.: $15.95
ISBN 0-88961-049-5 pa.: $7.95

1. Women – Canada – History. 2. Canada – Social conditions – 1867-1918.

Women's participation in social reform movements in Canada, over a forty-year period, are analysed by twelve historians. A well-chosen selection of papers which stresses the need for further research in the field. Women's studies collections.

4444 301.41'2
**Mazur, Carol,** comp.
Women in Canada, 1965 to 1975: A Bibliography. Compiled by Carol Mazur and Sheila Pepper. Hamilton, Ont.: McMaster University Library Press, c1976. 174p. Index. ISBN 0-919592-03-1 pa.: $5

1. Women – Canada – Bibliography.

A revised and expanded version of the 1972 edition. Items are listed under very specific headings, but not annotated; an author index is included. Useful because it provides access to individual articles, reports, etc. about Canadian women. Janice Zlatarits

4445 301.41'2
**Trofimenkoff, Susan Mann,** ed.
The Neglected Majority: Essays in Canadian Women's History. Edited by Susan Mann Trofimenkoff and Alison Prentice. Toronto: McClelland and Stewart, 1977. 192p. Bibliography: p. 146-152. (The Canadian Social History Series) ISBN 0-7710-8595-8 pa.: $4.95

1. Women – Canada – History.

A valuable addition to the increasing body of writing on the role of women in Canadian history, this collection of essays deals with both the world of ideas and action. Most of the papers were given at conferences and have been printed elsewhere. They are reprinted with the hope that the collection will spark interest in historical research on Canadian women. Excellent bibliography.

4446 301.41'57
**Lee, John Alan.**
Getting Sex: A New Approach: More Fun, Less Guilt. Don Mills, Ont.: Musson, 1978. 318p. Bibliography: p. 308-315. Index. ISBN 0-7736-1037-5 pa.: $8.95

1. Homosexuals.

Some patrons may object to the viewpoint (enjoyment of casual sex, promiscuity, homosexuality) in this easy reading, popular approach to the "gay" support system in Metropolis (Toronto). The author, a sociologist, admits to nothing new or scholarly as he culls pieces from the gay press, academic studies and mass media in his plea for wider acceptance of sexual mores labelled deviant. Claire England

4447 301.41'8
**Chernick, Beryl A.**
In Touch: Putting Sex Back into Love and Marriage, by Beryl A. Chernick and Avinoam B. Chernick. Adapted by Jeniva Berger. 182p. ill. Bibliography: p. 181-182.
ISBN 0-7705-1580-0 $9.95

1. Sex in marriage. 2. Sex therapy – Case studies.

A medical and marriage counselling team create a fictional couple who resolve their marital and sexual problems through increased communication. A non-sensationalized, good average guide with frank explanation, instruction and much sound general advice. Clear writing and popular topic will appeal to self-therapists. Claire England

## 301.42 Marriage and family

4448 301.42
**Schlesinger, Benjamin.**
Families: Canada. Rev. ed. Toronto: McGraw-Hill Ryerson, c1979. 194p. Bibliographies. ISBN 0-07-082897-0 pa.

1. Family – Canada.

First edition published in 1972 under title *Families: A Canadian Perspective.*

A well-known University of Toronto sociologist and his co-authors update introductory material on sex roles, family structure, abuse, alcoholism, occupations and child care. Mid-seventies statistics, clear summaries, questions and activities, references to further readings and films, reinforce the potential for secondary school, undergraduate use. Claire England

4449 301.42'7

**Eekelaar, John,** ed.

Family Violence: An International and Interdisciplinary Study. Edited by John Eekelaar and Sanford N. Katz. Introduction by Anthony Storr. Toronto: Butterworth, c1978. 572p. Bibliographies. ISBN 0-409-87460-4 pa.

1. Conjugal violence – Congresses.
2. Child abuse – Congresses.

Spousal and sibling violence, child abuse, incest, child suicide are covered in these proceedings from the second International Conference on Family Law, McGill University, 1977. Thirty-five well-documented papers by experts discuss psychological and sociological perspectives and consider various legal and social responses. Claire England

4450 301.42'7

**Gatley, Richard H.**

Single Father's Handbook: A Guide for Separated and Divorced Fathers, by Richard H. Gatley and David Koulack. 1st ed. Garden City, N.Y.: Anchor Books, c1979. 196p. Index. ISBN 0-385-13653-6 pa.: $6.50

1. Single parents.

Two Canadian psychologists, themselves separated fathers, have prepared a practical manual for men coping with marriage breakup and the concomitant effects upon relationships with their children, their parents, in-laws and friends. The third section addresses the problems of becoming a "houseperson". There is a dearth of material on this topic. Public libraries.

4451 301.42'7

**Hibbert, Joyce,** ed.

The War Brides. Toronto: PMA Books, c1978. 160p. ill., ports. ISBN 0-88778-185-3 $12.95

1. Wives – Canada. 2. World War, 1939-1945 – Women. 3. Canada – Emigration and immigration.

Bittersweet memories of whirlwind romances, long separations and adjustments to marriage and a new life in an unfamiliar country. Sixty of the more than forty thousand British and European wives of Canadian servicemen who arrived in Canada between 1945 and 1947 have taped their recollections. Of special interest to other immigrants.

4452 301.42'8

**Schlesinger, Benjamin.**

The One-parent Family: Perspectives and Annotated Bibliography. 4th ed. Toronto: University of Toronto Press, 1978. 224p. Bibliographies and Index. ISBN 0-8020-2335-5 $12.50

1. Single-parent family. 2. Single-parent family – Bibliography.

Third edition listed in *CS* no. 340.

Six essays deal with single-parent families which have resulted from broken marriages, death or unwed mothers. The second section has an annotated list of 750 items published to February, 1978. Like the earlier edition this one is useful for students in the fields of sociology and social work and for concerned general readers. Glenna Stevens.

4453 301.42'84

**Robson, Bonnie.**

My Parents Are Divorced, Too: What Teenagers Experience and How They Cope. Toronto: Dorset Publishing, 1979. 211p. ISBN 0-88893-010-0 pa.: $7.95

1. Children of divorced parents. 2. Divorce.
3. Adolescent psychology.

Twenty-eight teenagers voluntarily conversed with a child psychiatrist about their reactions to custody battles, parental ploys and problems. Brief anecdotes are followed by notes of advice for both children and parents. So, while written for youngsters, this paperback may also give divorcing parents some useful insight. Claire England

4454 301.42'84

**Troyer, Warner.**

Divorced Kids: Victims of Divorce and the Suicide of the Middle Class. Toronto: Clarke, Irwin, 1978. ISBN 0-7720-1222-9 $10.95

1. Children of divorced parents. 2. Broken homes.

An investigative reporter and a twice-divorced father of eight has assembled excerpts from interviews with children of divorced parents and supplemented them with personal commentary and conclusions. Although there is some careless use of language, the book is essentially well-organized and effective and of interest to parents, social workers and older teen-agers. Ille-Mai Gerdels

4455 301.42'86
**Wylie, Betty Jane.**
Beginnings: A Book for Widows. Toronto: McClelland and Stewart, c1977. 144p. Bibliography: p. 137-139. Index. ISBN 0-7710-9057-9 bd.: $7.95 ISBN 0-7710-9058-7 pa.

1. Widows.

Advice for widows written in response to requests following the author's article on how she dealt with her own widowhood, in a 1974 issue of "Maclean's Magazine". In addition to spiritual comfort it provides practical guidance on finances, employment, relationships with friends and children, and household repairs. For all libraries.

## 301.43 Specific age levels

4456 301.43'1
**Ishwaran, K.,** ed.
Childhood and Adolesence in Canada. Toronto: McGraw-Hill Ryerson, c1979. 386p. Bibliographies. (McGraw-Hill Ryerson Interdisciplinary Studies in Family and Marriage) ISBN 0-07-082935-7 pa.: $8.95

1. Children in Canada. 2. Child development – Canada. 3. Youth – Canada.

Of particular interest to people in education, university sociology courses, this text stands alone or complements two other titles, *Canadian Families: Ethnic Variations*, and *Marriage and Divorce in Canada,* in the same series. Nineteen diverse essays discuss research on socialization, social structure, models, media effects for specific groups of native, immigrant/non-immigrant, rural and urban youth. Claire England

4457 301.43'14
**Berkley, Heather,** ed.
Children's Rights: Legal and Educational Issues. Edited by Heather Berkley, Chad Gaffield and W. Gordon West. Toronto: Ontario Institute for Studies in Education, c1978. 177p. Bibliographies. (Symposium Series. The Ontario Institute for Studies in Education) ISBN 0-7744-0169-9 pa.: $7.25

1. Children's rights – Canada. 2. Children's rights – United States. 3. Education of children. 4. Children – Law – Canada.

A series of essays which provide a general overview of children's rights in Canada and the United States, including specific legal issues such as delinquency legislation and the educational issues of children and law. Academic articles, heavily footnoted, written for professionals in the field. Gail Dykstra

4458 301.43'14
**Michelson, William,** ed.
The Child in the City. Edited by William Michelson, Saul Levine and Ellen Michelson. Toronto: University of Toronto Press, 1979. 2v ISBN 0-8020-2134-2 bd.: $17.50 ISBN 0-8020-6337-3 pa.: $7.50

1. City children. 2. Child welfare.

Both volumes constitute an important collection of expert views on the impact of urban living on children. Volume Two deals in greater detail with issues raised in Volume One. Major issues discussed are legal ones affecting children, social and health services, daycare and delinquency. Bob Gardner

4459 301.43'5
**Allentuck, Andrew.**
The Cost of Age. Toronto: Fitzhenry & Whiteside, c1977. 183p. Bibliographical references and Index. (Modern Canadian Living) ISBN 0-88902-404-9 pa.: $5.95

1. Aged – Canada – Economic conditions.
2. Aged – Canada.

A well-written handbook offering solutions to the financial problems of retirement and old age. The author, a Winnipeg economist, discusses the costs of food, housing, insurance, pensions, debt, and medical and nursing care. Bob Gardner

4460 301.43'5
**Hunnisett, Henry S.**
Retirement Guide for Canadians: Planning Makes the Difference. 4th ed. Vancouver: International Self-Counsel Press, 1979. (Self-counsel Series) ISBN 0-88908-057-7 $4.95

1. Retirement – Canada. 2. Retirement income – Canada.

First edition published under title *How to Survive Retirement in Canada.* Listed CS no. 345.

Offers many useful suggestions on planning for retirement. Financial matters are emphasized, with brief discussions of psychological and social aspects. Writing style is chatty and easy to understand. Bob Gardner

## 301.44 Social classes

4461 301.44'42
**Abella, Irving Martin,** ed.
The Canadian Worker in the Twentieth Century. Edited by Irving Martin Abella and David Millar. Toronto: Oxford University Press, 1978. 310p. Bibliography: p. 307-310. ISBN 0-19-540250-2 pa.: $6.95

1. Labor and laboring classes – Canada – History.

Documentary anthology of eyewitness accounts of the daily lives of Canadian workers to 1940. Illuminating chapters on working conditions, the 1908-1916 depression, unions, homelife, and women in the workplace, taken from all over Canada. Excellent supplement to texts on working class history. Bibliographic notes suggest further readings. Nikki Lawrence

4462 301.44'42
**Piva, Michael J.**
The Condition of the Working Class in Toronto, 1900-1921. Ottawa: Ottawa University Press, 1979. 190p. ill. Bibliography: p. 175-183. Index. (Cahiers d'histoire de l'Université d'Ottawa) 2-7603-5009-6 pa.: $9

1. Labor and laboring classes – Ontario – Toronto – History. 2. Toronto, Ont. – Social conditions.

Turn of the century industrial growth in Toronto radically altered the wage rates, housing, health and employment patterns of urban workers. Piva parallels the landmark social history of Montreal recently published by J. T. Copp, *The Anatomy of Poverty* (*CS* no. 352). Barbara Stewart

## 301.45 Minorities

4463 301.45
**Gregorovich, Andrew.**
Ukraine and Ukrainian Canadians: Books for High School, College and Public Libraries. Toronto: Ucrainica Research Institute, 1979. 58p. pa.: $5

1. Ukrainians in Canada.

This annotated bibliography of over three hundred entries lists books, periodicals, maps and AV materials in the English language. With suppliers, addresses and prices it serves as a useful selection tool for librarians and also as a general bibliography. The author is a university librarian and is currently president of the Ukrainian Librarians Association of Canada.

4464 301.45'1
**Elliott, Jean Leonard,** ed.
Two Nations, Many Cultures: Ethnic Groups in Canada. Scarborough, Ont.: Prentice-Hall, 1979. 395p. graphs, map. Bibliographies. ISBN 0-13-935205-8 pa.: $9.95

1. Canada – Population – Ethnic groups.
2. Canada – Emigration and immigration.

Sociologists and anthropologists examine the complex Canadian cultural mosaic within the framework of Canadian nationhood, the survival of which hinges not on the solution to one or any of the Indian, French or European and Third World immigrant crises but on the successful interplay among these minorities and their relationship to main-stream Anglo-Saxon Canada. Frieda Ling

4465 301.45'1
**Kallen, Evelyn.**
Spanning the Generations: A Study in Jewish Identity. Toronto: Longman, c1977. 155p. Bibliography: p. 153-155. Index. (Canadian Social Problems Series) ISBN 0-7747-3036-6 $4.50

1. Jews in Canada – Identity. 2. Jews in Toronto, Ont. – Identity.

A useful study of the nature and expression of Jewish identity in Canada. The distinctive socialization mechanisms of Orthodox, Conservative, and Reform Jews are described to explain varying strengths of commitment to the Jewish identity. Bob Gardner

4466 301.45'1
**Krauter, Joseph F.**
Minority Canadians: Ethnic Groups, by Joseph F. Krauter and Morris Davis. Toronto: Methuen, c1978. 120p. Bibliographical references. (Canadian Sociology) ISBN 0-458-92240-4 pa.: $5.95

1. Canada – Population – Ethnic groups.
2. Canada – Race relations.

Brief, factual information, not easily located elsewhere, about the education, health, populations and employment of Indians, Blacks, Europeans, Métis, Inuit and Asians in Canada. Suitable for both students of sociology and the general reader. Marilyn Carr

4467 301.45'1'04
**Kovacs, Martin Louis.**
Ethnic Canadians: Culture and Education. Regina: Canadian Plains Research Center, University of Regina, 1978. 495p. Bibliographical references. (Canadian Plains Studies) ISBN 0-88977-009-3 $12

1. Ethnicity. 2. Minorities – Education – Canada. 3. Ethnology – Canada.

An extensive examination of Canadian multiculturalism, with a focus on the impact of the Canadian educational system on the expression of ethnicity. Articles were based on papers presented at a conference at the University of Regina in October 1976. A useful reference tool. Bob Gardner

4468 301.45'11
**Maxwell, Thomas R.**
The Invisible French: The French in Metropolitan Toronto. Waterloo, Ont.: Wilfrid Laurier University Press, c1977. 174p. graphs, maps. Bibliography: p. 169-174. ISBN 0-88920-029-7 bd.: $6.50
ISBN 0-88920-028-9 pa.: $4

1. Canadians, French-speaking – Ontario – Toronto metropolitan area. 2. French in Metropolitan Toronto, Ont.

Professor Maxwell has updated his study, prepared for the bilingual commission in 1965, and finds little improvement in the situation of the Toronto French-speaking community. The population is scattered and tends to speak little French in the home. Since the 1976 election its relationship with the English-speaking community has tended to cool.

4469 301.45'13
**Ishwaran, K.**
Family, Kinship and Community: A Study of Dutch Canadians, A Developmental Approach. Toronto: McGraw-Hill Ryerson, 1977. 181p. Bibliographical references. (Interdisciplinary Studies in Family and Marriage) ISBN 0-07-082552-1 $6.50

1. Dutch in Holland Marsh, Ont. 2. Holland Marsh, Ont. – Social conditions.

Students, researchers interested in integration of ethnic communities in Canadian life may find the methods and data of this social anthropologist rewarding. Intermittently, from 1961-1971, Ishwaran studied the structure and Calvinist values of an economically successful and socially well-knit Dutch community in Holland Marsh, north of Toronto. Claire England

4470 301.45'19
**Herman, Harry Vjekoslav.**
Men in White Aprons: A Study of Ethnicity and Occupation. Toronto: Peter Martin, 1978. 88p. map. Bibliography: p. 84-88. (Canadian Experience Series) ISBN 0-88778-178-0 pa.: $3.95

1. Macedonians in Toronto, Ont. 2. Restaurateurs – Ontario – Toronto.

Case studies are used to analyse Macedonian immigrants in Toronto, their history, economic conditions and family ties. Useful because of the dearth of comparable studies of ethnic minorities. Students in the social sciences and general readers. Marilyn Carr

4471 301.45'19
**Paine, Robert,** ed.
The White Arctic: Anthropological Essays on Tutelage and Ethnicity. St. John's, Nfld.: Institute of Social and Economic Research, Memorial University of Newfoundland, c1977. 418p. ill., maps, plans. Bibliographies. (Newfoundland Social and Economic Papers) ISBN 0-919666-14-0 $12

1. Eskimos – Northwest Territories. 2. Eskimos – Labrador. 3. Eskimos – Northwest Territories – Government relations. 4. Eskimos – Labrador – Government relations. 5. Northwest Territories – Race relations. 6. Labrador – Race relations.

Contrary to popular belief, anthropological research reveals that strained White-Inuit relations arise not from Indian inability to assimilate white culture but from the white man's failure to understand and change his misguided attitudes and behaviour towards the native peoples. A thorough self-examination and learning process by the "colonizers" is urged as the means of improvement. Frieda Ling.

4472 301.45'19
**Ward, William Peter.**
White Canada Forever: Popular Attitudes and Public Policy Towards Orientals in British Columbia. Montreal: McGill-Queen's University Press, c1978. 205p. ill. Bibliographical references and Index.
ISBN 0-7735-0318-8 bd.: $15
ISBN 0-7735-0319-6 pa.: $6.50

1. Chinese in British Columbia. 2. Japanese in British Columbia. 3. East Indians in British Columbia. 4. British Columbia – Race relations.

Drawing upon primary sources, a historian at the University of British Columbia examines factors underlying the racial hostility toward Asians during the period from 1850 to 1950. Emphasis is upon the attitudes and policies prevalent on the Pacific coast during the second World War. Of interest to both scholars and general readers.

## 301.5 Sociology of everyday activities

4473 301.5
**Haworth, Lawrence.**
Decadence and Objectivity. Toronto: University of Toronto Press, c1977. 169p. Bibliographical references and Index. ISBN 0-8020-5387-4 $12.50

1. Social values. 2. Social ethics.

A discussion, not specific to Canada, of leisure, and the professionalized society, the problems of modern life, and the changes that would enhance it. The author's views are worth the attention of sociology students. Documentation is scanty. Marilyn Carr

## 301.54 Housing sociology

4474 301.5'4
**Michelson, William M.**
Environmental Choice, Human Behaviour, and Residential Satisfaction. New York: Oxford University Press, 1977. 403p. ill. Bibliography: p. 379-398. Index. ISBN 0-19502-145-2 pa.: $7.50

1. Housing – Canada. 2. Residential mobility – Canada.

This work is the outcome of a research study, sponsored by the Central Mortgage and Housing Corporation, which examined high-rise and single-family housing in Toronto. The text has many tables and illustrations, an index and a lengthy bibliography. The subject has wide appeal but the academic style will make it of more interest to those with a background in sociology, geography, and urban planning. Margot Hewings

## 301.58 Religious sociology

4475 301.5'8
**Smucker, Donovan E.,** ed.
The Sociology of Canadian Mennonites, Hutterites and Amish: A Bibliography with Annotations. Waterloo, Ont.: Wilfrid Laurier University Press, c1977. 232p. Index. ISBN 0-88920-052-1 bd.: $7.50 ISBN 0-88920-051-3 pa.: $4.50

1. Mennonites in Canada – Bibliography. 2. Hutterite Brethren – Canada – Bibliography. 3. Amish in Canada – Bibliography.

A comprehensive, annotated bibliography of some eight hundred English language books, pamphlets, articles, theses, and unpublished manuscripts "on the recent social and cultural life of the Mennonites, Hutterites and Amish." Publication dates range from the 1930's to 1976. An important research resource for the social sciences.

## 301.59 Political socialization

4476 301.5'92
**O'Toole, Roger.**
The Precipitous Path: Studies in Political Sects. Toronto: Peter Martin, 1977. 119p. Bibliography: p. 98-119. (Canadian Experience Series) ISBN 0-88778-151-9 pa.: $3.95

1. League for Socialist Action. 2. Socialist Labor Party of Canada. 3. Political sociology. 4. Internationalists.

A well-written sociological study of three left-wing political movements in Canada: the League for Socialist Action, the Internationalists, and the Socialist Labour Party. Based on data gathered in 1968-69 through participant-observation. Includes a useful bibliography. Bob Gardner

## 301.6 Social conflict

4477 301.6'2
**Hagan, John.**
The Disreputable Pleasures: Crime and Deviance in Canada. Toronto: McGraw-Hill Ryerson, 1977. 254p. ill. Bibliography: p. 225-249. Index. (McGraw-Hill Ryerson Series in Canadian Sociology) ISBN 0-07-082447-9 pa.: $5.95

1. Deviant behavior. 2. Crime and criminals – Canada. 3. Social control.

An exceptionally well-written textbook examining theories of criminal and deviant behaviour. A very good introduction to the topic. Well illustrated with charts, and includes an extensive bibliography. Bob Gardner

4478 301.6'33
**Gammon, Mary Alice Beyer,** ed.
Violence in Canada. Toronto: Methuen, 1978. 286p. graphs. Bibliographies and Index. (Canadian Sociology) ISBN 0-458-93170-5 pa.: $10.95
1. Violence – Canada.
Articles contributed by experts, some reprinted from other sources, include aspects such as violence in the home and violence and the media. It is useful for a wider audience than the academic one for which it was designed. Marilyn Carr

4479 301.6'36
**Morris, Raymond N.**
Three Scales of Inequality: Perspectives on French-English Relations, by Raymond N. Morris and C. Michael Lanphier. Don Mills, Ont.: Longman, 1977. 300p. graphs. Bibliography: p. 283-300. Index. (Canadian Social Problems Series) ISBN 0-7747-3035-8 pa.: $4.95
1. Canada – English-French relations.
2. Canada – English-French relations – History.
A well-presented sociological study of minority rights in Canada with a particular focus on English-French relations. Covers from pre-Confederation to the present. Various solutions to the present English-French dilemma are discussed in detail. Includes an extensive bibliography. Bob Gardner

## 307 Community planning

4480 307.7'6
**Artibise, Alan F.,** ed.
The Usable Urban Past: Planning and Politics in the Modern Canadian City. Edited by Alan F. Artibise and Gilbert Al Stelter. Toronto: Macmillan; Ottawa: Institute of Canadian Studies, Carleton University, 1979. Bibliography. (The Carleton Library) ISBN 0-7705-1793-5 pa.: $10.95
1. Cities and towns – Canada. 2. Municipal government – Canada. 3. City planning – Canada.
"A collection of original essays which represents some of the innovative historical research being done in modern Canadian urban development." -Publisher's note. Editors provide an introductory setting for each essay, a useful guide to sources of information and a selected bibliography. The book will interest readers of history, geography, political science and urban planning. Margot Hewings

## 309 Social conditions

4481 309.171
**Canada. Statistics Canada. Office of the Senior Advisor on Integration.**
Perspective Canada II: A Compendium of Social Statistics, 1977. Prepared in the Office of the Senior Advisor on Integration, Statistics Canada. Ottawa: Statistics Canada, 1977. 335p. maps. Bibliography: p. 323-327. Index. pa.: $9.25 (Canada); $11 (foreign) DSS cat. no. CS 11-508E
Besides updating the first edition (*CS* no. 447), this companion volume adds much new material, such as statistics on older Canadians and leisure, and urban profiles of Montreal, Toronto and Vancouver. Although useful for the social scientist and marketer, it is designed primarily to meet the statistical needs of the non-specialist. Volume III expected in 1980.

4482 309.1'71
**Crysdale, Stewart.**
Sociology Canada: An Introductory Text, by Stewart Crysdale and Christopher Beattie. 2d ed. Toronto: Butterworth, c1977. 487p. ill., graphs. Bibliography: p. 435-471. Indexes. ISBN 0-409-82416-X pa.
1. Canada – Social conditions.
First edition listed *CS* no. 419. Complements *Sociology Canada: Readings*, 2d ed., edited by C. Beattie and S. Crysdale. -Canadiana.
This second edition clarifies, extends and updates the first edition by the addition of a new chapter.

4483 309.1'71
**Glenday, Daniel,** ed.
Modernization and the Canadian State. Edited by Daniel Glenday, Hubert Guindon and Allan Turowetz. Toronto: Macmillan, c1978. 456p. diagrs., graph, map. Bibliographical references. ISBN 0-7705-1626-2 pa.: $7.95
1. Canada – Social conditions – 1965-
2. Canada – Economic conditions – 1965-
This authoritative collection covers topics such as regionalism, the community, modernization and the urban poor. The notes and bibliographies at the end of each article are useful for university students. Marilyn Carr

4484 309.1'71

**Godfrey, Dave.**

Gutenberg 2: The New Electronics and Social Change. Victoria: Press Porcépic, 1979. ISBN 0-88878-171-7 $14.95

1. Mass media – Social aspects – Canada. 2. Data transmission systems. 3. Canada – Social conditions – 1965-

A good introduction to existing computer and communications technologies, with a particular focus on the economic, social, and political impacts of these technologies. Concentrates on technological innovations, and includes a useful glossary of media terms. Bob Gardner

4485 309.1'71

**Haas, Jack,** comp.

Shaping Identity in Canadian Society, compiled by Jack Haas and William Shaffir. Scarborough, Ont.: Prentice-Hall, 1978. 340p. Bibliography: p. 335-340. ISBN 0-13-808204-9 pa.: $9.95

1. Canada – Social conditions.

Canadian social and cultural conditions are subjected to a vigorous sociological analysis, from a symbolic interactionist perspective. Recommended as an introductory textbook. Includes extensive bibliographical references. Bob Gardner

4486 309.1'71

**Marsden, Lorna R.**

Fragile Federation: Social Change in Canada, by Lorna R. Marsden and Edward B. Harvey. Toronto: McGraw-Hill Ryerson, c1979. 242p. Bibliography: p. 228-235. Index. ISBN 0-07-082325-1 pa.: $7.95

1. Social change. 2. Canada – Social conditions.

Designed as a textbook, it applies sociological theories of social change to specific regional, demographic and cultural forces affecting change in Canada. Sometimes heavy going with jargon, it provides a useful discussion. Includes an extensive bibliography. Bob Gardner

4487 309.1'71

**McCready, Gerald B.**

Profile Canada: Social and Economic Projections. Georgetown, Ont.: Irwin-Dorsey, 1977. 413p. graphs. Bibliography: p. 375-395. Index. ISBN 0-256-01982-7 bd.: $12.95 ISBN 0-256-01703-4 pa.: $7.95

1. Social prediction. 2. Economic forecasting – Canada. 3. Canada – Social conditions – 1965- 4. Canada – Economic conditions – 1965-

A useful and interesting reference source on Canada's economic and social future, presenting the author's personal judgments on a variety of topics. Political and constitutional matters are not discussed. Bob Gardner

4488 309.17'14

**Québec (Province). Ministère d'État au Développement Culturel.**

A Cultural Develpment Policy for Quebec. Quebec: Editeur Officiel, 1978. 2v ill. Bibliographies. ISBN 0-77543-224-5 $2

1. Quebec (Province) – Social conditions. 2. Quebec (Province) – Social policy.

Contents: vol. 1. A General View: The Culture Under Consideration. vol. 2. The Three Aspects of the Policy: Ways of Life, Creative Activity, Education.

A comprehensive statement of the Quebec government's cultural policies, arguing the position of cultural sovereignty for the province of Quebec. The cultural history of Quebec is described in detail, and suggests proposals for future cultural development. Bob Gardner

4489 309.2'12

**Yelaja, Shankar A.,** ed.

Canadian Social Policy. Waterloo, Ont.: Wilfrid Laurier University Press, 1978. 321p. Bibliographies and Index. ISBN 0-88920-049-1 bd.: $9 ISBN 0-88920-050-5 pa.: $6

1. Canada – Social policy.

A collection of sixteen papers on topics such as housing, women, native people, and the government, all centre on social welfare. Contributing authors are all known in the field and the scholarly but readable style would make this a useful addition to academic sociology collections. Marilyn Carr

4490 309.2'6

**Roberts, Hayden.**

Community Development: Learning and Action. Toronto: University of Toronto Press, c1979. 201p. Bibliography: p. 189-197. Index. ISBN 0-8020-5437-4 bd.: $15 ISBN 0-8020-6351-9 pa.: $6.50

1. Underdeveloped areas. 2. Community development. 3. Adult education.

A general political analysis of community development planning in Canada and underdeveloped countries. Various theoretical models of development are presented, and a good bibliography is included. Bob Gardner

4491 309.2'62

**Lorimer, James,** ed.

The Second City Book: Studies of Urban and Suburban Canada. Edited by James Lorimer and Evelyn Ross. Toronto: James Lorimer, 1977. 180p. ill., maps. Index. ISBN 0-88862-141-8 bd.: $12 ISBN 0-88862-140-X pa.: $6.95

1. Cities and towns – Canada. 2. Cities and towns – Planning – Canada.

A sequel to *The City Book* listed *CS* no. 1842.

Another collection of case studies based upon articles which have been published in "City Magazine", illustrates some of the major issues in urban development in Canada. Arranged in four sections, the fourteen pieces analyze problems in land development, planning and demolition. Useful for the critical viewpoints on urban politics. Public and college libraries.

4492 309.2'62

**Russwurm, Lorne H.**

The Surroundings of Our Cities: Problems and Planning Implications of Urban Fringe Landscapes. Ottawa: Community Planning Press, 1977. 112p. ill. Bibliography: p. 101-112. pa.: $6

1. Cities and towns – Planning – Canada. 2. Land – Canada.

Problems relating to the use and management of land surrounding Canadian cities are examined in this well-written text. A good bibliography provides access to information on this little-researched topic. Bob Gardner

## 310 Statistics

4493 317.1

**Canada Handbook: The 48th Annual Handbook of Present Conditions and Recent Progress.**

Ottawa: Statistics Canada, 1979. 344p. ill. CS11-203/1979 ISBN 0-660-10203-X $6

46th edition listed in *CS* no. 451.

Metric measurements have been introduced where relevant. In future *Canada Handbook* will be published biennially rather than annually. An inexpensive, information-filled reference tool for all libraries.

4494 317.1

**Canada Year Book 1978-79: An Annual Review of Economic, Social and Political Development in Canada.**

Ottawa: Statistics Canada, 1978. 977p. tables. CS11-2-2-1978 $15

1. Canada – Statistics. 2. Canada – Economic conditions.

The 1975 edition is listed in *CS* no. 450.

Some chapters, such as those on health, education and energy have been completely revised. A useful feature is the inclusion, in an appendix, of a list of special articles published in previous editions. In the future *Canada Year Book* will be issued every two years instead of annually.

## 320 Political science

4495 320.

**Kontos, Alkis,** ed.

Powers, Possessions, and Freedom: Essays in Honour of C. B. Macpherson. Toronto: University of Toronto Press, 1979. 178p. Bibliography. ISBN 0-8020-5474-9 $20

1. Political science.

These essays in honour of the University of Toronto's world-renowned political theorist, were contributed by his fellow scholars from universities such as Oxford and Harvard. All relate to Macpherson's fields of interest, but primarily to reform of liberal-democratic theory. Included is a bibliography of his own publications to 1979. For the serious scholar.

4496 320.5'315

**McCormack, Andrew Ross.**

Reformers, Rebels, and Revolutionaries: The Western Canadian Radical Movement, 1899-1919. Toronto: University of Toronto Press, c1977. 228p. plates, ports. Bibliography: p. 211-220. Index. ISBN 0-8020-5385-8 bd.: $15 ISBN 0-8020-6313-6 pa.: $4.95

1. Socialism in Canada – History. 2. Radicalism – Canada – History. 3. Trade-unions – Canada – Political activity – History.

Comprehensive examination of radicalism focusing on the labour movement in the Prairies up to the time of the Winnipeg General Strike. Based on the analysis of three major groups within it: the moderate unionists, militant unionists, and the revolutionary Marxists. Portraits of the major leaders are included. Nikki Lawrence

4497 320.5'4
**Arnaud, Nicole.**
Nationalism and the National Question, by Nicole Arnaud and Jacques Dofny. Translated by Penelope Williams. Montreal: Black Rose Books, 1978. 133p. map. ISBN 0-919618-46-4 bd.: $12.95 ISBN 0-919618-45-6 pa.: $5.95

1. Nationalism – France, Southern. 2. Nationalism – Quebec (Province). 3. Occitan movement. 4. Quebec (Province) – History – Autonomy and independence movements.

An interesting analysis of the alliance between nationalist and socialist movements in Quebec and Occitan, a linguistic region of France. The work is arranged in the form of a dialogue between the two authors, sociologists teaching in the regions, and although somewhat rambling, a fresh, less parochial approach to our problem emerges. Nikki Lawrence

4498 320.5'4
**Cook, Ramsay.**
The Maple Leaf Forever: Essays on Nationalism and Politics in Canada. New ed. Toronto: Macmillan, 1977. 245p. Bibliographical references and Index. (Laurentian Library) ISBN 0-7705-1600-9 pa.: $4.95

1. Nationalism – Canada. 2. Nationalism – Quebec (Province). 3. Quebec (Province) – History – Autonomy and independence movements.

First edition listed *CS* no. 462.

This revision incorporates additional essays updating the work to the 1976 Quebec election of Lévesque and the Parti québecois. The thesis that Canada's problem is too much 'nationalism', with its tendency to produce a desire for homogeneity, is worked through the essays and the product is a thought-provoking classic of Canadian politics. Nikki Lawrence

4499 320.5'4
**Heron, Craig,** ed.
Imperialism, Nationalism and Canada: Essays From the Marxist Institute of Toronto. Introduction by John Saul and Craig Heron. Toronto: New Hogtown Press; Kitchener, Ont.: Between the Lines, c1977. 206p. graphs. Bibliographical references.
ISBN 0-919940-05-6 bd.: $13
ISBN 0-919940-06-4 pa.: $5.95

1. Nationalism – Canada. 2. Socialism in Canada. 3. Canada – Economic conditions – 1965-

The record of a series of lectures in the fall of 1974 on Canadian nationalism from the Marxist point of view. Of interest chiefly to the academic audience.

4500 320.9'71
**Bell, David V. J.**
The Roots of Disunity: A Study of Canadian Political Culture, by David V. J. Bell and Lorne Tepperman. Toronto: McClelland and Stewart, 1979. Bibliography. Index. (Canada in Transition Series)
ISBN 0-7710-1198-9 bd.: $16.95
ISBN 0-7710-1196-2 pa.: $8.95

1. Biculturalism – Canada. 2. Regionalism – Canada. 3. Canada – Politics and government.

Two English Canadian university professors postulate that the fragmentation of our country is rooted in the divergent cultural values of the founding provinces while trying to place Confederation and our subsequent evolution in historical perspective. Nikki Lawrence

4501 320.9'71
**Brown, Brian A.**
The New Confederation. Saanichton, B.C.: Hancock House, c1977. 158p. maps, ports. Index. ISBN 0-88839-001-7 $7.95

1. Federal government – Canada. 2. Canada – Politics and government – 1963-

The author promotes his idea of a federal/provincial structure based on five provinces in a "sovereignty association", a concept proposed earlier by W. A. C. Bennett. A United Church clergyman who broadcasts regularly on radio's "Challenge Canada", he credits grassroots discussion with citizens of Dawson Creek for clarifying his views. There is no evidence of scholarly research to support his position.

4502 320.9'71
**Butler, Rick,** ed.
The Trudeau Decade. Edited by Rick Butler and Jean-Guy Carrier. Toronto: Doubleday, 1979. 398p. plates, ports. Bibliography: p. 393. Index. ISBN 0-385-14806-2 bd.: $16.95
ISBN 0-385-15543-3 pa.: $9.95

1. Trudeau, Pierre Elliott, 1919- 2. Canada – Politics and government – 1968-

A well-chosen collection of articles on Prime Minister Trudeau's performance from 1968 to 1978, culled from a wide range of newspapers, including "Pravda", and a few journals. With the help of added background information, it traces the ebb and flow of public favour in Canada, Quebec and the world.

4503 320.9'71
**Campbell, Colin.**
Canadian Political Facts, 1945-1976. Toronto: Methuen, 1977. 151p. (Canadian Politics and Government) ISBN 0-458-92660-4 bd. ISBN 0-458-92430-X pa.: $5.50

1. Canada – Politics and government – 1935- – Handbooks, manuals, etc.

An interesting and useful package of political information of all kinds: executive, parliament, elections, political parties and pressure groups, judiciary, the provinces and federal-provincial relations; Canadian economy; population and language. No index, but the detailed listing of contents is helpful.

4504 320.9'71
**Canada. Task Force on Canadian Unity.**
A Future Together: Observations and Recommendations. Ottawa: Task Force on Canadian Unity, 1979. 152p.
ISBN 0-660-10154-8 pa.: $3.50 (Canada); $4.20 (Foreign) DSS cat. no. CP32-35/1979

1. Canada – Politics and government.

The first of the publications of the Pepin-Robarts Task Force, it examines the diverse governmental structures in Canada; what the governments do; how they are constituted and controlled. Includes a synopsis of evidence presented at public hearings. The second and third publications of the series are: *Coming to Terms: The Words of the Debate*, 1979; and *A Time to Speak: The Views of the Public*, 1979. Caroline Christie

4505 320.9'71
**Chandler, Marsha A.**
Public Policy and Provincial Politics, by Marsha A. Chandler and William M. Chandler. Toronto: McGraw-Hill Ryerson, c1979. Bibliography. Index. (McGraw-Hill Ryerson Series in Canadian Politics)
ISBN 0-07-082637-4 pa.: $6.95

1. Provincial governments – Canada.
2. Policy sciences.

Although intended as a university text this comparative approach to the development of provincial institutions and the design of their social and resource policies fills a vacuum in the analysis of the facets of government closest to us. An excellent bibliography and extensive notes. Nikki Lawrence

4506 320.9'71
**Crispo, John H. G.**
Mandate for Canada. Don Mills, Ont.: General Publishing, 1979. 144p. Index.
ISBN 0-7736-1051-0 pa.: $6.95

1. Canada – Politics and government – 1968-
2. Canada – Economic conditions – 1971-

An ambitious attempt at defining and solving Canada's major social, political, and economic problems. Contains some useful and often controversial ideas, and would be useful as supplementary reading. Bob Gardner

4507 320.9'71
**Hockin, Thomas A.,** ed.
Apex of Power: The Prime Minister and Political Leadership in Canada. 2d ed. Scarborough, Ont.: Prentice-Hall, 1977. 356p. Bibliographical references.
ISBN 0-13-038661-8 bd.: $9.95
ISBN 0-13-038653-7 pa.: $6.95

1. Prime ministers – Canada. 2. Canada – Politics and government – 1935-

First edition listed in *CS* no. 485.

This second edition adds nine new selections and revises and updates seven of the essays in the original landmark work. Outstanding among the new articles are Frederick Fletcher's "The Prime Minister as Public Persuader" and Gerald Lenoski's "Ministers' Staffs and Leadership Politics". For this timely topic, the extent of revision points to purchase by all but very small libraries.

4508 320.9'71
**Hodgins, Bruce W.,** ed.
Federalism in Canada and Australia: The Early Years. Edited by Bruce W. Hodgins, Don Wright and W. H. Heick. Waterloo, Ont.: Wilfrid Laurier University Press, c1978. 318p. maps. Bibliographical references and Index. ISBN 0-88920-061-0 $9

1. Federal government – Canada – History.
2. Federal government – Australia – History.
3. Canada – Politics and government.
4. Australia – Politics and government.

Canada and Australia are treated separately in these seventeen essays on the political structures of federal systems. Comparison emerges mainly in the introduction and conclusion. For large libraries.

4509 320.9'71
**Jenson, Jane.**
Canadian Politics: An Introduction to Systematic Analysis, by Jane Jenson and Brian W. Tomlin. Toronto: McGraw-Hill Ryerson, 1977. 168p. graphs. Bibliographical references and Index. (McGraw-Hill Ryerson Series in Canadian Politics)
ISBN 0-07-082456-8 pa.: $6.95

1. Political science – Methodology.
2. Canada – Politics and government.

A textbook for undergraduates prepared by two Carleton University professors uses a new approach to the study of politics. It provides elementary skills in political analysis as well as fact about political institutions.

4510 320.9'71
**Laxer, James.**
The Liberal Idea of Canada: Pierre Trudeau and the Question of Canada's Survival, by James Laxer and Robert Laxer. Foreword by George Grant. Toronto: James Lorimer, 1977. 234p. Bibliographical references.
ISBN 0-88862-123-X bd.: $15
ISBN 0-88862-124-8 pa.: $6.95

1. Trudeau, Pierre Elliott, 1919- 2. Liberal Party (Canada). 3. Nationalism – Quebec (Province). 4. Canada – Politics and government – 1963-

An important though depressing assessment of Canadian public policy in the past few decades. It suggests that Canada's present economic and constitutional crisis stems from Liberal ideology and policies. Whether or not one agrees completely with the Laxers' leftist interpretation, their ideas deserve wide attention.

4511 320.9'71
**McClellan, Grant S.,** ed.
Canada in Transition. New York: H. W. Wilson, 1977. 224p. map. Bibliography: p. 216-224. (The Reference Shelf)
ISBN 0-8242-0603-7.

1. Canada – Politics and government – 1963- 2. Canada – Economic conditions – 1965- 3. Canada – Foreign relations – 1945- 4. Quebec (Province) – History – Autonomy and independence movements.

Articles on Canadian economic, social and political affairs, many by Canadian scholars, which have appeared in American journals such as "Foreign Affairs" and "Atlantic". Designed for an American audience and stresses Canadian action independent of Great Britain or the United States. Has a useful bibliography.

4512 320.9'71
**McWhinney, Edward.**
Quebec and the Constitution, 1960-1978. Toronto: University of Toronto Press, c1979. 170p. Bibliographical references and Index.
ISBN 0-8020-5456-0 bd.: $15
ISBN 0-8020-6364-0 pa.: $5.95

1. Canada – Constitutional history.
2. Quebec (Province) – History – Autonomy and independence movements. 3. Quebec (Province) – Politics and government – 1960-1976.

The federal government, the constitution and Quebec are a popular triangle. This book examines the position, papers, legislation and politics of all three from 1960 to 1978. Written primarily for college students it is also useful for those with a serious interest in the question because it covers all relevant aspects, legal, social and political. Gail Dykstra.

4513 320.9'71
**Panitch, Leo,** ed.
The Canadian State: Political Economy and Political Power. Toronto: University of Toronto Press, c1977. 475p. Bibliographical references. ISBN 0-8020-2285-5 bd.: $25
ISBN 0-8020-6322-5 pa.: $7.50

1. Socialism in Canada. 2. Canada – Politics and government. 3. Canada – Economic policy.

A stimulating collection of writing on Canadian government and economics from the pens of Marxist scholars with differing points of view. Some of the conclusions may be extreme, but most of the arguments are based on historical fact. The book is "must" reading for anyone with a serious interest in Canadian political economy at the academic level.

4514 320.9'71
**Redekop, John H.,** ed.
Approaches to Canadian Politics. Scarborough, Ont.: Prentice-Hall, c1978. 377p. Bibliographies and Indexes.
ISBN 0-13-043729-8 pa.: $9.95

1. Canada – Politics and government.

These sixteen original essays, mostly by Canadian university professors, will stimulate the interest of beginning university students in the Canadian political system. It is unique in that it evaluates many approaches to studying the system.

4515 320.9'71
**Resnick, Philip.**
The Land of Cain: Class and Nationalism in English Canada 1945-1975. Vancouver: New Star Books, c1977. 297p. ill. Bibliography: p. 278-287. Index. ISBN 0-91988-867-4 bd.: $13.95 ISBN 0-91988-868-2 pa.: $6.50

1. Nationalism – Canada. 2. Social classes – Canada. 3. Canada – History – 1945- 4. Canada – Economic conditions – 1945- 5. Canada – Relations (general) with the United States. 6. United States – Relations (general) with Canada.

Based on the Ph.D. thesis of a professor at the University of British Columbia, this is a study of contemporary English-Canadian nationalism interesting for its analytical approach. Extensive appendices, notes and bibliography indicate its appropriateness to an academic audience.

4516 320.9'71
**Simeon, Richard E. B.,** ed.
Must Canada Fail? Montreal: McGill-Queen's University Press, 1977. 307p. ISBN 0-7735-0314-5 bd.: $13 ISBN 0-7735-0313-7 pa.: $5.95

1. Nationalism – Quebec (Province). 2. Canada – Politics and government – 1963- 3. Quebec (Province) – History – Autonomy and independence movements.

Twenty lucid essays, mostly by Queen's University political scientists, examine the national unity problem and especially the implications of the election of the Parti québecois in 1976, from the English-Canadian perspective. Designed for the general public and for students of public affairs.

4517 320.9'71
**Skidmore, Darrel R.**
You, and Your Government. Consulting authors Howard A. Doughty and Iain R. Munro. Rexdale, Ont.: John Wiley, 1978. 96p. ill. Index. (Canada, Origins and Options) ISBN 0-471-99766-8 pa.: $3.95

1. Canada – Politics and government.

An easy-to-read, lucid explanation of the organization, structure and function of the Canadian federal government system and some of the major issues which confront it. There is a glossary, and a summary following each chapter. Illustrated with political cartoons, graphs, charts, newspaper articles. Introductory level material for junior high up.

4518 320.9'71
**Watkins, Clem,** Jr.
Letters from Lilac, 1965-1973. Edited and selected by George Bain. Toronto: Macmillan, c1978. 187p. ill. ISBN 0-7705-1725-0 $10.95

1. Canada – Politics and government – 1963-

A collection of letters which appeared in the 'Globe and Mail' from 1965 to 1973 in which Clem Watkins of Lilac, Saskatchewan reports on local and national issues to his friend, George Bain, then Ottawa correspondent of the 'Globe and Mail'. Delightful political satire with cartoonist Duncan Macpherson's portraits of Lilac's leading citizens adding to the fun.

4519 320.9'71'064
**Swainson, Neil A.**
Conflict over the Columbia: The Canadian Background to an Historic Treaty. Toronto: Institute of Public Administration; Montreal: McGill-Queen's University Press, c1979. 476p. ill. Bibliography: p. 429-446. Index. (Canadian Public Administration Series) ISBN 0-7735-0325-0 bd.: $22 ISBN 0-7735-0326-9 pa.: $9.95

1. Columbia River Treaty, 1964. 2. Water resources development – Columbia River Valley. 3. Federal-provincial relations (Canada) – British Columbia. 4. Canada – Foreign relations – United States. 5. United States – Foreign relations – Canada.

This authoritative work analyses the twenty-year process of hammering out policy for the development of the Columbia River by the governments of the United States, Canada and British Columbia. It is of value not only for the content, but also as a case study of Canadian government decision-making. For the advanced scholar.

4520 320.9'711
**Persky, Stan.**
Son of Socred: Has Bill Bennett's Government Gotten B.C. Moving Again? Vancouver: New Star Books, 1979. 319p. Bibliography. ISBN 0-919888-90-9 bd.: $11.95 ISBN 0-919888-89-5 pa.: $2.95

1. Social Credit Party (British Columbia). 2. British Columbia – Politics and government – 1952-

A popular account of current British Columbia politics which deserves readership beyond the province despite its weakness in analysis. It not only records the failures of the Social Credit government but also points out the weaknesses of the New Democratic Party.

4521 320.9'712
**Thomas, Lewis H.**
The Struggle for Responsible Government in the North-West Territories, 1870-97. 2d ed. Toronto: University of Toronto Press, c1978. 304p. maps. Index. ISBN 0-8020-2287-1 bd.: $20 ISBN 0-8020-6327-6 pa.: $6.50

1. The West, Canadian – Politics and government – 19th century.

A chronological approach to constitutional history of the North West Territories recently expanded to include the years 1897 to 1970. Federal policies and their effects dominate the work but the increasing trend towards responsible government through the Executive Council is charted. This dry but useful reference work fills a vacuum in the record of our history. Nikki Lawrence

4522 320.9'7123
**Caldarola, Carlo,** ed.
Society and Politics in Alberta: Research Papers. Agincourt, Ont.: Methuen, c1979. 392p. Bibliographical references.

1. Alberta – Politics and government – 1905- 2. Alberta – Social conditions.

In a series of scholarly, carefully documented papers the interaction between politics and society in Alberta from 1905 to the present, is examined. Representative of recent research by political scientists, historians and sociologists, the book provides a useful synthesis of the factors which have shaped politics and society in the province. University and larger public libraries.

4523 320.9'7123
**Thomas, Lewis H.,** ed.
William Aberhart and Social Credit in Alberta. Toronto: Copp Clark, 1977. 175p. Bibliography: p. 173-174. (Issues in Canadian History) ISBN 0-7730-3128-6 pa.: $5.95

1. Aberhart, William, 1878-1943. 2. Social Credit Party. 3. Alberta – Politics and government – 1935- – Sources.

Although it includes little that is new, this collection of documents is of value to the non-specialist: selections from government publications, Alberta Premiers' papers, newspaper accounts and transcripts of Aberhart's radio broadcasts. The emphasis is on Aberhart's role as a humanitarian and social reformer.

4524 320.9'714
**Craig, Richard G.**
Two Nations: Problems and Prospects: Understanding Canada's Constitutional Crisis, by Richard G. Craig and Randy J. Noonan. Vancouver: New Star Books, 1979. Bibliography. ISBN 0-919888-94-1 bd.: $14.95 ISBN 0-919888-93-3 pa.: $5.95

1. Federal-provincial relations (Canada) – Quebec (Province). 2. Federal government – Canada. 3. Quebec (Province) – History – Autonomy and independence movements. 4. Quebec (Province) – Politics and government – 1960-1976. 5. Quebec (Province) – Politics and government – 1976-

Designed for high school students, yet useful for the general public, the authors examine the historical, legal and political perspectives on Canada's current constitutional debate. Illustrated, well written, offering numerous examples of newspaper and periodical commentary from 1867 to date, the problems and potential alternatives are fully examined. A teacher's guide is also available from the publishers. Gail Dykstra

4525 320.9'714
**Lévesque, René.**
My Québec. Toronto: Methuen, c1979. 191p. maps. ISBN 0-458-93980-3 $9.95

1. Parti québecois. 2. Quebec (Province) – Politics and government – 1960- 3. Quebec (Province) – History – Autonomy and independence movements.

Translation of *La Passion du Québec.*

Lévesque gives a personal account of his political development and that of the Parti québecois, discussing his beliefs within the context of sovereignty association for Quebec, and the referendum. The first five sections are presented as an interview with Jean-Robert Leselbaun. Although it adds little that is new the book provides an interesting view of Lévesque's position after two years in office. Caroline Christie

4526 320.9'714
**Milner, Henry.**
Politics in the New Quebec. Toronto: McClelland and Stewart, c1978. 257p. Bibliography: p. 254-257. ISBN 0-7710-6060-2 pa.: $6.95

1. Quebec (Province) – Politics and government – 1960-

From within a Marxist theoretical framework the author examines the political parties, the labour movement, and the Left in Quebec today. The section dealing with practical considerations is fairly clear; the theoretical analysis sometimes obscure. Caroline Christie

4527 320.9'714'04

**Ryan, Claude.**

A Stable Society. Edited and translated by Robert Guy Scully with Marc Plourde. Montreal: Editions Héritage, 1978. 398p. ISBN 0-7773-3816-5 pa.: $10.95

1. Quebec (Province) – Politics and government – 1960- 2. Quebec (Province) – Social conditions.

Translation of *Une Société Stable.*

Claude Ryan's aspirations for Quebec society are ably reflected in his addresses and articles written during the last fifteen years. Not limited to political views, the pieces encompass a range of issues crucial in the seventies: labour, education, language, and religion. An interesting and topical selection but a partisan one. General reading.

## 321 Forms of states

4528 321'.02

**Bercuson, David J.,** ed.

Canada and the Burden of Unity. Toronto: Macmillan, 1977. 191p. Bibliographical references. ISBN 0-7705-1487-1 bd.: $12.95 ISBN 0-7705-1488-X pa.: $6.95

1. Federal-provincial relations (Canada). 2. Regionalism – Canada. 3. Canada – Economic conditions.

These excellent essays by Maritime and Prairie academics trace the history of the grievances of the people of the Maritimes and Western Canada against economic and social inequalities they have suffered under the federal system. Solutions for strengthening federalism by reducing regional disparities are suggested: e.g., allowing the provinces more power in decision-making and decentralizing federal institutions. Quebec, British Columbia and Newfoundland are not considered. Advanced level.

4529 321'.02

**Byers, R. B.,** ed.

Canada Challenged: The Viability of Confederation. Edited by R. B. Byers and Robert W. Reford. Toronto: Canadian Institute of International Affairs, 1979. 375p. (Contemporary Affairs) ISBN 0-919084-33-8: $7.95

1. Federal-provincial relations (Canada). 2. Federal government – Canada. 3. Canada – Politics and government.

These essays make an important contribution to the ongoing debate on Confederation. The Canadian Institute of International Affairs commissioned experts in political science, economics and socio-cultural affairs to examine the probable effects of revising our current federal system by increasing decentralization of power or by strengthening centralization.

4530 321'.02

**Lalande, Gilles.**

In Defence of Federalism: A View from Quebec. Translated by Jo LaPierre. Toronto: McClelland and Stewart, 1978. 128p. Bibliography: p. 122-128. ISBN 0-7710-4563-8 pa.: $5.95

1. Federal government – Canada.

Translation of *Pourquoi le fédéralisme?*

The author contends that only within a federal system can the French cultural heritage survive. Didactic in intent, the book presents an informed and thorough response to the various objections to Confederation. The translation is good. Caroline Christie

4531 321'.02

**Meekison, J. Peter,** ed.

Canadian Federalism: Myth or Reality. 3d ed. Toronto: Methuen, c1977. 525p. Bibliographical references. ISBN 0-458-92400-8 pa.: $9.95

1. Federal government – Canada.

Second edition listed CS no. 515.

The focus of the series of articles has been adjusted to reflect the tensions and problems to which the Canadian federal system has been subjected between 1971 and 1977. There are a number of new contributors and many of the essays appear for the first time in this revised edition. A thoughtful examination of a timely topic.

4532 321'.02

**Rawlyk, George A.**

Regionalism in Canada: Flexible Federalism or Fractured Nation?, by George A. Rawlyk, Bruce W. Hodgins, and Richard P. Bowles. Scarborough, Ont.: Prentice-Hall, 1979. 244p. ill. Bibliography: p. 244. (Canada, Issues and Options) ISBN 0-13-7709-17-X pa.: $4.65

1. Regionalism – Canada. 2. Federal government – Canada. 3. Canada – Politics and government. 4. Canada – Economic conditions.

One of a series designed to encourage a thoughtful examination of important Canadian issues in both their contemporary and historical contexts. The contentious question of regionalism, its historical background, its contemporary manifestations and possible future patterns is introduced by three academics. The treatment of the subject and the writing style make it suitable for secondary school and public libraries.

4533 321.8
**Macpherson, C. B.**
The Life and Times of Liberal Democracy. Oxford, Eng.: Oxford University Press, 1977. 120p. Bibliography: p. 116-117. Index. ISBN 0-19-219120-9A0-19-289106-5 pa.: $3.95

1. Democracy.

An internationally respected Canadian political scientist discusses various models of democratic government, their history and limitations, as they have developed under capitalism and suggests new directions in which it can evolve as our economic system changes. An excellent analysis of the theories that have shaped our institutions, supplemented by a reading list for further study. Nikki Lawrence

## 322 State and social groups

4534 322'.3
**Finkel, Alvin.**
Business and Social Reform in the Thirties. Toronto: James Lorimer, 1979. Bibliography. Index. ISBN 0-88862-236-8 bd.: $19.95
ISBN 0-88862-235-X pa.: $8.95

1. Industry and state – Canada. 2. Canada – Economic policy. 3. Canada – Social policy.

Finkel argues that government and big business were instrumental in bringing about reform in the thirties as a desperate measure to support the capitalist system during the depression years. This interesting and novel thesis is supported by discussions of combines legislation, marketing boards, social insurance, the construction industry, the Bank of Canada and Dominion-Provincial relations. Barbara Schon

4535 322'.3
**Stanbury, W. T.**
Business Interests and the Reform of Canadian Competition Policy, 1971-1975. Agincourt, Ont.: Methuen, 1977. 227p. diagrs. Bibliographical references.
ISBN 0-458-92890-9 bd.: $16.95
ISBN 0-458-92900-X pa.: $6.95

1. Canada. Laws, statutes, etc. Combines investigation act. 2. Business and politics – Canada. 3. Competition, Unfair – Canada. 4. Pressure groups – Canada.

Professor Stanbury's study of the effects of the business community on Canadian legislation is fascinating and highly readable. He provides a chronological overview to show how business as a lobby group was able to stop legislation unfavourable to its interests, and to explain why consumers lack influence in political decisions. Each chapter has extensive bibliographical notes. Barbara Dance

4536 322.4'3
**McTaggart, David.**
Greenpeace III: Journey into the Bomb, by David McTaggart and Robert Hunter. New York: Morrow, 1979, c1978. 372p. ill., plates. ISBN 0-688-03385-7: $10.95

1. Atomic bomb – Testing.

A Vancouverite happily sailing his sloop to the South Pacific in 1972 encountered the French government's nuclear tests in the Pacific. Subsequently he set up the Greenpeace Foundation to fight nuclear testing.

## 323 State and its residents

4537 323.1'1
**Cardinal, Harold.**
The Rebirth of Canada's Indians. Edmonton: Hurtig Publishers, c1977. 222p.
ISBN 0-88830-119-7 bd.: $9.95
ISBN 0-88830-125-1 pa.: $4.95

1. Indians of North America – Canada – Government relations. 2. Indians, Treatment of – Canada.

An important work that provides the Native perspective on the problems of Indian-government relations. Outlined are the rights that Native Peoples demand concerning the Indian Act, economic programmes, education, aboriginal rights and treaties. This book is essential for an understanding of the need for Native Peoples to keep their identity and control their own affairs. Kathryn Walker

4538 323.1'19
**Ryan, Joan.**
Wall of Words: The Betrayal of the Urban Indian. Toronto: PMA Books, c1978. 117p. Bibliography: p. 99-117. ISBN 0-88778-181-0 pa.: $6.95

1. Small Legs, Nelson, d. 1976. 2. Indians of North America – Canada – Government relations. 3. Indians of North America – Alberta – Calgary.

The inside story of events that led to the bizarre suicide of Nelson Small Legs reveals the desperate effort of a poor people to assure survival in the face of a paternalistic, unresponsive, and mistrustful government. A timely case study with grave implications for future government policy on native peoples. Frieda Ling

4539 323.1'9707
**Watkins, M. H.,** ed.
Dene Nation, the Colony Within. Edited by M. H. Watkins for the University League for Social Reform. Toronto: University of Toronto Press, c1977. 189p. maps. Bibliographies. ISBN 0-8020-2264-2 bd.: $12.50
ISBN 0-8020-6315-2 pa.: $4.95

1. Tinne Indians – Government relations. 2. Indians of North America – Canada – Government relations. 3. Mackenzie Valley pipeline.

A compilation of opinions and statements made by the Indian People of the Mackenzie District at the Berger Inquiry, concerning the pipeline, land claims and aboriginal rights. Includes revealing statements not presented at the Inquiry. Presentations have been shortened and revised for the purpose of the book. Kathryn Walker

## 324 Electoral process

4540 324'.71
**Clarke, Harold D.**
Political Choice in Canada. Toronto: McGraw-Hill Ryerson, c1979. 445p. ill. Bibliographical references and Index. ISBN 0-07-082783-4 $24.95

1. Elections – Canada. 2. Political participation – Canada. 3. Voting – Canada.

A scholarly study based on surveys conducted in 1965, 1968, and 1974, concludes that Canadians vote on short term issues rather than party lines. The variables analyzed in this solidly documented work included media influences, leader image and regional consciousness. An excellent exploration of Canada's political thinking, with extensive notes for further study. Nikki Lawrence.

4541 324'.71
**Gargrave, Anthony.**
How to Win an Election: The Complete Practical Guide to Organizing and Winning Any Election Campaign, by Anthony Gargrave and Raymond Hull. Toronto: Macmillan, c1979. 228p. Bibliography: p. 225-228. ISBN 0-7705-1658-0 bd.: $14.95
ISBN 0-7705-1671-8 pa.: $7.95

1. Elections – Canada.

A veteran of many political campaigns gives practical advice to candidates for office at all levels of government, regardless of party: organizing the campaign, raising money, getting out the vote. Students and the general public will also profit from this insider's view of the election process.

## 325 Immigration

4542 325'.1
**Segal, Gary L.**
How to Immigrate into Canada. 2d ed. Vancouver: International Self-Counsel Press, 1977. 90p. ill., forms, map. (Self-counsel Series) ISBN 0-88908-029-1 pa.: $2.95

1. Canada – Emigration and immigration – Handbooks, manuals, etc.

First edition listed *CS* no. 552.

An updated version, taking into account new and more stringent immigration regulations. Step-by-step instructions designed for prospective immigrants. The book explains how the immigration system works. Prepared by a former lecturer in immigration law at York University. A third edition is in preparation.

4543 325.71
**Dirks, Gerald E.**
Canada's Refugee Policy: Indifference or Opportunism? Montreal: McGill-Queen's University Press, 1977. 316p. Bibliographical references and Index. ISBN 0-7735-0296-3 $18.95

1. Refugees – Canada. 2. Canada – Emigration and immigration.

Canada's record in accepting refugees is analysed systematically from the United Empire Loyalists to the Ugandan refugees of

1972-1973. Dirks concludes that government policy has depended as much on economic and political as on humanitarian considerations. This timely and interesting work should be in all libraries. Much research remains to be done on the topic.

4544 325.71

**Munro, Iain R.**

Immigration. Consulting authors: Howard A. Doughty and Darrell R. Skidmore. Toronto: John Wiley, c1978. 96p. ill., graphs, map, ports. Bibliographical references and Index. (Canada, Origins and Options) ISBN 0-471-99767-6 pa.: $3.95

1. Canada – Emigration and immigration – History.

Designed for secondary school students, it relates briefly the history of immigration policy in Canada. Included is discussion of patterns of immigration, changing attitudes of both the government and the citizens over the years and the problems of building a multicultural society. Many appropriate illustrations, tables and charts.

4545 325.712

**Gray, James H.**

Boomtime: Peopling the Canadian Prairies. Saskatoon: Western Producer Prairie Books, 1979. 148p. ill. ISBN 0-88833-020-0 bd.: $21 ISBN 0-88833-024-3 pa.: $14.95

1. Land settlement – Prairie Provinces.
2. Prairie Provinces – Emigration and immigration – History.

Alberta Non-Fiction Award.

The author brings to life with vivid text and 150 appropriate photographs, the human side of the settlement of the Canadian prairies, its excitement and frustrations. Recommended for all public libraries.

## 327 Foreign relations

4546 327.1'74

**Griffiths, Franklyn,** ed.

The Dangers of Nuclear War: A Pugwash Symposium, edited by Franklyn Griffiths and John Polanyi. Toronto: University of Toronto Press, 1979. 197p. ISBN 0-8020-2356-8 bd.: $15 ISBN 0-8020-6389-6 pa.: $5.95

1. Atomic weapons and disarmament.

Position papers prepared by experts from eleven countries were discussed at the thirtieth Pugwash Symposium held in Toronto in 1978. The discussions on nuclear war, arms control and proliferation, and nuclear terrorism, led to revision of the prepared papers and the writing of three additional chapters. Although the book adds little that is new, it does provide timely and authoritative information for advanced readers in all libraries.

4547 327.174

**Ranger, Robin.**

Arms and Politics, 1958-1978: Arms Control in a Changing Political Context. Toronto: Macmillan, 1979. Bibliography. Index. ISBN 0-7705-1627-0 $17.95

1. Arms control.

Arms control discussions over the past twenty years are analysed in this important work. The invasion of Afghanistan by the USSR lends credence to the author's argument that the Russians have used political arms control talks successfully to mask proliferation of their own arms, whereas attempts by the United States to control the technical aspects of arms control have been largely unsuccessful. For the informed layman and specialist. Extensive bibliography.

4548 327.41'071

**Wigley, Philip G.**

Canada and the Transition to Commonwealth: British-Canadian Relations, 1917-1926. Cambridge, N.Y.: Cambridge University Press, c1977. 294p. Bibliography: p. 284-291. Index. (Cambridge Commonwealth Series) ISBN 0-521-21157-3 $22

1. Great Britain – Foreign relations – Canada.
2. Canada – Foreign relations – Great Britain.
3. Great Britain – Foreign relations – 1910-1936. 4. Commonwealth of Nations – Foreign relations.

A Canadian who now teaches in Edinburgh provides fresh insights from British sources such as the Public Record Office in London, on a subject on which Canadian sources have already been tilled: the evolution of British attitudes towards Canada, 1917-1926. Recommended for large libraries.

4549 327.71
**Blanchette, Arthur E.,** ed.
Canadian Foreign Policy 1955-1965: Selected Speeches and Documents. Toronto: McClelland and Stewart; Ottawa: Institute of Canadian Studies, Carleton University, c1977. 424p. Bibliography: p. 421-424. (The Carleton Library) ISBN 0-7710-9804-9 pa.: $5.95

1. Canada – Foreign relations – 1945- – Sources.

A sequel to R. A. MacKay's *Canadian Foreign Policy: 1945-1954,* listed in *CS* no. 574.

4550 327.71
**Hillmer, Norman,** ed.
A Foremost Nation: Canadian Foreign Policy and a Changing World. Edited by Norman Hillmer and Garth Stevenson. Toronto: McClelland and Stewart, c1977. 296p. Bibliographical references. (A Carleton Contemporary) ISBN 0-7710-9911-8 pa.: $5.95

1. Canada – Foreign relations – 1945-

A constructive evaluation by eleven Canadian academics of recent Canadian foreign policy, in aspects such as multinational economics, world oil supplies, the sea, and in relation to specific areas such as Africa and China. Useful for serious students in Canadian studies courses.

4551 327.71
**Holmes, John W.**
The Shaping of Peace. Toronto: University of Toronto Press, 1979- 350p. Index. ISBN 0-8020-5461-7 $25 vol. 1.

1. Canada – Foreign relations – 1945-

Contents: vol. 1. 1943-1957 *Canada and the Search for World Power.*

The author, who was in the Department of External Affairs from 1943 to 1960, records the key events of Canada's participation in the World War II peace settlement and the organization of the United Nations, but emphasizes the philosophy the Department applied to world problems. It is the first of two volumes.

4552 327.71
**Johnson, Barbara,** ed.
Canadian Foreign Policy and the Law of the Sea. Edited by Barbara Johnson and Mark W. Zacher. Vancouver: University of British Columbia Press, c1977. 387p. Bibliographical references and Index. ISBN 0-7748-0073-9 bd.: $19 ISBN 0-7748-0076-3 pa.: $6.50

1. United Nations Conference on the Law of the Sea. 2. Maritime law. 3. Canada – Foreign relations – 1945-

As frequent newspaper headlines on fisheries disputes and oil spills indicate, Canada must be deeply involved with international developments in the law of the sea. This discussion relates particularly to the Third United Nations Conference on the Law of the Sea, and includes information on policies on fisheries and their boundaries, pollution and enforcement of maritime legal claims. Of interest to both layman and scholar.

4553 327.71
**Page, Donald M.,** comp.
A Bibliography of Works on Canadian Foreign Relations, 1971-1975. Toronto: Canadian Institute of International Affairs, 1977. 300p. Indexes. pa.: $9.25

1. Canada – Foreign relations – 1945- – Bibliography. 2. Canada – Military policy – Bibliography. 3. Canada – Foreign economic relations – Bibliography.

Continues the author's *A Bibliography of Works on Canadian Foreign Relations, 1945-1970,* (*CS* no. 576). Arrangement is the same as that in the earlier bibliography, by broad subject areas with author and subject indexes. Almost one half of this volume is cumulative index to 'International Canada', 1971-1975, published by the Canadian Institute of International Affairs. Glenna Stevens

4554 327.71
**Stacey, C. P.**
Canada and the Age of Conflict: A History of Canadian External Policies. Toronto: Macmillan, c1977. v ill. Bibliographical references and Index. ISBN 0-7705-1428-6 $19.95 vol. 1. 1867-1921. 1977.

1. Canada – Foreign relations.

An excellent introduction to Canada's external policy. It synthesizes past research and adds important new research drawn from diplomatic archives recently opened. Supersedes Glazebrook's *History of Canadian External Affairs.* Listed *CS* no. 566. All libraries.

4555 327.71'073
**Cuff, Robert D.**
Ties That Bind: Canadian-American Relations in Wartime, From the Great War to the Cold War, by Robert D. Cuff and J. L. Granatstein. 2d ed. Toronto: Samuel Stevens, 1977. 205p. plates, ports. Bibliographical references and Index. ISBN 0-88866-579-2 bd.: $12.95 ISBN 0-88866-580-6 pa.: $5.95

1. Canada – Foreign relations – United States. 2. United States – Foreign relations – Canada.

First edition published in 1975 under the title: *Canadian-American Relations in Wartime*. Listed *CS* no. 586.

A new introduction and illustrations have been added but the text has neither been revised nor enlarged. The chapter notes remain unchanged. Libraries which have the first edition may not wish to replace it.

4556 327.71'073

**Preston, Richard Arthur.**

The Defence of the Undefended Border: Planning for War in North America, 1867-1939. Montreal: McGill-Queen's University Press, 1977. 300p. ill., maps. Bibliographical references and Index. ISBN 0-7735-0291-2 $22

1. Canada – Foreign relations – United States. 2. United States – Foreign relations – Canada. 3. Canada – Military policy. 4. United States – Military policy. 5. Great Britain – Military policy.

Students of Canadian military history will applaud this study. It destroys for once and for all the myth of the "undefended border". The military on each side prepared numerous plans of attack, continuing into the 1930's. An important work for the serious student by a respected historian.

4557 327.71'098

**Griffiths, Franklyn.**

A Northern Foreign Policy. Toronto: Canadian Institute of International Affairs, 1979. 90p. maps. Bibliographical references. (Wellesley Papers) ISBN 0-919084-35-4 pa.: $4

1. Canada – Foreign relations – Arctic regions. 2. Arctic regions – Foreign relations – Canada.

As resources diminish and technology advances, the Canadian North is increasing in global importance. Professor Griffiths of the Political Economy Department at the University of Toronto pleads for an integrated approach to international relations in the North, considering factors such as sharing resources, security, economics, science and the environment.

## 328 Legislation

4558 328.71'05

**Canada. Parliament. House of Commons.**

Beauchesne's Rules and Forms of the House of Commons of Canada, with Annotations, Comments and Precedents. Prepared by Alistair Fraser, G. A. Birch and W. F. Dawson. 5th ed. Toronto: Carswell, 1978. 401p. Index. 0 459-32210-9

1. Canada. Parliament. House of Commons – Rules and practice.

The fifth edition of a standard guide to parliamentary procedure replaces the 1958 publication. The first four editions were prepared by Arthur Beauchesne. Glenna Stevens

4559 328.71'07'1

**Campbell, Edwin Colin.**

The Canadian Senate: A Lobby from Within. Toronto: Macmillan, 1978. 184p. Index. (Canadian Controversies Series) ISBN 0-7705-1695-5 bd.: $12.95 ISBN 0-7705-1631-9 pa.: $5.95

1. Canada. Parliament. Senate.

The case for the abolition of the Senate, based on careful study by a knowledgeable academic. He sees the Senate as serving primarily the interests of Canada's business community. His suggestion for a reformed Senate with provincial representation has already been included in Trudeau's proposals for a new constitution.

4560 328.71'072

**Kornberg, Allan.**

Influence in Parliament: Canada, by Allan Kornberg and William Mishler. Durham, N.C.: Duke University Press, 1976. 403p. Bibliographical references and Index. ISBN 0-82230-364-7 $14.75

1. Canada. Parliament. House of Commons. 2. Legislators – Canada. 3. Influence (Psychology).

Based on long interviews and quantitative analysis from 1968-1972, it studies both formal and informal behaviour of members of Parliament. It appears that reform of attitudes of members toward the House may be as important as reform of procedures. The project will be replicated in other countries. A significant contribution, which might be used as a supplement to Stewart's *Divide and Con* (*CS* no. 603).

4561 328.71'07'2
**Stewart, John B.**
The Canadian House of Commons: Procedure and Reform. Montreal: McGill-Queen's University Press, 1977. 337p. Bibliography: p. 327-331. Index.
ISBN 0-7735-0256-4 $16

1. Canada. Parliament. House of Commons – Rules and practice.

An authoritative analysis of parliamentary procedure in Canada by a professor of political science at St. Francis Xavier University, once a House member. Fundamental reforms are recommended to fit Canada's economic and social development. For all libraries.

4562 328'.713
**Shulman, Morton.**
Member of the Legislature. Toronto: Fitzhenry & Whiteside, c1979. 226p. ill.
ISBN 0-88902-417-0 $10.95

1. Legislators – Ontario – Biography.

Shulman's eight years in the Ontario Legislature, 1967 to 1975, are remembered for his antics as a self-appointed ombudsman. His crusades against corruption, exploitation, pollution and crime were not all successful but his investigative methods lacked nothing in drama, flamboyance and publicity potential. A maverick's chatty, sardonic view of provincial politics. Cartoon illustrations.

## 329 Political parties

4563 329.
**Mishler, William T. E.**
Political Participation in Canada: Prospects for Democratic Citizenship. Toronto: Macmillan, c1979. 167p. Bibliographical references and Index. (Canadian Controversies Series) ISBN 0-7705-1770-6 pa.: $6.95

1. Political participation – Canada.

Professor Mishler pulls together and evaluates evidence available on citizen involvement in politics, and speculates on the future of democratic citizenship. For the serious student.

4564 329'.00971
**Robin, Martin,** ed.
Canadian Provincial Politics: The Party System of the Ten Provinces. 2d ed. Scarborough, Ont.: Prentice-Hall, 1978. 316p. Bibliographical references.
ISBN 0-13-113233-4 pa.: $6.95

1. Political parties – Canada. 2. Provincial governments – Canada.

First edition listed in *CS* no. 618.

Contemporary provincial politics in each of the ten Canadian provinces is placed within a framework of historical background and the factors which shaped political development. A useful addition to political science collections in college, public and senior secondary school libraries.

4565 329'.023
**Camp, Dalton.**
Points of Departure. Ottawa: Deneau and Greenberg, 1979. 259p. Index.
ISBN 0-88879-020-1 $14.95

1. Canada. Parliament – Elections, 1979.

Camp himself is the central figure of this memorable and quotable collection of political reminiscences drawn from the years between the "dump Dief" era and the 1979 election. This is a fast, witty, clever piece of political journalism that hovers around the cruelty level in its deadly one-liners and shattering put-downs. Fun to read. Ille-Mai Gerdels

4566 329.9'71
**Avakumovic, Ivan.**
Socialism in Canada: A Study of the CCF-NDP in Federal and Provincial Politics. Toronto: McClelland and Stewart, 1978. 316p. Bibliography: p. 295-298. Index.
ISBN 0-7710-0978-X pa.: $6.95

1. Co-operative Commonwealth Federation.
2. New Democratic Party (Canada).
3. Socialism – Canada.

A useful introduction for students to the CCF-NDP from 1932 to 1961. It contributes little that is new. For critical analysis consult Walter Young's *The Anatomy of a Party* (*CS* no. 623) and Desmond Morton's *Social Democracy in Canada*, 2d ed. 1977.

4567 329.9'71
**English, John.**
The Decline of Politics: The Conservatives and the Party System, 1901-20. Toronto: University of Toronto Press, c1977. 237p. Bibliographical references and Index. (Canadian Government Series)
ISBN 0-8020-5386-6 $15

1. Borden, Robert Laird, Sir, 1854-1937.

2. Progressive Conservative Party (Canada) – History. 3. Canada – Politics and government – 1896-1911. 4. Canada – Politics and government – 1911-1921.

This thorough and well-written study fills a gap in the history of the Conservative Party. The country was undergoing vast changes and the Party attempted to restructure its organization and policies to fit the changing needs. All libraries.

4568 329.9'71

**Heggie, Grace F.,** ed.

Canadian Political Parties, 1867-1968: A Historical Bibliography. Toronto: Macmillan, c1977. 603p. Indexes. ISBN 0-7705-1341-7 $75

1. Political parties – Canada – Bibliography. 2. Canada – Politics and government – 1867- – Bibliography.

Canadian political history, government, and individual political parties from 1867 to 1968, are covered comprehensively in this carefully organized bibliography. The 8,850 entries, monographs, journal articles and theses, have full bibliographic descriptions and annotations. Detailed author and subject indexes. An expensive, but invaluable research tool for students, teachers and libraries.

4569 329.9'71

**Morton, Desmond.**

NDP: Social Democracy in Canada. 2d ed. Toronto: Samuel Stevens, 1977. 229p. ports. Bibliography: p. 214-218. Index.
ISBN 0-88866-581-4 bd.: $8.95
ISBN 0-88866-582-2 pa.: $4.95

1. New Democratic Party (Canada). 2. Canada – Politics and government – 1963-

The first edition published in 1974 under title: *NDP: The Dream of Power,* was listed in *CS* no. 615.

This second edition continues the tales of NDP fortunes across the country to 1977, with the addition of some sixty pages of information.

4570 329.9'71

**Whitaker, Reginald.**

The Government Party: Organizing and Financing the Liberal Party of Canada, 1930-58. Toronto: University of Toronto Press, c1977. 507p. Bibliographical references and Index. (Canadian University Paperbacks) ISBN 0-8020-6320-9 pa.: $7.95

1. Liberal Party (Canada) – History. 2. Canada – Politics and government – 1930-1935. 3. Canada – Politics and government – 1935-1957.

The first of two volumes, this major assessment of the federal Liberal party provides many fresh insights. It traces the development of party structure, financial support, relations of the federal and provincial parties, and the trend to the use of advertising agencies. All libraries should have it for serious students of Canadian politics. Beginners may find it too advanced and detailed.

4571 329.9'714

**Quinn, Herbert F.**

The Union Nationale: Quebec Nationalism from Duplessis to Lévesque. 2d enl. ed. Toronto: University of Toronto Press, 1979. Bibliography. Index. ISBN 0-8020-2318-5 bd.: $15 ISBN 0-8020-6347-0 pa.: $7.50

1. Union nationale (Canada). 2. Nationalism – Quebec (Province). 3 Quebec (Province) – Politics and government – 1936-1960. 4. Quebec (Province) – Politics and government – 1960-1976.

In this second edition, two additional chapters continue the story of the Union nationale from 1960 to 1973. The postscript gives information about the Biron revival of 1976 which the author considers outside the UN story. For those libraries that require up-to-date authoritative information on the UN in one place.

4572 329.9'714

**Saywell, John T.**

The Rise of the Parti Québecois, 1967-1976. Toronto: University of Toronto Press, c1977. 174p. ill. ISBN 0-8020-2275-8 bd.: $12.50 ISBN 0-8020-6317-9 pa.: $5.95

1. Parti québecois. 2. Quebec (Province) – Politics and government – 1960-

The author guides us through the development of the PQ by means of accounts originally published in *Canadian Annual Review* from 1967 to 1975, with the addition of a new essay on events of 1976. The pieces are pulled together by means of a prologue and epilogue. Useful to the general reader and student, and to the specialist who may wish to refresh his memory on the events of a particular year. Produced hastily after the election of 1976, it has no index.

## 330 Economics

4573 330.9'71
**Careless, Anthony G. S.**
Initiative and Response: The Adaptation of Canadian Federalism to Regional Economic Development. Montreal: McGill-Queen's University Press, 1977. 224p. Bibliographical references and Index. (Canadian Public Administration Series) ISBN 0-7735-0280-7 bd.: $13.50 ISBN 0-7735-0294-7 pa.: $6

1. Federal-provincial relations (Canada). 2. Regionalism – Canada. 3. Canada – Economic policy.

A survey of incentives to regional economic development provided by the federal system, designed to evaluate the balance between federal and provincial power. The growing influence of the federal bureaucracy in policy making is seen as a danger to responsible government. Academic level.

4574 330.9'71
**Cheveldayoff, Wayne.**
The Business Page: How to Read It for Profit, Politics and Peace of Mind. Ottawa: Deneau and Greenberg, 1978. 318p. graphs. Bibliographical references and Index. ISBN 0-88879-000-7 $15

1. Economics. 2. Canada – Economic conditions.

In clear, readable fashion the author tries to help readers understand the significance of economic developments in order to make informed purchases, investments, and voting decisions. Using specific examples from business and government publications he explains how to interpret GNP, consumer price index, unemployment figures, stock pages, annual reports, etc. Beth Goble

4575 330.9'71
**Clement, Wallace.**
A Practical Guide to Canadian Political Economy, by Wallace Clement and Daniel Drache. Toronto: James Lorimer, 1978. 183p. Index. ISBN 0-88862-184-1 bd.: $15 ISBN 0-88862-185-X pa.: $2.75

1. Canada – Economic conditions – Bibliography.

This bibliography is not annotated and is indexed by author only, but broad subject division is an aid to access. Its interdisciplinary approach makes it an essential aid to reading and research in both current and retrospective materials. Drache's introductory essay is an appropriate guide to scholarship in the field. Barbara Stewart

4576 330.9'71
**Dick, Trevor J. O.**
Economic History of Canada: A Guide to Information Sources. Detroit: Gale Research, c1978. 174p. Indexes. (Economics Information Guide Series) (Gale Information Guide Library) ISBN 0-8103-1292-1 $18

1. Canada – Economic conditions – Bibliography.

This indispensable research tool lists general sources, then is arranged by historical period, with subdivisions on regional sources, statistics, theses of economic growth, industries, economic organizations, technology, and resources. Helpful notes precede each subsection. Separate author, title and subject indexes.

4577 330.9'71
**McNiven, J. D.**
The Atlantic Vision – 1990: A Development Strategy for the 1980's. Halifax: Atlantic Provinces Economic Council, 1979. 172p. Index. ISBN 0-919040-15-2 $6

1. Atlantic Provinces – Economic conditions.

Based on three years of objective research unfettered by political interference, this report examines the past and the present economy of the region and points the general direction to progress. Future goals suggested include better information links, better industrial design, and better marketing of regional products. Essential for all economics collections. Available also on *Microlog* 79-1550.

4578 330.9'71'0622
**Fetherling, Doug.**
Gold Diggers of 1929: Canada and the Great Stock Market Crash. Toronto: Macmillan, 1979. Index. ISBN 0-7705-1824-9 $14.95

1. Depressions – 1929 – Canada. 2. Canada – History – 1918-1939.

A journalist's presentation of the mood and events leading up to the 1929 crash, concentrating on the Canadian experience in Toronto, Winnipeg and Montreal. Numerous anecdotes and black and white photos add interest. No bibliography or footnotes. Marilyn Koch

4579 330.9'71'064
**Armstrong, Muriel.**
The Canadian Economy and Its Problems. 2d ed. Scarborough, Ont.: Prentice-Hall, 1977. 388p. diagrs. Index. ISBN 0-13-113084-6 bd.: $10.95 ISBN 0-13-113076-5 pa.: $6.95

1. Canada – Economic conditions – 1945-

2. Canada – Economic policy.

A very clearly written book on Canadian economic policies, focusing on growth, income distribution, regional disparity, balance of payments, foreign investment and energy. No knowledge of economics is assumed, so the author, an economics professor at Concordia, has kept the theory to a minimum. Useful for readers at all levels. Beth Martin

4580 330.9'71'064

**Couchiching Conference, 47th, Geneva Park Ont., 1978.**

Growth in a Conserving Society: Based on Papers Prepared for the 47th Couchiching Conference of the Canadian Institute on Public Affairs. Edited by Dean Walker. Toronto: Yorkminster Publishing, c1979. 175p. ill. Index. ISBN 0-919692-03-6 pa.: $7.95

1. Conservation of natural resources – Canada – Congresses. 2. Economic history – 1945- – Congresses. 3. Social history – 1945- – Congresses. 4. Canada – Economic policy – Congresses.

"Thinkers from business, government, universities, labour, medicine, the church, and the arts plot alternate routes into post-industrial society. They searched for ways to achieve greater harmony between man, nature, technology, and the economy". -Publisher's note. The papers are short and lack bibliographies. An introduction to discussion.

4581 330.9'71'064

**Ruggeri, G. C.,** ed.

The Canadian Economy: Problems and Policies. Toronto: Gage Educational Publishing, c1977. 364p. ill. Bibliography: p. 357-364. ISBN 0-7715-5511-3 pa.: $2.95

1. Canada – Economic conditions – 1965-
2. Canada – Economic policy.

Provides a very cursory overview of many aspects of the Canadian economy. The articles and readings are short and to the point, and make good use of charts and tables. Because of this, the text is more likely to appeal to the student than the general reader. Beth Martin.

4582 330.9'71'0644

**Gordon, Walter L.**

What Is Happening to Canada. Toronto: McClelland and Stewart, c1978. 63p. ISBN 0-7710-3442-3 pa.: $2.95

1. Canada – Economic conditions – 1963-

A compilation of lectures present the author's views on the ills of the Canadian economy in a very forthright and thought-provoking manner. Gordon's own views on possible cures are also given in a very direct, point-by-point manner. Easy to read and interesting. Beth Martin

4583 330.9'71'0644

**Wayman, Morris.**

Health & Welfare: Every Canadian Can Be a Millionaire. Toronto: Griffin House, 1978. 146p. diagrs., graphs. ISBN 0-88760-093-X pa.: $5.95

1. Public welfare – Canada. 2. Canada – Economic policy. 3. Canada – Economic conditions – 1965-

Describes the roles of government, business, industry and agriculture in our economy and also presents new recommendations for the economic management of Canada. Margaret Covshoff

4584 330.9'714'04

**Joron, Guy.**

Minimum Salary: One Million Dollars: The Race Toward Madness. Translated by Mark Czarnecki. Don Mills, Ont.: Musson, c1978. 151p. Bibliography: p. 151. ISBN 0-7737-1023-X pa.: $7.95

1. Quebec (Province) – Economic conditions – 1945- 2. Quebec (Province) – Social conditions.

Guy Joron, Quebec's Energy minister, details in a highly readable style, how the Western world's race towards never-ending economic growth will eventually result in self-destruction. Joron's call for a return to a new basic lifestyle, ideally in an independent Quebec, could perhaps save the Western world as well. Beth Martin

## 331 Labour economics

4585 331.

**Smith, Trevor R.**

From Contract to Contract: A Study of Labour Relations in Canada, by Trevor R. Smith and Diane S. Smith. Toronto: Heath, c1977. 70p. ISBN 0-669-00552-5 pa.: $3.50

1. Industrial relations.

The personal narrative style of this book on arbitration, mediation and conciliation makes it an enjoyable and informative introduction to the collective bargaining process, but it is of little use to the researcher or professional. Barbara Stewart

4586 331'.0971

**Crispo, John H. G.**

The Canadian Industrial Relations System. Toronto: McGraw-Hill Ryerson, 1977. 570p. diagrs. Bibliographical references and Index. ISBN 0-07-082459-2 $13.95

1. Industrial relations – Canada.

Although designed as a university text Crispo's book satisfies a need for Canadian material on the collective bargaining process and labour relations in Canada. A blend of writings from various sources, the book is well-organized and the material clearly presented. A readable book on a complex subject that will be useful in a public library. Barbara Schon

4587 331'.0971

**Montero, Gloria.**

We Stood Together: First-Hand Accounts of Dramatic Events in Canada's Labour Past. Toronto: James Lorimer, 1979. Bibliography. ISBN 0-88862-268-6 bd.: $19.95
ISBN 0-88862-269-4 pa.: $9.95

1. Labor and laboring classes – Canada – History. 2. Trade-unions – Canada – History. 3. Strikes and lockouts – Canada – History.

A richly detailed account of ten watershed events in Canadian labour history from the Winnipeg General Strike to the 1970's. Montero travelled across the country to interview union leaders, providing a unique assessment of the worker's struggles. Numerous photographs are provided throughout, many from archival sources. Barbara Stewart

4588 331'.0971

**Phillips, Gerald E.**

The Practice of Labour Relations and Collective Bargaining in Canada. Toronto: Butterworth, 1976, c1977. 266p. Bibliographies and Index.

1. Industrial relations – Canada. 2. Collective bargaining – Canada.

Educators and general readers alike will find this text informative and well-researched. Phillips examines trade unions, employers and governments in interaction, elaborating on institutional, structural and statistical data determining the role of each in the process. The final chapter is a simulation game intended to provide experiential learning. Barbara Stewart

4589 331.1'0971

**Ostry, Sylvia.**

Labour Economics in Canada, by Sylvia Ostry, Mahmood A. Zaidi, and Gail Cook Johnson. 3d ed. Toronto: Macmillan, c1979. 418p. graphs. Bibliographical references and Indexes. ISBN 0-7705-1728-5 pa.: $12.50

1. Labor supply – Canada. 2. Wages – Canada. 3. Labor policy – Canada.

Second edition listed in *CS* no. 684.

This new edition of the most authoritative book of its kind in Canada is much expanded since 1976. Structural changes in the labour market and policy decisions like wage controls are examined, in addition to the influence of household economics and geography on the variables of labour supply and demand. Barbara Stewart

4590 331.1'27

**Grubel, Herbert G.**

The Brain Drain: Determinants, Measurement and Welfare Effects, by Herbert G. Grubel and Anthony Scott. Waterloo, Ont.: Wilfrid Laurier University Press, 1977. 165p. Bibliography: p. 157-165.
ISBN 0-88920-037-8 bd.: $7
ISBN 0-88920-036-X pa.: $4.50

1. Brain drain – Canada. 2. Brain drain – United States.

Presents theoretical and empirical information on the migration of highly skilled manpower. This study addresses itself to scholars and policy makers within governments who are trying to reduce or modify the "brain drain". Margaret Covshoff

4591 331.1'37971

**Gonick, Cy.**

Out of Work: Why There's So Much Unemployment and Why It's Getting Worse. Toronto: James Lorimer, 1978. 176p. graphs. (Economy in Crisis) ISBN 0-88862-208-2 pa.: $2.50

1. Unemployment – Canada. 2. Canada – Economic conditions – 1965- 3. Canada – Economic policy.

Discusses Canada's unemployment problem and tries to give the reasons for the failure of the Canadian economy to provide enough jobs for those who want to work. The government's role in handling the unemployment crisis is also covered. Margaret Covshoff

4592 331.2'1'01
**Walker, Michael,** ed.
Which Way Ahead?: Canada After Wage and Price Control. Contributors include Thomas Courchene, Richard Lipsey, Simon Reisman. Vancouver: Fraser Institute, 1977. 291p. graphs. Bibliographical references. ISBN 0-88975-010-6 pa.: $4.95

1. Wage-price policy – Canada. 2. Canada – Economic policy.

A collection of essays written by Canadian economists and scholars assessing the effectiveness of the government's programme of wage and price controls, and proposing alternative policies on how to deal with inflation when the controls are removed. Margaret Covshoff

4593 331.2'52
**Calvert, Geoffrey N.**
Pensions and Survival: The Coming Crisis of Money and Retirement. Toronto: Maclean-Hunter, c1977. 167p. graphs. (A Financial Post Book) ISBN 0-88896-057-3

1. Pensions – Canada.

Calvert's detailed look at the present funding of public and private pensions, along with our retirement institution, open up many questions about our ability to survive the future increased tax burden. His overall presentation and solutions make a penetrating study, whose appeal is limited to those interested in Canada's pension system. Beth Martin

4594 331.2'52
**Pesando, James E.**
Public and Private Pensions in Canada: An Economic Analysis, by James E. Pesando and S. A. Rea, Jr. Toronto: Published for the Ontario Economic Council by University of Toronto Press, c1977. 185p. graphs. Bibliography: p. 179-185. (Ontario Economic Council Research Studies) ISBN 0-8020-3347-4 pa.: $6

1. Old age pensions – Canada.

Analyzes the limitations and benefits of both private and public pension plans. Not directed to the general reader. Margaret Covshoff

4595 331.4'0971
**Armstrong, Pat.**
The Double Ghetto: Canadian Women and Their Segregated Work, by Pat Armstrong and Hugh Armstrong. Toronto: McClelland and Stewart, c1978. 199p. Bibliography: p. 183-199. ISBN 0-7710-0805-8 pa.: $5.95

1. Women – Employment – Canada.
2. Housewives – Canada.

A comprehensive study of 'women's work' at home and on the job, 1944-1974, which explains the phenomenon of sexual segregation in the work place. Based on previous studies, the authors of this well-documented piece of research are sociologists. Includes statistical tables, notes, and a bibliography. Not easy reading. Janice Zlatarits

4596 331.4'0971
**Collins, Kevin.**
Women and Pensions. Ottawa: Canadian Council on Social Development, 1978. 254p. Bibliography: p. 243-254. ISBN 0-88810-283-6 pa. Processed: $3.50

1. Women – Employment – Canada.
2. Pensions – Canada.

A thorough study of pensions which also covers related topics such as changing family structure and roles, changes in women's work patterns, discrimination in employment, and conditions of elderly women in Canada. Private and public pensions, RRSP's, etc. are examined and recommendations made for reform. Includes statistical tables and bibliography. Janice Zlatarits

4597 331.4'0971
**Connelly, Patricia.**
Last Hired, First Fired: Women and the Canadian Work Force. Introduction by Margaret Benston. Toronto: Women's Press, 1978. Bibliography. ISBN 0-88961-044-4 pa.: $3.50

1. Women – Employment – Canada.
2. Discrimination in employment – Canada.
3. Sex discrimination against women – Canada.

A slim volume tracing the pattern of women's participation in the labour market from 1901 to the 1970's. This book demonstrates that the Canadian economy has maintained a female reserve pool of labour to be activated as needed and shunted aside in economic downturn. Rich in tables and statistical data. Barbara Stewart

4598 331.4'0971
**Roberts, Wayne.**
Honest Womanhood: Feminism, Femininity and Class Consciousness Among Toronto Working Women, 1896-1914. Toronto: New Hogtown Press, 1977. 60p. ill. Bibliographical references. ISBN 0-919940-07-2 pa.: $2

1. Women – Employment – Ontario – Toronto – History. 2. Feminism – Ontario – Toronto – History.

The horrible working conditions facing women in female job ghettos at the turn of the century and the difficulties women encountered in unionizing are related in this social history. Roberts ably conveys the realities and expectations of working women's lives. Barbara Stewart

4599 331.4'81
**Shack, Sybil F.**
Saturday's Stepchildren: Canadian Women in Business. Toronto: Guidance Centre, Faculty of Education, University of Toronto, c1977. 184p. Bibliography: p. 181-184. ISBN 0-7713-0025-5 pa.: $4.95

1. Women in business – Canada.

A professional writer and educator gives an entertaining, subjective account of the career-related problems and attitudes of Canadian businesswomen. The book is based on personal interviews, contains some statistical data, and makes concrete suggestions for change. Primarily of interest to present and prospective career-women. Ille-Mai Gerdels

4600 331.6'3
**Knight, Rolf.**
Indians at Work: An Informal History of Native Indian Labour in British Columbia, 1858-1930. Vancouver: New Star Books, c1978. 317p. ill. Bibliography: p. 305-317.
ISBN 0-919888-78-X bd.: $13.95
ISBN 0-919888-77-1 pa.: $6.50

1. Indians of North America – Employment – British Columbia – History – 19th century. 2. Indians of North America – Employment – British Columbia – History – 20th century.

An extensively documented chronology of Indian contribution to the process of industrialization in the roles of ranchers, farmers, fishermen, loggers, longshoremen, miners, prospectors, sealers, and independent producers. It convincingly presents the Indian as the victim of post-Depression government policies rather than the irrelevant remnant of an archaic world unfit for the modern era. Frieda Ling

4601 331.88'092
**Lazarus, Morden.**
Up from the Ranks: Biographical Sketches of 115 Trade Union Leaders, Past and Present, Including Six Named to the Labour Hall of Honour; and "J. S. Woodsworth – Labour's Spokesman", A Biographical Article. Toronto: Co-operative Press, c1977. 133p. ports. pa.: $3.95

1. Trade-unions – Canada – Biography.

Brief biographies of 114 Canadian labour leaders, past and present. The biographies are uncritical and the selection is not always representative of the full breadth of labour office-holders. Nonetheless it is the only source for quick information of this kind. Barbara Stewart.

4602 331.88'0971
**Antonides, Harry.**
A Christian Union in Labour's Wasteland: Essays, by Harry Antonides and others. Edited by Edward Vanderkloet. Toronto: Wedge Publishing, 1978. 139p. Bibliography: p. 131-135. Index. ISBN 0-88906-101-7 pa.: $4.95

1. Christian Labour Association of Canada.

A collection of essays by advocates of desecularized trade unions. In particular, the book focuses on the development of the Christian Labour Association of Canada, recently charged with being a 'company union' by the mainstream of the labour movement. Barbara Stewart

4603 331.88'0971
**Bercuson, David J.**
Fools and Wise Men: The Rise and Fall of the One Big Union. Toronto: McGraw-Hill Ryerson, 1978. 300p. ill., map, plates, ports. Bibliography: p. 287-293. Index.
ISBN 0-07-082644-7 bd.: $12.95
ISBN 0-07-082645-5 pa.: $6.95

1. One Big Union – History. 2. Trade-unions – Canada – History.

Bercuson details the origins and development of this post World War I syndicalist movement which claimed the allegiance of immigrant workers in the mines and mills of the Canadian west. The OBU was founded in Canada in 1918 and until 1927 it represented workers in the fight against death and injury, and for revolutionary unionism. Barbara Stewart

4604 331.88'0971
**Caragata, Warren.**
Alberta Labour: A Heritage Untold. Toronto: James Lorimer, 1979. Bibliography. Index. ISBN 0-88862-264-3 $19.95

1. Trade-unions – Alberta – History.
2. Labor and laboring classes – Alberta – History.

A compelling history of the fierce struggle of labour in Alberta from the early days, during the building of the Canadian Pacific Railway, to the present. Portrayed are unions and their organization, governments and their role, and the police. Compiled from interviews with union members, original letters and documents, current newspapers and magazines. Ninety photographs illustrate the text. Barbara Schon

4605 331.88'0971
**Lazarus, Morden.**
The Long Winding Road: Canadian Labour in Politics. West Vancouver: Boag, 1978, c1977. 103p. ports. Bibliography: p. 71. ISBN 0-920638-00-7 pa.: $2.50

1. Trade-unions – Canada – Political activity – History. 2. Trade-unions – Canada – Biography.

The struggle to construct a political party based on the trade-union movement is briefly summarized from the 1870's to the New Democratic Party. Much less scholarly in its presentation than Martin Robin's comprehensive account, *Radical Politics and Canadian Labour, 1880-1930*. Biographies of sixteen leading worker-socialists supplement the text. A basic, readable chronicle. Barbara Stewart

4606 331.88'0971
**Scott, Jack.**
Canadian Workers, American Unions. Vancouver: New Star Books, cl978. 242p. Bibliographical references and Index. (Trade Unions and Imperialism in America)
ISBN 0-919888-82-8 bd.: $13.95
ISBN 0-919888-81-X pa.: $6.50

1. Trade-unions – Canada – History.
2. Trade-unions – United States.

This second volume of Scott's study of the history of unions in North America condemns the American international unions for not serving the interests of their Canadian members. The coverage of the relationship since 1956 is cursory. Analytical and critical. The viewpoint is Marxist.

4607 331.88'0973
**Scott, Jack.**
Yankee Unions, Go Home!: How the AFL Helped the U.S. Build an Empire in Latin America. Vancouver: New Star Books, c1978. 287p. Bibliographical references.
ISBN 0-919888-80-1 bd.: $13.95
ISBN 0-919888-79-8 pa.: $6.25

1. American Federation of Labour.
2. Trade-unions – United States – Political activity. 3. United States – Foreign relations – Latin America. 4. Latin America – Foreign relations – United States.

In this companion volume to his study of American Federation of Labour intrusions into Canada, *Canadian Workers, American Unions,* Scott decries the cooperation of labour leadership in the achievement of American imperialistic aims in the semi-colonial world. A thoughtfully researched segment of labour history. Barbara Stewart

4608 331.88'11
**Davidson, Joe.**
Joe Davidson, by Joe Davidson and John Deverell. Toronto: James Lorimer, 1978. 192p.
ISBN 0-88862-179-5 bd.: $12
ISBN 0-88862-180-9 pa.: $2.95

1. Canadian Union of Postal Workers.
2. Trade-unions – Postal service – Canada – Biography.

The former leader of the Canadian Union of Postal Workers has been noted as "the most hated man in Canada" for his central role at the head of militant struggles. This is the story of postal workers and the Post Office itself. Davidson presents the union's case forcefully and convincingly. Barbara Stewart

4609 331.88'11
**Stanton, John.**
The Life and Death of a Union: The Canadian Seamen's Union, 1936-1949. Toronto: Steel Rail Publishing, 1978. 182p. ill. Bibliography. Index. ISBN 0-88791-013-0 pa.: $6.95

1. Canadian Seamen's Union – History.

A good index and source notes are notable features of this chronology of the Canadian Seamen's Union. The Communist-led and nationalist CSU was unique in inspiring collaboration between international unions, employers and government directed at destroying the union. Stanton is not uncritical of the CSU but focuses his research on the storm of controversy which led to its demise. Barbara Stewart

4610 331.89'041

**Hennessey, Peter H.**

Schools in Jeopardy: Collective Bargaining in Education. Toronto: McClelland and Stewart, 1979. 205p. ISBN 0-7710-4067-9 pa.: $8.95

1. Collective bargaining – Teachers – Ontario.
2. Strikes and lockouts – Teachers – Ontario.

The author, a former principal and member of the Faculty of Education, Queen's University, traces the growth of teacher associations and the factors that led to increased teacher militancy in the 1970's. School board consolidation, Bill 100, the Education Relation Commission as well as specific strike situations are all examined for their role in creating an atmosphere of alienation and confrontation in the education system. Hennessy's solutions include a return to greater integrity, and a sense of public service. Ethel Auster

4611 331.89'0971

**Forrest, Anne.**

Unions and the Collective Bargaining Process. Toronto: Ontario Institute for Studies in Education, c1978. 77p. ill. Bibliography: p. 75-77. (Curriculum Series) ISBN 0-7744-0159-1 pa.: $3.95

1. Collective bargaining – Canada.
2. Trade-unions – Canada.

This pamphlet is intended for secondary school class study. It explains the institutions and processes involved in industrial relations and provides an objective assessment of the functions of trade-unions in society. Barbara Stewart

4612 331.89'283

**Cameron, Donald.**

The Education of Everett Richardson: The Nova Scotia Fishermen's Strike, 1970-71. Toronto: McClelland and Stewart, c1977. 239p. ill., maps, ports. ISBN 0-7710-1845-2 pa.:

1. Fishermen's Strike, Nova Scotia, 1970-1971.

This popular journalist offers an absorbing participant-observer's account of the experience of a rank and file unionist thrust into the leadership of a strike action. Barbara Stewart

4613 331.89'29

**Jantzi, Doris.**

Union Organizations and Strikes, by Doris Jantzi, Paul Craven and Gary Teeple. Toronto: Ontario Institute for Studies in Education, 1978. 103p. ill., graph, ports. (Curriculum Series) ISBN 0-7744-0160-5 pa.: $3.95

1. Strikes and lockouts – Canada – History.

Four significant strikes in the evolution of the present system of industrial relations are discussed in a self-study format including questions at the end of each chapter. The emphasis is on strikes in the post World War II period. Suitable for high school students and non-specialist adults. Barbara Stewart

4614 331.89'29

**Stewart, Walter.**

Strike! Toronto: McClelland and Stewart, c1977. 224p. Bibliographical references and Index. ISBN 0-7710-8351-3 bd.: $10 ISBN 0-7710-8352-1 pa.: $4.95

1. Strikes and lockouts – Canada. 2. Trade-unions – Canada.

A journalist who sympathizes with the union movement explores the dangers of using the strike as a bargaining tool. Despite inadequate research and analysis, the lively, anecdotal writing provokes interest in seeking better solutions to labour relations problems.

## 332 Financial economics

4615 332'.024

**Snyder, J. Christopher,** ed.

It's Your Money: The Complete Canadian Guide to Personal Financial Planning. Edited by J. Christopher Snyder and Brian E. Anderson. New ed., rev. and expanded. Toronto: Methuen, c1979. 195p. Index. ISBN 0-438-93950-1 pa.: $7.95

1. Finance, Personal.

The eight contributors, all financial consultants, have written a readable, practical guide to managing one's finances. They discuss budgeting, savings, insurance, tax shelters, and other relevant topics. Chapters are summarized with a list of planning hints. The book is worthwhile reading for those wanting to gain control of their money. A questionnaire, glossary and index are included. Barbara Dance

4616 332'.024
**Townson, Monica.**
The Canadian Woman's Guide to Money, by Monica Townson and Frank Stapenhurst. Toronto: McGraw-Hill Ryerson, 1979. 146p. Bibliography: p. 136-139. Index. ISBN 0-07-082939-X bd.: $12.95 ISBN 0-07-082875-X pa.: $7.95

1. Women - Canada - Economic conditions. 2. Finance, Personal.

Budgets, credit, pensions, life insurance and income tax are some of the topics clearly discussed, providing basic information for the woman wanting more control over the financial aspects of her life. A good bibliography is included. Marilyn Koch

4617 332.1'0971
**Benson, John Norman.**
Provincial Government Banks: A Case Study of Regional Response to National Institutions. Vancouver: Fraser Institute, 1978. 112p. Bibliographical references. ISBN 0-88975-020-3 pa.: $3.95

1. Banks and banking - Canada. 2. Government financial institutions - Canada.

This careful and well-written study will be of interest to banking students and economists. The case study centers around the B.C. Savings & Trust, called the 'super bank', but the book looks more deeply into the operating problems of national financial institutions in the various regions of Canada. Beth Martin

4618 332.1'0971
**Binhammer, H. H.**
Money, Banking and the Canadian Financial System. 3d ed. Toronto: Methuen, 1977 651p. graphs. Bibliographies and Index. ISBN 0-485-92730-9 $18.95

1. Finance - Canada. 2. Banks and banking - Canada. 3. Monetary policy - Canada.

Previous edition listed in CS no. 719.

This extensively documented work has again been revised to discuss issues dealt with in the 1977 Bank Act. Intended for students, it explains the functions and nature of money, the development of banking in Canada, the role of financial institutions, monetary theory, and international monetary systems. A basic text. Beth Goble

4619 332.4'1'0971
**Perry, Robert L.**
Treadmill to Ruin?: A Plain Guide to the Unseen Rot of Inflation. Toronto: Maclean-Hunter, c1977. 184p. ill. (A Financial Post Book) ISBN 0-88896-056-5 pa.: $5.95

1. Inflation (Finance) - Canada.

The author, an economic journalist, presents a grim picture of Canada in the future if inflation is allowed to continue: staggering unemployment, poverty despite high wages, and a stagnant economy because of the inability of Canadian industry to compete abroad. He defends business and places the blame on government deficit spending, expensive welfare programmes, and our own consumerism. Beth Goble

4620 332.4'1'0971
**Pesando, James E.**
The Impact of Inflation on Financial Markets in Canada. Montreal: Canadian Economic Policy Committee, 1977. 81p. Bibliographical references. ISBN 0-88806-025-4 pa.: $4

1. Inflation (Finance) - Canada.

A well-organized analysis, in non-technical terms, of the ways in which inflation affects interest rates, returns on common stocks, mortgages, pension plans, and taxation. The author concludes that neither equities nor fixed-income securities are adequate investments during high inflation, and that zooming real estate prices may be a result of our efforts to get higher returns on investments. Beth Goble

4621 332.4'1'0971
**Robinson, Lukin.**
Rising Prices. Toronto: James Lorimer, 1978. (Economy in Crisis) ISBN 0-88862-205-8 bd.: $10.95 ISBN 0-88862-204-X pa.: $2.50

1. Inflation (Finance) - Canada. 2. Wage-price policy - Canada. 3. Inflation (Finance).

A popularized treatment of inflation, which explains what it is, what causes it, why it has accelerated recently, and what the government has done to try to control it. The author gives his options about why wage-price controls failed, and how inflation can be reduced. Beth Goble

4622 332'.4'971
**Plumptre, A. F. Wynne.**
Three Decades of Decision: Canada and the World Monetary System, 1944-75. Toronto: McClelland and Stewart, c1977. 335p. ill., graphs, plates. Bibliography: p. 292-298. Index. ISBN 0-7710-7172-8 pa.: $6.95

1. International finance. 2. Monetary policy – Canada – History. 3. Foreign exchange problem – Canada – History. 4. Currency question – Canada – History.

A history, from a Canadian point of view, of the events leading from the opening of the International Monetary Fund in 1944 to the floating of the Canadian dollar, to the present situation where most currencies are afloat. A readable account of a complex subject. Beth Goble

4623 332.6'0971
**Canadian Securities Institute.**
How to Invest in Canadian Securities. Rev. and reprinted 1978. Toronto: Canadian Securities Institute, 1978, c1970. 339p. ill., forms, graphs, map. Bibliography: p. 315-316. Index. (Canadian Securities Institute Publication) $15

1. Investments – Canada. 2. Stocks – Canada. 3. Bonds – Canada.

Replaces *How to Invest Your Money in Stocks and Bonds* listed in CS no. 727.

An excellent book covering all the essential elements to teach the interested novice how to invest in Canadian securities. The book, well illustrated with many examples of financial tables and reports, will be very useful to all readers who want to be knowledgeable about investing. Beth Martin

4624 332.6'32
**Delaney, Tom.**
The Delaney Report on RRSP's. 2d ed. Toronto: McGraw-Hill Ryerson, c1978. 167p. ISBN 0-07-082811-3 pa.: $6.95

1. Pension trusts – Canada – Investments. 2. Retirement income – Canada.

A finance consultant answers many questions often asked about retirement plans. The report stresses the importance of flexibility, security of principal, and return on investment. The "Buyer's Guide" chapter ranks plans according to cost and return. A third edition is to be published in 1980. Beth Goble

4625 332.6'45
**Abrams, Don.**
The Profit-taker: The Proven Rapid Money-maker in Good and Bad Markets. Ottawa: Deneau and Greenberg, 1978. 117p. ill., graphs. ISBN 0-88879-010-4 $9.95

1. Convertible bonds. 2. Short selling. 3. Speculation.

Presents a system for doubling your money in six months, using convertible bonds, short selling, hedging, buying on margin, and the "Abrams automatic profit-taker" formula. The author claims it works whether the market goes up or down. Beth Goble

4626 332.6'78
**Mahoney, John E.**
Buy Low Sell High: Anyone Can Make Money in the Market: The Formula Way. Toronto: Pagurian Press, c1978. 224p. graphs. Bibliography: p. 216-217. Index. ISBN 0-88932-081-0 $14.95

1. Stocks – Canada. 2. Stocks – United States. 3. Investments. 4. Speculation.

Mahoney maintains that formula plans, which lost popularity in the 1940's, are the safest and most successful investment technique. He presents an analysis of thirty stocks over a fourteen year period to illustrate his premise. There are graphs, a bibliography, index and brief glossary. Mahoney works as an analyst at a large investment company. Barbara Dance

4627 332.6'78
**Shulman, Morton.**
Anyone Can Make Big Money Buying Art. Toronto: Fitzhenry & Whiteside, 1977. 136p. ill., plates. Index. ISBN 0-88902-427-8 $8.95

1. Art as an investment.

Another practical guide for the layman by the author of the best-selling, *Anyone Can Make a Million*. Shulman writes in his usual chatty style, unabashedly making his point by using his own experiences. Chapters tell what, when and how to buy, and how to sell. Art is a hedge against inflation, but Shulman advises us to buy beautiful things for pleasure as well as profit. Beth Goble

4628 332.6'78
**Shulman, Morton.**
How to Invest Your Money & Profit from Inflation. Edmonton: Hurtig Publishers, c1979. 151p. ill. ISBN 0-88830-158-8 $9.95

1. Investments. 2. Inflation (Finance).

A changed approach to investment is required as we are advised to buy equity with borrowed money. A wealthy example of his own philosophy, Shulman discusses the pros and cons of buying real estate, gold, commodities, foreign currencies, stocks, wine, art and antiques. Marilyn Koch

4629 332.7′2

**Steacy, Richard H.**

Practical Canadian Mortgage Guide: A Must for Owners, Buyers, or Anyone in Real Estate. Don Mills, Ont.: General Publishing, 1979. 158p. ill. ISBN 0-7736-1075-8 pa.: $5.95

1. Mortgage loans – Canada. 2. Mortgages – Canada.

The first edition was published in 1977 under the title: *Steacy's Practical Canadian Mortgage Guide.*

The author of several previous books on real estate offers a useful, clearly written guide to the different types of mortgages available to prospective homeowners. Definitions of real property terms are provided. Public libraries.

## 333 Land economics

4630 333.2′0971

**Aubin, Henry.**

City for Sale. Montreal: Editions l'Etincelle; Toronto: James Lorimer, 1977. 389p. ill., maps, ports. Bibliographical references and Index. ISBN 0-88515-094-5 bd.: $19.95 ISBN 0-88515-075-9 pa.: $10.95

1. Land tenure – Quebec (Province) – Montreal. 2. Real estate investment – Quebec (Province) – Montreal. 3. Investments, Foreign – Quebec (Province) – Montreal.

Aubin, a Montreal journalist, has written a unique account, exploring in fascinating detail, the international make up of the real estate development of Montreal. Although the book has a strong international flavour, it has nevertheless, application for all major Canadian cities. Well illustrated with maps, tables and pictures. For the serious reader and students of urban studies. Beth Martin

4631 333.3′3

**Kalymon, Basil A.**

Profits in the Real Estate Industry. Vancouver: Fraser Institute, 1978. 41p. ill., diagr. (Fraser Institute Housing and Land Economics Series) ISBN 0-88975-016-5 pa.: $2.95

1. Real estate business – Canada. 2. Real estate investment – Canada.

Professor Kalymon makes comparisons with other industries in an attempt to show that real estate companies are not making excessive profits. He maintains that there is a high level of risk and competition in real estate and inadequate rewards in reinvestment. There is a lengthy preface by Mark Ricketts, and an opposing viewpoint by Robert Decker. Barbara Dance

4632 333.3′3

**Steacy, Richard H.**

Canadian Real Estate: How to Make It Pay. 4th ed. Willowdale, Ont.: Real Estate Press, c1979. 303p. ISBN 0-9690470-5-3 $14.95

1. Real estate business – Canada.

Third edition listed in *CS* no. 741.

A revised edition of a standard work.

4633 333.3′8

**Lorimer, James.**

The Developers. Toronto: James Lorimer, 1978. 307p. Bibliographical references and Index. ISBN 0-88862-219-8 $12.95

1. Land use, Urban – Canada. 2. Real estate business – Canada.

The development of shopping malls, high-rise apartment and office buildings, industrial parks and suburban residential areas has resulted in huge profits for urban land developers such as Genstar and Cadillac Fairview and has permanently changed the lifestyles of major Canadian cities. Well documented. Marilyn Koch

4634 333.7

**Fine, Richard.**

Energy Sources for Today: The Renewable Energy Handbook. Prepared and edited by members of Energy Probe and Pollution Probe. Toronto: Tutor Press, c1978. 239p. ill., diagrs., maps, ports. Bibliographies. ISBN 0-7704-2557-3 pa.: $5.95

1. Power resources. 2. Energy conservation.

Describing the nature and use of energy in Canada, the book focuses on the technology of renewing energy. It includes "construction notes" on how to use renewable energy in the home, a good bibliography, and a trade index. Beth Martin

4635 333.7

**Krueger, Ralph R.,** ed.

Managing Canada's Renewable Resources. Edited by Ralph R. Krueger and Bruce Mitchell. Toronto: Methuen, 1977. 333p. ill., maps. Bibliographical references. ISBN 0-458-92350-8 pa.: $8.95

1. Renewable natural resources – Canada. 2. Environmental policy – Canada.

3. Conservation of natural resources – Canada.

The management of Canada's land and water resources is examined in twenty-two essays and case studies by geographers, environmentalists, planners and ecologists. An introductory essay provides an historical perspective; chapter notes, tables and figures support the jargon-free text. A useful overview for students, teachers and the general reader interested in environment and resource management.

4636 333.7'072

**Powell, Wyley L.,** comp.

The Ontario Energy Catalogue: A Directory of Who's Doing What in Energy in Ontario and a Bibliography of Materials on Energy Available in Ontario. Compiled by Wyley L. Powell and Walter F. Falby. Toronto: Ontario Library Association, 1977. 170p. Index. ISBN 0-88969-011-1 pa.: $9; Order of 10 copies or more, $6

1. Power resources – Research – Ontario – Directories. 2. Power resources – Bibliography.

Both individuals and organizations are listed in the directory. The indexing is very thorough including, for example, indexes to speakers and collections of materials. The selective annotated bibliography includes print and non-print materials published since 1973; the level of difficulty is indicated. Diane Hart

4637 333.7'0971

**Barker, Mary L.**

Natural Resources of British Columbia and the Yukon Territory. Vancouver: J. J. Douglas, 1977. 155p. maps. Bibliographical references and Index. ISBN 0-88894-122-6 pa.: $6.95

1. Natural resources – British Columbia. 2. Natural resources – Yukon Territory.

Derived from a class the author teaches at Simon Fraser University, this book looks at the discovery, distribution, and use of energy, land and wildlife resources in British Columbia and the Yukon. Much of the material is found in federal and provincial government reports and statistics. A geography background would be a definite asset to the reader. Beth Martin

4638 333.7'09713

**Crow, Robert.**

Energy Planning in a Conserver Society: The Future's Not What It Used to Be, by Robert Crow, Peter Szegedy-Maszak, and Christopher Conway. Toronto: Energy Probe, 1978. 97p. diagrs. Bibliography: p. 91-97. pa. Processed: $10

1. Energy policy – Ontario. 2. Energy consumption – Ontario.

Examines current energy planning practices in Ontario and analyzes their effectiveness. The report concludes by proposing an alternative energy policy for Ontario in 2025 based on conservation and renewable resources. Margaret Covshoff

4639 333.72

**Science Council of Canada.**

Canada as a Conserver Society: Resource Uncertainties and the need for New Technologies. Ottawa: Science Council of Canada, 1977. 108p. Bibliographical references and Index. (Science Council of Canada. Report: no. 27) ISBN 0-660-01400-9 pa.: $3 (Canada); $3.60 (Foreign)

1. Conservation of natural resources – Canada.

"It is now understood that in many fields the continuing expansion of current practices will not be possible in the future. This recognition is having a strong and stimulating effect; far form being restrictive, it is releasing creativity, imagination and initiative all around the world." -p. 6. This Report discusses Canada's possible contributions to the Conserver Society and makes recommendations which have been widely discussed.

4640 333.8'2

**Peacock, Donald.**

People, Peregrines and Arctic Pipelines: The Critical Battle to Build Canada's Northern Gas Pipelines. Vancouver: J. J. Douglas, c1977. 213p. maps. Bibliography: p. 208. Index. ISBN 0-88894-138-2 pa.: $5.95

1. Gas, Natural – Northwest, Canadian – Pipe lines. 2. Gas, Natural – Alaska – Pipe lines. 3. Gas, Natural – Pipe lines – Environmental aspects – Northwest, Canadian. 4. Gas, Natural – Pipe lines – Environmental aspects – Alaska.

An authoritative description of the proposals which have been made regarding the best method to transport natural gas from the north to the southern markets. Includes a chronology of events from 1967-1977. Margaret Covshoff

4641 333.8'2
**Turner, Dick.**
Sunrise on Mackenzie. Saanichton, B.C.: Hancock House, c1977. 175p. maps, port. ISBN 0-919654-98-3 pa.: $7.95

1. Indians of North America – Northwest Territories – Mackenzie – Claims. 2. Indians of North America – Northwest Territories – Mackenzie. 3. Mackenzie Valley pipeline.

A controversial book about Canada's North covering the social and economic problems that have to be dealt with if the North is to be developed. Margaret Covshoff

## 334 Cooperatives

4642 334.
**MacPherson, Ian.**
Each for All: A History of the Co-Operative Movement in English Canada, 1900-1945. Toronto: Macmillan, 1979. Bibliography. Index. (The Carleton Library) ISBN 0-7705-1771-4 pa.: $9.95

1. Cooperation – Canada – History.
2. Cooperative societies – Canada – History.

Surveys the English-Canadian co-operative movement describing its successes and failures. Includes detailed notes for each chapter and a good bibliography. Margaret Covshoff

4643 334.1'0971
**Laidlaw, Alexander F.**
Housing You Can Afford. Toronto: Green Tree Publishing, c1977. 234p. ill., diagrs., forms, plans. Bibliography: p. 229-232. Index. ISBN 0-919476-68-6 bd.: $10.95 ISBN 0-919476-69-4 pa.: $5.95

1. Housing, Cooperative – Canada.

Since the early 1970's, when housing became priced beyond the means of many Canadian families, co-operative housing has offered an attractive alternative. Laidlaw draws on his vast experience in this field to explain the what and how of co-operatives. Liberal use of illustrations enhances the book's appeal. Beth Martin

## 335 Socialism

4644 335.
**Penner, Norman.**
The Canadian Left: A Critical Analysis. Scarborough, Ont.: Prentice-Hall, c1977. 287p. Bibliography: p. 261-275. Index. ISBN 0-13-113126-5 pa.: $5.95

1. Socialism in Canada – History. 2. Communism – Canada – History.

A former Communist Party member looks at the continuity and unique features of the socialist tradition in Canada. Penner notes a persistent theme of attempts to Canadianize Marxism and social democracy. By far the most absorbing and thoughtful account of its kind. Barbara Stewart

4645 335'.02
**Suits, Bernard.**
The Grasshopper: Games, Life and Utopia. Toronto: University of Toronto Press, c1978. 178p. ill. Index. ISBN 0-8020-2301-0 $10

Aesop's redoubtable grasshopper and his disciples converse about the meaning of game-playing and the importance of games in a Utopian life. An unusually engaging philosophic discussion laced with wit and enlivened by the participation of a coterie of personable characters. Frank Newfeld's drawings contribute to a well-designed, visually interesting book.

4646 335.43'06
**Kolasky, John.**
The Shattered Illusion: The History of Ukrainian Pro-Communist Organizations in Canada. Toronto: PMA Books, 1979. 255p. Bibliography. Index. ISBN 0-88778-189-6 bd.: $15 ISBN 0-88778-190-X pa.: $7.95

1. Communism – Canada. 2. Ukrainians in Canada.

As the only work of its kind this study by an expert provides much information unavailable elsewhere. Kolasky, who lives in Toronto, is a teacher who was a member of the Communist Party of Canada for thirty years. In this fourth book he has combined careful research and good writing on a little known but significant aspect of Canadian history. A basic choice for libraries. Andrew Gregorovich

4647 335.43'092
**Beeching, William,** ed.
Yours Is the Struggle: Reminiscences of Tim Buck. Edited by William Beeching and Phyllis Clarke. Foreward by Tom McEwen. Toronto: NC Press, 1977. 414p. ill., plates, ports. Index. ISBN 0-919600-71-9 bd.: $17.95 ISBN 0-919600-70-0 pa.: $8.95

1. Buck, Tim, 1891-1973. 2. Communist Party of Canada. 3. Communists – Canada – Biography.

Interviews with the former general secretary of the Canadian Communist Party recorded in 1965 have been edited by two friends. The focus is upon Buck's role in the Party, its stance in the Depression, the Spanish Civil War, and relationships with the Soviet Union. Significant as a socialist perspective on major events of the twentieth century. Readable.

## 336 Public finance and taxation

4648 336.2
**Bird, Richard Miller.**
Charging for Public Service: A New Look at an Old Subject. Toronto: Canadian Tax Foundation, 1976. 269p. Bibliography: p. 241-259. Index. (Canadian Tax Papers) ISSN 0008-512X $7

1. Taxation – Canada. 2. Municipal service – Canada – Finances.

The author, an advocate of user charges, first explains what the benefit principle of taxation is and how public service can be priced. He then shows how it can be applied in Canada, using examples from the fields of transport, urban public services, health care, pensions and education. Beth Goble

4649 336.2'00971
**Pipes, Sally.**
Tax Facts: The Canadian Consumer Tax Index and You, by Sally Pipes and Michael Walker. 2d ed. Vancouver: Fraser Institute, 1979. 140p. ill., tables. Bibliography: p. 121-126. ISBN 0-88975-027-0 $3.95

1. Taxation – Canada. 2. Tax incidence – Canada.

First edition published 1976 under title: *How Much Tax Do You Really Pay?*

A non-technical explanation of the total tax burden, federal, provincial and municipal, borne by the average Canadian family. The statistics have been updated to 1978. Illustrative diagrams and figures, chapter notes and a glossary further clarify the clearly written text. Instructive reading for all Canadian taxpayers.

4650 336.2'42
**Johnston, Donald J.**
How to Survive Canada's Tax Chaos. Rev. and updated ed. Markham, Ont.: PaperJacks, 1977. 192p. ISBN 0-7701-0016-3 pa.: $1.95

1. Income tax – Canada – Popular works.

Third edition listed *CS* no. 771.

New material has been added on international tax planning, and on the future of tax reform.

4651 336.2'42
**McLeod, William E.**
Tax Savings Plans in Canada: How to Get the Most for Your Money! 2d ed. Vancouver: International Self-Counsel Press, 1978. 121p. (Self-counsel Series) ISBN 0-88908-039-9 pa.: $3.95

1. Tax planning – Canada – Popular works.
2. Income tax – Canada – Deductions – Retirement contributions – Popular works.
3. Income tax – Canada – Deductions – Popular works.

For the consumer in a quandry over the choice of an appropriate RRSP, RHOSP, annuity, or mutual fund, this book will be helpful in making a decision. The text is updated annually to reflect constantly changing legislation in this field. Makes a useful companion to McLeod's *Tax Shelters in Canada*. Beth Martin

4652 336.2'42
**McLeod, William E.**
Tax Shelters in Canada: Where are They? How do They Work? How to Get the Most for Your Money! 3d ed. Vancouver: International Self-Counsel Press, 1978. 157p. Bibliographical references. (Self-counsel Series) ISBN 0-88908-048-8 pa.: $4.50

1. Tax planning – Canada – Popular works.
2. Income tax – Canada – Deductions – Retirement contributions – Popular works.
3. Income tax – Canada – Deductions – Popular works.

A good basic book on RRSP's, mutual funds, life insurance policies, annuities and other tax shelters. The author illustrates how one can save money, choose an appropriate tax shelter, and avoid pitfalls. Can be understood easily by the layman. Beth Martin

4653 336.2'42
**Riehl, Gordon W.**
Reduce Your Personal Taxes. Rev. ed. Don Mills, Ont.: General Publishing; Markham, Ont. : PaperJacks, 1979. ISBN 0-7736-1044-8 pa.: $3.95 ISBN 0-7701-0066-X pa.: $1.95

1. Income tax – Canada – Popular works.
2. Tax planning – Canada – Popular works.

The author, a chartered accountant, contends that many Canadians pay more tax than necessary. He advocates planning throughout the year, and making use of tax shelters such as Registered Retirement Savings Plans, and using stock options. Detailed instructions for tax planning and worksheets are included. A useful companion to Wayne Beach's *Are You Paying Too Much Tax?* Beth Goble

4654 336.71
**Strick, J. C.**
Canadian Public Finance. 2d ed. Toronto: Holt, Rinehart and Winston, 1978. 198p. Bibliography: p. 188-192 Index. ISBN 0-03-928154-X pa.: $8.95

1. Finance, Public – Canada.

Second edition, published in 1973, listed *CS* no. 775.

The structure of the new edition remains unchanged but the content has been revised to incorporate new policy developments, the data in tables has been brought up to 1976, and the form of some of the tables has been altered. A list of selected readings for each chapter appears for the first time. Students and general readers.

4655 336.713
**Foot, David K.**
Provincial Public Finance in Ontario: An Empirical Analysis of the Last Twenty-five Years. Toronto: Published for the Ontario Economic Council by University of Toronto Press, c1977. 213p. graphs. Bibliography: p. 209-213. (Ontario Economic Council Research Studies) ISBN 0-8020-3350-4 pa.: $7.50

1. Finance, Public – Ontario. 2. Finance, Public – Ontario – Mathematical models.

Hailed as a major study on Canadian public finance, this text analyses Ontario's revenues and expenditures during the period 1950-1973. The heavy emphasis on economic analysis may limit interest primarily to economists, and, to a lesser extent, to historians and political scientists. Beth Martin

## 338 Production

4656 338'.0971
**Richards, John.**
Prairie Capitalism: Power and Influence in the New West, by John Richards and Larry Pratt. Toronto: McClelland and Stewart, c1979. 340p. Bibliographical references and Index. (Canada in Transition Series) ISBN 0-7710-7179-5 bd.: $16.95 ISBN 0-7710-7177-9 pa.: $6.95

1. Petroleum industry and trade – Alberta. 2. Gas, Natural – Alberta. 3. Potash industry and trade – Saskatchewan. 4. Alberta – Economic policy. 5. Saskatchewan – Economic policy.

Two academics, an economist and a political scientist, offer a carefully reasoned analysis of the economic, political and social changes in Alberta and Saskatchewan from the thirties to the present, as mineral wealth has transformed an agricultural economy. An important, timely study of an unprecedented shift in power. Academic and public libraries.

4657 338'.0971
**Starks, Richard.**
Industry in Decline: Why Canadian Industry Is So Weak, and What Can Be Done About It. Toronto: James Lorimer, 1978. 123p. Bibliographical references. (Economy in Crisis) ISBN 0-88862-210-4 pa.: $2.50

1. Canada – Industries.

A non-academic presentation, by a financial journalist, of Canada's industrial problems which include competition from developing nations, foreign ownership, low productivity and too few finished exports. Solutions offered by various national groups are discussed. Marilyn Koch

## 338.2 Mineral industries

4658 338.2'0971
**Taylor, Geoffrey W.**
Mining: The History of Mining in British Columbia. Saanichton, B.C.: Hancock House, 1977. 195p. ill. ports. Index. (The Resource Series) ISBN 0-919654-87-8 $17.95

1. Mineral industries – British Columbia – History.

Chronicles the history of mining in British Columbia from the nineteenth century to the present. Describes the gold rushes and copper and coal mining in detail. Includes a glossary. Margaret Covshoff.

4659 338.2'71'28
**Gould, Ed.**
Oil: The History of Canada's Oil and Gas Industry. Saanichton, B.C.: Hancock House, 1976. 288p. ill., maps, ports. Bibliography: p. 278-280. Index. ISBN 0-919654-55-X $17.95

1. Petroleum industry and trade – Canada – History. 2. Gas industry – Canada – History.

Records the history of the oil and gas industry covering the tar sands, pipelines, the role of government, etc. Includes a technical glossary, a chronology of "oil history events" and many black and white photographs. Margaret Covshoff

4660 338.2'7'282
**Foster, Peter.**
The Blue-Eyed Sheiks: The Canadian Oil Establishment. Don Mills, Ont.: William Collins, 1979. 320p. ISBN 0-00-216608-9 $17.95

1. Petroleum industry and trade – Canada.

A fascinating, but superficial inside look at the personalities and companies, including PetroCanada, that make up the new Canadian oil establishment. Foster, a senior editor with the Financial Post, concentrates rather heavily on the Calgary scene, but this in no way detracts from the general or national interest in the book. Includes several interesting appendices. Beth Martin

4661 338.2'7'282
**Watkins, Campbell,** ed.
Oil in the Seventies: Essays on Energy Policy. Edited by Campbell Watkins and Michael Walker. Vancouver: Fraser Institute, 1977. 283p. graphs. Bibliographical references and Index. ISBN 0-88975-018-1 bd.: $14.95 ISBN 0-88975-011-4 pa.: $5.95

1. Petroleum industry and trade. 2. Petroleum products – Prices. 3. Energy policy – Canada. 4. Energy policy – United States.

Includes essays by petroleum economists who analyze the entire range of the oil industry, covering such topics as OPEC, price changes, consumption, and government intervention. Margaret Covshoff.

## 338.4 Secondary industries

4662 338.4'3
**Blomqvist, Ake G.**
The Health Care Business: International Evidence on Private Versus Public Health Care Systems. Vancouver: Fraser Institute, 1979. 185p. Bibliography: p. 183-185. ISBN 0-88975-026-2 $5.95

1. Medical economics. 2. Insurance, Health. 3. Medical economics – Canada. 4. Insurance, Health – Canada.

Blomqvist, an economist, believes significant cost-effectiveness and improvements in health care delivery can be achieved by implementing free enterprise health insurance, combining minimum level of care for all, plus additional care for additional insurance. He compares the British, American, Canadian and Swedish systems. No index, but a detailed table of contents. Lucia Herwig

4663 338.4'7
**Allin, Janet,** comp.
Map Sources Directory. Toronto: Office of the Library Coordination, Council of Ontario Universities, 1978. 175p. in various pagings. Bibliographical references and Index. ISBN 0-88799-098-3 pa. Processed.

1. Map industry and trade – Directories. 2. Map industry and trade – Canada – Directories. 3. Map industry and trade – United States – Directories.

Sources useful in obtaining map materials are arranged in three geographical groupings: international, United States, and Canada, and within each are grouped by the issuing agent. There is an alphabetical index of sources, and a list of journals of interest to map libraries. The format is loose-leaf.

4664 338.4'7'60971
**Palda, Kristian S.**
The Science Council's Weakest Link: A Critique of the Science Council's Technocratic Industrial Strategy for Canada. Vancouver: Fraser Institute, 1979. Bibliography. ISBN 0-88975-031-9 $4.95

1. Technology and state – Canada.
2. Technological innovations – Canada.
3. Canada – Economic policy.

A professor of Business Economics at Queen's University appraises the Council's policy of technological sovereignty and offers suggestions for Canadian technological development.

4665 338.4'7'629
**Fredericks, H. A.**
Bricklin, by H. A. Fredericks and Allan Chambers. Fredericton, N.B.: Brunswick Press, c1977. 139p. ill., ports.
ISBN 0-88790-088-7 bd.: $12.50
ISBN 0-88790-087-9 pa.: $6.25

1. Bricklin, Malcolm. 2. Bricklin automobile. 3. New Brunswick – Politics and government – 1960-

Using little publicized documents, the authors, a management consultant and journalist, recount the fascinating story of Malcolm Bricklin and the New Brunswick government. Forming a partnership to produce a revolutionary car, the project ended in bankruptcy and left New Brunswick with a twenty-three million dollar debt. Of general interest. Beth Martin

4666 338.4'7'64
**Warnock, John W.**
Profit Hungry: The Food Industry in Canada. Vancouver: New Star Books, c1978. 276p. Bibliographies and Index.
ISBN 0-919888-86-0 bd.: $13.95
ISBN 0-919888-85-2 pa.: $6.50

1. Food industry and trade – Canada.

The sources of high food costs and declining nutritional levels are themes of Warnock's unrelenting research into the production, distribution and marketing of food in Canada. An excellent study suited to both the general and specialized collection. Barbara Stewart

4667 338.4'7'67
**Morton, James W.**
The Enterprising Mr. Moody, The Bumptious Captain Stamp: The Lives and Colourful Times of Vancouver's Lumber Pioneers. Vancouver: J. J. Douglas, 1977. 183p. ill., map, plates, ports. Bibliography: p. 177-180. Index. ISBN 0-88894-147-1 $13.95

1. Moody, Sewell Prescott, d. 1875. 2. Stamp, Edward, 1814-1872. 3. Lumber trade – British Columbia – Vancouver – History. 4. Vancouver, B.C. – History

Through its two colourful founders the author traces the development of the lumber industry in British Columbia before it joined Confederation. The shift in power from Vancouver Island to the new industrial hub on the mainland is described. Good popular history. Nikki Lawrence

## 338.6 Organization of production

4668 338.6'42
**Peterson, Rein.**
Small Business: Building a Balanced Economy. Erin, Ont.: Press Porcépic, 1977. 192p. ill., graphs. Bibliographical references.
ISBN 0-88878-140-7 bd.: $10
ISBN 0-88878-141-5 pa.: $2.95

1. Small business – Canada.

This small volume is a compelling theoretical and practical assessment of Canadian economic conditions and small business development policies. Equally suited to school, public and special library collections. Barbara Stewart

## 338.7 Corporations

4669 338.74
**The Blue Book of Canadian Business.**
Edited by Philip B. Guryich, Frances Caldwell and Edward W. Weigens. 4th ed. Toronto: Canadian Newspaper Services International, 1979. 1180p. ill., ports.
ISBN 0-9690116-3-6 $49.50

1. Corporations – Canada – Directories. 2. Canada – Industries – Directories.

1976 edition listed *CS* no. 814.

Information on approximately twenty-five hundred firms, including location, ownership, size, nature of business and chief executive officers. The top five hundred Canadian companies, one hundred advertisers and two hundred stocks are listed. Marilyn Koch

4670 338.7'4
**Clement, Wallace.**
Continental Corporate Power: Economic Elite Linkages Between Canada and the United States. Toronto: McClelland and Stewart, c1977. 408p. Bibliography: p. 374-384. Index. ISBN 0-7710-2150-X bd.: $14.95 ISBN 0-7710-2151-8 pa.: $6.95

1. Corporations – Canada. 2. Corporations – United States. 3. Elite (Social sciences) – Canada. 4. Elite (Social sciences) – United States. 5. Canada – Economic conditions – 1965- 6. United States – Economic conditions – 1971-

A sequel to his earlier study, *The Canadian Corporate Elite*, this book examines the inter-relationships between the corporate elite in Canada and the United States. Highly recommended. Margaret Covshoff

4671 338.7'4
**Gordon, Manuel.**
Researching Canadian Corporations. Toronto: New Hogtown Press, c1977. 74p. ISBN 0-919940-10-2 pa.: $2.50

1. Corporations – Information services – Canada. 2. Corporations – Canada – Bibliography.

This book is the only researcher's guide available on the topic. It misses several widely-used sources, is almost exclusively Ontario-centered and is poorly organized. Serious researchers should be advised to consult a special librarian. Not recommended for special libraries. Barbara Stewart

4672 338.7'62
**Smith, Philip.**
The Treasure-Seekers: The Men Who Built Home Oil. Toronto: Macmillan, c1978. 310p. ill., plates, ports. Index. ISBN 0-7705-1661-0 $14.95

1. Home Oil Company – History. 2. Petroleum industry and trade – Canada – History.

The author of *Brinco* (CS no. 759) brings to life the story of early oil exploration and discovery in Alberta in this first major history of a Canadian oil company. Since its production was supported by Home Oil funding, it is not unbiased, but nevertheless it is a useful contribution to Canadian business history.

4673 338.7'66
**Swift, Jamie.**
The Big Nickel: Inco at Home and Abroad. Foreward by Dave Patterson. Kitchener, Ont.: Between the Lines, c1977. 173p. ill., port. Bibliographical references.
ISBN 0-919946-06-2 bd.: $9.95
ISBN 0-919946-05-4 pa.: $5

1. International Nickel Company – History.
2. Nickel industry – Ontario – Sudbury.

An informative and timely book which traces the corporate and labour history of the International Nickel Company. While the study concentrates chiefly on the Sudbury basin, the company's current operations in Guatemala and Indonesia are also discussed. Margaret Covshoff

## 338.8 Combinations

4674 338.8
**Canada. Royal Commission on Corporate Concentration.**
Report. Ottawa: Ministry of Supply and Services, 1978. 450p. ISBN 0-660-01456-4 pa.: $10; Outside Canada: $12

1. Consolidation and merger of corporations.
2. Corporations.

One of the most important studies in Canada's history, it was commissioned to report on "the nature and role of corporate power in Canada, the economic and social implications for the public interest of such concentrations, and whether safeguards exist in the presence of such concentrations". Essential for all economics collections.

4675 338.8'8
**Antonides, Harry.**
Multinationals and the Peaceable Kingdom. Toronto: Clarke, Irwin, 1978. 248p. Bibliography: p. 225-235. Index.
ISBN 0-7720-1196-6 $13.95

1. International business enterprises.
2. Christianity and economics. 3. Canada – Economic conditions.

Antonides, writing from a religious and moral viewpoint, attempts to show that citizens' interests are harmed by multinational activities. He maintains that foreign ownership of Canadian companies has negative political, economic and cultural effects. He calls for a return to basic human values, reform of the work environment, and a decrease in technology. Many notes, a lengthy bibliography, and an index are included. The author is a trade unionist. Barbara Dance

4676 338.8'8
**Marchak, M. Patricia.**
In Whose Interests: An Essay on Multinational Corporations in a Canadian Context. Toronto: McClelland and Stewart, c1979. 317p. Bibliography: p. 299-303. Index. ISBN 0-7710-5488-2 pa.: $7.95

1. International business enterprises.
2. Corporations, Foreign – Canada.

Professor Marchak's study deals with the sociology and political economy of large corporations in Canada. She discusses class, ownership, control, and organizational structure in an attempt to illustrate the negative effects of the profit and power motivations of corporations on the public interest. Tables provide data on various companies. There are bibliographical notes for each chapter, and a bibliography of further readings. Barbara Dance

## 338.9 Industry and the state

4677 338.91'71
**Cuff, Robert D.**
American Dollars – Canadian Prosperity: Canadian-American Economic Relations, 1945-1950, by Robert D. Cuff and J. L. Granatstein. Toronto: Samuel Stevens, 1978. 286p. Bibliography. Index.
ISBN 0-88866-593-8 $14.95

1. Canada – Foreign economic relations – United States. 2. United States – Foreign economic relations – Canada.

Using many hitherto confidential documents, listed in a detailed index, two York University professors trace the events, between 1945 and 1950, which shifted Canada's dependence upon Britain to domination by the United States. A very timely study in light of today's interest in foreign control. It should appeal to the student of history and politics. Beth Martin

4678 338.971
**Canada. Board of Economic Development Ministers.**
ABC: Assistance to Business in Canada: The Federal Government's Directory of Business Assistance Programs, Services and Incentives. Ottawa: Ministry of Supply and Services, 1979. 283p. ISBN 0-662-10477-3 pa.: Free DSS Cat. no. ID31-61/1979

Designed to give the business community easier access to information on federal economic development programs, tax incentives and other services, it also supplies numbers of toll-free zenith telephone "hot lines" staffed by experienced officers. Arrangement is by problem area such as marketing. Especially useful for small business.

4679 338.971
**Phidd, Richard W.**
The Politics and Management of Canadian Economic Policy, by Richard W. Phidd and G. Bruce Doern. Toronto: Macmillan, c1978. 598p. diagrs. Bibliography: p. 577-593. Index. ISBN 0-7705-1611-4 pa.: $12.95

1. Canada – Economic policy. 2. Canada – Executive departments. 3. Canada – Politics and government – 1963-

Two political scientists scrutinize the economic policy-making of federal government departments and agencies to the end of 1976. An ambitious, detailed study with notes, useful appendices and a summary chapter proposing a mechanism for a carefully planned economy. For students and academics in the fields of political science and public administration.

4680 338.971
**Phillips, Paul A.**
Regional Disparities: Why Ontario Has So Much and the Others Can't Catch Up. Toronto: James Lorimer, 1978. 134p. graphs, maps. Bibliographical references. (Economy in Crisis) ISBN 0-88862-206-6 pa.: $2.50

1. Regional economics. 2. Canada – Economic conditions – 1965- 3. Canada – Economic policy.

Analyzes the origins of regional inequalities in Canada and explains these disparities in terms of inequalities of income, employment and industrial growth. Margaret Covshoff

## 339 Macroeconomics

4681 339.46
**Galbraith, John Kenneth.**
The Nature of Mass Poverty. Cambridge, Mass.: Harvard University Press, 1979. 150p. Index. ISBN 0-674-60533-0 $8.95

1. Poverty. 2. Rural poor. 3. Underdeveloped areas.

The noted economist argues that most of the world's poverty stems from attitudes of acquiescence among the poor, frustration at being caught in an unbreakable cycle. He urges education, and escape to the industrialized countries by migration. A pithy, provocative view which does not deal with the question of measures to aid the poor countries to develop their economies.

## 340 Law

4682 340.
**Shumiatcher, Morris C.**
Man of Law: A Model. Saskatoon: Western Producer Prairie Books, 1979. Index.
ISBN 0-88833-028-6 bd.: $14.95
ISBN 0-88833-034-0 pa.: $9.95

1. Lawyers. 2. Legal ethics.

The author, one of Canada's most famous

lawyers, comments on the law, the legal system and lawyers, with wit, charm and anecdotes. Of more than autobiographical interest, the book contains insight into lawyers' minds and training. Gail Dykstra

4683 340'.03

**Williams, J. Steven.**

Basic Canadian Legal Terminology. Toronto: McGraw-Hill Ryerson, c1979. 151p. Index. ISBN 0-07-082728-1 pa.: $4.95

1. Law – Canada – Terms and Phrases.

An expanded glossary of terms, is arranged by subject and defined in the Canadian context. Emphasis is on common terms used by businesses or legal secretaries. Does not include criminal or family law terms. An index is provided. Arranged by general topics. Useful only because a Canadian legal dictionary has not been published yet (1979). Gail Dykstra

4684 340'.07'1171

**Thompson, Duncan C.**

How to Become a Lawyer in Canada. Foreword by Thomas J. Walsh. Edmonton: Acorn Books, 1979. 617p. Bibliography: p. 593-603. Index. ISBN 0-920482-25-2 bd.: $22.50 ISBN 0-920482-27-9 pa.: $12.50

1. Law – Study and teaching – Canada – Handbooks, manuals, etc.

Describes becoming a lawyer in Canada in exhaustive detail, from applications to law schools, the taking of Law School Admission Tests, using a law library, studying, bar admission courses, etc. Very practical, often amusing and essential for all public and high school libraries. Handy charts. Gail Dykstra

4685 340'.0971

**Canadian Directory of Public Legal Information.**

Ottawa: Canadian Law Information Council, 1979. 13v (10 Provincial directories, 1 Index volume, 2 Federal volumes, 1 in English, 1 in French) $40 (complete set; Provincial volumes may be purchased separately)

1. Courts – Canada – Officials and employees – Directories.

Compiled by the Federal Department of Justice, this directory is essential for all libraries. Each province's directory lists all agencies (public, private, governmental) providing information or advice on the law. Names, addresses, description of programs and publications are included and indexed by subject, name, geographic location. The federal volume is available in English or French as is the general index. Gail Dykstra

4686 340'.0971

**Fitzgerald, Patrick.**

Looking at Law: Canada's Legal System, by Patrick Fitzgerald, and King McShane. Ottawa: Bybooks, c1979. 128p. Bibliographies and Index. ISBN 0-9690111-0-5 pa.: $7

1. Law – Canada.

Offering a concise, but excellent introduction to Canada's legal system and origins and development of Canadian law, this book covers everything from what is law, through the sources of law, to law and the future. Written with clarity and geared to the interested reader, the book also provides excellent charts, tables, diagrams and an excellent subject index. Gail Dykstra

4687 340'.0971

**Fitzgerald, Patrick.**

This Law of Ours. Scarborough, Ont.: Prentice-Hall, 1977. 365p. Indexes. ISBN 0-13-919274-3 $9.30

1. Law – Canada. 2. Sociological jurisprudence.

This is a book about the law ... not on the law. A high school text which explores the basic rule of law, sociological, historical and political considerations inherent in our legal system. Effective, well-written, by an established author, the book makes use of excellent charts, quotes, excerpts from fiction, newspaper articles and editorials. Study Guide available. Gail Dykstra

4688 340'.0971

**Foster, Hamar.**

Common Law for Common Folk. Vancouver: Legal Services Commission of British Columbia, 1977. 41p. ill.

1. Law – Canada – History. 2. Law – British Columbia – Popular works. 3. Common law – History.

Tracing the development of common law from its English origins to present day Canada, this well-written text with its clever cartoons creates the only easily understood book, or booklet, on common law ever published. A must for all libraries large or small. Gail Dykstra

4689 340'.0971

**Gall, Gerald L.**

The Canadian Legal System. Toronto: Carswell, 1977. 316p. Bibliographies and Index. ISBN 0-459-31720-2 $26.50

1. Law – Canada.

Covers the essentials of the Canadian legal system from historical roots, basic structure, personnel, functions, etc. Written primarily for law school students, university courses, etc. Standard academic approach; table of cases. Gail Dykstra

4690 340'.0971
**Harding, J. L.**
Your Legal Advisor. Edited by R. Rocchi. Toronto: Coles Publishing, c1978. 130p. ISBN 0-7740-2650-2 pa.: $3.98

1. Law – Canada – Popular works.

Title on cover: *A Guide to Canadian Law in Everyday Use.*

With an emphasis on business, or business related law, the book points out the essentials of Canadian law in outline form. The use of "legalese" and the narrow scope diminish the usefulness of this book. Best used by those in business as a guide to further research or information seeking. A glossary of terms is included. Gail Dykstra

4691 340'.0971
**Jennings, Winfield H.**
Canadian Law, by Winfield H. Jennings and Thomas G. Zuber. 3d ed. Toronto: McGraw-Hill Ryerson, c1979. 422p. ill. Index. ISBN 0-07-082772-9 $11.65

1. Law – Canada.

One of the standard textbooks on Canadian law provides an introductory overview for secondary school students. Using a subject approach to the law, the book covers contracts, torts, civil rights, family law, labour law, citizenship, business law, etc. Newspaper articles, pictures and tables are used to interest readers. Gail Dykstra

4692 340'.0971
**McDonald, M.**
Legal First Aid. Toronto: Coles Publishing, c1978. 175p. ISBN 0-7740-2661-8 pa.: $4.98

1. Law – Canada – Popular works.

The emphasis is on preventative law – if you know the pitfalls, you can avoid them. Covering a wide variety of legal topics without using jargon, written in an informative and interesting manner, the book would be useful for all people as a handy guide to Canadian law. It includes family, contracts, criminal, constitutional, real estate, court system, etc. Gail Dykstra

4693 340'.0971
**Waddams, S. M.**
Introduction to the Study of Law. Toronto: Carswell, 1979. 270p. Bibliographical references and Index. ISBN 0-459-32450-0 bd.: $11 ISBN 0-459-32440-3 pa.: $7.50

1. Law – Canada. 2. Law – Study and teaching – Canada.

A professor of law at the University of Toronto, Waddams has written an introduction to law featuring information on analyzing legal problems, structure of the courts, the legal profession, the origin and development of common and civil law, equity, public and private law, etc. An examination of the evolution of legal education and its development in Canada is included. Gail Dykstra

4694 340.1'15
**Greenaway, William K.,** ed.
Law and Social Control in Canada. Edited by William K. Greenaway and Stephen L. Brickey. Scarborough, Ont.: Prentice-Hall, c1978. 240p. Bibliographical references. ISBN 0-13-526244-5 pa.: $8.95

1. Sociological jurisprudence. 2. Social control. 3. Law – Canada.

Useful for university students or researchers, this collection of essays examines legislation and the administration of justice, psychiatry and social control, and social control organization. Examining how the law has been used or could be used as social control, the authors tie the three sections together with introductory notes and a final essay. Gail Dykstra

## 341 International law

4695 341.23'71
**Canada. Dept. of External Affairs.**
Canada and the United Nations, 1945-1975. Canada: Dept. of External Affairs, c1977. 202p. ill. Bibliography: p. 201-202. ISBN 0-660-00681-2 pa.: $4.50 (Canada); $5.40 (Foreign) DSS cat. no. E2-82/1977

1. United Nations – Canada.

This readable summary of Canada's active participation reflects the changes in both the membership and character of the United Nations. It records not only the successes but also the failures. Supersedes the 1966 edition.

## 342 Constitutional law

4696 342'.00971

**Hogg, Peter W.**

Constitutional Law of Canada. Toronto: Carswell, 1977. 548p. Bibliography: p. 477-485. Indexes. ISBN 0-459-31890-X bd.: $29 ISBN 0-459-31900-0 pa.

1. Canada - Constitutional law.

The most recent and most definitive work on Canadian constitutional law, the book covers the basic concepts of the constitution and constitutional process, distribution of powers and civil liberties/the Canadian Bill of Rights. Although lacking a bibliography, the citations to cases would provide researchers with additional sources of information. Gail Dykstra

4697 342'.71

**Campbell, Betty.**

Becoming a Canadian: A Guide Through Citizenship Court. Vancouver: International Self-Counsel Press, 1978. 123p. ill., forms, map. (Self-counsel Series) ISBN 0-88908-034-8 pa.: $3.50

1. Naturalization - Canada - Popular works.

Expands on the information provided by the government in the free pamphlet by explaining rules, procedures, possible questions and appeal procedure. Gail Dykstra

4698 342'.71'02

**McConnell, William H.**

Commentary on the British North America Act. Toronto: Macmillan, c1977. 469p. Bibliography: p. 455-457. Index. ISBN 0-7705-1376-X $24.95

1. Canada - Constitutional history.
2. Canada - Politics and government - 1867-
3. Canada - Constitutional law.

A law professor at the University of Saskatchewan examines the form of the British North America Act from 1867 to 1949 and the powers which it confers. He concludes that it provides a durable base for a viable form of federalism. A useful analysis for students of history and political science. College and public libraries.

4699 342'.71'02

**Scott, Frank R.**

Essays on the Constitution: Aspects of Canadian Law and Politics. Toronto: University of Toronto Press, c1977. 422p. Bibliography: p. 405-407. Indexes. ISBN 0-8020-2238-3 bd.: $25 ISBN 0-8020-6297-0 pa.: $7.50

1. Canada. Constitution. 2. Canada - Constitutional law. 3. Canada - Constitutional history.

Governor General's Literary Award.

McGill University's eminent professor of law evaluates Canada's constitutional, political and legal developments in twenty-nine essays and speeches prepared between 1928 and 1971. He defends Canada's federal system. Of special interest to students and others who are studying the Constitutional Amendment Bill of 1978. Well documented.

4700 342.7'106

**Canada. Committee on the Concept of the Ombudsman.**

Report of the Committee on the Concept of the Ombudsman. Ottawa: Government of Canada, 1977. 69p. Bibliographical references.

1. Ombudsman - Canada.

A well-organized and detailed examination of the role of an ombudsman tracing the growth of the concept, the jurisdiction and operation of the office. Summaries of cases illustrating the work of an ombudsman are included in the appendices. The English and French versions appear in inverted sections. A much-needed study. College and public libraries.

4701 342'.71'085

**Rankin, T. Murray.**

Freedom of Information in Canada: Will the Doors Stay Shut?: A Research Study Prepared for the Canadian Bar Association. Ottawa: Canadian Bar Association, 1977. 155p. Bibliographical references. pa. Processed: Free

1. Government information - Canada.
2. Government information - United States.

A critical evaluation of the Canadian government's Green Paper *Legislation on Public Access to Government Documents* of 1977. The author expresses his misgivings about the government's policy of clinging to ministerial responsibility and favours judicial review. No matter what the outcome in the legislation promised in 1980 by the new

Trudeau government, Rankin's statement is still worth purchasing for most libraries.

4702 342.71'087

**Jamieson, Kathleen.**

Indian Women and the Law in Canada: Citizen Minus. Ottawa: The Advisory Council on the Status of Women, 1978. 108p. ill. ISBN 0-662018540 Free

1. Women – Legal status, laws, etc. – Canada. 2. Indians of North America – Canada – Legal status, laws, etc.

Branding it as discriminatory, the author presents a well-researched case against the treatment of women under the Indian Act. Bibliographic footnotes provide an excellent source of information on books, articles, court cases and legislation on the topic. Useful for all libraries from large to small for information on native people. Gail Dykstra

4703 342'.714

**Roman, Andrew J.**

Guidebook on How to Prepare Cases for Administrative Tribunals. Ottawa: Consumers' Association, 1977. 157p. pa. Processed. Spiral binding.

1. Administrative courts – Quebec (Province). 2. Consumer education.

Prepared by an authority on administrative law, this manual shows public interest groups how to face administrative tribunals effectively. Very practical advice including how to approach the media and how to prepare information. Always defines legal terms and explains procedure. Should be useful in public libraries. Gail Dykstra

## 343 Miscellaneous public law

4704 343'.71'04

**Snyder, J. Christopher.**

How to Be Sure You Get the Right RRSP (or RHOSP or DPSP): The Comprehensive Guide to Registered Tax-shelter Plans. 1978 ed. Toronto: Maclean-Hunter, 1977. 120p. Index. (A Financial Post/Macmillan Book) ISBN 0-88896-068-9 pa.: $5.95

1. Tax planning – Canada – Popular works. 2. Income tax – Canada – Deductions – Retirement contributions – Popular works.

A partner in a Toronto financial consulting firm explains what Registered Retirement Savings Plans are, why everyone needs one, what types are available, and how to choose and invest in them as profitably as possible. Charts compare plans according to cost and returns. Further chapters discuss other tax-shelter plans. Beth Goble

4705 343'.71'052

**Coombs, J. J.**

Charities and Charitable Donations: An Evaluation of Canadian Tax Treatment. Don Mills, Ont.: CCH Canadian, c1978. 194p. Bibliographical references and Index. ISBN 0-88796-058-8 pa.: $15

1. Charitable uses, trusts, and foundations – Taxation – Canada. 2. Income tax – Canada – Deductions – Charitable contributions.

This work consolidates all the sections and revisions to the Income Tax Act and regulations relating to charities and charitable donations. While it deals only with federal legislation, related documents are included, as well as sample forms. A topical index is provided and numerous examples help to clarify the text. Lucia Herwig

4706 343'.71'052

**Ferguson, Thomas M.**

Tax Deductible Investments. Toronto: Coles Publishing, c1978. 179p. ISBN 0-7740-2692-8 pa.: $5.98

1. Investments – Taxation – Canada.

Written for the average taxpayers, the book explains the various types of tax deductible investments that are available, shows how to use them, hints on how to determine which one is right for you and a comparison guide for consumers. Very practical, very useful advice. Gail Dykstra

4707 343'.71'052

**Ingram, David.**

Self-counsel's Guide to Income Tax in Canada: (A Complete Step-by-Step Guide to Do-It-Yourself Income Tax). 6th ed. Vancouver: International Self-Counsel Press, c1979. 132p. (Self-counsel Series) ISBN 0-88908-049-6 pa.: $4.95

1. Income tax – Canada – Popular works.

Third edition published under title: *David Ingram's Guide to Income Tax in Canada* listed *CS* no. 768.

Written for the average taxpayer, this guide to income tax details all of the possible deductions in clear and concise terms. Instructions are easy to follow and samples are provided. Gail Dykstra

## 344 Social law

4708 344'.71'018
**Brown, Donald J. M.**
Canadian Labour Arbitration, by Donald J. M. Brown and David M. Beatty. Agincourt, Ont.: Canada Law Book, 1977. 551p. Bibliographical references and Indexes.
1. Arbitration, Industrial – Canada.
2. Collective labor agreements – Canada.
3. Arbitration, Industrial – Canada – Cases.
Special labour and business collections will benefit from this systematic explanation of labour law and established procedures in the area of arbitration of collective agreements. A one hundred page index to cases cited and an extensive subject index make it suitable for use as a reference handbook. Barbara Stewart

4709 344'.71'018
**Palmer, Earl E.**
Collective Agreement Arbitration in Canada, by Earl E. Palmer and B. Hovius. Toronto: Butterworth, c1978. 635p. Bibliographical references and Indexes. (Canadian Legal Text Series)
ISBN 0-409-85770-X $65
1. Arbitration, Industrial – Canada.
2. Collective labor agreements – Canada.
Palmer's text parallels Donald J. M. Brown's *Canadian Labour Arbitration*, 1977, in many ways. Both cite similar cases and are well-supported by indexes, detailed tables of contents and a concise narrative style. Recommended for special collections on labour law. Barbara Stewart

4710 344'.71'041
**Sharpe, Gilbert.**
Doctors and the Law, by Gilbert Sharpe and Glenn Sawyer. Toronto: Butterworth, c1978. 448p. ill. Bibliography: p. 437-438. Index. ISBN 0-409-86628-8 $25.95
1. Medical laws and legislation – Canada.
Written for health care professionals, the text covers subjects such as consent, hospital liability, confidentiality, and standard care, by providing a survey of the state of Canadian law. A comparative chart of provincial legislation is a very useful appendix as are the appendices on abortion and the index to health care cases by year. The writing eschews jargon and explains terms fully. Gail Dykstra

4711 344'.713
**Estrin, David.**
Environment on Trial: A Handbook of Ontario Environmental Law, by David Estrin and John Swaigen. Rev. ed. Edited by Mary Anne Carswell and John Swaigen. Toronto: Canadian Environmental Law Research Foundation, 1978. 587p. diagrs., form. Bibliographical references and Indexes.
ISBN 0-9690534-1-X pa.
1. Environmental law – Ontario.
First edition listed *CS* no. 894.
Although written for Ontario, the types of laws and overriding environmental concerns are applicable across Canada. Arranged by topic the book discusses pesticide use, waste disposal problems, environmental pollution such as oil, water, noise, etc. A handbook for the concerned citizen. Gail Dykstra

## 345 Criminal law

4712 345'.71
**Clarke, Kenneth L.**
Criminal Law and the Canadian Criminal Code, by Kenneth L. Clarke, Richard Barnhorst and Sherrie Barnhorst. Toronto: McGraw-Hill Ryerson, 1977. 286p. Bibliographical references and Index.
ISBN 0-07-082553-X pa.: $8.95
1. Canada. Laws, statutes, etc. Criminal code.
2. Criminal law – Canada.
Written for community college students and non-lawyers with a need for information on criminal law, the text covers general introductory material on the administration of criminal law and penalties and treatment of specific offenses. The use of legal jargon somewhat diminishes the effectiveness of the writing. Gail Dykstra

4713 345'.71
**Cohen, Stanley A.**
Due Process of Law: The Canadian System of Criminal Justice. Toronto: Carswell, 1977. 429p. Bibliography: p. 407-417. Indexes.
ISBN 0-459-31730-X $29
1. Criminal law – Canada.
Covering the definition of 'due process', the role and power of the police, pre-trial process, the prosecution judge and trial, the book explains current Canadian practice and points out abuses of due process and possible remedies. A scholarly work, yet of continuing interest to the non-lawyer. Gail Dykstra

4714 345'.71
**Mewett, Alan W.**
Criminal Law, by Alan W. Mewett and Morris Manning. Toronto: Butterworth, c1978. 577p. Bibliographical references and Index. (Canadian Criminal Law Series) ISBN 0-409-84920-0 $60
1. Criminal law – Canada.
Written for those studying the law, the text covers Canadian criminal law comprehensively. Since this is a legal text, economic, social or political issues in the treatment of criminals or criminal law are not covered. Included is information on criminal charges under the criminal code, their background, treatment by courts, all with the usual extensive case citations. Not for the casual reader. Gail Dykstra

4715 345'.71
**Parker, Graham.**
An Introduction to Criminal Law. Toronto: Methuen, 1977. 357p. Bibliography: p. 349-350. Indexes. ISBN 0-458-92620-5 bd.: $14.95 ISBN 0-458-92310-9 pa.: $9.95
1. Criminal law – Canada. 2. Criminal procedure – Canada.
Covering the philosophical, historical and procedural influences on Canadian criminal law, this text for high school/college students is comprehensive without being tedious, well-documented without drowning in case citations and fact situations. Very useful, the text has become a classic work in a very short time. Gail Dykstra

4716 345.71
**Rosenberg, Gertrude.**
Criminologie canadienne: Bibliographie commentée: La criminalité et l'administration de la justice criminelle au Canada. Canadian Criminology: Annotated Bibliography: Crime and the Administration of Criminal Justice in Canada. Prepared under the direction of Gertrude Rosenberg by Katia Luce Mayer, and Lise Brunet-Aubry. Ottawa: Solicitor General Canada, Research Division, 1977. 726p. pa.: Free DSS cat. no. JS22-41/1977
Includes 1463 entries for articles, monographs, government documents and reports, research reports and theses dealing with criminological research, issued between 1960 and 1976. Arranged topically; many entries are annotated. Separate contents and keyword indexes in French and English; author index. Diane Henderson

4717 345'.71'0247
**Purich, Donald.**
Drinking and Driving: What to Do if You're Caught. Vancouver: International Self-Counsel Press, 1978. 133p. diagrs. (Self-counsel Series) pa.: $4.50
1. Drunk driving – Canada – Popular works.
Detailed information on what can/will happen to a person charged with impaired driving. Covers everything from the initial contact with the police, through the courts, possible penalties, insurance premiums, etc. Sample forms are provided. The text spells out every detail in concise, understandable prose. Very, very useful. Gail Dykstra

4718 345'.71'0257
**MacFarlane, Bruce A.**
Drug Offences in Canada. Toronto: Canada Law Book, 1979. 607p. Bibliography: p. 591-593. Index. ISBN 0-88804-007-5 $42.50
1. Drug abuse – Canada. 2. Narcotics and crime – Canada.
Written for lawyers but useful as a research source, the book covers the legislation related to drug offences, specific offences, gathering of evidence, the defence of such cases and sentencing. Appendix E provides a useful bibliography on the testing of drugs. A subject index is provided. Gail Dykstra

## 346 Private law

4719 346'.013
**Baxter, Ian F. G.,** ed.
The Child and the Courts. Edited by Ian F. G. Baxter and Mary A. Eberts. Toronto: Carswell, 1978. 429p. diagrs. Bibliographical references. (Carswell's Family Law Series) ISBN 0-459-31990-6 $29.50
1. Children – Law. 2. Custody of children. 3. Parent and child (Law).
A collection of essays by experts in the field on the position of children in the court including custody (marriage breakdown), adoption, wardship, protection. Also included are essays on the legal status of the child. Useful for a full range of professionals concerned with children and child welfare. Gail Dykstra

4720 346.0482
**Keyes, Andrew A.**
Copyright in Canada: Proposals For a Revision of the Law, by Andrew A. Keyes and C. Brunet. Ottawa: Consumer and Corporate Affairs Canada, 1977. 245p. Bibliographical references.
ISBN 0-662-00564-3 pa. DSS cat. no. RG4-15/1977

1. Copyright – Canada.

Its stated purpose is "to expose for public discussion the proposals made to revise the law respecting copyright. On the basis of that discussion, it is anticipated that the preparation of new legislation for modernizing Canada's copyright law can proceed with a better understanding ..." -p. i. The proposals have been discussed widely, but at this writing no legislation has emerged. For all libraries.

4721 346'.71'012
**Mungall, Constance.**
Changing Your Name in Canada: How to Do It Legally. Vancouver: International Self-Counsel Press, 1977. 132p. forms.
ISBN 0-88908-035-6 pa.: $3.50

1. Names, Personal – Law – Canada – Popular works. 2. Married women – Canada.

Covers the many aspects of changing a name, either to a new name or resuming a previous name, from filing court forms to notifying necessary authorities. Step-by-step guide with sample forms. For all libraries. Gail Dykstra

4722 346.71'013
**Dranoff, Linda Silver.**
Women in Canadian Law. Introduction by Rosalie S. Abella. Toronto: Fitzhenry & Whiteside, 1977. 112p. ill. Bibliography: p. 108-110. Index. (Women in Canadian Life)
ISBN 0-88902-377-8 pa.: $3.95

1. Women's rights – Canada. 2. Women – Legal status, laws, etc. – Canada.

Illustrated and topical, the book examines the status of women in Canadian law as a single entity, wife, mother and citizen. Basically historical, the information has been prepared to be pertinent to high school studies, with questions for discussion, case studies, illustrations, case citations, etc. Well-written, concise. Includes a bibliography and a glossary of terms. Gail Dykstra

4723 346'.71'013
**McCaughan, Margaret M.**
The Legal Status of Married Women in Canada. Toronto: Carswell, 1977. 210p. Bibliographical references and Indexes. (Carswell's Family Law Series)
ISBN 0-459-31870-5 $23.50

1. Women – Legal status, laws, etc. – Canada.

Deals with topics such as personal property in marriage, the matrimonial home, divorce, custody, inheritance, etc. Although it is aimed primarily at people with a legal background some sections of this book will be useful to the lay person, and will supplement information found in more popular works. Janice Zlatarits

4724 346'.71'013
**Wilson, Jeffery.**
Children and the Law. Toronto: Butterworth, c1978. 367p. Bibliographies and Index. ISBN 0-409-87760-3 $30

1. Children – Law – Canada.

A children's legal expert provides a long-needed guide to Canadian laws affecting children such as adoption, child welfare, crime, financial support, driving, and education. Subject index and detailed table of contents. A first purchase for all libraries interested in providing legal information for readers.

4725 346'.71'013
**Wilson, Jeffery.**
Up against It: Children and the Law in Canada. Toronto: House of Anansi Press, 1979. ISBN 0-88784-076-0 pa.: $5.95

1. Children – Law – Canada.

Written by a leading advocate of children's rights, the book covers the status of children and the law in a number of important areas: the family in conflict (divorce, custody, etc.), financial support, crime (both against and by children), courts (testimony, evidence), education and immigration. Detailed, covering all jurisdictions in Canada, with a subject index, table of cases, wide-ranging appendices, combined with a well-written text make this an excellent survey. Gail Dykstra

4726 346'.71'015
**Amirault, Ernest James.**
Canadian Family Law. Ashburn, Ont.: P. & O. Business Publications, 1978. 350p. $13.95

1. Domestic relations.

A most comprehensive book on family law written for the non-lawyer, it covers every aspect of family law from adoption to social welfare. The section explaining Canadian law covers such usually ignored topics as equity. A detailed table of contents provides access in lieu of indexes. Case histories, articles and court cases highlight the text. Gail Dykstra

4727 346'.71'015

**Jahn, Penelope.**

The Self-Help Guide to Divorce, Children, Welfare, by Penelope Jahn and Charles Campbell. 2d ed. Toronto: House of Anansi Press, c1979. 116p. ISBN 0-88784-075-2 pa.: $4.95

1. Domestic relations – Canada – Popular works. 2. Divorce – Canada – Popular works. 3. Children – Law – Canada – Popular works. 4. Public welfare – Canada – Law – Popular works.

First edition listed *CS* no. 914.

The stress is on the commonsense, often preventive actions that can be taken to avoid unnecessary hassles with 'the law'. Covering divorce, custody, domestic contracts, eligibility for welfare, dealing with child welfare agencies and family courts, the text is easy to read. The book offers background, not a step-by-step guide to legal action. Gail Dykstra

4728 346'.71'015

**Kronby, Malcolm C.**

Canadian Family Law. Don Mills, Ont.: General Publishing, 1979. 203p. ISBN 0-7736-1045-6 pa.: $5.95

1. Domestic relations – Canada – Popular works.

General family law overview with emphasis on Ontario but legislation and judicial decisions are noted for other jurisdictions. Uses court cases to illustrate facts and presents a very easily understood and well organized text. The texts of the Divorce Act and the Family Law Reform Act are included in the appendix. Gail Dykstra

4729 346'.71'033

**Marshall, T. David.**

Patients' Rights: What You Should Know Before Seeing a Doctor. Vancouver: International Self-Counsel Press, c1976. 70p. (Self-counsel Series) ISBN 0-88908-022-4 pa.: $1.95

1. Sick – Legal status, laws, etc. – Canada. 2. Malpractice – Canada.

The author, a lawyer and a physician, has written a handy guide to the medical profession for laymen. Covering patients' rights, medical malpractice suits, the duties of the coroner, disciplinary actions against members of the medical profession, and the use of the criminal code in matters regarding health. Concentrates on physicians, barely mentioning dentists and nurses. Gail Dykstra

4730 346'.71'033

**Marshall, T. David.**

The Physician and Canadian Law. 2d ed. Toronto: Carswell, 1979. 130p. Bibliography: p. 119-120. Index. ISBN 0-459-32530-2 $15.75

1. Physicians – Malpractice – Canada. 2. Medical laws and legislation – Canada.

Physician, lawyer, coroner, professor, the author's qualifications are impressive. Even more impressive is the clear, concise explanation of medicine and the law. Covering a general introduction to the law, specific topics such as consent and explaining the coroners' system, the author writes for doctors and lawyers to provide both professions with the information needed to understand the other. Gail Dykstra

4731 346'.71'033

**Picard, Ellen I.**

Legal Liability of Doctors and Hospitals in Canada. Toronto: Carswell, 1978. 425p. Bibliographical references and Index. ISBN 0-459-32240-0 $32

1. Physicians – Malpractice – Canada. 2. Tort liability of hospitals – Canada.

Requiring some prior knowledge of law, the book concentrates on the legal liability of doctors and hospitals to their patients. Detailing the possible legal actions, and defenses, each chapter provides extensive, copiously footnoted information. Of particular note are the appendices listing cases by medical specialization and procedure. An examination of the current medical legal crises and alternatives to compensation are provided in Chapter 13. Gail Dykstra

4732 346'.71'048

**Burn, Peter.**

Guide to Patent, Trade Mark, & Copyright Law in Canada. Toronto: Coles Publishing, c1977. 267p. ill., forms. Index. ISBN 0-7740-2517-4 pa.: $4.98

1. Patent laws and legislation – Canada – Popular works. 2. Trade marks – Canada – Popular works. 3. Copyright – Canada – Popular works.

Useful as a guide through the maze of patent, trademark and copyright law in Canada for persons prior to seeking legal counsel. Outlines necessary requirements for holding a patent, etc., and indicates how one processes an application. A very general introduction to the topic for non-lawyers. Gail Dykstra

4733 346'.71'054

**Rocchi, Rosanne.**

Guide to Wills and Estate Planning in Canada. Toronto: Coles Publishing, c1978. 285p. diagrs., forms. Index. ISBN 0-7740-2621-9

1. Wills – Canada. 2. Inheritance and succession – Canada. 3. Estate planning – Canada.

Designed to provide the reader with essential information needed prior to seeing a lawyer to draw up the actual will. Covers all aspects of estate planning and includes sample forms. Strong Ontario bias is recognized by using symbols to indicate jurisdiction. Subject index and glossary of terms provided. Gail Dykstra

4734 346'.71'059

**Granger, Alix.**

Trust Companies in Canada: What You Need to Know to Avoid Getting Taken! Vancouver: International Self-Counsel Press, 1978. 92p. (Self-counsel Series) ISBN 0-88908-046-1 pa.: $3.95

1. Trusts and trustees – Canada – Popular works. 2. Trust companies – Canada – Popular works.

Trust companies and trustees are not only for the very rich. The author shows how and why all consumers can be affected and even shabbily treated by trusts. The use of case histories is both beneficial and illuminating. A book on a too often neglected topic offers practical advice. Gail Dykstra

4735 346'.71'0652

**Teckert, Harry E.**

You and the Law: What Every Small Business Owner Needs to Know, by Harry E. Teckert and Michael J. McDonald. Toronto: Financial Post; Macmillan, c1978. 324p. Index. (Canadian Small Business Series) (A Financial Post/Macmillan Book) ISBN 0-7705-1649-1 pa.: $5.95

1. Small business – Law and legislation – Canada. 2. Business law – Canada.

The text is well planned, full of valuable information, easy to use, and covers every possible aspect of running a small business. It uses checklists and outlines effectively and provides sample forms which are clear and concise. In general, a very useful guide to the legal ramifications of owning/running a small business. Gail Dykstra

4736 346'.71'0662

**Fayers, Heather.**

Federal Incorporation & Business Guide: How to Form Your Own Federal Corporation Under the Canada Business Corporations Act. Vancouver: International Self-Counsel Press, c1978. 115p. forms. (Self-counsel Series) ISBN 0-88908-036-4 pa.: $9.95

1. Incorporation – Canada – Popular works. 2. Corporation law – Canada – Popular works.

Fayers, the publisher's legal editor, gives a step-by-step guide for small business owners wanting to incorporate federally with minimal legal assistance. She discusses taxation, regulations, shares, company directors, records, and various procedures. The inclusion of thirty sample forms is useful. Barbara Dance

4737 346'.71'077

**Parker, Allan.**

Credit Law and Bankruptcy Handbook. 4th ed. Vancouver: International Self-Counsel Press, 1979, c1973. 143p. ill. (Self-counsel Series) ISBN 0-88908-053-4 pa.: $3.95

1. Debtor and creditor – Canada – Popular works. 2. Consumer credit – Law and legislation – Canada – Popular works. 3. Bankruptcy – Canada – Popular works.

Combines a general explanation of credit, what it is, how to obtain it, from whom, with practical advice on handling debt, debt pooling, payment, bankruptcy. Credit-giving institutions are described in some detail. Advice is practical and useful. Gail Dykstra

4738 346'.71'077

**Paulsen, Timothy R.**

Collecting Debts Successfully from Customers, Clients, and Former Friends. Vancouver: International Self-Counsel Press, 1978. 83p. (Self-counsel Series) ISBN 0-88908-045-3 pa.: $3.50

1. Debtor and creditor – Canada – Popular works.

The advice is practical and the strategies suggested detailed; sample collection letters, telephone conversations and reviews are provided. Very useful for public libraries or small businesses. The pros and cons of using collection agencies are examined. Gail Dykstra

## 347 Civil procedure

4739 347'.711'014

**Williams, David R.**

"The Man for a New Country": Sir Matthew Baillie Begbie. Sidney, B.C.: Gray's Publishing, 1977. 333p. ill., facsims., map, plates, ports. Bibliography: p. 309-323. Index. ISBN 0-88826-068-7 $15.95

1. Begbie, Matthew Baillie, Sir, 1819-1894. 2. Judges – British Columbia – Biography.

University of British Columbia Medal for Canadian Biography.

Appointed in 1858, the first Chief Justice of British Columbia regularly travelled throughout the new province, dispensing justice equitably, and firmly establishing British civil and criminal law to counter pro-American annexation sentiment. This well-documented biography of an eminent nineteenth century lawyer should find a place in western Canadian libraries. Ethel Kellen

## 348 Construction of statutes

4740 348'.71'04

**National Library of Canada. Resources Survey Division.**

Checklists of Law Reports and Statutes in Canadian Law Libraries. Listes de contrôle des recueils de jurisprudence et des statuts dans des bibliothèques de droit du Canada. Ottawa: National Library of Canada, 1977- v

0-662-00442-6 pa. Spiral binding: vol. 1. Canadian Law Reports. 1977. DSS cat. no. ISBN 3-66/1977 0-662-01054-X pa. Spiral binding: $5 (Canada); $6 (Foreign) vol. 3. United States Law Reports. 1978. DSS cat. no. ISBN 3-66/1977-3

1. Law reports, digests, etc. – Canada – Bibliography – Union lists. 2. Catalogs, Union – Canada.

Arranged by jurisdiction, federal and provincial, and sub-arranged by general law reports and topical reports, this checklist of holdings in Canadian law libraries would provide large public/research libraries with interlibrary loan information. The reports are listed by "popular title", as most commonly referred to by lawyers, etc. An alphabetical index is provided. Gail Dykstra

## 352 Local government

4741 352'.008

**Higgins, Donald J. H.**

Urban Canada: Its Government and Politics. Toronto: Macmillan, c1977. 322p. diagrs., map. Bibliography: p. 297-311. Index. ISBN 0-7705-1615-7 pa.: $8.95

1. Municipal government – Canada. 2. Cities and towns – Canada. 3. Political participation – Canada.

An overview of the variety of governments in twenty-two of our largest cities is illustrated by schematic diagrams to clarify structural details. This work focuses on the evolution of regional municipalities and the effects of reform politics on our urban systems. A comprehensive text with an extensive reading list. Nikki Lawrence

4742 352'.008

**Weaver, John C.**

Shaping the Canadian City: Essays on Urban Politics and Policy, 1890-1920. Toronto: Institute of Public Administration of Canada, 1977. 79p. Bibliography: p. 77-79. (Monographs on Canadian Urban Government) ISBN 0-91400-46-9 $3

1. Municipal government – Canada – History. 2. Urbanization – Canada – History. 3. Housing – Canada – History.

The dramatic surge in immigration at the end of the nineteenth century resulted in rapid urban and suburban growth. Various municipal institutions were formed to grapple with the resultant problems: inadequate zoning, housing, building codes, transportation and pollution. Tables, graphs and a detailed bibliography underscore the book's scholarly intent and suitability for larger collections. Ethel Kellen

4743 352.071

**Tindal, C. R.**

Local Government in Canada: An Introduction, by C. R. Tindal and S. Nobes Tindal. Toronto: McGraw-Hill Ryerson, c1979. 159p. Bibliography: p. 149-154. Index. (McGraw-Hill Ryerson Series in Canadian Politics)

1. Local government – Canada. 2. Municipal government- Canada.

A concise, well-organized overview of the history and development of local government in Canada, its various structures, its operation, problems and weaknesses. Attention is given to the government of small and rural communities as well as large urban centres. Each section of the book is summarized. A comprehensive, readable introduction to a topic of wide general interest. College and public libraries.

## 354 Canadian federal government

4744 354.71
**Kernaghan, W. D. K.,** ed.
Canadian Cases in Public Administration. Toronto: Methuen, c1977. 151p. Bibliographical references and Index. ISBN 0-45892-230-7 pa.: $4.95

1. Public administration – Case studies. 2. Civil service – Canada – Case studies.

This collection of case studies fills a gap in public administration literature. It is designed to be used with the third edition of Professor Kernaghan's *Public Administration in Canada,* 1977.

4745 354.71
**Kernaghan, W. D. K.,** ed.
Public Administration in Canada: Selected Readings. 3d ed. Toronto: Methuen, 1977. 372p. Bibliographies. ISBN 0-45892-410-5 $9.95

1. Public administration. 2. Canada – Politics and government.

This third edition updates the second edition which was published in 1971, with many new articles and revisions to the majority of others. Included are new articles on crown corporations, regulatory agencies, bilingualism, collective bargaining and federal-provincial administrative relations. Companion volume: *Canadian Cases in Public Administration.*

4746 354'.71
**Sinclair, Sonja.**
Cordial but Not Cosy: A History of the Office of the Auditor General. Toronto: McClelland and Stewart, c1979. 208p. plates, ports. Index. ISBN 0-7710-8157-X $19.95

1. Canada. Auditor General's Office – History.

A well-written and incisive account of the changing role and developing powers of the Auditor General's Office since 1878. Based upon interviews, research of government records and newspaper archives, the focus is on the colourful and sometimes controversial figures who have scrutinized federal government spending. Timely, interesting reading for every Canadian tax payer.

4747 354'.71'0074
**Lee, John Alan.**
RCMP: The Police Vs. the People, by John Alan Lee and William Edward Mann. Don Mills, Ont.: General Publishing, 1979. 290p. ISBN 0-7736-1046-4 $8.95

1. Canada. Royal Canadian Mounted Police.

Two sociologists use the methods of investigative journalism to study some questionable activities of the RCMP. With its tendency towards the sensational, it will not fail to hold the interest of the layman and the undergraduate sociology student for whom it was designed. Extensive bibliography.

4748 354'.71'0075
**French, Richard.**
The RCMP and the Management of National Security, by Richard French and André Béliveau. Toronto: Institute for Research on Public Policy, c1979. 79p. Bibliographical references. ISBN 0-920380-18-2 pa.: $6.95

1. Canada. Royal Canadian Mounted Police. Security Service – Management. 2. Canada – National security – Management.

The authors, management specialists, argue that inadequate personnel practices resulted in lack of communication between Force management and their political Ministers. Since the latter were unable/unwilling to provide policy guidelines the RCMP acted as it thought best. No index. Lucia Herwig

4749 354'.71'00827
**Hill, Olive Mary.**
Canada's Salesman to the World: The Department of Trade and Commerce, 1892-1939. Toronto: Institute of Public Administration of Canada; Montreal: McGill-Queen's University Press, 1977. 631p. ill., plates, ports. Bibliography: p. 609-615. Index. (Canadian Public Administration Series) ISBN 0-7735-0285-8 bd.: $17.50 ISBN 0-7735-0292-0 pa.: $7.50

1. Canada. Dept. of Trade and Commerce – History.

In this first comprehensive history of the Department, a long-time Department editor emphasizes the administrative structure: how the Department was established, its role, its expansion to meet growing needs. Based on primary sources, including restricted government files relating to the Department. Although it has been criticised for its lack of a theoretical orientation, it will be of interest to business, government, university students and laymen. First of a two-volume set.

4750 354'.71'0085

**Ostry, Bernard.**

The Cultural Connection: An Essay on Culture and Government Policy in Canada. Introduction by Robert Fulford. Toronto: McClelland and Stewart, c1978. 240p. Bibliographical references and Index. ISBN 0-7710-6900-6 pa.: $7.95

1. Arts – Canada – Management. 2. Art and state – Canada. 3. Canada – Intellectual life.

A high-ranking civil servant analyses, with historical perspective, the relationship between the federal government and culture, and the Quebec government and culture. He promotes the view that cultural policy should be based on public debate rather than on cabinet rulings, to ensure freedom for the artist. Of interest to all libraries.

4751 354'.71'0312

**Monet, Jacques.**

The Canadian Crown. Toronto: Clarke, Irwin, 1979. Index. ISBN 0-7720-1252-0 $9.95

1. Governors general – Canada. 2. Heads of state – Canada. 3. Executive power – Canada. 4. Canada – Constitutional history.

A well-documented history and discussion of the role and responsibilities of the crown's representatives in Canada. Although short, it is well-written, has 120 illustrations, a detailed index, and supplementary lists of all Canada's sovereigns, and all the Lieutenant Governors and Governors General. Lucia Herwig

4752 354'.71'0313

**Punnett, R. M.**

The Prime Minister in Canadian Government and Politics. Toronto: Macmillan, 1977. Bibliographical references and Index. (Canadian Controversies Series) ISBN 0-7705-1492-8 bd.: $11.95 ISBN 0-7705-1493-6 pa.: $4.95

1. Prime ministers – Canada. 2. Canada – Politics and government – 1867-

Based on sound research, it describes clearly the nature and powers of the Prime Minister's office, and how the work of the office is carried out. Designed for the university student, it is of interest also to the general reader and practising politician. It should help to clear away many misconceptions about the role of the Prime Minister.

4753 354'.71'04

**Campbell, Colin.**

The Superbureaucrats: Structure and Behaviour in Central Agencies, by Colin Campbell and George J. Szablowski. Toronto: Macmillan, 1979. 286p. Bibliographical references and Index. ISBN 0-7705-1767-6 pa.: $9.95

1. Government executives – Canada. 2. Canada – Executive departments.

A detailed examination of five key agencies in Canada's public service during Trudeau's regime, and the senior bureaucrats who influence government policy decisions from these strongholds of power. An important study based upon interviews with more than ninety senior executives. Proposals are made for reform. College and public libraries.

4754 354'.71'06

**Ferguson, Thomas M.**

What to Do When the Taxman Comes: The Inside Story on How to Cope with Canada's Tax Department. 2d ed. Vancouver: International Self-Counsel Press, 1979, c1976. 127p. (Self-counsel Series) ISBN 0-88908-047-X pa.: $3.50

1. Canada. Dept. of National Revenue, Taxation. 2. Tax administration and procedure – Canada – Popular works. 3. Income tax – Canada – Popular works.

First edition listed *CS* no. 970.

4755 354'.71'091

**Doern, G. Bruce,** ed.

The Regulatory Process in Canada. Toronto: Macmillan, c1978. 365p. diagr. Bibliography: p. 357-364. ISBN 0-7705-1610-6 pa.: $12.95

1. Independent regulatory commissions – Canada.

A useful guide to the current debate on the government's increasing role in regulating the economy. Respected economists, political scientists and lawyers analyse the regulatory process and then consider specific regulatory agencies as examples. Reforms are suggested. Although directed at the specialist, it also holds interest for any student of the subject.

4756 354'.713

**Sturgis, James.**

Adam Beck. Don Mills, Ont.: Fitzhenry & Whiteside, c1978. 64p. ill., ports. Bibliography: p. 64. (The Canadians) ISBN 0-88902-246-1 pa.: $2.25

1. Beck, Adam, Sir, 1857-1925. 2. Ontario Hydro – Biography.

Like others in the series, the biography of Adam Beck is easy to read, informative and well illustrated. This would be a useful book to introduce a study of the history of Ontario Hydro. Paula de Ronde

## 355 Military science

4757 355.03'1
**Hill, Roger.**
Political Consultation in NATO. Toronto: Canadian Institute of International Affairs; Kingston, Ont.: Centre for International Studies, Queen's University, c1978. 143p. diagrs. Bibliography: p. 139-143. (Wellesley Papers) pa.: $3.75

1. North Atlantic Treaty Organization.

NATO performs a vital peacekeeping function by providing an international forum for information exchange, consultation and co-ordinated policy formation. This volume offers a detailed analysis of its hierarchical structure, and an assessment of the past and present performance and future potential. There is a detailed bibliography. Suitable for university or special collections. Ethel Kellen

4758 355.03'1
**Reid, Escott.**
Time of Fear and Hope: The Making of the North Atlantic Treaty, 1947-1949. Toronto: McClelland and Stewart, 1977. 315p. Bibliography: p. 257-263. Index. ISBN 0-7710-7440-9 $13.95

1. North Atlantic Treaty Organization.
2. North Atlantic treaty, 1949.

The author, who was second in command to Lester Pearson, presents a personal account of the delicate four-stage diplomatic negotiations which culminated in the creation of NATO. He captures the immediate post-war Canadian and western geopolitical perceptions regarding potential Russian aggression. Recommended for larger libraries and specialized collections. Ethel Kellen

4759 355.03'35'71
**Cuthbertson, Brian.**
Canadian Military Independence in the Age of the Superpowers. Toronto: Fitzhenry & Whiteside, c1977. 282p. Bibliographical references and Index. ISBN 0-88902-429-4 $15.95

1. Canada – Military policy.

A former Canadian Army officer with a doctorate in war studies from King's College, England, looks critically at Canada's defence policy in the past, and in the present. He concludes that Canada is capable of moving toward less military reliance upon the United States and Great Britain. A useful, well-documented analysis. College and public libraries.

4760 355.03'35'71
**Porter, Gerald.**
In Retreat: The Canadian Forces in the Trudeau Years. Ottawa: Deneau and Greenberg, 1978. 232p. Bibliographical references and Index. ISBN 0-88879-007-4 $12.95

1. Canada – Military policy. 2. Canada. Armed forces.

A hard-hitting, partisan view of Canada's defence policy between 1968 and 1978. Porter's premise is that Trudeau's government so emasculated the Armed Forces as to render them incapable of functioning effectively. Persuasive rhetoric conceals the dearth of objective analysis. University and public libraries.

4761 355.2'236
**Granatstein, J. L.**
Broken Promises: A History of Conscription in Canada, by J. L. Granatstein and J. M. Hitsman. Toronto: Oxford University Press, 1977. 281p. Bibliography: p. 270-274. Index. ISBN 0-19-540258-8 pa.: $6.95

1. Military service, Compulsory – Canada – History.

An examination of the controversial question of compulsory military service in wartime, from Frontenac's day to the Cold War years. Extensive research of primary sources, careful documentation and an index make this detailed study an important one for the Canadian history collections in public and college libraries. Well-written but not impartial.

4762 355.3'45
**Nicholson, Gerald W. L.**
Seventy Years of Service: A History of the Canadian Army Medical Corps. Ottawa: Borealis Press, 1977. 388p. ill., maps, plates. Bibliographical references and Indexes. ISBN 0-919594-61-1 $18.95

1. Canada. Armed Forces. Royal Canadian Army Medical Corps – History.

Nicholson, author of eight military histories, has written a very thorough, scholarly history of the Army Medical Corps, providing both the broad overview of events and a detailed recounting of operations in the field. Well-documented with extensive notes, maps, photographs, seven appendices and three indexes. Lucia Herwig

4763 358.4
**Kostenuk, Samuel.**
R.C.A.F. Squadron Histories and Aircraft, 1924-1968, by Samuel Kostenuk and John Griffin. Toronto: Samuel Stevens, 1977. 255p. ill. Index. (Historical Publications) ISBN 0-88866-577-6 $19.95

1. Canada. Royal Canadian Air Force – History. 2. Airplanes, Military – History. 3. Aeronautics, Military – Canada – History.

A carefully researched pictorial and narrative history of the individual squadrons which served in Canada, overseas during the Second World War, and in post-war years in Europe and at home. The operational history, achievements, honours, mottoes and badges for each unit are recorded. A detailed, well-illustrated, and thoroughly indexed reference work. Highly recommended.

4764 358.4'3
**Dow, James.**
The Arrow. Toronto: James Lorimer, 1979. Bibliography. Index. ISBN 0-88862-282-1 $15.95

1. Avro Arrow (Fighter planes). 2. Canada – Politics and government – 1957-1963.

The author unfolds the story of the controversial two-engined, supersonic fighter, The Arrow, from its appearance in 1958 to the cancellation of the programme by government decision. Gwen Liu

## 360 Social services

4765 361.8
**Wharf, Brian,** ed.
Community Work In Canada. Toronto: McClelland and Stewart, 1979. 272p. ISBN 0-7710-8826-4 $7.95

1. Community organization. 2. Community development – Canada.

In order to relate theory to practice, case studies of Canadian community-oriented services and organizations such as Regent Park Community Services Unit are clearly presented and analyzed. Recommendations are based on trends derived. A useful, informative collection of articles for anyone interested in community development. Diane Hart

## 362 Social problems

4766 362.'0971
**Harrison, Phyllis,** ed.
The Home Children: Their Personal Stories. Winnipeg: Watson & Dwyer Publishing, 1979. 271p. ill. ISBN 0-920486-02-9 bd.: $14.95 ISBN 0-920486-04-5 pa.: $8.50

1. Children – Employment – Canada. 2. Canada – Emigration and immigration.

Presents mostly first-hand accounts of the experiences of British orphans shipped to Canada as farm labourers between 1870 and 1930. The many contributions are uneven in quality and interest, but they still constitute a moving and absorbing chapter in Canada's social history. Carefully researched and edited by an interested social worker. Ille-Mai Gerdels

4767 362'.1
**Allentuck, Andrew.**
Who Speaks for the Patient?: The Crisis in Canadian Health Care. Toronto: Burns & MacEachern, c1978. 111p. Bibliography: p. 107-108. Index. ISBN 0-88768-079-8 pa.: $5.95

1. Medical care – Canada.

Discussing the fundamental rights of patients in law and possible types of legal actions, the book examines the current medical-legal debate from the patient's point of view. The author provides a balanced and far-ranging examination of the entire health care system. Useful and easy to read, the book is one of the few to speak for the patient. Gail Dykstra

4768 362.1
**Culyer, A. J.**
Measuring Health: Lessons for Ontario. Toronto: Published for the Ontario Economic Council by University of Toronto Press, c1978. 189p. graphs. Bibliography: p. 183-189. (Ontario Economic Council Research Studies) ISBN 0-8020-3354-7 pa.: $10

1. Medical care – Evaluation. 2. Medical care – Ontario – Evaluation.

Culyer has produced a quite technical synthesis of the literature relating to Ontario, identifying the need for the development of better and more comprehensive health measurement tools to be used by public sector planners and politicians in the design and provision of health care delivery. No index, but graphs and tables. Lucia Herwig

4769 362.1
**Soderstrom, Lee.**
The Canadian Health System. London, Eng.: Croom Helm, c1978. 271p. Bibliography: p. 254-261. Index.
ISBN 0-85664-534-6 bd.: $23
ISBN 0-85664-658-X pa.
1. Medical care – Canada.
This ambitious work is the first to attempt to describe Canada's health services comprehensively. The assessment of public financing is of great relevance to the on-going arguments between the medical profession and governments. Useful suggestions are made for improving the system. All libraries.

4770 362.1
**Wilcox, Lewis DeWitt.**
Where Is My Doctor? Toronto: Fitzhenry & Whiteside, c1977. 246p. Index.
ISBN 0-88902-042-6 $12.50
1. Physician and patient. 2. Medical care.
Based on his own wide experience, a practising physician, educator and researcher, Wilcox details the selection, the inadequate training, and options available for medical students, and deplores the continuing shift from general practice to specialization. Well-written, for the interested layman, citing many examples to make his case. Lucia Herwig

4771 362.1'04'22
**Horrobin, D. F.**
Medical Hubris: A Reply to Ivan Illich. Montreal: Eden Press, 1977. 146p. Index.
ISBN 0-88831-001-3 $9
1. Social medicine. 2. Medical care.
3. Medicine – Philosophy.
A British doctor, now Director of the Pathophysiology Laboratory at the Clinical Research Institute of Montreal, agrees with much of Illich's criticism of the medical establishment, (*Limits to Medicine*, Pantheon, 1976), but disagrees with the solutions he suggests, and offers solutions of his own. He is hopeful that the medical profession will initiate radical changes. Of interest to both laymen and the medical profession.

4772 362.1'9
**Brown, Tom.**
Jeannette: A Memoir. Toronto: Lester and Orpen, c1978. 217p. ISBN 0-919630-92-8 $9.95
1. Brown, Jeannette. 2. Cancer – Biography.
A moving story which focuses on the last nine days in the life of the author's wife, a victim of pancreatic cancer. Flashbacks provide background information about the couple. The book deserves a wide audience for the insights it provides into cancer treatments and the effect of knowledge of a terminal illness on the individual and the family. Diane Hart

4773 362.2'92
**Amit, Zalman.**
Guide to Intelligent Drinking, by Zalman Amit, E. Ann Sutherland, and Andrew Weiner. Toronto: Fitzhenry & Whiteside, c1977. 269p. forms. Bibliography: p. 265-269.
ISBN 0-88902-424-3 $8.95
1. Alcoholism – Treatment. 2. Alcoholism – Prevention. 3. Alcoholics – Rehabilitation.
Written as a self-help manual for "problem drinkers", as defined by the authors. After a general discussion of alcoholism, the authors provide a series of charts for self-monitoring and consequent behaviour modification. Lucia Herwig

4774 362.2'93
**Weisman, Marilee.**
Drug Alert!: A Provocative Look at Street Drugs. Toronto: John Wiley, c1979. 127p. ill. Bibliography: p. 111. Index.
ISBN 0-471-99819-2 pa.: $6.95
1. Drugs and youth. 2. Drug abuse.
An objective, unemotional exposition of the problem of non-medical drugs written for parents, teachers and youth workers. Intoxicants, stimulants, barbituates, tranquillizers, narcotics and hallucinogens, their use and effects are factually described. Trafficking and the issue of decriminalization are discussed. A plea for understanding when coping with suspected drug abuse is made. Contains an excellent glossary and directory of agencies. Secondary school, college and public libraries.

4775 362.3
**Cormack, Barbara Villy.**
George. Downsview, Ont.: Canadian Association for the Mentally Retarded, 1978. 67p. ISBN 0-919648-14-2 $2
1. Mentally handicapped.
A pioneer in the provision of services for the mentally retarded presents the human, factual account of the life of a multihandicapped mental retardate and the history of Canadian services over the last thirty years. Highly readable, it provides observations on current concepts. Anecdotes add humanness to a subject inundated with research reports. Linda Pulver

4776 362.4
**Brown, Joan C.**
A Hit-and-Miss Affair: Policies for Disabled People in Canada. Ottawa: Canadian Council on Social Development, 1977. 508p. Bibliography: p. 483-508. ISBN 0-8810-268-2 pa.: $8

1. Handicapped – Canada. 2. Handicapped – Research – Canada.

This well-documented reference tool analyzes existing data and literature and leads to supplementary materials obtainable through contact with organizations and concerned individuals. The presentation highlights policy deficiencies and improvements needed rather than describing details of the present situation. The table of contents provides access to sections on prevention, minimizing of disability and assistance programs. Linda Pulver

4777 362.6'15
**Baum, Daniel Jay.**
Warehouses for Death: The Nursing Home Industry. Toronto: Burns & MacEachern, c1977. 191p. ports. Bibliography: p. 182-185. Index. ISBN 0-88768-072-0 pa.: $4.95

1. Nursing homes – Canada. 2. Old age homes – Canada. 3. Aged – Canada.

The decline of the nuclear family leaving the elderly to shift for themselves, has led to a thriving nursing home industry in Canada. The author's research found it grossly lacking in sensitivity to the needs of its clientele, and he suggests alternatives. Of interest to all libraries.

4778 362.7
**Task Force on the Child as Citizen.**
Admittance Restricted: The Child as Citizen in Canada. Interdit aux mineurs: la place de l'enfant dans la société canadienne. Ottawa: Canadian Council on Children and Youth, 1978. 172, 195p. ill., ports. Bibliographical references. ISBN 0-920786-00-6 pa.: $8.95

1. Children in Canada. 2. Child welfare – Canada.

The report of the Council's Task Force examines the role of children in Canadian society and their needs and rights. Of interest to both the general public and students. Text in English and French; French text on inverted pages. Marilyn Carr

4779 362.7'1
**Flint, Betty M.**
New Hope for Deprived Children. Toronto: University of Toronto Press, c1978. 200p. diagrs. Bibliography: p. 193-200. ISBN 0-8020-5394-7 $12.50

1. Children – Institutional care – Canada – Longitudinal studies. 2. Children, Adopted – Canada – Longitudinal studies.

This Institute of Child Study project was earlier discussed in *The Security of Infants* (1959), *The Child and the Institution* (1966). Flint studied twenty-eight adopted children who experienced institutional deprivation. Dry reporting of findings on mental and physical development will perhaps be of interest to other researchers but not to those patrons wanting explanation and generalization. Claire England

4780 362.7'1
**Krashinsky, Michael.**
Day Care and Public Policy in Ontario. Toronto: Published for the Ontario Economic Council by University of Toronto Press, c1977. 139p. Bibliography: p. 135-139. (Ontario Economic Council Research Studies) ISBN 0-8020-3349-0 pa.: $6.50

1. Day care centers – Ontario. 2. Day care centers – Ontario – Finance.

Two issues, subsidy and regulation, underlie the discussions in this paperback. An economist discusses development of private demand and public subsidy in day care. Present policies are evaluated as background to theory, optimal subsidy formula and suggestions for future change. Information, ideas and bibliography are useful to researchers and policy-makers. Claire England

4781 362.7'1
**Ross, Kathleen Gallagher,** ed.
Good Day Care: Fighting for It, Getting It, Keeping It. Toronto: Women's Press, c1978. 223p. ill. Bibliography: p. 205-221.
ISBN 0-88961-043-6 bd.: $15.95
ISBN 0-88961-041-X pa.: $7.95

1. Day care centers – Canada. 2. Day care centers.

A comprehensive overview of day care in the Canadian context comprised of articles by parents, social workers and others involved. The importance of day care, the various types available and practical advice on organizing services are included. Suitable for students, parents, social workers and others interested in the subject. Diane Hart

4782 362.7'1
**Silverman, Peter.**
Who Speaks for the Children: The Plight of the Battered Child. Don Mills, Ont.: Musson, 1978. 224p. Index. ISBN 0-7737-1022-1 pa.: $8.95

1. Child abuse – Canada.

An advocate's review of recent and well-publicized cases of child abuse, examining the role and actions of courts, social service agencies and doctors, from a critical perspective. Pointing out that the child has no one to act as his/her advocate, the author proposes possible solutions to this problem. Well written and of great interest to parents and to everyone who cares about/for children. Gail Dykstra

4783 362.7'1
**Van Stolk, Mary.**
The Battered Child in Canada. Rev. ed. Toronto: McClelland and Stewart, c1978. 178p. Bibliographical references. ISBN 0-7710-8712-8 pa.: $7.95

1. Child abuse – Canada. 2. Child welfare – Canada.

First edition listed *CS* no. 1015.

A well-documented update of a major work contributes to advancement in the field. New material on the roles of school and police is added, along with remedies rooted in changes involving legislation and professional training. Includes appendices on child welfare legislation and recent statistics. Linda Pulver

4784 362.7'34
**Marcus, Clare.**
Adopted?: A Canadian Guide for Adopted Adults in Search of Their Origins. Vancouver: International Self-Counsel Press, 1979. 108p. Bibliography: p. 103. (Self-counsel Series) ISBN 0-88908-050-X pa.: $3.95

1. Adoption – Canada. 2. Genealogy.

Outlining the steps for adopted adults to follow in searching for birth parents, the book uses case histories and a very practical writing style to confront the anxieties of the search, and attempts to put the pros and cons into a realistic perspective. A detailed guide on a very topical point of continuing concern. Gail Dykstra

4785 362.7'8
**Schaefer, Nicola.**
Does She Know She's There? Toronto: Fitzhenry & Whiteside, c1978. 235p. ISBN 0-88902-433-2 $9.95

1. Mentally handicapped children – Canada – Biography.

Eschewing institutionalization of their severely retarded daughter, a Winnipeg couple incorporated her as fully as possible into family life. The strains and discouragements are not minimized, but there was also satisfaction and pleasure. An unusually candid and warmly humorous account of efforts to improve conditions for Cath and other abnormal children. Absorbing reading.

4786 362.8'3
**Ross, Anne G.**
Pregnant and Alone. Toronto: McClelland and Stewart, c1978. 144p. ill. Bibliography: p. 141-143. ISBN 0-7710-7728-9 pa.: $5.95

1. Pregnancy, Unwanted. 2. Unmarried mothers. 3. Contraceptives.

Pro-life groups might criticize the view on abortion of this nurse/counsellor. Others might criticize tone or presentation which, however, would appeal to young adolescent girls. Brief case stories capture interest for the simply-put information on birth control, venereal disease, pregnancy, adoption, etc. Diagrams, some further reading and addresses for Planned Parenthood of Canada. Claire England

## 363.2 Police services

4787 363.2
**Sallot, Jeff.**
Nobody Said No: The Real Story About How the Mounties Always Get Their Man. Toronto: James Lorimer, 1979. 224p. Index. ISBN 0-88862-286-4 $15.95

1. Canada. Royal Canadian Mounted Police. 2. Police corruption – Canada.

The author, a Pulitzer Prize winner, has written an absorbing, well-documented account of the illegal and anti-terrorist activities carried out by the Security Unit of the RCMP in the name of national security. Although based on testimony presented at the McDonald Commission, it reads like a fast-paced thriller. Lucia Herwig

4788 363.3'1
**Birdsall, Peter.**
Mind War: Book Censorship in English Canada, by Peter Birdsall and Delores Broten. Victoria, B.C.: CANLIT, 1978. 66p. Index. ISBN 0-920566-01-4 pa.: $5

1. Censorship – Canada – History.

Covers newspaper accounts of censorship in British Columbia and Ontario for the period 1935-1978. Although produced in typescript the book is nevertheless valuable as an account of changes in attitudes from the thirties through the seventies. The books and reasons for banning them make fascinating reading including as they do, *Ulysses, The Bible, Women in Love* and *Alice in Wonderland.* Barbara Schon

## 363.6 Public utilities

4789 363.6
**Dotto, Lydia.**
The Ozone War, by Lydia Dotto and Harold Schiff. Toronto: Doubleday, 1978. 342p. Index. ISBN 0-385-12927-0 $11.95

1. Atmospheric ozone. 2. Ozone – Environmental aspects.

A detailed account of the continuing controversy between scientists, government and big business over the role and importance of the earth's ozone layer, and the need to protect it from deterioration brought about as a result of modern technology. A fascinating, well-written study which entertains as it informs and educates. Indexed. Lucia Herwig

4790 363.6
**Troyer, Warner.**
No Safe Place. Toronto: Clarke, Irwin, 1977. 267p. ill., plates. Bibliography: p. 246-257. Index. ISBN 0-7720-1117-6 $13.95

1. Mercury – Environmental aspects – Ontario. 2. Mercury – Environmental aspects. 3. Pollution. 4. Environmental policy.

A well-researched book on the mercury pollution in Northwestern Ontario that has affected the Native Peoples of Grassy Narrows and White Dog Reserve. A journalist reveals disturbing evidence about the actions of government and industry. Includes some discussion of parallel incidents in other parts of the world. Kathryn Walker

## 364 Crime

4791 364.12'092
**Murray, John Wilson.**
Memoirs of a Great Detective: Incidents in the Life of John Wilson Murray. Toronto: Totem Books, 1979. 226p. port. ISBN 0-00-216168-0 pa.: $2.25

1. Crime and criminals – Ontario. 2. Detectives – Ontario – Biography.

Originally published 1904. First Canadian edition published 1977 under title: *Memoirs of a Great Canadian Detective.*

Thirty years of tenacious crime detection in late nineteenth century Ontario are recalled by the first provincial detective. Cases of fraud, violence and counterfeiting reveal interesting glimpses of the social milieu of the time. A period piece with a Victorian flavour abridged from the 1904 edition. Entertaining. For detective story enthusiasts.

4792 364.1'522
**Rabkin, Brenda.**
Growing Up Dead. Toronto: McClelland and Stewart, c1978. 188p. Bibliographical references. ISBN 0-7710-7230-9 pa.: $7.95

1. Youth – Suicidal behavior.

A readable account, considering suicide as a human expression rather than in terms of statistics. Parts appear in the words of those who have attempted suicide, parts have been contributed by parents, teachers and friends. The author analyzes the cases and leaves the reader with some valid suggestions concerning practical courses of action. For teenagers, their parents and professionals working with young people. Linda Pulver

4793 364.1'523
**Cobb, Chris.**
Rape of a Normal Mind, by Chris Cobb and Bob Avery. Markham, Ont.: PaperJacks, 1977. 189p. ISBN 0-7701-0025-2 pa.: $1.95

1. Poulin, Robert. 2. Murder – Ontario – Ottawa.

In October 1975 Robert Poulin fired off a shotgun into a crowded classroom. Two reporters have written a concise account of the events leading to the tragedy and of the investigation which followed. They speculate at some length on the influence of the media, parental supervision, pornography, the availability of guns and the school system on the mind of an apparently normal boy. Catharine MacKenzie

4794 364.1'523
**Hambleton, Ronald.**
A Master Killing. Toronto: Green Bushell (J. M. Dent), 1978. 200p. ill., plates, ports. ISBN 0-9690786-1-7 $8.95

1. Kinnear, Thomas, d. 1843. 2. Murder – Ontario – Toronto. 3. Trials (Murder) – Ontario – Toronto.

An account, which reads like fiction, of the murder of Thomas Kinnear in 1843 and the trial of the accused. After a slow start, the action moves quickly but the tale is most interesting for its picture of life in Toronto in the 1840's. More illustrations, including a map of Toronto, would have been useful. Peggy Sinclair

4795 364.1'523
**Jonas, George.**
By Persons Unknown: The Strange Death of Christine Demeter, by George Jonas and Barbara Amiel. Toronto: Macmillan, 1977. 349p. plates, ports. ISBN 0-7705-1437-5 $11.95

1. Demeter, Christine, 1940-1973. 2. Demeter, Peter, 1933- 3. Uxoricide – Ontario – Mississauga. 4. Trials (Murder) – Ontario – Mississauga.

Periodical Distributors of Canada Author Award.

In following the Demeter trial the authors provide insight into the investigation of a complex murder case and evaluate the effectiveness of the legal system. A readable account including some speculation on the part of the authors. Linda Pulver

4796 364.1'523
**Miller, Orlo.**
Twenty Mortal Murders: Bizarre Murder Cases from Canada's Past. Toronto: Macmillan, 1978. 226p. Bibliography: p. 210-215. Index. ISBN 0-7705-1713-7 $12.95

1. Murder – Canada.

Miller has applied his playwriting skills to a dramatic recounting of twenty Canadian murder cases ranging in time from the Vikings to the present. Although several cases may not involve murder, the vignettes are fast-paced, fact-filled and entertaining. No index. Lucia Herwig

4797 364.1'523
**Robin, Martin.**
The Bad and the Lonely: Seven Stories of the Best – and Worst – Canadian Outlaws. Toronto: James Lorimer, 1976. 221p. ill., maps, plates. ISBN 0-88862-121-3 $10.95

1. Outlaws – Canada. 2. Crime and criminals – Canada. 3. Brigands and robbers – Canada.

A collection of true stories with popular appeal. Included are accounts of Donald Morrison, the Donnellys and Bill Miner. A section of "Notes" concludes each chapter, including references used and some evaluative comments. Diane Hart

4798 364.1'53
**Clark, Lorenne M. G.**
Rape: The Price of Coercive Sexuality, by Lorenne M. G. Clark and Debra J. Lewis. Toronto: Women's Educational Press, c1977. 222p. Bibliography: p. 219-222.
ISBN 0-88961-033-X bd.: $12.95
ISBN 0-88961-032-0 pa.: $5.95

1. Rape – Canada.

A unique, informative work of major general concern. Findings from a study of rape cases reported to the Toronto police in 1970 are discussed. Included are a theoretical analysis of rape in its historical and social context and the need for changes in attitudes, related laws and police action. Diane Hart

4799 364.1'55
**Fazakas, Ray.**
The Donnelly Album: The Complete and Authentic Account Illustrated with Photographs of Canada's Famous Feuding Family. Toronto: Macmillan, 1977. 311p. ill., ports. Bibliographical references and Index.
ISBN 0-7705-1439-1 bd.: $30
ISBN 0-7705-1440-5 pa.: $12.95

1. Donnelly family (James Donnelly, 1815?-1880). 2. Crime and criminals – Ontario – Lucan.

Well-written, exhaustively documented account of the Donnellys which adds to information contained in previous accounts and permits a glimpse of Canadian frontier life. Information and photographs collected from private, government, library and media sources during fifteen years of research. Thoroughly indexed and useful as resource material or interest reading. Linda Pulver

4800 364.1'62
**Waller, Irvin.**
Burglary: The Victim and the Public, by Irvin Waller and Norman Okihiro. Toronto: University of Toronto Press; Centre of Criminology, University of Toronto, c1978. 190p. map. Bibliography: p. 175-186. Index. (Canadian Studies in Criminology)
ISBN 0-8020-5421-8 $12.50

1. Burglary – Ontario – Toronto. 2. Victims of crimes – Ontario – Toronto.

Based on surveys, police records, interviews

and census data – the authors examine the effect of burglary on the victim, the courts, the police, the correction system, the criminal and the general public. Of great use to researchers, the analysis and conclusions of the authors provide unusual insight into the effect of crime on society. Gail Dykstra

4801 364.36

**Hackler, James C.**

The Prevention of Youthful Crime: The Great Stumble Forward. Toronto: Methuen, 1978. 252p. Bibliography: p. 227-246. Indexes. (Canadian Sociology) ISBN 0-458-93180-2 pa.: $10.95

1. Juvenile delinquency – Canada – Prevention. 2. Rehabilitation of juvenile delinquents – Canada.

What to do about youthful crime rather than why it is – is the author's intention. Detailing the usual pitfalls – expensive correctional institutions, inexpert experts, vested interests, etc. – the author recommends a pot-pourri of possible solutions ranging from the old-fashioned to the very new. Gail Dykstra

4802 364.36

**Leyton, Elliott.**

The Myth of Delinquency: An Anatomy of Juvenile Nihilism. Toronto: McClelland and Stewart, c1979. 220p. Bibliography: p. 207-208. ISBN 0-7710-5307-X pa.: $7.95

1. Juvenile delinquency – Atlantic Provinces – Case studies. 2. Juvenile delinquency – Case studies.

Beginning with a literature review and a reference to sociological theory, this anthropologist considers cases of incarcerated delinquents and presents a synthesis and recommendations to the government. Cases are descriptive and evaluative from the point of view of society, the family, and the offender. A readable, sympathetic account which fosters understanding. Linda Pulver

4803 364'.971

**Baum, Daniel Jay.**

Discount Justice: The Canadian Criminal Justice System. Toronto: Burns & MacEachern, c1979. 148p. Bibliographical references and Index. ISBN 0-88768-080-1 $6.95

1. Criminal justice, Administration of – Canada.

A law professor explains the law and the vital role individuals should play in defining and seeking justice. Factual, readable approach includes statements from reports, commissions, recent cases. Suggestions for reform of the tradition-bound legal system advocate more citizen input. Linda Pulver

4804 364.971

**Parizeau, Alice Poznanska.**

The Canadian Criminal-Justice System. Translation revised and edited by Dorothy E. Crelinsten. Toronto: D. C. Heath, c1977. 219p. ill. Bibliography: p. 191-211. Index. ISBN 0-66901-448-6 $18

1. Criminal justice, Administration of – Canada.

An overview of the criminal justice system designed to explain objectively how the system works. It includes discussion of jurisdictions, criminal proceedings, police services, detention, probation and social rehabilitation. Readily understandable by the layman. Gail Dykstra

4805 364'.971

**Tepperman, Lorne.**

Crime Control: The Urge Toward Authority. Toronto: McGraw-Hill Ryerson, 1977. 256p. graphs. Bibliography: p. 238-253. Index. (McGraw-Hill Ryerson Series in Canadian Sociology) ISBN 0-07-082449-5 pa.: $5.95

1. Crime and criminals – Canada. 2. Criminal justice, Administration of – Canada.

A somewhat scholarly treatment of institutional reaction to crime as it arises from distribution of power within society. Uses historical statistics to consider biases in reporting incidences of criminal activity, representing the first cumulation of such information. Concern from alternating points of view – process of criminal justice and social organization of criminals – makes it valuable for readers with an interest in applied social theories. Linda Pulver

4806 364'.971

**Vaz, Edmund W.,** ed.

Crime and Delinquency in Canada. Edited by Edmund W. Vaz and Abdul Q. Lodhi. Scarborough, Ont.: Prentice-Hall, 1979. 390p. graphs. Bibliography: p. 379-390. ISBN 0-13-192708-6 pa.: $11.95

1. Crime and criminals – Canada. 2. Juvenile delinqency – Canada.

A collection of articles for those with some sociology/psychology background. Organized in three parts, it includes background information and statistics plus theory and research on juvenile delinquency and crime viewed as a type of work. Many United States sources are cited, but Canadian research is included when available. Diane Hart

4807 364.973
**Silberman, Charles E.**
Criminal Violence, Criminal Justice. Toronto: Random House, c1978. 540p. Bibliography: p. 498-524. Index.
ISBN 0-394-4830-6 bd.: $18.95
ISBN 0-394-7414-7 pa.: $4.95

1. Crime and criminals – United States. 2. Criminal justice, Administration of – United States. 3. Violence – United States.

Examining the reality of violence and its treatment in the criminal justice system. Covering all aspects and ranging from the western to the eastern world for examples, the author is reformist without being revolutionary. Analyzes and places in context the current sociological, political and legal attitudes toward violence. Gail Dykstra

## 365 Penal institutions

4808 365'.6'0924
**Caron, Roger.**
Go-boy!: Memoirs of a Life Behind Bars. Toronto: McGraw-Hill Ryerson, c1978. 264p.
ISBN 0-07-082535-1 $10.95

1. Caron, Roger, 1938- 2. Prisoners – Canada – Biography.

Governor General's Literary Award.

A true account of double imprisonment is recorded by the prisoner himself. He was repeatedly incarcerated in Canadian prisons for robbery, jailbreak and parole violation but also unwittingly he reveals a mind in thrall. Catharine MacKenzie

4809 365'.971
**McNeil, Gérard.**
Cruel and Unusual, by Gérard McNeil and Sharon Vance. Ottawa: Deneau and Greenberg, c1978. 179p. ill., plates.
ISBN 0-88879-005-8 pa.: $6.95

1. Prisons – Canada. 2. Criminal justice, Administration of – Canada.

A Parliamentary Press Gallery reporter toured the prisons in 1976 and 1977 with the House of Commons Subcommittee on the Penitentiary System in Canada. What he found passes judgement on a nation; it documents Canadians' inhumanity to Canadians. Catharine MacKenzie

## 368 Insurance and pensions

4810 368.3
**Pedoe, Arthur.**
Life Insurance Annuities & Pensions: A Canadian Text. 3d ed. Revised by Colin E. Jack. Toronto: University of Toronto Press, c1978. 468p. ill., diagr., graphs. Bibliographical references and Index.
ISBN 0-8020-2316-9 $25

1. Insurance, Life – Canada. 2. Annuities – Canada. 3. Pensions – Canada.

Second edition listed in *CS* no. 1057.

A detailed, authoritative text intended for the employees of life insurance companies, but also useful for students and the interested layman. In a lucid presentation of a complicated topic basic and more advanced information is provided; terms are clearly defined. Retains the format of the second edition. Diane Hart

4811 368.3'2
**Rogers, James Edward.**
Life Insurance for Canadians: How Much? What Kind? From Whom? Vancouver: International Self-Counsel Press, 1978. 71p. form, graphs. (Self-counsel Series)
ISBN 0-88908-032-1 pa.: $2.95

1. Insurance, Life. 2. Insurance, Life – Canada.

A basic easy-to-follow guide to life insurance for the novice, including a step-by-step method of evaluating one's need for insurance. Also considered are disability insurance, retirement savings plans and other aspects such as child insurance. Includes a short glossary. Diane Hart

4812 368.4'2
**Evans, Robert G.**
Extending Canadian Health Insurance: Options for Pharmacare and Denticare, by Robert G. Evans and M. F. Williamson. Toronto: Published for the Ontario Economic Council by University of Toronto Press, c1977. 276p. graphs. Bibliography: p. 265-276. (Ontario Economic Council Research Studies)
ISBN 0-8020-3353-9 pa.: $12

1. Insurance, Health – Canada. 2. Insurance, Dental – Canada. 3. Insurance, Pharmaceutical services – Canada.

A detailed, technical analysis of the various factors and combinations of these which must be considered in any plan to extend Medicare in Ontario to include universal pharmaceutical and dental coverage. The study provides costing for various options, using 1975 base figures and concludes total coverage is too costly. No index. Lucia Herwig

4813 368.4'2

**Taylor, Malcolm G.**

Health Insurance and Canadian Public Policy: The Seven Decisions That Created the Canadian Health Insurance System. Toronto: The Institute of Public Administration of Canada; Montreal: McGill-Queen's University Press, 1978. 473p. Bibliographical references and Index. (Canadian Public Administration Series) ISBN 0-7735-0307-2 bd.: $18.95 ISBN 0-7735-0308-0 pa.: $7.95

1. Insurance, Health – Canada – History.

A member of the Royal Commission on Health Services (1964), now a professor at York University, explains lucidly the policy decision making behind Canada's system of public health insurance, sometimes called the best in the world. For all those interested in the health-care problem or in public policy-making.

4814 368.4'4

**Grubel, Herbert G.,** ed.

Unemployment Insurance: Global Evidence of Its Effects on Unemployment. Edited by Herbert G. Grubel and Michael A. Walker. Vancouver: Fraser Institute, 1978. 388p. ill., graphs. Bibliographical references. ISBN 0-88975-008-4 pa.: $12.95

1. Insurance, Unemployment – Congresses. 2. Unemployed – Congresses.

A collection of thirteen detailed conference papers, and responses to them, which examines the relationship between the provision and subsequent liberalization of unemployment. The conclusion is that there is a positive correlation. Countries include the United States, Canada, New Zealand, and six European countries. No index. Lucia Herwig

4815 368.4'4

**Schneider, William James.**

A Practical Guide to Unemployment Insurance, by William James Schneider and Lawrence Solomon. Toronto: Fitzhenry & Whiteside, c1977. 246p. forms, graphs, map. Index. ISBN 0-88902-405-7 pa.: $5.95

1. Insurance, Unemployment – Canada – Handbooks, manuals, etc.

Essential information on the Unemployment Insurance Commission, what it is, how to apply, how to appeal. What sets this book apart from the others is the practical organization of the information. Extensive use of checklists, outlines, charts, forms, step-by-step guides, tables, etc. Buy two copies, one for reference and one for circulation. Gail Dykstra

## 370 Education

4816 370.19

**Chaiton, Alf,** ed.

Canadian Schools and Canadian Identity. Edited by Alf Chaiton and Neil McDonald. Agincourt, Ont.: Gage Educational Publishing, 1977. 189p. Bibliography: p. 184-185. Index. ISBN 0-7715-5719-1 bd.: $7.95 ISBN 0-7715-5718-3 pa.: $4.50

1. Nationalism and education – Canada – History. 2. Education – Canada – History.

While political treatises on nationalism abound, little has been published examining the role of the school in the search for Canadian identity. This collection of eleven articles presents a primarily historical perspective that will be a useful supplement to introductory courses on Canadian history. Ethel Auster

4817 370.19'3

**Martin, Wilfred B. W.**

Canadian Education: A Sociological Analysis, by Wilfred B. W. Martin and Allan J. Macdonell. Scarborough, Ont.: Prentice-Hall, 1977. 354p. Bibliography: p. 303-341. Indexes. ISBN 0-13-113092-7 pa.: $7.95

1. Educational sociology – Canada. 2. Education – Canada.

Among the topics treated by this textbook are the characteristics of the Canadian educational structure, the teacher in the school, education and social mobility, the labour market, and social change. Appendices present the development of the sociology of education and the British North America Act. Name and subject indexes conclude the volume. Ethel Auster

4818 370'.971

**Channon, Geraldine L.**

Education, A Continuing Priority, by Geraldine L. Channon and Wilfred J. Brown. Ottawa: Canadian Teachers' Federation, 1978. 88p. ill. Bibliography: p. 87-88. (CTF Publication) ISBN 0-88989-030-7 pa.: $3

1. Education – Canada.

Originally prepared for a conference

sponsored by the International Teachers Trade Union Cooperation Committee, this work outlines the conditions under which teachers have worked during the past two decades. Tables show birth rates, enrolment levels, expenditures, and pupil-teacher ratios by province for selected years from 1960 to 1974. Appendices provide examples of provisions affecting workload and job security in contracts negotiated by teachers and boards. Ethel Auster

4819 370'.9713
**Prentice, Alison L.**
The School Promoters: Education and Social Class in Mid-nineteenth Century Upper Canada. Toronto: McClelland and Stewart, c1977. 192p. ill. Bibliographical references and Index. (The Canadian Social History Series) ISBN 0-7710-7181-7 pa.: $5.95

1. Education – Ontario – History. 2. Educational sociology – Ontario – History.

The mid-nineteenth century was a time of profound change in education in Upper Canada. While most histories emphasize the contributions of men like Ryerson and outline the legislation introduced, this monograph examines the effect the educational innovations had on the children, their families, the reformers and society. The well-documented volume is meant for students and the general public. Ethel Auster

## 371 Teaching

4820 371'.02
**Gossage, Carolyn.**
A Question of Privilege: Canada's Independent Schools. Toronto: Peter Martin, c1977. 301p. ill., ports. Bibliography: p. 289-293. Index. ISBN 0-88778-156-X $15

1. Private schools – Canada – History.

This study brings together for the first time extensive information on the history of Canada's private schools. The introduction and conclusion provide an overview and discussion of trends in education. The bulk of the text consists of individual essays on each of forty-eight schools opened before 1950. Although interesting to alumni and parents seeking alternatives to the public educational system the analysis needs strengthening in future studies.

4821 371.2
**Gue, Leslie R.**
An Introduction to Educational Administration in Canada. Toronto: McGraw-Hill Ryerson, 1977. 230p. ill. Bibliographies and Indexes. ISBN 0-07-082379-0 pa.: $6.95

1. School management and organization – Canada.

One of the few Canadian treatments of educational administration, this text will be especially useful in training teachers for the elementary and secondary grades while providing a useful synthesis for the general public of the work of experts in the field. A summary and bibliography conclude each chapter. Ethel Auster

4822 371.3'7
**Watson, Walter.**
How to Give an Effective Seminar: A Handbook for Students and Professionals, by Walter Watson, Luis Pardo and Vladislav Tomovic. Don Mills, Ont.: General Publishing, 1978. 158p. Bibliography: p. 125-158. ISBN 0-7736-1043-X pa.: $5.95

1. Seminars.

A step-by-step guide to effective oral communication pilots the neophyte through the preparation, presentation, and participation in seminars. Written in a simple, conversational style by three Sociology professors at Brock University, this manual can be used by secondary school students, university undergraduates, and non-academics in business and government.

## 371.9 Special education

4823 371.9'7
**Enns, Carol,** comp.
The Education of New Canadians: An Annotated Bibliography. Toronto: Library, Reference and Information Services, Ontario Institute for Studies in Education, 1978. 50p. Indexes. (Current Bibliography – The Library, Reference and Information Services, the Ontario Institute for Studies in Education) pa.: $3.95

1. Children of immigrants – Education – Canada – Bibliography. 2. Minorities – Education – Canada – Bibliography.
3. Canada – Population – Ethnic groups – Education – Bibliography.

This bibliography of 162 items annotates the

relevant literature concerning the teaching of Canadian immigrants for the years 1960-1978. Annotations are unsigned, roughly 25 to 200 words in length, and often with quotations from ERIC and ONTERIS abstracts. Two indexes and an explanatory introduction are included. Carl Spadoni

## 372 Elementary education

4824 372.6'4

**Hazzard, Russ.**

It Scares Me But I Like It. Don Mills, Ont.: Fitzhenry & Whiteside, 1979. 128p. Bibliography: p.128. ISBN 0-88902-568-1 $6.95

1. Poetry – Study and teaching (Elementary). 2. Creative writing (Elementary education). 3. Children's writings, Canadian (English) – Ontario – Ottawa.

An innovative experiment to encourage eight-to-ten year olds to improve their language skills by expressing themselves in poetry. Hazzard outlines his approach, and is openly critical of it, but his enthusiasm in awakening the latent creativity of children is infectious. The forward is by Dennis Lee. School and public libraries.

4825 372.6'5'41

**Desjarlais, Lionel.**

The Costs of Providing Instruction in French Language Instructional Units: In-depth Study of Eight Areas Where There Exists a High Concentration of Francophones. Toronto: Ministry of Education, 1977. 265p.

1. French language – Study and teaching.

This volume is representative of an extensive publication series of final reports of contractual research projects funded by the Ministry of Education, Ontario. Access to these reports as well as research-in-progress is available through the manual and online versions of the Ontario Educational Research Information System (ONTERIS) index at OISE. Ethel Auster

4826 372.9'712

**Charyk, John C.**

Those Bittersweet School Days. Saskatoon: Western Producer Prairie Books, c1977. 322p. ill. Index. ISBN 0-919306-87-X $11.50

1. Rural schools – Prairie Provinces.

The vanishing one-room prairie schoolhouse serves as a focus for an unpretentious, nostalgic portrait of rural life and education in Alberta and Saskatchewan in the early part of the twentieth century. Although rambling and anecdotal in style, the reality of time and place are conveyed successfully. An attractive format. Secondary school and public libraries.

4827 372.9'718

**Sawyer, Don.**

Tomorrow Is School and I'm Sick to the Heart Thinking About It. Vancouver: Douglas & McIntyre, 1979. 205p. ill. ISBN 0-88894-228-1 $10.95

1. Education – Newfoundland. 2. Teachers – Newfoundland – Biography.

Teaching positions in a small Newfoundland outport thrust two young Americans into a rigidly structured educational system irrelevant to the needs of the students, and into a community in the throes of socio-economic change. With sensitivity Sawyer writes of the value conflicts and the questioning of mores within the school and the village. Thought-provoking reading for educators and parents.

## 374 Adult education

4828 374.9'712

**Jameson, Sheilagh S.**

Chautauqua in Canada, by Sheilagh S. Jameson and Nola B. Erickson. Calgary: Glenbow-Alberta Institute, 1979. 161p. ill., ports. Bibliography: p. 157. Index. ISBN 0-919224-07-5 $12.50

1. Erickson, John M., 1882-1963. 2. Chautauquas – History.

Years before radio and television networks brought the world into every living room Chautauqua tent shows introduced small Canadian prairie communities to music, theatre, lectures, travelogues and elocutionists. The Chief Archivist of the Glenbow-Alberta Institute has reconstructed the heyday of the summer circuit, between 1917 and 1935, from archives and interviews. Authoritative social history.

4829 375'.00971

**Barrow, Robin.**

The Canadian Curriculum: A Personal View. London, Ont.: Faculty of Education, University of Western Ontario, c1979. 118p. Bibliographical references. ISBN 0-920354-04-1 pa.: $4.95

1. Education – Canada – Curricula. 2. Education – Curricula.

Philosophical reflections of an educational

scholar concerning commonly held traditions and practices that permeate the present-day school system. After examining radical and progressive positions, he advocates the adoption of a core curriculum across Canada. Ethel Auster

## 376 Education of Women

4830 376'.65

**Vickers, Jill.**

But Can You Type?: Canadian Universities and the Status of Women, by Jill Vickers and June Adam. Toronto: Clarke, Irwin, 1976. 142p. Index. ISBN 0-7720-1056-0 pa.: $5.95

1. Higher education of women – Canada.
2. Women college teachers – Canada.

The authors set forth the statistical evidence that clearly delineates the problems (additional to those faced by men) faced by women entering higher education as undergraduates, graduate students and teachers. They deplore the fact that "Canadian university structure reflects the social and moral value structure of society and does little to ameliorate." Catharine MacKenzie.

## 378 Higher education

4831 378.

**Cameron, James M.**

On the Idea of a University. Toronto: University of St. Michael's College; University of Toronto Press, 1978. 92p. Bibliographical references.
ISBN 0-8020-2300-2 bd.: $15
ISBN 0-8020-6335-7 pa.: $5

1. Universities and colleges.

This volume is comprised of the four lectures that Professor Cameron delivered to commemorate the 125th anniversary of St. Michael's College and the 150th anniversary of the Universary of Toronto. Using Cardinal Newman's *The Idea of a University* as his point of departure, Cameron eloquently re-examines the purpose, form, and future of the university in contemporary society. Ethel Auster

4832 378.1'22

**Knapper, Christopher K.,** ed.

If Teaching Is Important ...: The Evaluation of Instruction in Higher Education. Toronto: Clarke, Irwin; Canadian Association of University Teachers, c1977. 230p. Bibliographies and Index. (A CAUT Monograph Series) ISBN 0-7720-1035-8 pa.: $5.95

1. College teachers, Rating of.

The second in a series published by the Canadian Association of University Teachers, this monograph treats the purposes, methods, and criteria for evaluating teaching at the post-secondary level. Student evaluation, self-assessment, evaluation of functions outside the classroom are some of the issues examined in "state of the art" reviews. Of interest not only to academics but to those interested in the effectiveness of university teaching. Ethel Auster

4833 378.71

**Directory of Canadian Universities.**

Répertoire des universités canadiennes. Edited by Gloria Royce. Ottawa: Association of Universities and Colleges of Canada, 1979. Annual. 362p. ISBN 0-88676-059-0 $7

1. Universities and colleges – Canada.

1973 edition listed *CS* no. 1158.

This twenty-second edition of the directory features an introductory article on university life by Dr. Edward Sheffield, University of Toronto. A standard reference tool for Canadian libraries.

4834 378.713'72

**Neatby, Hilda.**

Queen's University: To Strive, to Seek, to Find, and Not to Yield. Edited by Frederick W. Gibson and Roger Graham. Montreal: McGill-Queen's University Press, 1978- v ill., ports. Bibliography: p. 337-339. Index.

1. Queen's University, Kingston, Ont. – History.

Contents: vol. 1. 1841-1917. 1978.

Intended as a two-volume study, this first volume by a distinguished historian chronicles the founding and development of Queen's University between 1841 and 1917. Included in the text are many illustrations and notes, a bibliography, and an index. Ethel Auster

## 379 Education and the state

4835 379.71

**McDonald, Neil,** ed.

Egerton Ryerson and His Times: Essays on the History of Education. Edited by Neil McDonald and Alf Chaiton. Toronto: Macmillan, c1978. 319p. Bibliographical references. ISBN 0-7705-1706-4 bd.: $14.95 ISBN 0-7705-1707-2 pa.: $8.95

1. Ryerson, Egerton, 1803-1882. 2. Education – Canada – History – 19th century.

Ryerson's influence on the development of education in mid-nineteenth century Ontario is examined by thirteen prominent educators in relation to the social, economic, political, and educational milieu of his times. The thirteen carefully documented papers were prepared for a symposium in 1976, marking the centennial of the educator's retirement. A significant contribution to educational historiography.

## 380 Commerce

4836 380.1'41'31

**Wilson, Charles F.**

A Century of Canadian Grain: Government Policy to 1951. Saskatoon: Western Producer Prairie Books, c1978. 1138p. Bibliography: p. 1109-1118. Index. ISBN 0-919306-79-9 pa.: $25

1. Grain trade – Canada – History.

The author, a former Dominion Bureau of Statistics official associated with the institutions of the grain trade at home and abroad, reviews a century of Canadian government grain policy. How are decisions in high places made? Who makes them and why, etc. A "must" for agricultural libraries, while optional for school or neighbourhood libraries. Gwen Liu

4837 381.

**Priamo, Carol.**

The General Store. Toronto: McGraw-Hill Ryerson, 1978. 104p. ill. ISBN 0-07-082780-X $15.95

1. General stores – Ontario, Southern – Pictorial works.

Good photography by the author of *Mills of Canada*, makes this an interesting picture book, but the accompanying narrative is superficial and supplies a minimal amount of information about the general store in Canada. An excellent opportunity for treating an aspect of our social history has been missed. Compare *Building a House in New France*, by Peter N. Moogk. Nancy Cohen

## 383 Postal communication

4838 383.

**Robert W. Lyman (Canada) Company.**

Lyman's Standard Catalogue of Canada – BNA Postage Stamps. 30th ed. Toronto: The Author, 1979. 128p. ISSN 0318-3629 $3.50

1. Postage-stamps – Catalogues.

A completely revised, full-colour edition which includes postage stamps of Canada, British North America and Newfoundland. Published annually. An inexpensive and reliable guide for the stamp enthusiast. Schools and public libraries.

4839 383.4'971

**Canada. Study group to the Postmaster General.**

Considerations Which Affect the Choice of Organization Structure for the Canada Post Office. Report of a Study group to the Postmaster General. Ottawa: Canada Post Office, 1978. 105p. Bibliographical references. ISBN 0-660-10038-X $3.25

1. Canada. Post Office Department.

This report attempts to provide a balanced, objective picture of the possible effects of changing the status of the Canadian Post Office from Department to Crown Corporation. The views of labour unions representing Post Office employees are included. Because of the great public interest in the topic, this study deserves a place in all libraries.

## 384 Telecommunication

4840 384.54

**Schell, Winston G.**

Reading, Writing and Radio, by Winston G. Schell and Marstan E. Woollings. Don Mills, Ont.: Longman, c1977. 208p. ill. ISBN 0-7747-1112-4 pa.: $3.95

1. Radio broadcasting.

An invaluable primer for the neophyte. Chapter nine, "Getting into Radio" should be required reading for all guidance counsellors in schools. The list of source materials is comprehensive as well as very useful. Gwen Liu

4841 384.54'0971
**Ellis, David.**
Evolution of the Canadian Broadcasting System: Objectives and Realities, 1928-1968. Ottawa: Ministry of Supply and Services, 1979. 86p. Bibliography: p. 85-86. ISBN 0-660-1044-X $3.25

1. Canadian Broadcasting Corporation. 2. Broadcasting policy – Canada. 3. Canada. Dept. of Communications.

Analyses some of the main themes that have tended to dominate the policy debate on Canadian broadcasting from the establishment of the Aird Commission in 1928 to the proclamation of the Broadcasting Act in 1968. -Foreword. A chronology covers the period 1919-1968.

4842 384.54'0971
**Hallman, Eugene S.**
Broadcasting in Canada, by Eugene S. Hallman and H. Hindley. Don Mills, Ont.: General Publishing, c1977. 90p. ill., map. (Case Studies on Broadcasting Systems) ISBN 0-7736-6001-1 pa. Processed: $5.95

1. Radio broadcasting – Canada. 2. Television broadcasting – Canada.

This easy-to-read case study sponsored by the International Institute of Communications can be used as a handbook on radio and television in Canada. It includes governmental organization and regulations, statistical summaries and some history. The author's twenty-four years of varied experience with the CBC contributes to the success of the work. Gwen Liu

4843 384.55'4
**Peers, Frank W.**
The Public Eye: Television and the Politics of Canadian Broadcasting, 1952-1968. Toronto: University of Toronto Press, c1979. 459p. Index. ISBN 0-8020-5436-6 $25

1. Canadian Broadcasting Corporation – History. 2. Television broadcasting – Canada – History.

The author's earlier work, *The Politics of Canadian Broadcasting 1920-1951*, is listed in CS no. 1182.

An objective and thoughtful examination of Canadian broadcasting from the coming of television to the passing of the Broadcasting Act in 1968. Based upon research of official records, personal papers, and interviews, Professor Peers documents the problems, the policy shifts, the controversies and the public investigations which have studded this period of broadcasting history. An important and readable survey.

4844 384.6'065
**Ogle, E. B.**
Long Distance Please: The Story of the TransCanada Telephone System. Don Mills, Ont.: William Collins, 1979. Bibliography. Index. ISBN 0-00-216167-2 $13.95

1. Trans-Canada Telephone System – History. 2. Telephone – Canada – History. 3. Telecommunication – Canada – History.

The fascinating story of the creation of Canada's long-distance telephone network from a conglomeration of public and private telephone systems.

---

## 385 Railroad transportation

---

4845 385'.06'571
**Lamb, W. Kaye.**
History of the Canadian Pacific Railway. Toronto: Macmillan; Don Mills, Ont.: Collier Macmillan, 1977. 491p. ill. Bibliography: p. 467-476. Index. (Railroads of America) ISBN 0-02-567660-1 $17.95

1. CP Rail – History.

The author, formerly librarian of the National Library of Canada, presents this corporate history covering approximately one hundred years. It is a scholarly book essential for anyone who wishes to be informed about Canada's transport history. Gwen Liu

4846 385'.065'713
**Helm, Norman S.**
In the Shadow of Giants: The Story of the Toronto, Hamilton & Buffalo Railway. Cheltenham, Ont.: Boston Mills Press, c1978. 257p. ill., maps, ports. Bibliography: p. 257. ISBN 0-919822-22-3 $27.95

1. Toronto, Hamilton and Buffalo Railway – History.

Sketches, maps and photographs enhance this history of the railways in southern Ontario, the most densely populated and heavily industrialized region. Should be in public and school libraries in southern Ontario. Gwen Liu

4847 385'.06'5713
**Tucker, Albert.**
Steam into Wilderness: Ontario Northland Railway 1902-1962. Toronto: Fitzhenry & Whiteside, c1978. 214p. ill., maps, plates, ports. Bibliographical references and Index. ISBN 0-88902-444-8 bd.: $19.95 ISBN 0-88902-558-4 pa.: $9.95

1. Ontario Northland Railway – History. 2. Ontario – History – 20th century.

A significant book on Northeastern Ontario history and the development of Canadian transportation. While describing how the railway served the social needs of the northern country, the author vividly portrayed the men and women who settled there. Gwen Liu

4848 385'.0971
**Legget, Robert F.**
Canadian Railways in Pictures. Vancouver: Douglas, David & Charles, 1977. 118p. ill., maps. ISBN 0-88914-052-9 $14.95

1. Railroads – Canada – Pictorial works.

An historical album of 118 black and white photographs in 15 sections which cover the history of Canadian railways from the beginning to the present. Although it may be treasured by many a railway buff, the lack of an index, bibliography, or suggested readings, limits its usefulness in a school or public library. Gwen Liu

4849 385'.09712
**Liddell, Ken.**
I'll Take the Train. Saskatoon: Western Producer Prairie Books, c1977. 196p. ill., plates, ports. ISBN 0-919306-06-3 bd. ISBN 0-919306-84-5 pa.: $4.95

1. Railroads – The West, Canadian – History.

This collection of nostalgic reminiscences about trains and the people associated with them is readable and entertaining. Readers can learn and enjoy the history of western Canada from the many interesting anecdotes. Chapters are short and almost independent. Rare photographs enhance this inexpensive, soft-cover edition. Gwen Liu

4850 385'.09713
**Jackson, John N.**
Railways in the Niagara Peninsula: Their Development, Progress and Community Significance, by John N. Jackson and John Burtniak. Belleville, Ont.: Mika Publishing, 1978. 240p. ill., facsims., maps. Bibliographical references and Index. ISBN 0-919303-27-7 bd.: $20

1. Railroads – Ontario – Niagara Peninsula – History.

The author examines the establishment and growth of the railroad network in the Niagara Peninsula of southwestern Ontario from about 1850 to 1900. Many illustrations and photographs enliven the book. Libraries in Ontario will wish to add this to their collections. Gwen Liu

4851 385'.09713
**Willmot, Elizabeth A.**
Faces and Places along the Railway. Toronto: Gage Publishing, c1979. 126p. ill. ISBN 0-7715-9472-0 $17.95

1. Railroads – Ontario – History. 2. Railroads – Ontario – Stations.

As an extension of her earlier book, *Meet Me at the Station*, the author presents this collection of new and old photographs of Ontario's railways and stations with anecdotes about the people who financed and built them. Interesting and pleasant reading but not for the serious student. Gwen Liu

4852 385'.314
**Bohi, Charles.**
Canadian National's Western Depots: The Country Stations in Western Canada. Toronto: Railfare Enterprises, c1977. 127p. ill., map, plans. Bibliography: p. 128. ISBN 0-919130-28-3 $19.95

1. Canadian National Railways. 2. Railroads – The West, Canadian – Stations.

Of great interest to railway enthusiasts, the book covers the historical context, the origin of station names, architectural plans and design criteria, and detailed tables of the types of depots built. Illustrated with black and white photographs. Nancy Cohen

## 386 Inland waterway transportation

4853 386'.22'40971
**Charlebois, Peter.**
Sternwheelers & Sidewheelers: The Romance of Steamdriven Paddleboats in Canada. Toronto: NC Press, 1978. 142p. ill., diagrs. Bibliography: p. 141. Index. ISBN 0-919600-73-5 bd.: $20 ISBN 0-919600-72-7 pa.: $9.95

1. Paddle steamers – History. 2. Steam navigation – Canada – History.

This lavishly illustrated history of steamboats in Canada is the first comprehensive book on the subject. The author's anecdotal style is a delight to both the boat buff and the general reader. Gwen Liu

4854 386'.22'409712
**Barris, Theodore.**
Fire Canoe: Prairie Steamboat Days Revisited. Toronto: McClelland and Stewart, c1977. 304p. ill., maps, ports. Bibliography: p. 278-284. Index. ISBN 0-7710-1025-7 $16.95

1. River steamers – Prairie Provinces –

History. 2. Lake steamers – Prairie Provinces – History.

A history of prairie steamboats from 1859 when the first vessel arrived on the Red River to the early part of the twentieth century when they were replaced by diesel engines and railroads. Detailed descriptions of boats and people involved in the industry add interest. Gwen Liu

4855 386'.22'409713

**Tatley, Richard.**

Steamboating on the Trent-Severn. Belleville, Ont.: Mika Publishing, 1978. 220p. ill., maps, ports. Bibliography: p. 209-211. Index. ISBN 0-919303-24-2 $22.50

1. Steamboats – History. 2. Steam navigation – Ontario – Trent Canal – History. 3. Trent River Valley, Ont. – History.

Steam vessels in the Trent-Kawartha Lakes region of southern Ontario during the period 1832-1951. The book will be of special interest to libraries in eastern Ontario and those with special collections in steam navigation. The author, a history major, presents the adventures of steamers chronologically, and provides a generous number of illustrations and maps. Gwen Liu

4856 386'.5

**Legget, Robert F.**

The Seaway. Toronto: Clarke, Irwin, 1979. ISBN 0-7720-1270-9 $15.95

1. St. Lawrence Seaway – History.

The author of *Canals of Canada* presents this attractive volume to mark the twentieth anniversary of the St. Lawrence Seaway's opening in 1959. Readable, informative and interesting. Gwen Liu

4857 386'.6'097

**Payzant, Joan M.**

Like a Weaver's Shuttle: A History of the Halifax-Dartmouth Ferries, by Joan M. Payzant and Lewis J. Payzant. Halifax, N.S.: Nimbus Publishing, c1979. 214p. ill., ports. Bibliographical references and Index. ISBN 0-920852-00-9 $19.95

1. Halifax, N.S. – Ferries – History.
2. Dartmouth, N.S. – Ferries – History.

Regional history at its best, carefully researched and readable. The ferry's tale is set in a political, economic and social context with the Halifax explosion as a highlight. Of interest beyond Nova Scotia. Excellent illustrations.

4858 386'.6'09715

**Bruce, Harry.**

Lifeline: The Story of the Atlantic Ferries and Coastal Boats. Toronto: Macmillan, c1977. 249p. ill., map, plates. ISBN 0-7705-1608-4 $12.95

1. Ferries – Atlantic Provinces – History.
2. Coastwise shipping – Atlantic Provinces – History.

Evelyn Richardson Award.

Divided into three sections, the book covers the Newfoundland-Labrador-Nova Scotia coastal services, the Prince Edward Island connection, and the Bay of Fundy-New England routes. Although the book deals mainly with ships railway enthusiasts will also enjoy the readable prose and anecdotal details. The lack of an index and a bibliography is a drawback for serious readers. Gwen Liu

## 387 Shipping

4859 387.7'06

**Collins, David H.**

Wings across Time: The Story of Air Canada. Toronto: Griffin House, 1978. 93p. ill., facsim., map, plates, ports. Bibliography: p. 75. Index. ISBN 0-88760-090-5 pa.: $8.95

1. Air Canada – History.

A succinct but informative and profusely illustrated history of Air Canada from 1937 to 1977. As popular, non-analytical history outlining the development of the airline, the types of planes and the air routes used, it is recommended for all types of libraries. Gwen Liu

4860 387.7'36

**Stewart, Walter.**

The Paper Juggernaut: The Story of Pickering Airport. Toronto: McClelland and Stewart, 1979. 207p. ISBN 0-7710-0972-0 $14.95

1. Airports – Ontario – Toronto metropolitan area. 2. Airports – Ontario – Pickering.

A well-researched and documented story of two airports, the Mirabel, having cost possibly one and one quarter billion dollars, is underused and losing one million dollars a week. The Pickering, planned and shelved, has cost two hundred million. The indignant author painstakingly points out how the paper juggernaut has victimized all tax payers. Gwen Liu

## 388 Road transportation

4861 388'.09714
**Tulchinsky, Gerald.**
The River Barons: Montreal Businessmen and the Growth of Industry and Transportation 1837-53. Toronto: University of Toronto Press, c1977. 310p. ill., map. Bibliography: p. 267-283. Index.
ISBN 0-8020-5339-4 $20

1. Businessmen – Quebec (Province) – Montreal – History. 2. Railroads – Canada – History. 3. Shipping – Canada – History. 4. Montreal, Que. – Industries – History. 5. Montreal, Que. – Commerce – History.

This business history focuses on Montreal with particular interest in its influential business personnel from 1837 to 1853. As a re-written doctoral dissertation it caters only to readers with special interests, and as such, does not appeal to the mass. Gwen Liu

## 388.5 Pipeline transportation

4862 388.5
**Bregha, François.**
Bob Blair's Pipeline. Toronto: James Lorimer, 1979. 220p. maps. Index.
ISBN 0-88862-280-5 $16.95

1. Blair, Bob. 2. Petroleum – Alaska – Pipe lines. 3. Gas, Natural – Alaska – Pipe lines. 4. Petroleum – Canada, Northern – Pipe lines. 5. Gas, Natural – Canada, Northern – Pipe lines.

An independent researcher, Bregha makes a critical analysis of government policy as it has affected the planning and building of natural gas pipelines in the north. An important, meticulously researched study in which criticisms are substantiated. Public and college libraries.

4863 388.5'09719
**Gray, Earle.**
Super Pipe: The Arctic Pipeline, World's Greatest Fiasco? Toronto: Griffin House, 1979. 262p. maps. Index. ISBN 0-88760-099-9 pa.: $7.95

1. Gas, Natural – Northwest, Canadian – Pipe lines. 2. Petroleum – Northwest, Canadian – Pipe lines. 3. Gas, Natural – Alaska – Pipe lines. 4. Petroleum – Alaska – Pipe lines.

Dealing with the confrontation between the Canadian Arctic Gas Pipe Line Limited and the Alberta Gas Trunk Line Limited, the author's bias is in favour of the former. The book should be read with one representing another viewpoint. Gwen Liu

## 389 Metrology and standardization

4864 389'.152
**The Canadian Metric Conversion Handbook.**
Edmonton: Hurtig Publishers, c1977. 98p.
ISBN 0-88830-149-9 pa.: $1.45

1. Metric system – Conversion tables.

A pocket-sized guide to metric measurements used in driving, cooking, weather, sewing and shopping. The meaning of terms used in the metric system are defined, and both quick metric conversion tables, and comprehensive conversion tables are given. An easy-to-use handbook for students and the general public.

4865 389.6
**Standards Council of Canada.**
Directory and Index of Standards. Répertoire des normes. Ottawa: Standards Council of Canada, 1977. 705p.
ISBN 0-920360-00-9 $10

1. Materials – Standards – Canada – Indexes. 2. Standardization – Canada – Indexes.

The two parts, the first is an explanation of the National Standards System and its components, and a listing with abstracts, of National Standards of Canada. The second is an index of standards published by Canadian standards writing organizations, and includes a KWOC index of standards. Diane Henderson

## 394 Customs

4866 394.26
**Allen, G. P.**
Days to Remember: Observances of Significance in Our Multicultural Society. Toronto: Multicultural Development Branch, 1978. 78p. (Multicultural Ontario) pa.

"Information on holidays that are celebrated in Ontario by residents of the various ethnocultural backgrounds ... to provide knowledge on which to base understanding." -Preface. Arrangement under ethnic group is by date.

## 400 Language and dictionaries

4867 423.

**Funk & Wagnalls Standard College Dictionary.**

Canadian ed. Don Mills, Ont.: Fitzhenry & Whiteside, 1978. 1590p. ill.
ISBN 0-88902-440-5 $12.95

1. English language – Dictionaries.

The 1976 edition listed CS no. 1270.

The 1978 Canadian edition contains some 152,000 entries and several extraneous lists: Canadian universities and community colleges, a table of metric weights and measures, the Canadian Bill of Rights, etc. A number of Canadian words are clearly defined. School, college and public libraries which purchased the 1976 edition may not need to replace it.

4868 423'.1

**Green, James.**

A First Thesaurus: The Word-hunter's Companion, by James Green and Arthur Thomas. Agincourt, Ont.: Book Society, 1977. 100p. Index. ISBN 0-7725-5024-7 pa.: $2.95

1. English language – Synonyms and antonyms.

Young adults and individuals approaching English as a second language will find this thesaurus very helpful. The text is broadly divided into four sections covering nouns, adjectives, verbs and adverbs, arranged alphabetically within each section. Access to terms is provided through an index to numbered keywords. Gartly Wagner

4869 427.

**Sherk, Bill.**

Brave New Words: The Newest, Funniest and Most Original Dictionary in the World. Illustrated by Leah Taylor. Toronto: Doubleday, 1979. 174p. Bibliography.
ISBN 0-385-15552-2 bd.: $12.95
ISBN 0-385-15331-7 pa.: $6.95

1. Words, New – English – Dictionaries.
2. English language – Dictionaries.

Bill Sherk's illustrated dictionary of new words presents a light-hearted look at one hundred words created by Canadians. The etymology of each new word is presented with its definition and the name of its creator. Sherk has taught a course in word power at York University. Gartly Wagner

4870 427'.9'71

**McConnell, Ruth E.**

Our Own Voice: Canadian English and How It Came to Be. Toronto: Gage Publishing, 1978. 276p. ill., maps. Bibliography: p. 245-270. Index.
ISBN 0-7715-9904-8 $14.95

1. English language in Canada. 2. Canadianisms (English).

Ruth McConnell, professor of Education at the University of British Columbia, discusses the characteristics of Canadian English in this study of the development of the language. The vocabulary, grammar and dialect of Newfoundland, the Maritimes, the Central Provinces, the Prairie Provinces, the Canadian North and British Columbia are examined in depth. The book's fresh approach makes it a welcome addition to any library shelf. Gartly Wagner

4871 427'.9'71

**Sandilands, John.**

Western Canadian Dictionary and Phrase Book. Facsimile of the 1913 edition. Introduction by John Orrell. Edmonton: University of Alberta Press, 1977. 51p.
ISBN 0-88864-021-8 $5

1. English language – Provincialisms – Canada. 2. English language – Slang.
3. Canadianisms (English).

Some of the picturesque speech of western Canada prior to the first World War is to be found in this facsimile of a 1913 publication. Readers will enjoy Sandilands humorous look at the language of the cowboy and the sodbuster. Gartly Wagner

4872 427'.9'71

**Scargill, M. H.**

A Short History of Canadian English. Victoria: Sono Nis Press, 1977. 63p. Bibliography: p. 61-62. ISBN 0-919462-31-6 pa.: $4

1. English language in Canada – History.
2. Canadianisms (English).

The Director of the Lexicographical Centre for Canadian English at the University of Victoria identifies Canadian contributions to the English language. Students and general readers will enjoy discovering how trappers, miners, homesteaders, sportsmen, and early settlers, have enriched our speech. Gartly Wagner

4873 428'.2
**Colter, Rob.**
Grammar to Go. Toronto: House of Anansi Press, 1978. 160p. ISBN 0-88784-063-9 pa.: $3.95

1. English language - Grammar - 1950-

This guide to English grammar will appeal to those busy people who require information which is clear, concise, and easy to find. Arranged alphabetically, it covers many typical grammatical problems but its usefulness is diminished by the lack of an index and a system of cross references. Gartly Wagner

4874 428'.2
**Cunningham, Murray.**
Communication: From Principles to Practice. Toronto: McGraw-Hill Ryerson, c1978. 292p. ill. Index. ISBN 0-07-082663-3 $9.50

1. English language - Grammar - 1950-
2. English language - Rhetoric.

All aspects of communication from body language to telecommunication are covered in this guide. Grammar, vocabulary and the mechanics of language are discussed in part two; the writings of résumés, letters, memoranda and telecommunications in part three. Information on the preparation of essays and research reports is also included. Gartly Wagner

4875 440.71'071
**Where to Learn French or English: A Directory of Canadian Institutions Offering Adults Second Language Training Courses in French and/or English.**
Ottawa: Dept. of the Secretary of State, 1979. 105p. ISBN 0-662-50286-8 Free

1. English language - Study and teaching - Canada. 2. French language - Study and teaching - Canada.

Arranged by province, from west to east, and within each province, by city and town, more than 480 courses in the French and English languages are detailed. The courses are of three types: general, intensive, and specialized. The French section of the Directory appears on inverted pages. An invaluable guide. Public and college libraries.

4876 443.2
**Collins-Robert French-English English-French Dictionary.**
By Beryl T. Atkins and others. Don Mills, Ont.: William Collins, c1978. 717, 781p. ISBN 0-00-433479-5 $22.95

1. French language - Dictionaries - English
2. English language - Dictionaries - French

A new two-part bilingual dictionary with emphasis on contemporary language, written and spoken. In both the French and the English sections of the dictionary the meanings of words, idioms and phrases are well defined, and examples cited. Lists of commonly used abbreviations are included in both language sections. A good, general purpose dictionary.

4877 447.
**Stanfield, David.**
How to Live in French in Ontario. Toronto: The Ontario Educational Communications Authority, 1978. 125p. ill. $3.50

1. French in Ontario. 2. French language - Ontario.

An interesting and well-organized guide to enjoying French cultural, educational and social opportunities in the province. Theatres, clubs, restaurants, and opportunities for study and entertainment in the French language are identified for the province generally, and for cities and towns in three Ontario regions: eastern, northern, and southwestern. A much needed reference.

## 500 Pure sciences

4878 500.9'71
**Karstad, Aleta.**
Aleta Karstad's Canadian Nature Notebook. Toronto: McGraw-Hill Ryerson, c1979. 144p. ill. Index. ISBN 0-07-082782-6 $12.95

1. Natural history - Canada. 2. Animals, Habitations of - Canada. 3. Nature study.

A field naturalist and artist explores plant and animal life in twenty-five different habitats. Vivid descriptions, line drawings and watercolours reveal the often overlooked natural world of beaches, marshes, prairie sloughs, tundra, forest and northern lakes. A pleasure to read. For school and public library natural history collections and for backpackers, campers and cottagers.

4879 500.9'71

**Reader's Digest Association (Canada).**

Outdoors Canada. Montreal: Reader's Digest Association (Canada); Ottawa: Canadian Automobile Association, 1977. 384p. ill., maps, plates, port. Index. ISBN 0-88850-052-1 $19.95

1. Natural history – Canada. 2. Outdoor life – Canada. 3. Parks – Canada – Guide-books.

This glossy overview of natural history and outdoor life in Canada encompasses everything from birds and plants to camp cooking and map reading. Profusely illustrated with photographs, charts and diagrams. While useful for the outdoorsman one might wish that the subject range had been more restricted and the coverage of each topic more detailed. School and public libraries.

4880 500.9'711

**Russell, Andy.**

Alpine Canada, by Andy Russell and Janis Kraulis. Edmonton: Hurtig Publishers, 1979. 143p. ill. ISBN 0-88830-153-7 $27.50

1. Natural history – Rocky Mountains, Canadian. 2. Rocky Mountains, Canadian.

The spectacular beauty of each of the four seasons in the Canadian Rockies is captured in Russell's facile prose and Kraulis' superb photographic studies. The waterfalls and the meadows, the glaciers and the streams, the wild life and delicate alpine plants are portrayed in quality colour plates. A beautiful coffee-table book for libraries which can afford it.

4881 507.2

**Canada. Parliament. Senate. Special Committee on Science Policy.**

A Science Policy for Canada: Report of the Special Committee of the Senate on Science Policy. Ottawa: Special Committee of the Senate on Science Policy, 1970- v ill.

Volumes 1-3 are listed in *CS* no. 1305.
vol. 4. *Progress and Unfinished Business*, 1977.

In the fourth volume of this important report the committee under the chairmanship of M. Lamontagne, points out that most of the findings of the first three volumes are still valid but that implementation of the recommendations has been discouragingly slow. A summary is provided of all the recommendations formulated in volumes one to three. Glenna Stevens

4882 507'.2071

**Eggleston, Wilfrid.**

National Research in Canada: The NRC, 1916-1966. Toronto: Clarke, Irwin, 1978. 470p. ill., diagr., graph, plates, ports. Bibliographical references and Index. ISBN 0-7720-1181-8 $22.50

1. National Research Council of Canada – History. 2. Research – Canada – History.

Covers the first fifty years of the National Research Council of Canada. Concentrates heavily on the people and projects surrounding the war years. An excellent record of the development of scientific research and science policies in Canada. Arch Stewart

4883 509.711

**Lawrence, Ronald D.**

The North Runner. Toronto: Holt, Rinehart and Winston, c1979. 287p. maps. ISBN 0-03-041551-9 $8.95

1. Natural history – British Columbia.
2. Outdoor life – British Columbia.
3. Dogs – Legends and stories.

The wilderness of northern Ontario and British Columbia provide the setting for a well-written account of the unusual bond which developed between a naturalist and an ill-used sled dog. There are fine descriptions of the wilderness and perceptive observations about man's relationship to nature. For thoughtful readers in secondary schools and public libraries.

## 520 Astronomy and surveying

4884 523.

**Newton, Jack.**

Deep Sky Objects: A Photographic Guide for the Amateur Astronomer. Toronto: Gall Publications, c1977. 160p. ill., maps. ISBN 0-88904-081-8 $9.50

1. Astronomy – Observers' manuals.

Contains an Observing Program, a glossary, full-page photographs, and instructions on how to use the accompanying charts. Useful for beginning astronomers. Recommended. Carol Rhodes

4885 523'.0074

**Gall, James.**

Astronomical Directory: Planetariums, Amateur Clubs, Observatories, Publications, Suppliers: Over 3000 World Listings. Toronto: Gall Publications, 1978. 144p. ill. ISBN 0-88904-082-6 pa.: $8

1. Planetaria – Directories. 2. Astronomy – Societies, etc. – Directories.

An easy to use directory compiled by an amateur astronomer who recognized the need for such a publication. Entries are well organized by country and category. Should be of use to amateur and professional astronomers alike. Arch Stewart

4886 523'.0074

**King, H. C.**

Geared to the Stars: The Evolution of Planetariums, Orreries and Astronomical Clocks, by H. C. King and R. Millburn. Toronto: University of Toronto Press, c1978. 442p. ill., diagr., ports. Bibliography: p. 405-428. Index. $50

1. Planetaria. 2. Astronomical clocks.

A comprehensive and authoritative reference work, containing numerous illustrations and photographs. Included are copious notes to the text as well as a twenty-four page bibliography. This book should interest not only the serious astronomer, but also the neophyte. Recommended for medium-sized astronomy collections. Carol Rhodes

4887 526.9'092

**Fraser, Esther.**

Wheeler. Banff, Alta.: Summerthought, 1978. 164p. ill. Index. ISBN 0-919934-07-2 $14.95

1. Wheeler, Arthur O., 1860-1943. 2. Surveyors – Canada – Biography. 3. Mountaineers – Canada – Biography. 4. Rocky Mountains, Canadian – Discovery and exploration. 5. Selkirk Mountains – Discovery and exploration.

A well-written biography, based on Wheeler's diaries and papers for anyone interested in the history of the exploration of the Rockies and western Canada. Contains reproductions of good archival photographs of people and places. A fine complement to Fraser's earlier book on the history of the Rockies. Arch Stewart

4888 529'.75

**Thomson, Malcolm M.**

The Beginning of the Long Dash: A History of Timekeeping in Canada. Toronto: University of Toronto Press, c1978. 190p. ill., diagrs., facsim., plates, ports. Bibliography: p. 179-183. Index. ISBN 0-8020-5383-1 $17.50

1. Time – Systems and standards.

The history of timekeeping in Canada, from the use of the stars to its development as an exacting branch of physics. The book is well-researched and provides an extensive bibliography and numerous plates of the people, places, and instruments involved. Arch Stewart

## 530 Physics

4889 530.

**Buckley, Paul.**

A Question of Physics: Conversations in Physics and Biology, by Paul Buckley and F. David Peat. Toronto: University of Toronto Press, c1979. 159p. (Canadian University Paperbacks) ISBN 0-8020-6331-4 pa.: $6

1. Physicists – Interviews. 2. Biologists – Interviews.

Interviews with eleven physicists, chemists and biologists are recorded in question and answer format. The discussions centre around theoretical physics, with an emphasis on quantum theory and relativity; a chapter on theoretical biology is also included. Familiarity with scientific concepts is required on the part of the reader. Diane Hart

4890 534.

**Schafer, Raymond Murray.**

The Tuning of the World. Toronto: McClelland and Stewart, c1977. 301p. ill., diagrs. Bibliographical references and Index. ISBN 0-7710-7965-6 $12.95

1. Sound. 2. Noise pollution. 3. Music – Philosophy and aesthetics.

The world of sounds and their effects on our lives form the subject matter of this pioneering study by one of Canada's most distinguished composers and authors. A fascinating critique of the sound environment. Don Sedgwick

## 549 Mineralogy

4891 549.
**Ince, Bill.**
Collecting Minerals: A Handbook for the Amateur. Toronto: McClelland and Stewart, c1977. 136p. ill. Bibliography: p. 128-131. Index. ISBN 0-7710-4316-3 pa.: $4.95

1. Mineralogy – Collectors and collecting.

A practical book for the layman written in a simple, non-technical style, with accompanying illustrations, some in color. Included are tips for the beginner on where to begin, and how, tools and techniques to use, plus a useful bibliography. Recommended for all general collections. Carol Rhodes

## 550 Earth sciences

4892 550'.92'4
**Inglis, Alex I.**
Northern Vagabond: The Life and Career of J. B. Tyrrell. Toronto: McClelland and Stewart, c1978. 256p. ill., maps, ports. Index. ISBN 0-7710-4357-0 $14.95

1. Tyrrell, J. Burr, 1858-1957. 2. Geologists – Canada – Biography.

An almost forgotten Canadian explorer, surveyor and mining geologist who played a major role in the development of the north in the late nineteenth and early twentieth century. Based upon archival records, illustrations and the Tyrrell papers, Inglis' work is factual, objective but not exciting. Writing is mediocre but subject matter warrants general purchase.

4893 551.2'1
**Lambert, Maurice B.**
Volcanoes. Vancouver: Douglas & McIntyre, c1978. 64p. ill. Bibliography: p. 62. ISBN 0-88894-226-5 bd.: $11.95
ISBN 0-88894-227-3 pa.: $6.95

1. Volcanoes.

Written by a volcanologist with the Geological Survey of Canada, this book sets out a reasonably simple explanation of what volcanoes are and how they affect us. Included are photographs from various parts of the world, diagrams, maps and a bibliography. Of particular interest is the information on geothermal energy. Recommended for public collections. Carol Rhodes

4894 551.4
**Canadian National Committee for the International Hydrological Decade.**
Hydrological Atlas of Canada. Atlas hydrologique du Canada. Ottawa: Fisheries and Environment Canada, 1978.
ISBN 0-660-01591-9 $35 (Canada); $42 (Other countries)

1. Hydrology – Canada – Maps.

Although this large format, coloured, loose-leaf atlas is heavily based on previous climatic publications, it brings together in one volume, for the researcher and the public, climatic and hydrologic maps and texts, with additional data and references. Of special interest are new hydrological maps such as 28A: Hardness of surface water. Mary Armstrong

## 551.5 Meteorology

4895 551.5'52
**Kennedy, Betty.**
Hurricane Hazel. Toronto: Macmillan, 1979. 176p. ill. ISBN 0-7705-1821-4 $12.95

1. Ontario – Hurricane, 1954.

A popularly written, journalistic report of the hurricane which devastated Toronto and environs on October 15, 1954. Anecdotes and recollections of persons whose lives were touched by the disaster appear in their own words. School and public libraries.

## 551.6 Climatology

4896 551.6'9
**Hare, F. Kenneth.**
Climate Canada, by F. Kenneth Hare and Morley K. Thomas. 2d ed. Toronto: John Wiley, 1979. 230p. ill., figures, maps, tables. Bibliographies and Indexes.
ISBN 0-471-99796-X $12.95

1. Canada – Climate.

First edition listed *CS* no. 1344.

Planned for college students, geographers, environmental and soil scientists, and readers concerned with environmental management, the second edition of this important work is more attractive in format than the earlier one. Few changes appear to have been made in the text but the bibliographies and the statistical data in the tables have been updated.

## 553 Economic geology

4897 553'.282
**Fitzgerald, John Joseph.**
Black Gold With Grit. Sidney, B.C.: Gray's Publishing, 1978. 264p. ill., plates, ports. Bibliography: p. 238-243. Index. ISBN 0-88826-075-X $10

1. Oil sands – Alberta.

A fascinating historical account of the Alberta tar sands, with good descriptions of the Great Canadian Oil Sands Company, Syncrude, Fort McMurray, and explanations with diagrams, of the technical aspects of the oil recovery process and the problems encountered. Includes photographs and a glossary. Recommended. Carol Rhodes

## 557 Geology of Canada

4898 557.1
**Janes, J. Robert.**
The Great Canadian Outback. Vancouver: Douglas & McIntyre, c1978. 144p. ill., maps. ISBN 0-88894-225-7 $19.95

1. Geology – Canada.

The geological processes which have created Canada's well-known geographical features, waterfalls, glaciers, tar sands, tidal flats, and potash mines, are lucidly explained by a geologist. A glossary, excellent photographs, maps and figures further clarify the readable text. For geology and geography collections in public and secondary school libraries.

4899 568.19
**Russell, Dale A.**
A Vanished World: The Dinosaurs of Western Canada. Photographs by Susanne M. Swibold; paintings by Eleanor M. Kish. Ottawa: National Museum of Natural Sciences, c1977. 142p. ill., ports. Bibliography: p. 137-142. (National History Series) ISBN 0-660-00011-3 DSS cat. no. NM 95-17/4

1. Dinosauria.

This vivid textual and visual presentation of the Canadian prehistoric world includes an intriguing theory linking the mysterious extinction of dinosaurs to high-energy radiation from a supernova. It also offers fascinating glimpses into the bustling world of archaeologists digging and reassembling to make reconstructions possible. For dinosaur enthusiasts of all ages. Frieda Ling

## 570 Life sciences

4900 572.8'034
**Bradley, Michael.**
The Iceman Inheritance: Prehistoric Sources of Western Man's Racism, Sexism and Aggression. Introductions by Imre Nemeth and Judith Posner. Toronto: Dorset Publishing, 1978. 229p. ill., maps. Bibliography: p. 227-229. ISBN 0-88893-000-3 bd.: $12.95 ISBN 0-88893-006-2 pa.: $6.95

1. Caucasian race. 2. Physical anthroplogy. 3. Human evolution.

The author's contention, in this provocative book, is that the aggressiveness and sexism of white males can be traced to their Neanderthal ancestors. Written for the general reader, Bradley's arguments will stimulate mixed reactions.

4901 574.5'222
**Sherbin, I. Griff.**
Mercury in the Canadian Environment. Ottawa: Environmental Protection Service, Environment Canada, 1979. 359p. figs., map, tables. Bibliography: p. 63-72. (Economic and Technical Review Report – Environment Protection Service: EPS 3-EC-79-6) ISBN 0-66210-467-6 Free.

1. Mercury – Environmental aspects – Canada.

The sources of mercury, and the areas in which the level of mercury pollution are unacceptably high are documented and tabulated. Federal regulations governing the control of mercury discharge are examined. For larger collections.

4902 574.9713
**Stewart, Darryl.**
Point Pelee: Canada's Deep South, by Darryl Stewart and Don Ross. Foreword by Pierre Berton. Toronto: Burns and MacEachern, c1977. 112p. ill., maps. Bibliography: p. 110-111. ISBN 0-88768-073-9 pa.: $5.95

1. Natural history – Ontario – Point Pelee National Park. 2. Point Pelee National Park, Ont.

An interesting and informative introduction to the range of plant and animal life which inhabit the sandy peninsula thrusting into Lake Erie. Mammals, birds, reptiles and amphibians, fish and insects are described and illustrated with line drawings and photographs. A checklist of birds is provided. Invaluable for visitors to this unique National Park.

## 580 Botanical sciences

4903 581.6'32
**Domico, Terry.**
Wild Harvest: Edible Plants of the Pacific Northwest. Photographs by Terry Domico; drawings by Hannah Jones. Saanichton, B.C.: Hancock House, 1978. 89p. Bibliography: p. 88. Index. ISBN 0-88839-022-X $4.95

1. Wild plants, Edible – Northwest, Pacific – Identification. 2. Poisonous plants – Northwest, Pacific – Identification. 3. Cookery (Wild foods).

Arranged according to season this attractively illustrated small book provides a guide to the identification and use of edible wild plants. Cautions are given about several plants which may be toxic.

4904 581.6'32
**Scott, Peter John.**
Some Edible Wild Fruit and Herbs of Newfoundland. St. John's, Nfld.: Breakwater Books, 1978. 76p. ill. Bibliography: p. 74. Index. ISBN 0-919948-58-8 pa.: $4.25

1. Wild plants, Edible – Newfoundland – Identification. 2. Fruit – Newfoundland – Identification. 3. Herbs – Identification.

A variety of herbs and wild fruits native to Newfoundland, but found also in the Atlantic provinces and in other regions of Canada, are identified by full-page, clear line drawings and discussed in readable text. Only vascular plants are included. Basic recipes are found in the introductory section. Another choice is *Edible Garden Weeds of Canada* by A. F. Szczawinski and N. J. Turner.

4905 581.6'32
**Turner, Nancy J.**
Wild Coffee and Tea Substitutes of Canada, by Nancy J. Turner and Adam F. Szczawinski. Ottawa: National Museum of Natural Sciences, 1978. 111p. ill. Bibliography: p. 105-107. Index. (Edible Wild Plants of Canada) ISBN 0-660-00090-3 pa. Spiral binding: $6.95 DSS cat. no. NM95-40/2

1. Wild plants, Edible.

A succinct, carefully researched guide to the identification, collection, preparation and use of twenty-five wild plants for beverages, for food or medication. Plants are described and illustrated with line drawings or colour photographs. Others in the same series are: *Edible Garden Weeds of Canada*, 1978; *Edible Wild Fruits and Nuts of Canada*, 1979; and *Edible Wild Greens of Canada*, 1980. For wild food enthusiasts.

4906 581.6'32
**Williams, Kim.**
Eating Wild Plants. Surrey, B.C.: Antonson Publishing, c1977. 180p. ill. Bibliography: p. viii. Index. ISBN 0-919900-23-2 pa.: $5.95

1. Wild plants, Edible. 2. Poisonous plants.

Contains descriptions and illustrations of numerous edible wild plants with instructions for their use and preparation. Also includes a chapter on poisonous plants. Unfortunately, some of the author's drawings and descriptions lack sufficient detail for identifying the plants if the user is not already familiar with them. Arch Stewart

4907 582'.0467
**Montgomery, Frederick H.**
Seeds and Fruits of Plants of Eastern Canada and Northeastern United States. Toronto: University of Toronto Press, c1977. 232p. ill. Bibliography: p. 209-212. Index. ISBN 0-8020-5341-6 $25

1. Seeds – Identification. 2. Fruit – Identification. 3. Botany – Canada. 4. Botany – Northeastern States.

Written by an eminent botanist, this authoritative work is "primarily intended for taxonomists and those teaching seed identification ... students of archaeology studying seed remains, ecologists studying bog formations, and seed analysts ..." Contains photographic descriptions, a glossary, seed chart and key, plus a lengthy bibliography. Recommended for large collections. Carol Rhodes

4908 582'.13
**Cormack, R. G. H.**
Wild Flowers of Alberta. Edmonton: Hurtig Publishers, c1977. 415p. ill. Bibliography: p. 404. Index. ISBN 0-88830-127-8 $10

1. Wild flowers – Alberta – Identification.

First published Edmonton: Queen's Printer, 1967.

A reissue of the popular field guide for amateur botanists, with a new colour index, glossary and colour photographs of over four hundred common flowering plants of Alberta. The author's intention was to provide a good non-technical aid for the newcomer to plant identification, and this book should assist those who wish to explore Alberta's countryside. Carol Rhodes

4909 582'.13
**Vance, Fenton R.**
Wildflowers across the Prairies, by Fenton R. Vance, James R. Jowsey and James S. McLean. Saskatoon: Western Producer Prairie Books, 1977. 214p. map. Bibliography: p. 199. Index. ISBN 0-919306-74-8 bd.: $14.95 ISBN 0-919306-73-X pa.: $8.95

1. Wild flowers – Prairie Provinces – Identification.

Some 270 flowering plants of western Canada and adjacent states are identified by descriptive notes, colour illustrations and detailed line drawings. Arrangement is by plant family with a glossary, indexes of common and scientific names, plant families, and plant colours. An invaluable field guide for all ages. All libraries.

4910 582'.16
**McKay, Sheila M.**
Trees, Shrubs and Flowers to Know in Ontario, by Sheila M. McKay and Paul M. Catling. Illustrated by Betsy Gordon. Don Mills, Ont.: J. M. Dent, c1979. 208p. ill. Bibliographies and Index. ISBN 0-460-95304-4 pa.: $6.95

1. Trees – Ontario – Identification.
2. Shrubs – Ontario – Identifcation.
3. Wild flowers – Ontario – Identification.

Concise descriptions of characteristic features and clear line drawings identify some four hundred trees, flowers and shrubs of the province. An authoritative guide for the summer cottage shelf and a companion for nature hikes.

4911 589'.2
**Brodie, Harold J.**
Fungi: Delight of Curiosity. Toronto: University of Toronto Press, c1978. 131p. ill. Bibliography: p. 127-128. Index. ISBN 0-8020-2289-8 $10

1. Fungi.

An invitiation for the uninitiated to share the beauty found in living organisms. The text is not highly technical and is informative and readable for the lay person. It is not intended for use as a field guide, and the black and white illustrations emphasize the form, beauty and structure rather than serve as identifiers. A basic glossary and selected references are included. Suitable for budding naturalists and general readers. Carol Rhodes

4912 589.2
**Jackson, Henry A. C.**
Mr. Jackson's Mushrooms. Edited and with an introduction by Mimi Cazort. Ottawa: National Gallery of Canada, 1979. 161p. ill., plates. ISBN 0-88884-364-X $35

1. Mushrooms.

A great botanical artist, the brother of A. Y. Jackson of the Group of Seven, painted exquisite watercolours of Canadian mushrooms in actual size, on field trips near Montreal between 1931 and 1954. This remarkable folio volume reproduces his work and includes notes from his diary which reflect his joy at discovering rare varieties. For all libraries that can afford the price.

4913 589'.222
**Canada. Dept. of Agriculture.**
Edible and Poisonous Mushrooms of Canada. Rev. ed. Ottawa: Dept. of Agriculture, 1979. 326p. ill. Bibliography: p. 270-279. A43-112/1979 $9.95

The 1975 revision was listed in *CS* no. 1388.

An authoritative, well-illustrated guide. A glossary is included.

## 590 Zoological sciences

4914 591.
**Russell, Andy.**
Andy Russell's Adventures with Wild Animals. Illustrated by Harry Savage. Edmonton: Hurtig Publishers, c1977. 183p. ill. ISBN 0-88830-143-X $9.95

1. Animals, Legends and stories of.

Alberta Non-fiction Award.

From his experience and observation of animal and bird life in the Rocky Mountains a perceptive nature writer has constructed appealing and very readable stories. Harry Savage's attractive line drawings contribute to the authenticity of the tales. For natural history collections in public and school libraries.

4915 591'.04
**Grainger, David.**
Animals in Peril: A Guide to the Endangered Animals of Canada and the United States. Toronto: Pagurian Press, c1978. 192p. ill. Bibliography: p. 190-192. (A Christopher Ondaatje Publication) ISBN 0-88932-082-9 $14.95

1. Rare animals – Canada. 2. Rare animals – United States.

Twenty fur-bearing mammals whose existence is threatened by indiscriminate hunting, trapping and pollution, are portrayed by the Guelph wildlife artist. Physical appearance, habitat, life cycle and survival potential are described. Excellent colour illustrations and black and white sketches. A well-organized reference tool for school and public libraries.

4916 591'.04

**Stewart, Darryl.**

From the Edge of Extinction: The Fight to Save Endangered Species. Toronto: McClelland and Stewart, c1978. 191p. ill. Bibliography: p. 187-191. ISBN 0-7710-8300-9 $12.95

1. Rare animals – North America. 2. Wildlife conservation – North America.

Full-page drawings and succinct notes describing habitat, life cycle, and migratory routes are provided for twenty-three North American birds and animals which have been saved from extinction. Successful protective programmes are described. Useful if additional material needed in school and public libraries.

4917 591'.05

**James, R. D.**

Annotated Checklist of the Birds of Ontario, by R. D. James, P. L. McLaren and J. C. Barlow. Toronto: Royal Ontario Museum, 1976. 80p. ill., maps. (Life Sciences Miscellaneous Publications) ISBN 0-88854-190-2 $2.50

1. Zoology – Periodicals.

Contains information on breeding, common and scientific names, seasonal distribution, and migratory status. Maps for southern and northern Ontario are included. Checklist covers 394 species of living birds, one extinct species, and thirty-four of hypothetical occurrence. Extensive references are given. Recommended for collections with a strong interest in ornithology. Carol Rhodes

4918 591.9'711

**Hancock, Lyn.**

There's a Raccoon in My Parka. Toronto: Doubleday; McClelland and Stewart-Bantam, 1977. 231p. ill., plates. ISBN 0-385-12755-3 $8.95 ISBN 0-7704-1532-6 pa.: $2.25

1. Zoology – Pacific coast (North America). 2. Pacific coast (North America) – Description and travel.

On a trip to the Pacific Northwest to film a colony of sea otters, the pet raccoon is only one of the wild creatures about whom the author writes engagingly. Personal adventures, descriptions of scenic beauty, people and wildlife are combined with observations on conservation in this readable travelogue. School and public libraries.

4919 591.9'713

**MacCrimmon, Hugh R.**

Animals, Man and Change: Alien and Extinct Wildlife of Ontario. Illustrated by Uta Strelive. Toronto: McClelland and Stewart, c1977. 160p. ill., maps. Bibliography: p. 154-156. Index. ISBN 0-7710-5420-3 $10

1. Animal introduction – Ontario. 2. Extinct animals – Ontario.

The author highlights the historical background and current status of twenty-eight species of wildlife, including fourteen fish species, which have been added to or eliminated from Ontario since the early settlers. Each chapter is accompanied by a line drawing and a map indicating the former or present range of the species. Suitable for the general reader. Diane Hart

## 597 Fishes

4920 597'.55

**Childerhose, R. J.**

Pacific Salmon & Steelhead Trout, by R. J. Childerhose and Marj Trim. Vancouver: Douglas & McIntyre, c1979. 158p. ill. ISBN 0-88894-218-4 $22.50

1. Pacific salmon. 2. Steelhead (Fish). 3. Fishery management – British Columbia.

Looking at the problems related to future depletion of our west coast salmon stocks the book covers the history of Pacific salmon fishing, biology, environment, and the enhancement of the stocks. There is also discussion of programmes and projects for conservation. Apart from a good and informative text, the book is well worth purchasing for the 115 beautiful colour photographs, particularly those of the magnificent salmon run. Maps are included. Recommended for reference use. Carol Rhodes

## 598.2 Birds

4921 598.2
**Baker, Ross H.**
Reflections of a Bird Watcher. Hantsport, N.S.: Lancelot Press, 1979. 258p. ill., plates. ISBN 0-88999-096-4 pa.: $7.95

1. Birds – Nova Scotia. 2. Bird watching – Nova Scotia.

The joys of bird-watching are shared by a Nova Scotia enthusiast from his experiences in his own backyard and on field trips. Pictures are from coloured transparencies. For both the serious bird watcher and the beginner.

4922 598.2'0971
**James, Ross D.**
Glen Loates' Birds of North America. Scarborough, Ont.: Prentice-Hall, 1979. 112p. ill. ISBN 0-13-357103-3 $24.95

1. Birds – Canada – Pictorial works.
2. Birds – United States – Pictorial works.

Twenty-four full page bird portraits by the renowned wildlife artist are accompanied by detailed descriptions of natural habitat, physical appearance, nesting habits and geographical distribution, written by the Canadian ornithologist. A large, handsomely designed book which will be enjoyed for its superb colour illustrations and accurate text. For all libraries which can afford it.

4923 598.2'97
**Mackenzie, John P. S.**
Birds in Peril: A Guide to the Endangered Birds of Canada and the United States. Illustrated by Terence Shortt. Toronto: McGraw-Hill Ryerson; Pagurian Press, c1977. 191p. ill. Bibliography: p. 189-191. ISBN 0-07-082538-6 $14.95 ISBN 0-88932-084-5 pa.: $7.95

1. Birds – Canada. 2. Birds – United States. 3. Birds, Protection of – Canada. 4. Birds, Protection of – United States. 5. Rare birds.

Terence Shortt's full-colour plates and black and white sketches lend vitality to Mackenzie's informative studies of twenty endangered bird species. The habitat, life cycle, and the destructive factors which threaten each bird are discussed as well as protection programmes. Highly recommended for bird lovers and conservationists.

4924 598.2'97
**Shortt, Terry.**
Wild Birds of Canada and the Americas. Toronto: Published by Pagurian Press for John Wiley, c1977. 271p. ill. Indexes. ISBN 0-88932-057-8 $14.95

1. Birds – North America. 2. Birds – South America.

Sixty-seven colour studies and more than one hundred black and white sketches by the widely travelled ornithologist. The scientifically accurate illustrations depict natural habitat, the readable text describes characteristics and habits of each species. An aesthetically pleasing, interesting volume for natural history enthusiasts from junior high to adult.

4925 598'.41
**Turner, Trudy.**
Fogswamp: Living with Swans in the Wilderness, by Trudy Turner and Ruth M. McVeigh. Saanichton, B.C.: Hancock House, c1977. 255p. ill., map. ISBN 0-919654-63-0 $10.95

1. Trumpeter swan. 2. Birds, Protection of – British Columbia.

Carrying on the work of Ralph Edwards, her father, of caring for the once-endangered trumpeter swans, the author and her family have built a satisfying life on a remote homestead in the Chilcotin area of British Columbia. Colour plates and a map. An engaging account of the rewards and handicaps of wilderness living. Popular reading.

4926 598.8
**Rising, Trudy L.**
Songbirds of Eastern Canada: Manitoba, Ontario, Quebec, Atlantic Provinces. Paintings by Kathryn DeVos-Miller. Montreal: Tundra Books, 1977. 96p. ill. Indexes. ISBN 0-88776-037-6 pa.: $3.95

1. Passeriformes. 2. Birds – Canada, Eastern.

The use of fascinating behavioral information in addition to basic facts relating to breeding, nesting and feeding make this book particularly appealing to the novice. The forty-five songbirds included are grouped by families and illustrated in colour reproductions of paintings. Despite its quality, the book may go unnoticed on the shelf due to its small size. Diane Hart

4927 598.8'64
**Angell, Tony.**
Ravens, Crows, Magpies, and Jays. Foreword by J. F. Lansdowne. Vancouver: Douglas & McIntyre, 1978. 111p. ill. Bibliography: p. 107-112. ISBN 0-88894-178-1 $16.95

1. Ravens. 2. Crows. 3. Magpies. 4. Jays.

A personalized and sympathetic look at the family Corvidae, with details concerning physical characteristics and behavioral traits common to these oft-maligned birds. Angell's black and white line drawings complement an informative text. Recommended for public libraries. Carol Rhodes

4928 598.9
**Tufts, Robie W.**
Nova Scotia: Birds of Prey. Hantsport, N.S.: Lancelot Press, 1978. 88p. ill. ISBN 0-88999-085-9 pa.: $2.95

1. Birds of prey – Nova Scotia.

Twenty-nine varieties of vultures, owls, hawks and eagles, their nesting and hunting practises and their habitat are described by an authority on ornithology. Tufts stresses the importance of birds of prey in the cycle of nature and decries their wanton destruction. Written for the amateur. Black and white illustrations. School and public libraries.

## 599 Mammals

4929 599.09'263
**Haley, Delphine,** ed.
Marine Mammals of Eastern North Pacific and Arctic Waters. Vancouver: Pacific Search Press, 1978. 256p. ill., plates. Bibliography: p. 246-249. ISBN 0-914718-35-5

1. Marine mammals – North Pacific Ocean.
2. Marine mammals – Arctic Ocean.
3. Mammals – North Pacific Ocean.

Useful addition to a marine collection. Covers cetaceans and pinnipeds as well as other marine-adapted species, such as the polar bear, sea otter, and stellar sea cow. Includes photographs, most of which are black and white, a classification, and a bibliography. Recommended for public libraries. Carol Rhodes

4930 599'.3232
**Lawrence, Ronald D.**
Paddy: A Naturalist's Story of an Orphan Beaver. Illustrated by Bill Elliot. New York: Random House, 1977. 240p. ill. ISBN 0-394-40403-3 $8.95

1. Beavers. 2. Natural history – Ontario.

Serving unexpectedly in loco parentis for a motherless beaver kit intensified the author's interest not only in the master dam-builders he had gone to study, but in the other wildlife which shared the same habitat. A very readable and interesting record of a naturalist's four months in the north woods of Ontario. Schools and public libraries.

4931 599'.882
**Hancock, Lyn.**
An Ape Came Out of My Hatbox: The Story of Gypsy, a Gibbon. Toronto: McClelland and Stewart, c1979. 224p. ill. Bibliography: p. 224. ISBN 0-7710-3805-4 $12.95

1. Gibbons – Behavior.

Useful information about the gibbon, the smallest of the apes is conveyed in this popularly written account of its behaviour and development as it frolics with other wild animals in the Hancock ménage. Factually accurate and easy to read. Young people and adults.

## 610 Medical sciences

4932 610.73
**LaSor, Betsy,** ed.
Issues in Canadian Nursing. Edited by Betsy LaSor and M. Ruth Elliott. Scarborough, Ont.: Prentice-Hall, 1977. 205p. Bibliographical references and Index. ISBN 0-13-506220-9 bd.: $9.95
ISBN 0-13-506238-1 pa.: $6.25

1. Nursing – Canada. 2. Nurses – Canada.

Significant concerns of Canadian nurses, education, the practice of nursing, and legislation and political issues, are examined by established members of the nursing profession in this first of three planned studies. Some of the original papers fill gaps in the existing literature. An important addition to health care collections in college and university and public libraries.

4933 610.73'9
**Shapiro, Martin.**
Getting Doctored: Critical Reflections on Becoming a Physician. Kitchener, Ont.: Between the Lines, c1978. 221p. Bibliographical references.
ISBN 0-919946-10-0 bd.: $12.95
ISBN 0-919946-09-7 pa.: $6.95

1. Medical students. 2. Medical education.

The author presents a revealing yet negative analysis of the medical profession based on his own experiences and a study of related literature. Included is a consideration of the socialization process through which a student becomes a "Doctor". Karl Marx's theory of alienation and Erich Fromm's concept of authoritarianism provide a framework for the problems explored. Diane Hart

4934 610'.92'4
**Copland, Dudley.**
Livingstone of the Arctic. Foreword by A. Y. Jackson. Lancaster, Ont.: Canadian Century Publishers, 1978. 183p. ill., maps, ports. ISBN 0-920738-00-1 pa.: $7.95

1. Livingstone, Leslie David, d. 1964.
2. Physicians – Canada – Biography.
3. Arctic regions.

A reprint of a volume first published in 1967.

Dairy farming and the Arctic are not synonymous in most minds, but to a physician concerned with improving the health and welfare of the Inuit in Canada's Arctic, they were closely linked. Dr. Livingstone's efforts to teach the Eskimos to farm were as important to him as his doctoring of them. An excellent biography paying tribute to Dr. Livingstone's contribution. Paula de Ronde

4935 610'.92'4
**Repka, William.**
Howard Lowrie, M.D.: Physician, Humanitarian. Toronto: Progress Books, 1977. 104p. (Portraits of Canadians In Struggle Series) ISBN 0-919396-43-7 pa.: $3.95

1. Lowrie, Howard, 1888- 2. Physicians – Canada – Biography.

A biography of Dr. Lowrie, physician and humanitarian is used as the vehicle to present Repka's political views. Paula de Ronde

4936 610'.92'4
**Selye, Hans.**
The Stress of My Life: A Scientist's Memoirs. Toronto: McClelland and Stewart, c1977. 272p. ill., ports. ISBN 0-7710-8050-6 $12.95

1. Physicians – Canada – Biography.

Engaging anecdotal reminiscences of the well-known medical researcher who has devoted almost half a century to the study of the effects of stress on human beings. Interesting and amusing vignettes of the world of the scientist for the non-specialist.

## 613 Personal health

4937 613.043'8
**Morf, Gustav.**
Let's Face It: We're All Growing Older, by Gustav Morf and Lucjan Dobrowolski. Foreword by Hans Selye; drawings by Dorothy Irwin. Markham, Ont.: PaperJacks, 1977. 158p. ill., graphs. ISBN 0-7701-0002-3 pa.: $1.95

1. Aging. 2. Aged – Conduct of life.

The physical and mental aspects of aging are examined by two physicians who are in their seventies. An objective discussion with a positive tone. Public libraries.

4938 613.2'6
**Cohlmeyer, David.**
A Guide to Vegetarian Living in Toronto. Toronto: Pythagorean Press, c1979. 152p. ill. Index. ISBN 0-9690906-0-9 pa.: $4.95

1. Vegetarianism – Directories. 2. Toronto, Ont. – Restaurants – Directories.

Owner of a vegetarian catering firm and restaurant, both in Toronto, the author explains how and what to order in restaurants, where to buy vegetarian ingredients. Information about cookbooks, cooking classes and recipes. Restaurants are categorized as to ethnic background. Frances Clutton

4939 613.7
**Percival, Jan.**
The Complete Guide to Total Fitness, by Jan Percival, Lloyd Percival and Joe Taylor. Scarborough, Ont.: Prentice-Hall, 1977. 224p. ill. Bibliographical references and Index. ISBN 0-13-160770-7 pa.: $7.95

1. Exercise. 2. Physical fitness.

An excellent addition to any fitness collection. Contains a self-test section, nutritional information, and useful exercises for all parts of the body. Also included is a philosophy of fitness and help in overcoming a sedentary life-style. Recommended for all public libraries. Carol Rhodes

4940 613.7
**Shephard, Roy J.**
Endurance Fitness. 2d ed. Toronto: University of Toronto Press, c1977. 380p. ill. Bibliography: p. 285-367. Index.
ISBN 0-8020-2250-2 bd.: $17.50
ISBN 0-8020-2251-0 pa.: $9.95

1. Physical fitness.

First published 1969.

This scholarly monograph, a scientific examination of general theories of physical fitness, is designed for university courses in exercise physiology. The second edition is a complete revision of the first in the light of recent advances in the field of sports medicine. Included are a glossary of symbols and abbreviations and a bibliography of over thirteen hundred items. Carl Spadoni

4941 613.7'1
**Michener, Leslie.**
The Exercise Book, by Leslie Michener and Gerald Donaldson. Photography and design by Peter Christopher. Agincourt, Ont.: Gage Publishing, c1978. 100p. ill., port.
ISBN 0-7715-9459-3 pa.: $8.95

1. Exercise.

A sequence of forty-eight coordinated movement patterns has been designed to exercise the body's various muscle groups. It incorporates a series of relaxing exercises. Each group of movements is illustrated and instructions given for following them. A persuasive invitation to physical fitness. Will find enthusiastic users in school and public libraries.

4942 613.7'1
**Steen, David.**
The Canadian Pilot's Fitness Manual. David Steen, in cooperation with the Fitness Institute and the Canadian Air Line Pilots Association. Toronto: Fitzhenry & Whiteside, 1978. 203p. ill., tables. ISBN 0-88902-410-3 $10.95

1. Exercise. 2. Physical fitness.

A practical guide to becoming and remaining physically fit. Instructions are given for measuring one's fitness, and there are training tables for every age, diet and nutrition tables, and tension-relieving exercises. Well illustrated.

## 614 Public health

4943 614'.19
**Emson, H. E.**
The Doctor and the Law: A Practical Handbook for the Canadian Physician. Toronto: Macmillan, c1979. 226p. Bibliography: p. 227. Index.
ISBN 0-7705-1786-2 pa.: $9.95

1. Medical jurisprudence – Canada.
2. Medical laws and legislation – Canada.

Containing valuable instructions to doctors regarding legal responsibilities in cases of abortion, rape, child abuse, gun shot wounds, and on record keeping, court testimony, autopsies, etc. Information on malpractice, and a general discussion of Canadian law and health personnel are also included. Clear writing and an index add to the usefulness of the text for all health care personnel. Gail Dykstra

4944 614.5'42'09
**Wherrett, George Jasper.**
The Miracle of the Empty Beds: A History of Tuberculosis in Canada. Toronto: University of Toronto Press, 1977. 299p. ill., tables. Bibliography: p. 267-280. Index.
ISBN 0-8020-2269-3 $12.50

1. Tuberculosis – Canada – History.
2. Tuberculosis – Prevention – History.

Canada's remarkable success in reducing the incidence of death from tuberculosis is chronicled by a leader in the fight against the disease. The first part of this well-researched, carefully documented social history focuses on the national campaign to improve health care, the second describes provincial achievements in control. An important study. Public health personnel and general readers.

## 614.7 Environmental pollution

4945 614.7
**Soyka, Fred.**
The Ion Effect: How Air Electricity Rules Your Life and Health, by Fred Soyka and Alan Edmonds. Toronto: Lester and Orpen; McClelland and Stewart-Bantam, 1978, c1977. 181p. Bibliography: p. 165-169. Index.
ISBN 0-919630-84-7 $7.95 pa.: $1.95

1. Air, Ionized – Physiological effects.
2. Man – Influence of environment.
3. Environmentally induced diseases.

An easy to read, well-researched explanation

of how the air around us can influence our physical or mental well-being. Based on personal experiences and international reports, this book will be of interest to anyone concerned with how aspects of our environment may affect our lives. Arch Stewart

## 615 Pharmacology

4946 615'.1

**Leonard, Geraldine T.**

The Canadian Consumer's Guide to Prescription Drugs. Rexdale, Ont.: John Wiley, c1979. 147p. Index. ISBN 0-471-99818-4 pa.: $6.95

1. Drugs. 2. Drugs – Side effects.

Brand name drugs are grouped generically into more than 130 entries indicating, as applicable, when the drugs are prescribed, when not prescribed and precautions to be taken. Adverse effects are also given, but with no indication of probability. The index is the prime means of access and includes both generic and trade names. Diane Hart

## 616 Diseases

4947 616.3'98

**Laverty, Frank T.**

The O.K. Way to Slim: Weight Control Through Transactional Analysis. Scarborough, Ont.: Prentice-Hall, 1977. 240p. ill. Bibliography: p. 236. Index. ISBN 0-13-633727-9 $8.95

1. Reducing. 2. Reducing – Psychological aspects. 3. Transactional analysis.

A rational, clearly stated explanation of the reasons why people overeat, and a guide to weight control through a change in mental attitudes. A practical manual for the general reader.

4948 616.7'2

**Robinson, Harold Speers,** ed.

You Asked about Rheumatoid Arthritis. Vancouver: Douglas & McIntyre, c1978. 120p. ill. ISBN 0-88894-177-3 pa.: $4.95

1. Rheumatoid arthritis.

A straightforward question and answer format addresses the concerns of patients and their families about this widespread disease. The symptoms, diagnosis, prognosis, types of treatment, research, and the incidence of quackery are each discussed. Clear diagrams, a glossary and a list of volunteer agencies augment the lucid explanation. Sponsored by the British Columbia Division of the Arthritis and Rheumatism Society. Public libraries.

4949 616.8'582

**Richmond, Guy.**

Shadows of a Violent Mind. Surrey, B.C.: Antonson Publishing, 1978. 223p. ISBN 0-919900-29-1 pa.: $6.95

1. Violence. 2. Psychology, Pathological.

An excellent and very readable examination of violence in individuals, groups, and society. The author draws on his extensive experience and on authorities in criminology to provide insight into the violent, psychopathic mind. Some case histories are included. Criticisms of the criminal code and penal system are well presented. Arch Stewart

4950 616.8'588

**Ministry of Community and Social Services. National Institute on Mental**

Retardation. Orientation Manual on Mental Retardation. 2d rev. ed. Downsview, Ont.: National Institute on Mental Retardation, 1977. 118p. $3

1. Mental deficiency. 2. Mentally handicapped.

An informative readable introduction to mental retardation including the history, definitions and causes, the parent movement, normalization, community services and recent developments. Intended as a training manual for students, volunteers and staff, but useful to anyone with an interest in the topic. An "Information Services and Reading List" concludes each chapter. Diane Hart

4951 616.9'803

**Tataryn, Lloyd.**

Dying for a Living. Ottawa: Deneau and Greenberg, c1979. Index. ISBN 0-88879-018-X $12.95

1. Occupational diseases – Canada.
2. Industrial hygiene – Canada.

A well-researched and reported look at health hazards imposed on workers and the environment by industry. The frustrations of trying to obtain information from government and industrial sources are well described. A timely topic that should be of interest to a wide range of readers. Arch Stewart

4952 616.9'94
**MacDonald, John A.**
When Cancer Strikes: A Book for Patients, Families and Friends. Toronto: McClelland and Stewart, c1979. 144p. Bibliography: p. 143-144. ISBN 0-7710-5424-6 pa.: $7.95
1. Cancer.
All cancer patients and their doctors should read this book by a surgeon who himself waged a courageous battle with the disease. He explains in lay terms what cancer is and the state of knowledge about treating it, and he offers wise counsel about handling its psychological effects on both patients and their friends. An intensely human book for all. Excellent bibliography.

## 618 Gynecology and obstetrics

4953 618.1'453
**Gifford-Jones, W.,** pseud.
What Every Woman Should Know About Hysterectomy. Toronto: Fitzhenry & Whiteside, c1977. 228p. Index. ISBN 0-88902-421-9 $8.95
1. Hysterectomy.
Written by the popular syndicated columnist-physician, this book is a *must* for all women to read. The explanations are straightforward, and the author allays some of the myths surrounding this common surgery, as well as dispelling the notion that today, hysterectomies are "minor" surgery. For all public library collections. Carol Rhodes

## 620 Engineering

4954 621.48
**Peat, F. David.**
The Nuclear Book. Ottawa: Deneau and Greenberg, c1979. ISBN 0-88879-017-1 $7.95
1. Nuclear technology.
The near-tragedy at Harrisburg alerted the public to the possibility of a large-scale nuclear accident. Prompted by this incident, the author has written a succinct but readable book. Special emphasis is directed at Canada's participation in the sale of nuclear reactors. Carl Spadoni

4955 621.48
**Wyatt, Alan.**
The Nuclear Challenge: Understanding the Debate. Toronto: Book Press, c1978. 224p. ill., diagrs., graphs. Bibliography: p. 203-212. Index. ISBN 0-920650-00-9 bd.: $12.95 ISBN 0-920650-01-7 pa.: $6.95
1. Atomic power.
A spokesman for the Canadian Nuclear Association expounds the advantages of nuclear energy as a form of power. A glossary, a list of abbreviations used in nuclear literature, and a bibliography arranged by subject, and by opposing views on nuclear power, supplement the text. The commentary at times becomes technical. One viewpoint on a controversial issue.

4956 621.48'0971
**Glen, Ron.**
Critical Choice: Nuclear Power in Canada, The Issues Behind the Headlines, by Ron Glen and Charles Law. Toronto: Corpus Information Services, c1978. 268p. ill., diagrs. Bibliographical references and Indexes. ISBN 0-919217-05-2 pa.: $9.95
1. Atomic power. 2. Atomic power-plants – Environmental aspects – Canada.
An attempt is made here to analyse the many-sided arguments concerning nuclear power in Canada. The reader is initially given an explanation of its technology – fission and fusion processes – and its history. The dilemma between the solution to the energy crisis and the problems of waste management and public danger is considered unresolvable in simplistic terms. Carl Spadoni

4957 623.44
**Barnes, Leslie W. C. S.**
Canada's Guns: An Illustrated History. Ottawa: National Museum of Man, 1979. 112p. ill. ISBN 0-660-00137-3 pa.: $9.95
1. Firearms – Canada.
The author traces the effect of the gun on the course of military history from the earliest times. Special attention is paid to the role of Canadian artillery in the Boer War and the First and Second World Wars. For both the general reader interested in weaponry and the student of military affairs. Copiously illustrated.

4958 623.74'64
**Peden, Murray.**
Fall of an Arrow. Stittsville, Ont.: Canada's Wings, 1978. 182p. ill., ports. ISBN 0-920002-04-8 $14.95
1. Arrow (Turbojet fighter planes).

An angry denunciation of the government decision which not only cancelled the production programme for the interceptor aircraft but ordered the destruction of the completed Arrows and those on the production line and abolished the jobs of some thirteen thousand skilled Canadian workers. Of general interest.

4959 623.82'8

**MacKean, Ray.**

The Little Boats: Inshore Fishing Craft of Atlantic Canada. Models, Ray MacKean; paintings, Robert Percival. Fredericton, N.B.: Brunswick Press, c1979. 109p. ill. ISBN 0-88790-104-2 pa.: $12.95

1. Fishing boats – Atlantic Provinces.

Replicas of twenty-one small boats indigenous to the Atlantic fishing industry have been constructed by modelmaker Ray MacKean and painted in appropriate settings by Robert Percival. The informative commentary, spiced with anecdotes, the paintings, drawings and photographs, evoke a vanishing phase of maritime life. A glossary is included. Recommended for schools and public libraries.

4960 628.1'686

**McLeod, Joseph.**

And the Rivers Our Blood. Toronto: NC Press, 1977. 179p. ill., maps. Bibliography: p. 186-187. Index. ISBN 0-919600-78-6 bd.: $14.98 ISBN 0-919600-77-8 pa.: $6.98

1. Water – Pollution – Canada. 2. Pollution – Canada.

The writer interviewed residents of the Grassy Narrows/White Dog Reserves about their feelings towards the mercury pollution of their villages. Included are taped conversations showing the frustrations, anger, and apathy of living with that ever-present danger. This is not a scientific book, but an account written from a poet's perspective of a serious ecological problem. It also contains poems by the author. Recommended as an addition to environmental collections. Carol Rhodes

## 629.13 Aeronautics

4961 629.13

**Milberry, Larry.**

Aviation in Canada. Toronto: McGraw-Hill Ryerson, 1979. 272p. Index. ISBN 0-07-082778-8 $16.95

1. Aeronautics – Canada – History.

A general survey of Canadian aviation history from the first balloon flight in 1840 to the present. The role of aviation in Canada's commercial, government, military and developmental activities is chronicled, and the growth of the aviation industry detailed. Photographs from government, military and corporate archives and private collections provide a parallel pictorial history. All libraries.

4962 629.13'091'1

**Rowe, Percy.**

The Great Atlantic Air Race. Toronto: McClelland and Stewart, c1977. 224p. ill., ports. Bibliography: p. 223-224. ISBN 0-7710-7739-4 $10

1. Transatlantic flights.

A former member of the Royal Air Force and an experienced journalist, Rowe recreates vividly the drama and excitement of the first non-stop transatlantic flight in June, 1919. The intrepid airmen and their fragile aircraft hold centre stage in this popular, well-illustrated account of one segment of early Canadian aviation history. School and public libraries.

4963 629.13'092'2

**Sutherland, Alice Gibson.**

Canada's Aviation Pioneers: 50 Years of McKee Trophy Winners. Foreword by Fred W. Hotson. Toronto: McGraw-Hill Ryerson, c1978. 304p. ill., maps, ports. Index. ISBN 0-07-082704-4 $19.95

1. Air pilots – Canada – Biography.
2. Aeronautics – Canada – History.
3. Trans-Canada Trophy (Aeronautics).

Fifty years of flight history are mirrored in the profiles of the pilots, navigators, engineers, researchers and cartographers whose contribution to Canadian aviation has won for them the coveted McKee Trophy. Carefully researched and well-illustrated, this useful reference source covers the period 1927-1977. All libraries.

## 629.2 Motor vehicles

4964 629.22

**Edmonston, Phil.**

Lemon-aid. Rev. ed. Don Mills, Ont.: Musson, 1979. 464p. ISBN 0-7737-1029-9 $5.95

1. Automobile purchasing.

The 1976 edition listed *CS* no. 1552.

A revised version of a popular consumer

guide to intelligent shopping for new and used cars. There are chapters on car repair rackets, using the courts to redress complaints, and an analysis of individual models for specific years. Public libraries.

## 630 Agriculture

4965 630'.971
**Anderson, Allan.**
Remembering the Farm: Memories of Farming, Ranching, and Rural Life in Canada, Past and Present. Toronto: Macmillan, c1977. 287p. ill., plates, ports. ISBN 0-7705-1572-X bd.: $12.95 ISBN 0-7705-1827-3 pa.: $8.95

1. Farm life – Canada. 2. Farmers – Canada – Biography. 3. Canada – Rural conditions.

Several hundred Canadians from every part of the country have recorded recollections of life on the family farm. A nostalgic patch-work of anecdotes reveal the joys and discouragements, the fun and hard work of rural life. Readable oral social history for both urbanites and exiles from the farm.

4966 630'.971
**Lawrence, James,** ed.
The Harrowsmith Reader: An Anthology from Canada's National Award Winning Magazine of Country Life and Alternatives to Bigness. Camden East, Ont.: Camden House, c1978. 287p. ill. Index. ISBN 0-920656-01-3 bd.: $12.50 ISBN 0-920656-00-5 pa.: $8.95

1. Country life – Canada. 2. Agriculture – Canada.

A collection of the best articles from the first two years of Canada's highly successful magazine of country and alternative life style. Arranged under the broad topics: land, country careers, shelter, the garden, husbandry, the pantry, and rural life. Excellent, profuse illustrations plus a short index help to make this a first choice. Peter Moffet

4967 630'.9713
**Ladell, John.**
Inheritance: Ontario's Century Farms Past & Present, by John Ladell and Monica Ladell. Illustrated by Bert Hoferichter. Toronto: Macmillan, 1979. Index. ISBN 0-7705-1792-7 $16.95

1. Family farms – Ontario – History.
2. Ontario – Rural conditions.

Based on interviews with the current holders of forty-two farms that have been owned by generations of the same family for at least one hundred years, this book comprises a popular history of rural Ontario. Good bibliography, useful index, well illustrated. Peter Moffet

4968 631.
**Winter, Eric.**
Recreational Farming: Finding and Working Your Own Place in the Country. Toronto: McGraw-Hill Ryerson, 1978. 162p. ill., maps. Bibliography: p. 146-162. ISBN 0-07-082708-7 $12.95

1. Part-time farming.

An excellent introduction to the subject. Concentrates on eastern Canada, but much of the advice can be applied to other areas. Includes a useful, annotated list of government publications. Current references and illustrations are also provided. Arch Stewart

## 634.9 Forests and forestry

4969 634.9'82
**MacKay, Donald.**
The Lumberjacks. Toronto: McGraw-Hill Ryerson, c1978. 319p. ill., diagrs., maps, ports. Bibliography: p. 312-313. Index. ISBN 0-07-082727-3 $19.95

1. Logging – Canada – History. 2. Loggers – Canada – Biography.

The saga of Canada's logging industry in eastern and western Canada, from the beginning of the nineteenth to the middle of the twentieth centuries is enlivened by the memories of pioneer loggers and lumberjacks. Contemporary photographs have been garnered from government and commercial archives, museums, and private collections. Readable, informative social history with a good glossary. General reading.

## 635 Gardening

4970 635'.03
**The Weekend Magazine Practical Gardening Encyclopedia.**
Edited by Roy Hay. Montreal: Optimum Publishing, c1977. 351p. ill., map. Index. ISBN 0-88890-070-8 $19.95

1. Gardening – Dictionaries.

This comprehensive guide to all aspects of

gardening is very well indexed and illustrated. A basic reference work. Brenda Hughes

4971 635.7
**Jacobs, Betty E. M.**
Profitable Herb Growing at Home. Illustrated by Charles H. Joslin. Charlotte, Vt.: Garden Way Publishing, c1976. 225p. ill. Bibliography: p. 205-206. ISBN 0-88266-087-X pa.: $6.95

1. Herb gardening.

A useful guide for the serious herb gardener, with tips on growing and selling herbs and herb products. Brenda Hughes

4972 635.9′32
**Buckley, Arthur R.**
Canadian Garden Perennials. Saanichton, B.C.: Hancock House; Ottawa: Research Branch, Agriculture Canada: Publishing Centre, Supply and Services Canada, 1977. 212p. ill. Index. ISBN 0-919654-78-9 $17.50 DSS cat. no. A-22-84-1977

1. Perennials. 2. Perennials – Canada.

Comprehensive coverage of the care, propagation and recommended varieties of perennials for Canadian gardens. Extensive plant lists, excellent illustrations, and plans for seasonal borders. Brenda Hughes

4973 635.9′65
**Arnold, Jud.**
The Weekend Magazine Illustrated Encyclopedia of House Plants. Montreal: Optimum Publishing, c1979. 223p. ill. Index. ISBN 0-88890-052-X $19.95

1. House plants – Handbooks, manuals, etc. 2. Indoor gardening.

In Part One, over one hundred and fifty plants are listed alphabetically, with concise information about care, feeding and propagation. Part Two covers general topics such as soil, plant pests, hydroponics, bonsai and greenhouse gardening. Brenda Hughes

4974 635.9′65
**Collins, Marnie.**
Green Things in Small Spaces: Apartment Gardening Indoors, Outdoors, on-the-Cheap. Toronto: Methuen, 1977. 154p. ill. Bibliography: p. 137-139. Index. ISBN 0-458-93070-9 bd.: $9.95 ISBN 0-458-92770-8 pa.: $5.95

1. House plants. 2. Balcony gardening.

A useful guide for the beginning indoor gardener, with emphasis on overcoming the dry, overheated growing conditions of most apartments. Practical, basic instructions on light, temperature and soil, plus suggestions for plant displays and balcony gardening. Brenda Hughes

4975 635.9′65
**Reeves, Ken.**
Plants: Answers That Work. Toronto: Clarke, Irwin, c1978. 157p. ill. Index. ISBN 0-7720-1214-8 pa.: $6.95

1. House plants.

Problems in growing house plants are explained in a straightforward question-and-answer format, and unusually clear diagrams, by the CBC horticulturalist. Optimum conditions for potting, fertilizing, propagating and lighting are described and a glossary and a list of poisonous plants included. Will be read enthusiastically by indoor gardeners. Public libraries.

4976 635.9′7
**Pouliot, Paul.**
A Guide to Trees, Shrubs and Hedges. Montreal: Habitex Books, c1978. 343p. ill., diagrs., map, plates. ISBN 0-88912-041-2 pa.: $6.95

1. Ornamental woody plants – Canada.

This clearly presented and very readable source will aid the home gardener in choosing and caring for trees and shrubs. A detailed table of contents serves as an index, but does not consistently provide access to individual plants. The illustrations, particularly the photographs, would be more effective and clearer if greater use was made of colour. Diane Hart

## 636 Animal husbandry

4977 636.2′1
**Gould, Ed.**
Ranching: Ranching in Western Canada. Saanichton, B.C.: Hancock House, 1978. 165p. ill., ports. Bibliography: p. 164-165. Index. ISBN 0-919654-79-9 $14.95

1. Ranches – The West, Canadian – History. 2. Cattle trade – The West, Canadian – History. 3. The West, Canadian – History.

A nostalgic pictorial and narrative sketch of the old West as it was, by a native Albertan. Information about individual ranches, and an index, add to the usefulness for school and public libraries.

4978 636.7

**Cochrane, Brian M.**

Your Pets, Your Health and the Law: The Dog and Cat Owner's Guide. Preface by John S. Bennett. Toronto: John Wiley, c1979. 135p. ill. Index. ISBN 0-471-99817-6 pa.: $6.95

1. Dogs. 2. Cats. 3. Dogs as carriers of disease. 4. Animals as carriers of disease. 5. Pets – Law and legislation – Canada.

The responsibilities of pet ownership, the potential health hazards, and common legal problems involving pets and their owners are examined by a medical doctor and a lawyer. A factual exploration of a problem which concerns not only pet owners but their friends and neighbours. Of general interest.

4979 636.7'08'87

**Nowell, Iris.**

The Dog Crisis. Toronto: McClelland and Stewart, c1978. 270p. Bibliography: p. 263-266. Index. ISBN 0-7710-6795-X pa.: $7.95

1. Dogs. 2. Pets.

Substantiating her premise that the escalating dog population is becoming an acute and costly social problem, the author makes a frontal attack on irresponsible pet owners and the profit-hungry pet industry. Rational corrective measures are proposed. A contentious issue has been well researched. School and public libraries.

## 639.2 Fisheries

4980 639'.2'00497

**Stewart, Hilary.**

Indian Fishing: Early Methods on the Northwest Coast. Vancouver: J. J. Douglas, c1977. 181p. ill. Bibliography: p. 178-179. Index. ISBN 0-88894-120-X $15.95

1. Indians of North America – Northwest coast of North America – Fishing. 2. Indians of North America – Northwest coast of North America – Implements.

Minute descriptions of fishing tools, techniques, and cooking methods, and a short but penetrating account of the spiritual and social significance of such activities unravel a fascinating way of life centred around the sea and its resources. Profusely illustrated with quality photographs and hundreds of exquisite, original drawings. An important work for specialists and laymen alike. Frieda Ling

4981 639'.27'55

**Landale, Zoe.**

Harvest of Salmon: Adventures in Fishing the B.C. Coast. Saanichton, B.C.: Hancock House, c1977. 222p. ill. ISBN 0-919654-75-4 $9.95

1. Pacific salmon fishing – British Columbia.

Detailed accounts of life as a commercial fishing couple in British Columbia. Part of the interest lies in the fact that both were young and inexperienced when they began. Included are photographs and illustrations of vessels and fish. For general interest and larger collections. Carol Rhodes

4982 639.29'097

**Coish, E. Calvin.**

Season of the Seal: The International Storm Over Canada's Seal Hunt. St. John's, Nfld.: Breakwater Books, 1979. 296p. Bibliography: p. 271-280. Index. ISBN 0-919948-626 pa.: $4.95

1. Sealing – Newfoundland.

A Newfoundlander presents a history of the seal hunt and the pros and cons of the current controversy surrounding it. The tale begins objectively, but as it proceeds, a Newfoundland pro-hunt bias becomes increasingly apparent in a point of view seldom presented by the mass media. Extensive bibliography. Of interest to all libraries.

## 639.9 Conservation

4983 639'.9

**Foster, Janet.**

Working for Wildlife: The Beginning of Preservation in Canada. Toronto: University of Toronto Press, c1978. 283p. ill., maps, ports. Bibliography: p. 265-271. Index. ISBN 0-8020-5399-8 $19.95

1. Wildlife conservation – Canada. 2. Wildlife conservation – Canada – History.

This first comprehensive, thoroughly researched history of the development of the wildlife conservation movement in Canada, traces it from 1885 to the 1920's. The well-known naturalist and photographer pays tribute to the far-sighted senior civil servants who saw the need for national parks and protective legislation. Well illustrated. College and larger public libraries.

4984 639'.97'95
**Hunter, Robert.**
To Save a Whale: The Voyages of Greenpeace. Photography by Rex Weyler; introduction by Paul Spong. Vancouver: Douglas & McIntyre, c1978. 119p. ill. ISBN 0-88894-188-9 pa.: $6.95

1. Greenpeace Foundation. 2. Whaling – Russia. 3. Wildlife conservation.

A day-by-day account of the confrontation between a small halibut seiner and the large Russian and Japanese whaling ships off the coast of California, as the Greenpeace crew struggled to protect the sperm whale population from indiscriminate killing. Excellent photographs and a readable story will attract readers. Conservation collections in school and public libraries.

## 640 Budgeting and consumer information

4985 640'.2'02
**Conran, Shirley.**
Superwoman: Everything You Need to Know About Running a Home in Canada Today. Illustrated by Jan Mitchener. Markham, Ont.: Penguin Books, 1978. 378p. ill. Index. ISBN 0-14-00-4880-4 $2.95

1. Home economics – Handbooks, manuals, etc.

Advice on accomplishing household tasks in less time, and eliminating others completely. Conran covers a multitude of topics including shopping, decorating, cleaning, combining motherhood and career, handling sexual aggression, and more. The British bestseller now edited by Ruth Fremes for use in Canada. Lively narrative with some useful information. Janice Zlatarits

4986 640.73
**Trebilcock, Michael J.**
Help! Handbook of Consumer Rights in Canada. Toronto: CBC Learning Systems, c1978. 84p. ill. ISBN 0-8879400846 $2.50

1. Consumer education. 2. Consumer protection.

Written for the CBC's television program "Marketplace", this book covers consumer law for the non-lawyer. Covering all aspects of contracts, warranties, defective goods and services, credit, insurance, etc., the book provides you with information as well as names and addresses for complaints. Gail Dykstra

## 641.1 Nutrition

4987 641.2'2
**Rowe, Percy.**
Red, White and Rosé: Enjoying Wines in Canada. Don Mills, Ont.: Musson, 1978. 230p. Bibliography: p. 228-230. ISBN 0-7737-1024-8 pa.: $8.95

1. Wine and wine making – Canada. 2. Wine and wine making.

Background information about wines in Canada, domestic as well as imported, their history, manufacture and marketing. Guidelines on buying, storing and serving them. The book has a glossary and a bibliography but the lack of an index limits its usefulness as a reference source. Frances Clutton

4988 641.2'2
**Sharp, Andrew.**
Vineland 1000: A Canadian View of Wine. Toronto: Andrew Sharp Publications, c1977. 200p. ill. Index. $6.95

1. Wine and wine making. 2. Wine and wine making – Canada.

Using the year Leif Ericsson discovered Canada and the name he gave it as title, syndicated columnist Sharp discusses the major aspects of wine in Canada. Question and answer format are used to present information about buying, storing and serving wine. Frances Clutton

4989 641.3'7'3
**Wells, Joyce.**
The Cheese Stands Alone: Guide to Home Cheesemaking. Illustrated by Jocelyn Curry. Saanichton, B.C.: Hancock House, 1978. 142p. ill., diagrs., map. Bibliography: p. 138. Index. ISBN 0-88839-004-1 pa.: $3.95

1. Cheese. 2. Cheese – Varieties.

The first half of this book gives details on how to make cheese – ingredients, equipment, recipes. The second part is to encourage the appreciation of cheese: how to buy, store, serve, with a few recipes. Highly informative, clear, concise instructions with Imperial and metric measures and a good index. Frances Clutton

## 641.5 Cooking

4990 641.5
**Benoit, Jehane.**
Madame Benoit Cooks at Home. Toronto: McGraw-Hill Ryerson, c1978. 335p. ill., plates, ports. Index. ISBN 0-07-082775-3 $14.95

1. Cookery.

Mme. Benoit's memories of growing up and developing her love of food and knowledge about cooking. Pleasures and enthusiasms are evident throughout. Detailed recipes with commentaries, information about cooking terms, definitions, discussions of food. Ingredients listed in Imperial and metric measures. Frances Clutton

4991 641.5
**The Best of Canadian Cooking: The Best and Most Exciting Recipes from Canada's Most Famous Cooks.**
Introduction by Jeremy Brown. Toronto: Pagurian Press, c1977. 192p. ill. Index. ISBN 0-88932-062-4 $12.95

1. Cookery.

A collection of recipes from Canadian chefs, writers and celebrities to illustrate the foods characteristic of Canadian cuisine from wild edibles to elegant, high-calorie desserts. Recipes from popular restaurants across Canada and from well-known cookbooks. Frances Clutton

4992 641.5
**McPherson, Ruth.**
With a Pinch of Pine Cones and Chipmunks: A Cookbook for the Cottage. Illustrated by Marilyn Cassidy. Thorold, Ont.: The Author, 1978. 116p. ill. Index. ISBN 0-9690864-0-7 pa. Spiral binding: $4.95

1. Cookery.

How to make cottage vacations more enjoyable with interesting variations in standard holiday fare. Conversational instructions and emphasis on ease of preparation with use of mixes and labour-saving appliances. Ingredients are in Imperial measure only. Frances Clutton

4993 641.5
**Oliver, Margo.**
Margo Oliver's Most Treasured Recipes. Montreal: Optimum Publishing, 1977. 192p. ill. Index.

1. Cookery.

The usual beautiful photographs illustrating this author's cookbooks accompany over 450 recipes. Featured are those for special occasions as well as others for family meals. Includes a good general index. Frances Clutton

4994 641.5
**Pattinson, Nellie Lyle.**
Nellie Lyle Pattinson's Canadian Cook Book. Revised by Helen Wattie and Elinor Donaldson Whyte. Metric ed. Toronto: McGraw-Hill Ryerson, 1978. 391p. ill., plates. Index. ISBN 0-07-082612-9 $14.95

1. Cookery, Canadian.

Previous edition listed CS no. 1661.

A revised edition of the standard Canadian cookbook, providing metric measurements as well as Imperial. Useful sections on home canning, freezing and preparation of mixes for breads with whole grains and reduced salt. Frances Clutton

4995 641.5'3
**Brimacombe, Karen.**
The Best of Bridge: Royal Treats for Entertaining. Calgary: Best of Bridge Publishing, 1976. 216p. ill. Index. pa. Processed. Spiral binding: $9.95

1. Luncheons. 2. Suppers. 3. Desserts.

Recipes collected by the eight members of a bridge club over the eleven years they have been playing together. Emphasis is on luncheons, buffets and desserts. Imperial measure only. Colourful, attractive, with excellent illustrations, an enthusiastic presentation. Indexed by section only. Frances Clutton

4996 641.5'3
**Brimacombe, Karen.**
Enjoy! More Recipes from the Best of Bridge. Written and published by Karen Brimacombe and others. Hand lettered by Norm W. Hodgins. 2d ed. Calgary: Best of Bridge Publishing, 1979. 206p. ill., plates. Index. $11

1. Desserts. 2. Luncheons. 3. Suppers.

Beautiful photographs of tempting food illustrate this second offering of the group. Plastic spine may not stand up to library use; index is by section with no general one; ingredients are in Imperial measure only. Highly recommended as a useful, attractive collection of recipes for family as well as for entertaining. Frances Clutton

4997 641.5'3
**Wallace, Maureen.**
Kick the Junk Food Habit with Snackers, by Maureen Wallace and Jim Wallace. Vancouver: Douglas & McIntyre, c1978. 136p. ill. Index. ISBN 0-88894-193-5 pa.: $4.95

1. Cookery. 2. Snack foods. 3. Food, Junk.

Another book explaining the problems caused by food additives, white sugar, refined foods, while praising the virtues of honey, "pure" foods for nutritious snacks. The many recipes stressing the use of honey, which is a sugar, may encourage love of sweets. Imperial measures only. Good general index. Francis Clutton

4998 641.5'52
**Wylie, Betty Jane.**
Encore: The Leftovers Cookbook. Toronto: McClelland and Stewart, c1979. 140p. Index. ISBN 0-7710-9054-4 $12.95

1. Cookery.

A folksy, chatty cookbook giving ideas and recipes for using leftovers. Food processors are necessary for many recipes, a drawback for readers without that appliance. An interesting cookbook by a Canadian author who obviously loves cooking and finding delicious ways of preparing ordinary foods. Frances Clutton

4999 641.5'61
**Beaulieu, Mirelle.**
Cooking for Myself. Agincourt, Ont.: Gage Publishing, 1978. 237p. ill. Index. ISBN 0-7715-9435-6 pa.: $5.95

1. Cookery.

Translation of *Je cusine pour moi.*

Recipes for uncomplicated, easy-to-prepare foods from hors d'oeuvres to desserts. Ingredients are given in Imperial measure for single servings. Useful suggestions for leftovers and the storage of unused portion of ingredients. Index by section only. Frances Clutton

5000 641.5'61
**Beaulieu, Mirelle.**
Cooking for You and Me. Agincourt, Ont.: Gage Publishing, 1979. 145p. ISBN 0-7715-9437-2 pa.: $7.95

1. Cookery.

Translation of *Cuisine pour nous deux*

For the cook who wants recipes resulting in only two servings, this book may be especially useful for the novice. The offerings are rather ordinary. Imperial measures only, no index, although a detailed table of contents for browsing. Well illustrated by sketches and excellent colour photographs. Frances Clutton

5001 641.5'636
**Smith, Elizabeth.**
Vegetarian Meal-planning Guide: A Lacto-ovo-vegetarian Diet. Winnipeg: Hyperion Press, c1979. 104p. ill. Bibliography: p. 97-98. Index. ISBN 0-920534-04-X pa.: $5.95

1. Vegetarianism. 2. Cookery (Vegetables).

More than one-half of this book consists of valuable information about how to plan vegetarian meals to enjoy a nutritionally sound diet. Advice on protein requirement, vitamin supplements, sample menus from a qualified specialist in nutrition makes it an especially important book. Recipes in metric measures with a good general index. Frances Clutton

5002 641.5'68
**Murray, Rose.**
The Christmas Cookbook: Great Canadian Recipes. Toronto: James Lorimer, 1979. 96p. Bibliography. Index. ISBN 0-88862-276-7 $12.95

1. Christmas cookery. 2. Cookery, Canadian.

A slim book of recipes for traditional Canadian Christmas foods. The ninety-six pages are a browsing treat. Special cakes, breads, menus for seasonal feasts. Good general index. Metric and Imperial measures. Although not illustrated, a very attractive addition to Christmas collections. Frances Clutton

5003 641.5'753
**Burkhardt, Barbara.**
Sailors & Sauerkraut: Or, Recipes from Paradise: Or, Making Do with What You Have, by Barbara Burkhardt, Barrie Angus McLean and Doris Kochanek. Sidney, B.C.: Gray's Publishing, c1978. 198p. ill., maps, ports. Index. ISBN 0-88826-076-8 pa.: $4.95

1. Cookery, Marine.

For information about Cook's voyages, these journal excerpts, maps and recipes provide a colourful source of material. Not a practical cookbook for general use. Small type, paperback format would make it difficult to use for other than general interest. Frances Clutton

5004 641.5'8
**Barber, James.**
Fear of Frying. Vancouver: Douglas & McIntyre, c1978. 96p. ill. ISBN 0-88894-215-X $6.95

1. Frying. 2. Cookery.

A humorous defence of frying as a method of cooking by the author of *Ginger Tea Makes Friends*, and in the same format as that book. Cartoon-like illustrations by the author give instructions for the recipes. Explicit directions are given for amounts, temperatures. A relaxed, casual attitude toward cooking rules. Frances Clutton

5005 641.5'89
**Stern, Bonnie.**
Food Processor Cuisine. La cuisine tourbillon. Toronto: Methuen, c1978. 118p. ill., plates. Index. ISBN 0-458-93790-8 $6.95

1. Food processor cookery.

The author, who has her own cooking school, writes in the Toronto 'Sun' and 'Canadian Living'. Measurements are in both metric and Imperial. Suggestions for using this appliance for recipes from appetizers to desserts. English and French versions appear on facing pages. Frances Clutton

5006 641.5'9411
**Hay, Gordon.**
The Commonsense Scots Cookery Book. Scarborough, Ont.: Prentice-Hall, c1978. 117p. ill., plates. Index. ISBN 0-13-152645-6 $9.95

1. Cookery, Scottish.

Published simultaneously in Canada, this is truly a cookbook of Scotland. Traditional recipes have been brought up to date, many of them illustrated in colour photographs. Measures are given in both Imperial and metric although in several cases ingredients, such as flour, by weight rather than volume, will be frustrating for the average cook. Frances Clutton

5007 641.5'944
**Sancton, Pamela.**
French Recipes North Americans Love Best. Illustrations by Bruce Johnson. Montreal: Tundra Books, c1977. 126p. ill. Index. ISBN 0-88776-027-9 pa.: $4.95

1. Cookery, French. 2. Montreal, Que. – Restaurants.

Fifty chefs of Montreal's French restaurants have contributed recipes for their most popular dishes. Tested by the author in her home kitchen, the recipes appear uncomplicated to prepare and with ingredients generally available. Notes included give origins of recipes and background of restaurants. Frances Clutton

5008 641.5'971
**Breckenridge, Muriel.**
Every Day a Feast: Over 360 Delicious Old-time Special-occasion Recipes from Canadian Country Kitchens. Toronto: McGraw-Hill Ryerson, c1978. 244p. ISBN 0-07-082776-1 $14.95

1. Cookery, Canadian.

Festive traditions and customs in many parts of early Canada are represented in these recipes which have been located in journals, newspapers and family cook books. Tested and adapted for modern families, the ingredients are given in metric and Imperial measures. Comments on the origin or special feature of recipes, and two introductory chapters on social life in early Canada add to the interest. Frances Clutton

5009 641.5'9713
**Bates, Christina.**
Out of Old Ontario Kitchens: A Collection of Traditional Recipes of Ontario and the Stories of the People Who Cooked Them. Toronto: Pagurian Press, c1978. 190p. ill. Bibliography: p. 181-185. Index. (A Christopher Ondaatje Publication) ISBN 0-88932-073-X $9.95

1. Cookery, Canadian – Ontario.

Quotations taken from books and diaries kept by women of pre-Confederation Ontario accompany authentic recipes from that time. Recipes appear in original form, and consist of those tested for use by to-day's cooks and those with historical or curiosity value. Likely to have more appeal for the social historian than the cook. Frances Clutton

5010 641.5'9713
**Staebler, Edna.**
More Food That Really Schmecks. Toronto: McClelland and Stewart, c1979. 318p. Index. ISBN 0-7710-8295-9 $12.95

1. Cookery, Mennonite. 2. Cookery, Canadian – Ontario – Waterloo (County).

Easy-to-follow recipes with clear instructions using only Imperial measures in this second book of Mennonite recipes gathered mainly from Waterloo County in Ontario. Variations of recipes from her first cookbook as well as new ones in the same tradition as the first book of food that "schmecks". Recommended. Frances Clutton

5011 641.5'9716
**Gill, Janice Murray.**
Nova Scotia Down-home Cooking. Toronto: McGraw-Hill Ryerson, 1978. 208p. ill. Index. ISBN 0-07-082777-X $14.95

1. Cookery, Canadian – Nova Scotia.

Scottish-Canadian influence in this collection of favourite recipes from Pictou County, Nova Scotia, with author's memories of food of her youth. Well detailed recipes, enthusiastic discussion of metrication, ingredients in both metric and Imperial measure. Frances Clutton

5012 641.6
**Berglund, Berndt.**
The Complete Outdoorsman's Guide to Edible Wild Plants, by Berndt Berglund and Claire E. Bolsby. Toronto: Pagurian Press, c1977. 189p. ill. ISBN 0-88932-048-9 $8.95

1. Cookery (Wild foods). 2. Wild Plants, Edible.

A guide to a variety of edible nuts, roots, tubers and wild fruits which are nutritious and tasty in a range of foods from casseroles to desserts. Although wild plants form the basic ingredients this is not designed for outdoor cooking but for experimenting in a well-stocked kitchen. Well indexed and attractively illustrated.

5013 641.6'4
**Baird, Elizabeth.**
Apples, Peaches & Pears. Toronto: James Lorimer, 1977. 96p. ill. Index.
ISBN 0-88862-129-9 bd.: $11.95
ISBN 0-88862-128-0 pa.: $5.95

1. Cookery (Fruit). 2. Cookery, Canadian.

Traditional and imaginative treatments of the three most widely produced fruits of Canada. Regional recipes, history of the cultivation of the fruits in this country. Summary of special varieties with uses for each. Indexed according to type of food. Frances Clutton

5014 641.6'4'76
**Buszek, Beatrice Ross.**
The Cranberry Connection: Cranberry Cookery with Flavour, Fact and Folklore, from Memories, Libraries and Kitchens of Old and New Friends, and Strangers. Granville Centre, N.S.: The Author, 1977. 222p. ill., map. pa. Spiral binding: $5.95

1. Cookery (Cranberries).

Historical anecdotes accompany suggestions for serving cranberries in various forms in all parts of the meal from punches to baked goods. Contents are listed by the type of food. Lacks an index. Hand-lettered by the author. An interesting variety of uses for the fruit. Frances Clutton

5015 641.65
**Szczawinski, Adam F.**
Edible Garden Weeds of Canada, by Adam F. Szczawinski and Nancy J. Turner. Ottawa: National Museum of Natural Sciences, c1978. 184p. ill. Bibliography: p. 176-178. Index. (Edible Wild Plants of Canada)
ISBN 0-660-00026-1 pa. Spiral binding: $8.95
DSS cat. no. NM-95-40/1

1. Wild plants, Edible – Canada.

Directions for converting more than forty common flowering weeds into nutritious and palatable foods are offered in this well-organized guide. Line drawings and photographs aid identification, an appendix lists dangerous weeds. Simple recipes which can be used by campers and city cooks, amateurs or experts. In the same series and format: *Edible Wild Fruits and Nuts of Canada*, 1979.

5016 641.6'5'655
**Mallard, Gwen.**
Soy Bean Magic: Delicious Recipes with Soy Beans, Flour, & Grits. Saanichton, B.C.: Hancock House, 1976. 80p. Index.
ISBN 0-919654-64-9 pa.: $1.50

1. Cookery (Soybeans).

The author writes from a background as a manager of a health food store and restaurant, with a basic concern about world protein supply and the environment. She presents information and recipes for using soy beans and their commercial forms in all parts of the meal to substitute for animal protein. Frances Clutton

5017 641.6'6'3
**Benoit, Jehane.**
Madame Benoit's Lamb Cook Book. Toronto: McGraw-Hill Ryerson, c1979. 122p. ill., plates. Index. ISBN 0-07-082944-6 $9.95

1. Cookery (Lamb and mutton).

This competent author covers all aspects of lamb cookery to encourage its use. Bits of historical information, how to buy, prepare, cook, use leftovers, and with recipes from shish kebabs to lamburgers. Colour photographs, a good index and inclusion of both Imperial and metric measures add to the book's usefulness. Frances Clutton

5018 641.7'1
**Rey, René.**
The Art of Baking. West Vancouver, B.C.: R. J. Watts, 1978. 152p. ill., diagrs. Index. ISBN 0-920072-05-4 $14.95

1. Baking.

Colour and black and white photographs illustrate steps of instructions for recipes as well as finished product. Even complicated baked items look easy; reader will want to try them. Highly recommended for both professional and home bakers. Imperial measure, metric volumes as well as metric weights provided. Good general index. Frances Clutton

5019 641.8'13
**Binet, Suzanne.**
Diabetic Soups. Agincourt, Ont.: Gage Publishing, 1977. 172p. Index.
ISBN 0-7715-9370-8 bd.: $8.95
ISBN 0-7715-9371-6 pa.: $5.95

1. Cookery for diabetics. 2. Soups.

Translation of *Soupes pour diabétiques et pour ceux qui veulent se bien porter.*

Soups, from light to substantial, to provide variety for a diabetic diet. Calories and exchange values per recipe and per serving are given for each. An additional useful feature is a list of exchange values for commercial soups. Frances Clutton

5020 641.8'3
**Binet, Suzanne.**
Salads for Diabetics and Dieters. Toronto: Gage Publishing, c1979. 191p. Indexes. ISBN 0-7715-9487-9 pa.: $6.95

1. Salads. 2. Cookery for diabetics.

Translation of *Salades – Santé.*

As in her other books, the recipes are carefully calculated, using ingredients available all year, featuring freshness and colourful results. Clear, attractive instructions, recommended for the general cook as well as dieters. Exchange values and nutritive content of each recipe clearly shown. Frances Clutton

5021 641.8'6
**Binet, Suzanne.**
Desserts for Diabetics. Agincourt, Ont.: Gage Publishing, 1977. 128p. Index.
ISBN 0-7715-9366-X bd.: $8.95
ISBN 0-7715-9367-8 pa.: $5.95

1. Cookery for diabetics. 2. Desserts.

Translation of *Desserts pour diabétiques.*

Primarily for diabetic diets, recipes give measurements of ingredients by weight, the number of calories per serving as well as in the whole recipe, and diabetic exchange value. A variety of desserts from basic rice puddings to sophisticated meringues, for family meals entertaining. Frances Clutton

## 641.87 Beverages

5022 641.8'75
**Binet, Suzanne.**
Beverages for Diabetics and Dieters. Toronto: Gage Publishing, c1979. 191p. Indexes. ISBN 0-7715-9485-2 pa.: $6.95

1. Beverages. 2. Cookery for diabetics.

Translation of *Breuvages pour diabétiques.*

The author who is diabetic herself presents recipes for low calorie beverages, showing nutritive content of each. Spices, interesting fruits, readily available ingredients in attractive, easy to follow recipes. Well indexed, both Imperial and metric measures, as well as weights by grams for diabetic diets. Frances Clutton

## 643 The home and its equipment

5023 643.
**Clarke, John.**
Condominiums: What Are You Really Buying? Toronto: McGraw-Hill Ryerson, 1977. 205p. ISBN 0-07-082573-4 pa.: $4.95

1. Condominium (Housing) – Ontario.

A comprehensive, clearly-written and well-organized book, especially useful to those contemplating buying a residential condominium. Advantages, problems and complexities unique to this recent alternative for home ownership are considered. Legal matters are mainly discussed relative to Ontario legislation. Marilyn Koch

5024 643.
**Moysey, JoAnn.**
Your Move! Toronto: Maclean-Hunter, c1977. 119p. ill. (A Financial Post Book) ISBN 0-88896-067-0 $3.95

1. Moving, Household.

"How to transplant yourself, your family and your worldly goods without anguish. From the experience of a business wife." -Cover. Covers the major problems to be resolved in organizing a move within the same city, across Canada or abroad. Concise and sensible. Public libraries.

5025 646.7'26
**Slatt, Bernard J.,** ed.
The Naked Face. Don Mills, Ont.: General Publishing, 1979. 186p. ill. ISBN 0-7736-0073-6 $12.95

1. Face – Care and hygiene. 2. Beauty, Personal. 3. Cosmetics.

A Canadian ophthalmologist and twelve specialists in psychiatry, dermatology, plastic and cosmetic surgery discuss the potential of modern surgery in correcting facial imperfections. The book offers suggestions on the choice of a surgeon, includes a consumer's guide to plastic surgery, and warns of possible complications in surgery. There is no index or bibliography. A readable introduction for the lay person.

5026 647'.9471
**Thompson, John Beswarick.**
Country Bed and Breakfast Places in Canada. Ottawa: Deneau and Greenberg, c1979. 224p. ill., maps. ISBN 0-88879-014-7 pa.: $5.95

1. Tourist camps, hostels, etc. – Canada – Directories.

Every Canadian province is represented in this useful guide to inexpensive accommodation in private homes. Grouped by province, from east to west, outline maps indicate the location of each listing. Descriptions include rates, directions and mileage. A handy reference for the motoring tourist.

5027 647'.95713
**Epicure.**
Epicure's Toronto Food Book. Toronto: Greey de Pencier, 1978. 255p. ill., plates. Index. ISBN 0-919872-39-5 pa.: $10.95

1. Cookery. 2. Food industry and trade – Ontario – Toronto. 3. Toronto, Ont. – Restaurants.

Thirty-three of Epicure's food columns in 'Toronto Life' have been updated and revised, each dealing with one category of food. The book recommends where to eat and buy ingredients in Toronto, and gives recipes for preparation at home. Separate indexes for restaurants and recipes. Frances Clutton

## 649.1 Child care

5028 649'.15'283
**Johnson, Margaret Anne.**
Teaching Your Retarded Child: A Parent's Manual. Toronto: Gage Publishing, c1978. 163p. ill. Bibliography: p. 155-162. ISBN 0-7715-9463-1 pa.: $5.95

1. Mentally handicapped children – Education. 2. Domestic education.

This simply written guide for the parents of handicapped children focuses upon planned activity programmes commensurate with each child's ability, during the important pre-school years. The characteristics of the mentally retarded child, and his place in the family, are examined. Straightforward, common-sense suggestions for improving the development pattern of the trainable pre-schooler. Public libraries.

5029 649'.51
**Cass-Beggs, Barbara.**
Your Baby Needs Music: A Music-sound Book for Babies Up to Two Years Old. Vancouver: Douglas & McIntyre, c1978. 144p. ill., music, ports. Bibliography: p. 134-136. Discography: p. 128-130. Index. ISBN 0-88894-213-3 $8.95

1. Music, Influence of. 2. Infants. 3. Children's songs. 4. Music in the home.

Cass-Beggs, author of three previous books on music, presents a lively collection of songs, rhymes, rhythmic exercises and musical games for infants up to two years of age. There are many musical examples, a bibliography, and a discography of children's materials. Don Sedgwick

## 650 Business services

5030 650.
**Land, Brian.**
Sources of Information for Canadian Business. 3d ed. Montreal: Canadian Chamber of Commerce, 1978. 76p. Index. pa.: $3.95

1. Reference books – Business – Bibliography. 2. Business – Bibliography.

The second edition listed as out-of-print in *CS* no. 1702.

More than double the length of the second edition which was published in 1972, this third revision of a basic guide has expanded and revised some sections and added new ones on 'Directories' and 'Business, Economic and Financial Services'. An index is a new feature. An invaluable guide for the businessman and libraries serving him.

5031 650.

**Newman, Dorothy M.**

Canadian Business Handbook, by Dorothy M. Newman and Jean P. Newman. 3d ed. Toronto: McGraw-Hill Ryerson, 1979. 673p. Bibliography. Index. ISBN 0-07-082964-0 $24.95

1. Business – Handbooks, manuals, etc.

The second edition listed *CS* no. 1703.

This new edition of a standard work has undergone a complete revision and added a new chapter on computers. Other chapters deal with stocks and bonds, financial statements, banks, trust companies and credit unions, taxes, insurance, trade, communications, law, federal and provincial government aids to business, and business information, as well as miscellaneous almanac-type information. Brian Land

5032 650'.03

**MacInnes, J. Lyman.**

A Handbook of Business Terminology. Don Mills, Ont.: General Publishing, 1978. 110p. ISBN 0-7736-1042-1 pa.: $4.95

1. Business – Terminology.

Although a few definitions in this dictionary are difficult to locate elsewhere, there is little need for this work in specialized business collections. Public libraries, however, may find the book's popular approach useful for their reference collections. Barbara Stewart

5033 650'.07

**Moreland, Paul A.**

A History of Business Education. Toronto: Pitman Publishing, c1977. 208p. ill., ports. Bibliography: p. 207-208. ISBN 0-273-04241-6 $14.95

1. Business education – History. 2. Business education – Canada – History.

Two-thirds of this authoritative text describes the development of Canadian business education in all provinces and highlights some of the outstanding leaders. Black and white illustrations and explanatory footnotes add interest. An index would be useful. Marilyn Koch

5034 651'.3741

**Canadian Secretary's Handbook.**

Don Mills, Ont.: Collier Macmillan, 1979. 378p. Bibliography: p. 351-361. Index. ISBN 0-02-973090-2 $8.95

1. Secretaries – Handbooks, manuals, etc.
2. Office practice – Handbooks, manuals, etc.

A clearly organized but not comprehensive guide to English usage and office procedures illustrated with figures, tables and sample letters. The bibliography is organized by types of work, from almanacs to legal references. A useful supplement to standard references.

5035 657.

**Leonard, W. G.**

Canadian Accountant's Handbook. 3d ed. Toronto: McGraw-Hill Ryerson, c1978. 618p. Bibliography. Index. ISBN 0-07-082748-6 $39.95

1. Accounting – Handbooks, manuals, etc.

The second edition, published in 1972, listed *CS* no. 1710.

5036 657'.839

**Husack, Glen A.**

More Profit from Your Retail Business: A Way to Achieve It and to Maintain It. Toronto: Maclean-Hunter, c1977. 84p. ill. (A Financial Post Book) ISBN 0-88896-066-2 pa.

1. Inventories – Accounting. 2. Inventories, Retail.

The small businessman will benefit appreciably from this handbook on greater sophistication in inventory, bookkeeping and forecasting methods. Space is provided in the text for notes and calculations. Barbara Stewart

## 658 General management

5037 658.

**Preshing, William A.**

Business Management in Canada: An Introduction. 2d ed. Toronto: John Wiley, c1979. 587p. ill. Bibliographical references and Index. ISBN 0-471-99795-1 $14.95

1. Industrial management.

First edition, published in 1974, listed in *CS* no. 1725.

A revision of a standard work.

5038 658'.022
**Archer, Maurice.**
Starting and Managing Your Own Small Business, by Maurice Archer and Jerry White. Toronto: Macmillan, c1978. 291p. ill. (Canadian Small Business Series) (A Finanial Post/Macmillan Book) ISBN 0-7705-1629-7 pa.: $5.95

1. Small business – Canada – Management.

This is a detailed, well-organized book progressing through realistic sequences for the businessman wanting to make an idea a reality. Checklists, business ratios, financing sources and examples of planning and record-keeping charts make the book an essential handbook. Barbara Stewart

5039 658'.022
**James, Jack D.**
Starting a Successful Business in Canada. 4th ed. Vancouver: International Self-Counsel Press, 1978, c1974. 207p. ill. Bibliography: p. 202-207. (Self-counsel Series) ISBN 0-88908-042-9 pa.: $4.50

1. Small business – Canada – Management.

Second edition listed *CS* no. 1727.

Basic, comprehensive and easily-read information for those with minimal knowledge of, or experience in starting or buying a business. Marilyn Koch

5040 658'.022
**Scott, Donald S.,** ed.
The Technical Entrepreneur: Inventions, Innovations and Small Business. Edited by Donald S. Scott and Ronald M. Blair. Victoria, B.C.: Press Porcépic, 1979. 192p. ISBN 0-88878-169-5 $18.95

1. Small business – Canada – Management.
2. Inventions – Canada.

Scott, an engineering professor, and Blair, a consultant, present readings on aspects of initiating small technology-based businesses. They cover the Canadian environment, inventions, marketing, finance, planning, management and government aid. Chapters include references and illustrations. The book is suitable for university students with some economic knowledge and for engineers and other technical specialists who are considering establishing a small business. Barbara Dance

5041 658'.022
**Szonyi, Andrew J.**
Small Business Management Fundamentals, by Andrew J. Szonyi and Dan Steinhoff. 1st Canadian ed. Toronto: McGraw-Hill Ryerson, 1978, c1974. 408p. Bibliographies and Index. ISBN 0-07-082916-0 $12.95

1. Small business – Management. 2. Self-employed. 3. Small business – Canada – Management. 4. Self-employed – Canada.

The authors, both professors with experience in small business, present a valuable overview of small business for students and practitioners. They cover the essential aspects of planning and running a small firm: accounting, financing, location, merchandising, control. Abundant illustrations, tables, and headings, and a consultant's checklist, enhance the well-written text. Chapters include summaries, questions, and bibliographies. Barbara Dance

5042 658.1'148
**Fisher, John.**
Money Isn't Everything: A Survival Manual for Non-profit Organizations. Toronto: Management and Fund Raising Centre, 1977. 213p. ill. Bibliographical references. ISBN 0-920432-00-X pa.: $8.95

1. Corporations, Non-profit – Management.
2. Associations, institutions, etc. – Management.

Fisher's personal experience has enabled him to write a practical, extensive guide to management of nonprofit organizations. He discusses seven functional areas, including planning, administration, promotion and lobbying. Each brief chapter has relevant quotations, cartoons, charts, numerous useful checklists, annotated bibliographies and other sources of information, including libraries. This book is valuable to all community-oriented individuals. Barbara Dance

5043 658.1'5
**Mumey, Glen A.**
Canadian Business Finance. Georgetown, Ont.: Irwin-Dorsey, 1977. 481p. Bibliographical references and Index. ISBN 0-256-01787-5 $14.50

1. Corporations – Canada – Finance.
2. Corporations – Finance.

Professor Mumey covers the theory and practice of financial decision-making, including cash flow, budgeting, risk, ratios, profits, debt, and social aspects of finance. Each chapter includes a summary, questions, and a bibliography. The intended audience is university students and others with some knowledge of accounting, economics and statistics. Barbara Dance

5044 658.1'5
**Niosi, Jorge E.**
The Economy of Canada: A Study of Ownership and Control. Translated by Penelope Williams and Hugh Ballem. Montreal: Black Rose Books, c1978. 179p. Bibliography: p. 177-179. (Black Rose Books) ISBN 0-919618-49-9 bd.: $16.95
ISBN 0-919618-75-8 pa.: $5.95

1. Corporations – Canada – Finance.
2. Capitalists and financiers – Canada.
3. Canada – Industries.

Niosi discusses three traditional theories of corporate ownership and control. He rejects these in favour of his premise that Canadian corporations are controlled by a ruling class. He identifies and presents data on specific Canadian families and companies to support his theory. The book is quite readable and will appeal to the lay person interested in big business in Canada. Barbara Stwewart

5045 658.1'527
**Boersema, John M.**
Capital Budgeting Practices Including the Impact of Inflation. Toronto: Canadian Institute of Chartered Accountants, c1978. 226p. Bibliographical references.
ISBN 0-88800-033-2 pa.: $12.50

1. Capital budget. 2. Capital investment.
3. Inflation (Finance) and accounting.
4. Business enterprises – Canada – Finance.

This study is of interest to accountants and managers as a comprehensive guide to the current accounting theories and practices of twenty-five of the top one hundred Canadian corporations. Suitable only for large business collections. Barbara Stewart

5046 658.3
**Kuyek, Joan Newman.**
The Phone Book: Working at the Bell. Illustrated by Luc Robert. Kitchener, Ont.: Between the Lines, c1979. 95p.
ISBN 0-919946-14-3 bd. ISBN 0-919946-13-5 pa.: $5.95

1. Bell Canada – Personnel management.
2. Industrial relations – Canada – Case studies. 3. Technological innovations – Canada – Case studies.

Rapid changes in technology and a spectacular growth pattern, coupled with outmoded personnel practices, are analysed in terms of the effect upon company employees. A former service representative for Bell Canada has meshed employee comments with her carefully researched history of the corporation. An interesting and informative study.

5047 658.3
**Martin, Anne.**
Your Personnel Handbook: A Practical Guide to Finding, Hiring and Keeping Productive Employees. Don Mills, Ont.: General Publishing, 1979. 141p. forms.
ISBN 0-7736-1050-2 pa.: $5.95

1. Personnel management – Handbooks, manuals, etc. 2. Small business – Personnel management – Handbooks, manuals, etc.

First edition published in 1977 under title *Info-personnel*.

Martin, a supervisor and consultant, provides a basic overview of recruiting, interviewing, hiring and managing of support staff. The primary audience is people who work in small firms and handle personnel matters, but are not personnel specialists. Included are twelve useful exhibits, including sample advertisements and application forms. Barbara Dance

5048 658.3
**Smith, Ross E.**
Successful People Management: How to Get and Keep Good Employees. Toronto: Macmillan, c1978. 221p. Index. (Canadian Small Business Series) (A Financial Post/Macmillan Book) ISBN 0-7705-1648-3 pa.: $5.95

1. Personnel management.

Smith's successful addition to the Canadian Small Business Series tells employers how to effectively manage their personnel. The author, a community college teacher, gives practical information on hiring, compensation, records, staff problems such as absenteeism and discipline, and current issues such as flextime and industrial relations. The many valuable worksheets, questionnaires and forms are attractively presented. Barbara Dance

5049 658.31'52
**Crispo, John H. G.**
Industrial Democracy in Western Europe: A North American Perspective. Toronto: McGraw-Hill Ryerson, 1978. 181p. Bibliography: p. 175-176. Index. ISBN 0-07-082700-1 pa.: $6.95

1. Employees' representation in management – Europe, Western.

The author examines the status of industrial democracy in Western Europe, and contrasts the North American situation. He discusses collective bargaining, and innovations in labour-management relations such as works councils, codetermination, and unions and national policy. Professor Crispo's research in Europe and Canada has resulted in a knowledgeable and timely study relevant to all Canadians. Includes a bibliography and index. Barbara Dance

5050 658.31'52
**Sanderson, George,** ed.
Industrial Democracy Today: A New Role for Labour. Associate editor: Frederick Stapenhurst. Toronto: McGraw-Hill Ryerson, 1978. 288p. ISBN 0-07-082721-4 $14.95

1. Employees' representation in management – Canada.

Contributions by thirty-three of the most prominent commentators on the Canadian labour movement review arguments favouring worker participation in the management of industry and general democratization of the workplace as a means to achieve an improved quality of working life. Barbara Stewart

5051 658.4
**Archer, Maurice,** ed.
An Introduction to Canadian Business. 3d ed. Toronto: McGraw-Hill Ryerson, 1978. 644p. ill., diagrs., forms, plans. Index. ISBN 0-07-082641-2 $13.95

1. Industrial management – Canada.
2. Industrial organization – Canada.
3. Business.

Second edition listed *CS* no. 1724.

5052 658.4
**Bilyea, C. G.**
The Canadian Manager. Toronto: John Wiley, 1979. Bibliography. Index. ISBN 0-471-99820-6 $13.95

1. Management. 2. Business.

Bilyea gives brief information on a wide range of management topics, including planning, leadership, marketing, finance, personnel management, and the business environment. Some charts, tables, cases, cartoons and an index are included. The book is suitable for high school and undergraduate students, and anyone wanting a basic introduction to Canadian management. Barbara Dance

5053 658.4
**Sexty, Robert W.**
Issues in Canadian Business. Scarborough, Ont.: Prentice-Hall, 1979. 430p. Bibliography. Index. ISBN 0-13-506212-8 $16.95

1. Business. 2. Canada – Commerce.

Professor Sexty presents basic information on personnel, marketing, innovation, and finance. Particular attention is given to business-government-social interactions, and to the decision-making process. Chapters explore key issues, and contain reprints, illustrations and questions. The useful bibliographies include listings of relevant subject headings in *Canadian Business Periodicals Index*. The book is suitable for students and the general public. Includes a good index. Barbara Dance

5054 658.4
**Spikes, Brian.**
Boss Is a Four Letter Word!: How to Become a Creative and Successful Leader. Don Mills, Ont.: General Publishing, 1977. 143p. Bibliography: p. 142-143. ISBN 0-7736-1028-6 pa.: $5.95

1. Management. 2. Leadership. 3. Supervisors.

Spikes, a teacher and consultant, distinguishes between bosses and leaders, and shows why the latter are more effective in motivating and developing employees. The short chapters discuss human needs, communication, performance, time management and organizational structure. Checklists and examples of typical work situations are useful for increasing awareness of leadership characteristics. This is a basic introduction for managers and employees. Barbara Dance

5055 658.4'008
**Jain, Harish C.,** ed.
Behavioural Issues in Management: The Canadian Context. Edited by Harish C. Jain and Rabindra N. Kanungo. Toronto: McGraw-Hill Ryerson, 1977. 586p. Bibliographies. ISBN 0-07-082455-X $9.95

1. Management. 2. Organization.

The authors emphasize the interaction of individuals, groups, and organizations. They cover the human aspects of motivation, performance, attitudes, communication, leadership, and organizational change. Each section has an overview, cases, bibliographies, and useful tables and charts. An appendix lists twelve relevant films. This book will appeal to a broad audience: university students, present and future managers, and anyone curious about human resource management. Barbara Dance

5056 658.4'08
**Banner, David K.**
Business and Society: Canadian Issues. Toronto: McGraw-Hill Ryerson, c1979. 388p. Bibliographies. ISBN 0-07-082868-7 pa.: $9.95

1. Industry – Social aspects – Canada.

Professor Banner deals in depth with several timely aspects of business in Canada, including corporate concentration, minority group employees, pollution, foreign investment, changing technologies and lifestyles, and business/government relations. Chapters include reprints from Canadian periodicals. The book is useful for university students, managers, and others interested in business and society. Includes footnotes and a good index. Barbara Dance

5057 658.4'56
**Drain, Robert H.**
Successful Conference and Convention Planning, by Robert H. Drain and Neil Oakley. Toronto: McGraw-Hill Ryerson, 1978. 205p. ill., form. Bibliography: p. 202-203. Index. ISBN 0-07-082609-9 $14.95

1. Congresses and conventions.

The authors present detailed procedures for organizing a large-scale conference so as to make it a public relations and educational success. The clearly-written text is enhanced by many checklists, charts and timetables of each step in the planning process. They discuss budgets and the division of responsibilities among committees. This book will be invaluable for anyone involved in convention planning. Barbara Dance

## 658.8 Marketing

5058 658.8
**Banting, Peter M.**
Canadian Marketing: A Case Approach. Toronto: McGraw-Hill Ryerson, 1977. 305p. ill. Bibliography: p. 297-305. ISBN 0-07-082458-4 pa.: $6.95

1. Marketing – Canada – Case studies.

Professor Banting provides a well-organized problem-solving approach to Canadian marketing. He covers the Canadian environment, research, consumers, products, pricing, planning, and international aspects. The book discusses case study technique and presents forty-eight cases, well-illustrated with exhibits, to demonstrate marketing principles. University students and business people are the primary audience. The appendix is a selected annotated list of references. Barbara Dance

5059 658.8
**Barnes, James G.,** comp.
Current Topics in Canadian Marketing. Compiled by James G. Barnes and Montrose S. Sommers. Toronto: McGraw-Hill Ryerson, 1978. 402p. ill., graphs. Bibliographies. ISBN 0-07-082640-4 pa.: $8.95

1. Marketing – Canada.

Major areas of marketing discussed include the Canadian scene, products, pricing, distribution, and advertising. Each main section has an overview of the topic, a summary of the key articles which follow, key questions that the reader should examine, and bibliographies. The book is geared towards university students and others interested in Canadian marketing. The editors, both university professors, have produced a well-organized, physically pleasing book. Barbara Dance

5060 658.87'1
**Bryant, James.**
Department Store Disease. Toronto: McClelland and Stewart, c1977. 192p. ISBN 0-7710-1720-0 $10

1. Department stores – Canada.

An opportunity to view department stores form the other side of the counter. Bryant tells of the joys and frustrations of operating a department store using amusing and illustrative anecdotes drawn from his many years and levels of experience, particularly at Simpsons where he ultimately became a vice-president. Marilyn Koch

5061 658'.91
**Kneider, A. P.**
How to Make Money in a Retail Store of Your Own. Toronto: Financial Post; Macmillan, c1978. 250p. ill., graphs. Bibliography: p. 246-247. Index. (Canadian Small Business Series) ISBN 0-7705-1645-9 pa.: $5.95

1. Retail trade – Canada – Management.
2. Stores, Retail.

Professor Kneider's book is a useful addition to the Canadian Small Business Series. He provides independent retailers with basic principles and advice on trends and practices of day-to-day management of a retailing business: the Canadian scene, planning, consumers, location, purchasing, merchandising, pricing, advertising. Clearly-presented charts and forms illustrate and summarize important points. Includes a bibliography and index. Barbara Dance

5062 658.91
**Tooke, Gerald.**
Crafts Are Your Business. Ottawa: Canadian Crafts Council, 1976. 83p. ill. Bibliography: p. 81. ISBN 0-88980-002-2 pa.: $3.50

1. Handicraft – Marketing. 2. Small business.

Covers all aspects of establishing a small crafts business, including marketing and administration. Sources of loans and grants are listed, plus major craft organizations and government agencies. A very useful guide for both beginning and established craftsmen. Brenda Hughes

## 660 Chemical technology

5063 663'.22
**Rannie, William F.**
Wines of Ontario: An Industry Comes of Age. Beamsville, Ont.: W. F. Rannie, 1978. 171p. ill., port. Bibliographical references and Index. bd.: $7 pa.: $5

1. Wine and wine making – Ontario – History.

Traces the evolution of Ontario's wine-making industry during its first hundred years. Individual firms are discussed. Appendix I places all the commercial wineries into a chronological framework. For all business collections.

5064 664'.06
**Pim, Linda R.**
Additive Alert: A Guide to Food Additives for the Canadian Consumer. Illustrated by Iain Baines. Toronto: Doubleday, 1979. 116p. ill. Bibliographies and Index.
ISBN 0-385-15060-1 pa.: $2.95

1. Food additives – Handbooks, manuals, etc.

A necessary handbook for today's Canadian consumer, guiding through a maze of additives contained in our foods. It provides a listing by types and indicates those considered unsafe. Also included is information on Canadian food laws, and avenues open to the consumer for complaints. Although in paperback only, this is an important purchase for public libraries. Carol Rhodes

5065 667'.26
**Lathrop-Smit, Hermine.**
Natural Dyes. Toronto: James Lorimer, 1978. 72p. ill. Bibliography: p. 70. Index.
ISBN 0-88862-227-9 bd.: $13.95
ISBN 0-88862-226-0 pa.: $5.95

1. Dyes and dyeing, Domestic. 2. Dye plants – Canada.

An introductory manual for extracting dyes from plants commonly found in many parts of Canada. The author, an Albertan, who teaches dyeing, weaving and batik, guides the beginner through the collecting, drying, storing and preparation of the plants and recommends necessary equipment. Recipes for dyes are in colour groups. Clear instructions. School and public libraries.

5066 667'.26
**McGrath, Judy.**
Dyes From Lichens & Plants. Toronto: Van Nostrand Reinhold, 1977. 144p. ill., plates. Bibliography: p. 139. Indexes.
ISBN 0-442-29858-7 $14.95

1. Dyes and dyeing, Domestic. 2. Dye plants.

An experienced craftswoman who has experimented with the extracting of natural dyes from a variety of Arctic flora, shares her knowledge. The processes, which are applicable to plants grown anywhere, are clearly explained and well illustrated. An informative, unusually well-organized and indexed handbook for hobbyists. Recommended.

## 674.88 Woodenware

5067 674'.88
**Morgan, Carl.**
Early Woodenware in Canada. Cheltenham, Ont.: Boston Mills Press, c1977. 96p. ill. (Collector Series) ISBN 0-919822-88-6 pa.: $5.95

1. Treenware – Collectors and collecting – Canada. 2. Woodwork – Canada – History.

In this practical guide to collecting the wooden utensils used in everyday life by Canadian pioneers a collector and dealer describes the various utensils and the kinds of wood from which they were fashioned and suggests how to judge the age and value. Nancy Cohen

## 690 Building

5068 692.8

**Moogk, Peter N.**

Building a House in New France: An Account of the Perplexities of Client and Craftsmen in Early Canada. Toronto: McClelland and Stewart, c1977. 144p. ill., maps, plans. Bibliography: p. 130-136. Index. ISBN 0-7710-5466-1 $9.95

1. Architecture, Domestic – New France – History. 2. House construction – Contracts and specifications – New France.

Sainte-Marie prize in history.

Diagrams and building plans illustrate this scholarly study in which the author explains exactly how the houses were built and what materials were used. An interesting account of one aspect of social and industrial life in seventeenth century Canada. Nancy Cohen

5069 694.

**Mann, Dale.**

The Complete Log House Book, by Dale Mann and Richard Skinulis. Photography by Nancy Shanoff. Illustrated by Jane Nelson. Toronto: McGraw-Hill Ryerson, 1979. 175p. ill. Bibliography: p. 171-172. Index. ISBN 0-07-082817-2 $9.95

1. Log cabins.

The craft of building with hewn or round logs, and the merits of different methods are explained and illustrated. The clear line drawings and photographs clarifying the construction details are supplemented by visual and descriptive glossaries. A practical guide for the novice, from design and planning to log preservation. Dreaming pleasure for the armchair builder.

5070 697.

**Argue, Robert.**

The Sun Builders: A People's Guide to Solar, Wind and Wood Energy in Canada, by Robert Argue, Barbara Emanuel and Stephen Graham. Editor: Rick Wilks; designer: Lawrie Raskin; illustrator: Dave Butt. Toronto: Renewable Energy in Canada, c1978. 254p. ill., diagrs., maps, plans, ports. ISBN 0-920456-12 X pa.: $7.50

1. Dwellings – Canada – Power supply. 2. Dwellings – Power supply – Case studies. 3. Solar heating.

A necessary source of information on renewable energy. The authors travelled across Canada, interviewing and checking over seventy projects. Included is a consumers' guide, manufacturers' listings, a resource/bibliography listing, and an extremely helpful glossary. Recommended. Carol Rhodes

5071 697'.22

**Flagler, Gordon.**

The Canadian Wood Heat Book: A Complete Guide and Catalogue. Ottawa: Deneau and Greenberg, 1979. 295p. ill. Bibliography: p. 278-280. Index. ISBN 0-88879-015-5 pa.: $8.95

1. Wood as fuel. 2. Stoves, Wood. 3. Chimneys. 4. Heating.

Written in a straightforward style, this consumer's guide is designed for the Canadian market and provides details on everything from purchasing the right stove to getting the best results from wood. Included is a catalogue, as well as addresses of forestry departments, a bibliography, and index. Useful for all general collections. Carol Rhodes

## 700 Fine and decorative arts

5072 700.971

**Fulford, Robert.**

An Introduction to the Arts in Canada. Toronto: Copp Clark, c1977. 135p. ill., ports. ISBN 0-77304-028-5 $3.95

1. Arts – Canada.

The purpose of this book is to provide new Canadians with an introduction to the arts in Canada. Robert Fulford adequately covers native arts, literature in French and English, music, theatre, painting, sculpture, dance, film, architecture, and broadcasting. The book's language is descriptive and simple and the text is short. Several sections of the book need to be updated. It does not have an index. Janice Zlatarits

## 706.5 Art dealers

5073 706'.5

**Laing, G. Blair.**

Memoirs of an Art Dealer. Toronto: McClelland and Stewart, 1979. 264p. ISBN 0-7710-4569-7 $24.95

1. Art dealers – Canada – Biography.

City of Toronto Book Award.

Blair Laing's tome on art collecting and collectors is a coffee table item. The glimpses he gives are sketchy, anecdotal and reveal very little about them. If one has money the book might be worth purchasing for the beautiful colour plates of great Canadian paintings. Paula de Ronde

## 709 Art

5074 709'.0'1

**Brodzky, Anne Trueblood,** ed.

Stones, Bones and Skin: Ritual and Shamanic Art. Edited by Anne Trueblood Brodzky, Rose Danesewich and Nick Johnson. Toronto: Society for Art Publications, 1977. 180p. ill. Bibliographical references and Index. ISBN 0-919902-03-0 $27.50

1. Indians – Art. 2. Magic in art. 3. Shamanism.

"The marks or musical instruments, the ceremonial robes, or the instruments of healing, the architecture or the sacred dances used by the shaman and others from the beginning of recorded time to the present". -Publisher's note. Essays by twenty anthropologists, folklorists, art historians and musicians are complemented by beautiful black and white and colour plates. Well indexed.

## 709.011 Indian and Eskimo art

5075 709'.01'1

**Bradley, Ian L.**

A Bibliography of Canadian Native Arts: Indian and Eskimo Arts, Craft, Dance and Music, by Ian L. Bradley and Patricia Bradley. Agincourt, Ont.: GLC Publishers, c1977. 107p. ports. Index. ISBN 0-88874-051-4 $19.95

1. Indians of North America – Canada – Art – Bibliography. 2. Indians of North America – Canada – Industries – Bibliography.

3. Eskimos – Canada – Art – Bibliography.

A listing of fifteen hundred entries. Indian and Eskimo arts are listed separately under format and topical headings: arts and crafts, dance and music. Includes a subject index by type of art form. Diane Henderson

5076 709'.01'1

**Ray, Dorothy Jean.**

Eskimo Art: Tradition and Innovation in North Alaska. Vancouver: J. J. Douglas, 1977. 298p. ill., map. Bibliography: p. 277-285. Index. ISBN 0-88894-130-7 $27.50

1. Eskimos – Alaska – Art.

An impressive volume on the history of Eskimo arts in North Alaska, with references to the Canadian Eskimo. Over three hundred photographs and illustrations are arranged chronologically, each entry accompanied by full descriptive details. A map, bibliography, glossary of special terms and an index contribute to the usefulness of the work. A valuable contribution in terms of historical significance. Andrea Trudel

5077 709'.01'1

**Stewart, Hilary.**

Looking at Indian Art of the Northwest Coast. Vancouver: Douglas & McIntyre, c1979. 111p. ill., map. Bibliography: p. 110. Index. ISBN 0-88894-229-X pa.: $6.95

1. Indians of North America – Northwest coast of North America – Art. 2. Indians of North America – British Columbia – Art.

This thorough and beautifully illustrated book introduces everyone from the casual observer to the serious collector of silkscreen prints to the forms, themes, sources of inspiration and elements of style of the indigenous art of the Northwest Coast. Stylistic elements are described, myths and legends explained by Stewart, a professional and sensitive authority. Includes an index and bibliography. Andrea Trudel

## 709.22 Collected artists

5078 709'.2'2

**Lives and Works of the Canadian Artists.**

Toronto: Dundurn Press, 1977- ill., ports. Bibliographies. $12

1. Artists – Canada.

Contents: Andre Belier. William Cruikshank. Daniel Fowler. John Hammond. Robert Holmes. Frances Anne Hopkins. Charles W. Jefferys. Ernest Lindner. Charles M. Manly. Paul Peel. Peter Rindisbacher. Robert Sinclair. Michael Snow. Homer Watson. Joyce Wieland. F. M. Bell-Smith. William Critchlow Harris. Frances Loring. Tony Tascona. Florence Wylie.

A continuing series of folders on individual Canadian artists compresses essential information on each one into a four-page leaflet. Comments by the artist on his own work, and comments by others, are supplemented by a chronology. The loose-leaf format of this useful quick reference material may place it in the closed stacks.

5079 709'.2'2

**Wolff, Hennie,** ed.

The Index of Ontario Artists. Toronto: Visual Arts Ontario: Ontario Association of Art Galleries, c1978. 337p. Bibliographies and Indexes. pa.: $6.95

1. Artists – Ontario – Directories. 2. Artists – Ontario – Biography.

Compiled from questionnaires, this work is designed as a comprehensive listing of contemporary Ontario visual artists. Arrangement is alphabetical by artist; biographical information includes addresses, exhibitions, dealer/agents, medium, style, awards and bibliographies. There are also listings of professional organizations, dealers and public galleries. Despite omissions a useful working tool. Judy Bialkowski

5080 709'.438'6

**Balawyder, Aloysius.**

The Odyssey of the Polish Treasures. Antigonish, N.S.: St. Francis Xavier University Press, 1978. 107p. ill., plates, ports. Bibliography: p. 105-107. pa.: $7.95

1. Art, Polish. 2. Art treasures in war.
3. World War, 1939-1945 – Art and the war.
4. Poland – Foreign relations – Canada.
5. Canada – Foreign relations – Poland.

Polish art treasures, tapestries and jewelry were smuggled out of Poland at the onset of the Second World War and concealed in Ottawa. The return of the pieces took until 1960, and not before triggering a series of political disputes. Well-researched, but written in an awkward and somewhat unimaginative style. Andrea Trudel

## 709.7 Canadian art

5081 709.7'1

**Hudson, Andrew,** comp.

14 Canadians: A Critic's Choice. Washington: Smithsonian Institute Press, 1977. 80p. ill. Bibliographies and Index. $3.25

1. Art, Canadian – Exhibitions. 2. Art, Modern – 20th century – Canada – Exhibitions.

Contents: Dorothy Knowles. Bruce O'Neill. William Perehudoff. Alan Reynolds. David Boldue. Jack Bush. Alex Cameron. Paul Fournier. K. M. Graham. Howard Simkins. Paul Sloggett. Daniel Solomon. Charles Gagnon. Jean Paul Lemieux.

Representative works of thirteen painters and one sculptor were selected by Hudson for an exhibition of Canadian art at the Hirshhorn Museum and Sculpture Garden in Washington in 1977. The Maritimes and British Columbia are not represented. There is a bibliography and an index.

5082 709'.71

**Mellen, Peter.**

Landmarks of Canadian Art. Toronto: McClelland and Stewart, c1978. 260p. ill. Bibliography: p. 257. Index.
ISBN 0-7710-5828-4 $39.95

1. Art, Canadian – History. 2. Artists – Canada.

The works in this handsome book were selected by a panel of experts to illustrate the development of Canadian art from the first Indian and Inuit craftsmen to the present. Peter Mellen's detailed descriptive notes accompany the reproductions of painting, sculpture and visual arts. Well produced colour plates. Judy Bialkowski

5083 709'.71

**National Gallery of Canada. Library.**

Artists in Canada, Files in the National Gallery Library. Artistes au Canada, dossiers à la Bibliothèque de la Galerie nationale. Ottawa: Library, National Gallery of Canada, 1975- v ISSN 0705-7342

First edition listed in *CS* no. 1828.

A new edition to supersede that of 1975, and the first to be computer-produced. Artists of the fine and applied arts are listed alphabetically with birth date, province of residence, medium in which they work and dealer/gallery affiliation. Indicates if file is available on microform. Text in English and French. Judy Bialkowski

5084 709'.71

**Ontario Heritage Foundation.**

Firestone Art Collection. Photography by John Evans. Toronto: McGraw-Hill Ryerson, 1978. 167p. ill. Bibliographical references. ISBN 0-07-082747-8 pa.: $14.95

1. Firestone, O. J. – Art collections.
2. Art, Canadian – Catalogs.

A catalogue of twelve hundred Canadian art works, chiefly from the twentieth century, donated to the Ontario Heritage Foundation. In addition to providing an inventory of the collection the text includes a history of it, an analysis of the Canadian art scene and brief biographical sketches. Twenty of the one hundred reproductions are in colour. Judy Bialkowski

5085 709'.711
**Tippett, Maria.**
From Desolation to Splendour: Changing Perceptions of the British Columbia Landscape, by Maria Tippett and Douglas Cole. Toronto: Clarke, Irwin, 1977. 159p. ill. Bibliographical references and Index. ISBN 0-7720-1048-X $19.95

1. British Columbia in art. 2. Landscape in art. 3. British Columbia – Description and travel.

Eaton's British Columbia Book Award.

For the scholar, student and layman, an interesting study of the artists who have painted the British Columbia landscape, and their reactions to it. Well-researched with bibliographic notes and illustrated with familiar and unfamiliar works, some in colour. Introduction by Jack Shadbolt. Judy Bialkowski

## 720 Architecture

5086 720.
**Cardinal, Douglas.**
Of the Spirit: Writings. Edited by George Melnyk. Edmonton: NeWest Press, c1977. 126p. ill., plates. ISBN 0-920316-06-9 bd.: $6.95 ISBN 0-920316-04-2 pa.: $3.95

1. Architecture.

In a series of highly personal essays adapted from his speeches, interviews and working papers, the controversial architect from Alberta pits all that is wrong with contemporary life in Canada against North American Indian philosophy. Eight black and white photographs are not well integrated into the text. Jan Greenwood

5087 720.28
**Denhez, Marc C.**
Heritage Fights Back: Legal, Financial and Promotional Aspects of Canada's Efforts to Save Its Architecture and Historic Sites. Introduction by Pierre Berton. Ottawa: Heritage Canada; Toronto: Fitzhenry & Whiteside, c1978. 286p. ill. ISBN 0-88902-563-0 $5.95

1. Historic buildings – Canada – Conservation and restoration. 2. Historic sites – Canada – Conservation and restoration. 3. Gastown, Vancouver, B.C.

The story of Canada's youthful heritage movement is unfolded in this work which concludes with a detailed case study of the renaissance of the Gastown area in Vancouver. The text is indexed and profusely illustrated. The paucity of material available, the author's qualifications and comprehensive treatment make it important reading for any individual or organization interested in preserving architecture and historic sites. Margot Hewings

5088 720'.92'4
**Reksten, Terry.**
Rattenbury. Victoria, B.C.: Sono Nis Press, 1978. 204p. ill., plates, ports. Bibliography: p. 197-199. Index. ISBN 0-919462-58-8 $12.95

1. Rattenbury, Francis Mawson. 2. Architects – Canada – Biography.

Francis Mawson Rattenbury is best known as the architect who designed the British Columbia legislative buildings and the Empress Hotel. What is less known is the stormy history of the man, from his arrival in Canada in 1892, culminating in his grisly death in England in 1935. Terry Reksten has prepared a well-researched and very readable biography, documented by an index, bibliography, and some illustrations. Andrea Trudel

5089 720'.92'4
**Tuck, Robert C.**
Gothic Dreams: The Life and Times of a Canadian Architect, William Critchlow Harris, 1854-1913. Toronto: Dundurn Press, c1978. 252p. ill., ports. Bibliographical references and Index. ISBN 0-919679-31-8 $12.50

1. Harris, William Critchlow, 1854-1913.
2. Architects – Canada – Biography.

The author has drawn upon a wide variety of sources, including the architect's notebook and diary to produce a well-documented and informative biography of an architect who did most of his work in Prince Edward Island. A useful addition to Canadian architectural history. Jan Greenwood

5090 720'.9713
**Campbell, Dorothy.**
Toronto: Cabin to Highrise. Toronto: House of Grant, c1977. 64p. ill., map. ISBN 0-460-95270-6 pa.: $3.95

1. Architecture – Ontario – Toronto.
2. Historic buildings – Ontario – Toronto.

3. Toronto, Ont. – Buildings.

In this small paperback, architectural historian Dorothy Campbell traces the growth of Toronto through the changing architectural styles as the city developed. Fifty black and white photographs refer to particular European and American trends that influenced this architectural development. Explanatory marginal drawings, a glossary, and map explain terms and provide direction for the interested urban observer. Andrea Trudel

5091 720'.9713

**Stokes, Peter John.**

Old Niagara-on-the-Lake. Drawings by Robert Montgomery. Toronto: University of Toronto Press, 1977, c1971. 152p. ill., maps. Bibliography: p. 132-133. Index. (Canadian University Paperbooks) ISBN 0-8020-1773-8 bd.: $20 ISBN 0-8020-6318-7 pa.: $7.95

1. Architecture – Ontario – Niagara-on-the-Lake – History. 2. Historic buildings – Ontario – Niagara-on-the-Lake. 3. Niagara-on-the-Lake, Ont. – Dwellings.

A well-designed tribute and guide to this old Ontario town comprises largely full-page drawings of individual buildings, each with facing text and map. The illustrated glossary draws attention to individual architectural details which might be overlooked by the novice. Includes historical background, selected bibliography and index of buildings. Jan Greenwood

5092 721'.0448

**Clemson, Donovan.**

Old Wooden Buildings. Saanichton, B.C.: Hancock House, c1978. 95p. ill., maps. ISBN 0-919654-90-8 pa.: $4.95

1. Building, Wooden – British Columbia.
2. Church architecture – British Columbia.
3. Architecture – British Columbia.

Clemson has combined good quality black and white photographs with lucid narrative in this pictorial record of old houses, stores, hotels and barns. It adds up to a pleasing picture of the countryside in the interior of British Columbia. Sketch maps are provided for each area included. Nancy Cohen

5093 725.31

**Willmot, Elizabeth.**

Meet Me at the Station. Toronto: Gage Publishing, 1976. 114p. ill. Index. ISBN 0-7715-9976-5 $14.95

1. Railroads – Ontario – Stations.

A childhood interest in trains inspired this study of railway stations and flagstops in southern Ontario. A history of the community and railway anecdotes are interwoven with the information about each station. Most of the fifty-five stations described are contemporary. Good quality illustrations. Nancy Cohen

5094 726'.5

**De Visser, John.**

Pioneer Churches. Photographs by John de Visser; text by Harold Kalman. Toronto: McClelland and Stewart, c1976. 192p. ill. Bibliography: p. 185-189. Index. ISBN 0-7710-2700-1 $29.50

1. Churches – Canada – History. 2. Churches – United States – History. 3. Church architecture – Canada. 4. Church architecture – United States.

A handsomely illustrated and well-documented survey of selected North American pioneer churches containing descriptions of building styles and of the social and cultural setting of individual churches. Archival pictures, and plans and drawings illustrate churches erected in Canada and the United States from the beginning of the seventeenth to the close of the nineteenth century.

5095 726'.5

**Veillette, John.**

Early Indian Village Churches: Wooden Frontier Architecture in British Columbia, by John Veillette and Gary White. Commentaries by Harold Kalman, Robin Fisher, and Warren Sommer. Vancouver: University of British Columbia Press, c1977. 195p. ill., maps, plans, ports. Bibliography: p. 193-194. ISBN 0-7748-0074-7 bd.: $29 ISBN 0-7748-0075-5 pa.: $15

1. Rural churches – British Columbia.
2. Church architecture – British Columbia.
3. Indians of North America – British Columbia – Missions.

An ethnologist with the British Columbia Provincial Museum, and an antique dealer, have produced a scholarly and thorough study of late nineteenth century wooden churches in the province. Construction and architecture are discussed; church history is summarized; and a brief introduction to missionary work among the Indians is given. Nancy Cohen

## 728 Domestic architecture

5096 728'.09713
**Ondaatje, Kim.**
Old Ontario Houses, by Kim Ondaatje and Lois Mackenzie. Agincourt, Ont.: Gage Publishing, c1977. 192p. ill., map. Bibliography: p. xi. Index. ISBN 0-7715-9350-3 bd.: $29.95 ISBN 0-7715-9351-1 pa.

1. Architecture, Domestic – Ontario – History.

The importance of this book lies in the handsome photographs by an award-winning artist; the text is slight and contributes little to the social or architectural history of the province. Nancy Cohen

5097 728'.09714
**Mather, Edith.**
Les rues de Montréal, façades et fantaisie. Touches of Fantasy on Montreal Streets. Photographs by Edith Mather; text by René Chicoine. Montreal: Tundra Books, c1977. 96p. ill. ISBN 0-88776-038-4 pa.: $9.95

1. Architecture, Domestic – Quebec (Province) – Montreal. 2. Architecture – Quebec (Province) – Montreal. 3. Decoration and ornament – Quebec (Province) – Montreal.

Excellent black and white photographs capture unerringly the architectural whimsy that is so much a feature of Old Montreal. The accompanying bilingual text traces the historical influences that shaped these unique landmarks and calls for a halt to the forces of "progress" that threaten their existence. Jan Greenwood

5098 728.6
**Mackie, B. Allan.**
Log House Plans. Prince George, B.C.: Log House Publishing, 1979. 167p. ill., plans. ISBN 0-920270-28-X pa.

1. Architecture, Domestic – Designs and plans. 2. Building, Wooden.

Detailed floor plans and black and white photographs of thirty-seven log house designs may be supplemented by blueprints available from the publisher. Clear, informative text addresses itself to log house enthusiasts, particularly those interested in building such a home. Includes good table of contents, legend, glossary and many diagrams. Public libraries. Jan Greenwood

5099 728'.8
**Gill, Brendan.**
Summer Places, by Brendan Gill and Dudley Witney. Toronto: McClelland and Stewart, c1978. 223p. ill. Index. ISBN 0-7710-9031-5 $30

1. Summer homes – United States.
2. Summer homes – Canada.

The imaginative photography of Canada's Dudley Witney and Brendan Gill's descriptive text are combined in a salute to vacation homes. Pretentious mansions and modest cottages from the Gulf Coast to Maine, from the Maritimes to the Rockies, are illustrated. Coffee-table format. Arm-chair enjoyment for winter evenings.

## 730 Sculpture

5100 731.453
**Roukes, Nicholas.**
Sculpture in Plastics. Rev. ed. New York: Watson Guptill, 1978. 192p. ill. Bibliography: p. 189. Index. ISBN 0-82304-701-6 $29.95

1. Plastic sculpture.

Step-by-step demonstrations of the various working methods in plastics, both traditional and abstract. Contains a useful appendix on safety precautions. Brenda Hughes

## 737 Medals and coins

5101 737.4'971
**Charlton, J. E.**
Standard Catalogue of Canadian Coins: The Standard Reference. 30th ed. Toronto: The Charlton Press, c1980. Annual. 128p. ill. ISBN 0-88968-002-7 $3

1. Coins, Canadian.

The twenty-fifth edition is listed in *CS* no. 1880.

"An historical background of Canadian coins, patterns, essais, commemorative issues, specimen coins & sets". -Title page. Published annually, this standard guide for philatelists includes coins of Canada, Newfoundland, Prince Edward Island, Nova Scotia and New Brunswick.

5102 737.4'971
**Charlton, J. E.**
The 1980 Charlton Coin Guide. 20th ed. Toronto: Charlton International Publications, 1979. Annual. 156p. ill. ISBN 0-88968-000-0 pa.: $1.50

1. Coins, Canadian. 2. Paper money – Canada – Catalogues.

"Includes dealers' buying prices for Canadian, Newfoundland & Maritime coinage, Canadian tokens & paper money, United States coinage & paper money, English coinage." -Title page.

## 738 Ceramic arts

5103 738.
**Weinrich, Peter H.**
A Bibliographical Guide to Books on Ceramics. Guide bibliographique des ouvrages sur la céramique. Ottawa: Canadian Crafts Council, 1976. 272p. Index. ISBN 0-88980-000-6 $12.50

1. Pottery – Bibliography.

Divided into sections such as General Works, Africa, America, Asia and Europe. Articles in serial publications are not included. Brenda Hughes

5104 738.0971
**Antonelli, Marylu.**
Pottery in Alberta: The Long Tradition, by Marylu Antonelli and Jack Forbes. Edmonton: University of Alberta Press, 1978. 189p. ill., ports. ISBN 0-88864-023-4 $12.50

1. Pottery – Alberta.

A fascinating study of the Alberta clay products industry, with emphasis on the history of two companies – Alberta Clay Products and Medalta. Very well illustrated. Brenda Hughes

5105 738.3'0971
**Newlands, David L.**
Early Ontario Potters: Their Craft and Trade. Toronto: McGraw-Hill Ryerson, 1979. Bibliography. Index. ISBN 0-07-082972-1 $29.95

1. Potters – Ontario. 2. Pottery – 19th century – Ontario. 3. Pottery, Canadian – Ontario.

A comprehensive history of the potters of early Ontario. Contains over 350 illustrations, a glossary of ceramic terms, and an illustrated checklist of pottery marks. Brenda Hughes

## 741 Drawing and drawings

5106 741.5'971
**Desbarats, Peter.**
The Hecklers, by Peter Desbarats and Terry Mosher. Toronto: McClelland and Stewart, 1979. Index. ISBN 0-7710-2686-2 $19.95

1. Canadian wit and humor, Pictorial – History and criticism. 2. Cartoonists – Canada.

Traces the development of political cartooning in Canada from the work of John Bengough in the nineteenth century to Macpherson, Donato and other greats of today. The informed commentary of Desbarats and Mosher, whose cartoons appear under the pseudonym "Aislin", are supplemented by a useful section of biographies. A splendid, illustrated history of the craft. Annemarie Toth

5107 741.5'971
**Hutchings, Trevor.**
Some of Our Best Friends Are in Business: An Irreverent but Sympathetic Study of an Endangered Species. Cartoons by Trevor Hutchings; text by Robert L. Perry. Toronto: Financial Post Macmillan, c1978. 128p. ill. ISBN 0-88896-078-6 pa.: $5.95

1. Business – Caricatures and cartoons.
2. Canada – Economic conditions – 1965- – Caricatures and cartoons.

Presents a delightful review of the economic follies and foibles of the Trudeau era, and satirizes its subversive effect on business and the work ethic. Narrated with tongue-in-cheek naiveté by a journalist skilled in the art of understatement and irony, and developed in complete harmony with cartoons previously published in "The Financial Post". Ille-Mai Gerdels

5108 741.5'971
**Johnston, Lynn Franks.**
Do They Ever Grow Up?: 101 Cartoons About the Terrible Twos and Beyond. Don Mills, Ont.: Musson, 1978. 107p. ill. ISBN 0-7737-1026-4 pa.: $3.50

1. Children – Caricatures and cartoons.
2. Canadian wit and humor, Pictorial.

A lively look at the joys and traumas of parenting the toddler set. The third in a series of books on family life by this popular Canadian cartoonist. Annemarie Toth

5109 741.5'971

**Johnston, Lynn Franks.**

Hi Mom! Hi Dad!: 101 Cartoons. Foreword by Mary Blum. Toronto: Peter Martin, 1977. 107p. ill. ISBN 0-88778-157-8 pa.: $2.95

1. Parent and child – Caricatures and cartoons. 2. Canadian wit and humor, Pictorial.

A sequel to the very popular collection of cartoons, *David We're Pregnant*. Johnston's fresh subtle humour gives us a joyful depiction of baby and parents' first year together. Annemarie Toth

5110 741.5'971

**Macpherson, Duncan Ian.**

Editorial Cartoons 1978: 136 Selected Cartoons. Introduction by Christina McCall Newman. Toronto: Macmillan, c1978. 150p. ill. ISBN 0-7705-1733-1 pa.: $4.95

1. World politics – 1975-1985 – Caricatures and cartoons. 2. Canada – Politics and government – 1963- – Caricatures and cartoons.

This annual collection of the best of Macpherson, noted political cartoonist for the "Toronto Star" may be the last. Readers who have enjoyed his wit will regret his retirement. Annemarie Toth

5111 741.5'971

**Mosher, Terry.**

150 Caricatures. Edmonton: Hurtig Publishers, c1977. 100p. ill. ISBN 0-88830-145-6 pa.: $3.95

1. Canada – Politics and government – 1963- – Caricatures and cartoons. 2. Quebec (Province) – Politics and government – 1960- – Caricatures and cartoons.

Title on cover: *O.K. Everybody Take a Valium.*

Aislin's satiric wit flourishes in this collection of cartoons, some of which appear for the first time. Some of the drawings and the language in the previously unpublished cartoons may prove offensive to a few readers. Annemarie Toth

5112 741.5'971

**Peterson, Roy.**

The World According to Roy Peterson, by Roy Peterson, with the Gospel according to Allan Fotheringham. Vancouver: Douglas & McIntyre, 1979. 160p. ISBN 0-88894-254-0 bd.: $16.95 ISBN 0-88894-246-X pa.: $8.95

1. Canadian wit and humor, Pictorial.
2. Editorial cartoons – Canada.

One of Canada's top editorial cartoonists finds his match in the acerbic wit of the well-known columnist for "Maclean's Magazine". An excellent retrospective collection of the best of Peterson's work. Annemarie Toth

5113 741.5'971

**Roschkov, Vic.**

Roschkov Editorial Cartoons. Introduction by Gary Lautens. Scarborough, Ont.: Prentice-Hall, 1979. 150p. ill. ISBN 0-13-783316-4 pa.: $3.95

1. Canadian wit and humor, Pictorial.
2. World politics – 1975-1985 – Caricatures.

A fresh perception of political machinations at every level of government can be found in this first collection of cartoons. All have originally appeared in the "Toronto Star" and "Windsor Star". Annemarie Toth

5114 741.5'971

**Wicks, Ben.**

Ben Wicks' Book of Losers. Toronto: McClelland and Stewart, 1979. 127p. ISBN 0-7710-8993-7 $9.95

1. Canadian wit and humor, Pictorial.

Culled from newspapers around the globe, Wicks has produced an anthology of anecdotes about losers in life's everyday battles. The humour leans towards the scatological and is illustrated by Wick's distinctive line drawings. Annemarie Toth

5115 741.5'971

**Wicks, Ben.**

Ben Wicks' Women. Toronto: McClelland and Stewart, c1978. 160p. ill. ISBN 0-7710-8982-1 $8.95

1. Women – Caricatures and cartoons.
2. Women – Anecdotes, facetiae, satire, etc.

Wicks, the well-known cartoonist, flaunts his misogynist tendencies in this comic examination of "God's Biggest Blunder". Written in epigrammatic prose and illustrated with Wick's drawings, and photographs, this work may have limited appeal. Annemarie Toth

5116 741.6

**MacGregor, A. J.**

Graphics Simplified: How to Plan and Prepare Effective Charts, Graphs, Illustrations, and Other Visual Aids. Toronto: University of Toronto Press, c1979. 64p. ill. Bibliography: p. 59-62. Index. (Canadian University Paperbooks) ISBN 0-8020-6363-2 pa.: $2.50

A clear and concise guide to designing and effective use of visual aids for teachers, scientists, artists, photographers and students. For all libraries.

## 741.9 Collections of drawings

5117 741.9'713
**Rickard, George P.**
Sketching Rambles in Ontario: A Collection of Pen and Ink Drawings. London, Ont.: George Rickard Studio, c1977. 96p. ill.
1. Buildings in art. 2. Ontario in art.
Sepia-toned, full-page drawings are annotated and preserve for posterity a variety of landmarks that are fast disappearing from the Ontario countryside. Jan Greenwood

## 745 Antiques and crafts

5118 745.1'0971
**Arnett, Janet.**
Antiques & Collectibles: Starting Small. Cobalt, Ont.: Highway Book Shop, c1978. 59p. ill. Bibliography: p. 58-59.
ISBN 0-88954-164-7 pa.: $3
1. Antiques – Canada.
Originally published as a series of magazine articles, this book offers advice to the beginner on how to start collecting without attempting large pieces such as furniture, which are usually too expensive for the new enthusiast. A selective bibliography is included. Nancy Cohen

5119 745.5
**Hungry Wolf, Adolf,** comp.
Blackfoot Craftworker's Book, compiled by Adolf Hungry Wolf and Beverly Hungry Wolf. Invermere, B.C.: Good Medicine Books, c1977. 79p. ill. Bibliography: p. 2. (Good Medicine Books) pa. Processed: $6
1. Siksika Indians – Costume and adornment. 2. Indians of North America – Costume and adornment.
This collection of photographs of traditional Blackfoot craftwork is supplemented by descriptions of the history and production methods of various items. Crafts illustrated include clothing, ornaments, toys, gun cases, horse gear and utensils. Some basic craftwork techniques, such as beadwork, hide tanning and quillwork are described. Brenda Hughes

5120 745.59'22
**Wiseman, Adele.**
Old Woman at Play. Toronto: Clarke, Irwin, c1978. 148p. ill., port.
ISBN 0-7720-1230-X $13.95
1. Wiseman, Chaika, 1896- 2. Dollmakers – Canada – Biography.
Wiseman explores the process of creativity by examining a collection of dolls produced by her mother. The dolls discussed in the narrative are pictured in the margins. Focuses on the "why" of crafts, rather than the "how". Brenda Hughes

5121 745.6'7
**Bird, Michael S.**
Ontario Fraktur: A Pennsylvania-German Folk Tradition in Early Canada. Toronto: M. F. Feheley Publishers, c1977. 144p. ill., map, ports. Bibliography: p. 141-142. Index.
ISBN 0-919880-08-8 $18
1. Illumination of books and manuscripts, Pennsylvania German – Ontario.
Dr. Bird, a professor of religious studies at the University of Waterloo, examines fraktur, a religious-ethnic art form combining calligraphy and decoration, in the three founding Mennonite settlements of southern Ontario, tracing it back to its North American roots in Pennsylvania. Many of the superb illustrations are from private collections. An excellent, scholarly introduction to one of Ontario's nineteenth century folk arts. Merike Koger

## 746 Textile arts and handicrafts

5122 746.
**Gervers, Veronika,** ed.
Studies in Textile History: In Memory of Harold B. Burnham. Toronto: Royal Ontario Museum, c1977. 371p. ill., diagrs., maps, ports. Bibliography: p. x-xii.
ISBN 0-88854-192-9 $25
1. Textile fabrics – History.
Textile specialists from around the world have contributed twenty-five scholarly articles as a tribute to the former Curator of Textiles at the Royal Ontario Museum. Well-illustrated and carefully documented, the book is most suitable for large fine arts collections.

5123 746.1
**Morrison, Phyllis.**
Spiders' Games: A Book for Beginning Weavers. Foreword by Joanne Segal Brandford. Toronto: Douglas & McIntyre, 1979. 112p. ill. ISBN 0-88894-219-2 $16.95

1. Weaving.

This introduction to weaving explains how to make and use the essential tools, and gives directions for each of the basic techniques, with clear step-by-step illustrations and examples of traditional weaving styles. Brenda Hughes

5124 746.9'7
**McKendry, Ruth.**
Quilts and Other Bedcoverings in the Canadian Tradition, by Ruth McKendry, and Blake McKendry. Toronto: Van Nostrand Reinhold, 1979. 454p. Index.
ISBN 0-442-29778-5 $39.95

1. Coverlets – Ontario. 2. Bedding.
3. Quilting – Ontario.

Published in the United States under title, *Traditional Quilts and Bedcoverings.*

This study of nineteenth century handmade bedding in Ontario should be of interest to all collectors of textiles and antiques. Well illustrated with over 450 photographs. Brenda Hughes

## 749 Furniture and accessories

5125 749.2'11
**Webster, Donald Blake.**
English-Canadian Furniture of the Georgian Period. Foreword by Charles Hummel. Toronto: McGraw-Hill Ryerson, c1979. Bibliography. Index.
ISBN 0-07-082980-2 $27.50

1. Furniture, Georgian – Canada. 2. Furniture – Canada.

More than three hundred examples of fine Canadian furniture produced before 1830 are described and illustrated. Included are introductory chapters on the characteristics of the furniture (styles, wood usage, proportion, hardware) and a brief discussion of the early Canadian cabinet-makers. Brenda Hughes

5126 749.2'113
**Nykor, Lynda Musson.**
Mennonite Furniture: The Ontario Tradition in York County, by Lynda Musson Nykor and Patricia D. Husson. Foreword by Nancy-Lou Patterson; photographs by Martha Kuehner. Toronto: James Lorimer, 1977. 95p. ill. Bibliography: p. 93-95.
ISBN 0-88862-148-5 bd.: $15
ISBN 0-88862-149-3 pa.: $6.95

1. Furniture, Mennonite – Ontario – York (County).

By tracing the history of York County Mennonites the authors have provided a sensitive interpretation of the influences on their furniture-making. The works of several craftsmen are identified and illustrated in black and white. Not all of the furniture shown is uniquely Mennonite and the work is flawed by inaccurate use of terminology. Nancy Cohen

5127 749.2'113
**Pain, Howard.**
The Heritage of Upper Canadian Furniture: A Study in the Survival of Formal and Vernacular Styles from Britain, America and Europe, 1780-1900. Foreword by Dean A. Fales, Jr.; introduction by William Kilbourn. Toronto: Van Nostrand Reinhold, 1978. 548p. ill., map. Bibliography: p. 544. Index.
ISBN 0-442-29829-3 bd.: $49.95
ISBN 0-442-29830-7 (limited ed.): $200

1. Furniture – Ontario – History.

Containing 1450 plates (249 in colour) which illustrate the finest examples of Upper Canadian furniture, this handsome work is a major contribution to the subject. The furniture is grouped in sections on Anglo-American, German, Polish and French Canadian designs. A glossary and bibliography are included. Nancy Cohen

5128 749.2'115
**Foss, Charles H.**
Cabinetmakers of the Eastern Seaboard: A Study of Early Canadian Furniture. Photography by Richard Vroom. Toronto: M. F. Feheley Publishers, c1977. 156p. ill. Bibliography: p. 155-156. Index.
ISBN 0-919880-09-6 $29

1. Furniture – New Brunswick. 2. Cabinet-workers – New Brunswick.

A well-written, beautifully illustrated discussion of the various influences on early furniture-making in New Brunswick. The Loyalist influence is identified, and chapters devoted to thirteen of the province's fine cabinetmakers. Large, attractive format deriving from quality paper, pleasing page layout, and clear black and white illustrations. Nancy Cohen

5129 749'.3

**Ingolfsrud, Elizabeth.**

All About Ontario Cupboards. Photographs by John Willard. Toronto: House of Grant, c1978. 95p. ill. ISBN 0-460-90084-6 pa.: $5.95

1. Cupboards. 2. Furniture – Ontario.

Other titles in the series on Ontario antiques were listed in *CS* nos. 1961, 1962, 1963 and 1964.

The fifth book in a series on Ontario furniture offers a short history of Ontario cupboards, advice on decoration, restoration and assessment of age and condition. Numerous pictures supplement the detailed descriptions of the article which give date, provenance and relative value on today's market. Nancy Cohen

5130 749.3

**Ingolfsrud, Elizabeth.**

All About Ontario Desks. Photographs by John Willard. Toronto: House of Grant, 1979. 79p. ill. ISBN 0-460-90085-4 pa.: $5.95

1. Desks. 2. Furniture – Ontario.

Sixth in the "All About" series. Twenty-five antique desks found in Ontario are illustrated, with information about style, construction and value. Brenda Hughes

## 750 Painting and paintings

5131 751.4'22

**Szabo, Zoltan.**

Zoltan Szabo Paints Landscapes: Advanced Techniques in Watercolor. Don Mills, Ont.: General Publishing, 1977. 175p. ill., port. Bibliography: p. 171. Index. ISBN 0-7736-0057-4 $19.95

1. Water-color painting – Technique.
2. Landscape painting – Technique.

All components of a landscape – rocks, trees, buildings, flowers, etc. – are discussed, and techniques are demonstrated by colour illustrations. Several of Szabo's landscapes are reproduced with lifesize details on the facing page as an aid to study. Brenda Hughes

5132 751.4'5

**Reid, Dave.**

My Book on Oil Painting. Vancouver: The Author, c1977. 90p. ill. Index. pa.: $9.95

1. Painting – Technique.

Written for the beginner, with emphasis on the basic techniques of oil painting. Includes chapters on perspective, materials, colour mixing, and detailed instructions for painting a still life, landscape, seascape and portrait. Brenda Hughes

5133 759.

**Szabo, Zoltan.**

Zoltan Szabo, Artist at Work. Don Mills, Ont.: General Publishing, 1979. 144p. ill. ISBN 0-7736-0077-9 pa.: $24.95

1. Water-color painting – Technique.

An exploration of the philosophy, working method and materials of this popular and prolific artist. Several of his favourite paintings are reproduced, with a detailed explanation of how they were executed. Brenda Hughes

## 759.11 Canadian painting

5134 759.11

**Adamson, Jeremy.**

Lawren S. Harris: Urban Scenes and Wilderness Landscapes, 1906-1930: Art Gallery of Ontario, January 14-February 26, 1978. Toronto: Art Gallery of Ontario, c1978. 231p. ill. Bibliography: p. 216-218. ISBN 0-919876-35-8 pa.: $15

1. Harris, Lawren, 1885-1970 – Exhibitions.
2. Harris, Lawren, 1885-1970 – Expositions.
3. Painters – Canada – Biography.

A full range of the artist's work is discussed and illustrated in this exhibition catalogue. The 175 illustrations, 15 in colour, relate well to the text. A chronology and extensive bibliographic footnotes are included. Judy Bialkowski

5135 759.11

**Bell, Michael.**

Painters in a New Land: From Annapolis Royal to the Klondike. Toronto: McClelland and Stewart, 1978. 224p. ISBN 0-7710-0954-2 pa.: $10.95

1. Paintings, Canadian. 2. Canada in art.
3. Canada – Description and travel.

Clothbound edition listed *CS* no. 1975.

5136 759.11
**Bobak, Molly Lamb.**
Wild Flowers of Canada: Impressions and Sketches of a Field Artist. Toronto: Pagurian Press, c1978. 96p. ill. (A Christopher Ondaatje Publication) ISBN 0-88932-077-2 $19.95

1. Women painters – Canada – Biography.

A delightful, very personal combination of autobiography and comment on the Canadian art world of the last thirty years, by the daughter of H. Mortimer Lamb. Memories are recalled through the discussion of wild flowers. The author's meticulous water colour paintings are beautifully reproduced. Judy Bialkowski

5137 759.11
**Bolt, Ron.**
The Inner Ocean. Paintings and drawings by Ron Bolt; edited by David Bolt; introduction by Hugh MacLennan. Toronto: Merritt Publishing, 1979. 159p. Bibliography: p. 154-157. Index. ISBN 0-920886-00-0 $24.95

1. Sea in art. 2. Ocean – Literary collections.

A sensitively conceived and pleasingly designed visual and verbal exploration of the many moods of the sea. Bolt's realistic marine paintings and drawings are complemented by carefully selected writings about the sea. Comments on Bolt's artistic status, a biographical sketch, and a chronology of exhibitions and list of awards is included. A book to be savoured and enjoyed on several levels.

5138 759.11
**Bridges, Marjorie Lismer,** ed.
A Border of Beauty: Arthur Lismer's Pen and Pencil. Toronto: Red Rock Publishing, 1977. 156p. ill., ports. ISBN 0-920178-04-9 $16.95

1. Lismer, Arthur, 1885-1969. 2. Painters – Canada – Biography.

A personal glimpse of this Group of Seven painter revealed through his family correspondence. Text, not illustrations are emphasized, as the majority of the fifty-three illustrations are simple sketches originally enclosed within letters. Includes four colour plates. Judy Bialkowski

5139 759.11
**Duval, Paul.**
The Art of Glen Loates. Scarborough, Ont.: Prentice-Hall, c1977. 189p. ill. Index. ISBN 0-920016-05-7 $35

1. Loates, Martin Glen. 2. Animal painters – Canada – Biography. 3. Animals in art.

The work of one of Canada's foremost nature artists is explored through text and 130 full-colour plates of remarkable quality. Includes an index to works, a statement by the artist, but lacks a bibliography. Good quality paper. Judy Bialkowski

5140 759.11
**Duval, Paul.**
The Tangled Garden: The Art of J. E. H. Macdonald. Toronto: Prentice-Hall, 1978. 192p. ill. Index. ISBN 0-920016-18-1 $42.50

1. Macdonald, James Edward Hervey, 1873-1932. 2. Painting, Canadian. 3. Painters, Canadian.

A selection of over 150 quality reproductions, the majority of which are in colour, highlight this study of the influential Group of Seven painter. Text, drawn from letters and family history, is interspersed. An index to works gives date, medium and provenance but there are no references and no bibliography. Judy Bialkowski

5141 759.11
**Fenton, Terry.**
Modern Painting in Canada: Major Movements in Twentieth Century Canadian Art, by Terry Fenton and Karen Wilkin. Edmonton: Hurtig Publishers; Edmonton Art Gallery, c1978. 119p. ill. Bibliography: p. 117-118. ISBN 0-88830-162-6 $18.95

1. Painting, Canadian. 2. Painting, Modern – 20th century – Canada.

Major twentieth century art movements and painters are studied in this catalogue of an exhibition sponsored by the Edmonton Art Gallery and held during the 1978 Commonwealth Games. Organized by subject, each chapter includes a well-documented introductory essay and quality colour reproductions. Includes biographical notes. Judy Bialkowski

5142 759.11
**Gray, Margaret.**
Carl Schaefer, by Margaret Gray, Margaret Rand and Lois Steen. Agincourt, Ont.: Gage Publishing, c1977. 65p. ill., ports. Bibliography: p. 65. (Canadian Artists) ISBN 0-7715-9340-6 $14.95

1. Schaefer, Carl, 1903- 2. Painters – Canada – Biography.

Drawing upon personal interviews the authors discuss the life and artistic techniques of the well-known Ontario painter. Text is augmented by numerous photographs. Twenty-four of the excellent reproductions are in colour. Includes a chronology. Judy Bialkowski

5143 759.11
**Gribbon, Michael J.**
Walter J. Phillips: A Selection of His Works and Thoughts. Un choix de son oeuvre et des réflexions. Ottawa: National Gallery of Canada; National Museums of Canada, 1978. 125p. ill., ports. Bibliography. ISBN 0-8884-365-8 $7.95

1. Phillips, Walter Joseph, 1884-1963.
2. Artists – Canada – Biography.

More than fifty reproductions of his watercolours and colour woodcuts , each of which is dated and captioned in French and in English, illustrate the artistic development of the talented Canadian. Excerpts from Phillips' works, published and unpublished, add interest to Gribbon's critical analysis. A chronology is included. Public and college libraries.

5144 759.11
**Harper, John Russell.**
Krieghoff. Toronto: University of Toronto Press, c1979. 204p. ill. Bibliography: p. 187-188. Index. ISBN 0-8020-2348-7 $29.95

1. Krieghoff, Cornelius, 1815-1872.
2. Painters – Canada – Biography.

Canada's eminent art historian, J. Russell Harper has skillfully documented the life of one of the country's best-loved painters. A superb collection of almost two hundred colour and black and white reproductions illustrates the essential elements of Krieghoff's work: his wit and charm in portraying nineteenth century habitant life. Of special interest is the chapter on forgeries and imitators. Andrea Trudel

5145 759.11
**Harper, John Russell.**
Painting in Canada: A History. 2d ed. Toronto: University of Toronto Press, 1977, c1966. 463p. ill., ports. Bibliography: p. 439-443. Index. (Canadian University Paperbooks) ISBN 0-8020-2271-5 bd.: $29.50 ISBN 0-8020-6307-1 pa.: $12.50

1. Painting, Canadian – History.

First edition listed *CS* no. 1990.

A revised and expanded history of Canadian painting includes the author's recent research. There are no colour plates but 45 of the 175 black and white illustrations are new. Includes brief biographies of artists, extensive notes, and a selective bibliography. Judy Bialkowski

5146 759.11
**Harper, John Russell.**
A People's Art: Primitive, Naîve, Provincial, and Folk Painting in Canada. Toronto: University of Toronto Press, c1974. 176p. ill. Bibliographical references and Index. (Canadian University Paperbooks) ISBN 0-8020-2153-0 pa.: $9.95

1. Paintings, Canadian. 2. Primitivism in art – Canada. 3. Folk art – Canada.

Clothbound listed in *CS* no. 1991.

5147 759.11
**Kuhns, William.**
Sam Borenstein, by William Kuhns and Leo Rosshandler. Toronto: McClelland and Stewart, c1978. 144p. ill., ports. Index. ISBN 0-7710-4553-0 $35

1. Borenstein, Sam, 1908-1969. 2. Painters – Quebec (Province) – Biography.

The life and work of this recently recognized Laurentide painter is explored through text and illustration. Of the eighty quality reproductions, twenty are in colour, with date, size and provenance indicated. Includes a list of exhibitions but no bibliography. Judy Bialkowski

5148 759.11
**Kurelek, William.**
Kurelek's Canada. Toronto: Pagurian Press, c1978. 127p. ill. (A Christopher Ondaatje Publication) ISBN 0-88932-076-4 pa.: $8.95

1. Canada in art.

Clothbound edition listed in *CS* no. 2004.

This paperback version of the best-selling book by the late William Kurelek captures the artist's delightfully personal view of Canada. Province by province, thirty colour and several black and white paintings are presented, with accompanying text by Kurelek, elaborating his experiences and influences. The simplistic yet evocative style expresses a great love for his country. Andrea Trudel

5149 759.11
**Kurelek, William.**
The Last of the Arctic. Toronto: Pagurian Press, c1978. 94p. ill. (A Christopher Ondaatje Publication) ISBN 0-88932-074-8 pa.: $8.95

1. Eskimos – Canada – Pictorial works.
2. Eskimos – Canada – Social life and customs.

Clothbound listed in *CS* no. 2005.

5150 759.11
**McDougall, Anne.**
Anne Savage: The Story of a Canadian Painter. Montreal: Harvest House, c1977. 215p. ill., plates, ports. ISBN 0-88772-182-6 $19.95

1. Savage, Anne, 1896-1971. 2. Painters – Canada – Biography.

A biographical account of the artist and art educator who was closely allied to the Group of Seven. Written by the artist's niece, the core of the work is based on correspondence between Anne Savage and A. Y. Jackson. Photographs, black and white reproductions and eight colour plates illustrate the text. Judy Bialkowski

5151 759.11
**Reid, Dennis.**
"Our Own Country Canada": Being an Account of the National Aspirations of the Principal Landscape Artist in Montreal and Toronto, 1860-1890. Ottawa: National Gallery of Canada, 1979. 384p. ill. ISBN 0-88884-360-7 $29.95

1. Landscape painting, Canadian.

Canada's foremost art historian examines landscape painting in the social, political and economic setting of the period. The influence of photography, and especially of the Notman studios, is emphasized. It draws attention to neglected artists such as Lucius O'Brien and Otto Jacobi. Black and white illustrations.

5152 759.11
**Robert, Guy.**
Lemieux. Translated by John David Allan. Toronto: Gage Publishing, c1978. 303p. ill., ports. Bibliography: p. 296-301. ISBN 0-7715-9352-X $50

1. Lemieux, Jean-Paul, 1904- 2. Painters – Quebec (Province) – Biography.

A scholarly and detailed study of the life and artistic development of a major Quebec artist. The French edition won the Montreal Grand Prix for Literature in 1976. Despite a sometimes involved style and a dearth of colour reproductions the book is a significant addition to Canadian art history.

5153 759.11
**Robertson, Heather,** ed.
A Terrible Beauty: The Art of Canada at War. Toronto: James Lorimer; Oshawa, Ont.: Robert McLaughlin Gallery; Ottawa: National Museum of Man, 1977. 239p. ill. ISBN 0-88862-144-2 $29.95

1. Painting, Canadian. 2. Painting, Modern – 20th century – Canada. 3. War in art. 4. European War, 1914-1918 – Personal narratives, Canadian. 5. World War, 1939-1945 – Personal narratives, Canadian.

One hundred colour plates depicting Canadians in two world wars are reproduced from the collections at the Canadian War Museum and the National Gallery. Excerpts from memoirs, diaries, letters, novels, songs and poetry are interwoven, but neither sources nor writers are identified. An attempt to personalize the reality of war for the general reader. For casual browsing rather than for information. Nancy Cohen

5154 759.11
**Sapp, Allen.**
A Cree Life: The Art of Allen Sapp. Introduction by John Anson Warner and Thecla Bradshaw. Vancouver: J. J. Douglas, c1977. 126p. ill., port. Bibliography: p. 121-122. ISBN 0-88894-149-8 $24.95

1. Cree Indians – Pictorial works. 2. Indians of North America – Saskatchewan – Pictorial works.

The talented native painter whose canvas records the life of his people on a northern Saskatchewan reservation thirty years ago, is introduced in a biographical essay. The comments on each painting are in the artist's own words. The ninety examples of Sapp's work are nicely reproduced. Judy Bialkowski

5155 759.11
**Schleicher, Edythe Hembroff.**
Emily Carr: The Untold Story. Saanichton, B.C.: Hancock House, c1978. 408p. ill., ports. Bibliography: p. 405. Index. ISBN 0-88839-003-3 $14.95

1. Carr, Emily, 1871-1945. 2. Painters – British Columbia – Biography.

A close friend and sketching partner attempts to correct errors and misinterpretations which exist in published accounts about the West Coast artist and her work. Few illustrations, but an extensive chronology, and a history of the artist's exhibiting career. Useful as a supplement to other works. Judy Bialkowski

5156 759.11
**Shadbolt, Doris.**
The Art of Emily Carr. Vancouver: Douglas & McIntyre, 1979. 224p. Bibliography. ISBN 0-88894-244-3 $39.95

1. Carr, Emily, 1871-1945.

The major periods in the artist's life, and the influences which shaped her artistic development, are treated sequentially. Lucid comments on the two hundred beautiful reproductions are interwoven with excerpts from Carr's own writing. A handsomely designed, carefully researched and objective assessment which pays tribute to the individuality and stature of the West Coast painter. Recommended for first purchase.

5157 759.11
**Sinclair, Lister Shedden.**
The Art of Norval Morrisseau, by Lister Shedden Sinclair and Jack Pollock. Agincourt, Ont.: Methuen, 1979. 200p. Bibliography. Index. ISBN 0-458-93820-3 (trade ed.): $60 ISBN 0-458-94230-8 (gallery ed.): $1000

1. Morrisseau, Norval, 1933- 2. Painters – Canada – Biography.

This is an impressive and comprehensive collection and commentary on the work of the well-known Ojibway artist. There are 130 colour reproductions, outstanding in their quality, accompanied by numerous black and white illustrations. Lister Sinclair provides a critical appraisal of Morrisseau's style, while Jack Pollock contributes personal reminiscences. Morrisseau adds some descriptive commentary on particular paintings. Andrea Trudel

5158 759.11
**Tippett, Maria.**
Emily Carr, A Biography. Toronto: Oxford University Press, 1979. 314p. Index. ISBN 0-19-540314-2 $16.95

1. Carr, Emily, 1871-1945. 2. Painters – British Columbia – Biography.

Governor General's Literary Award.

This first major biography of Carr traces, illustrates and elucidates the complex development of her life and art. The author, a teacher of cultural history at Simon Fraser University, has written a pleasingly unaffected, richly detailed book that retains a personally sympathetic but critically objective stance throughout. Does full justice to a challenging subject. Ille-Mai Gerdels

5159 759.11
**Town, Harold.**
Tom Thomson: The Silence and the Storm, by Harold Town and David P. Silcox. Toronto: McClelland and Stewart, c1977. 240p. ill., ports. Bibliography: p. 237-238. Index. ISBN 0-7710-8482-X $29.95

1. Thomson, Tom, 1877-1917.

A beautifully designed and superbly illustrated tribute to the Canadian painter. Harold Town's introductory essay and comments on individual paintings are complemented by David Silcox's notes on Thomson's life and artistic development. A landmark publication illustrating the range of the artist's creative talent and a critical analysis of it. Highly recommended.

5160 759.11
**University of Western Ontario.**
The Image of Man in Canadian Painting, 1878-1978. L'image de l'homme dans la peinture canadienne, 1878-1978. London, Ont.: University of Western Ontario, 1978. 91p. ill. Bibliographical references. ISBN 0-7714-0031-4 pa.: $8.50

1. Painting, Canadian – Exhibitions.
2. Human figure in art.

Exhibition catalogue providing a historical look at Canadian painting. Bilingual text surveys the century, followed by a catalogue of fifty works representing forty painters. Biographies, and a detailed index to the paintings provide notes, exhibitions, and bibliographies for each. The majority of the illustrations are in black and white. Judy Bialkowski

5161 759.11
**20 Painters/20 Paintings: Contemporary Canadian Art.**
Selected by Marci Lipman and Louise Lipman. Toronto: Lester and Orpen Dennys, 1979. 48p. ill. ISBN 0-91963-010-3 $14.95

1. Paintings, Canadian. 2. Painting, Modern – 20th century – Canada.

A visual survey of contemporary Canadian art through the reproduction of twenty paintings by twenty painters. The colour reproductions are large, however the book lacks adequate descriptive text, though brief biographical notes are included. Artists include Bush, Colville, Pachter, Loates and others, representing a wide scope of Canadian talent both geographically and stylistically. Andrea Trudel

5162 759.11'074
**Art Gallery of Ontario. Extension Dept.**
The Laurentians: Painters in a Landscape. Toronto: Art Gallery of Ontario, c1977. 88p. ill., map, ports. Bibliography: p. 83-86. ISBN 0-919876-23-4 pa.

1. Paintings, Canadian – Quebec (Province) – Exhibitions. 2. Paintings, Modern – 20th century – Canada – Exhibitions. 3. Laurentides region, Que. in art.

How fifteen painters over the last fifty years have viewed the Laurentian landscape. The entry for each artist includes a portrait, short biography, descriptive essay and documented reproductions. Included are sixty-one plates, twelve of which are in colour, and a catalogue raisonné for each artist. Judy Bialkowski

5163 759.11'074
**McMichael Canadian Collection.**
A Heritage of Canadian Art: The McMichael Collection. Biographies by Paul Duval. Toronto: Clarke, Irwin, c1979. 208p. ill. ISBN 0-7720-1209-1 $19.95

1. Paintings, Canadian. 2. Art, Canadian.

1976 edition listed *CS* no. 2030.

A slightly expanded version of the 1976 catalogue, with a new introduction by D. G. Carmichael and some new reproductions. Handsomely designed and beautifully illustrated. A first purchase if a library does not have the earlier publication.

5164 759.9494
**Burnett, David.**
A Tribute to Paul Klee, 1879-1940. Hommage à Paul Klee, 1879-1940. Ottawa: National Gallery of Canada, 1979. 123p. ill. Bibliography: p. 122-123. Index. ISBN 0-88884-381-X pa.: $19.95

1. Klee, Paul, 1879-1940.

The first exhibition of Paul Klee's works to originate in Canada was arranged to mark the centenary of his birth. Seventy-seven plates, a carefully documented review of his life and artistic development, and a chronology of the principal exhibitions of Klee's works comprise the catalogue. A useful addition to the available material on an important Canadian artist.

5165 769.5
**Dimson, Theo.,** ed.
Great Canadian Posters. Toronto: Oxford University Press, 1979. Unpaged. ill. ISBN 0-19-540343-6 pa.: $8.95

1. Posters, Canadian.

A poster designer's selection of favourite posters from 1880 to 1979. Interesting but not essential for general collections.

5166 769'.5
**Stacey, Robert H.**
The Canadian Poster Book: 100 Years of the Poster in Canada. Toronto: Methuen, 1979. Bibliography: p. 81-84. Index. ISBN 0-458-93850-5 $14.95

1. Posters, Canadian.

Posters are examined in relation to their social, political and economic setting. The selection of examples, based on an exhibition organized for the Art Gallery of Ontario by the editor, is arranged by subjects, such as circus, politics and sports. Not a definitive work, but the best available on the topic.

## **769.56** Postage stamps

5167 769.56
**Patrick, Douglas.**
The Stamp Bug: An Illustrated Introduction to Stamp Collecting, by Douglas Patrick and Mary Patrick. Toronto: McGraw-Hill Ryerson, 1978. 95p. ill., plates. ISBN 0-07-082779-6 $8.95

1. Postage-stamps – Collectors and collecting.

A highly readable, attractively presented introduction to the many aspects of stamp collecting. Patrick is an authority in the field, and has written a stamp column for the Toronto "Globe and Mail" for many years. The book should appeal to young people and adults. A glossary is included. Annemarie Toth

5168 769'.569
**Morin, Cimon N.**
Canadian Philately: Bibliography and Index, 1864-1973. Philatélie canadienne: Bibliographie et index, 1864-1973. Ottawa: National Library of Canada, 1979. 281p. ill. Indexes. ISBN 0-660-50175-9 pa.: $9.80 DSS cat. no. SN3-108/1979

1. Postage-stamps – Canada – Bibliography.
2. Postmarks – Canada – Bibliography.
3. Postal service – Canada – History – Bibliography.

An inventory of Canadian philatelic works, it "brings together the body of literature dealing with the postage stamp, postal stationery, postal history and postal markings". Includes 3481 entries for monographs, brochures, specialized catalogues and auction catalogues and articles. Author and subject indexes. Diane Henderson

## 769.9 Eskimo prints

5169 769.92'4

**Stewart, Hilary.**

Robert Davidson, Haida Printmaker. Vancouver: Douglas & McIntyre, 1979. 117p. ill. ISBN 0-88894-242-7 $24.95

1. Davidson, Robert, 1946- 2. Printmakers – British Columbia – Biography. 3. Haida Indians – Art.

Robert Davidson is a young Northwest Coast Indian who is following the traditions and revitalizing the heritage of his ancestors through his work as an artist. Davidson's artistic strengths as a silkscreen printmaker are powerfully presented through text and reproductions. Stewart traces his development as an artist, carver, jeweller and principally, printmaker, placing his work within the social framework from which it emerged. Andrea Trudel

5170 769.9'719

**National Museum of Man.**

The Inuit Print: A Travelling Exhibition of the National Museum of Man, National Museums of Canada and the Department of Indian and Northern Affairs. L'estampe inuit: Une exposition itinérante du Musée national de l'homme, Musée nationaux du Canada et du Ministère des affaires indiennes et du Nord. Ottawa: National Museum of Man, c1977. 267p. ill., map. Bibliography: p. 266. ISBN 0-660-00082-2 pa.: $12.95 DSS cat. no. NM 92-58/1977

1. Eskimos – Canada – Art. 2. Prints, Eskimo.

The first 20 years of Inuit printmaking are attractively displayed in this bilingual exhibition catalogue. The development of Inuit printmaking is traced in concise commentary; representative works from 5 communities are reproduced. English and French captions identify the artist, the size and medium of 155 reproductions. An important survey illustrative of the richness of Inuit graphic art.

## 770 Photography and photographs

5171 770.

**Greenhill, Ralph Ackland.**

Canadian Photography, 1839-1920, by Ralph Ackland Greenhill and Andrew Birrell. Toronto: Coach House Press, c1979. 171p. ill. ISBN 0-88910-134-5 $27.50

1. Photography – Canada – History – 19th century. 2. Photography – Canada – History – 20th century. 3. Photographers – Canada – History. 4. Canada – Description and Travel – Views.

A revised and slightly expanded version of Green's *Early Photography in Canada*, published in 1965, but out of print for several years. More than one hundred excellent duatone plates complement the historical perspective of the text. An important and authoritative work for college and public libraries. Jan Greenwood

5172 770.

**Patterson, Freeman.**

Photography and the Art of Seeing. Toronto: Van Nostrand Reinhold, c1979. 156p. ill. ISBN 0-44229-780-7 $24.95

1. Photography.

The author of *Photography for the Joy of It* stresses the importance of careful observation, imagination and good visual design in creative photography. Patterson illustrates his techniques with some sixty colour photographs and analytic commentary. For technically competent photographers. College, school and public libraries.

5173 770'.28

**Patterson, Freeman.**

Photography for the Joy of It. Toronto: Van Nostrand Reinhold, 1977. 168p. ill. Index. ISBN 0-442-29883-8 bd.: $19.95
ISBN 0-442-29893-5 pa.: $9.95

1. Photography.

The well-written, clearly organized text interspersed with beautiful and instructive photographs taken by the author should inspire near-novice and experienced photographer alike. Includes index and bibliographical note. Jan Greenwood

5174 778.5'3'0924
**Reid, Alison.**
Richard Leiterman. Ottawa: Canadian Film Institute, c1978. 120p. ill., ports. Bibliography: p. 118-119. (Canadian Film Series) ISBN 0-919096-02-6 $5.50
1. Leiterman, Richard.
A discussion and analysis of the work of one of Canada's most well-known cinematographers, and a rambling interview with Leiterman in which he discusses the development of his career, his feelings about film-making, and problems he has encountered on various projects. Includes filmography and bibliography. Janice Zlatarits

5175 779'.092'4
**Resnick, Marcia.**
Re-visions. Toronto: Coach House Press, 1978. 100p. ill. ISBN 0-88910-080-2 pa.: $9.95
1. Photography, Erotic.
One woman's view of the feminine rites of passage is presented with humour, artistry and some eroticism in the sparse, tongue-in-cheek text and black and white photographs of Marcia Resnick. Jan Greenwood

5176 779'.2'0924
**Harper, Jennifer,** comp.
City Work at Country Prices: The Portrait Photographs of Duncan Donovan. Toronto: Oxford University Press, 1977. 64p. ill., ports. ISBN 0-19-540275-8 pa.: $6.95
1. Photography – Portraits. 2. Donovan, Duncan, 1857-1933.
Fifty-three photographs of the residents of Glengarry County, Ontario between the years 1901-1921 have been selected by a Montreal photographer and photographic historian. Reproduced in duotone they are numbered and indexed. The introductory text traces Donovan's professional career and assesses its significance within the context of his era. Jan Greenwood

5177 779'.2'0924
**Karsh, Yousuf.**
Karsh Canadians. Toronto: University of Toronto Press, c1978. 203p. ports. ISBN 0-8020-2317-7 $27.50
1. Photography – Portraits. 2. Canada – Biography – Portraits.
Seventy-nine photographic portraits of creative and performing artists, authors, scientists, churchmen, politicians and athletes taken since 1932. Arranged alphabetically, each full-page black and white photograph is dated and accompanied by Karsh's informal impressions of his subject. Beautifully reproduced studies of distinguished Canadians.

5178 779'.4
**Clery, Val.**
Doors. Photographs by Gordon Beck and others. Toronto: Macmillan, c1978. 150p. ill. ISBN 0-7705-1737-4 pa.: $9.95
1. Doors. 2. Doorways. 3. Photography, Artistic.
This companion volume to the author's *Windows* explores another aspect of wall openings. The photographs express a certain social and historical analysis about this work, introducing various forms, decorations, uses and contexts in which doors come to play a part. High quality colour photographs are combined with a descriptive text in an imaginative and pleasant fashion. Andrea Trudel

5179 779'.4
**Clery, Val.**
Windows. Photographs by Gordon Beck and others. Toronto: Macmillan, c1978. 150p. ill. ISBN 0-7705-1583-5 pa.: $8.95
1. Photography, Artistic. 2. Windows.
Windows are portrayed in exquisite colour photographs as not only expressing men's desire to gaze upon the world outside of their homes, but as symbols of the social world of those men. This collection of 150 full-colour photographs is accompanied by thoughtful and perceptive text. Andrea Trudel

5180 779'.9
**Harmon, Carole,** ed.
Great Days in the Rockies: The Photographs of Byron Harmon, 1906-1934. Edited by Carole Harmon and the Peter Whyte Foundation; with a biography by Bart Robinson and an appreciation by Jon Whyte. Toronto: Oxford University Press, 1978. 109p. ill., ports. ISBN 0-19-540288-X $14.95
1. Harmon, Byron, 1876-1934. 2. Photography, Artistic. 3. Rocky Mountains, Canadian – Description and travel – Views.
Eighty-six black and white prints have been selected as representative of the photographic art of the distinguished alpine photographer. A biographical portrait and a note of appreciation are testimony to almost thirty years of recording the beauty of the mountains on film. The book should bring pleasure to those with an interest in

photography or Canadian history. Jan Greenwood.

5181 779'.9
**Sugino, Shin.**
The Rockies: High Where the Wind Is Lonely. Text by Jon Whyte. Toronto: Gage Publishing, c1978. 96p. ill. ISBN 0-7715-9326-0 bd.: $8.95 ISBN 0-7715-9327-9 pa.

1. Photography, Artistic. 2. Rocky Mountains, Canadian – Description and travel – Views.

The talents of an award-winning photographer and a poet from Banff have been combined to relate this history of the Rocky Mountains and those who have explored them. Jan Greenwood

5182 779'.9'3
**Cunningham, Imogen.**
After Ninety. Introduction by Margaretta Mitchell. Vancouver: J. J. Douglas, 1977. 111p. ill., ports. Bibliography: p. 109. ISBN 0-88894-150-1 $16.95

1. Aged – Portraits. 2. Photography, Artistic.

A stunning collection of black and white photographs pays moving tribute to the aged and reveals much of Cunningham's own overwhelming commitment to life and humanity during her ninety-third and last year. An introductory biographical essay includes photographs of the feisty lady herself. Selected bibliography and list of plates. Jan Greeenwood

## 780 Music

5183 780.7
**Wilson, Renate.**
For the Love of Music: A Guide for the Parents of Young Musicians. Vancouver: Douglas & McIntyre, c1978. 167p. ill., diagrs., plates. Bibliography: p. 161-163. Index. ISBN 0-88894-214-1 pa.: $7.95

1. Music – Instruction and study – Canada. 2. Music – Analysis, appreciation. 3. Music – Canada.

Information on music schools, careers in music, festivals, competitions and examinations are included in this rather general guide to music. There are errors of both omission and commission and some of the material is now outdated. Moderately helpful, but to be used advisedly. Don Sedgwick

5184 780'.8
**Schafer, Raymond Murray,** ed.
Ezra Pound and Music: The Complete Criticism. Toronto: McClelland and Stewart, 1978. 530p. ill. Index. ISBN 0-8112-0668-8 $42

1. Music. 2. Pound, Ezra, 1885-1972.

Edited by the Canadian composer, this excellent book brings together for the first time all of Pound's writings about music. Literary and music scholars will appreciate the poet's acerbic style and may look forward to a second volume to be devoted to his musical composition. Includes index and a glossary of musical personalities. Jan Greenwood

5185 780'.9
**Menuhin, Yehudi.**
The Music of Man, by Yehudi Menuhin and Curtis W. Davis. Toronto: Methuen, 1979. Bibliography. Index. ISBN 0-458-93830-0 $19.95

1. Music – History and criticism.

A highly illustrated history of music from the prehistoric period to the present, *The Music of Man* is based on the lengthy television series of the same name. Written by two renowned figures in the field, it provides a good general overview but not a comprehensive history. Don Sedgwick

5186 780'.92'2
**Bradley, Ian L.**
Twentieth Century Canadian Composers. Victoria: University of Victoria, c1977- v music, ports. Bibliography: p. 218-221. Discography: p. 221-222. ISBN 0-88874-052-2 bd.: $16.95

A biographical sketch and an analysis of several works are provided for ten prominent composers including Healey Willan, Sir Ernest MacMillan, Harry Freedman, and R. Murray Schafer. A non-critical, general text suitable for secondary school and first year university students. Includes a bibliography, a glossary of musical terms and a discography. Don Sedgwick

5187 781.97
**Bradley, Ian L.**
A Selected Bibliography of Musical Canadiana. Rev. ed. Victoria: University of Victoria, c1976. 177p. ISBN 0-88874-050-6 bd.: $19.95

1. Music – Canada – Bibliography.

The first edition was listed in *CS* no. 2074.

Approximately seven hundred new entries

have been added to this revised and updated edition. Invaluable as a reference and research text. Don Sedgwick

5188 782.8'1'2
**Ursell, Geoffrey.**
Superwheel. Script by Rex Deverell; songs by Geoffrey Ursell. Moose Jaw, Sask.: Coteau Books, 1979. 72p. ill., ports.
ISBN 0-919926-07-X pa.: $5

1. Musical revues, comedies, etc. – Librettos.
2. Traffic safety – Drama.

A play about cars, their function and their style, *Superwheel* is a humorous and entertaining musical originally produced for a high school audience. Hilary Elliott

## 784 Vocal music

5189 784.3'06'1
**Byrne, Pat,** ed.
The Ryan's Fancy Song and Other Stuff Book. St. John's, Nfld.: Breakwater Books, 1977. 122p. ill., music, ports.
ISBN 0-919948-26-X pa.: $6

1. Ryan's Fancy (Musical group). 2. Music, Popular (Songs, etc.).

A lively collection of traditional and contemporary songs and stories influenced by the Irish popular idiom and the folklore of Canada's east coast. Melody, chords and lyrics for thirty-one songs. Includes a history of Ryan's Fancy and a discography. Don Sedgwick

5190 784.4'9'4114
**Fergusson, Donald A.,** ed.
From the Farthest Hebrides. Bho na h-innse gall as iomallaiche. Gaelic editor, Aonaghus Iain MacDhomhnuil; musical editor, Jean F. Gillespie London. Toronto: Macmillan, 1978. 321p. ill. Bibliography: p. 316-318. Index.
ISBN 0-7705-1342-5 $25

1. Folk-songs, Gaelic – Scotland – Hebrides.

Thorough research, attractive presentation and fascinating material make this one of the finest Canadian books on folk music published in recent years. Music for 108 Gaelic songs, accompanied by original texts and contemporary translations. A wealth of material about folklore, mythology, history and folk music. Bibliography and index of first lines. Don Sedgwick

5191 784.4'971
**Usher, Bill,** ed.
"For What Time I Am in This World": Stories from Mariposa. Edited by Bill Usher and Linda Page-Harpa. Toronto: Peter Martin, 1977. 226p. ill., music, ports. Bibliography: p. 219-221. Discography: p. 221. Index. ISBN 0-88778-166-7 bd.: $15
ISBN 0-88778-167-5 pa.: $8.95

1. Mariposa Folk Festival. 2. Music – Anecdotes, facetiae, satire, etc.

Essentially an oral history of the Mariposa Folk Festival, *For What Time I Am in This World* also celebrates the lives and musical traditions of the common folk. Stories and reminiscences of past participants are accompanied by numerous illustrations, some in colour. An important document in the history of North American folk music. Don Sedgwick

5192 784.4'9'711
**Thomas, Phil J.**
Songs of the Pacific Northwest. Saanichton, B.C.: Hancock House, 1979. Bibliography. Index. ISBN 0-919654-89-4 $17.95

1. Folk-songs, Canadian – British Columbia.
2. Music, Popular (Songs, etc.) – British Columbia.

The life of the British Columbia people is depicted in an important collection of folk songs. Copious notes and photographs provide fascinating background for each of the forty-nine songs. Melodies, lyrics, and guitar and piano chords are included for each selection. An index of titles and first lines. Don Sedgwick

5193 784.4'9718
**Ryan, Shannon,** comp.
Haulin' Rope and Gaff. Compiled by Shannon Ryan and Larry Small. St. John's, Nfld.: Breakwater Books, c1978. 176p. ill., maps, music, port. Bibliography: p. 173-176. Index. (Folklore & Folklife) (Studies of the Newfoundland and Labrador Fishery: Historical and Cultural Series)
ISBN 0-919948-53-7 bd.: $13.95
ISBN 0-919948-52-9 pa.: $6.95

1. Sealing – Newfoundland – Songs and music.

Over ninety songs and numerous photographs document the controversial Newfoundland sealing industry from 1867 to the present. In addition to its musical value, *Haulin' Rope and Gaff* is also a valuable historic document which will interest students of folklore. Maps, bibliography, notes, title and first line indexes. Don Sedgwick

5194 784.6'8'94053
**Hopkins, Anthony.**
Songs From the Front and Rear: Canadian Servicemen's Songs of the Second World War. Edmonton: Hurtig Publishers 1979. 192p. ISBN 0-88830-172-3 bd.: $18.95 ISBN 0-88830-171-5 pa.: $12.95

1. World War, 1939-1945 – Songs and music, Canadian.

Words and music for more than 120 humorous and often bawdy songs have been collected by the co-editor of "The English Quarterly". Not intended for children or those offended by raunchy language. Don Sedgwick

5195 784.9'3'0924
**McCullagh, Harold.**
The Man Who Made New Brunswick Sing. St. Stephen, N.B.: Print'N Press, c1978. 97p. ill., plates, port. ISBN 0-920732-08-9 pa.: $4.95

1. Thomson, David, 1895- 2. Conductors (Music) – New Brunswick – Biography. 3. Music teachers – New Brunswick – Biography.

The life and works of David Thomson, the New Brunswick choral director, adjudicator, teacher and provincial supervisor of music. An interesting story, but somewhat limited in its scope and appeal. Don Sedgwick

5196 785'.092'4
**Cline, Beverly Fink.**
The Lombardo Story. Don Mills, Ont.: Musson, 1979. 158p. ill., ports. Index. Discography: p. 153. ISBN 0-7737-0042-0 $10.95

1. Lombardo, Guy, 1902-1977. 2. Lombardo family. 3. Lombardo, Carmen, 1903-1971 – Bibliography. 4. Royal Canadians (Musical group). 5. Musicians – Canada – Biography.

The author provides a personal look at the legendary Canadian bandleader, complete with photographs, some published for the first time, and a discography. A well-researched, though somewhat nostalgic biography. Don Sedgwick

5197 785'.092'4
**Robinson, Paul.**
Solti. Discography by Bruce Surtees. Toronto: Lester and Orpen, 1979. 168p. plates, ports. Bibliography: p. 165. Discography: p. 151-164. Index. (The Art of the Conductor) ISBN 0-919630-72-3 $9.95

1. Solti, Georg, Sir, 1912- 2. Conductors (Music) – Biography.

Robinson adopts a slightly more critical stance in his study of the fiery leader of the Chicago Symphony. Another well-researched biography with a first-class discography. Don Sedgwick

5198 785'.092'4
**Robinson, Paul.**
Stokowski. Discography by Bruce Surtees. Toronto: Lester and Orpen, c1977. 154p. ill., plates, ports., music. Bibliography: p. 121. Discography: p. 123-152. Index. (The Art of the Conductor) ISBN 0-354-04232-7 $8.95

1. Stokowski, Leopold, 1882-1977.
2. Conductors (Music) – United States – Biography.

Robinson chronicles the life and work of the eccentric and innovative conductor of the Philadelphia Orchestra in the second volume of "The Art of the Conductor" series. Includes a comprehensive discography. Don Sedgwick

5199 786.1'092'4
**Payzant, Geoffrey.**
Glenn Gould, Music and Mind. Toronto: Van Nostrand Reinhold, 1978. 192p. ill., plates, ports. Bibliography: p. 173-175. Discography: p. 177-183. Filmography: p. 176. Index. ISBN 0-442-29802-1 $14.95

1. Gould, Glenn, 1932-

A somewhat philosophical look at Canada's most renowned and intriguing pianist. Includes biographical material, essays on Gould's aesthetics and a critique of his performing style. Photographs, a bibliography, and a discography. Don Sedgwick

5200 787'.1'0924
**Adaskin, Harry.**
A Fiddler's World. Vancouver: November House, 1977- v ill., facsims., ports. ISBN 0-920156-02-0 $14.95

1. Violinists, violoncellists, etc. – Canada – Biography.

Contents: vol. 1. Memoirs to 1938. 1977.

Broadcaster and violinist Harry Adaskin traces his early career as one of the Hart House Quartet, a Canadian ensemble which achieved international recognition. Filled with personal anecdotes, humorous asides and the author's own philosophical musings. Don Sedgwick

## 790 Recreational and performing arts

5201 791.1'092
**Elves, Hazel.**
It's All Done with Mirrors: A Story of Canadian Carnival Life. Victoria: Sono Nis Press, 1977. 131p. ill., plates, ports. ISBN 0-919462-35-9 pa.: $3.95

1. Amusement parks. 2. Circus – Canada.

Canadian carnival life is described in a breezy, colloquial style by a woman who grew up in a "carnie" family. Undemanding leisure reading for young people and adults.

## 791.4 Motion pictures, radio, television

5202 791.404
**Canadian Film Digest Yearbook.**
Toronto: Film Publications, 1979. Annual. 199p. Spiral binding.

1. Moving-picture industry – Canada – Directories. 2. Moving-picture industry – Canada – Yearbooks. 3. Moving-picture theatres – Canada – Directories.

A key reference book for the Canadian film industry. Published annually, it includes directories of film-makers, production and distribution companies, studios, labs, theatres across Canada, film institutes, courses, co-operatives, publications, awards, festivals, TV networks, etc., as well as a list of films currently in production and release, and statistics of the industry. Janice Zlatarits.

5203 791.43'01
**Harcourt, Peter.**
Movies and Mythologies: Towards a National Cinema. Toronto: Canadian Broadcasting Corporation, c1977. 171p. Bibliographies. ISBN 0-88794-080-3 pa.: $3.95

1. Canadian Broadcasting Corporation.

Based upon his series of eight broadcasts prepared for CBC in 1975, Harcourt, a film critic, deplores the long-term exposure of Canadian audiences to American cinematic styles and values and pleads for the development of Canadian cinema. For readers concerned about the future of Canadian cinema. College and public libraries.

5204 791.43'023
**Beveridge, James A.,** comp.
John Grierson, Film Master. Toronto: Macmillan, 1978. 361p. ill., ports. Index. ISBN 0-02-510530-2 $17.95

1. Grierson, John, 1898-1972. 2. Grierson (Motion picture). 3. Moving-picture producers and directors – Great Britain – Biography.

The primary source materials, correspondance, speeches, film clips, melded so effectively in the 1973 film honouring the founder of the National Film Board, are the basis for this print tribute. Through recollections of film-makers around the world the dynamic Scot and his influence on visual communication comes vibrantly to life. For all libraries.

5205 791.43'023
**Hardy, Forsyth.**
John Grierson: A Documentary Biography. Toronto: Oxford University Press, 1979. 298p. ill. Index. ISBN 0-571-10331-6 $27.95

1. Grierson, John, 1898-1972. 2. Moving-pictures, Documentary – Production and direction.

The achievements of the innovative Scot known as the father of the documentary film, and the first director of the National Film Board, are assessed by a long-time friend and film critic. Hardy offers a detailed, carefully researched and readable biography covering Grierson's contribution to film and television on three continents. Chapter notes and fifty-one photographs support the narrative. College and public libraries.

5206 791.43'0233
**Handling, Piers.**
The Films of Don Shebib. Ottawa: Canadian Film Institute, c1978. 148p. ill., ports. Bibliography: p. 140-147. (Canadian Film Series) ISBN 0-919096-01-8 pa.: $5.95

1. Shebib, Don, 1938-

A thorough, eighty-page analysis of a well-known Canadian film-maker's work, and a forty-page interview in which Shebib discusses his films and his experiences in the industry. Included are a Shebib filmography, a bibliography of articles and reviews of his work, and still photographs from his films. Janice Zlatarits

5207 791.43'02'9
**Colombo, John Robert.**
Colombo's Hollywood. Don Mills, Ont.: William Collins, 1979. 192p. Index. ISBN 0-00-216606-2 $8.95

1. Moving-pictures – Quotations, maxims, etc.

An entertaining collection of three thousand remarks and observations made by the greats of the motion picture industry. The chapter on malapropisms of Sam Goldwyn is a gem. Lack of an index makes this work difficult to use. Annemarie Toth.

5208 791.43'09
**Yost, Elwy.**
Magic Moments from the Movies. Toronto: Doubleday, 1978. 246p. ill., plates. Index. ISBN 0-385-13691-9 $9.95

1. Moving-pictures – Miscellanea.

Written with unbounded enthusiasm this book will have more appeal for fans of television's inimitable movie host than for those with a serious interest in the subject. 150 films are discussed in chronological order and the text is interspersed with black and white illustrations. Index of film titles. Jan Greenwood

5209 791.43'0971
**Feldman, Seth,** ed.
Canadian Film Reader. Edited by Seth Feldman and Joyce Nelson. Toronto: Peter Martin, c1977. 405p. Bibliography: p. 388-400. Index. ISBN 0-88778-158-6 bd.: $15 ISBN 0-88778-159-4 pa.: $6.95

1. Moving-pictures – Canada – History.
2. Moving-pictures – Canada.

Expository and critical articles by film-makers, critics and academics survey the Canadian film industry from its beginnings, through the influence of the National Film Board, the growth of the feature film industry and experimental film-making. A useful and authoritative anthology for film courses and general reading.

5210 791.43'0971
**Knelman, Martin.**
This Is Where We Came In: The Career and Character of Canadian Film. Toronto: McClelland and Stewart, c1977. 176p. Index. ISBN 0-7710-4533-6 pa.: $5.95

1. Moving-pictures – Canada.

A brief, descriptive overview of the development of the feature film industry from the heyday of the documentary to the seventies. Knelman, a film critic, comments upon the major feature films, well-known Canadian film-makers, and film-making in French and in English Canada. Based upon interviews and previously published film reviews. Anecdotal, easy to read.

5211 791.43'0971
**Morris, Peter.**
Embattled Shadows: A History of Canadian Cinema, 1895-1939. Montreal: McGill-Queen's University Press, c1978. 350p. ill., ports. Filmography: p. 251-273. Bibliographical references and Indexes. ISBN 0-7735-0322-6 bd.: $19.95 ISBN 0-7735-0323-4 pa.: $7.95

1. Moving-pictures – Canada – History.

This authoritative, well-documented and colourful account of the previously unrecorded history of the Canadian film industry prior to the foundation of the Canadian Film Board should appeal to lovers of film and those with a special interest in Canadian history. Ilustrated with production stills, posters and portraits. Jan Greenwood

5212 791.43'0973
**Jowett, Garth.**
Film: The Democratic Art. 1st ed. Toronto: Little, Brown, c1976. 518p. Bibliography: p. 487-505. Index. (The American Film Institute Series) ISBN 0-316-47370-7 $19.95

1. Moving-pictures – United States.
2. Moving-pictures – Social aspects.

An extensive sociological analysis of the impact of film on North American society, based on the history of American cinema. Includes discussion of film content, audiences, censorship, production, the phenomenon of Hollywood, and the impact of television. Valuable to academics but also very readable for film buffs. Tables, bibliography, and index. Janice Zlatarits

5213 791.4'38
**Worsnop, Brenda M.,** ed.
The Film Users' Guide to Canadian Short Films. Edited by Brenda M. Worsnop and Chris M. Worsnop. Mississauga, Ont.: Wright Communications, 1979. 624p. ISBN 0-920028-44-6 $13.50 vol. 1.

1. Moving-pictures – Canada. 2. Moving-pictures – Catalogues.

Volume 2 is in preparation for publication in 1981.

Reviews of some four hundred films, most of which have appeared in the Ontario Film Association's "A Newsletter Called Fred", are listed alphabetically. Technical data, a descriptive paragraph and a critique, which suggests audience interest and the use of the film, are included in each review. There is a subject index and a list of distributors. For all film collections.

5214 791.45'7
**Rowland, Wade.**
Making Connections. Agincourt, Ont.: Gage Publishing, c1979. 226p. ill.
ISBN 0-7715-9442-9 $10.95

1. Connections (Television program). 2. Television – Canada – Production and direction – Case studies. 3. Television broadcasting of news – Canada.

Canadians who were chilled by the inroads of organized crime in Canada as revealed in the two ninety minute television documentaries, "Connections", will be fascinated by the exploits of the three-man team which gathered the material upon which the programmes were based. A briskly-paced, engrossing account of modern investigative journalism.

## 792 Theatre

5215 792'.016
**Ball, John L.,** ed.
The Bibliography of Canadian Theatre History: Supplement, 1975-1976. Edited by John Ball and Richard Plant. Toronto: Playwrights Co-op, c1979. 75p. Index.
ISBN 0-88754-170-4 bd. ISBN 0-88754-136-4 pa.: $3.95

1. Theatre – Canada – History – Bibliography.

*A Bibliography of Canadian Theatre History, 1583-1975*, listed *CS* no. 2124.

This supplement is a valuable bibliographical addition for Canadian theatre historians. Indexed and illustrated with photographs, it contains twelve hundred new entries. Hilary Elliott

5216 792'.0226
**Doolittle, Joyce.**
A Mirror of Our Dreams: Children and the Theatre in Canada, by Joyce Doolittle and Zina Barnieh; with a chapter on theatre in Québec by Hélène Beauchamp. Vancouver: Talonbooks, 1979. 214p. ill. Bibliography: p. 188-197. Index. ISBN 0-88922-161-8 pa.: $6.95

1. Children's plays – Presentation, etc. – Canada.

This history of children's theatre in Canada includes information about children's plays and their presentation, concepts of childhood, television, and education. A bibliography of titles and authors is also provided. Hilary Elliott

5217 792'.07'1
**Kemp, David.**
Theatre for Young Audiences, by David Kemp and Eva Russel. Toronto: Simon & Pierre Publishing, 1979. 180p.
ISBN 0-88924-043-4 bd.: $9.95
ISBN 0-88924-062-0 pa.: $6.95

1. Theatre – Canada.

This book includes an overview of the types of children's theatre, a section for those involved in theatre, philosophies of all the major companies, a critical assessment of the companies, and an analysis of the methods of funding, the relationship between theatre and education, and the future. Hilary Elliott

5218 792.07'17
**A Directory of Canadian Theatre Schools.**
Edited by Don Rubin and Allison Cranmer-Byng. Downsview, Ont.: CTR Publications, c1979. 52p. ill.
ISBN 0-92064-471-6 pa.: $2.50

1. Acting – Study and teaching – Canada – Directories. 2. Theatre – Study and teaching – Canada – Directories.

One of a series of service booklets, this directory lists conservatories, graduate and undergraduate theatre programs, community colleges, dramatic arts studios, and mime schools, a total of eighty schools, offering theatre training. The booklet brings together basic information such as address and program description for the person interested in studying theatre. Hilary Elliott

5219 792.0971
**Canadian Theatre Checklist.**
Edited by Don Rubin and Mimi Mekler. 1979-80 ed. Downsview, Ont.: CTR Publications, 1979. 47p. ISBN 0-920644-64-3 pa.: $2.50

1. Theatre – Canada – Directories.

The third edition of this checklist is expanded to cover Canada's more than 170 theatre companies. This booklet provides address, phone number, names of personnel, theatre type, seating capacity, year of founding, union status, an overview of the theatre's philosophy and program and a "Useful Addresses" section which includes theatre suppliers. Hilary Elliott

5220 792.0971
**Rubin, Don,** ed.
Canada on Stage: Canadian Theatre Review Yearbook 1978. Downsview, Ont.: CTR Publications, 1978. Annual. 438p. ill. Index. ISBN 0-920644-06-6 $16.95

1. Theatre – Canada – Yearbooks.

Continues *Canadian Theatre Review Yearbook.*

The fifth edition in the series, this reference book documents professional stage activity in Canada on a province-by-province basis for 1978. Included are a 6,000 entry index, six overview critical essays, performance records for over 160 theatres, and photographs. Hilary Elliott

5221 792'.0973
**Shaw, Grace Lydiatt.**
Stratford Under Cover: Memories on Tape. Foreword by Harry J. Boyle. Toronto: NC Press, 1977. 126p. ill., ports.
ISBN 0-919600-68-9 bd.: $20
ISBN 0-919600-67-0 pa.: $9.95

1. Stratford Festival – History.

Published in honour of the twenty-fifth season of the Canadian Stratford Festival, this oral history traces the development of the Stratford theatre from the first ideas and small beginnings to the present reality through the words of directors, producers, designers, and actors such as Tyrone Guthrie and Dora Mavor Moore. Hilary Elliott

5222 792.8
**Crabb, Michael,** ed.
Visions, Ballet and Its Future. Foreword by Frederick Ashton; introduction by Vincent Tovell. Toronto: Simon & Pierre Publishing, 1979. Bibliography. Index. ISBN 0-88924-079-5 pa.: $8.95

1. Ballet – Congresses. 2. Ballet – Canada – Congresses.

In this selection of the major speeches given at the National Ballet of Canada's 25th Anniversary Conference held in Toronto in 1976, each chapter is preceded by a well-written summary and followed by indications of audience reaction. Non-technical language and biographical notes on the contributors will appeal to the general reader. Merike Koger

5223 792.8'08
**Jackson, Graham.**
Dance as Dance: Selected Reviews and Essays. Drawings by Albert Forister. Scarborough, Ont.: Catalyst, c1978. 128p. ill. Bibliographical references and Index.
ISBN 0-920000-22-3 pa.: $6.95

1. Ballet. 2. Ballet – Reviews.

A collection of sixty reviews and articles by the Toronto dance critic reflect the heightened interest in dance in the Toronto area in the last decade. Stressing eroticism in dance, his impressions, mostly of ballet performances, and the stinging criticisms delivered in bold, provocative language, make for consistently lively reading. For dance aficionados. Merike Koger

5224 792.8'092
**Darling, Christopher.**
Kain & Augustyn: A Photographic Study. Text by John Fraser. Toronto: Macmillan, 1977. 160p. ill., ports. ISBN 0-7705-1622-X bd.: $14.95 ISBN 0-7705-1612-2 pa.: $4.95

1. Kain, Karen, 1951- – Portraits, etc.
2. Augustyn, Frank, 1953- – Portraits, etc.
3. Ballet – Pictorial works.

An admiring tribute to two young National Ballet of Canada dancers whose talent has gained international recognition. Fraser briefly summarizes their background and training, Darling captures their artistry in some 150 fine photographs, the dancers' reflections on ballet add the personal perspective. The introduction is by Rudolf Nureyev. School and public libraries.

5225 792.8'092
**Street, David.**
Karen Kain: Lady of Dance. Text by David Mason. Toronto: McGraw-Hill Ryerson, 1978. 127p. ill., ports. ISBN 0-07-082705-2 $14.95

1. Kain, Karen, 1951- – Portraits, etc.

A visually beautiful portrait of Canada's talented young ballerina in rehearsal, on stage and at leisure. Multi-exposure colour shots and black and white photographs will give pleasure to ballet devotees of all ages. Street's adulatory narrative affords glimpses of the dancer's personality and motivation. Recommended for junior high to adult readers.

5226 792.8'0971
**Bell, Ken.**
The National Ballet of Canada: A Celebration. Photographs by Ken Bell and a memoir by Celia Franca. Toronto: University of Toronto Press, c1978. 284p. ill., plates, ports. ISBN 0-8020-2303-7 $24.95

1. National Ballet of Canada – History.

The artistic director who, for a quarter of a century shared the vicissitudes of a fledgling ballet group, has collaborated with an outstanding photographer in a salute to the company's maturity. The difficulties and successes are recalled in a chatty, candid narrative; excellent photographs form a pleasing visual history. For everyone who enjoys ballet and fine photography.

5227 792.8'0971
**Wyman, Max.**
The Royal Winnipeg Ballet, The First Forty Years. Toronto: Doubleday, 1978. 275p. ill., ports. Index. ISBN 0-385-14009-6 $17.95

1. Royal Winnipeg Ballet – History.

The theatre and dance critic for the 'Vancouver Sun' examines objectively the history, personalities and performance record of Canada's first ballet company. Based upon careful research the smoothly flowing narrative is supported by good quality photographs. A list of choreographers and their ballets, and a chronology enhance the book's reference value. Significant Canadiana.

5228 792.9
**Reaney, James.**
14 Barrels from Sea to Sea. Erin, Ont.: Press Porcépic, 1977. 176p. ill., ports. Bibliography: p. 176. ISBN 0-88878-150-4 bd.: $8.95 ISBN 0-88878-151-2 pa.: $4.95

1. Reaney, James, 1926- 2. NDWT Company. 3. Theatre – Canada.

Reaney's documentation of the NDWT company's cross-Canada tour with the Donnelly trilogy is rich with anecdotes and observations about the Canadian theatre scene. Reaney's qualities as accomplished story-teller, zealous historian and committed nationalist make him an admirable tour guide. Annette Wengle

## 793 Indoor games and amusements

5229 793.3'19'71
**Oxenham, Andrew.**
Dance Today in Canada, by Andrew Oxenham and Michael Crabb. Toronto: Simon & Pierre Publishing, 1977. 228p. ill. Index. ISBN 0-88924-059-0 $34.95

1. Dancing – Canada – Pictorial works.
2. Dancing – Canada – History.

Michael Crabb's overview of the history of dance in Canada and Andrew Oxenham's sensitive and beautiful photographs make this publication a very useful and informative work. However, the text is somewhat short and poorly integrated with the photographs. A second problem is the placement of the description of each photograph at the end of the book. Included are a list of Canadian dance companies and an index. Janice Zlatarits

## 796 Athletic and outdoor sports and games

5230 796.
**Bowering, George,** ed.
Great Canadian Sports Stories. Ottawa: Oberon Press, 1979. 147p. ISBN 0-88750-319-5 bd.: $12.95 ISBN 0-88750-320-9 pa.: $5.95

1. Sports.

A typically uneven collection of twelve previously published short stories with sports themes by such authors as Hugh Hood, Hugh Garner, Morley Callaghan, and Dave Godfrey. Women writers are not represented. Peter Moffet

5231 796'.01
**Shephard, Roy J.**
The Fit Athlete. Don Mills, Ont.: Oxford University Press, 1978. 214p. ill., graphs, port. Bibliographical references and Index. ISBN 0-19-217549-1 $11.95

1. Athletes. 2. Athletic ability. 3. Physical fitness. 4. Sports – Psychological aspects. 5. Sports – Physiological aspects.

This introduction to some of the complex factors impinging on the Olympic-level athlete is documented with scientific studies and several Canadian examples. It briefly covers the needs of different types of athletes, the handicapped and female contestants, and such current problems in sports as drugs and professionalism. For young adults planning careers in sports, and for coaches. Janet Frost

5232 796'.019'4
**Cochrane, Jean.**
Women in Canadian Sports, by Jean Cochrane, Abby Hoffman, and Pat Kincaid. Toronto: Fitzhenry & Whiteside, c1977. 96p. ill., ports. Bibliograhies and Index. (Women in Canadian Life) ISBN 0-88902-376-X pa.: $4.95

1. Sports for women – Canada.

The participation of women in sports from ancient times to the present is traced as a background to commentary on the accomplishments of outstanding Canadian women athletes. Well illustrated. Suggested study topics and bibliographies are geared to school use. Others in the same series and format: Dranoff, L. *Women in Canadian Life: Law;* McClung, M. G. *Women in Canadian Life: Literature.*

5233 796'.092'2
**Ferguson, Bob.**
Who's Who in Canadian Sport. Scarborough, Ont.: Prentice-Hall, c1977. 310p. Index. ISBN 0-13-958421-8 $10

1. Athletes – Canada – Biography. 2. Sports – Canada – Biography.

Short sketches of the great and not so great in Canadian sports are presented in Ferguson's book. One does not have to be Canadian nor to be great, to be included. For sports enthusiasts this will be a handy reference tool. Well-indexed, with cross references by sport to each entry. Paula de Ronde

5234 796'.0971
**The Corpus Almanac's Canadian Sports Annual.**
Toronto: Corpus Information Services, 1977. Annual. v ill. ISSN 0704-7274 $9.95

1. Sports – Canada – Yearbooks.

A handy source of information on organized sport in Canada. Outlines the role of government and associations as well as summarizing the history of over eighty sport governing bodies, mostly amateur, with their 1976 or 1977 champions. Includes a directory of sport associations; however, there are no plans to update it. Janet Frost

5235 796'.0971
**McRae, Earl.**
Requiem for Reggie and Other Great Sports Stories. Introduction by Trent Frayne. Toronto: Chimo Publishing, c1977. 149p. ISBN 0-920344-01-1 $9.95

1. Athletes – Canada. 2. Athletes – United States.

A collection of articles previously published in 'The Canadian' and 'Sport' magazine. Bobby Orr, George Chuvalo, Mark Fidrych, Derek Sanderson are some of the athletes profiled, not always in a flattering manner. Above average sports writing for adults. Peter Moffet

5236 796'.0971
**Patterson, Gerry.**
Behind the Superstars: The Business Side of Sports. Scarborough, Ont.: Prentice-Hall, c1978. 173p. ill., ports. ISBN 0-13-074153-1 $9.95

1. Professional sports – Canada.

The former business manager for such top stars as Gordie Howe, Nancy Green and Guy Lafleur relates his experiences with aspects such as player contract negotiations and commercial endorsements. Anecdotal style entertains but reveals few real secrets. Peter Moffet

5237 796.33'4
**Lebow, Jared.**
All About Soccer. Scarborough, Ont.: Prentice-Hall, 1978. 240p. ill. Index. ISBN 0-13-022236-4 $14.95

1. Soccer.

A comprehensive, lavishly illustrated work written with the North American sports fan in mind. Covers all aspects of the game: history, rules, soccer around the world, etc. Enough detail here to interest the more experienced fan. Little Canadian emphasis. Includes a glossary and index. Annemarie Toth

5238 796.33'5
**Gabriel, Tony.**
Double Trouble, by Tony Gabriel and Stanley Fillmore. Toronto: Gage Publishing, c1978. 199p. ill., plates. ISBN 0-7715-9382-1 $9.95

1. Football players – Canada – Biography.

Autobiography of the Ottawa Rough Rider tight end who has been named the outstanding Canadian player in the Canadian Football League three times. Includes a diary of the 1977 season plus the author's comparisons of Canadian and American football. Nothing exciting is revealed but a good read nonetheless. For teens and adults. Peter Moffet

5239 796.34'2
**Platt, Don.**
Tennis: Playing a Winning Game with Don Platt. Photography by Rick Radelja. Toronto: McGraw-Hill Ryerson, 1977. 103p. ill. ISBN 0-07-082511-4 pa.: $5.95

1. Tennis.

An accomplished Canadian tennis player presents the principal strokes in numerous black and white photographs. Emphasis is on his personal philosophy of simplicity, rhythm, and concentration. For those who are dissatisfied with their style and want another opinion. Janet Frost

5240 796.34'3
**McKay, Heather.**
Heather McKay's Complete Book of Squash, by Heather McKay and Jack Batten. Toronto: Macmillan, c1977. 143p. ill. ISBN 0-7705-1582-7 pa.: $5.95

1. Squash rackets (Game).

Frank insights into international court soft-ball squash by a world champion now living in Toronto. Stop-action black and white photographs clarify essential strokes for the beginner. Advice on strategy and diagrams of practice drills for the more skilled. Informally written so that it is both inspiring and enjoyable to read. Janet Frost

5241 796.352'02
**Huston, Mervyn J.,** ed.
Great Golf Humour: A Collection of Stories & Articles. Edmonton: Hurtig Publishers, c1977. 287p. ISBN 0-88830-141-3 $11.95

1. Golf – Anecdotes, facetiae, satire, etc.

For the golf enthusiast who has everything – an anthology of proverbial tall tales. Disappointing because truly funny moments are scattered through much inconsequential material. Janet Frost

5242 796.352'02
**Kiehl, Bob.**
Duffer Golf: Or, How to Break a Hundred. Illustrated by James Simpkins; introduction by Robert F. Nielson. Hamilton, Ont.: Potlatch Publications, c1979. 64p. ill. ISBN 0-919676-13-8 pa.: $3.95

1. Golf – Anecdotes, facetiae, satire, etc.

The absolute basics of the game are given for beginners by an amateur rather than by a professional player. Anecdotal in style and reassuring for the average, weekend golfer. Amusing illustrations. Peter Moffet

5243 796.4'1
**Hunn, David.**
The Complete Book of Gymnastics. Rexdale, Ont.: John Wiley, c1978. 200p. ill. Bibliography: p. 197. Index. ISBN 0-471-99804-4 $11.95

1. Gymnastics.

Contains a short history of the sport highlighting its popular breakthrough at the Olympics, brief biographies of major gymnasts, chapters on individual men's and women's exercises plus related sports such as trampolining. Excellent illustrations and competition results. No Canadian content. Peter Moffet

5244 796.4'1'092
**Boulogne, Jean.**
The Making of a Gymnast. Toronto: Macmillan, 1978. 96p. ill. ISBN 0-7705-1694-7 bd.: $11.95 ISBN 0-7705-1673-4 pa.: $5.95

1. Kelsall, Karen. 2. Gymnasts – Canada – Biography. 3. Gymnastics.

Karen Kelsall's career from beginner through contender to Canadian National Women's Gymnastics Champion is used as an inspirational example for young girls contemplating taking up this demanding sport. Lacks substance but good for intended audience and fans. Well illustrated. Peter Moffet

5245 796.4'26
**Batten, Jack.**
The Complete Jogger. Don Mills, Ont.: Musson; Markham, Ont.: PaperJacks, c1977. 145p. ill. Bibliography: p. 145. ISBN 0-7737-1014-0 pa.: $4.95 ISBN 0-7701-017-0 pa.: $1.95

1. Jogging.

A practical manual for those contemplating or already involved in this popular activity. Sensible advice complete with do's and don'ts is presented concisely and with enthusiasm. A first choice for adult collections. Peter Moffet

5246 796.5
**Berglund, Berndt.**
The Complete Guide to Orienteering in North America: A Comprehensive Manual for the Outdoorsman. Toronto: Pagurian Press, 1979. 160p. ill. ISBN 0-88932-101-9 pa.: $7.95

1. Orientation.

Drawing upon forty years of experience in Canada and Sweden, Berglund introduces map-reading, land navigation by compass, and the outdoor pleasures of recreational and competitive orienteering. Complemented by several drawings and photographs, a glossary and index. Good chapter on how to organize a meet. Janet Frost

5247 796.5

**Schuh, Dwight R.**

Modern Survival: Outdoor Gear and Savvy to Bring You Back Alive. Edmonton: Hurtig Publishers, 1979. Index. ISBN 0-88830-177-4 $11.95

1. Wilderness survival. 2. Outdoor life – Safety measures.

Not a manual but a coherent examination of some potential hazards in North American outdoor recreation. Offers reasonable solutions to emergency situations based on recent research, outdoor survival principles, and personal experience. Several Canadian references, with a good introduction to map and compass use and selective first-aid information. Janet Frost

5248 796.5'22

**Dowling, Phil.**

The Mountaineers: Famous Climbers in Canada. Edmonton: Hurtig Publishers, 1979. Index. ISBN 0-88830-170-7 $13.95

1. Mountaineers – Canada – Biography.

Biographical background and accounts of the most important climbs of the nine men and one woman the author, a Past President of the Alpine Club of Canada, considers the greatest climbers of Canada's mountains. Includes a glossary of mountaineering terms. For adults. Peter Moffet

5249 796.54

**Durst, Douglas.**

The Outdoorsman's Guide to Wilderness Camping: A Complete Manual for the Adventurous Camper, Including Plans for Tent Making and Camping in the Snow. Toronto: McGraw-Hill Ryerson, c1977. 186p. ill., diagrs. Bibliography: p. 185-186. ISBN 0-07-082539-4 pa.: $4.95

1. Camping.

From outfitting and trip planning to on-the-site campcraft, a common sense approach to basic tent camping in layman's terms. Tent-making patterns included for the advanced camper-sewer. Sections on winter camping and compass use need to be supplemented. Janet Frost

## 796.9 Ice and snow sports

5250 796.9'1

**Gross, George.**

Donald Jackson: King of Blades. Toronto: Queen City Publishing, 1977. 156p. ill., ports. ISBN 0-9690508-1-X $10.50

1. Jackson, Donald, 1940- 2. Skaters – Biography.

A simple, straightforward account of the hard work, failures and successes of a Canadian figure skating champion. The talented skater's progress is followed through the series of coaches who groomed him for success. A readable sports biography for young people.

5251 796.9'2

**Wolfram, Gerry.**

Walk into Winter: A Complete Guide to Snow-shoeing & Winter Camping. Rexdale, Ont.: John Wiley, c1977. 127p. ill., ports. ISBN 0-471-99777-3 bd.: $9.95
ISBN 0-471-99763-3 pa.: $5.95

1. Snowshoes and snowshoeing. 2. Snow camping.

A practical handbook on equipment selection and rudimentary skills written by a seasoned outdoorsman-journalist. Bonuses include a brief history of snowshoeing in Canada, many black and white photographs, and addresses of suppliers, recreation agencies and organizations. Author's personal style makes it pleasurable reading for young people and adults. Janet Frost

5252 796.9'3

**Athans, Greg.**

Ski Free. Photographs by Allan de la Plante. Toronto: Clarke, Irwin, 1978. 126p. ill., ports. ISBN 0-7720-1156-7 pa.: $7.95

1. Skis and skiing.

For the virtuoso skier, a free-style guide to mogul, ballet and aerial skiing. Annotated photographic segments of both fundamental and exotic manoeuvres, highlighted with spectacular colour photographs. Emphasis is on succinct description rather than instruction. Good tips on equipment, judging criteria, and off-season training camps. Janet Frost

5253 796.9′3
**Baldwin, Edward R.**
Skiing Cross Country. Toronto: McGraw-Hill Ryerson, 1977. 174p. ill. Bibliography: p. 173. ISBN 0-07-082490-8 pa.: $5.95

1. Cross-country skiing.

An excellent guide to the techniques of cross-country skiing, the equipment and the clothing required. Line drawings and photographs, and a glossary of terms supplement the easy-to-understand explanations. For both the novice and the committed enthusiast.

5254 796.9′3
**Keating, Michael.**
Cross-country Ontario. Foreword by Jack Rabbit Johannsen. Toronto: Van Nostrand Reinhold, 1979. 111p. ill. ISBN 0-442-29781-5 $3.95

1. Cross-country skiing – Ontario – Guide-books. 2. Ontario – Description and travel – Guide-books.

An up-to-date guide to over two hundred Ontario trails, and a handbook to cross-country skiing endorsed by the Canadian Ski Association. Though there is no index, much useful information is logically organized and skillfully presented in this slim volume. An Ontario counterpart to *Cross-country Canada*. Janet Frost

5255 796.93
**Rees, David.**
Cross-country Skiing: Touring and Competition. Rev. ed. Toronto: Copp Clark, 1977. 207p. ill. Index. ISBN 0-77304-031-5 pa.: $4.95

1. Cross-country skiing.

First edition listed in *CS* no. 2209.

A revised edition replacing a work first published in 1975. Cross-country skiing for fun and competitive cross-country skiing are discussed. Illustrated with photographs, clear diagrams and tables. For young people and adults.

5256 796.9′3
**Ritchie, David.**
Ski the Canadian Way. David Ritchie and members of the Canadian National Ski Team. Scarborough, Ont.: Prentice-Hall, 1979. ISBN 0-13-809780-1 $7.95

1. Canadian National Ski Team. 2. Ski racing.

A chronicle of the Canadian ski team's experience of current World Cup downhill competition. The book covers the exhilarating lifestyle and sophisticated technique, training and equipment. Photo-sequences of the team in action, and descriptions of seven courses including Lake Louise and Lake Placid, compensate for the mediocrity of the writing. Janet Frost

5257 796.93025
**Enzel, Robert G.**
The White Book of Ski Areas, United States and Canada, by Robert G. Enzel and John R. Urcioli. 3d. ed. Washington: Inter-ski Services, c1978. 410p. maps. ISBN 0-52884-635-3 $9.95

1. Skis and skiing – United States – Guide-books. 2. Winter resorts – United States – Guide-books.

This edition is the first to include Canadian ski areas. There are over two hundred, mostly for downhill skiing, and for each resort a questionnaire format displays brief information on conditions, rates, equipment rental, instruction, availability of accommodation, and travel directions with telephone numbers. Contains key maps, index, and a chapter on helicopter skiing. Janet Frost

5258 796.9′6
**Kalchman, Lois.**
Safety on Ice. Toronto: Totem Books, 1979. 153p. ill. Index. ISBN 0-00-216604-6 pa.: $9.95

1. Hockey – Safety measures.

A guide to hockey equipment emphasizing safety aspects. Also discusses common injuries, nutrition and conditioning, rink safety, girls and hockey. For parents and young hockey players. Author is a parent and a reporter on minor hockey for the "Toronto Star". Peter Moffet

5259 796.9′6
**Thiessen, Roy D.**
Curling Handbook: For Curlers, Teachers and Coaches. Saanichton, B.C.: Hancock House, 1977. 88p. ill. Bibliography: p. 88. ISBN 0-919654-71-1 pa.: $5.95

1. Curling.

From an explanation of curling terminology through the art of sweeping and game strategy, the reader is guided in this well-organized, easy-to-follow instructional manual. Illustrated with line drawings. A popular acquisition for school and public library sports collections.

5260 796.9'62
**Spencer, David.**
The New Professional Hockey Almanac: Histories of the NHL and Stanley Cup, Up-dated Records, Statistics and Results. Toronto: Pagurian Press, c1978. 192p. ill., ports. ISBN 0-88932-087-X pa.: $4.95

1. National Hockey League. 2. Hockey.

A brief historical background introduces a mass of statistical information concerning the National Hockey League. Covers team and individual records, regular season and Stanley Cup playoff figures, trophies, all-star teams and rules of the professional game. Useful for quick reference. Peter Moffet

5261 796.9'62
**Taylor, Joe.**
Lloyd Percival's Total Conditioning for Hockey. Toronto: Fitzhenry & Whiteside, c1978. 192p. ill. Bibliography: p. 191-192. ISBN 0-88902-439-1 $10.95

1. Hockey. 2. Exercise.

Percival's long-time collaborator updates his work with an exercise and training program for year-round fitness stressing total physical capacity. Primarily intended for coaches, it is also useful for the individual player. Peter Moffet

5262 796.9'62'016
**Thom, D. J.**
The Hockey Bibliography: Ice Hockey Worldwide, by D. J. Thom, Tom Watt and others. Toronto: Ontario Institute for Studies in Education; Ministry of Culture and Recreation, Ontario, 1978. 153p. ill. (OISE Bibliography Series) ISBN 0-7744-0166-4 pa.: $6.95

1. Hockey – Bibliography.

Both amateur and professional hockey are covered in the books, theses, articles, reports, and films cited in the twenty-five hundred items included in this important bibliography. The arrangement is by author within broad subject categories. Entries in languages other than French or English appear in the original language, with an English title. There is no index. Peter Moffet

5263 796.9'62'0207
**Nicol, Eric.**
The Joy of Hockey, by Eric Nicol and Dave More. Edmonton: Hurtig Publishers, c1978. 158p. ill. ISBN 0-88830-156-1 $8.95

1. Hockey – Anecdotes, facetiae, satire, etc.
2. Hockey – Canada – Anecdotes, facetiae, satire, etc.

A tongue-in-cheek spoof on Canada's national sport. Calgary artist Dave More's amusing drawings enhance Nicol's satiric observations on the game. Light-hearted nonsense to be taken in small doses. Adults.

5264 796.9'62'09
**McFarlane, Brian.**
Stanley Cup Fever: The Incredible Story of the Men and the Teams Who Have Fought for Hockey's Most Prized Trophy. Toronto: Pagurian Press, c1978. 256p. ill., ports. (A Christopher Ondaatje Publication) ISBN 0-88932-094-2 $9.95

1. Stanley Cup (Hockey) – History.
2. Hockey – History.

Published in 1970 under the title *The Stanley Cup*.

A year-by-year description of the annual battle for National Hockey League supremacy. A chapter of statistics concludes this easy-to-read, well illustrated history. A first choice. Peter Moffet

5265 796.9'62'0924
**Whitehead, Eric.**
Cyclone Taylor: A Hockey Legend. Toronto: Doubleday, 1977. 205p. ill., plates, ports. ISBN 0-385-13063-5 $7.95

1. Taylor, Fred, 1884- 2. Hockey players – Canada – Biography.

The career of one of the great figures in the formative years of professional hockey is described for modern hockey fans by a Vancouver sports columnist. Whitehead's account, reconstructed from contemporary records and interviews, recreates the excitement of a period of rapid development and peoples it with some of hockey's colourful pioneers. Junior and senior high school students.

## 797 Aquatic sports

5266 797.1'22
**Franks, Charles E. S.**
The Canoe and White Water: From Essential to Sport. Toronto: University of Toronto Press, c1977. 237p. ill., diagrs., ports. Bibliographical references and Index.
ISBN 0-8020-2236-7 bd.: $15
ISBN 0-8020-6294-6 pa.: $7.95

1. White-water canoeing. 2. Canoes and canoeing – Canada.

An experienced white water canoeist offers a carefully organized and clearly written guide to the challenging sport. Techniques of paddling, canoe safety, and the organization of successful trips are explained and illustrated with diagrams and photographs. A concise history of canoeing in Canada is included. Can be read for pleasure and consulted for information. Schools and public libraries.

5267 797.1'22
**Sloan, A. Tony.**
Blackflies and White Water. Toronto: McClelland and Stewart, c1977. 191p. ISBN 0-7710-8210-X $10

1. Canoes and canoeing – Canada.

A colourful description of memorable moments while canoe tripping in various regions of Canada. Underlying the light and entertaining approach is sound outdoor wisdom. Uses an occasional expletive in keeping with the circumstances at hand. Janet Frost

5268 797.1'24
**Cook, Peter,** ed.
The Complete Book of Sailing. Edited by Peter Cook and Barbara Webb; consultant editor, Theodore A. Jones. Toronto: Doubleday, 1977. 304p. ill. Index. ISBN 0-385-11531-8 $14.95

1. Sailing.

This introduction to the sport includes chapters on sailing in various parts of the English-speaking world such as Canada, Great Britain and Australia, types of boats, preparation and safety, weather and navigation, racing and cruising. Well illustrated with photographs and distinct diagrams. Peter Moffet

## 799 Fishing, hunting and shooting

5269 799.1'7'55
**Thornton, Barry M.**
Steelhead: The Supreme Trophy Trout. Saanichton, B.C.: Hancock House, 1978. 159p. ill. Index. ISBN 0-88839-019-X $14.95

1. Steelhead fishing. 2. Steelhead fishing – British Columbia – Vancouver Island.

How and where to catch this highly rated gamefish. Contains the life cycle, habits and management of the fish plus a guide to Vancouver Island streams. The author's environmental conservation viewpoint and fishing tips are relevant cross-Canada. For beginning and expert anglers. Peter Moffet

5270 799.2'97
**Knap, Jerome J.**
The Complete Hunter's Almanac. Toronto: Pagurian Press, c1978. 291p. ill., diagrs., ports. Index. (A Christopher Ondaatje Publication) ISBN 0-88932-060-8 $14.95

1. Hunting. 2. Hunting – North America. 3. Game and game-birds – North America.

Covers aspects of hunting in North America such as weapon selection and use, dress, the choice of a dog, life histories of game, provincial and state regulations and limits. Although essentially a revised edition of the author's *Hunter's Handbook* (*CS* no. 2281) fuller information and more illustrations make this title a better selection. Peter Moffet

## 801 Philosophy and theory

5271 801'.95
**Denham, Robert D.**
Northrop Frye and Critical Method. University Park: Pennsylvania State University Press, c1978. 262p. Bibliographical references and Index. ISBN 0-271-00546-7 $15.30

1. Frye, Northrop, 1912- 2. Criticism.

A detailed explication of Frye's *Anatomy of Criticism* and an assessment of his stature in the field of literary criticism. Illustrated by diagrams which the author acknowledges oversimplify rather than enhance meaning. Includes an index. Suitable for post-secondary school students of criticism. Patricia O'Sullivan

5272 801'.95
**Shouldice, Larry,** comp.
Contemporary Quebec Criticism. Toronto: University of Toronto Press, 1979. 320p. Bibliography. (Canadian University Paperbooks) ISBN 0-8020-2344-4 bd.: $25 ISBN 0-8020-6376-4 bd.: $7.95

1. Criticism – Quebec (Province). 2. Canadian literature (French) – Quebec (Province) – History and criticism.

This anthology of original articles and essays by notable Quebec critics and poets provides an introduction to Quebec literary criticism and cultural commentary written during the past two decades. Sheila Latham

5273 801'.95'0924
**Frye, Northrop.**
Northrop Frye on Culture and Literature: A Collection of Review Essays. Edited and with an introduction by Robert E. Denham. Chicago: University of Chicago Press, 1978. 264p. Bibliographical references and Index. ISBN 0-22626-647-8 $13

1. Books – Reviews.

Some twenty review articles, written by Northrop Frye in the decade from 1947 to 1957 have been selected to illustrate the clarity and analytic depth of his critical writings. A useful compilation of the eminent scholar's work for students of Canadian literature.

## 807.9 Literary competitions and awards

5274 807.9
**Canada. Statistics Canada. Fine Arts and Media Section.**
Literary and Journalistic Awards in Canada. Les Prix de littérature et de journalisme au Canada, 1923-1973. Ottawa: Information Canada, 1976. 276p. ill.

1. Literary prizes. 2. Journalism – Awards.

Each award is described in French and English, and winners are listed chronologically. The value of the work is enhanced by the appendices which contain chronological lists of journalistic and literary awards by category, alphabetical lists of the awards, and an alphabetical list of award winners. A useful reference tool for all libraries.

## 808 Rhetoric and collections

5275 808.
**Ricoeur, Paul.**
The Rule of Metaphor: Multi-disciplinary Studies of the Creation of Meaning in Language. Translated by Robert Czerny, Kathleen McLaughlin and John Costello. Toronto: University of Toronto Press, c1977. 384p. Bibliography: p. 369-380. Index. (University of Toronto Romance Series) ISBN 0-8020-5326-2 $22.50

1. Metaphor.

A scholarly study of the meaning and use of metaphor from Aristotle to the present. Encompassing the fields of philosophy, history, theology and linguistics, Ricoeur examines, in eight separate studies, classical rhetoric, semantics and metaphor, and hermeneutics. Has extensive notes, a bibliography of works cited and an index. Patricia O'Sullivan

## 808.02 Authorship and editorial techniques

5276 808'.02
**Birdsall, Peter.**
Who's(e) Who: The English Canadian Literary Scene, by Peter Birdsall and Delores Broten. Victoria: Canlit, 1979. ISBN 0-920566-03-0 $5

1. Authors and publishers – Canada.
2. Publishers and publishing – Canada.
3. State encouragement of science, literature and art – Canada.

A concise guide to governmental and professional organizations and assistance programmes of interest to writers, publishers, booksellers, and libraries. Sheila Latham

5277 808'.02
**Cameron, Bill.**
A Way with Words: A Light-hearted Look at the Agony of Writing. Saskatoon: Western Producer Prairie Books, 1979. ISBN 0-88833-026-X $4.95

1. Authorship. 2. Journalism.

A journalist's guide to prose writing presents a refreshingly different approach to communication. The book stresses the importance of simplicity, offering the novice practical advice on avoiding some of the pitfalls of writing. A popular introduction for the general reader. Gartly Wagner

5278 808'.02
**Canadian Authors Association.**
The Canadian Writer's Guide: Official Handbook of the Canadian Authors Association. 7th ed. Toronto: Fitzhenry & Whiteside, c1979. 149p. ISBN 0-88902-000-0 pa.: $5.95

1. Authorship. 2. Canadian periodicals (English) – Directories.

Sixth edition listed *CS* no. 2289.

A revised and updated edition of an authoritative reference guide for free-lance writers in Canada. Following fifteen chapters on researching and writing the manuscript are lists of possible markets for it: periodicals, book publishers, films, television and radio.

5279 808'.02
**Coggins, Gordon.**
A Guide to Writing Essays & Research Papers. Toronto: Van Nostrand Reinhold,

1977. 94p. ill. Index. ISBN 0-442-29862-5 pa.: $3.95

1. Report writing.

The step-by-step approach to conducting research, outlining a topic, and preparing a first draft will appeal to students faced with the task of writing their first paper. A sample essay and research paper are provided as examples of completed works. Gartly Wagner.

5280 808'.02

**Goodman, Eileen.**

The Canadian Writer's Market. 5th ed., rev. Toronto: McClelland and Stewart, c1978. 233p. ISBN 0-7710-3380-X pa.: $6.95

1. Authorship – Handbooks, manuals, etc. 2. Publishers and publishing – Canada – Directories. 3. Canadian periodicals – Directories. 4. Advertising agencies – Canada – Directories. 5. Journalism – Study and teaching – Canada – Directories.

Fourth edition listed in *CS* no. 2290.

5281 808'.025

**Drobot, Eve,** ed.

Words for Sale: More than Two Dozen Professionals Show How You Can Make Money in the Fast-growing Canadian Magazine Market. Edited by Eve Drobot and Hal Tennant for the Periodical Writers Association of Canada. Toronto: Macmillan, 1979. ISBN 0-7705-1831-1 bd.: $12.95 ISBN 0-7705-1832-X pa.: $6.95

1. Authorship.

This informative guide to writing offers selections from more than two dozen writers in an easy style suitable for the general reader. The advice given is useful for anyone wishing to become a successful free-lance writer. Gartly Wagner

5282 808'.042

**Bell, James B.**

The Little English Handbook for Canadians, by James B. Bell and Edward P. J. Corbett. Toronto: John Wiley, c1977. 207p. facsims. Index. ISBN 0-471-99853-2 pa.: $3.95

1. English language – Rhetoric.

Students will appreciate the model research paper, bibliography and footnotes; the general reader will find the information on letter writing especially helpful. Grammar, punctuation and style are emphasised in this book which will be useful in many collections. Gartly Wagner

5283 808'.042

**Corder, Jim W.**

Handbook of Current English. Canadian ed. Prepared by Walter S. Avis. Toronto: Gage Educational Publishing, 1979. 494p. Index. ISBN 0-7715-1758-0 pa.: $9.45

1. English language – Rhetoric. 2. English language – Grammar – 1950-

This guide to grammar, punctuation, usage and composition serves as a handbook for both the student preparing an essay and the individual seeking advice when composing a business letter or résumé. Helpful exercises at the end of each section provide the user with the opportunity to test each newly acquired skill. Gartly Wagner

5284 808'.042

**David, Jack,** ed.

Playback: Canadian Selections, edited by Jack David and Michael Park. Toronto: McClelland and Stewart, c1978. 237p. ill., ports. ISBN 0-7710-2560-2 pa.: $5.95

1. Creative writing.

Forty short essays on a range of contemporary issues, grouped thematically, and illustrated with cartoons, have been assembled as a resource for the teaching of creative writing at the community college level. A number of the pieces have been published previously in the popular press. A stimulating introduction to Canadian writing. College, school and public libraries.

5285 808'.042

**Dawe, Alan.**

Copyright Canada: A Prose Rhetoric and Sampler. Toronto: Macmillan, c1978. 243p. ill., graphs. ISBN 0-7705-1670-X pa.: $5.95

1. English language – Rhetoric. 2. College readers.

The focus is on the narrative and expository essay, using passages from works by Canadian authors in this guide to writing. The rudiments of good grammar, rhetorical devices, and the mechanics of the language are covered. Students and adults interested in writing will find the book helpful. Gartly Wagner

5286 808'.042

**Gehle, Quentin L.**

The Writing Process, by Quentin L. Gehle and Duncan J. Rollo. Toronto: Macmillan, 1977. 268p. Index. ISBN 0-7705-1491-X pa.: $6.95

1. English language – Rhetoric.

All aspects of essay writing are covered in this

text designed for a student audience. The mechanics of language, grammar and sentence structure are discussed at length. Exercises are provided to help the student evaluate progress. Gartly Wagner

5287 808.1
**Skelton, Robin.**
Poetic Truth. Agincourt, Ont.: Book Society, 1978. 131p. Bibliographical references and Index. ISBN 0-435-18821-6 bd.: $19.25
ISBN 0-435-18822-4 pa.: $8.95

1. Poetry.

Essential questions about the nature, value and significance of poetry are outlined in this critical and theoretical text. Sample chapters include "Metaphor and Emotion" and "Poetry and Explanation". The third and equally important volume in the author's trilogy begun with *The Poet's Calling* and *The Craft of Poetry*. Don Sedgwick.

## 808.851 Speeches - Collections

5288 808.88'2
**McPhee, Nancy.**
The Book of Insults Ancient and Modern: An Amiable History of Insult, Invective, Imprecation & Incivility (Literary, Political & Historical) Hurled Through the Ages & Compiled as a Public Service. Toronto: Van Nostrand Reinhold, 1978. 160p. ill. Indexes.
ISBN 0-442-29832-3 $6.95

1. Invective.

Roughly one thousand insults are presented in this history of the art of invective in Canada, Great Britain, the United States and Europe by Toronto researcher Nancy McPhee. Illustrations by David Shaw accompany this collection which highlights literary, geographic and political malevolence. A highly entertaining work which will appeal to readers of all ages. Gartly Wagner

## 809 History and criticism

5289 809.
**Frye, Northrop.**
Spiritus Mundi: Essays on Literature, Myth and Society. Toronto: Fitzhenry & Whiteside, c1976. 296p. Bibliographical references.
ISBN 0-253-35432-3 $13.25

1. Literature.

This collection of Frye's more recent essays reflects both his personal views and the experiences in his life which fostered them. Arranged in three sections, the essays deal with "Contexts of Literature", "The Mythological Universe" and "Four Poets" (Milton, Yeats, Blake and Stevens). Information about the essays, many of which were initially delivered as speeches, is supplied in the author's introduction. Glenna Stevens

5290 809.
**New, William H.,** ed.
A Political Art: Essays and Images in Honour of George Woodcock. Vancouver: University of British Columbia Press, 1978. 249p. ill. Bibliography: p. 209-249.
ISBN 0-7748-0095-X $15

1. Woodcock, George, 1912- 2. Woodcock, George, 1912 – – Bibliography.

This collection of scholarly essays pays tribute to Woodcock's contribution to Canadian literature, criticism and social commentary. Arranged in three parts, the book includes essays on Woodcock's own work; contributions from old friends such as Margaret Laurence and Jack Ludwig; and a bibliography of Woodcock's writing by Ivan Avakumovic. The result of this collaboration is a valuable study of Woodcock's literary and political presence. Andrea Trudel.

5291 809'.04
**Bessai, Diane,** ed.
Figures in a Ground: Canadian Essays on Modern Literature Collected in Honor of Sheila Watson. Edited by Diane Bessai and David Jackel. Saskatoon: Western Producer Prairie Books, 1978. 365p. ill., port. Index.
ISBN 0-919306-89-6 bd.: $14.50
ISBN 0-919306-90-X pa.: $7.50

1. Literature, Modern – 20th century – History and criticism.

Essays in this collection include both scholarly criticism and works of a less specialized nature. Subject matter is not restricted to the idea of Canadian literature as an isolated entity, rather, Canadian writing is studied in recognition of its position in the collective literature of the world. Footnotes, notes on contributors and an index follow text. Glenna Stevens

5292 809'.933'2
**Chadbourne, Richard,** ed.
The New Land: Studies in a Literary Theme. Edited by Richard Chadbourne and Hallvard Dahlie. Waterloo, Ont.: Published for the Calgary Institute for the Humanities by Wilfrid Laurier University Press, c1978. 160p. Bibliographical references. ISBN 0-88920-065-3 pa. Processed: $4.50

1. North America in literature – Congresses.

A stimulating, well-written collection of essays by scholars of Canadian literature which re-examines the concept of the new land as explored in the works of such diverse authors as McClung, Lowry and Wiebe. Provides a fresh look at an overworked approach to the study of Canadian literature. Patricia O'Sullivan

## C810.16 Bibliography

5293 C810.16
**Gnarowski, Michael.**
A Concise Bibliography of English-Canadian Literature. Rev. ed. Toronto: McClelland and Stewart, c1978. 145p. ISBN 0-7710-3362-1 pa.: $6.95

1. Canadian literature (English) – Bibliography.

First edition listed *CS* no. 2317.

1975 is the cut-off date for this revision of the 1973 publication. The same format is followed, authors arranged alphabetically with the publications of each, and pertinent critical works in chronological order. No indexes. Glenna Stevens

5294 C810.16
**Hamilton, K. A.,** ed.
Canada Writes: The Member's Book of the Writer's Union of Canada. Toronto: The Union, 1977. 399p. ports. $2.50

1. Canadian literature – Bio-bibliography. 2. Authors, Canadian.

A brief biographical sketch submitted by the author, a photograph, and a chronologically arranged bibliography identify some two hundred Canadian writers of prose and poetry. A useful quick reference tool for public and high school libraries.

5295 C810.16
**Moyles, Robert G.**
English-Canadian Literature to 1900: A Guide to Information Sources. Detroit: Gale Research, c1976. 346p. Indexes. (Gale Information Guide Library) (American Literature, English Literature and World Literature in English) ISBN 0-8103-1222-0 $22

1. Canadian literature (English) – Bibliography. 2. Canadian literature (English) – History and criticism – Bibliography.

Attempts "to provide a list of all the important primary and secondary sources necessary for a thorough study of this literature." Includes general reference guides, literary history and criticism, anthologies, bio-bibliographies of major and minor authors, the literature of exploration, travel and description. Author and title indexes. Diane Henderson

## C810.8 Collections

5296 C810'.8
**Daymond, Douglas,** ed.
Literature in Canada. Edited by Douglas Daymond and Leslie Monkman. Toronto: Gage Educational Publishing, 1978- 2v Indexes. ISBN 0-7715-1156-6 $8.95 vol. 1. ISBN 0-7715-1157-4 $13.95 vol. 2.

1. Canadian literature.

A two-volume anthology of Canadian narrative, fiction, drama and poetry from the sixteenth century to the present. Emphasis is on work of major English-Canadian writers but some lesser-known and French authors in translation are featured as well. Coverage is more comprehensive than previous anthologies. Should be a standard in library collections. Patricia O'Sullivan

5297 C810'.8
**Wolfe, Morris,** ed.
Aurora: New Canadian Writing 1978. Toronto: Doubleday, 1978. 248p. ISBN 0-385-13646-3 $7.95

1. Canadian literature (English) – 20th century.

The sixty-nine items of this book include poems, short stories, reminiscences. Works of both known and unknown contemporary Canadian authors; many reflect the Canadian themes of survival and violence. There is no French material in this initial issue of what is intended as an annual publication. Notes on contributors appended. Glenna Stevens

5298 C810'.8
**Wolfe, Morris,** ed.
Aurora: New Canadian Writing 1979. Toronto: Doubleday, 1979. 256p. ISBN 0-385-14610-8 $7.95
1. Canadian literature (English) – 20th century.
Formerly unpublished poems, stories, and essays by new and established Canadian writers comprise a well written, readable anthology that will appeal to a broad, general audience. Sheila Latham

5299 C810'.8'032
**Chalmers, John W.,** ed.
The Alberta Diamond Jubilee Anthology. Edmonton: Hurtig Publishers, 1979. 335p. ISBN 0-88830-176-6 $14.95
1. Canadian literature (English) – Alberta.
Choice stories, essays, poems, and prose pieces by Alberta's best writers, including W. O. Mitchell, James Gray, Rudy Wiebe, Sheila Watson, and many others, provide a welcome creative portrait of the people, history, landscape, and culture of Alberta. Sheila Latham

5300 C810'.8'032
**Hale, Alice K.,** ed.
Nearly an Island: A Nova Scotia Anthology. Edited by Alice K. Hale and Sheila A. Brooks. St. John's, Nfld.: Breakwater Books, 1979. ISBN 0-919948-65-0 bd.: $7.95 ISBN 0-919948-64-2 pa.: $4.95
1. Canadian literature (English) – Nova Scotia. 2. Nova Scotia – Literary collections.
This anthology attempts to reveal "the blood and spirit of what has been written by Bluenosers." -Introduction. Included is writing by native Nova Scotians no longer residing in the province and by residents who are not Nova Scotian by birth. Contributors include well-known writers such as Hugh MacLennan, Ernest Buckler, Alden Nowlan, Helen Creighton and Charles Bruce. A well-chosen collection, which would represent the province well in all libraries.

5301 C810'.8'032
**Mitchell, Ken,** ed.
Horizon: Writings of the Canadian Prairie. Toronto: Oxford University Press, 1977. 288p. ill., ports. Bibliographical references. ISBN 0-19-540262-6 pa.: $6.95
1. Canadian literature (English) – Prairie Provinces. 2. Prairie Provinces – Literary collections.
Mitchell has edited a chronological anthology of stories, poems and historical observations by sixty western Canadian writers and historical figures. Selections from explorers' records, to Wiebe, Bowering, Laurence and Valgardson, illustrate the particularly prairie experience with the land itself. A creative collection from both a social and literary standpoint. Andrea Trudel.

5302 C810'.8'0352
**Hesse, M. G.,** ed.
Childhood and Youth in Canadian Literature. Edited by M. G. Hesse. Toronto: Macmillan, c1979. 122p. ill. Bibliography: p. 120-122. (Themes in Canadian Literature) ISBN 0-7705-1598-3 pa.: $3
1. Children – Literary collections. 2. Youth – Literary collections. 3. Canadian literature (English) – 20th century.
The thrills and enchantment of childhood are recaptured in the multiple brief selections of prose and poetry in this anthology. Contributors are well-known Canadian authors who approach the subject with a perspective which creates a refreshing, nostalgic experience for the reader. Glenna Stevens

5303 C810'.8'0352
**Saint-Pierre, Gaston,** ed.
The French Canadian Experience. Toronto: Macmillan, 1979. Bibliography. (Themes in Canadian Literature) ISBN 0-7705-1363-8 pa.: $3.40
1. Canadians, French-speaking – Literary collections. 2. Canadian literature. 3. Canadian literature (French) – Translations into English. 4. English literature – Translations from French.
A slim volume of selected poetry and prose in translation covers French Canadian literature from the days of New France to the present, with emphasis on the twentieth century. Some writing on Quebec themes by English-speaking authors is included. A good introduction to Quebec literature for the uninitiated, with study questions and a bibliography. Patricia O'Sullivan

5304 C810'.8'0928
**Morgan, Bernice,** ed.
From This Place: A Selection of Writings by Women of Newfoundland and Labrador. Edited by Bernice Morgan, Helen Porter and Geraldine Rubia. St. John's, Nfld.: Jesperson Press, c1977. 194p. ill. ISBN 0-92052-02-4 $4.99
1. Canadian literature (English) –

Newfoundland. 2. Canadian literature (English) – Labrador. 3. Canadian literature – Women authors.

An engaging collection of poems, short stories, essays, and excerpts from books, illustrative of the range and vitality of the creative writing being done by women in Newfoundland and Labrador. An interesting addition to Canadian literature shelves in college, public and secondary school libraries.

## C810.9 History and criticism

5305 C810'.9

**Cappon, Paul,** ed.

In Our Own House: Social Perspectives on Canadian Literature. Toronto: McClelland and Stewart, c1978. 207p. Bibliography: p. 207. ISBN 0-7710-1899-1 pa.: $5.95

1. Canadian literature (English) – History and criticism. 2. Literature and society.

English-Canadian literature is examined from a sociological perspective in the essays by five Canadian authors. Criticism in Marxist terms is the platform upon which each builds his composition. A substantial introduction to the text and to each section by the editor merit him recognition as a major contributor. Glenna Stevens

5306 C810'.9

**Dudek, Louis.**

Selected Essays and Criticism. Ottawa: Tecumseh Press, 1978. 380p. Bibliographical references. ISBN 0-919662-60-9 pa.: $6.95

1. Canadian literature – History and criticism.

This collection of critical articles from one of Canada's foremost poets and critics covers the period from 1944 to 1977. Gleaned chiefly from magazines, the selections include studies on individual poets as well as reflections on the Canadian literary scene. Dudek's respected viewpoint provides an important perspective in chronicling the development of Canadian poetry as a whole. Andrea Trudel

5307 C810'.9

**Helwig, David,** ed.

The Human Elements: Critical Essays. Ottawa: Oberon Press, c1978. 163p.
ISBN 0-88750-281-4 bd.: $15
ISBN 0-88750-282-2 pa.: $6.95

1. Canadian literature – 20th century – History and criticism.

Directed to the average reader, this book includes eight essays on diverse topics thought to comprise the cultural landscape of Canada. Criticism of writers and their material, analyses of film and of the theatre, and an examination of the literature of Quebec forn a representative sample of the subject matter. Brief notes on contributors follow text. Glenna Stevens

5308 C810.9

**Mandel, Eli.**

Another Time. Erin, Ont.: Press Porcépic, 1977. 160p. Bibliographical references. (Three Solitudes, Contemporary Literary Criticism in Canada) ISBN 0-88878-076-1 bd.: $15
ISBN 0-88878-077-X pa.: $4.95

1. Canadian literature (English) – 20th century – History and criticism.

A collection of materials which the author contends "are reflections rather than arguments", these fifteen essays are grouped in three sections: one to display Mandel's position, one in which his theories are defined by reference to Canada's West, and one on the problems of contemporary Canadian writing. Essays are liberally illustrated by quotations for which full footnote references are provided. Glenna Stevens

5309 C810'.9

**Mathews, Robin.**

Canadian Literature: Surrender or Revolution. Edited by Gail Dexter. Toronto: Steel Rail Publishing, 1978. 250p. Bibliographical references and Index.
ISBN 0-88791-014-9 bd.: $12.95
ISBN 0-88791-012-2 pa.: $5.95

1. Canadian literature (English) – History and criticism. 2. Politics and literature – Canada.

This book is more a collection of damning essays than of objective criticism. Mathews contends that American anarchism has had severe effects on Canadian authors; few emerge as having withstood either American pressures or the British colonialist attitude. Mathews' criterion of judgement is his political view, consequently he finds little in Canadian literature and few Canadian writers worthy of his praise. Glenna Stevens

5310 C810.9
**McClung, Molly G.**
Women in Canadian Literature. Preface by George Woodcock. Toronto: Fitzhenry & Whiteside, c1977. 96p. ill., facsims., ports. Bibliography. Index. (Women in Canadian Life) ISBN 0-88902-378-6 pa.: $2.95

1. Canadian literature – History and criticism. 2. Women in literature.

One of a series of brief introductions to the place women have carved for themselves in various spheres of Canadian life. Outlines the development of creative writing and provides profiles of a number of women writers. Attractive format. Designed for schools but useful for general reading. In the same series and format: Cochrane, J. *Women in Canadian Life: Sports;* Dranoff, L. S. *Women in Canadian Life: Law.*

5311 C810'.9
**Staines, David,** ed.
The Canadian Imagination: Dimensions of a Literary Culture. Cambridge, Mass.: Harvard University Press, 1977. 265p. Bibliographical references and Index. ISBN 0-674-09355-0 $10

1. Canadian literature – History and criticism.

David Staines presents a collection of essays by nine Canadian writers: Frye, Atwood, Brian Parker, Marine Leland, McLuhan, Peter Buitenhuis, George Woodcock, and Douglas Bush. *The Canadian Imagination* is an introduction to Canadian literature for a foreign audience. The essays vary in approach and direction and may not satisfy a student of Canadian literature. Includes bibliographic references and an index. Janice Zlatarits

5312 C810'.9
**Sutherland, Ronald.**
The New Hero: Essays in Comparative Quebec/Canadian Literature. Toronto: Macmillan, c1977. 118p. Bibliography: p. 100-113. Index. ISBN 0-7705-1613-0 pa.: $5.95

1. Canadian fiction – 20th century – History and criticism.

In four essays, Sutherland further examines ideas advanced in his earlier publication, *Second Image* (1971). He contends and illustrates that distinct similarities exist between English and French-Canadian literature, regarding both themes and subjects. Sutherland's expression is clear and direct, to read his essays is an enjoyable pastime. Bibliography, notes and index appended. Glenna Stevens

5313 C810'.9'32
**Harrison, Dick,** ed.
Crossing Frontiers: Papers in American and Canadian Western Literature. Edmonton: University of Alberta Press, 1979. 174p. Bibliographical references. ISBN 0-88864-058-7 pa.: $10

1. Literature, Comparative – Canadian (English) and American – Congresses. 2. The West, Canadian, in literature – Congresses. 3. The West in literature – Congresses.

Conference papers presented by American and Canadian scholars, poets and novelists examine historical and cultural similarities and differences of the West as reflected in the literature of the two countries. Lively debate on the relative merits of an historical versus a mythological rendering of reality provides stimulating reading. Patricia O'Sullivan

5314 C810'.99716
**Milner, Philip,** comp.
Nova Scotia Writes. Antigonish, N.S.: Formac Publishing, 1979. 100p. ports. ISBN 0-88780-036-X pa.: $4.95

1. Canadian literature (English) – Nova Scotia – Bio-bibliography. 2. Canadian literature (English) – 20th century – Bio-bibliography. 3. Nova Scotia – Bio-bibliography.

An identification list of eighty-six contemporary Nova Scotia writers and publishers. Arranged alphabetically by author, the one-page entries include a biographical note, a bibliography of the writer's work and a photograph.

5315 C810'.9'9718
**O'Flaherty, Patrick.**
The Rock Observed: Literary Responses to Newfoundland and its People. Toronto: University of Toronto Press, 1979. Index. ISBN 0-8020-5419-6 $15

1. Canadian literature (English) – Newfoundland – History and criticism. 2. Newfoundland in literature. 3. Newfoundland – History – Sources.

An important critical survey ranging from sixteenth-century explorer's narratives to novels of the 1970's. The literature is viewed in the context of Newfoundland's historic, economic, and cultural foundations. Sheila Latham

## C811 Poetry

5316 C811.
**Abbey, Lloyd.**
Braindances: Poems. Ottawa: Oberon Press, c1979. 80p. ISBN 0-88750-316-0 bd.: $11.95 ISBN 0-88750-317-9 pa.: $4.95

Through the precise, detailed rendering of striking natural metaphors, Abbey's poems resound with multiple meanings. Exploring the pleasures and painful difficulties inherent in relationships, these well-crafted poems reveal a small but highly charged landscape. Janet Fraser

5317 C811.
**Acorn, Milton.**
Jackpine Sonnets. Toronto: Steel Rail Publishing, 1977. 109p. ISBN 0-88791-007-6 bd.: $10.95 ISBN 0-88791-005-X pa.: $4.95

These are hard-hitting poems from a master of the literary craft. Acorn, often referred to as "the people's poet", deals with such contemporary problems as social injustice and misguided politics. To borrow one of his own lines, Acorn aims at "Making my fellow person real, not abstract!". Don Sedgwick

5318 C811.
**Allen, Robert.**
The Assumption of Private Lives. La Salle, Que.: New Delta. 58p. ISBN 0-919162-48-7 $2.50

Focusing on the unusual and the exotic, Allen creates vivid contemporary myths and legends. The curious mixture of tragedy and satire and the strained metaphors are not always successful. This is the first Canadian publication of a poet gaining recognition in the United States. Janet Fraser

5319 C811.
**Amabile, George.**
Flower and Song. Ottawa: Borealis Press, 1977. 41p. ISBN 0-919594-63-8 pa.: $3.95

A work of startling contrasts – terrible poverty and incredible riches, cascades of azaleas and human filth – describes the poet's experience of Mexican life and culture. Catharine MacKenzie

5320 C811.
**Anderson, Patrick.**
Return to Canada: Selected Poems. Toronto: McClelland and Stewart, c1977. 110p. ISBN 0-7710-0705-1 pa.: $4.95

Grouped in three thematic sections, Ways of Seeing, Notes from an Old Montreal Wartime, and An Expanding Neighbourhood, these poems show the development and influence of a poet famous for his work in *Preview* during the postwar period in Montreal. Contains his lengthy "Poem on Canada". Don Sedgwick

5321 C811.
**Atwood, Margaret.**
Two-headed Poems. Toronto: Oxford University Press, c1978. 112p. ISBN 0-19-540292-8 pa.: $3.95

Questions and answers and opposing viewpoints carry the two-headed image through a broad range of themes, including questions of national identity, uncertain relationships and political violence. A powerful work by one of Canada's major poets. Don Sedgwick

5322 C811.
**Aubert, Rosemary.**
Two Kinds of Honey: Poems. Ottawa: Oberon Press, c1977. 144p.
ISBN 0-88750-240-7 bd.: $9.95
ISBN 0-88750-241-5 pa.: $4.95

Scenes of children, elderly men and figures from Russian history are to be found in Aubert's first full-length book. Previously her work appeared in *Storm Warning 2,* edited by Al Purdy. Although the thoughts may not be profound, the images remain vivid. Don Sedgwick

5323 C811.
**Avison, Margaret.**
Sunblue. Hantsport, N.S.: Lancelot Press, 1978. 105p. ISBN 0-88999-088-3 pa.: $3.95

Winner of the Governor General's Award for poetry in 1960, Avison is a thoughtful poet with a strong Christian conviction. "*Sunblue* fulfills all the promises and extends all the boundaries of her previous books in terms of vocabulary, technique, intellectual challenge and emotional impact" (Dr. J. R. C. Perkin, Dean of Arts, Acadia University). Essential reading. Don Sedgwick

5324 C811.
**Bauer, William A.**
The Terrible Word. Fredericton, N.B.: Fiddlehead Poetry Books, 1978. 93p. (Fiddlehead Poetry Books)
ISBN 0-920110-09-6 pa.: $5

Joyful exuberance is the dominant tone of this first major collection by a Fredericton poet, previously published in two chapbooks. His humour has been described as "reminiscent of

Mark Twain". Not a major poet, but one whose work is certainly pleasant to read. Don Sedgwick

5325 C811.

**Beardsley, Doug.**

Play on the Water: Poems. Erin, Ont.: Press Porcépic, 1978. 60p. ill. ISBN 0-88878-154-7 pa.: $4.95

Beardsley's poems are based on and accompanied by the marvellous drawings of Swiss artist Paul Klee. Although the poetry is deft and delicate, the overall conception of the book has bothered some critics and may likewise disappoint a few readers. What can the poems tell us that the pictures can't? Don Sedgwick

5326 C811.

**Bennet, Jim.**

Jim Bennet's Verse. Halifax: Petheric Press, 1979. Unpaginated. ISBN 0-919380-32-8 pa.: $4.95

A collection of light verse deals with human quirks, the ironies of life, current issues, and there is some social criticism. The tone is sprightly, satiric. Catharine MacKenzie

5327 C811.

**Berrouard, Leon.**

The Green Damsel & The Silver Doctor. Charlottetown: Square Deal Publications, 1978. 50p. ISBN 0-920078-16-8 $3.95

This Prince Edward Island poet's deceptively simple poems capture the subtle ironies of everyday life and the absurd humour of unusual predicaments. Sheila Latham

5328 C811.

**Birney, Earle.**

Alphabeings & Other Seasyours. London, Ont.: Pikadilly Press, 1976. 32p. ill. ISBN 0-919878-17-2 pa.: $3.50

A slim volume of playful images and concrete poetry by the dean of Canadian writing. Don Sedgwick

5329 C811.

**Birney, Earle.**

Fall by Fury & Other Makings. Toronto: McClelland and Stewart, c1978. 96p. ill. ISBN 0-7710-1430-9 pa.: $5.95

Sound, visual and concrete poems are part of a varied collection by one of the foremost Canadian poets. At times lively, humorous or poignant, Birney shows his mastery of form and expression. Central to any collection of poetry. Don Sedgwick

5330 C811.

**Birney, Earle.**

Ghost in the Wheels: Selected Poems, 1920-1976. Toronto: McClelland and Stewart, c1977. 159p. Index. ISBN 0-7710-1408-2 pa.: $4.95

A retrospective selection of poems by a writer often described as the "Dean" of Canadian literature. Contains some of the author's best-known works, including "David", "The Bear on the Delhi Road" and the witty poem "Billboards Build Freedom of Choice". Central to any collection of Canadian poetry. Don Sedgwick

5331 C811.

**Bissett, Bill.**

Sailor. Vancouver: Talonbooks, 1978. 98p. ill. ISBN 0-88922-139-1 pa.: $4.95

A linguistic innovator and radical bard, Bill Bissett continues his tirades against established poetic and social norms. His sound poems, chants and sixties rhetoric are popular on the high school reading circuit but are likely to bore or infuriate more mature readers. Don Sedgwick

5332 C811.

**Blodgett, Edward D.**

Sounding. Edmonton: Tree Frog Press, c1977. 60p. ISBN 0-88967-053-6 pa.: $5.95

Dream-like and metaphysical, *Sounding* is a series of brief, pointillistic images directed to Vincent van Gogh, an ever-present companion in this volume. Pastoral and pleasant, but likely to be somewhat ethereal for a general audience. Don Sedgwick

5333 C811.

**Bowering, George.**

Allophanes. Toronto: Coach House Press, c1976. 55p. ISBN 0-88910-192-2 pa.: $3.50

Bowering's serial poem is a metaphysical study of "allo", meaning "all" and "phanes", meaning "appearances". "I had gathered about me all gods/ because I believed in none," ponders the narrator at one point. Challenging material from an innovative writer. Don Sedgwick

5334 C811.

**Bowering, George.**

Another Mouth. Toronto: McClelland and Stewart, c1979. 96p. ISBN 0-7710-1590-9 pa.: $7.95

Witty, entertaining and imaginative, this is Bowering at his provocative best. He examines, in his own words, "love, death, violence, travel, nature, fatherhood, politics, art, the cosmos and fate." A strong and direct voice in Canadian writing. Don Sedgwick

5335 C811.
**Bowering, George.**
The Concrete Island: Montreal Poems, 1967-1971. Montreal: Véhicule Press, c1977. 64p. ISBN 0-919890-05-9 pa.: $3

The author describes these chronicles of his daily experiences in Montreal as "desperate poems". He seems lost in the "placelessness" of the city and frequently longs for a west coast vista. A modern volume, *The Concrete Island* should not be purchased before Bowering's other more widely acclaimed works. Don Sedgwick

5336 C811.
**Bowering, Marilyn.**
The Killing Room. Victoria, B.C.: Sono Nis Press, 1977. 74p. ISBN 0-919462-37-5 bd.: $8.95 ISBN 0-919462-43-X pa.: $4.95

Blood, bones, wild creatures and drowning children are a few of the images in Bowering's macabre poetry. She is searching for "a means to bring together the two worlds of inner and outer experience ... to kill what needs killing" -Publisher's Note. Strong, imaginative work, which captures the primitive qualities of Canada's west coast. Don Sedgwick

5337 C811.
**Brady, Elizabeth.**
Tintype. Vancouver: Fiddlehead Poetry Books, 1977. 36p. (Fiddlehead Poetry Books) ISBN 0-920110-12-6 pa.: $3

A very small collection presents a new poet whose work is thoughtful and thought-provoking. A photograph album launches her on a voyage into her personal and cultural past. Catharine MacKenzie.

5338 C811.
**Brewster, Elizabeth.**
Sometimes I Think of Moving: Poems. Ottawa: Oberon Press, c1977. 123p. ISBN 0-88750-221-0 bd.: $8.95 ISBN 0-88750-222-9 pa.: $4.50

A collection of very engaging poems by a prolific and widely published poet. Reflections on landscapes, people, dreams and love are presented in five thematic sections: "The Silent Scream", "Where I Come From", "Map of the City", "The Dancers", and "Renewal". Contains the haunting eulogy, "For Pat Lowther". Don Sedgwick

5339 C811.
**Callaghan, Barry.**
The Hogg Poems and Drawings. Don Mills, Ont.: General Publishing, c1978. 143p. ill., ports. ISBN 0-7736-0066-3 bd.: $75 ISBN 0-7736-1036-7 pa.: $10

Callaghan's mini-epic depicts Hogg's search for meaning as he travels through Jerusalem and experiences sensual delight and then rejection in love. A series of sixteen erotic paintings precedes Hogg's encounter with some unusual characters in the Toronto-Hogtown subway. Callaghan's book investigates the realm of the unconscious for discerning readers. Don Sedgwick.

5340 C811.
**Carmichael, Michael.**
Oyster Wine. Lantzville, B.C.: Oolichan Books, 1978. 64p. ISBN 0-88982-12-0 $4.95

This anecdotal prose poem focuses on the character of 'Dirty Bob', a fisherman on the B.C. coast. Carmichael matches depictions of pain and violence with crude language and authentic dialogue. "Oyster wine" becomes a poignant symbol of momentary pleasure in a brutal life. A realistic regional study, the book lacks a distinctive poetic voice or imagination. Janet Fraser

5341 C811.
**Cohen, Leonard.**
Death of a Lady's Man. Toronto: McClelland and Stewart, c1977. 216p. ISBN 0-7710-2177-1 bd.: $10

A long-awaited opus, *Death of a Lady's Man* has received mixed reviews. It is essentially an autobiographical romance in which poems are followed by editorial journal entries commenting on the themes of love, art, and politics. Alternately witty, lyrical, boring or dramatic, these poems are usually engaging, if somewhat enigmatic. Don Sedgwick

5342 C811.
**Coles, Don.**
Anniversaries: Poems. Toronto: Macmillan, 1979. ISBN 0-7705-1745-5 $5.95

Author of *Sometimes All Over* (1975), the poet's second collection uses a variety of subjects to broach the themes of time: past, present and future. Artifacts and people carefully illustrate the quixoticism of human accomplishment when pitted against the unpredictable events of society and future. Beth Marcilio

5343 C811.
**Colombo, John Robert.**
Variable Cloudiness: New Poems. Willowdale, Ont.: Hounslow Press, c1977. 77p. ISBN 0-88882-018-6 pa.: $3.95

A pot-pourri of original, found and translated poetry, *Variable Cloudiness* is an uneven collection: sometimes witty, at times imaginative, occasionally self-indulgent. Colombo touches on a myriad of subjects including love, sex, nationalism and culture. Students of poetics may be intrigued by the variety of formal structures. Don Sedgwick

5344 C811.
**Cooperman, Stanley.**
Canadian Gothic and Other Poems. Vancouver: Intermedia Press, c1976. 127p. Index. ISBN 0-88956-006-4 pa.: $6

The last book of poems by Stanley Cooperman has been carelessly arranged and the very small print may be discouraging. This does not do justice to a fine collection of poems. The rich use of metaphor, strength of style, questioning and often tortured introspection make the way worthwhile. Beth Marcilio

5345 C811.
**Couzyn, Jeni.**
Monkey's Wedding. North Vancouver, B.C.: Douglas & McIntyre, 1979. 96p. ISBN 0-88894-197-8 $5.95

An important and popular young poet intensely concerned with the perplexities of the human condition, Couzyn writes urgent, brutally honest poems. Angry social criticism is tempered by lyricism and sensuous imagery derived from the poet's native South Africa. This is the Canadian paperback edition of a collection first published in England in 1972. Janet Fraser

5346 C811.
**Crawford, Isabella Valancy.**
Hugh and Ion. Edited with an introduction and notes by W. Glenn Clever. Ottawa: Borealis Press, 1977. 33p. Bibliographical references. ISBN 0-919594-77-8 pa.: $3.95

Critics have pointed out that the poet was first to use an extensive imagery drawn from the Canadian environment. This collection is taken from the original manuscript, edited by Glenn Clever, and contains some previously unpublished work. The Hugh of the title is the representative of hope; Ion the voice of despair. Catharine MacKenzie

5347 C811.
**Currie, Robert.**
Diving into Fire: Poems. Ottawa: Oberon Press, c1977. 87p. ISBN 0-88750-212-1 bd.: $8.95 ISBN 0-88750-214-8 pa.: $3.95

The sections of this volume entitled "The Way Across", "The Divers", "Fire", "Flood", and "A Sudden Radiance", are arranged to re-enforce a recurring theme: rites of passage. Bridges, crossings, taking chances, arriving – the metaphors are simple in poems that are generally anecdotal. Metaphors aside, the simplicity (not always commendable) and style make the work also suitable for young readers and listeners. Beth Marcilio

5348 C811.
**Day, David.**
The Cowichan. Madiera Park, B.C.: Harbour Publishing, 1976. Unpaginated. $3.95

This collection concerned with the author's logging experiences in the Cowichan area of British Columbia is clearly in the current of contemporary worker poetry in its authenticity, clear, natural narration, and prosaic rhythms. At times passion and imaginative insight combine to make this document approach myth. The well-designed cover and layout and the photographs add to the value of the book. Janet Fraser

5349 C811.
**Di Cicco, Pier Giorgio.**
A Burning Patience. Ottawa: Borealis Press, 1978. 82p. ISBN 0-919594-96-4 pa.: $4.95

A poet known for his flair with images and metaphor, Di Cicco nevertheless displays a noticeable lack of depth in this collection of poems about immigrant strivings, relationships (amorous and platonic) and the nature of poetry itself. Don Sedgwick

5350 C811.
**Di Cicco, Pier Giorgio.**
The Circular Dark. Ottawa: Borealis Press, 1977. 65p. ISBN 0-919594-62-X pa.: $3.95

Divided into four thematic sections: La Gente; January Parks; Her Only Sons; and The Circular Dark, Di Cicco's poetry speaks of his Italian heritage, his views on writing, and his perception of amorous and family relationships. A second choice to the author's *The Tough Romance.* Don Sedgwick

5351 C811.
**Di Cicco, Pier Giorgio.**
The Tough Romance. Toronto: McClelland and Stewart, 1979. 96p. ISBN 0-7710-2710-9 pa.: $5.95

Di Cicco is a young Toronto poet of Italian origin whose work has been published in over one hundred magazines and in several chapbooks. His poems are image-filled and intense: prose commentaries on the author's own world. A trifle verbose but always imaginative. Don Sedgwick

5352 C811.
**Domanski, Don.**
Heaven. Toronto: House of Anansi Press, c1978. 62p. (House of Anansi Poetry) ISBN 0-88784-069-8 pa.: $4.95

After his acclaimed *Cape Breton Book of the Dead,* the skill and economical style of this poet is sustained in this second book of verse. Nature poems, human and botanical, in new and unusual depths suggest another dimension with every read. Beth Marcilio

5353 C811.
**Downes, G. V.**
Out of the Violent Dark: Poems and Translations. Victoria: Sono Nis Press, 1978. 149p. ISBN 0-919462-64-2 $10

1. Canadian poetry (French) – Translations into English. 2. English poetry – Translations from French.

The style and philosophy of this Canadian author are well represented in this fine selection of her own poems and her translations of French-Canadian poets. While many of the works have been published in earlier collections, anthologies and journals, or broadcast on radio, they are assembled here in one convenient source. Merike Koger

5354 C811.
**Everson, R. G.**
Carnival. Ottawa: Oberon Press, c1978. 58p. ISBN 0-88750-272-5 bd.: $9.95 ISBN 0-88750-273-3 pa.: $4.50

An interesting, though uneven, collection from the well-known Montreal poet whose style is anecdotal, often prosy, and whose subjects include almost everything, great and small. Catharine MacKenzie

5355 C811.
**Fairley, Barker.**
Poems. Toronto: Yonge Street Press, 1977. 42p. ill., ports. bd. limited edition: $10 pa.: $4.50

Vivid verbal landscapes by this contemporary of the Group of Seven will interest those who know Fairley as the celebrated Goethe scholar, painter, and founding editor of the "Canadian Forum". Sheila Latham

5356 C811.
**Filip, Raymond.**
Somebody Told Me I Look Like Everyman. Vancouver: Pulp Press, 1978. 74p. ISBN 0-88978-058-7 $3.50

The title of this collection capsulizes its central concern with the individualist in a conformist society. Combining bitter social satire with fierce self-analysis, Filip wittily exposes his values, fear, and loneliness. A tendency to overload language and an unevenness in the quality of the poems flaw the work of this talented newcomer. Janet Fraser

5357 C811.
**Finnigan, Joan.**
A Reminder of Familiar Faces. Toronto: NC Press, 1978. 128p. ill. ISBN 0-919600-91-3 bd.: $10 ISBN 0-919600-90-5 pa.: $3.95

An award-winning and prolific writer, Finnigan has been described by Fred Cogswell as both a "poet's poet" and a writer whose work will appeal to "the crowd of non-poets". *A Reminder of Familiar Faces* is witty, incisive, lyrical, and above all, a delight to read. Don Sedgwick

5358 C811.
**Fraser, Dawn.**
Echoes From Labour's War: Industrial Cape Breton in the 1920's: Narrative Verse. Introduction by David Frank and Donald MacGillivray. Toronto: New Hogtown Press, c1976. 93p. ISBN 0-919940-08-0 bd.: $8 ISBN 0-919940-09-9 pa.: $2

1. Labor and laboring classes – Nova Scotia – Cape Breton Island – Poetry.

This collection of songs and poems chronicles the anger and anguish of workers' lives and their conflicts with management in the coal mines of eastern Canada. Barbara Stewart

5359 C811.
**Fry, Joseph.**
Old Wives' Lake. Saskatoon: Thistledown Press, 1978. 74p. ill., maps.
ISBN 0-920066-18-6 bd.: $12
ISBN 0-920066-17-8 pa.: $5

Although in places marred by a somewhat stale use of language this verse drama is moving in its ultimate effect. A Cree legend tells how Old Wives' Lake got its name. Catharine MacKenzie

5360 C811.
**Garnet, Eldon.**
A Martyrdom of Jean de Brébeuf. Erin, Ont.: Press Porcépic, 1977. 144p. ill.
ISBN 0-88878-137-7 pa.: $4.95

1. Brébeuf, Jean de, Saint, 1593-1649 – Poetry.

Experimental poems explore the story of Jean de Brébeuf, the Jesuit Missionary whose attempt to bring Christianity to the Indians ended in his own torture and death. Sheila Latham.

5361 C811.
**Gasparini, Len.**
Moon Without Light. Toronto: York Publishing, 1978. 53p. ill. ISBN 0-920424-08-2 bd.: $8.50 ISBN 0-920424-09-0 pa.: $3.95

Gasparini, a frequent contributor to Canadian literary magazines, writes in a powerful manner about his personal experiences – divorce, travel, falling in love, and death. Described by Irving Layton as a collection of "fine and moving poems". Don Sedgwick

5362 C811.
**Gatenby, Greg.**
The Salmon Country: A Book of Poems. Windsor, Ont.: Black Moss Press, c1978. 80p.
ISBN 0-88753-045-1 pa.: $4.95

Satiric, witty poems about Canadian writers combine with serious personal poems to provide an entertaining, competent collection. Sheila Latham

5363 C811.
**Gool, Reshard.**
In Medusa's Eye. Introduction by Ronald Baker. Charlottetown: Square Deal Publications, 1979. 62p. ISBN 0-920078-17-6 $3.95

These impressionistic poems rich in allusion, are seriously concerned with a wide variety of subjects: friendship, politics, memory, desire, time. The author is well-known for his political and publishing involvements and his award-winning novel *Price*. An unprofessional layout does not serve the publication well. Janet Fraser

5364 C811.
**Gotlieb, Phyllis.**
The Works: Collected Poems. Toronto: Calliope Press, c1978. 254p.
ISBN 0-9690774-0-8 pa.: $10.50

A collection of lyric and dramatic poetry written over twenty-one years, *The Works* includes three previously published titles: *Within the Zodiac, Ordinary, Moving* and *Doctor Umlaut's Earthly Kingdom*. Gotlieb, an internationally renowned science-fiction writer, also incorporates the language of science into some of these lively and inventive poems. Difficult but rewarding literature from an established Canadian writer. Don Sedgwick

5365 C811.
**Grier, Eldon.**
The Assassination of Colour. Fredericton, N.B.: Fiddlehead Poetry Books, 1978. 101p. (Fiddlehead Poetry Books)
ISBN 0-920110-60-6 pa.: $5

An interesting poet who is also a painter examines the work of many artists, some of them Canadian, in his search for truth in art. Catharine MacKenzie

5366 C811.
**Gustafson, Ralph.**
Corners in the Glass. Toronto: McClelland and Stewart, c1977. 92p. ISBN 0-7710-3705-8 pa.: $4.95

A fine collection from a mature poet, these poems contain more personal experience and evocative imagery than his earlier collections. They are in many instances gentler, more touching, less intellectual and grand. Catharine MacKenzie

5367 C811.
**Gustafson, Ralph.**
Soviet Poems, Sept. 13 to Oct. 5, 1976. Winnipeg: Turnstone Press, 1978. 47p. (Turnstone Poetry Series Two)
ISBN 0-88801-010-9 bd.: $7
ISBN 0-88801-008-7 pa.: $4

Nineteen poems written on a twenty-one day journey to the USSR document the movement and impressions of this poet who won the Governor General's Award in 1974 for his poetry collection, *Fire on Stone*. These poems are not philosophical or deeply reflective but are well-crafted, humorous and graceful in the dark Russian-red print of a well-designed book. Beth Marcilio

5368 C811.
**Gutteridge, Don.**
A True History of Lambton County. Ottawa: Oberon Press, c1977. 138p. ISBN 0-88750-245-8 bd.: $12.95 ISBN 0-88750-246-6 pa.: $4.95

1. Lambton, Ont. – Poetry.

In a long narrative poem, the lines interspersed with prose accounts of exploration by Champlain, Radisson and others, the poet discovers his sense of continuity with the people who knew before him the environment that shaped him. Catharine MacKenzie.

5369 C811.
**Hawley, Helen.**
Gathering Fire: Poems. Saskatoon: Thistledown Press, 1977. 52p. ill. ISBN 0-920066-12-7 bd.: $9.50 ISBN 0-920066-11-9 pa.: $4

Libraries specializing in poetry may wish to consider for purchase this interesting collection of poems and illustrations by a poet who grew up on the prairies and is now exiled in London. The poetry is subjective and reflects her attachment to her beginnings. Catharine MacKenzie

5370 C811.
**Helwig, David.**
A Book of the Hours: Poems. Ottawa: Oberon Press, c1979. 90p. ISBN 0-88750-295-4 bd.: $11.95 ISBN 0-88750-296-2 pa.: $4.95

Quiet but important statements from a poet with different perspectives. This volume includes the poignant, "Dumbells", one of the rare poems with Canadian allusions. Well-published, unaffected poetry in clear honest print. Beth Marcilio

5371 C811.
**Henderson, Brian.**
The Expanding Room. Oakville, Ont.: Mosaic Press/Valley Editions, 1977. 93p. ISBN 0-88753-036-2 $3.95

Henderson is part of a uniquely Canadian poetic trend that fuses contemporary angst with the terrors of the natural world. In his use of the mythopoeic and his playfulness with language and perception, Henderson may be compared with Atwood. This collection uses many cultural sources and personae to vividly chart the progress of a probing mind. Janet Fraser

5372 C811.
**Henderson, Brian.**
Paracelsus: A Poem in Forty Parts, With a Prologue. Erin, Ont.: Porcupine's Quill, 1977. 24p. ISBN 0-88984-034-2 bd.: $10.95 ISBN 0-88984-032-6 pa.: $4.95

1. Paracelsus, 1493-1541 – Poetry.

Using deeply different rhythms and content from other modern Canadian poets, Brian Henderson uses the alchemist's search for purity as the central metaphor for a search for the true self. This outstanding poem in forty parts, carefully and beautifully published gives a new perspective with each reading. Beth Marcilio

5373 C811.
**Henderson, Brian.**
The Viridical Book of the Silent Planet. Calligraphy, Ann Housden; illustrations, Stephen Wohleber. Toronto: Aya Press, 1978. 89p. ill. ISBN 0-920544-06-1 bd.: $20 ISBN 0-920544-05-3 pa.: $5.95 ISBN 0-920544-07-X deluxe (in slipcase): $80

In his third collection, Henderson finds a unifying frame of reference for his continuing exploration of human perception and language and the cosmos: the science fiction fantasy. Philosophical yet passionate, these poems indicate a growing complexity and assurance. The imaginative illustrations may broaden the book's appeal. Janet Fraser

5374 C811.
**Hicks, John V.**
Now Is a Far Country: Poems Selected from the Works of John V. Hicks. Saskatoon: Thistledown Press, 1978. 113p. port. ISBN 0-920066-20-8 bd.: $12 ISBN 0-920066-19-4 pa.: $5

The poet's work has been published for many years in Canadian and American magazines but this is his first collection. He is a craftsman, generous in his perceptions, frequently traditional in form. Those who believe that poetry should be a "celebration of life" should look into this volume. Catharine MacKenzie

5375 C811.
**Jaques, Edna.**
Prairie Born, Prairie Bred: Poetic Reflections of a Pioneer. Saskatoon: Western Producer Prairie Books, c1979. 86p. Index. ISBN 0-88833-012-X $8.95

A native of Saskatchewan describes the "little things" in pioneering life on the prairies in rhymed verses which teeter on the edge of doggerel. Catharine MacKenzie

5376 C811.
**Jones, Douglas Gordon.**
Under the Thunder the Flowers Light Up the Earth. Toronto: Coach House Press, c1977. 110p. pa.: $4.50

Critic-author of the brilliant *Butterfly on Rock,* D. G. Jones won the 1977 Governor General's Award for this collection of poetry, written over a span of ten years. The A. J. M. Smith award was won for the section entitled, "The Lampman Poems". Beth Marcilio

5377 C811.
**Kearns, Lionel.**
Practicing Up to Be Human. Toronto: Coach House Press, c1978. 84p.
ISBN 0-88910-101-9 $4

A very substantial collection of poetry in many forms. Kearns alliterates, concretes and formalizes with graphic humour and occasional beauty. The strongest poem, "Private Poem for a Manitoulin Island Canada Day", justifies this first major collection in nine years. Beth Marcilio

5378 C811.
**Kelly, Michael T.**
Country You Can't Walk To. Moonbeam, Ont.: Penumbra Press, 1979. 47p. ill.
ISBN 0-920806-00-7 pa.: $3.50

This slim collection of verse with its clean, economical language and sharp, visual imagery leaves the reader begging for more poems. Taken separately or as a group, the poems are an indictment of the perverse, destructive nature of man. Most outstanding are the intensely felt portraits of martyred animals. Janet Fraser

5379 C811.
**Kogawa, Joy.**
Jericho Road. Toronto: McClelland and Stewart, c1977. 112p. ISBN 0-7710-4527-1 pa.: $4.95

The poems deal with life in the city and the agonies of personal relationships. Particularly the short poems thrum with energy like telegraph wires and the images are sharp as the razor's edge. A very fine collection. Catharine MacKenzie

5380 C811.
**Kroetsch, Robert.**
The Ledger. 2d ed. Ilderton, Ont.: Brick/Nairn, 1979. 32p. ill., maps.
ISBN 0-919626-11-4 $3

A re-issue of the long documentary poem first published in 1975. The daily record of the transactions at his grandfather's sawmill provides the metaphor, managed with grace and skill, for the poet's search for the balance in life. Catharine MacKenzie

5381 C811.
**Kroetsch, Robert.**
Seed Catalogue: Poems. Winnipeg: Turnstone Press, c1977. 75p. ill.
ISBN 0-88801-005-2 bd.: $12
ISBN 0-88801-004-4 pa.: $5.95

The long title poem, comprising more than half of this collection, is a series of thoughtful reflections on life on the prairies. Well-crafted and inventive work from a former winner of the Governor General's Award for fiction. Don Sedgwick

5382 C811.
**Lane, Patrick.**
Albino Pheasants. Madeira Park, B.C.: Harbour Publishing, c1977. 32p.
ISBN 0-920080-16-2 pa.: $2.95

A small book of twenty-one lyrics from a poet who controls his material, knows how to choose the perfect work, and to keep the sound of his lines running in one's mind. The subjects in this volume are nature and working people. Catharine MacKenzie

5383 C811.
**Lane, Patrick.**
Poems, New and Selected. Toronto: Oxford University Press, 1978. 112p.
ISBN 0-19-540296-0 pa.: $4.95

Winner of the Governor General's Award for poetry in 1978, *Poems, New and Selected* is one of the landmarks of poetry in the last decade. Lane creates stark images in these accounts of his travels and experiences. Don Sedgwick

5384 C811.
**Layton, Irving.**
The Covenant. Toronto: McClelland and Stewart, c1977. 112p. ISBN 0-7710-4832-7 pa.: $4.95

In this book the poet again implicates Christianity in anti-Semitism and holds it ultimately responsible for the Holocaust. Though this book is rougher and more brutal than the earlier one, those libraries which have *For My Brother Jesus* will want to purchase this complementary volume. Some typical Layton love poems are included here as well. Catharine MacKenzie

5385 C811.
**Layton, Irving.**
Droppings From Heaven. Toronto: McClelland and Stewart, c1979. 111p. ISBN 0-7710-4944-7 pa.: $5.95

Another surge of energy from life-by-the-throat Layton. Slight, never boring poems live amid the beautiful and new, "Senile My Sister Sleeps" and "Divorce". Not all the droppings are from heaven but the downpour is worthwhile. The wordy foreward includes a vivid Layton testament, "I want to go into the sunset with both pitchforks blazing". Beth Marcilio

5386 C811.
**Layton, Irving.**
The Poems of Irving Layton. Edited and with an introduction by Eli Mandel. Toronto: McClelland and Stewart, c1977. ISBN 0-7710-9516-3 pa.: $1.95

Fifty poems from Layton's many volumes were selected by poet-professor Eli Mandel. A good collection to introduce the reader to the brilliance, "A Tall Man Executes a Jig", the beauty, "Keine Lazarovitch 1870-1959", the acerbity, "Golfers", and human insight, "Lillian Roxon" of the great Canadian. Beth Marcilio

5387 C811.
**Layton, Irving.**
The Selected Poems of Irving Layton. Toronto: McClelland and Stewart, c1977. 63p. ISBN 0-8112-0641-6 bd. ISBN 0-8112-0642-4 pa.: $1.95

A tidy little book of the poet's best-known and most popular poems, with a useful introduction by a poet admirer, would serve very well to introduce Layton to a new reader. Catharine MacKenzie

5388 C811.
**Layton, Irving.**
The Tightrope Dancer. Toronto: McClelland and Stewart, c1978. 112p. ISBN 0-7710-4871-8 pa.: $5.95

Poetic balancing acts featuring male and female relationships and erotic sex and death. Sheila Latham

5389 C811.
**Lee, Dennis.**
The Gods. Toronto: McClelland and Stewart, c1979. 63p. ISBN 0-7710-5214-6 pa.: $6.95

The theme of the collection is the absence of the gods, the religious dimension, from our everyday life and the consequent devaluation of life. The book includes the long poem "The Death of Harold Ladoo" published separately in 1976. Catharine MacKenzie

5390 C811.
**Livesay, Dorothy.**
The Woman I Am. Erin, Ont.: Press Porcépic, c1977. 96p. ISBN 0-88878-139-3 pa.: $2.95

In a selection of poems published between 1926 and 1977 by a winner of two Governor General's awards, Dorothy Livesay's themes remain constant; sex, ageing, love, loneliness and death. These large themes are often diminished by a soft monotonous touch. The lyricism of the early, lovely "Serenade for Strings" is often diluted to the facile rather than the wise. Beth Marcilio

5391 C811.
**Lowther, Pat.**
A Stone Diary. Toronto: Oxford University Press, 1977. 96p. ISBN 0-19-540261-8 pa.: $3.95

This is the fourth and last book of a talented young poet who died in 1975. Her poems deal with personal relationships largely, though some are political. Both her celebrations and her denunciations are intense, passionate. Catharine MacKenzie

5392 C811.
**MacPhee, Rosalind.**
Scarecrow. Fredericton, N.B.: Fiddlehead Poetry Books, 1979. 64p. port. (Fiddlehead Poetry Books) ISBN 0-920110-78-9 pa.: $4.50

Widely published in journals, MacPhee is one of a long line of promising poets introduced in the Fiddlehead series. These poems which probe knowledge of love and the self are candid, flowing, and lyrical. Her focus is narrow but clear; it is hoped that she will branch out in future works. Janet Fraser

5393 C811.
**Madoff, Mark.**
Dry Point. Drawings by Bryan Wert. Vancouver: Pulp Press, c1979. 86p. ill. ISBN 0-88978-060-9 pa.: $3.50

Nature themes permeate this collection of poems which record Madoff's impressions of British Columbia. The poet is a writing and literature instructor at the University of British Columbia. The simple, direct language makes an advanced level of poetic appreciation unnecessary for the enjoyment of this selection. Merike Koger

5394 C811.
**Mandel, Eli.**
Out of Place: Poems. Preface and photographs by Ann Mandel. Erin, Ont.: Press Porcépic, 1977. 77p. ill. Bibliography: p. 77. ISBN 0-88878-075-3 pa.: $4.95

An inexpensive but imaginative publication shows Eli Mandel's limitless poetic boundaries. Using a return to the land of his childhood, Jewish farming settlements in Saskatchewan, with stark photographs by Ann Mandel, the poet skillfully crafts styles and moods that evoke elusive memories, mirror-images and the knowledge that time makes the image and the memory out of place. Beth Marcilio

5395 C811.
**Mandel, Miriam.**
Station 14. Edmonton: NeWest Press, 1977. 40p. ill. ISBN 0-920316-08-5 $4.95

Winner of the Governor General's Award for Poetry in 1973, Mandel in her second book documents the various stages of a nervous breakdown. The confessional nature of the poetry is saved from self-indulgence by the poet's precise analysis and touches of black humour. Richly metaphoric details contribute to the overall poignance of the narration. Janet Fraser

5396 C811.
**McCracken, Kathleen.**
Reflections. Fredericton, N.B.: Fiddlehead Poetry Books, 1978. 51p. (Fiddlehead Poetry Books) ISBN 0-920110-64-9 pa.: $4

The young (and others) will enjoy the work of this very young poet, where they will find a great deal to think about and admire. The maturity of her thought and craft make this book outstanding. Catharine MacKenzie

5397 C811.
**McFadden, David.**
On the Road Again. Toronto: McClelland and Stewart, c1978. 112p. ISBN 0-7710-5510-2 pa.: $5.95

Good-natured reporting of experiences and thoughts are simply expressed in many narrative poems, making them accessible to readers and listeners of all ages. David McFadden is also the author of, *Intense Pleasure, The Great Canadian Sonnet,* and other books. Beth Marcilio

5398 C811.
**McFadden, David.**
The Poet's Progress. Toronto: Coach House Press, 1977. 63p. port. ISBN 0-88910-006-3 pa.: $4

A large outstanding poem in a small insignificant book moves between real and surreal, urbanity and the sublime. The free verse, in twenty-two sections, goes intuitively and intellectually in and out of the poet's life processes with tenderness, exuberance and wit. Beth Marcilio

5399 C811.
**McFadden, David.**
The Saladmaker. Montreal: Cross Country Press, c1977. 37p. ISBN 0-916696-03-0 pa.: $2

First published in "Imago" the verse in this volume is re-issued with deletions and "further simplification" of some lines. In his introduction the poet writes about the origins of his poems in the events of his own life, frequently ordinary, familiar, domestic, delivered with wit and without pretension. Catharine MacKenzie.

5400 C811.
**McKay, Gail.**
The Pat Lowther Poem. Toronto: Coach House Press, c1978. 72p. ISBN 0-88910-105-1 pa.: $4

1. Lowther, Pat, 1935-1975 – Poetry.

Winner of the CBC Radio Literary Competition's second prize for the best long poem of 1978.

This personal account of the death of poet Pat Lowther, the author's friend and teacher, poetically incorporates newspaper reports about the murder and trial. Sheila Latham

5401 C811.
**McLeod, Joseph.**
Protect My House. Ottawa: Borealis Press, 1977. 54p. ISBN 0-919594-68-9 pa.: $3.95

Fifty-four brittle, economical poems in McLeod's distinctive style generate a multitude of images of farms, family, blood-ties and loves. Themes also extend beyond the "house" but only to emphasize its significance. Stravinsky/ will always/possess/the tickle and itch/of spring/I/possess/the old Cornwall Farm. Beth Marcilio

5402 C811.
**McNamara, Eugene.**
Screens. Toronto: Coach House Press, 1977. 66p. ill. ISBN 0-88910-016-0 pa.: $4

Movie screen stars are used to screen time,

maturity, evoke feelings of inadequacy and humour in an interesting treatment. Sympathy toward humanity is presented through the instruments of popular culture. The best poems are in the section, "Running to Daylight", and do not use movie stars as an evocative base line. Recurring television screen graphics remind the reader of a current medium that can recall the past. Beth Marcilio

5403 C811.
**Moir, James M.**
Family Chronicle: Poems and Photographs of the Canadian West. Toronto: Gage Publishing, 1978. 64p. ill. ISBN 0-7715-9465-8 pa.: $5.95

The interesting clear old photographs in this book are of a better quality than the poems they illustrate. However, there is enough clarity of style, characterization and conventional rhyme to make this work from the West a suitable introduction to poetry for younger readers. Beth Marcilio

5404 C811.
**Moisan, Clément.**
A Poetry of Frontiers. Translated by George Lang. Victoria: Press Porcépic, 1979. Bibliography. Index. (Three Solitudes, Contemporary Literary Criticism in Canada) ISBN 0-88878-078-8 $15

1. Literature, Comparative – Canadian (English) and Canadian (French). 2. Canadian poetry – 20th century – History and criticism.

Translation of *Poésies des frontières.*

"A survey of Quebec poetry as well as of English-Canadian poetry, essays on themes important for comparison and many insightful cultural comparisons." -Publisher's note. Includes critical commentaries on poets Anne Hébert, P. K. Page, Margaret Avison, Irving Layton, Raymond Souster, John Newlove, Margaret Atwood, and others. Sheila Latham

5405 C811.
**Mouré, Erin.**
Empire, York Street. Toronto: House of Anansi Press, 1979. 91p. (House of Anansi Poetry) ISBN 0-88784-072-8 pa.: $5.95

Erin Mouré's first book of well-crafted and lovely poems was nominated for a 1980 Governor General's Award. Some affectations by the young artist do not mar an outstanding work. Not only has the poet great promise, she has already much to give. Attention should be paid to any future works. Beth Marcilio

5406 C811.
**Musgrave, Susan.**
Becky Swan's Book. Erin, Ont.: Porcupine's Quill, c1977. 32p. ill.
ISBN 0-88984-026-1 bd.: $40
ISBN 0-88984-024-5 pa.: $4.95

Eleven short poems reveal Becky Swan's inner world, partly through her own experience and partly through the experience of other women, all of whom are in some way victimized. The reader must have a taste for the gothic in order to appreciate fully this talented poet's work. Catharine MacKenzie

5407 C811.
**Musgrave, Susan.**
A Man to Marry, A Man to Bury. Toronto: McClelland and Stewart, c1979. 125p.
ISBN 0-7710-6655-4 pa.: $6.95

Profoundly disturbing in its stark grizzliness, *A Man to Marry, A Man to Bury* is a truly haunting collection of poems. Her mythical and often surreal images make Musgrave one of Canada's most compelling authors. This selection of her poems is, quite simply, essential reading. Don Sedgwick

5408 C811.
**Musgrave, Susan.**
Selected Strawberries and Other Poems. Victoria: Sono Nis Press, 1977. 164p.
ISBN 0-919462-39-1 bd.: $10
ISBN 0-919462-41-3 pa.: $4.95

Musgrave creates haunting images in this selection of poems divided into four thematic sections: Fire-Feast, Kistatinaw Songs, Witchery Way, and Selected Strawberries. Unusual, vivid writing from a prolific west coast poet. Don Sedgwick

5409 C811.
**Newlove, John.**
The Fat Man: Selected Poems, 1962-1972. Toronto: McClelland and Stewart, c1977. 127p. ISBN 0-7710-6733-X pa.: $4.95

John Newlove has revised a number of poems from five previous books, bringing together a selection from the work of a decade. This collection, by the 1973 Governor General's Award winner, is important because many poems are included from volumes now out of print. Moreover, they show the range of this fine poet from poignancy and negation in, "Then If I Cease Desiring", to the still great but more affirmative, "The Pride". Beth Marcilio

5410 C811.
**Nowlan, Alden.**
Smoked Glass. Toronto: Clarke, Irwin, c1977. 71p. ISBN 0-7720-1194-X $7.95

Canadian Authors' Association Literary Award.

An award-winning poet and novelist, Nowlan is a keen observer of the human condition and a poet with that rare commodity, a sense of humour. *Smoked Glass* is a delight to read and a pleasant antidote to some of our more academic and abstruse poetry. Don Sedgwick

5411 C811.
**Ondaatje, Michael.**
There's a Trick with a Knife I'm Learning to Do: Poems 1963-1978. Toronto: McClelland and Stewart, c1979. 107p. ISBN 0-7710-6882-4 pa.: $5.95

Governor General's Literary Award.

Ondaatje's poetry is intense, challenging and often profound. Patient readers will want to linger over these haunting images and admire their many layers of meaning. A necessary addition to any poetry collection. Don Sedgwick

5412 C811.
**Pittman, Al.**
Once When I Was Drowning: Poems. St. John's, Nfld.: Breakwater Books, 1978. 79p.
ISBN 0-919948-49-9 bd.: $10.95
ISBN 0-919948-48-0 pa.: $5.95

The author of the award-winning collection of children's poems, *Down by Jim Long's Stage* has produced a tender but slight collection of poems for adults. Recurring themes of death, shooting, drowning, freezing, falling, sleeping, cancer and old-age are drawn lightly, almost good-naturedly and thus inappropriately. A likeable light-weight from Newfoundland. Beth Marcilio

5413 C811.
**Plantos, Ted.**
The Universe Ends at Sherbourne & Queen. Photographs by Angeline Kyba. Toronto: Steel Rail Publishing, 1977. 125p. ill., map. ISBN 0-88791-011-4 bd.: $10.95
ISBN 0-88791-009-2 pa.: $5.95

Poetry, prose and perhaps deliberately under-exposed photographs by Angela Kyba document darkness, despair, tough humour and raw truth through life in Toronto's tenderloin. Included is the much-praised, "Legend of Red Ryan", a true story from the thirties of an infamous bank robber. This poem reflects Plantos' sympathy with the down-and-out, the social outcast and his cynicism toward the would-be reformers. Beth Marcilio

5414 C811.
**Purdy, Al.**
At Marsport Drugstore. An appreciation by Charles Bukowski; drawings by Hugh LeRoy. Sutton West, Ont.: Paget Press, 1977. 62p. ill. ISBN 0-920348-00-9 pa.: $6

Purdy writes eloquently of the joy, passion and pain of love. "Woman is", the first of the fifteen poems, sets the tone: "Woman is image of woman/ woman is she/ whom even if I had never known/ could never forget." The book unfortunately contains numerous uninspired drawings by artist Hugh LeRoy. Don Sedgwick

5415 C811.
**Purdy, Al.**
Being Alive: Poems, 1958-1978. Toronto: McClelland and Stewart, c1978. 208p. Index. ISBN 0-7710-7207-4 pa.: $7.95

Selected poems dating from 1958 to 1978 are presented in this representative collection by a major Canadian poet. Purdy writes eloquently about our nation's past: the people, the places and the awesome qualities of life and death. Powerful, evocative and often humorous, Purdy is a central voice in our poetic tradition. Don Sedgwick

5416 C811.
**Purdy, Al.**
A Handful of Earth. Coatsworth, Ont.: Black Moss Press, 1977. 62p.
ISBN 0-88753-023-0 bd.: $8
ISBN 0-88753-022-2 pa.: $2.50

At times gruff, on occasion witty, Purdy deals with beauty and suffering in "Starlings" and with our sense of place and history in "A Handful of Earth", two of the strongest poems in this collection. Not all his best work, Purdy himself admits, but still very powerful poetry. Don Sedgwick

5417 C811.
**Pyke, Linda.**
Prisoner. Toronto: Macmillan, 1978. ISBN 0-7705-1715-3 $4.95

A bold metaphysical wit and graphic sexual imagination mark this study of frustrated desire. A series of addresses to an imprisoned murderer whose past has aroused the poet's passions, the book must be read like a novel for its full impact. Widely published in magazines, Pyke published this one collection before she died suddenly in 1979. Janet Fraser

5418 C811.
**Rapoport, Janis.**
Winter Flowers. Willowdale, Ont.: Hounslow Press, c1979. 87p. ISBN 0-88882-028-3 pa.: $4.95

Poems about landscapes, about motherhood and prenatal life, family poems, poems inspired by her children's paintings make up this collection. They are affectionate though not sentimental, rich in imagery, and occasionally obscure in meaning. Catharine MacKenzie

5419 C811.
**Rikki.**
Knife Notebook. Fredericton, N.B.: Fiddlehead Poetry Books, 1977. 36p. $4

The subject matter, the intense emotions of a victimized lover, and the structure, the design of a "notebook" or diary, clearly designate this collection as an expression of personal experience. Within severe limitations of theme and style, the poet creates original images of a woman hopelessly drawn to a man who torments and betrays her. Janet Fraser

5420 C811.
**Rogers, Linda.**
This Is a List. Fredericton, N.B.: Fiddlehead Poetry Books, 1977. 36p. ill. (Fiddlehead Poetry Books) ISBN 0-919197-98-1 pa.: $3

The author's fourth book presents dominant images of creation, birth, and motherhood in poems that ponder the natural cycle of life and death. Sheila Latham

5421 C811.
**Rosenblatt, Joe.**
Loosely Tied Hands: An Experiment in Punk. Oakville, Ont.: Black Moss Press, 1978. 48p. ISBN 0-88753-042-7 pa.: $3.95

Joe Rosenblatt is unconventional, never easy but fun to read. This book celebrates the snake and shows him in many guises. Catharine MacKenzie

5422 C811.
**Saunders, Thomas.**
Beyond the Lakes: Selected Poems. Winnipeg: Peguis Publishers, 1978. 57p. ISBN 0-919566-70-7 $7.50

Poems about the prairie landscape and its inhabitants describe rural life during the thirties to the sixties. Some are written in blank verse, some in free verse and some in a rhyme scheme which the poet felt "might reflect something of the unobtrusive nature of prairie beauty which, unlike the beauty of the mountains, does not rush out to meet us ..." Catharine MacKenzie

5423 C811.
**Skelton, Robin.**
Because of Love. Toronto: McClelland and Stewart, c1977. 98p. ISBN 0-7710-8189-8 pa.: $4.95

Skelton, a prolific author and respected editor, has divided this collection into six thematic sections: Prologue, The Awakening, Seasons of Love, The Space Between, The Hold of Our Hands, and Epilogue. These are passionate works, even erotic, and a tribute to the sensual pleasures of love. Don Sedgwick

5424 C811.
**Skelton, Robin.**
Landmarks. Lantzville, B.C.: Oolichan Books, 1979. ISBN 0-88982-024-4 bd.: $8.95 ISBN 0-88982-028-7 pa.: $5.95

An Englishman who considers Canada his spiritual home, Skelton in this collection discovers and recreates the legends and peoples of his adopted Vancouver Island. Like the mythopoeic poets, he is concerned with how man inhabits and is inhabited by his environment. A prolific poet, he has developed a natural narrative voice, tense rhythms, and compelling images taken from many sources. Janet Fraser

5425 C811.
**Smith, A. J. M.**
The Classic Shade: Selected Poems. Introduction by M. L. Rosenthal. Toronto: McClelland and Stewart, c1978. 96p. ISBN 0-7710-8213-4 pa.: $5.95

Highly regarded as a critic and literary editor, Smith is also a respected poet, a master of the sonnet and other verse forms. *The Classic Shade* deals with such themes as the poetic muse, death and nature. Some of the poems are formalistic and impersonal, but many of Smith's classics are reprinted here. Don Sedgwick

5426 C811.
**Smith, Kay.**
When a Girl Looks Down. Fredericton, N.B.: Fiddlehead Poetry Books, 1978. 132p. (Fiddlehead Poetry Books) ISBN 0-920110-03-7 pa.: $5

There are more than one hundred poems in this collection. They are not obscure in language nor inaccessible in thought. They are on subjects and about feelings which are familiar to the common reader. They are also fully professional in craft. Catharine MacKenzie

5427 C811.
**Sorestad, Glen A.**
Ancestral Dances. Saskatoon: Thistledown Press, 1979. 69p. ISBN 0-920066-26-7 bd.: $12 ISBN 0-920066-25-9 pa.: $5.95

Some reviewers believe that this poet will eventually give the world a volume of outstanding poetry. Poetry lovers who would like to know what he is capable of will find this book interesting though some of the poems are disappointing. Catharine MacKenzie

5428 C811.
**Souster, Raymond.**
Extra Innings: New Poems. Ottawa: Oberon Press, c1977. 176p. ISBN 0-88750-217-2 pa.: $4.50

*Extra Innings* demonstrates Souster's ability to deal with melancholic remembrances of the two World Wars and reflections on daily events in Toronto in a very poignant manner. Thoughtful, compelling and imaginative, Souster is an accomplished poet. Oberon Press has failed here and elsewhere to include an index. Don Sedgwick

5429 C811.
**Souster, Raymond.**
Hanging In: New Poems. Ottawa: Oberon Press, c1979. 141p. port. ISBN 0-88750-305-5 bd.: $15 ISBN 0-88750-306-3 pa.: $6.95

The City of Toronto Book Award.

Strong, evocative poems, mainly about Toronto, by one of the best established figures of the Canadian literary scene. The book concludes with "Pictures From a Long-Lost World", a narrative poem about World War II which some critics consider one of the best creations of Souster's long and illustrious career. Don Sedgwick

5430 C811.
**Stevens, Peter.**
The Bogman Pavese Tactics. Fredericton, N.B.: Fiddlehead Poetry Books, 1977. 71p. ISBN 0-920110-00-2 pa.: $4.50

Supernatural poems presenting images of bone, decay and frightened animals are balanced by poems depicting the ironies and frustrations of everyday life. Sheila Latham

5431 C811.
**Suknaski, Andrew.**
East of Myloona. Saskatoon: Thistledown Press, 1979. 68p. ISBN 0-920066-22-4 bd.: $14.95 ISBN 0-920066-21-6 pa.: $6.95

In this collection Suknaski has shifted his focus from the prairies to the north. Using authentic dialogue and incident, he shapes a powerful vision of a region, its peoples and its problems. The form is experimental; the moral messages are not subtle. The publication is enhanced by the poet's sensitive drawings. Janet Fraser

5432 C811.
**Suknaski, Andrew.**
The Ghosts Call You Poor. Toronto: Macmillan, 1978. 117p. port. ISBN 0-7705-1656-4 pa.: $5.95

Canadian Authors' Association Literary Award.

"The ghosts call us poor" because we impoverish ourselves by allowing ourselves to forget our beginnings. But the poet celebrates the heritage of the West: the Romanians, Ukrainians, Chinese, Métis, Indians, the early explorers. He listens to the stories the elders tell and shapes them for our enrichment. Catharine MacKenzie

5433 C811.
**Thompson, John.**
Stilt Jack. Toronto: House of Anansi Press, c1978. 48p. (House of Anansi Poetry) ISBN 0-88784-055-8 pa.: $6.95

In his foreward the poet has explained the form which he uses. The ghazal originated in Persia and is a series of five couplets linked by a tone rather than subject. This collection has been published just as it was found after the poet's death at the age of thirty-eight. It is a striking book, sombre, with many images of despair. Catharine MacKenzie

5434 C811.
**Virgo, Seán.**
Deathwatch on Skidegate Narrows and Other Poems. Victoria: Sono Nis Press, 1979. 142p. ISBN 0-919462-70-7 pa.: $5.95

The title poem is a long ambitious poem, powerful in its effect, a journey to self discovery through the Canadian landscape, nature and Indian themes. Unhappily the remainder of the collection does not attain the same power. Catharine MacKenzie

5435 C811.
**Waddington, Miriam.**
Mister Never. Winnipeg: Turnstone Press, c1978. 35p. (Turnstone Press Poetry Series One) ISBN 0-88801-001-7 pa.: $4.95

Poetry, as the poet states in her preface, on the "theme of absence, of unreturned love, or to put it differently, of a one-sided projection of the self". The projection is "Mister Never", the man of one's dreams who has his existence only in the imagination. The poet catches glimpses of him in Paris, Moscow, Toronto, but alas he never becomes corporeal. Catharine MacKenzie

5436 C811.
**Watson, Wilfred.**
I Begin with Counting. Edmonton: NeWest Press, c1978. 104p. ISBN 0-920316-22-0 pa.: $9.95

An attractive book, printed in two colours, featuring experimental concrete and sound poems with words and syllables arranged according to a numbered grid system. Sheila Latham

5437 C811.
**Wayman, Tom.**
Free Time: Industrial Poems. Toronto: Macmillan, 1977. 128p. ISBN 0-7705-1522-3 pa.: $5.95

The work of this socially committed poet skirts the edge of prosiness. In this volume there are poems on loggers, factory workers, suburban housewives, on Pablo Neruda, George Brown and the Indians of Lytton, B.C. as well as poems about his loves, fears, feelings of triumph and inadequacy. Catharine MacKenzie

5438 C811.
**West, David S.**
Franklin and McClintock: Poems. Vancouver: Intermedia Press, 1977. 78p. ill., maps, ports. ISBN 0-8895-605-44 pa.: $6.95

The story of the ill-fated Franklin expedition of 1845-1848 to find the Northwest Passage, and the McClintock search mission of 1857-1859, is told in poetry. Vignette after vignette brings to life the two major characters and the reader is left with a feel for Arctic exploration seldom achieved by history books. The poetry is supplemented by maps and illustrations from McClintock's own account.

## C811.008 Poetry - Collections

5439 C811'.008
**Allison, Gay,** ed.
Landscape. Edited by Gay Allison, Karen Hood and Janis Rapoport. Toronto: Women's Writing Collective, c1977. 123p. ISBN 0-9690680-0-X pa.: $4

1. Canadian poetry (English) – 20th century. 2. Canadian poetry (English) – Ontario – Toronto – Women authors.

Sixty-five Toronto-based women present a wide range of poetic form, content, and craftsmanship. Sheila Latham

5440 C811'.008
**Bayard, Caroline.**
Out-posts. Avant-postes. By Caroline Bayard and Jack David. Erin, Ont.: Press Porcépic, 1977. Bibliographies.
ISBN 0-88878-102-4 bd.: $15
ISBN 0-88878-103-2 pa.: $6.95

1. Poets, Canadian (English) – 20th century – Interviews. 2. Poets, Canadian (French) – 20th century – Interviews.

This is the fourth volume in the series *Three Solitudes: Contemporary Literary Criticism in Canada*.

An interesting collection of interviews with, and poetry by, eight avant-garde Canadian poets. The experimental format includes four interviews in French, without translation. Includes selected bibliographies of the poets' works and critical writings on each artist. Patricia O'Sullivan

5441 C811'.008
**Clement, Tom,** ed.
Poems for Sale in the Street: A Daring New Anthology. Edited by Tom Clement and Ted Plantos. Toronto: Steel Rail Publishing, c1979. 119p. ISBN 0-88791-017-3 pa.: $4.95

1. Canadian poetry (English) – 20th century.

While most works in this collection are forthright in their treatment of the fundamental realities of life, "daring" is too strong an adjective. The recurring theme is politics in this selection of the work of fourteen poets. There are biographical notes. Merike Koger

5442 C811'.008
**Clever, W. Glenn,** ed.
Poets of the Capital II, edited by W. Glenn Clever and Frank M. Tierney. Ottawa: Borealis Press, 1978. 136p. plates, ports. ISBN 0-919594-94-8 pa.: $5.95

1. Canadian poetry (English) – 20th century.

2. Canadian poetry (English) – Ontario – Ottawa.

Editors Glenn Clever and Frank M. Tierney have collected the work of forty-six living Canadian poets from the Ottawa area. Brief biographies and bibliographies are given for each of the authors. Although selections by Joy Kogawa and Robin Mathews have been included, most of the poets are lesser-knowns. Don Sedgwick

5443 C811'.008

**Colombo, John Robert.**

Mostly Monsters. Willowdale, Ont.: Hounslow Press, c1977. 126p. ISBN 0-88882-014-3 pa.: $2.95

1. Poetry – Collections. 2. Monsters in literature.

Another in an ongoing series of "found poetry" books, *Mostly Monsters* is a collection of literary curiosities culled from comic books, monster films, radio scripts and horror novels. Wonder Woman, Werewolf, Buck Rogers and Jekyll and Hyde are a few of the featured fantasies. The final epithets are the real poetic gems in this collection. Don Sedgwick

5444 C811'.008

**Colombo, John Robert,** ed.

The Poets of Canada. Edmonton: Hurtig Publishers, c1978. 303p. Index. ISBN 0-88830-150-2 $12.95

1. Canadian poetry.

The "Master Gatherer" has herein gathered the work of two hundred Canadian poets whose work ranges in date from 1606 to 1978. One representative work by poets as diverse as Jean de Brébeuf and Margaret Atwood is presented with a brief biography and bibliography. A highly recommended introduction to our literary history. Don Sedgwick

5445 C811'.008

**Currie, Robert,** ed.

Number One Northern: Poetry From Saskatchewan. Photographs of Saskatchewan places and people by Richard Gustin. Moose Jaw, Sask.: Thunder Creek Publishing, c1977. 155p. ill. ISBN 0-919926-04-5 pa.: $5

1. Canadian poetry (English) – 20th century.
2. Canadian poetry (English) – Saskatchewan.

This visually appealing anthology captures the traditions and character of Saskatchewan with poems by Elizabeth Brewster, Ken Mitchell, Suknaski, Sorestad, and thirty-seven others. Sheila Latham

5446 C811'.008

**Davis, N. Brian,** ed.

The Poetry of the Canadian People: Volume II, 1900-1950. Toronto: NC Press, 1978. 224p. ill. ISBN 0-919600-98-0 bd.: $16.95 ISBN 0-919600-97-2 pa.: $8.95

1. Labor and laboring classes – Poetry.
2. Canadian poetry.

*The Poetry of the Canadian People, 1720-1920: Two Hundred Years of Hard Work* listed *CS* no. 2555.

Davis has assembled a unique collection of working-class poetry: limericks, songs and other verse by miners, lumbermen, soldiers and railwaymen. Many of the poems are accompanied by fascinating notes on the incidents or people involved. Also includes an introduction on working-class culture and its place within the Canadian cultural mosaic. Don Sedgwick

5447 C811'.008

**Day, David,** ed.

Many Voices. Edited by David Day and Marilyn Bowering. Vancouver: J. J. Douglas, 1977. 98p. ISBN 0-88894-134-X pa.: $5.95

1. Canadian poetry (English) – Indian authors. 2. Canadian poetry (English) – 20th century.

Familiar names such as Duke Redbird and George Clutesi and lesser-known but deserving young writers are included in this collection of works by thirty-four Canadian Indian poets. Readers will be impressed by the variety and power of these poems which depict the various tribes and locales. An important addition to any representative collection of Canadian poetry. Don Sedgwick

5448 C811'.008

**Dempster, Barry,** ed.

Tributaries, An Anthology, Writer to Writer. Oakville, Ont.: Mosaic Press/Valley Editions, c1978. 112p. ISBN 0-88962-092-X bd.: $8.95 ISBN 0-88962-091-1 pa.: $4.95

1. Canadian poetry (English).

Sixty-six modern Canadian poets, including Atwood, Purdy, Livesay, and Lane write poems about fellow-poets. Sheila Latham

5449 C811'.008

**Di Cicco, Pier Giorgio,** ed.

Roman Candles: An Anthology of Poems by Seventeen Italo-Canadian Poets. Willowdale, Ont.: Hounslow Press, c1978. 85p. ISBN 0-88882-030-5 pa.: $4.95

1. Canadian poetry (English) – Italian Canadian authors. 2. Canadian poetry (English) – 20th century.

5450 C811'.008

**Gatenby, Greg,** ed.

Whale Sound: An Anthology of Poems About Whales and Dolphins. Vancouver: J. J. Douglas, 1977. 96p. ill. ISBN 0-88894-135-8 $5.95

1. Whales – Poetry. 2. Canadian poetry (English) – 20th century.

Inspired by the desire to end the whale slaughter, this visually appealing anthology of poems and drawings highlights the history, mythology, and intelligence of whales. Sheila Latham

5451 C811'.008

**Giant Canadian Poetry Annual. 1977-**

Erin, Ont.: Press Porcépic. v ill. Annual. ISSN 0703-1416 $2.95

1. Canadian poetry (English) – 20th century – Periodicals.

Supersedes: *Canadian Poetry Annual*. ISSN 0383-1574.

The pulp format of this periodical might trap a comic-cut fan into reading a poem. The less-than-giant periodical gives less-than-gigantic poetry. However, the different form, less formidable, reasonably priced and containing contributions from sea to sea, make a good acquisition to detract from the literary elitist myth of poetry. Beth Marcilio

5452 C811'.008

**Klassen, Ingrid,** ed.

D'Sonoqua: Women Poets of British Columbia. Vancouver: Intermedia Press, 1979. ISBN 0-88956-060-9 bd.: $12.95 vol. 1. ISBN 0-88956-059-5 pa.: $6.95 vol. 1. ISBN 0-88956-084-6 bd.: $12.95 vol. 2. ISBN 0-88956-083-8 pa.: $6.95 vol. 2.

1. Canadian poetry (English) – British Columbia. 2. Women poets, Canadian – 20th century. 3. Canadian poetry (English) – 20th century.

Except for the curious omission of Dorothy Livesay, (living on Galiano Island, B.C.,) this two-volume anthology provides an enjoyable, commendable survey of British Columbia women poets. Each of the thirty-two authors is represented by three or four selections. Sheila Latham

5453 C811'.008

**Norris, Ken,** ed.

Montreal: English Poetry of the 70's. Edited by Ken Norris and Andre Farkas. Montreal: Véhicule Press, c1977. 149p. ill. Bibliographies. Index. ISBN 0-919890-13-X bd.: $4 ISBN 0-919890-12-1 pa.: $3.95

1. Canadian poetry (English) – 20th century. 2. Canadian poetry (English) – Quebec (Province) – Montreal.

More than one hundred poems written by twenty-two English poets in Montreal are accompanied by brief biographical notes on each poet. Differing in form from earlier movements these new poets stress language as a means of expressing political and social consciousness. For readers interested in a regional selection of modern Canadian poetry. Merike Koger

5454 C811'.008

**Ondaatje, Michael,** ed.

The Long Poem Anthology. Toronto: Coach House Press, 1979. 343p. ISBN 0-88910-177-9 $7.95

1. Canadian poetry (English) – 20th century – Collections.

Writer and editor Michael Ondaatje has drawn together a unique collection of epic poems by such noted authors as Robert Kroetsch, George Bowering, Daphne Marlatt, and B.P. Nichol. A variety of styles are represented and each author writes briefly on the structure and purpose of the long poem. Challenging material for Canadian literature courses. Don Sedgwick

5455 C811'.008

**Page, P. K.,** ed.

To Say the Least: Canadian Poets from A to Z. Victoria: Press Porcépic, 1979. ISBN 0-88878-174-1 pa.: $5.95

1. Canadian poetry.

More than two hundred thematically arranged short poems by Canada's top one hundred contemporary poets prove to be entertaining, provocative, and memorable. Sheila Latham

5456 C811'.008

**Peck, Edward,** ed.

Transitions III: Poetry: A Source Book of Canadian Literature. Vancouver: CommCept Publishing, 1978. 340p. ill., ports. Indexes. ISBN 0-88829-026-8 $7.95

1. Canadian poetry (English) – 20th century. 2. Canadian poetry (English) – 20th century – History and criticism.

Similar in design and format to companion volumes edited by Edward Peck: *Transitions I: Short Plays*, and *Transitions II: Short Fiction*, this third anthology contains works of thirty-five English Canadian poets. Succinct biographies, photographs and the poets' comments on their own writing add to the book's value for high school and public libraries.

5457 C811.008

**Poems of French Canada.**

Translated by F. R. Scott. Burnaby, B.C.: Blackfish Press, 1977. 59p. pa.: $4.95

1. Canadian poetry (French) – Translations into English. 2. Canadian poetry (English) – Translations from French.

Poet F. R. Scott has been translating verse from his native province for more than three decades. This selection, dating back to Lescarbot is introduced by the translator and presented in a handsomely printed limited edition. Merike Koger

5458 C811'.008

**Western Windows: A Comparative Anthology of Poetry in British Columbia.**

Vancouver: CommCept Publishing, 1977. 294p. ill. ISBN 0-88829-000-4 pa.: $8.25

1. Canadian poetry (English) – 20th century. 2. Canadian poetry (English) – British Columbia.

A well-illustrated anthology of the works of some forty-four British Columbia poets of the last ninety years. Interesting prose articles by some of the poets, and brief biographies, are included. Especially suitable for senior high school students and readers interested in a regional collection of modern Canadian poetry. Merike Koger

---

**C811.009** Poetry - History and criticism

---

5459 C811'.009

**Brown, E. K.**

Responses and Evaluations: Essays on Canada. Edited with an introduction by David Staines. Toronto: McClelland and Stewart, c1977. 314p. (New Canadian Library) ISBN 0-7710-9252-0 pa.: $3.50

1. Canadian literature (English) – History and criticism.

This is an important work which presents a collection of the writings of a pioneer critic of Canadian literature. Included are E. K. Brown's important essays and reviews from 1929 to 1951, his first chapter from *On Canadian Poetry* and the memoir of D. C. Scott which prefaced Brown's edition of Scott's *Selected Poems*. David Staines summarizes Brown's career and provides an admiring evaluation of his work. The essays are primarily in chronological order. Unfortunately the book does not have an index. Janice Zlatarits

5460 C811'.009

**Marshall, Tom.**

Harsh and Lovely Land: The Major Canadian Poets and the Making of a Canadian Tradition. Vancouver: University of British Columbia Press, 1978. 184p. Bibliographical references and Index. ISBN 0-7748-0107-7 $18.50

1. Canadian poetry (English) – History and criticism. 2. Poets, Canadian (English).

Marshall's concern for the "poem that is Canada and Canadians" is examined through the works of major Canadian poets writing in English, from the middle of the nineteenth century to the present. This survey offers a fresh insight into Canadian poetry, from the academic viewpoint, focusing on the persisting "obsession with space, with enclosure and openness." Andrea Trudel

5461 C811'.009

**Smith, A. J. M.**

On Poetry and Poets: Selected Essays of A. J. M. Smith. Toronto: McClelland and Stewart, c1977. 122p. Bibliography: p. vi. (New Canadian Library) ISBN 0-7710-9257-1 pa.: $2.95

1. Canadian poetry (English) – History and criticism.

Reprints Smith's introductions to several important poetry anthologies, along with critical essays on Layton, Pratt, A. G. Bailey, and Duncan Campbell Scott. Sheila Latham

---

**C811.4** Poets - 19th century - Criticism and interpretation

---

5462 C811'.4

**Connor, Carl Y.**

Archibald Lampman: Canadian Poet of Nature. Foreward by Ray Palmer Baker. 2d ed. Ottawa: Borealis Press, 1977. 210p. port. Bibliography: p. 203-206 Index. ISBN 0-919594-75-1 pa.: $7.95

1. Lampman, Archibald, 1861-1899.
2. Poets, Canadian (English) – 19th century – Biography.

Neither the introduction nor the text of the original biography, published in 1929, have been revised for this second edition. The florid prose of this romanticized account will annoy some, but delight others who are interested in a period piece on the life and work of the nature poet. Patricia O'Sullivan

5463 C811'.4
**Klinck, Carl F.**
Wilfred Campbell: A Study in Late Provincial Victorianism. Ottawa: Tecumseh Press, 1977. 289p. Bibliography: p. 283-284. Index. ISBN 0-919612-58-7 pa.: $5.95

1. Campbell, Wilfred, 1861-1918. 2. Poets, Canadian (English) – Biography.

First published Toronto, Ryerson Press, 1942.

This is a reprint of one of a long out-of-print series on Canadian literary figures. The well-respected authority of Klinck is evident in his critical biographical approach to Campbell and his poetry. Klinck places Campbell's work within the social frame of Victorian Ontario in an enthusiastic style. A highly recommended addition to a Canadian literature collection. Andrea Trudel

## C811.5 Poets - 20th century - Criticism and interpretation

5464 C811'.5
**Clever, W. Glenn,** ed.
The E. J. Pratt Symposium. Ottawa: University of Ottawa Press, 1977. 172p. facsim., port. Bibliography: p. 141-169. (Reappraisals, Canadian Writers) ISBN 0-7766-4384-3 pa.: $4.80

1. Pratt, Edwin J., 1883-1964 – Criticism and interpretation – Congresses.

Teacher, critic, editor and poet Glenn Clever takes a critical look at E. J. Pratt in four essays entitled Pratt: The Essential Myth; The Narrative Impropriety of Pratt's "Brébeuf"; Pratt as War Poet; and a Critical Reading of *The Iron Door: An Ode.* Don Sedgwick

5465 C811'.5
**David, Jack,** ed.
Brave New Wave. Windsor, Ont.: Black Moss Press, c1978. 226p. Bibliographical references. ISBN 0-88753-051-6 pa.: $8.75

1. Canadian poetry (English) – 20th century – History and criticism.

A collection of critical essays, exploring the craft and poetic principles of eleven top Canadian poets who have gained prominence in the sixties and seventies. Poets included were chosen for their distinctive styles and unique gifts, thus giving the reader an overview of the range of poetic expression in Canada. Patricia O'Sullivan

5466 C811.5
**Lee, Dennis.**
Savage Fields: An Essay in Literature and Cosmology. Toronto: House of Anansi Press, 1977. 125p. Bibliographical references.
ISBN 0-88784-059-0 bd.: $11.95
ISBN 0-88784-058-2 pa.: $5.95

1. Ondaatje, Michael, 1943- 2. Cohen, Leonard, 1934-

A major critical study which attempts "to understand the world [civilization] and the earth [nature] in the images that several writers give them." Ondaatje's *Collected Works of Billy the Kid* and Cohen's *Beautiful Losers* are analyzed in detail, with specific references to planetary structure and the rise of technology. Sheila Latham

5467 C811'.5
**Livesay, Dorothy.**
Right Hand, Left Hand: A True Life of the Thirties: Paris, Toronto, Montreal, the West and Vancouver: Love, Politics, the Depression and Feminism. Erin, Ont.: Press Porcépic, c1977. 280p. ill., ports. Bibliography: p. 258-287. Index.
ISBN 0-88878-104-0 bd.: $15
ISBN 0-88878-105-9 pa.: $6.95

1. Women poets – Canada – Biography.
2. Canada – History – 1918-1939.

A montage of letters, poems, speeches and odd memorabilia is the way Dorothy Livesay chooses to present her avant-garde life and times. At first there is a feeling of bombardment, of being overwhelmed but soon the rightness of the method asserts itself. An unorthodox concept for an unorthodox woman. Paula de Ronde

5468 C811.5
**Mayne, Seymour,** ed.
Irving Layton: The Poet and His Critics. Toronto: McGraw-Hill Ryerson, c1978. 291p. Bibliography: p. 287-291. (Critical Views on Canadian Writers) ISBN 0-07-082711-7 bd.: $12.95 ISBN 0-07-082717-6 pa.: $8.95

1. Layton, Irving, 1912- – Criticism and interpretation.

"Essays on Layton's poetry from his early works to the present by A. J. M. Smith, Louis Dudek, Al Purdy, Susan Musgrave, Gwendolyn MacEwan and others."

-Publisher's note. Equally interesting and essential to a student are the other essays. Beth Marcilio

5469 C811.5
**Oliver, Michael Brian.**
Poet's Progress: The Development of Alden Nowlan's Poetry. Fredericton, N.B.: Fiddlehead Poetry Books, 1978. 46p. (Fiddlehead Poetry Books)
ISBN 0-920110-19-3 pa.: $5

1. Nowlan, Alden, 1933- – Criticism and interpretation.

This useful introduction, aimed at high school students and university undergraduates, surveys the criticism published prior to 1978 and provides detailed analyses of specific poems chosen from Nowlan's ten published collections. Sheila Latham

5470 C811.5
**Scobie, Stephen.**
Leonard Cohen. Vancouver: Douglas & McIntyre, c1978. 192p. Bibliography: p. 187-192. (Studies in Canadian Literature)
ISBN 0-88894-194-3 pa.: $3.95

1. Cohen, Leonard, 1934- – Criticism and interpretation.

High school and university students will welcome this readable critical monograph which analyses the novels, poems, and songs, etc., published by Cohen between 1956 and 1977. Sheila Latham

5471 C811.5
**Woodcock, George.**
Thomas Merton, Monk and Poet: A Critical Study. Vancouver: Douglas & McIntyre, c1978. 200p. port. Bibliography: p. 189-192. Index. ISBN 0-88894-189-7 bd.: $12.95
ISBN 0-88894-190-0 pa.: $5.95

1. Merton, Thomas, 1915-1968. 2. Poets, American – 20th century – Biography. 3. Trappists – Biography.

This lucid portrait of the prolific twentieth-century religious poet will appeal to students and general readers interested in poetry, theology, and mysticism. Sheila Latham

5472 C811'.5'4
**Lawrance, Scott.**
Names of Thunder. Toronto: McClelland and Stewart, c1978. 95p. ISBN 0-7710-4740-1 pa.: $5.95

An unusual first collection. Lawrence combines the mystic and modern with verse both experimental and traditional. The mixture of styles and themes suggests something tentative, gentle experiment and self-effacement rather than the passions of a dogged craftsman. Beth Marcilio

5473 C811.5'4'016
**Stevens, Peter,** ed.
Modern English-Canadian Poetry: A Guide to Information Sources. Detroit: Gale Research, c1978. 216p. (American Literature, English Literature and World Literature in English) (Gale Information Guide Library)
ISBN 0-8103-1244-1 $22

1. Canadian poetry – 20th century – History and criticism – Bibliography. 2. Canadian poetry (English) – 20th century – Bibliography.

A checklist of reference sources, literary histories, anthologies, periodicals, primary poetical works, and criticism published between 1900 and 1973. Sheila Latham

5474 C811'.5'408
**Candelaria, Fred,** ed.
New: West Coast: New Poems by British Columbia Writers with Their Own Commentaries and Autobiographical Sketches. Vancouver: Intermedia Press, 1977. 258p. ill. Index. ISBN 0-88956-068-4 bd.: $50
ISBN 0-88956-065-X pa.: $15.95

1. Canadian poetry (English) – British Columbia. 2. Canadian poetry (English) – 20th century.

An attractive book of contemporary verse and poetics compiled by the editor of "West Coast Review". Works by such established writers as Earle Birney, Dorothy Livesay and George Woodcock are presented alongside poetry by many new and emerging authors, seventy-two in total. The unique qualities of the west coast are the recurring leitmotivs. Don Sedgwick

5475 C811'.5'408
**Glistening in the Sun: An Anthology of Y.C. Verse Originally Published in the Western Producer.**
Saskatoon: Western Producer Prairie Books, 1977. 122p. Index. ISBN 0-919306-78-0 pa.: $3.25

1. Canadian poetry (English) – 20th century.

Poems published between 1927 and 1976 in "The Young Co-operators' Club" pages of the farm weekly "The Western Producer" provide a poetic history of Canada from the young person's viewpoint. Sheila Latham

## C812 Plays

5476 C812.
**Angel, Leonard.**
After Antietam and Isadora and G. B.: Two Short Plays. Toronto: Playwrights Co-op, 1978. 59p. ISBN 0-88754-095-3 pa.: $3.50
*After Antietam* stages an encounter between a soldier of the Confederate army and a woman, during the Civil War in the United States. *Isadora and G. B.* is an evening of Shavian intellect combined with Isadora Duncan's beauty. Hilary Elliott

5477 C812.
**Baglole, Harry.**
The Chappell Diary, by Harry Baglole and Ron Irving. Belfast, P.E.I.: Ragweed Press, c1977. 60p. ill., map. ISBN 0-920304-02-8 pa.: $2.50
1. Prince Edward Island – History – 1763-1873 – Drama.
The play, based on 'found' material, and evolved through improvisation, tells the story of the settlement of New London, Prince Edward Island. Its regional and historical appeal is supported by the inclusion of photographs of archival materials. Well illustrated by production photographs. Annette Wengle

5478 C812.
**Birney, Earle.**
The Damnation of Vancouver. Introduction by Wai Lan Low. Toronto: McClelland and Stewart, c1957, 1977 printing. 79p. (New Canadian Library) ISBN 0-7710-9515-5 pa.: $1.95
Noted Canadian poet Birney examines the effects of progress in a whimsical poetic drama in which early settlers called as witnesses to a trial of Vancouver provides the opportunity for a virtuoso display of dialects and verse forms. Puns and word-plays suggest the play is intended for reading but the small typeface makes reading difficult. Annette Wengle

5479 C812.
**Bolt, Carol.**
One Night Stand. Toronto: Playwrights Co-op, c1977. 52p. ISBN 0-88754-084-8 pa. Processed: $3.50
A "comedy thriller" of limited scope set in a highrise apartment owned by Daisy, a Toronto woman who has gone out alone to a bar and picked up Rafe, a guitar-playing young man. Their "one-night stand" concludes with Rafe provoking Daisy into stabbing him. Hilary Elliott

5480 C812.
**Bruyere, Christian.**
Walls: A Play. Vancouver: Talonbooks, 1978. 131p. ISBN 0-88922-140-5 pa.: $4.95
*Walls* is a documentary-drama based on the Andy Bruce-Mary Steinhauser hostage-taking incident at a British Columbia penitentiary in 1975 which resulted in the death of Mary Steinhauser. A first play by Christian Bruyere, it is a powerful drama exploring the background, motivations, and relationships of the characters. Hilary Elliott

5481 C812.
**Colley, Peter.**
The Donnellys: A Drama With Music. Composer Berthold Carrière. Toronto: Simon & Pierre Publishing, 1976, c1974. 110p. ill., diagrs., maps, ports. (Canplay Series) ISBN 0-88924-058-2 $4.95
1. Donnelly family (James Donnelly, 1815?-1880) – Drama.
*The Donnellys* is the fourth Canadian play to be inspired by the legend of the Donnellys of south-western Ontario. The legend has painted the Donnellys very black, but Canadian dramatists, including Peter Colley, have emphasized the fear and hatred of the townspeople of Lucan. The play concludes with the brutal massacre. Hilary Elliott

5482 C812.
**Cone, Thomas.**
Three Plays. Vancouver: Pulp Press, c1976. 105p. ill. ISBN 0-88978-038-2 bd.: $8.95 ISBN 0-88978-036-6 pa.: $3.50
In this collection of short, theatrical, sometimes obscure plays, Tom Cone, an established playwright of the West Coast, ranges from a mysterious study of the relationship between two women in *Cubistique,* to a one-man medicine show and vaudeville act in *Herringbone,* to an elegant Henri Rousseau tableau in *Beautiful Tigers.* Hilary Elliott

5483 C812.
**Cook, Michael.**
Three Plays. St. John's, Nfld.: Breakwater Books, 1977. 101p. ISBN 0-919948-30-8 pa.: $5.95
These three plays are all set in Newfoundland. *On the Rim of the Curve* is about the effects of the arrival of Europeans on the Beothuks of Newfoundland, *The Head, Guts and Soundbone Dance* is about the fishermen of Newfoundland, and *Theresa's*

*Creed*, a monologue, is about a fisherman's widow. Hilary Elliott

5484 C812.
**Cook, Michael.**
Tiln & Other Plays. Vancouver: Talonbooks, 1976. 111p. ISBN 0-88922-107-3 pa.: $3.50
Cook's three short plays are all set in Newfoundland and each focuses on the consciousness of the title character. *Tiln* is a play between two characters – the powerful Tiln and the frail Fern, two lighthouse keepers. *Quiller* and *Therese's Creed* are monologues of a retired fisherman and a fisherman's widow respectively. Hilary Elliott

5485 C812.
**Coulter, John.**
François Bigot: A Rediscovery of Dramatic Form of the Fall of Quebec. Toronto: Hounslow Press, c1978. 78p. (An Orenda Book) ISBN 0-88882-027-5 pa.: $4.95
1. Bigot, François, 1703-ca. 1777 – Drama.
A two-act play about François Bigot, the last Intendant of New France, who brought Quebec to the brink of ruin and aided General Wolfe in the conquest of Quebec. The action of the play is an imaginary trial of Bigot at which witnesses such as Madame de Pompadour and the Marquis de Montcalm appear. Hilary Elliott

5486 C812.
**Crisp, Jack H.**
A Wife in the Hand: A Farce. Toronto: Simon & Pierre Publishing, 1976, c1968. 126p. ill., port. (Canplay Series) ISBN 0-88924-046-9 pa.: $4.95
A lively, fast-paced farce about love, marriage, success, and best laid plans going awry, this play revolves around James Henderson who has just been appointed President of Universal Trust and his wife, Lydia, who in her spare time and unbeknownst to James, has been writing sex novels. Hilary Elliott

5487 C812.
**DeFelice, James.**
Take Me Where the Water's Warm: A Summer Comedy in Three Acts. Toronto: Playwrights Co-op, 1978. 87p. ISBN 0-88754-102-X pa. Processed: $3.50
This comedy-romance is set on Vancouver Island during the summer. Hilary Elliott

5488 C812.
**Deverell, Rex.**
Boiler Room Suite: A Play. Vancouver: Talonbooks, 1978. 93p. ISBN 0-88922-137-5 pa.: $4.95
Canadian Authors' Association Literary Award.
Three characters, Aggie Rose, Sprugg, and Pete, who do not understand how they have become failures, discover each other in the boiler room of an abandoned hotel on the prairies. A tragicomedy which combines fantasy and reality, the play provides no illumination for the characters but concludes with a little human kindness. Hilary Elliott

5489 C812.
**Deverell, Rex.**
Uphill Revival; Shinbone General Store; Underground Lake: Three Plays. 1st ed. Toronto: Playwrights Co-op, 1977. 102p. ISBN 0-88754-053-8 $3.50
These three plays by Rex Deverell are suitable for school audiences, *Underground Lake* for kindergarten to grade three, *Shinbone General Store* for grades four to seven, and *Uphill Revival* for high school students. All three plays are imaginative and employ varied theatrical techniques such as performance in the round. Hilary Elliott

5490 C812.
**Doucet, Clive.**
A Very Desirable Residence. Toronto: Playwrights Co-op, 1978. 77p. ISBN 0-88754-117-8 pa. Processed: $3.50
Set in Ottawa, this play focuses on a young couple whose marriage is threatened by a landlady, children, and a mother-in-law, all of whom create problems which are resolved in the end. Hilary Elliott

5491 C812.
**Fennario, David,** pseud.
Balconville. Vancouver: Talonbooks, 1979. 128p. ISBN 0-88922-145-6 $4.95
The Chalmers Canadian Play Award.
A bitter comedy about three families sitting on their balconies in the Montreal summer, *Balconville* takes place during election time. The realistic, working-class characters are both English and French-Canadian, united against the Establishment. Hilary Elliott

5492 C812.
**Fennario, David,** pseud.
Nothing to Lose: A Play. Vancouver: Talonbooks, 1977. 136p. ISBN 0-88922-121-9 pa.: $3.95

Fennario's second play is set in 1976, in a tavern in the Point Saint Charles working-class district of Montreal. The play brings together two old friends, Jerry, a writer, and Jackie, a warehouse worker, who begin by reminiscing about the past and conclude by precipitating a workers' sit-down strike. Hilary Elliott

5493 C812.
**Fielden, Charlotte.**
One Crowded Hour. Toronto: Playwrights Co-op, c1976. 71p. (Women Write for Theatre: v. 2) ISBN 0-88754-048-1 pa.: $3.95

One of the winning full-length plays in the Women Write for Theatre competition of 1976, *One Crowded Hour* is a one-woman play about the recently widowed Mabel Harrison and her personal journey towards knowledge of herself. By the end of the play Mabel is moving on to find her own place. Hilary Elliott

5494 C812.
**Findley, Timothy.**
Can You See Me Yet?: A Play. Vancouver: Talonbooks, 1977. 166p. ISBN 0-88922-119-7 pa.: $4.95

Physically set in 1938, in an Ontario insane asylum, Findley's play also takes place in the mind of Cassandra Wakelin who confuses her fellow inmates with members of her family. Questions about alienation and involvement, and fantasy and reality lead Cassandra to her desperate question, "Can you see me yet?" Hilary Elliott

5495 C812.
**Fineberg, Larry.**
Eve. Toronto: Theatrebooks, 1977. 68p. ISBN 0-920382-00-2 pa.: $4.95

The Chalmers Award.

Fineberg has taken Constance Beresford-Howe's novel *The Book of Eve* and turned it into a spare but compelling play about a grandmother who flees her respectable marriage for the squalor of a Montreal rooming house, finally finding that, although there are complications, she has her own life to live. Hilary Elliott

5496 C812.
**Fineberg, Larry.**
Four Plays. Toronto: Playwrights Co-op, 1978. 180p. ISBN 0-88754-092-9 pa.: $5.95

Contents: Death. Stonehenge. Hope. Human Remains.

These four early works by Larry Fineberg, three of which are comedies, deal with the theme of alienation. Sparse dialogue, bitter comedy and violent images create visions of a cruel and chaotic universe. Hilary Elliott

5497 C812.
**Fineberg, Larry.**
Medea. Toronto: Theatrebooks, 1978. 34p. ISBN 0-920382-00-4 pa.: $3.50

The play was commissioned by the Stratford Festival. To be performed on a bare stage with no props, music, or sound effects, this verse adaptation is contemporary in language but remains true to the classic Greek drama. Hilary Elliott

5498 C812.
**French, David.**
Jitters: A Comedy. Toronto: Playwrights Co-op, 1979. 95p. ISBN 0-88754-158-5 pa. Processed: $3.50

This insider's look at the problems, anxieties and clashes of temperament which beset the cast of a new play moves from dress rehearsal through the players' reactions to the first reviews. "*Jitters* is witty, affectionate, bitchy, bitterly touching." -Publisher's note. Annette Wengle

5499 C812.
**Fruet, William.**
Wedding in White. Toronto: Simon & Pierre Publishing, 1977. 63p. ill. ISBN 0-88924-054-X pa.: $4

The play takes place in a Canadian town, near the end of the second World War. Jeanie, a young girl, is raped by her brother's friend, becomes pregnant, and is forced to marry an old army buddy of her father's for the sake of her family's reputation. Hilary Elliott

5500 C812.
**Garneau, Michel.**
Four to Four. Translated by Christian Bédard and Keith Turnbull. Toronto: Simon & Pierre Publishing, 1978. A46p. ill.

Translation of *Quatre—à quatre.*

Also included in: Kalman, Rolf, ed. *A Collection of Canadian Plays.* Vol. 5.

A cast of four women portray four generations of a Quebec family at different times in their lives. Daughter, mother, grandmother, and great-grandmother examine their lives and the feminine condition. Psychological, realistic, mythical, and poetic, the play is a series of monologues and conversations between the women. Hilary Elliott

5501 C812.
**Gervais, Charles H.**
Baldoon, by Charles H. Gervais and James Reaney. Erin, Ont.: Porcupine's Quill, c1976. 119p. ill. ISBN 0-88984-018-0 bd.: $8.95 ISBN 0-88984-016-4 pa.: $3.95

Set in Baldoon and Long Point, Upper Canada, in the nineteenth century, *Baldoon* dramatizes a legend of a community disturbed by poltergeists. Puppets, magic tricks, and religious ceremonies add to the theatricality of this play based on actual occurrences between two families which led to a series of mysterious persecutions. Hilary Elliott

5502 C812.
**Gourlay, Elizabeth.**
Isabel: The Continuous Dream of the Former Prime Minister: A Play in Three Acts. Toronto: Playwrights Co-op, 1979. 50p. ISBN 0-88754-119-4 pa. Processed: $3.50

1. King, William Lyon Mackenzie, 1874-1950 – Drama.

An aging Mackenzie King is visited on his birthday by apparitions of his former fiancée, his mother, and other deceased family members. The hold which the ambitious, selfish, manipulative Isabel exerts over her son is revealed through flashbacks in this gripping if somewhat simplistic psychological study. Annette Wengle

5503 C812.
**Hamer, Maimie.**
A Living Thing, by Maimie Hamer and Helen Lustig. Dinner Party, by Via Sarossy. Wheelchair, by Margaret Penman. Edited by Madeline Thompson. Toronto: Playwrights Co-op, c1976. 105p. (Women Write for Theatre: v. 1) ISBN 0-88754-054-6 pa.: $3

1. Canadian drama (English) – 20th century.
2. Women's writings.

The first volume of a four-volume series, these one-act plays, "A Living Thing", "Wheelchair", and "Dinner Party" are winners of a competition, Women Write for Theatre, held during International Women's Year, for plays written by and about women. Hilary Elliott

5504 C812.
**Hardin, Herschel.**
Great Wave of Civilization: A Play. Vancouver: Talonbooks, 1976. 121p. music. ISBN 0-88922-106-5 pa.: $3.95

Hardin's play about the destruction of the Blackfoot Confederacy in nineteenth century Montana and Alberta attacks the white free traders and liquor merchants who represented "civilization" to the Indians. A theatrical combination of history, arguments, and songs, the play presents this cultural clash in episodic form. Hilary Elliott

5505 C812.
**Havard, Lezley.**
Victims. Toronto: Playwrights Co-op, 1976. 81p. (Women Write for Theatre: v. 4) ISBN 0-88754-052-X pa.: $3.95

*Victims* is a winner of the Women Write for Theatre competition. The volume contains three short plays, "Claws", "Forfeits", and "Despair" which deal with terror, cruelty, and suffering. Hilary Elliott

5506 C812.
**Kenny, George.**
October Stranger, by George Kenny and Denis Lacroix. Toronto: Chimo Publishing, c1978. 77p. ISBN 0-920344-04-6 pa.: $3.95

A one-act play created and performed by native people, *October Stranger* was Canada's entry at Monaco for the Sixth International Theatre Festival. The painful 'October' changes facing the young generation of Indians are evoked through an Indian poet's recollections of the day he left his Ojibway reservation in Northern Ontario. Based on the author's *Indians Don't Cry*. Annette Wengle

5507 C812.
**Lambert, Betty.**
Sqrieux-de-dieu: A Play. Vancouver: Talonbooks, 1976. 122p. ISBN 0-88922-105-7 pa.: $4.95

Lambert, a British Columbia professor of English, lampoons contemporary hang-ups and the quest for self-fulfillment. "A sophisticated sexual comedy of manners, which has been described as 'a nasty play about nice people,' *Sqrieux-de-dieu* (pronounced 'screw-dee-doo') has been a great success with audiences in Vancouver and Festival Lennoxville." -Publisher's note

5508 C812.
**Mathews, Robin.**
Selkirk. Toronto: Steel Rail Publishing, 1977. 126p. ill. (Canadian Historical Plays) ISBN 0-88791-008-4 pa: $3.95

1. Red River Settlement, Man. – Drama.

The struggle of Lord Selkirk to establish the Red River Colony despite the opposition of the North West Company is vividly recreated. The drama highlights many interesting aspects of life in the early settlements. Annette Wengle

5509 C812.
**Mitchell, Ken.**
Cruel Tears. Vancouver: Talonbooks, 1977. 145p. ill. ISBN 0-88922-120-0 pa.: $3.95

1. Humphrey and the Dumptrucks (Musical group).

"Imagine the *Othello* story played to its conclusion in Saskatoon by a group of truckers and their women, and then set it all *Three Penny Opera-style* to country and western music and you have *Cruel Tears*, a country opera." -Publisher's note. Well illustrated by numerous production photographs, but does not include music for the songs. Annette Wengle

5510 C812.
**Mitchell, Ken.**
Davin, The Politician: A Play. Introduction by C. B. Koester. Edmonton: NeWest Press, c1979. 122p. (Prairie Play Series)
ISBN 0-920316-22-0 bd.: $11.95
ISBN 0-920316-24-7 pa.: $5.95

1. Davin, Nicholas Flood, 1843-1901 – Drama.

Nicholas Flood Davin, the flamboyant Irish-Canadian journalist and poet who founded the "Regina Leader" and served in John A. MacDonald's parliament, is brought vividly to life, as are some of the key issues of his time. This edition includes an excellent historical introduction. Annette Wengle

5511 C812.
**Nichol, James W.**
Gwendoline: A Play in Two Acts. Toronto: Playwrights Co-op, 1978. 63p.
ISBN 0-88754-099-6 pa.: $3.50

A sensitive drama in which the gentle innocence of the town 'crazy lady' brings to life the repressed violence of the small-minded 'righteous' folk of the town. Set in southern Ontario in 1907. Annette Wengle

5512 C812.
**Nichol, James W.**
Sainte-Marie among the Hurons: A Play. Toronto: Playwrights Co-op, 1977. 48p.
ISBN 0-88754-057-0 pa. Processed: $3

1. Jesuits – Missions – Ontario – Drama.
2. Huron Indians – Missions – Drama.

A gripping, dramatically effective rendering of the spiritual conflict of a Jesuit priest who cannot accept the conditions necessary for the 'salvation' of the Hurons. "... based on the disastrous mission by French Jesuits to the Huron Indians in the seventeenth century." -Publisher's note. Annette Wengle

5513 C812.
**Pinsent, Gordon.**
John and the Missus: A Play. Toronto: Playwrights Co-op, 1977. 62p.
ISBN 0-88754-059-7 pa.: $3.50

Pinsent, a native of Newfoundland who is a well-known Canadian actor and playwright, has fashioned an affecting drama which focuses on the end of a way of life in a Newfoundland mining community. Annette Wengle

5514 C812.
**Ravel, Aviva.**
Dispossessed. 2d ed. rev. Toronto: Playwrights Co-op, 1978, c1976. 91p. (Women Write for Theatre: v. 3) pa.: $3.95

A winner of the Women Write for Theatre competition, *Dispossessed* is about three characters, Roochel Abrams, her husband, and her son who drift apart after the death of Roochel's former lover. Hilary Elliott

5515 C812.
**Reaney, James.**
The Dismissal: Or, Twisted Beards & Tangled Whiskers. Erin, Ont.: Press Porcépic, c1978. 63p. ill., ports. ISBN 0-88878-147-4 pa.: $3.95

1. University of Toronto – Strike – Drama.

Commissioned for 1977's sesquicentennial of the University of Toronto, *The Dismissal* deals with the student strike of 1895. "Reaney in this revue/satire/comedy of manners puts his finger on Ontario quirks and stupidities that still plague us." -Publisher's note. Enriched by a bibliography of reviews and numerous photographs of the production, the college architecture, and the historic figures involved. Annette Wengle

5516 C812.
**Reaney, James.**
Wacousta: A Melodrama. Victoria: Press Porcépic, 1979. 105p. Bibliography. ISBN 0-88878-175-X $5.95

1. Richardson, John, 1796-1852.

A three-act play based upon the historical romance of the nineteenth century Canadian novelist, John Richardson. The British forts of Detroit and Michilimackinac in 1763 are the setting for a melodrama which has liberal dollops of intrigue, treachery and love. Reaney includes a summary of the workshops out of which the play was developed.

5517 C812.
**Rosen, Sheldon.**
Frugal Repast and The Grand Hysteric: Two One-Act Plays. Toronto: Playwrights Co-op, 1978. 53p. ISBN 0-88754-132-1 pa.: $3.50

Both of these unconventional one-act plays for two characters by the author of *Ned and Jack* display a sharp ear for dialogue, and both deal with characters at an extreme in the spectrum of human experience. *Frugal Repast* presents two derelicts celebrating their anniversary, while *The Grand Hysteric* shows a young psychotic and his therapist. Annette Wengle

5518 C812.
**Rosen, Sheldon.**
Ned and Jack: A Play. Toronto: Playwrights Co-op, 1978. 54p. ISBN 0-88754-130-5 pa. Processed: $3.50

This warm, witty, touching drama by American expatriate Sheldon Rosen is set in New York in 1922. The popular playwright Ned Sheldon was stricken with incurable crippling arthritis. In the course of a late night visit from his dear friend John Barrymore he begins to come to terms with his situation. Annette Wengle

5519 C812.
**Roussin, Claude.**
Looking for a Job. Une job. Translated by Allan van Meer. Toronto: Simon & Pierre Publishing, 1978. E32p. ill. ISBN 0-88924-023-X pa.: $4.95

Also included in: Kalman, Rolf, ed., *A Collection of Canadian Plays*, vol. 5.

This comedy is about a Quebec family made up of father, mother, and son who is looking for a job. Hilary Elliott

5520 C812.
**Ryga, George.**
Captives of the Faceless Drummer. Vancouver: Talonbooks, c1977. 78p. ISBN 0-88922-041-7 pa.: $4.95

A combination of political philosophy, humour, music, choral passages, and psychological studies, Ryga's play is about an assassin and his victim. Although not a radical piece of political propaganda, *Captives* gained some notoriety as such after being banned by the Board of Directors of the Vancouver Playhouse in 1970. Hilary Elliott

5521 C812.
**Ryga, George.**
Ploughmen of the Glacier: A Play. Vancouver: Talonbooks, 1977. 79p. ISBN 0-88922-118-9 pa.: $4.95

In this play, meetings between an aged prospector, Volcanic, and an alcoholic newspaperman, Lowery, permit Ryga to examine the nature of life and death, hope and despair. The setting is "possibly surrealistic to suggest a mountainside," up and down which a third character, Poor Boy, struggles with leaking water buckets. Hilary Elliott

5522 C812.
**Ryga, George.**
Seven Hours to Sundown: A Play. Vancouver: Talonbooks, 1977. 110p. ISBN 0-88922-124-3 pa.: $4.95

In this play, Ryga examines the nature of politics in a small community. Sid Kiosk, the newly elected mayor, and Jerry Goyda, an ex-schoolteacher and craftsman, are manipulated by an alderman and journalist who understand power. Goyda's conflict with City Hall provides a platform for Ryga's moral and political ideas. Hilary Elliott

5523 C812.
**Salutin, Rick.**
Les Canadiens: A Play, by Rick Salutin and Ken Dryden. Vancouver: Talonbooks, 1977. 176p. ISBN 0-88922-122-7 pa.: $4.95

The Chalmers Canadian Play Award.

A clever political history play, "*Les Canadiens* begins on the Plains of Abraham in 1759 when a French-Canadian soldier throws his rifle to his son and it becomes a hockey stick." The ending, in the Montreal Forum on November 15, 1976, turns the hockey game into a victory rally for the Parti québecois. Hilary Elliott

5524 C812.
**Simard, André.**
Waiting for Gaudreault. En attendant Gaudreault. Translated by Henry Beissel and Arlette Francière. A little bit left. Encore un peu, by Serge Mercier. Translated by Allan van Meer. Toronto: Simon & Pierre Publishing, 1978. C48p. ill.
ISBN 0-88924-026-4 pa.: $4.95

Translations of *En attendant Gaudreault* and *Encore un peu.*

These two French-Canadian plays, translated into English, are set in Quebec, and deal with the monotony of the lives of the characters in a humorous way. Hilary Elliott

5525 C812.
**Szanto, George H.**
After the Ceremony. Toronto: Playwrights Co-op, 1978, c1977. 89p. ISBN 0-88754-112-7 pa. Processed: $3.50

Returned prisoners-of-war, cult-followers, misfits and strikers people this impressionistic drama which offers a jarring vision of the difficulties in readjustment which face a Vietnam veteran when he attempts to begin a new life in Montreal. Annette Wengle

5526 C812.
**Theatre Passe Muraille.**
I Love You Baby Blue. Edited by Connie Brissenden. Erin, Ont.: Press Porcépic, 1976. 77p. ill. ISBN 0-88878-086-9 bd.: $11.95
ISBN 0-88878-087-7 pa.: $4.95

A play about sex, this edition contains sixty-four photos from the Toronto production which was closed by the Toronto police. The performers wrote the show in the Passe Muraille documentary manner. Hilary Elliott

5527 C812.
**Theatre Passe Muraille.**
The Last Best West Show and If You're So Good Why Are You in Saskatoon? Edited by Connie Brissenden. Erin, Ont.: Press Porcépic, 1977. 64p. ISBN 0-88878-143-1 $4.95

*The Last Best West Show* deals with the history of Western Canada while *If You're So Good, Why Are You in Saskatoon?* deals with the present problems of people in the West. Hilary Elliott

5528 C812.
**Tremblay, Michel.**
La Duchesse de Langeais & Other Plays. Translated by John Van Burek. Vancouver: Talonbooks, 1976. 123p. port.
ISBN 0-88922-104-9 pa.: $3.95

These five plays, "La Duchesse de Langeais", "Berthe", "Johnny Mangano and His Astounding Dogs", "Gloria Star", and "Surprise, Surprise", are minor works of Quebec's best-known playwright.
Hilary Elliott

5529 C812.
**Tremblay, Michel.**
Sainte Carmen of the Main. Montreal: Leméac, c1976. 88p. ISBN 0-7761-0055-6 $4.50

The Chalmers Canadian Play Award.

Carmen, from *Forever Yours, Marie-Lou,* returns from Nashville to teach the Québecois their own songs. The play ends with her death and a return to despair for the people who loved her. Hilary Elliott

5530 C812.
**Wade, Bryan.**
Blitzkrieg and Other Plays: Alias, Lifeguard, Underground, Electric Gunfighters. Toronto: Playwrights Press, 1979. 161p. ISBN 0-88754-122-4 pa.: $5.95

This collection of some of Wade's early work contains such varied characters as Adolf Hitler, the Lone Ranger, two swimmers representing death, and television cowboys, but all these isolated characters enact fantasies and all the plays deal with relationships built on tension and a struggle for power. Hilary Elliott

5531 C812.
**Wade, Bryan.**
Tanned: A Three Act Play. Toronto: Playwrights Co-op, c1977. 89p.
ISBN 0-88754-071-6 pa. Processed: $3.50

Sunning themselves on a dock, three women talk about their men, their lives, and their fears. Sometimes humorous and witty, there is an underlying desperation in the lives of these women. Hilary Elliott

5532 C812.
**Wade, Bryan.**
This Side of the Rockies: A Play. Toronto: Playwrights Co-op, 1977. 108p.
ISBN 0-88754-047-3 pa. Processed: $3.50

Three men, Ronny, Dave, and Tom, who are on a camping trip, meet up with Dianne, a hippie, and two hunters. They argue, play tricks on each other, and talk about their fears. Hilary Elliott

5533 C812.
**Walker, George F.**
Three Plays. Toronto: Coach House Press, 1978. 190p. ill. ISBN 0-88910-078-0 pa.: $6.50
The settings of *Bagdad Saloon, Beyond Mozambique,* and *Ramona and the White Slaves* are an Arabian desert, an African jungle, and the port of Hong Kong. Episodic, ironic, witty, absurdist, and populated with mad characters, these plays reflect the futility of the pursuit of heroism and morality.
Hilary Elliott

5534 C812.
**Walker, George F.**
Zastrozzi: The Master of Discipline: A Melodrama. Toronto: Playwrights Co-op, 1979. 66p. ISBN 0-88754-081-3 pa. Processed: $3.50
Witty, vigorous, and powerful, *Zastrozzi* deals with the nature of man and good and evil in a melodramatic theatrical style. In the play, set in Europe in the 1890's, Zastrozzi, the master criminal of all Europe, seeks revenge and triumphs over Verezzi, an impressionist painter. Hilary Elliott

5535 C812.
**Walmsley, Tom.**
The Jones Boy: A Play in One Act. Vancouver: Pulp Press, 1978. 48p. ISBN 0-88978-054-4 pa.: $2.95
Walmsley's second one-act play deals with aggression, violence, sex, and heroin. Set in a high-rise apartment, the characters are victims of society, barely surviving in a hostile world. Hilary Elliott

5536 C812.
**Wiebe, Rudy.**
Far as the Eye Can See: A Play, by Rudy Wiebe and Theatre Passe Muraille. Edmonton: NeWest Press, c1977. 125p. ill.
ISBN 0-920316-12-3 bd.: $9.95
ISBN 0-920316-10-7 pa.: $4.95
The first playscript from NeWest Press in a projected series, this collaboration of Rudy Wiebe and Theatre Passe Muraille is a humorous look at the events surrounding the Dodds-Round Hill Power Development controversy. A combination of historical persons such as Crowfoot and invented characters and situations captures the spirit of Alberta. Hilary Elliott

5537 C812.
**Wiesenfeld, Joe.**
Spratt: A Play. Vancouver: Talonbooks, 1978. 104p. ISBN 0-88922-142-1 pa.: $4.95
A raw, hard-hitting drama, set in Vancouver, about a vulgar, abrasive, improvident and insensitive salesman. Wiesenfeld's considerable achievement lies in presenting him, with all his flaws, as a human being who inspires both terror and pity. "... a powerful, moving play about a man locked into the macho world." -Publisher's note.
Annette Wengle

5538 C812.
**Wismer, Leslie E.**
Marry Harry: A Play. Cornwall, Ont.: Vesta Publications, c1979. 164p. ISBN 0-919806-45-7 pa.: $5
An amusing spoof pivoting on the formulating of a marriage contract between two sophisticated young moderns. Three acts and a large cast. General purchase where there is an interest in amateur theatricals.

5539 C812.
**Woodcock, George.**
Two Plays. Vancouver: Talonbooks, 1977. 109p. ISBN 0-88922-123-5 pa.: $4.95
This volume contains two stories of exile, one of romantic lovers, the other of Gabriel Dumont. *The Island of Demons* takes place on a return journey from Canada to France in 1545. *Six Dry Cakes* is set during the Rebellion of 1885. In both plays the exile is a result of idealism and nonconformity. Hilary Elliott

## **C812.008** Drama - Collections

5540 C812'.008
**Beissel, Henry,** ed.
Cues and Entrances: Ten Canadian One-act Plays. Toronto: Gage Educational Publishing, c1977. 185p. ISBN 0-7715-1191-4 pa.: $2.35
1. One-act plays, Canadian. 2. Canadian drama – 20th century.
Ten one-act plays by Robertson Davies, Ken Mitchell, George Ryga, Isabelle Foord, Mavor Moore, Michel Tremblay, Henry Beissel, Michael Cook, Carol Bolt, and James Reaney are compiled in this anthology which captures the range and variety of Canadian drama. Four of the plays are suitable for use in high schools. Hilary Elliott

5541 C812'.008

**Five Canadian Plays.**

Toronto: Playwrights Co-op, 1978. 152p.
ISBN 0-88754-118-6 pa.: $3.50

1. Canadian drama (English) – 20th century.

Contents: Mitchell, K. *Heroes*. Lazarus, J. *Babel Rap*. Shein, B. *Cowboy Island*. Gass, K. *Hurray for Johnny Canuck*. Hubert, C. *The Twin Sinks of Allan Sammy*.

The plays in this collection of recent Canadian works are similar in theme dealing with legends and heroes but vary in theatrical style from realism to satire, fantasy, absurdism, and surrealism. Particularly recommended for young performers, they provide good material for student actors and students of Canadian drama. Hilary Elliott

5542 C812'.008

**Kalman, Rolf,** ed.

A Collection of Canadian Plays. Toronto: Simon & Pierre Publishing, 1972- v ill.
ISBN 0-88924-020-5 $19.95 vol. 5.

1. Canadian drama (English) – 20th century – Collections.

Contents: vol. 5. Seven Authors from Quebec. 1978. Garneau, M. *Four to Four*. Tremblay, R. *Greta, The Divine*. Simard, A. *Waiting for Gaudreault*. Mercier, S. *A Little Bit Left*. Sirois, S. *Dodo*. Roussin, C. *Looking for a Job*. Lavigne, L. D. *Are you Afraid of Thieves?*

Volumes 1-4 listed *CS* no. 2707. Seven plays from Quebec are translated into English in this volume. An introduction by Claude Des Landes provides background for the scripts. Hilary Elliott

5543 C812'.008

**Wagner, Anton,** ed.

Canada's Lost Plays, edited by Anton Wagner and Richard Plant. Downsview, Ont.: CTR Publications, 1978- v ill. Bibliographical references.
ISBN 0-920644-46-5 bd.: $11.95
ISBN 0-920644-48-1 pa.: $6.95

1. Canadian drama (English).

Contents: vol. 1. The Nineteenth Century. 1978. Candidus, C. *The Female Consistory of Brockville*. Scribble, S. *Dolorsolatio*. Bush, T. *Santiago*. Davin, N. F. *The Fair Grit; or, The Advantages of Coalition*. Fuller, W. H. *H.M.S. Parliament; or, The Lady Who Loved a Government Clerk*. McIlwraight, J. N. *Ptarmigan; or, A Canadian Carnival*.

This anthology is an important source book for Canadian theatre historians. It contains six scripts previously unavailable in print. The plays, five of which are comedies, are from the period 1856-1895. The volume includes an essay by the editors examining the theatre and the society for which these plays were written. Hilary Elliott

5544 C812'.008

**Wagner, Anton,** ed.

Canada's Lost Plays, edited by Anton Wagner and Richard Plant. Downsview, Ont.: CTR Publications, 1978-1979. v ill.
ISBN 0-920644-50-3 bd.: $13.95
ISBN 0-920644-52-X pa.: $7.95

1. Canadian drama (English) – 20th century – Collections.

Contents: vol. 2. Women Pioneers. 1979. Cushing, E. L. *The Fatal Ring*. Curzon, S. A. *Laura Secord: The Heroine of 1812*. Merritt, C. N. *The Sweet Girl Graduate*. Ringwood, G. P. *When George the Third Was King*. Joudry, P. *Teach Me How to Cry*. Ringwood, G. P. *Pasque Flower*.

Six plays, only one a comedy, written by women between 1840 and 1955, present a variety of female characters from a sixteenth-century French countess to Laura Secord, and a prairie farmer's wife. To a greater or lesser degree, all the plays examine the role of women in the family and society. Hilary Elliott

5545 C812'.008

**Wilson, Marian M.,** ed.

Popular Performance Plays of Canada. Toronto: Simon & Pierre Publishing, 1976- v ill., diagrs., maps, ports. (Canplay Series)
ISBN 0-88924-044-2 $19.95

1. Canadian drama (English) – 20th century.

Contents: vol. 1. Colley P. The Donnellys. Crisp, J. H. *A Wife in the Hand*. Campbell, P., Skolnik, W. *Hoarse Muse*. McMaster, B. *Put on the Spot/When Everybody Cares*. Grant, D. *What Glorious Times They Had*. 1976.

This volume is the first in a series of Canadian plays which have had success in production. The plays, which range from tragedy to comedy, are also available individually in paperback. Hilary Elliott

## C812.016 Drama - Bibliography

5546 C812'.016
**A Directory of Canadian Plays and Playwrights.**
Toronto: Playwrights Co-op, 1977- v ill. ISSN 0707-5456 Limited free distribution.

1. Playwrights Co-op – Bibliography – Catalogs – Periodicals. 2. Playwrights Co-op – Directories. 3. Canadian drama (English) – 20th century – Bibliography – Catalogs - Periodicals. 4. Canadian drama (English) – 20th century – Bio-bibliography – Periodicals.

Includes a list of about 250 plays published by Playwrights Co-op, arranged alphabetically by playwright, with brief plot synopsis and first production information. There is an annotated list of reference works for Canadian drama, a list of children's plays published by the firm, about 100 brief biographies of members, and an index. A supplement was published in September, 1979, and a new edition will be available in 1980. Annette Wengle

5547 C812'.016
**O'Neill, Patrick B.**
Canadian Plays: A Supplementary Checklist to 1945. Halifax, N.S.: Dalhousie University, University Libraries, School of Library Service, 1978. 69 leaves. Index. (Occasional Paper – Dalhousie University Libraries and Dalhousie School of Library Service) pa. Processed. Spiral binding: $3

1. Canadian drama (English) – Bibliography.

Over 750 titles of Canadian drama are compiled by author, with a title index. The plays include both published items and those in typescript and manuscript forms, many of which are unavailable. Hilary Elliott

5548 C812'.016
**Wagner, Anton,** ed.
The Brock Bibliography of Published Canadian Plays in English, 1766-1978. Toronto: Playwrights Canada, 1979. Index. ISBN 0-88754-093-7 $6.95

1. Canadian drama (English) – Bibliography.

*The Brock Bibliography of Canadian Stage Plays in English, 1900-1972* is listed *CS* no. 2712.

An annotated bibliography of English-Canadian drama and French-Canadian drama in translation, this book is a valuable research tool for the theatre historian and the student of Canadian literature. It contains more than two thousand entries, is indexed, and illustrated with photographs. Hilary Elliott

## C812.5 Playwrights - Criticism and interpretation

5549 C812.5
**Anthony, Geraldine.**
John Coulter. Boston: Twayne Publishers, c1976. 176p. port. Bibliography: p. 159-172. Index. (Twayne's World Authors Series) ISBN 0-8057-6240-X $8.25

1. Coulter, John, 1888- – Criticism and interpretation.

A biographical and critical interpretation of the life and works of John Coulter, this study traces Coulter's development as a playwright from the early influence of the Irish literary renaissance to his mature plays based on Canadian history. Hilary Elliott

5550 C812'.5
**Anthony, Geraldine,** ed.
Stage Voices: Twelve Canadian Playwrights Talk about Their Lives and Work. Toronto: Doubleday, 1978. 318p. ports. Bibliographies and Index. ISBN 0-385-12643-3 bd.: $12.50 ISBN 0-385-13540-8 pa.: $7.95

1. Dramatists, Canadian – 20th century. 2. Canadian drama – 20th century – History and criticism. 3. Theatre – Canada.

John Coulter, Herman Voaden, Robertson Davies, Gwen Pharis Ringwood, Tom Grainger, James Reaney, John Herbert, Michael Cook, David French, David Freeman, Michel Tremblay and Michel Garneau write about their experiences as playwrights. These twelve essays are supplemented by Geraldine Anthony's introductions, a chronology of each playwright's life, and selected bibliographies. Hilary Elliott

5551 C812'.5
**Peck, Edward,** ed.
Transitions I: Short Plays: A Source Book of Canadian Literature. Vancouver: CommCept Publishing, 1978. 306p. ill., ports. ISBN 0-88829-022-5 $10.20

1. Canadian drama (English) – 20th century.

Fifteen short plays representative of contemporary drama and its various forms are followed by the playwrights' comments on their work. An outline of Canadian theatre, full-page photographs and brief biographical sketches of the dramatists enhance the value of this useful introduction to Canadian drama. Students and general readers. High school and public libraries. Similar in design and format: Peck, E., ed. *Transitons II: Short Fiction*, 1978, and *Transitions III: Poetry*, 1978.

## C813 Novels and short stories

5552 C813.
**Adams, Ian.**
End Game in Paris. Toronto: Doubleday, 1979. 216p. ISBN 0-385-14935-2 $9.95
A rather weak philosophical thriller about a disoriented news photographer who tries to track down his double in Toronto, Montreal, Algiers and Paris. Interesting for the glimpses it provides of the intelligence field and also for its hypothetical explanation of events during the Quebec crisis in 1970. Peggy Sinclair

5553 C813.
**Adams, Ian.**
Portrait of a Spy: RCMP Intelligence: The Inside Story: A Novel. Agincourt, Ont.: Gage Publishing, c1977. 178p. ISBN 0-7715-9354-X $8.95
An exciting story of international intrigue involving RCMP Intelligence. The hints, both subtle and blatant, of actual Canadian events and characters add to its fascination. Jean Dodd

5554 C813.
**Anderson, Doris.**
Two Women: A Novel. Toronto: Macmillan, c1978. 243p. ISBN 0-7705-1653-X $9.95
Despite a rather pedestrian beginning, this novel of two mature women, one dreaming of a perfect marriage and the other faced with reality, develops into an authentic appraisal of today's lifestyles. Interesting story-line and honest characterization make it worthwhile reading. Jean Dodd

5555 C813.
**Annett, R. Ross.**
Especially Babe. Introduction by Rudy Wiebe. Edmonton: Tree Frog Press, 1978. 187p. ISBN 0-88967-080-3 bd.: $9.95 ISBN 0-88967-081-1 pa.
First published 1942 by Appleton-Century, New York and London.
Pleasant easy reading, these thirteen stories first appeared in the "Saturday Evening Post". Big Joe, Little Joe and irascible Uncle Pete dote on blonde, angelic Little Babe, who during the grim depression years represented their hope for the future. Jean Dodd

5556 C813.
**Aquin, Hubert.**
Hamlet's Twin. Translated by Sheila Fischman. Toronto: McClelland and Stewart, 1979. 208p. ISBN 0-7710-0800-7 $12.95
Translation of *Neige noire.*
There are many parallels between this novel and the play from which it takes its English title. It tells of the honeymoon journey of a modern young couple as they travel to Norway and to lands beyond the Arctic circle – a "cold desert" without night. A dense, complex, alarming novel. Catharine MacKenzie

5557 C813.
**Askey, Derek C.**
The Goat and the Tiger. Markham, Ont.: PaperJacks, c1977. 239p. ISBN 0-7701-0011-2 pa.: $1.95
An average, middle-aged veterinarian in Oakville is stalked by a psychopathic killer. A well written thriller, suspenseful and believable. Jean Dodd

5558 C813.
**Atwood, Margaret.**
Dancing Girls and Other Stories. Toronto: McClelland and Stewart; McClelland and Stewart-Bantam, 1978, c1977. 254p. ISBN 0-7710-0810-4 bd.: $10.95 pa.: $2.25
These fourteen stories, some of which have been previously published, demonstrate Atwood's cool appraisal of people and situations. Both humorous and painful incidents are described with a sure, deft touch. Jean Dodd

5559 C813.
**Atwood, Margaret.**
Lady Oracle. Toronto: McClelland and Stewart-Bantam, 1977, c1976. 345p. (Seal Books) pa.: $2.25
Clothbound edition listed *CS* no. 2733.

5560 C813.
**Atwood, Margaret.**
Life Before Man. Toronto: McClelland and Stewart, c1979. 317p. ISBN 0-7710-0807-4 $12.95
City of Toronto Book Award. Governor General's Literary Award.
A prehistoric monster, with an extra claw for disembowelling which may have made sex cruelly painful, is the apt metaphor in this cool novel about humans who fail to evolve emotionally. Relationships of many kinds are probed with the precision of a scalpel and without the analgesic of pity or love.

Interesting but as depressing as a sigh of resignation. Jean Dodd

5561 C813.
**Bacque, James.**
The Queen Comes to Minnicog. Agincourt, Ont.: Gage Publishing, 1979. 177p. ill. ISBN 0-7715-9488-7 $9.95

The author has read his stories about a fictional small Ontario town with success over Don Harron's morning show on CBC radio. This collection loses something in not having the accompaniment of his voice, but they are still funny in a hearty, unsubtle but sharp, matey fashion. Catharine MacKenzie

5562 C813.
**Bailey, Don.**
The Sorry Papers. Ottawa: Oberon Press, c1979. 144p. port. ISBN 0-88750-321-7 bd.: $15 ISBN 0-88750-322-5 pa.: $6.95

Two of the eight short stories in this new collection have been broadcast on CBC's "Anthology", and two have been previously published in periodicals. Four have a unifying theme of guilt. Good characterization and wit leaven, somewhat, the depressing picture of the exploitation of society's losers.

5563 C813.
**Ballem, John Bishop.**
The Moon Pool. Toronto: McClelland and Stewart; McClelland and Stewart-Bantam, 1979, c1978. 236p. map. ISBN 0-7710-1004-4 bd.: $12.95 ISBN 0-7704-1608-X pa.: $2.25

A timely, exciting story of terrorist activity in the Canadian North where a foreign power develops a plot to use Native Peoples as pawns in international intrigue. Authentic description of a drillship in the Beaufort Sea adds to the interest. Jean Dodd

5564 C813.
**Barfoot, Joan.**
Abra: A Novel. Toronto: McGraw-Hill Ryerson; Scarborough, Ont.: New American Library, 1978. 199p. ISBN 0-07-082740-0 $9.95 pa.: $2.25

Books in Canada First Novel Award.

Ridding herself of family and society to live as a hermit without mirrors or clocks, Abra finds an acceptance of herself without the labels imposed by others. The gentle, simple style is well suited to the theme of being at peace with aloneness and at one with nature. Jean Dodd

5565 C813.
**Bauer, William A.**
A Family Album. Ottawa: Oberon Press, 1979. 150p. ISBN 0-88750-299-7 bd.: $12.95 ISBN 0-88750-300-4 pa.: $5.95

Six short stories set in New England during the recent past. Somewhat uneven in quality but each has an interesting perspective. The book itself is very handsomely produced. Peggy Sinclair

5566 C813.
**Beaulieu, Victor-Lévy.**
Don Quixote in Nighttown. Translated by Sheila Fischman. Erin, Ont.: Press Porcépic, 1978, c1977. 192p. ISBN 0-88878-080-X $10

Translation of *Don Quichotte de la démanche.*

A Quebec writer is feverishly glutted with ideas and teeming, unwanted memories. His inability to tame the words to express them is almost too painful to bear. A masterly work, full of a rich fireworks of allusion, puns, imagery. A brilliant, dazzling novel requiring careful reading and depth of perception. Jean Dodd

5567 C813.
**Bénoit, Jacques.**
The Princes. Translated by David Lobdell. Ottawa: Oberon Press, 1977. 123p. ISBN 0-88750-242-3 bd.: $12.95 ISBN 0-88750-243-1 pa.: $5.95

Translation of *Les princes.*

The world of this novel is inhabited by humans, sub-humans, dogs and monsters. It is a world where men eat dogs and dogs eat men, and the political and moral implications are disturbing in the extreme. Although there are no direct references Quebec appears to be the country and Montreal "the City". The author won the Prix de la Province de Québec for his first novel, *Jos Carbone.* Catharine MacKenzie

5568 C813.
**Beresford-Howe, Constance.**
A Population of One: A Novel. Toronto: Macmillan; Macmillan-NAL Publishing, 1978, c1977. 201p. ISBN 0-7705-1575-4 bd.: $9.95 ISBN 0-7723-0007-0 pa.: $2.25

Thirty-year-old Wilhelmina Doyle, having led a sheltered life, gets her first job as professor of English and makes plans to find a lover. Her slightly absurd hesitancy in both endeavours creates a story of charm and light humour. Jean Dodd

5569 C813.
**Birney, Earle.**
Big Bird in the Bush: Stories & Relations. Ottawa: Mosaic Press/Valley Editions, 1979. 96p. ISBN 0-88962-085-7 bd.: $10 ISBN 0-88962-086-5 pa.: $4.95

A collection of ten prose pieces originally published between 1941 and 1955 displays the author's marvellous ear for speech and capacity to entertain. The title story is about a Kootenay rancher who tries to capture a phoenix; the other pieces deal with duelling, student illiteracies, an obnoxious Canadian tourist in South America; and there is an excerpt from the novel, *Down the Long Table*. Catharine MacKenzie

5570 C813.
**Blais, Marie-Claire.**
The Fugitive. Translated by David Lobdell. Ottawa: Oberon Press, c1978. 96p. ISBN 0-88750-283-0 bd.: $12.95 ISBN 0-88750-284-9 pa.: $5.95

Translation of *L'insoumise.*

A subtle account of a young man's fragmented relationships with mother, father, friend and lover. Two rather delicate themes intertwine – how one does not recognize oneself except through the eyes of another and the resultant "avarice of the heart". For the sophisticated reader. Jean Dodd

5571 C813.
**Blais, Marie-Claire.**
A Literary Affair. Translated by Sheila Fischman. Toronto: McClelland and Stewart, 1979. 160p. ISBN 0-7710-1559-3 $12.95

Explores the conflict of French-Québecois values as experienced by a young French-Canadian writer involved in an affair with a Parisian authoress. A humourless approach and tedious characters further weaken an already weak and trivial narrative. Originally published in French in 1975, subsequent to the author's stay in Brittany. Ille-Mai Gerdels

5572 C813.
**Blais, Marie-Claire.**
Nights in the Underground: An Exploration of Love. Translated by Ray Ellenwood. Don Mills, Ont.: Musson, c1979. 199p. ISBN 0-7737-1031-0 pa.: $8.95

Translation of *Les nuits de l'underground.*

In the closed world of a bar for women, sheltered from the winter cold, with its camaraderie, jealousy, good-natured banter, Genevieve Aures, a sculptress, falls in love with Lali Dorman, a doctor. In tone the novel is tender, meditative, hopeful Genevieve emerges from this unsatisfying love into the springtime of a happier one. Catharine MacKenzie

5573 C813.
**Blaise, Clark.**
Lunar Attractions. Toronto: Doubleday, 1979. 305p. ISBN 0-385-13318-9 $11.50

Books in Canada First Novel Award.

A precocious, alienated boy learns about life vicariously and each lesson provokes intense, agonizing self-examination. The writing is good, the theme cleverly created, but a bizarre sexual incident flaws what could have been a realistic and honest portrait. Interesting but disappointing in the final analysis. Jean Dodd

5574 C813.
**Bonnie, Fred.**
Squatter's Rights. Ottawa: Oberon Press, c1979. 129p. ISBN 0-88750-327-6 bd.: $12.95 ISBN 0-88750-328-4 pa.: $5.95

The universal concerns and emotions of humanity are experienced by the memorable characters who people the small communities in the New Brunswick-Maine border region in which Bonnie's stories are set. Well crafted, with convincing dialogue and revealing incident, the seven stories run the gamut from tragedy to comedy. Recommended.

5575 C813.
**Bowering, George.**
Protective Footwear: Stories and Fables. Toronto: McClelland and Stewart, c1978. 175p. ISBN 0-7710-1595-X pa.: $6.95

Ranging from the mere anecdotal, the meaning of which is frequently elusive, to the fanciful and familiar, these short stories present a broad scope of characters, sometimes recognizable, sometimes enigmatic. The human psyche is held up for examination in a variety of attitudes and settings from the Canadian West to Mexico. Pat George

5576 C813.
**Bowering, George.**
A Short Sad Book: A Novel. Vancouver: Talonbooks, 1977. 191p. ISBN 0-88922-127-8 pa.: $4.95

This strange blend of Canadian history and Canadian literature will not appeal to many readers, and yet it is an interesting experiment. It is the author's attempt, apparently, to understand why he loves this country. Select with care. Catharine MacKenzie

5577 C813.
**Bowering, Marilyn.**
The Visitors Have All Returned. Erin, Ont.: Press Porcépic, 1979. 86p. ISBN 0-88878-164-4 pa.: $5.95
Prose vignettes illustrated by photographs delicately suggest rather than state the essential isolation of a young woman, in spite of husband, child, and lover. V. M. Gill

5578 C813.
**Boyarsky, Abraham.**
A Pyramid of Time. Erin, Ont.: Porcupine's Quill, 1978. 76p. ISBN 0-88984-009-1 bd.: $10.95 ISBN 0-88984-007-5 pa.: $5.95
A boy, who has survived a German concentration camp, describes his life as an immigrant in Montreal's Jewish section, in a collection of short stories. The stories, prefaced by unnecessary, enigmatic introductions, and written in a precise and cynical style, show man's instincts for survival and point a finger at Jews who have forgotten their heritage. Pat George

5579 C813.
**Boyle, Harry J.**
The Luck of the Irish: A Canadian Fable. Scarborough, Ont.: Macmillan-NAL Publishing, 1979, c1975. 166p. (A Signet Book) ISBN 0-7723-0018-6 pa.: $2.25
Clothbound listed in *CS* no. 2775.

5580 C813.
**Bradley, Michael.**
Imprint: A Novel. Toronto: Dorset Publishing, 1978. 233p. ISBN 0-88893-002-X $10.95
Energy and environment problems are related to American politics and Canadian/American relations in this unusual suspense story. The potential audience includes not only mystery buffs, but also those interested in ecology.

5581 C813.
**Braithwaite, Max.**
The Commodore's Barge Is Alongside. Toronto: McClelland and Stewart, c1979. 193p. ISBN 0-7710-1610-7 $12.95
The misadventures of a brash young naval recruit as he bumbles his way through three months of basic training aboard a make-shift training "ship" on the Saskatchewan prairie. Light-hearted nonsense fashioned from stock situations and stereotyped characters. Ephemeral entertainment.

5582 C813.
**Braithwaite, Max.**
Lusty Winter. Toronto: McClelland and Stewart, c1978. 207p. ISBN 0-7710-1609-3 $12.95
A sixty-five-year-old man tries to live in a country-dream setting only to find the machine-dominated world encroaching. A mixture of adventure and romanticism with realistic characters and a vivid description of Canadian winter. Jean Dodd

5583 C813.
**Branden, Victoria.**
Mrs. Job. London: Victor Gollancz (Clarke, Irwin), 1979. 238p. ISBN 0-575-02529-8 $16.50
An amusing first novel in which a clutch of strongly individualistic characters, a heroine who thinks God dislikes her, several plots, and wry wit are blended with some success. Undemanding escape reading.

5584 C813.
**Brewster, Elizabeth.**
It's Easy to Fall on the Ice: Ten Stories. Ottawa: Oberon Press, c1977. 127p. ISBN 0-88750-247-4 bd.: $9.95 ISBN 0-88750-248-2 pa.: $4.95
The heroines of these stories are intelligent, observant, superficially calm, but ineffectual. They seem unable to make their lives satisfying. So the stories are concerned with chance encounters, failure to make contact, failure to deal with those whose style is different from one's own. Nevertheless there is nothing tentative about the writing which catches and holds the interest. Catharine MacKenzie

5585 C813.
**Brown, Jamie.**
Shrewsbury. Scarborough, Ont.: New American Library, 1978, c1977. 218p. (A Signet Book) ISBN 0-451-08368-7 pa.: $2.25
Sequel to *So Free We Seem*.
Those libraries which already have *Stepping Stones* and *So Free We Seem* will want this third part of the chronicle of the Moncrieff family. The series is a competent portrayal of three generations of social history in Ontario and of the building of a large automotive company, but this novel is old-fashioned in manner, the dialogue and characterization are uninspired. Catharine MacKenzie

5586 C813.
**Bruneau, André.**
Moving Out: A Novel. Don Mills, Ont.: Musson, 1978. 240p. ISBN 0-7737-0040-4 bd.: $12.95 ISBN 0-7737-1025-6 pa.: $7.95

Michael Armstrong, married to a French Canadian, is forced to move his business headquarters out of the Province of Quebec because of political unrest. A straightforward story suitable for a television script. The characters lack subtlety and the insight into the Quebec situation is superficial.
Jean Dodd

5587 C813.
**Brycht, Andrew.**
Zoom: A Novel. Translated from the Polish by Kevin Windle. Toronto: Simon & Pierre Publishing, c1978. 154p. ISBN 0-88924-070-1 $10.95

Against the spectre of a concentration camp, the themes of ambition, heroism and martyrdom are explored. Told in the first person by an unnamed young photographer, the novel focuses on his and several others' lives. Un-Canadian in mood and setting, the author, well known in his native Poland, has now settled in Ontario. Peggy Sinclair

5588 C813.
**Burnford, Sheila.**
Bel Ria: Dog of War. Toronto: McClelland and Stewart; McClelland and Stewart-Bantam, 1978, c1977. 203p. ISBN 0-7710-1785-5 bd. $10 pa.: $2.25

A simple story of the courage of a dog during World War II. The humans he meets are good and kind, the wartime background authentic. Competently written. Suitable for all ages.
Jean Dodd

5589 C813.
**Callaghan, Morley.**
Close to the Sun Again: A New Novel. Toronto: Macmillan; Scarborough, Ont.: Macmillan-NAL Publishing, 1978, c1977. 169p. ISBN 0-7705-1574-6 bd.: $9.95 ISBN 0-7723-0008-9 pa.: $2.50

As he lies dying Ira Groome returns in memory to the self he used to be when he was "close to the sun", and the scenes which led to the dramatic change in his personality. This part of the novel takes place on board a corvette in the North Atlantic during World War II. Catharine MacKenzie

5590 C813.
**Callaghan, Morley.**
No Man's Meat and The Enchanted Pimp. Toronto: Macmillan, c1978. 170p. ISBN 0-7705-1726-9 $9.95

One very short story which first appeared in 1931 in a limited edition and a long short story written in 1978 deal with two kinds of love, neither well-regarded in respectable society but treated here with compassion.
Catharine MacKenzie

5591 C813.
**Callaghan, Morley.**
A Passion in Rome. Toronto: Macmillan, 1978. 352p. (Laurentian Library) ISBN 0-7705-1663-7 pa.: $5.95

Clothbound edition listed *CS* no. 2807.

5592 C813.
**Carrier, Jean-Guy.**
A Cage of Bone. Ottawa: Oberon Press, c1978. 175p. ISBN 0-88750-287-3 bd.: $15 ISBN 0-88750-288-1 pa.: $6.95

Sequel to *My Father's House* and to *Family.*

The third book about the Vallaire family in Ste. Camille, Quebec. Unfortunately, in an attempt to exemplify the meaning in the title, the author has created bloodless characters and lifeless incidents. The writing is stilted and awkward. Perhaps a reading of the first two novels would ameliorate this. Jean Dodd

5593 C813.
**Carrier, Roch.**
The Garden of Delights. Translated by Sheila Fischman. Toronto: House of Anansi Press, c1978. 173p. (Anansi Fiction Series) ISBN 0-88784-066-3 pa.: $6.95

Translation of *Le jardin des délices.*

Like a modern morality play, this delightful novel, with its motley of characters in a Quebec setting, reveals the frailties and evils of all humanity. The humour may be black, but the style, the insight, the joy of living pure gold. Jean Dodd

5594 C813.
**Carrier, Roch.**
The Hockey Sweater and Other Stories. Translated by Sheila Fischman. Toronto: House of Anansi Press, 1979. (Anansi Fiction Series) ISBN 0-88784-078 pa.: $6.95

Translation of *Les enfants du bonhomme dans la lune.*

Twenty vignettes about the life of a boy growing up in a Quebec village in the 1940's.

Humorous, poignant, well-written, these stories make comments about situations which have a present-day appropriateness. Ably translated. Peggy Sinclair

5595 C813.
**Carroll, Joy.**
Proud Blood. Rexdale, Ont.: Dell International, 1978. 603p. ill.
ISBN 0-440-11562-0 pa.: $1.95

The romance of an English woman and French man in Montreal at the turn of the century, and the family split that their marriage caused. A costume piece with slight historical background, written for the mass market. Jean Dodd

5596 C813.
**Childerhose, R. J.**
Wild Blue. Victoria: Hoot Productions, c1978. 346p. ISBN 0-919994-02-4 bd.: $12.95
ISBN 0-919994-03-2 pa.: $6.95

From his experiences as an RCAF fighter pilot with NATO during the 1950's, the author has drawn a number of anecdotes and fashioned them into a readable, personal view of this era of flight. Humour and a writer's license to embellish add icing to true incidents. For aviation buffs of any age.

5597 C813.
**Clarke, Austin C.**
The Prime Minister: A Novel. Don Mills, Ont.: General Publishing, 1977. 191p.
ISBN 0-7736-0060-4 bd.: $10.95
ISBN 0-7736-1030-8 pa.: $6.95

Explores the political ignorance, viciousness and corruption of a newly independent Caribbean state. Particular strengths are Clarke's honesty, his caustic humour, his handling of the native idiom, and the lyrical and narrative power of his prose. Complex and controversial, but relevant and enlightening in view of Canada's expanding third world population. Ille-Mai Gerdels

5598 C813.
**Cohen, Matt.**
The Colours of War. Toronto: McClelland and Stewart, c1977. 234p. ISBN 0-7710-2175-5 $10

An imaginative but partly naive account of next-generation Canada disintegrating into political chaos and civil disorder. The hero, in search of his past amidst revolution, is interesting, but fails to rescue the novel from one-dimensional minor characters and a slow plot. Ille-Mai Gerdels

5599 C813.
**Cohen, Matt.**
Night Flights: Stories New and Selected. Toronto: Doubleday, 1978. 180p.
ISBN 0-385-13333-2 $7.95

An eclectic group of stories which reveal Cohen's considerable talent for both realism and fantasy, his sure touch with characterization and his skill with the perfectly apt phrase to delight and surprise the reader. Jean Dodd

5600 C813.
**Cohen, Matt.**
The Sweet Second Summer of Kitty Malone. Toronto: McClelland and Stewart, c1979. 233p. ISBN 0-7710-2221-2 $12.95

Kitty Malone and Pat Frank have been lovers/haters for twenty years and their story is told with a discerning eye for the authentic incident and revealing detail. A clear honest appraisal of people caught up in a relationship of passion, inevitably full of light and dark. Jean Dodd

5601 C813.
**Copeland, Ann.**
At Peace: Stories. Ottawa: Oberon Press, c1978. 164p. ISBN 0-88750-270-9 bd.: $15
ISBN 0-88750-271-7 pa.: $6.95

The charm of these stories, set in a convent, lies in the style which is perfectly suited to the themes of unexpressed love and anger, the subtlety of disciplined emotions and the wry humour at their recognition. Jean Dodd

5602 C813.
**Copeland, Ann.**
The Back Room. Ottawa: Oberon Press, c1979. 149p. ISBN 0-88750-307-1 bd.: $15
ISBN 0-88750-309-8 pa.: $6.95

These simple stories are clear-eyed examinations of banal events in the lives of ordinary people. They point out the fact that toward life most of us seem to have a "learning disability". The images and events have a crystal quality and the emotions expressed are as gentle as a sigh. Jean Dodd

5603 C813.
**Craig, John.**
Chappie and Me: An Autobiographical Novel. Toronto: Dodd, 1979. 247p.
ISBN 0-396-07660-2 $11.50

A white Canadian, Don Shoeblack, plays baseball with a team of Negro barnstormers. Humorous and poignant, an insight is provided into what it was like to be black during the thirties. Peggy Sinclair

5604 C813.
**Creighton, Donald.**
Takeover. Toronto: McClelland and Stewart, c1978. 196p. ISBN 0-7710-2368-5 $12.95

A murder story from the distinguished historian opens in the mid-sixties with Hugh Stuart, the head of a proud family of whisky distillers, trying to jettison his business responsibilities and find someone to take command. The offer for the firm comes from a gentleman from Kentucky. Catharine MacKenzie

5605 C813.
**Davies, Robertson.**
World of Wonders. New York: Penguin Books, 1977, c1975. 315p. ISBN 0-14-004389-6 pa.: $1.95

Reprint of the 1976 edition published in New York by Viking Press. Clothbound listed *CS* no. 2855.

5606 C813.
**Dennison, Shane.**
Sidehill Gouger or, What's So Deadly about Caterpillars? Toronto: Doubleday, 1977. 312p. ISBN 0-385-12515-1 $8.95

An iconoclastic young teacher takes on the educational establishment and the unimaginative residents of a small British Columbia village. Although the author has a tendency to preach, his writing contains large elements of humour, suspense and romance, and it is a promising first novel. Peggy Sinclair

5607 C813.
**Deverell, William.**
Needles. Toronto: McClelland and Stewart, c1979. 351p. ISBN 0-7710-2727-3 $12.95

Seal Books First Novel Award.

A Vancouver lawyer, hooked on drugs, and failing in his marriage and law practice, gets a chance to change his luck by acting for the crown in the murder trial of a notorious Oriental drug dealer and torturer. The action and suspense entrap the reader to the final page despite some stereotyping and the author's inability to portray female characters. Pat George

5608 C813.
**Dewdney, Selwyn.**
Christopher Breton: A Novel. Toronto: McClelland and Stewart, c1978. 367p. ISBN 0-7710-2698-6 $14.95

In style this novel about a young artist's struggle for freedom and sanity seems to belong to an earlier generation of writers. In spite of this the book impresses by its sense of experience deeply felt. Catharine MacKenzie

5609 C813.
**Dorland, Michael.**
The Double-cross Circuit: A Novel. Toronto: Lester and Orpen, c1978. 222p. ISBN 0-919630-91-X $10.95

A complex thriller in which a huge communications corporation plans to trade to the Russians the secret of a new system which has been developed for NATO. The plan is discovered by a French counter agent. The business of the corporation is believable and interesting; the action is fast, if sometimes brutal. Catharine MacKenzie

5610 C813.
**Doucet, Clive.**
Disneyland, Please. Toronto: Fitzhenry & Whiteside, c1978. 239p. ISBN 0-88902-435-9 $9.95

Guy Leblanc, from Cape Breton, believes in the American dream, according to Disney and gets to California on a football scholarship. The contrast between dream and reality is well developed. No need to be a football fan to enjoy this one. Jean Dodd

5611 C813.
**Dow, David Stuart.**
The Cliff Hanger House. Antigonish, N.S.: Formac Publishing, c1978. 176p. ISBN 0-88780-026-2 pa.: $5.95

The McNeil clan emigrates from Scotland to an isolated coast on Cape Breton in the seventeen hundreds where they and their descendants grow wealthy through crime and piracy. The large cast of characters, while thinly drawn, is entertaining. The unembellished prose style carries the reader forward with interest and affection despite the family's questionable activities. Pat George

5612 C813.
**Drábek, Jan.**
Report on the Death of Rosenkavalier: A Novel. Toronto: McClelland and Stewart, 1977. 224p. ISBN 0-7710-2880-6 $8.95

Antonin Klima feels compelled to return to Prague to publicly execute an evil official. The contrast between everyday life in Canada and that in a totalitarian state is pointed out with telling anecdote. A politically sophisticated story related with a simple clarity and an exciting plot. Jean Dodd

5613 C813.

**Dragland, Stan.**

Peckertracks: A Chronicle. Toronto: Coach House Press, c1978. 140p. ISBN 0-88910-136-1 pa.: $5.50

Another book about a boy growing up in a small town manages to be genuinely readable, funny and a little bit different. The difference is the way in which the author captures the voices of the people who make up Percy Lewis' world in his final year in high school. Catharine MacKenzie

5614 C813.

**Dunmore, Spencer.**

Means of Escape. London, Eng.: Peter Davies (William Collins), 1978. 216p. ISBN 0-432-03504-4 $11.95

A stirring tale told in skillful prose of the escape to Britain of a British airman who had been shot down, and a German officer involved in a plot against Hitler, in 1944. For war story enthusiasts.

5615 C813.

**Eggleston, Wilfrid.**

Prairie Symphony. Ottawa: Borealis Press, 1978. ISBN 0-919594-99-9 $9.95

This romantic novel about a young Alberta man torn between his love and his ambition to become a major poet expounds Eggleston's favourite thesis that frontier art cannot flourish in an uncultured environment. Contains some sensitive descriptions of the southern Alberta rangeland. Sufficiently uncomplicated to attract the younger teen-ager. Ille-Mai Gerdels

5616 C813.

**Engel, Marian.**

The Glassy Sea. Toronto: McClelland and Stewart; McClelland and Stewart-Bantam, 1979, c1978. 167p. ISBN 0-7710-3084-3 bd.: $10.95 ISBN 0-7704-1555-5 pa.: $2.25

An interesting subject is treated in a rather disappointing epistolary novel which reads like the first trial for a larger, more substantial and important work. The narrator is an Anglican nun recalled to her vocation and placed in charge of re-opening a long-closed convent. Catharine MacKenzie

5617 C813.

**Evans, Florence.**

A Man Without Passion. Toronto: Clarke, Irwin, 1979. 194p. ISBN 0-7720-1268-7 $13.95

Published in England under the title *The Headmaster*.

Relates the experiences of the unpopular and cynical headmaster of an Oxfordshire primary school, and illuminates his character and the current trend of his life by flashbacks to his formative years in Manitoba. Skillfully written in first person, this is an accomplished and successful first novel by a Canadian author living and teaching in England. Ille-Mai Gerdels

5618 C813.

**Faessler, Shirley.**

Everything in the Window: A Novel. Toronto: McClelland and Stewart, c1979. 331p. ISBN 0-7710-3110-6 $13.95

City of Toronto Book Award. Books in Canada First Novel Award.

A vivid portrait of Toronto's immigrant Jewish community in the 1930's emerges from this tale of a girl who marries a gentile. The author has previously written short stories and this may account for some of the weaknesses of the writing. The ending is somewhat unsatisfactory, but the whole is enjoyable reading. Peggy Sinclair

5619 C813.

**Ferguson, Trevor.**

High Water Chants: A Novel. Toronto: Macmillan, c1977. 268p. ISBN 0-7705-1568-1 $10.95

This promising first novel about personal commitment unravels the past histories of several characters engaged in a desperate chase through the British Columbia rain forest. Although events are needlessly obscure, and the style overly explicit and verbose, the author writes convincingly and exhibits an impressive, if overworked descriptive talent. Ille-Mai Gerdels

5620 C813.

**Ferron, Jacques.**

Quince Jam. Translated by Ray Ellenwood. Toronto: Coach House Press, c1977. 262p. (Coach House Quebec Translations) ISBN 0-88910-031-4 pa.: $6.50

Translation of *Les confitures de coings et autres textes*.

Contents: Papa Boss. Quince Jam. Credit Due. Appendix to Quince Jam, or, The Sacking of Frank Archibald Campbell.

An engrossing English-language edition by an infrequently translated, infuential exponent of Quebec independence. "Papa Boss" attacks the commercialized, exploitative institutions of North American finance and technology. The three remaining texts are autobiographical explorations of individual and national self-definition. Ironic, incisive, and politically relevant. Ille-Mai Gerdels

5621 C813.
**Findlay, David K.**
King Winter. Ottawa: Deneau and Greenberg, 1978. 214p. ISBN 0-88879-008-2 $9.95

Findlay's fourth novel centers on a planeload of American tourists trapped in a small Canadian village by a month-long cataclysmic snowstorm. The plot involves their struggle to survive themselves, each other and the elements. Entirely plausible and exciting, and magnificent in depicting the awesome beauty and evil power of the storm. Ille-Mai Gerdels

5622 C813.
**Findley, Timothy.**
The Wars. Toronto: Clarke, Irwin; Markham, Ont.: Penguin Books, 1978, c1977. 226p. ISBN 0-7720-1188-5 bd.: $8.95 ISBN 0-14-005011-6 pa.: $2.25

City of Toronto Book Award. Governor General's Literary Award.

The story of a young C.E.F. officer in Canada, France and England in the year 1915 is a fine novel of the Great War. With marvellous economy – not a wasted word, not a scene too much – the full inhumanity of that conflict is forced upon the reader's cringing sensibility. Catharine MacKenzie

5623 C813.
**Fletcher, Peggy.**
When the Moon Is Full. Cornwall, Ont.: Vesta Publications, c1977. 115p. ISBN 0-919806-28-7 pa.: $4

The first collection of fifteen short stories by a Newoundland poet and editor. The work is unified by rural settings, simple characters and a thematic concentration on the survival of love and individual dignity in the face of generally tragic human experience. Realistic, but unrelieved by humour, hope or joy. Ille-Mai Gerdels

5624 C813.
**Fraser, Raymond.**
The Bannonbridge Musicians. Portugal Cove, Nfld.: Breakwater Books, c1978. 136p. ISBN 0-919948-33-2 bd.: $11 ISBN 0-919948-32-4 pa.: $5.95

Fraser's second novel is an episodic, loosely structured, bawdy tale about the defeated lives of rural New Brunswick youth around 1960. There is merit in the regional flavour of the dialogue and in the sporadic humour of outrageous events, but the characters are unattractive, their language obscene, and their tragedy unmoving. Ille-Mai Gerdels

5625 C813.
**Fraser, Sylvia.**
A Casual Affair: A Modern Fairy Tale. Toronto: McClelland and Stewart, c1978. 287p. ISBN 0-7710-3180-7 $12.95

Lacks the power, wit and sophistication of Fraser's earlier novels. The narrative, punctuated by interpretative parables, consists of a series of frustrating confrontations between a pair of unlikeable lovers. Of popular appeal because of its romantic and sexual promise and theme of rebellion against marriage and the establishment. Ille-Mai Gerdels

5626 C813.
**Fraser, Sylvia.**
The Emperor's Virgin. Toronto: McClelland and Stewart, 1980. 384p. ISBN 0-7710-3175-0 $14.95

Rome is at its most corrupt in this novel depicting a near-mad emperor and the intrigues surrounding him. Bordering on the pornographic, a moderately interesting story can be discerned between the numerous scenes of depraved sexuality. But the characters are not as well drawn as in Fraser's other books. Perhaps the single viewpoint would have been better. Pat George

5627 C813.
**Fraser, William Douglas.**
Nor'east for Louisburg. Scarborough, Ont.: Amethyst Publications, 1978. 221p. ill., maps, plans, plates, ports. ISBN 0-920474-01-2 pa.: $5.95

Historical fiction focusing upon the two sieges of Louisburg in 1745 and 1758, but set within the context of a Massachusetts boy's life from age eighteen to seventy-three. The story line has too many coincidences to be believable, but the historical detail is fascinating. Includes photographs and illustrations. Peggy Sinclair

5628 C813.
**Gallant, Mavis.**
From the Fifteenth District: A Novella and Eight Short Stories. Toronto: Macmillan, c1979. 243p. ISBN 0-7705-1813-3 $12.95

These superbly crafted stories, which appeared originally in "The New Yorker", relate incidents in European settings from the thirties to the seventies. The unusual mixture of incisive clarity and subtle undertones demands careful reading, but the rewards are worthwhile. Jean Dodd

5629 C813.
**Gane, Margaret Drury.**
Parade on an Empty Street. Toronto: Clarke, Irwin, c1978. 219p. ISBN 0-7720-1169-9 $10.95

A charming and competent first novel about a twelve-year-old boy's life and relationships in a dreamy Toronto neighbourhood of 1939-40. Realistic characters and dialogue, and the author's keen eye for detail make the book enjoyable reading for both adults and teen-agers. Ill-Mai Gerdels

5630 C813.
**Garner, Hugh.**
A Hugh Garner Omnibus. Toronto: McGraw-Hill Ryerson, 1978. 752p. ISBN 0-07-082701-X $14.95

Contains the complete novel *Cabbagetown*, thirteen favourite short stories and excerpts from Garner's best fiction and non-fiction works, all in the tradition of social realism. The recurrent theme is that of individual helplessness in the face of class structures and tensions. An inviting selection for the initiate, and a memorial volume for Garner fans. Ille-Mai Gerdels

5631 C813.
**Garner, Hugh.**
The Intruders: A Novel. Toronto: Totem Books, 1977, c1976. 328p. pa.: $2.25

Clothbound listed *CS* no. 2920.

5632 C813.
**Garner, Hugh.**
Murder Has Your Number: An Inspector McDumont Mystery. Toronto: McGraw-Hill Ryerson, c1978. 263p. ISBN 0-07-082703-6 $9.95

This is Garner's third murder mystery with the hardboiled, street-wise Inspector McDumont in the lead role. The plot is intricate and has an unexpected ending, but is weakened by cumbersome dialogue and extraneous detail about the Toronto setting. The hero's addiction to a proletarian boiler-room philosophy of life grates on the intellect. Ille-Mai Gerdels

5633 C813.
**Gedge, Pauline.**
Child of the Morning. Toronto: Macmillan, 1977. 403p. ISBN 0-7705-1520-7 $9.95

1. Hatshepsut, Queen of Egypt – Fiction. Search-for-a-New Alberta-Novelist-Award.

A traditional historical novel with highly romantic overtones that chronicles the life of Hatshepsut, Egypt's only female Pharaoh. The book is painstakingly researched and so full of intrigue and incest, passion and pageantry, that it is easy to overlook the surface characterization and the lack of message and meaning in the narrative. Ille-Mai Gerdels

5634 C813.
**Gedge, Pauline.**
The Eagle and the Raven: A Novel. Toronto: Macmillan, 1978. ISBN 0-7705-1714-5 $12.95

Gedge's second published novel is a heroic saga of the Celtic struggle against the Roman invasion of Britain in the first century. The book is rich in atmosphere and action, but the hero Caradoc is unsympathetic, the dialogue is unnatural, and the novel is intellectually and thematically weak. Marred by some historical inaccuracies. Ille-Mai Gerdels

5635 C813.
**Gibbs, Robert.**
I've Always Felt Sorry for Decimals: Stories. Selected by John Metcalf; design by Michael Macklem. Ottawa: Oberon Press, c1978. 147p. ISBN 0-88750-268-7 bd.: $12.95 ISBN 0-88750-269-5 pa.: $5.95

Six lengthy stories chronicle the real and make-believe lives of two small brothers growing up in a New Brunswick town in the 1930's. Eight-year-old Hutchie's eye-popping accounts of fundamentalist sects, astonishing relatives, and enterprising schoolmates are discursive and overly crammed, but natural and warmly humorous. Ille-Mai Gerdels

5636 C813.
**Gibson, Margaret.**
Considering Her Condition. Toronto: Gage Publishing, c1978. 120p. ISBN 0-7715-9324-4 $8.95

Gibson's second collection, consisting of seven short stories, depicts women as victimized losers driven to the edge of madness by the brutal and insane world around them. More uneven in quality and generally less precise and powerful than *The Butterfly Ward*, the book still contains some of Gibson's finest writing. Ille-Mai Gerdels

5637 C813.
**Giguère, Diane.**
Wings in the Wind. Translated by Alan Brown. Toronto: McClelland and Stewart, 1979. 108p. ISBN 0-7710-3310-9 $10.95

Translation of *Dans les ailes du vent.*

A delightfully truculent and hopelessly single-minded professional dragon hunter sets out to save his beloved Quebec from the destructive grip of American technological greed. Effervescent satire and climactic imagery contribute to the fun and stylistic originality of this allegorical adult fairy tale. Ille-Mai Gerdels

5638 C813.
**Girard, Rodolphe.**
Marie Calumet. Translated by Irène Currie. Montreal: Harvest House, 1976. 167p. (The French Writers of Canada Series)
ISBN 0-88772-230-X bd.: $9.95
ISBN 0-88772-167-2 pa.: $2.50

Centred around a famous figure in French-Canadian folklore, this hilarious novel, at times bordering on the ribald, raised a few eyebrows when originally published in 1904. Presented in folktale style, it portrays life in 1860 in a fictitious Catholic parish in rural Quebec. This smooth translation will make delightful reading for all. Merike Koger

5639 C813.
**Godbout, Jacques.**
Dragon Island. Translated by David Ellis. Don Mills, Ont.: Musson, c1978. 118p. ISBN 0-7737-1027-2 pa.: $8.95

Translation of *L'isle au dragon.*

Godbout's long waited third novel is an intellectually demanding and emotionally dark poetic vision of two women whose lives are a synthesis of the despair of meaningless existence. The sensitive translation leaves the evocative and complex interweaving of religious allegory, allusion and imagery unimpaired. Ille-Mai Gerdels

5640 C813.
**Godfrey, Dave.**
Dark Must Yield. Erin, Ont.: Press Porcépic, c1978. 190p. ISBN 0-88878-100-8 bd.: $12 ISBN 0-88878-101-6 pa.: $6.95

Fifteen stories, of which nine have been previously published. Represented are the folkloric, the stridently nationalistic and polemical, and the stylistically experimental strains of Godfrey's writing. The richness of dialogue, metaphoric vividness, and impressionistic vitality fail to compensate entirely for the lack of discipline and focus, and the occasionally resultant confusion of purpose and meaning. Ille-Mai Gerdels

5641 C813.
**Godfrey, Ellen.**
Murder among the Well-to-do. Erin, Ont.: Press Porcépic, 1977. 187p.
ISBN 0-88878-155-5 $7.95

Though much in need of better editing this book provides an evening's light entertainment in which Rebecca Rosenthal, an old lady of spunk and decided opinions, tries to discover who is blackmailing her sister-in-law and runs into murder. Catharine MacKenzie

5642 C813.
**Gordon, Richard L.**
The Lady Who Loved New York. Toronto: Fitzhenry & Whiteside, c1977. 277p.
ISBN 0-88902-422-7 $10.95

In a series of flashbacks a former New York socialite recalls her life amidst the city's vanishing aristocracy. The author is a retired Canadian teacher whose superficial knowledge of New York has resulted in an unsatisfactory mood piece more accurately resembling a character novel. Structurally controlled and easily readable, but banal in characterization and content. Ille-Mai Gerdels

5643 C813.
**Gotlieb, Phyllis.**
O Master Caliban! Toronto: McClelland and Stewart-Bantam, 1979. 276p. (Seal Books)
ISBN 0-7704-1549-0 pa.: $1.95

Clothbound listed in *CS* no. 2938.

5644 C813.
**Gotlieb, Sondra.**
True Confections: Or, How My Family Arranged My Marriage. Don Mills, Ont.: Musson, c1978. 187p. ISBN 0-7737-0038-2 $12.95

Stephen Leacock Memorial Medal.

A fat Jewish girl grows up in the north end of Winnipeg in the fifties amid mountains of "true confections" which make her life bearable but aggravate her problem. The heroine is a comic character, not a pathetic one. The strange assortment of friends and family together with her own awareness of the humour of her situation make this an entertaining light novel. Catharine MacKenzie

5645 C813.
**Gould, Jan.**
The Boathouse Question. Sidney, B.C.: Gray's Publishing, 1978. 207p. port. ISBN 0-88826-073-3 pa.: $5.95

The world of these stories – the Gulf Islands of British Columbia – is an idyllic setting into which the politics, the economics of the real world scarcely intrudes, but it is not without its own violence. Not a collection for first purchase but still interesting and in the best stories exhibiting a fresh viewpoint. Catharine MacKenzie

5646 C813.
**Govier, Katherine.**
Random Descent: A Novel. Toronto: Macmillan, c1979. 228p. ISBN 0-7705-1719-6 $12.95

Jennifer Beecham's search for her forebears is the subject of a well-made novel which contains some memorable characters, many vivid scenes and effective use of historical detail. An impressive first novel. Catharine MacKenzie

5647 C813.
**Grignon, Claude-Henri.**
The Woman and the Miser. Translated by Yves Brunelle. Montreal: Harvest House, c1978. 99p. (The French Writers of Canada Series) ISBN 0-88772-180-X pa.: $4.95

Translation of *Un homme et son péché.*

Prix David.

Originally published in 1933, this moralistic tale about the life and death of a habitant money-lender is essentially a parable about the deadly sin of avarice. The characters, though exaggerated, are interesting, and the Laurentian setting is beautifully conveyed, but sophisticated readers may find the book predictable, simplistic or old-fashioned. Ille-Mai Gerdels

5648 C813.
**Guèvremont, Germaine.**
The Outlander. Translated by Eric Sutton. An introduction by Anthony Mollica. Toronto: McClelland and Stewart, 1978, c1950. 290p. (New Canadian Library) ISBN 0-7710-9266-0 pa.: $3.50

Translation of *Le survenant* and *Marie-Didace.* Clothbound listed in *CS* no. 2949.

5649 C813.
**Gurr, David.**
Troika: A Novel. Toronto: McClelland and Stewart, c1979. 271p. ISBN 0-7710-3660-4 $12.95

This is an authentic, gripping spy thriller that involves its two protagonists in a British-Russian tug-of-war over their potential defection. The writing is intelligent and highly talented, and the plot expertly structured and paced. A superior first novel by a former naval officer. Ille-Mai Gerdels

5650 C813.
**Hall, Chipman.**
Lightly. Toronto: McClelland and Stewart, c1977. 127p. ISBN 0-7710-3770-8 $8.95

The empathy between a lonely, fatherless boy and his grandfather, a retired sea captain, is handled with sensitivity in this story which won the 1976 Nova Scotia Novel-in-Manuscript competition. Told from the view point of the boy the isolated fishing village, which is his world, and the omnipresent sea which governs it, are very real. A whimsical, moving first novel.

5651 C813.
**Hambleton, Ronald.**
The Love & Death of Orpheus. Toronto: Green Bushell (J. M. Dent), 1979. 192p. ill. ISBN 0-9690786-2-5 $10

The myths relating to Orpheus, the legendary father of song, have been collected, organized and presented as narrative fiction. Although the author's style is uneven, it is an unusual approach, and the mythical characters come alive. Parallels with contemporary life are implicit. Includes eight black and white illustrations as well as a map. Peggy Sinclair

5652 C813.
**Hardy, W. G.**
The Scarlet Mantle: A Novel of Julius Caesar. Toronto: Macmillan, c1978. 462p. ISBN 0-7705-1567-3 $12.50

Followed by *The Bloodied Toga.*

A robust, sweeping novel of Roman politics, military campaigns and political intrigue peopled by a stellar cast of historical figures. A carefully researched work by a classics scholar.

5653 C813.
**Hartley, Norman.**
Quicksilver. Don Mills, Ont.: William Collins, 1979. 239p. ISBN 0-00-221-684-1 $11.95

A fast-paced, entertaining, escapist novel

with lots of violence and sex, set in this age of computers and slick operators. Catharine MacKenzie

5654 C813.
**Heaps, Leo.**
The Quebec Plot. Don Mills, Ont.: William Collins; Toronto: McClelland and Stewart-Bantam, 1979. 245p.
ISBN 0-432-06600-4 bd.: $11.95
ISBN 0-7704-1559-8 pa.: $2.25

Predictable and written to formula, this is nonetheless an exciting tale about the possiblity of Quebec suddenly declaring its independence by force. It can be enjoyed as a thriller but not on any deeper level.
Peggy Sinclair

5655 C813.
**Hébert, Anne.**
Children of the Black Sabbath. Translated by Carol Dunlop-Hébert. Markham, Ont.: PaperJacks, 1978, c1977. 198p.
ISBN 0-7701-0073-2 pa.: $2.25

Translation of *Les enfants du sabbat*.
Clothbound listed *CS* no. 2966.

5656 C813.
**Helwig, David.**
Jennifer. Ottawa: Oberon Press, 1979. 179p.
ISBN 0-88750-324-1 bd.: $15
ISBN 0-88750-326-8 pa.: $6.95

This is a pleasant piece of solid fiction about a divorced woman who copes cheerfully, intelligently with her life and creates an orderly existence. Catharine MacKenzie

5657 C813.
**Henley, Gail.**
Where the Cherries End Up. Toronto: McClelland and Stewart, c1978. 244p.
ISBN 0-7710-4065-2 $10.95

This first novel has some bad things about it and some good: it lacks development and direction, but it contains persuasive dialogue and convincing descriptions of small town wretchedness and some good characterization. It is the story of Genia growing up Polish in a backwoods Polish-Canadian town, going through university in Montreal and Toronto and returning home to her family. Catharine MacKenzie

5658 C813.
**Hodgins, Jack.**
The Invention of the World: A Novel. Toronto: Macmillan, 1977; Scarborough, Ont.: Macmillan-NAL Publishing, 1978, c1977. 354p. ISBN 0-7705-1518-5 bd.: $10.95
ISBN 0-7723-0005-4 pa.: $2.50

A colony of Irish men and women mesmerized by a weird messianic figure named Donal Brendan Keneally emigrate to Vancouver Island at the turn of the century. Long after Keneally's death a new colony is gathered in the same place by Maggie Kyle. The author sets up correspondences between the past and the present to explore at length the nature of myth and reality. An ambitious, exuberant novel, not to every reader's taste. Catharine MacKenzie

5659 C813.
**Hodgins, Jack.**
The Resurrection of Joseph Bourne: or, A Word or Two on Those Port Annie Miracles. Toronto: Macmillan, c1979. 271p.
ISBN 0-7705-1717-X $12.95

Governor General's Literary Award.

A fantastical novel, set in a small mill town on Vancouver Island with a cast of drifters and failures of various kinds not to mention castaways tossed ashore by a tidal wave, proves to be a curious and compelling work. Catharine MacKenzie

5660 C813.
**Hodgins, Jack.**
Split Delaney's Island: Selected Stories. Toronto: Macmillan, 1977, c1976. 199p. (Laurentian Library) ISBN 0-7705-1607-6 pa.: $3.95

Clothbound listed in *CS* no. 2979.

5661 C813.
**Hood, Hugh.**
A New Athens. Ottawa: Oberon Press, c1977. 226p. ISBN 0-88750-233-4 bd.: $17.50
ISBN 0-88750-234-2 pa.: $7.95

The narrative core of the second part of *The New Age* recounts the young manhood of Matt Goderich and his marriage to Edie Codrington; but the memorable substance of the novel is past life in the small towns of southeastern Ontario recollected not out of a wish to return but with a desire to understand. Catharine MacKenzie

5662 C813.
**Hood, Hugh.**
Reservoir Ravine. Ottawa: Oberon Press, c1979. 238p. ISBN 0-88750-297-0 bd.: $17.50 ISBN 0-88750-298-9 pa.: $7.95

City of Toronto Book Award.

Some very long digressions notwithstanding, the story is essentially about the meeting, courtship and marriage of Matt Goderich's parents. Although it is the third part of *The New Age*, the events described here take place in Toronto of the twenties before Matt was born. Catharine MacKenzie

5663 C813.
**Hood, Hugh.**
Selected Stories. Ottawa: Oberon Press, c1978. 232p. ISBN 0-88750-279-2 bd.: $17.50 ISBN 0-88750-280-6 pa.: $7.95

A fine selection of the best from four previous collections, published over a period of sixteen years, is notable for the variety of styles which the author has at his command. As always his work unobtrusively suggests the complexity of life's decisions and of human actions. Some libraries may already have these stories scattered through the earlier collections. If not, this book is well worth buying. Catharine MacKenzie

5664 C813.
**Horwood, Harold.**
Only the Gods Speak: Ten Tales From the Tropics, Seven Pieces From the North. St. John's, Nfld.: Breakwater Books, 1978? 130p. ISBN 0-919948-41-3 pa.: $4.95

This collection contains some very good work, particularly in setting the scene, but taken as a whole the didactic purpose gets in the way of the storytelling. The stories are a condemnation of materialism and the drug culture of the sixties. Catharine MacKenzie

5665 C813.
**Houston, James.**
Spirit Wrestler. Toronto: McClelland and Stewart, 1980. 306p. ISBN 0-7710-4250-7 $12.95

An ambiguously rendered, but intriguing narrative of the anguished life of an Inuit shaman. The ancient power bestowed upon him with imperfect understanding conflicts with the power of white culture, causing fear and destruction on both sides. Houston's knowledge of Inuit culture and language brings a tone of realism to this tale of magic. Patricia O'Sullivan

5666 C813.
**Hubert, Cam.**
Dreamspeaker and Tem Eyos Ki and the Land Claims Question. Toronto: Clarke, Irwin, c1978. 137p. ISBN 0-7720-1220-2 $10.95

1. Indians of North America – Canada – Fiction.

The first of these remarkable stories tells of an elderly Indian, the dreamspeaker, and a disturbed eleven-year-old foster child. Their love and understanding is set against the obtuseness of authority. The second is a monologue by Tem Eyos Ki, a young Nootka woman, who brilliantly recreates a farcical event in the life of the reserve. Catharine MacKenzie

5667 C813.
**Hyde, Christopher.**
The Wave: A Novel. Toronto: McClelland and Stewart, c1979. 226p. ISBN 0-7710-4274-4 $12.95

The world's largest dam, built on the Columbia River, is blown up during an unusually heavy rainfall. The resultant wave wipes out all the other dams on the system and threatens to pollute the Pacific Ocean with radioactive waste from a nuclear plant located in its path. This well researched and possible story keeps the reader turning pages until the end. Pat George

5668 C813.
**Kaplan, Bess.**
Malke, Malke. Winnipeg: Queenston House, 1976. 232p. ISBN 0-919866-19-0 $11.95

The delightful tale of a sixty-five-year old Jewish widow who advertises in the personals column of the Winnipeg newspaper for a fourth husband. Includes a glossary of Yiddish words which are liberally sprinkled throughout the text. Peggy Sinclair

5669 C813.
**Kattan, Naîm.**
Paris Interlude. Translated from the French by Sheila Fischman. Toronto: McClelland and Stewart, 1979. 208p. ISBN 0-7710-4471-2 $12.95

Translation of *Les fruits arrachés.*

An Iraqi Jew studying in Paris in the late 1940's juggles three simultaneous love affairs, as he debates his future and his identity. The sense of time and place are not sharply drawn, and there is a certain superficiality in the protagonist's relationships, but his quest is universal and its description will appeal to most readers. Peggy Sinclair

5670 C813.
**Keenleyside, David.**
Where the Mountain Falls. Toronto: Nelson, Foster and Scott, c1977. 192p. ISBN 0-919324-29-0 $8.95

The theme of this novel is the primitive past of the North struggling with the technological future. The setting is a remote Eskimo village named "where the mountain falls". The action moves quickly and the descriptions of an unfamiliar life style and environment are compelling, but the plot is melodramatic and the people unconvincing. An interesting book for an undemanding reader. Catharine MacKenzie

5671 C813.
**Keenleyside, T. A.**
The Common Touch. Toronto: Doubleday, 1977. 230p. ISBN 0-385-12275-6 $8.95

Misplaced Canadian aid to a fictional Southeast Asian country is the subject of this novel. Although the author has obvious knowledge of what it is like to work in the foreign service, and though the political situation set forth is credible, the action is unfocused and the characters lack the breath of life. Catharine MacKenzie

5672 C813.
**Kilian, Crawford.**
Icequake: A Novel. Vancouver: Douglas & McIntyre, 1979. 229p. ill. ISBN 0-88894-231-1 $11.95

A group of scientists at the Commonwealth Scientific Research Station at New Shackleton in Antarctica is studying movements in the ice cap when a massive earthquake sets off a chain reaction for catastrophe. The strength of the thriller lies in its compelling descriptions and accurate-sounding technical details. Catharine MacKenzie

5673 C813.
**Kinsella, W. P.**
Dance Me Outside. Ottawa: Oberon Press, c1977. 158p. ISBN 0-88750-223-7 bd.: $11.95 ISBN 0-88750-224-5 pa.: $4.95

The sixteen stories in the collection are all narrated by Silas Ermineskin, an eighteen-year-old Cree. They are funny, sometimes verging on slapstick and occasionally becoming violent. The tables are turned and it is the white man and his civilization that are shown to be absurd. Catharine MacKenzie

5674 C813.
**Kinsella, W. P.**
Scars: Stories. Ottawa: Oberon Press, c1978. 154p. ISBN 0-88750-285-7 bd.: $12.95 ISBN 0-88750-286-5 pa.: $5.95

These sixteen stories describe how the interesting but unpretentious men and women of the Hobbema reserve cope with life. The reader who is not Indian may find himself shaken by the stereotype which in this instance may well be himself and his kind. Catharine MacKenzie

5675 C813.
**Knickerbocker, Earl L.**
The Merger. Markham, Ont.: PaperJacks, 1978. 166p. ISBN 0-7701-0065-1 pa.: $2.25

A young woman avenges the death of her father and the crippling of her brother by a triumvirate in control of a powerful multi-national corporation. A bit hard to follow in parts where the author fails to lay the groundwork for the ensuing events, but an intriguing read for those who like an international mystery. Pat George

5676 C813.
**Knox, Alexander.**
The Kidnapped Surgeon. Toronto: Macmillan, 1977. 214p. maps. ISBN 0-333-21304-1 $9.95

A modest novel of life at a Hudson's Bay Company factory in the eighteenth century tells a dramatic story uncomplicated by profound message or psychological complexity, and in language not very far above that of light romances or pulp thrillers. Catharine MacKenzie

5677 C813.
**Koch, Eric.**
Good Night Little Spy. Toronto: Virgo Press, c1979. 181p. map. ISBN 0-920528-03-1 $9.95

A lightweight spy spoof, in which a well-meaning public relations man from Toronto gets mixed up in the events following the overthrow of an African dictatorship, provides a possible choice for a library requiring additional material which combines suspense and comedy. Catharine MacKenzie

5678 C813.
**Koch, Eric.**
The Last Thing You'd Want to Know. Toronto: Tundra Books, 1976. 190p. ISBN 0-88776-066-X $8.95

A satire on twentieth-century life and values

in America has a witch for the 40th president of the United States and a former Nazi for hero. The conflict between these two represents a struggle between primitive emotionalism on the one hand and rational humanism on the other. Humorous in a sardonic vein. Catharine MacKenzie

5679 C813.
**Kroetsch, Robert.**
What the Crow Said. Don Mills, Ont.: General Publishing, 1978. 218p. ISBN 0-7736-0067-1 $12.95

Big Knife is the sort of place where hard-drinking men play a game of cards which lasts for 151 days. Everything is on the heroic scale: the events are magical; the humour is thigh-slapping. The author's style is so matter of fact that one is half inclined to believe him. Catharine MacKenzie

5680 C813.
**Kroetsch, Robert.**
The Words of My Roaring. Markham, Ont.: PaperJacks, 1977. ISBN 0-7701-003-0-9 pa.: $1.95

Clothbound edition listed *CS* no. 3018 as out-of-print.

5681 C813.
**Kruper, Jack.**
Child of the Holocaust. Markham, Ont.: PaperJacks, 1978. ISBN 0-7701-0082-1 pa.: $2.50

Jacob Kuperblum, the child of the title, was nine years old at the beginning of World War II. From a child's point of view he recounts the adventures of the four years during which he eluded the Nazis in occupied Poland. One sees what it cost him to do it. Catharine MacKenzie

5682 C813.
**Kurisko, Joan.**
Interlude: The Story of Elliot Lake. Cobalt, Ont.: Highway Book Shop, c1977. 242p. ISBN 0-88954-128-0 $12

A combination love story and social history set during the boom and bust period of this Ontario uranium mining town. The descriptions are sometimes overblown, but the characters are sympathetically drawn and the story fills a void concerning this time and place. Peggy Sinclair

5683 C813.
**Laberge, Albert.**
Bitter Bread. Translated by Conrad Dion. Montreal: Harvest House, c1977. 128p. port. (The French Writers of Canada Series) ISBN 0-88772-205-9 bd.: $9.95
ISBN 0-88772-166-4 pa.: $3.95

Translation of *La Scouine.*

The author's only novel is a masterpiece of French Canadian fiction in the naturalist tradition, and a very disturbing book. The plot follows two generations of the Deschamps family and portrays Quebec peasant life as bleak and brutal, although the author views his people with compassion. An important work which some readers may find repellent. Catharine MacKenzie

5684 C813.
**Laidlaw, Robert.**
The McGregors: A Novel of an Ontario Pioneer Family. Toronto: Macmillan, c1979. 166p. ISBN 0-7705-1711-0 $12.95

A posthumous novel by the father of Alice Munro describes the years which transformed Huron County from raw pioneer country into a prosperous land of comfortable farms and towns. An unpretentious book which gives Ontarians an idea of how their "home and native land" was won from the wilderness. Catharine MacKenzie

5685 C813.
**LaMarsh, Judy.**
A Very Political Lady: A Novel. Toronto: McClelland and Stewart, c1979. ISBN 0-7710-4622-7 $12.95

This roman à clef requires very little expertise to unlock its secrets. It is about life among the people at the top in Ottawa by someone who was there. The author writes best when she is describing the everyday details of political life in the House of Commons. Catharine MacKenzie

5686 C813.
**Lampert, Gerald.**
Chestnut/Flower/Eye of Venus. Edited by B. P. Nichol. Toronto: Coach House Press, 1978. 162p. ISBN 0-88910-079-9 pa.: $4.50

Lampert's last novel examines the separate inner worlds of a husband and wife confronting the emotional crises of a disintegrating marriage. Stereotyped in its presentation of the middle-class lifestyle, but incisive and witty and indicative of the author's linguistic virtuosity. Ille-Mai Gerdels

5687 C813.
**Levi, Helen.**
Honour Your Partner. Winnipeg: Queenston House, 1979. 150p.
ISBN 0-919866-43-3 bd.: $12.95
ISBN 0-919866-44-1 pa.: $4.95

The tranquility of life in the small prairie town of Plum Bluff is disrupted when the wife of a retired bishop chooses the community as a suitable home for her retirement years. The choice of incident, the interplay of personalities, and dialogue are deftly handled. Readers who enjoyed the light touch and subtle humour of the first two parts of the trilogy, *A Small Informal Dance* and *Tangle Your Web and Dosey-do,* will not be disappointed in the third part. School and public libraries.

5688 C813.
**Levi, Helen.**
A Small Informal Dance: A Novel. Winnipeg: Queenston House, 1977. 165p.
ISBN 0-919866-21-2 $10.95

The small events in the daily lives of nice people and their only slightly less admirable neighbours are told with affection, humour and touches of irony that keep the interest in an inconsequential plot alive. Many of the characters are middle-aged and live in a quiet Manitoba town. Catharine MacKenzie

5689 C813.
**Levi, Helen.**
Tangle Your Web and Dosey-do. Winnipeg: Queenston House, c1978. 148p.
ISBN 0-919866-36-0 bd.: $10.95
ISBN 0-919866-37-9 pa.: $4.95

An unimportant but very enjoyable book about the inhabitants of Plum Bluff, some of whom have already appeared in *A Small Informal Dance.* They are ordinary people, basically kindhearted, going about their small adventures and petty concerns, observed by a writer with a good ear and a sharp eye for humorous detail. Catharine MacKenzie

5690 C813.
**Levine, Norman.**
Thin Ice. Ottawa: Deneau and Greenberg, c1979. 160p. ISBN 0-88879-016-3 $10.95

These beautifully observed people and places – in England and Canada – are recorded in a lean prose which projects an unrelenting sensitivity to light and shade in human relations. Catharine MacKenzie

5691 C813.
**Lotz, Jim.**
Death in Dawson. Markham, Ont.: PaperJacks, 1978. 183p. ISBN 0-7701-0075-9 pa.: $1.95

What distinguishes this mildly interesting crime story are the setting and the author's exposition of the fascinating history of the Yukon. Catharine MacKenzie

5692 C813.
**MacNeill, James A.**
Under the Sweetgrass Sky. Saskatoon: Western Extension College, c1978. 121p. ill., map. Bibliography: p. 121.
ISBN 0-920284-04-3 pa.: $4.75

Many of these fifteen stories deal with real people and actual events on the prairies in the last quarter of the nineteenth century. An outbreak of smallpox, the Riel Rebellion, the arrival of Sitting Bull in Canada after the Custer massacre are some of the events on which the plots are based. Catharine MacKenzie

5693 C813.
**Maillard, Keith.**
Two Strand River. Erin, Ont.: Press Porcépic, 1976. 267p. ISBN 0-88878-088-5 $8.95

An unusual, intriguing story of a man and a woman confused about their sexual identities. This theme of androgyny, set against the background of urban Vancouver and the forest of British Columbia takes on mythic proportions. Well written and satisfying. Jean Dodd

5694 C813.
**Maillet, Antonine.**
La Sagouine. Translated by Luis de Céspedes. Toronto: Simon & Pierre Publishing, c1979. 183p. ill.
ISBN 0-88924-100-7 pa.: $6.95

Prix littéraire de la Presse.

This translation from the Acadian French of prize-winning author Antonine Maillet brings La Sagouine, the Acadian scrubwoman, to English-speaking readers. Her monologues, which reveal an incredibly deprived way of life and the stubborn endurance, humour and native wit with which it is faced, have made La Sagouine something of a folk heroine. Annette Wengle

5695 C813.
**Maillet, Antonine.**
The Tale of Don l'Orignal. Translated by Barbara Godard. Toronto: Clarke, Irwin, c1978. 107p. ISBN 0-7720-1216-4 $9.95

Translation of *Don l'Orignal.*

Governor General's Literary Award.

An amusing, improbable fantasy about a mysterious island which appears to threaten an Acadian fishing village. Zany characters, tongue-in-cheek irony and gentle satire mark this novel by a major French-Canadian author. It was a runner-up for the Prix Goncourt in 1977.

5696 C813.
**Major, André.**
The Scarecrows of Saint-Emmanuel. Translated by Sheila Fischman. Toronto: McClelland and Stewart, c1977. 176p. ISBN 0-7710-5471-8 $10

Translation of *L'épouvantail.*

Governor General's Literary Award.

A small-town ex-con, recently arrived in Montreal from prison, wakes up one morning to find his knife in his girlfriend's back. Stark realism is successfully combined with the murder-mystery genre, resulting in a harsh but compassionate portrayal of the underbelly of Quebec society. Patricia O'Sullivan

5697 C813.
**Major, Kevin.**
Hold Fast. Toronto: Clarke, Irwin, c1978. 170p. ill. ISBN 0-7720-1175-3 $7.95

Canada Council Award for Children's Literature. CACL Bronze Medal. The Ruth Schwartz Children's Book Award.

Suddenly orphaned, fourteen-year-old Michael is forced to leave his home in the Newfoundland outport and face life in new, often unfriendly surroundings. Written in a gentle dialect, but using some strong language nonetheless, this fast-paced story will appeal to young people and even adults. Peggy Sinclair

5698 C813.
**Marshall, Tom.**
Rosemary Goal. Ottawa: Oberon Press, c1978. 149p. ISBN 0-88750-255-5 bd.: $15 ISBN 0-88750-256-3 pa.: $6.95

A novelist is unable to separate himself from his created characters and flounders in his real relationships. Contemporary themes and ideas are cleverly played within a terse, wry style. Jean Dodd

5699 C813.
**Marty, Sid.**
Men for the Mountains. Toronto: McClelland and Stewart, c1978. 270p. ISBN 0-7710-5852-7 $12.95

Canadian Authors' Association Literary Award.

The author draws on personal experience to record the intriguing history of park wardens in the Canadian Rockies, and to make a moving ecological statement that mourns our violation of nature's beauty and integrity. Philosophical in tone and poetic in style, rich in humour, earthiness and human drama. Attractive to a varied readership. Ille-Mai Gerdels

5700 C813.
**McRae, Garfield.**
A Room on the River. Winnipeg: Queenston House, c1977. 135p. ISBN 0-919866-20-4 $8.95

All eleven of the stories are loosely connected by means of the narrator, Willie-John MacNie, and Oraloo, the Manitoba setting. When his family moves to Oraloo in the mid-forties Willie-John is eight, and eighteen when he leaves for the city. These years shape the man and lead him to a hard decision. Catharine MacKenzie

5701 C813.
**Metcalf, John.**
Girl in Gingham. Ottawa: Oberon Press, c1978. 154p. ISBN 0-88750-266-2 bd.: $12.95 ISBN 0-88750-267-0 pa.: $5.95

Comprises two novellas, unrelated, but developing similar themes about discrepancies between art and life, dream and reality. *Private Parts* is a succession of explicit autobiographical fragments about boyhood's feverish obsession with sex. In the title story a divorced man searches for love through a computer dating service. Skilled, entertaining writing, full of humour and pathos. Ille-Mai Gerdels

5702 C813.
**Mills, John.**
Skevington's Daughter. Ottawa: Oberon Press, c1978. 195p. ISBN 0-88750-253-9 bd.: $15 ISBN 0-88750-254-7 pa.: $6.95

An unremitting satire of modern manners written by a professor of English in the style of the eighteenth century epistolary novel. The intricate plot revolves around academic infighting over a donation of letters detailing the sexual exploits of a fictitious explorer and his daughter. Enjoyable reading in spite of the dark humour and typecast characters. Ille-Mai Gerdels

5703 C813.

**Mitchell, Ken.**

The Con Man: A Novel. Vancouver: Talonbooks, 1979. ISBN 0-88922-168-5 pa.: $7.95

The misadventures of an artless, good-looking half-breed Indian as he bumbles his way in and out of petty crime on the Saskatchewan prairies in the 1960's. Realistic settings, wry humour, and a fast-paced narrative engage the reader. Recommended.

5704 C813.

**Mitchell, Ken.**

Everybody Gets Something Here: Stories. Toronto: Macmillan, 1977. 122p. ISBN 0-7705-1495-2 bd.: $11.95 ISBN 0-7705-1541-X pa.: $4.95

Of the fourteen entertaining short stories in Mitchell's first major collection, ten have been previously published. Most are raunchy tales set in rural Saskatchewan, with likeable rogues, punks and hustlers for heroes. Of wide appeal because of its fast, slangy style, and constant, often wild, occasionally black humour. Ille-Mai Gerdels

5705 C813.

**Montgomery, L. M.**

The Doctor's Sweetheart and Other Stories. Selected and with an introduction by Catherine McLay. Toronto: McGraw-Hill Ryerson, c1979. 190p. Bibliographies. ISBN 0-07-082790-7 $7.95

Contains fourteen previously uncollected short stories, published between 1899 and 1935 in popular journals of the time. The stories follow the standard pattern of formula romance and are insignificant from a literary standpoint. Sentimental and uncomplicated reading, except for McLay's lengthy, scholarly introduction. Ille-Mai Gerdels

5706 C813.

**Moore, Brian.**

The Doctor's Wife. Toronto: McClelland and Stewart-Bantam, 1977, c1976. 217p. (Seal Books) ISBN 0-7704-1506-7 pa.: $2.25

Clothbound listed in *CS* no. 3084.

5707 C813.

**Moore, Brian.**

The Mangan Inheritance. Toronto: McClelland and Stewart, c1979. 335p. ISBN 0-7710-6423-3 $12.95

A search for roots, and the transmission of poetic ability as well as destiny through genes, are two themes developed in this brooding account of one man's quest for his identity. Written by a two-time winner of the Governor-General's Award for fiction. Peggy Sinclair

5708 C813.

**Moore, Phyllis S.**

Williwaw! St. John's, Nfld.: Breakwater Books, 1978. 457p. ISBN 0-919948-54-5 bd.: $10.95 ISBN 0-919948-55-3 pa.: $5.95

An illegal separatist army from Quebec invades newly independent Labrador and triggers the formation of a local resistance force. The novel expounds an intriguing blend of political ideas and fully exploits the entertainment potential of action, heroism, sex and violence. Stylistically flawed, but gripping and convincing. Ille-Mai Gerdels

5709 C813.

**Mosher, Howard Frank.**

Disappearances. Markham, Ont.: Penguin Books, 1977. 255p. ISBN 0-670-27358-9 $9.50

Attempts to parody the heroic male quest story in the guise of father-son adventures in the Quebec-Vermont border country of 1932. Contains mythological and semi-mystical elements and some pleasing and tangible descriptive writing, but the narrative remains implausible, and the American author has not emphasized its Canadian aspects. Ille-Mai Gerdels

5710 C813.

**Mowat, Farley.**

The Snow Walker. Toronto: McClelland and Stewart-Bantam, 1977, c1975. 209p. (Seal Books) ISBN 0-7704-1507-5 pa.: $1.95

Clothbound listed in *CS* no. 3091.

5711 C813.

**Munro, Alice.**

Who Do You Think You Are?: Stories. Toronto: Macmillan; Scarborough, Ont.: Macmillan-NAL Publishing, 1979, 1978. 206p. ISBN 0-7705-1712-9 bd.: $9.95 pa.: $2.25

Governor General's Literary Award.

Published by Knopf under the title *Beggarmaid*.

Ten stories follow the heroine's life from her

childhood in a small Ontario town through her married life in Vancouver and its breakup, her career as television broadcaster and actress to her eventual return to her home town. Brilliant selection of detail and startlingly recognizable speech give these stories more depth than their ordinary events would lead one to expect. Catharine MacKenzie

5712 C813.
**Myers, Martin.**
Izzy Manheim's Reunion. Don Mills, Ont.: General Publishing, c1978. 327p.
ISBN 0-7736-0059-0 bd.: $10
ISBN 0-7736-1033-2 pa.: $4.95

The author's third novel recounts a glue magnate's comic efforts to stage a class reunion with a cast of bizarre college classmates. Parodies the media's interpretation of life through slick quips, incredible puns and one-line jokes. A clever, polished adult novel by a talented satirist. Ille-Mai Gerdels.

5713 C813.
**Nichol, B. P.**
Journal. Toronto: Coach House Press, c1978. 80p. ISBN 0-88910-120-5 pa.: $4.25

Interior struggles and the problems associated with writing are explored in this novel using the stream of consciousness technique combined with lyrical repetition. It is the first novel in ten years by the 1970 winner of the Governor General's Literary Award. Explicit sexual sections and a theme of incest may offend some readers. Merike Koger

5714 C813.
**Nichols, Ruth.**
The Left-handed Spirit. Toronto: Macmillan, c1978. 220p. ISBN 0-7705-1701-3 $7.95

The story of Mariana the artisan, who has the gift of healing, and the Chinese ambassador, who abducts her from her father's home in tenth century Rome, and of their journey along the Silk Road to China. Catharine MacKenzie

5715 C813.
**Nicol, Clive.**
The White Shaman. Toronto: McClelland and Stewart, 1979. 248p. ISBN 0-7710-6767-4 $12.95

A young man on an Arctic expedition experiences a change of awareness in his relationship with the Inuit. The characters are stiff and their dialogue awkward and adolescent, but the author's feeling for the land, life and spirit of the Inuit is conveyed with intensity and conviction. The first adult novel by an accomplished writer of children's books. Ille-Mai Gerdels

5716 813.
**Oates, Joyce Carol.**
Son of the Morning: A Novel. Agincourt, Ont.: Gage Publishing, c1978. 382p.
ISBN 0-8149-0793-8 $13.50

Explores the spiritual and material life of a proselytizing evangelist in Born-Again America. This is an excellent topical novel, real and living in its detailing of events and setting, psychologically convincing in its characterizations, and lyrically compelling in its visionary passages. By a respected American author with an academic career in Canada. Ille-Mai Gerdels

5717 C813.
**O'Connell, Dorothy.**
Chicolet Gomez. Ottawa: Deneau and Greenberg, 1978. 150p. ISBN 0-88879-001-5 $4.95

Contains twenty-seven simple short stories meant to provide a humorous social commentary on life in public housing. Although some have been well received on the CBC's Morningside show, these tales are essentially hackneyed, devoid of wit, often silly and rarely amusing. Not for sophisticated readers. Ille-Mai Gerdels

5718 C813.
**Ogle, Bob.**
When the Snake Bites the Sun. Saskatoon: Texchuck Enterprises, c1977. 205p. ill.
ISBN 0-920478-00-X pa.: $4.95

Sixteen short stories by a Roman Catholic priest mirror his personal experiences in the field of international co-operation and development. The theme, involving the practical and humanitarian aspects of the role of Canadian money in human development, is unusual, and the writing, though not exceptional, is competent and pleasing. Ille-Mai Gerdels

5719 C813.
**O'Hagan, Howard.**
The School-marm Tree: A Novel. Vancouver: Talonbooks, 1977. 245p.
ISBN 0-88922-129-4 pa.: $4.95

O'Hagan's second novel is the expanded version of an earlier unpublished short story. It centers on the loves and destiny of a girl who dreams of escaping from life in a dismal Alberta railroad town. Typical of O'Hagan's writing in its narrative and poetic strength and its mythical implications of the mountain "presence". Ille-Mai Gerdels

5720 C813.

**O'Hagan, Howard.**

Wilderness Men: Stories. Vancouver: Talonbooks, 1978. 189p. ISBN 0-88922-141-3 pa.: $5.95

First published Garden City, N.Y., Doubleday, 1958.

This first Canadian edition contains nine of the original ten stories about lone men struggling against the wilderness. The biographical and historical element is strong, but O'Hagan's narrative and descriptive intensity and gift for characterization have endowed the stories with legendary and mythical qualities. Well-told, riveting tales. Ille-Mai Gerdels

5721 C813.

**O'Hagan, Howard.**

The Woman Who Got on at Jasper Station & Other Stories: Short Stories. Vancouver: Talonbooks, 1977. 132p. ISBN 0-88922-130-8 pa.: $4.95

First published in 1963.

The eleven short stories in this volume are all set in the savage mountain territory of Alberta or British Columbia. All but the title story depict male characters at war with themselves, each other, or the wilderness. Economical and exact writing, appealing to both adults and adolescents. Ille-Mai Gerdels

5722 C813.

**Paci, F. G.**

The Italians: A Novel. Ottawa: Oberon Press, c1976. 205p. ISBN 0-88750-264-6 bd.: $15 ISBN 0-88750-265-4 pa.: $6.95

An immigrant Italian family settles in a small Ontario town and suffers through the conflicts of merging with a new culture. The inevitable clash between the generations pervades the story. Told with sympathy and insight by an author who is, himself, of similar background, the story is highly readable despite some minor flaws in style and structure. Pat George

5723 C813.

**Pape, Gordon.**

Chain Reaction: A Novel, by Gordon Pape and Tony Aspler. Toronto: McClelland and Stewart-Bantam, 1979, c1978. 246p. (Seal Books) ISBN 0-7704-1553-9 pa.: $2.25

An imaginative novel set in the near future when the Parti québecois demands immediate separation. The political intrigue involves international business, the United States, United Kingdom and France. An exciting adventure mixed with frightening possibilities. Jean Dodd

5724 C813.

**Percy, Herbert R.**

Flotsam. St. John's, Nfld.: Breakwater Books, 1978. 223p. ISBN 0-919948-57-X bd.: $10.95 ISBN 0-919948-56-1 pa.: $5.95

A tale of seamen and the sea told by an experienced writer of short stories who served in the Canadian navy until 1971. A series of flashbacks explains the circumstances which brought chaos to the personal and working life of a commander in the Royal Canadian Navy. The controversy over the integration of Canada's three armed forces plays a major role in the commander's resignation, as it did in the author's own. A "good read" which promises well for the author's future writing.

5725 C813.

**Person, Lloyd H.**

No Foot in Heaven. Saskatoon: Western Producer Prairie Books, c1978. 222p. ISBN 0-919306-98-5 $9.25

Unsentimental stories of ordinary life in a small Canadian town during the 1930's. Their charm lies in their very simplicity and their true insight into everyday people. Jean Dodd

5726 C813.

**Plaut, W. Gunther.**

Hanging Threads. Toronto: Lester and Orpen, c1978. 155p. ISBN 0-919630-99-5 $8.95

Well told stories concerning personal relationships and the irony in many situations. The interesting international flavour and crisp style makes for good, easy reading. Jean Dodd

5727 C813.

**Reeves, John.**

Murder by Microphone. Toronto: Doubleday, 1978. 214p. ISBN 0-385-14217-X $8.95

A light-hearted whodunnit set amid the bureaucracy of the CBC and dotted with jokes about Canadian places, institutions and character. Good light reading. Jean Dodd

5728 C813.
**Rippon, Marion.**
Lucien's Tombs. Toronto: Doubleday, 1979. 232p. ISBN 0-385-14429-6 bd.: $9.95

After four years in France, a Victoria author sets a series of mystery novels in France. In this one, a retired gendarme, Maurice Ygrec, returns from retirement in a small rural village to the Paris area for a visit, but finds himself involved in a murder mystery. A tale well told, for all mystery fans.

5729 C813.
**Robinson, Spider.**
Stardance, by Spider Robinson and Jeanne Robinson. New York: The Dial Press/James Wade (Doubleday), c1977. 278p. (Quantum Science Fiction) ISBN 0-8037-8232-2 $11.95

Winner of the John W. Campbell Memorial Award as the best new writer of science fiction in 1973, Robinson, who lives in Halifax, received the Hugo and Nebula awards for the novella which is the first part of this book. A good example of the genre.

5730 C813.
**Rohmer, Richard H.**
Separation. Toronto: McClelland and Stewart; McClelland and Stewart-Bantam, 1977, c1976. 240p. ISBN 0-7710-7704-1 bd.: $9.95 pa.: $1.95

Canadian unity is threatened by an agreement to accept mass immigration from Britain during an economic crisis there. Except for Rashida, a Palestinian Liberation Fighter, the characters are poorly sketched. But if the reader can wade through the highly technical details of government operations and the involved dialogue, the book aptly fulfills the author's intent – to inform and provoke. Pat George

5731 C813.
**Rooke, Leon.**
The Love Parlour: Stories. Ottawa: Oberon Press, c1977. 157p. ISBN 0-88750-231-8 bd.: $9.95 ISBN 0-88750-232-6 pa.: $4.95

Short stories, some of which have appeared elsewhere, dealing with love, age, death and general anomie. They vary from a claustrophobia of the mind to cool, rather distanced examination. For large collections. Jean Dodd

5732 C813.
**Rosenstock, Janet.**
Riel. Toronto: NC Press, 1979. 202p. ISBN 0-919601-42-1 $9.95

1. Riel, Louis David, 1844-1885 – Fiction.

A novel based on the original screenplay by Roy Moore with illustrations from the production. A good example of the genre. Jean Dodd

5733 C813.
**Roy, Gabrielle.**
Children of My Heart. Translated by Alan Brown. Toronto: McClelland and Stewart, c1979. 171p. ISBN 0-7710-7838-2 $12.95

Translation of *Ces enfants de ma vie.*

Governor General's Literary Award.

An exquisite work about a teacher's love for her pupils, and hence for all humanity. The milieu of the Depression years in Manitoba is perfectly drawn. The wonder – of a snow flake, a bird's song – is reflected in the eyes of the children. A lovely celebration of living and loving, in a style as gentle as thistledown. Jean Dodd

5734 C813.
**Roy, Gabrielle.**
Garden in the Wind. Translated by Alan Brown. Toronto: McClelland and Stewart, c1977. 175p. ISBN 0-7710-7834-X $10

Translation of *Un jardin au bout du monde.*

Like so much of the author's work these stories, so simple in their events and so profound in their understanding of the human condition, make much other writing seem unnecessarily pretentious. Catharine McKenzie

5735 C813.
**Rule, Jane.**
Desert of the Heart: A Novel. Vancouver: Talonbooks, 1977. 251p. ISBN 0-88922-131-6 pa.: $2.95

A college teacher flies to Reno for a divorce where, during her stay, she falls in love with a younger woman. The marriage relationship is explored and the rapport that often occurs between women. While the writer handles the female character with expertise, the men are faceless and the plot a little contrived toward the end of the novel. A worthwhile read. Pat George

5736 C813.
**Rule, Jane.**
The Young in One Another's Arms. Toronto: Doubleday; Don Mills, Ont.: Totem Books, 1978, c1977. 204p. ISBN 0-385-11660-8 bd.: $6.95 ISBN 0-00-222018-0 pa.: $2.25

Canadian Authors Association Literary Award.

A group of disparate characters live together in a boarding house in Vancouver, each one caught in a struggle for survival. The interplay between them and society is interestingly and capably told in a cool, objective manner well suited to the theme of adapt or perish. Jean Dodd

5737 C813.
**Sallot, Lynne.**
Bearwalk, by Lynne Sallot and Tom Peltier. Don Mills, Ont.: Musson, 1977. 213p. ISBN 0-7737-0034-X bd.: $10.95 ISBN 0-7737-1017-5 pa.: $6.95

A melodramatic account of an Indian who has forsaken his roots but is forced to learn about his heritage in order to break an ancient family curse. Not particularly well written, but an interesting introduction to shamanism. Peggy Sinclair

5738 C813.
**Saul, John Ralston.**
The Birds of Prey. Toronto: Macmillan; Don Mills, Ont.: Totem, 1979, c1977. 247p. ISBN 0-7705-1609-2 bd.: $9.95 ISBN 0-00-222023-7 pa.: $2.50

Competent story of political intrigue based on the actual event, an aeroplane crash on an island in the Indian ocean. Good insight into the different factions of France and the realities of being "on the winning side and lose". Jean Dodd

5739 C813.
**Scott, Chris.**
To Catch a Spy. Markham, Ont.: Penguin, 1978. 291p. ISBN 0-670-71663-4 bd.: $12.95 pa.: $2.50

Too literary to be mistaken for a routine spy thriller, though not of the first rank, this work exhibits wit and originality enough to merit a wide readership. Without reconstructing the Burgess-Maclean and the Kim Philby defections the novel nevertheless develops its action from those affairs. Catharine MacKenzie

5740 C813.
**Sears, Dennis T. Patrick.**
Aunty High Over the Barley Mow. Toronto: McClelland and Stewart, c1977. 303p. ISBN 0-7710-8026-3 $12.50

Amid a rough, harsh, hardworking group of farmers in Ontario in the 1930's, a brother and sister find solace in their love for each other. Carefully written with good characterization and description. The mixture of joy and sorrow in their relationship creates a story of unusual tenderness. Jean Dodd

5741 C813.
**Sears, Dennis T. Patrick.**
The Lark in the Clear Air. Toronto: McClelland and Stewart-Bantam, 1978, c1974. 177p. ISBN 0-7704-1508-3 pa.: $1.95

Clothbound listed in *CS* no. 3163.

5742 C813.
**Seitz, Mary Ann.**
Shelterbelt. Saskatoon: Western Producer Prairie Books, 1979. 218p. ISBN 0-88833-023-5 $12.95

Winner of Saskatchewan Novel Competition.

A perceptive first novel of a Ukrainian girl's growing up on a large Saskatchewan farm. Frynca's world was circumscribed not only by the poverty of the thirties and the impact of the Second World War, but by the tensions of family life dominated by an authoritarian father. From the minutiae of rural life the author has fashioned a convincing aura of reality. School and public libraries.

5743 C813.
**Shaffer, Ivan.**
The Sixth Day Is the Day of Death. Toronto: McClelland and Stewart, 1978. 302p. ISBN 0-7710-8130-8 $12.95

A young American idealist is involved with a band of Mexican guerrillas out to assassinate their president. Violence, bloodshed, kidnapping, and a host of characters, sometimes difficult to keep in order, hold the reader's interest. At the somewhat hurried ending an attempt is made to pull all the threads together; the success is only modest. Pat George

5744 C813.
**Shields, Carol.**
The Box Garden: A Novel. Toronto: McGraw-Hill Ryerson; Don Mills, Ont.: Totem Books, 1979, c1977. 213p. ISBN 0-07-082547-5 $9.95

A thirty-eight-year-old woman, who prides herself on lacking "the most debilitating of diseases, subjectivity", examines with wry humour her life as both mother and daughter. Her discovery that "rhythms of life are random and irreducible" is revealed in a quiet, straightforward style. Jean Dodd

5745 C813.
**Simonds, Peter.**
David and Max: Based on a Bizarre and Tragic Incident of the Second World War. Don Mills, Ont.: J. M. Dent, c1977. 265p. ill., maps, plates. ISBN 0-87695-174-4 $10.75

1. World War, 1939-1945 – Fiction.

A former communications officer with the First Canadian Army tells the controversial and tragic story of Canada's complicity in the court-martial and execution of two German corporals. The factual style does not charm, but the story, based on a real World War II occurrence, presents intriguing insights into the painful effects of bureaucratic crime. Ille-Mai Gerdels

5746 C813.
**Simpson, Leo.**
Kowalski's Last Chance. Toronto: Clarke, Irwin, 1980. 200p. ISBN 0-7720-1281-4 $12.95

A policeman from the mythical Ontario town of Bradfarrow frees a robber and triggers a leprechaun plot to rid the force of an ineffectual police chief and reward the "good guys" in this satirical look at modern middle-class morals. A good chuckle that borders on the slapstick in parts, but entirely readable. Pat George.

5747 C813.
**Skoggard, Bruno.**
China Hand. Toronto: McClelland and Stewart, c1979. 276p. ISBN 0-7710-8196-0 $10.95

An adventurous pilot uses both sides in the Chinese Civil War to make money, betraying each and himself. Full of action and romance. Simple and easy to read. Jean Dodd

5748 C813.
**Slater, Ian.**
Firespill. Toronto: McClelland and Stewart-Bantam, c1977. 309p. (Seal Books) ISBN 0-7704-1504-0 $1.95

Adventure, mystery, romance and political intrigue are combined in this first novel which became a best-seller. Two supra-tankers collide off the coast of Alaska and the spilled oil causes a colossal fire. Fast-paced escape reading for all library collections.

5749 C813.
**Slater, Ian.**
Sea Gold. Toronto: McClelland and Stewart-Bantam, 1979. 274p. ISBN 0-7704-1525-3 pa.: $2.50

More polished than the author's first novel, *Fire Spill*, it reflects the author's knowledge of oceanography and the Canadian west coast. In the competition for riches at the bottom of the sea, the protagonists encounter greed, ambition, espionage, sabotage, murder and storms. An engrossing tale for adventure-suspense fans.

5750 C813.
**Smart, Elizabeth.**
The Assumption of the Rogues & Rascals. Toronto: Clarke, Irwin, 1978. 123p. ISBN 0-224-01566-5 $11.95

Smart's second novel after thirty years of non-productivity is an autobiographically flavoured succession of fragments, short reflections, stories and excerpts from journals. It deals with personal survival in the face of drudgery, sacrifice, and lovelessness. Characterized by tight imagery and metaphor and natural talk. Ille-Mai Gerdels

5751 C813.
**Solomon, Michael.**
The Struma Incident: A Novel of the Holocaust. Translated by Carol Dunlop-Hébert. Toronto: McClelland and Stewart, 1979. 174p. ISBN 0-7710-8218-5 $10.95

Through the experiences of one Jewish family seeking to escape the virulent anti-Semitism of a Hitler-dominated Europe in 1942, the reader shares the anguish of hundreds of Jewish people risking death to reach a refuge in Palestine. A moving and engrossing novel based upon an actual incident.

5752 C813.
**Soucy, Jean-Yves.**
Creatures of the Chase. Translated by John Glassco. Toronto: McClelland and Stewart, 1979. 161p. ISBN 0-7710-8216-9 $12.95

Powerful writing invigorates the old theme of the attraction and incompatibility of a free male and a civilized female (here a trapper and a schoolmarm). V. M. Gill

5753 C813.
**Sutherland, Ronald.**
Where Do the MacDonalds Bury Their Dead? Don Mills, Ont.: General Publishing; Markham, Ont.: PaperJacks, 1977, c1976. 258p. ISBN 0-7736-00043-4 bd.: $5.95 ISBN 0-7737-7128-X pa.: $2.50

A tough, scrapping half-Scots, half-French Canadian gets involved with an American commune devoted to sex and violence, and suffers a change in his macho self-image. Capably written for this genre. Jean Dodd

5754 C813.
**Suthren, Victor J. H.**
The Black Cockade: Paul Gallant's Louisbourg Command. Don Mills, Ont.: William Collins, 1977. 246p. maps. ISBN 0-00-222012-1 $10.95

A swashbuckling story of a corvette running through the blockade of English ships during the siege of Louisbourg in 1745. The battles are exciting, the hero romantic and the girl, of course, is beautiful. For all ages. Jean Dodd

5755 C813.
**Templeton, Charles B.**
Act of God: A Novel. Toronto: McClelland and Stewart; McClelland and Stewart-Bantam, 1978, c1977. 319p. ISBN 0-7710-8549-4 bd.: $10.95 pa.: $2.50

A well-written, gripping novel in which mystery, intrigue and church politics are intertwined with questions of ethics and morality. Jean Dodd

5756 C813.
**Thériault, Yves.**
Agoak: The Legacy of Agaguk. Translated by John David Allan. Toronto: McGraw-Hill Ryerson, 1979. 160p. ISBN 0-07-082947-0 bd.: $9.95 ISBN 0-07-082934-9 pa.

Sequel to *Agaguk*.

A brilliant, stark exposé of the primitive savagery close to the surface of humanity. Against the background of bleak Arctic cold, violent and primitive instincts are laid bare, as a young man is forced to flee the law. The despair, the savagery, the crude emotions may be disconcerting and distasteful to some readers. Jean Dodd

5757 C813.
**Thériault, Yves.**
Ways of the Flesh. Illustrations by Louise Nicole. Translated by Jean David. Agincourt, Ont.: Gage Publishing, c1977. 177p. ill. ISBN 0-7715-9363-5 pa.: $5.95

Pornographic short stories which juxtapose the appetite for sex with that for food. Heterosexual and homosexual combinations are described without reservation and the drawings are explicit. Jean Dodd

5758 C813.
**Thomas, Audrey.**
Ladies & Escorts. Edited by Gail Low. Ottawa: Oberon Press, c1977. 159p. ISBN 0-88750-219-9 bd.: $11.95 ISBN 0-88750-220-2 pa.: $4.95

These stories, some of which have appeared elsewhere, are poignant evocations of human emotions, some overt, some subliminal. The theme of the sadly unbridgeable distance between people is woven into a brilliant pattern of unusual style. Jean Dodd

5759 C813.
**Thomas, Audrey.**
Latakia: A Novel. Vancouver: Talonbooks, 1979. ISBN 0-88922-167-7 pa.: $7.95

A woman novelist examines the convolutions of a deteriorating romance with a younger man. The realization of the woman as an artist and the ambiguities of effective communication are subverted by the novelist's excessive passion for her egocentric and unworthy lover. Patricia O'Sullivan

5760 C813.
**Thomas, Audrey.**
Ten Green Bottles. Ottawa: Oberon Press, 1977, c1967. 177p. ISBN 0-88750-215-6 bd.: $11.95 ISBN 0-88750-216-4 pa.: $4.95

First published Indianapolis, Bobbs Merrill Co., 1967.

In this first collection of stories, Audrey Thomas displays great skill in describing confrontations between people in widely diverse locations, Africa, England, Scotland, America. Delicate and sensitive, with flashes of humour. Jean Dodd

5761 C813.
**Torgov, Morley.**
The Abramsky Variations. Toronto: Lester and Orpen, 1977. 175p. ISBN 0-919630-80-4 $8.95

Three generations of the Abramsky family dream of heroic exploits but remain mired in the humdrum, middle-class, materialistic society of Toronto. Enjoyable, light reading. Jean Dodd

5762 C813.
**Trengove, John.**
Mr. September. Don Mills, Ont.: General Publishing, 1979. 192p. ISBN 0-7736-0071-X $10.95

The separate worlds of White and Black in South Africa fail to destroy the friendship of two men caught in each. Authoritatively written from personal experience of the local political facts. Straightforward and unsentimental. Jean Dodd

5763 C813.
**Van Herk, Aritha.**
Judith: A Novel. Toronto: McClelland and Stewart, c1978. 190p. ISBN 0-7710-8700-4 $10

Seal Books First Novel Award.

To expiate her past and prove her independence, a young Alberta woman sheds her city image and becomes a pig farmer. Competently written, but in studied and portentous prose, and cliché-ridden in the current vein of feminist literature. Transcends the ordinary only in expert descriptions about pigs and pig farming. Ille-Mai Gerdels

5764 C813.
**Van Rjndt, Philippe.**
Blueprint. Toronto: Lester and Orpen; Don Mills, Ont.: Totem Books, 1979, c1977. 267p. ISBN 0-919630-76-6 bd.: $9.95 ISBN 0-00-222028-8 pa.: $2.50

A story of espionage and counterespionage with realistic characters and frighteningly possible ideas. Jean Dodd

5765 C813.
**Walker, David.**
Ash. Don Mills, Ont.: William Collins; Totem Books, 1977, c1976. 256p. ISBN 0-00-221042-8 bd.: $9.95 ISBN 0-00-618004-3 pa.: $1.95

A neatly paced story of a romantic hero – bush pilot, renegade, nature-lover – who is unable to control his zestful and intemperate character, and places himself above the law. The descriptions of landscape, animals and birds gives added dimension to the rather juvenile action. Jean Dodd

5766 C813.
**Watson, Patrick.**
Alter Ego: A Novel. Toronto: Lester and Orpen, c1978. 255p. ISBN 0-919630-05-7 $10.95

An experiment in teleportation results in a clone of the hero. A simple science fiction story without technical jargon. Jean Dodd

5767 C813.
**Watson, Sheila.**
Four Stories. Toronto: Coach House Press, 1980. 62p. ISBN 0-88910-135-3 $6.50

Sheila Watson's only published fiction other than *The Double Hook* yields resonance rather than resolutions in a combination of myth and modern life. V. M. Gill

5768 C813.
**Weintraub, William.**
The Underdogs. Toronto: McClelland and Stewart, c1979. 225p. ISBN 0-7710-9012-9 $12.95

Although set in Montreal twenty years after a successful referendum for independence, this delightful political satire could take place anywhere. Good fun. Jean Dodd

5769 C813.
**Wiebe, Rudy.**
The Scorched-wood People: A Novel. Toronto: McClelland and Stewart, c1977. 351p. ISBN 0-7710-8979-1 $12.95

1. Riel, Louis David, 1844-1885 – Fiction.
2. Dumont, Gabriel, 1838-1906 – Fiction.

An epic novel about the Northwest Rebellions. Although the contrast between Louis Riel's mysticism and Gabriel Dumont's realism is well drawn, the story as a whole lacks dramatic tension. Heavy going for the average reader, but perhaps interesting for the history buff. Jean Dodd

5770 C813.
**Woods, Grahame.**
Bloody Harvest. Toronto: McClelland and Stewart; McClelland and Stewart-Bantam, 1978, c1977. 335p. ISBN 0-7710-9049-8 bd.: $12.95 ISBN 0-7704-1539-3 pa.: $2.25

A middle-aged man, who had been a teen-aged hockey star and a war hero, struggles for a living as a migrant farm labourer in Ontario. A competent account of harsh reality replacing dreams. Jean Dodd

5771 C813.
**Woods, Grahame.**
A Gift to Last: A Novel. Toronto: McClelland and Stewart-Bantam, c1978. 215p. (Seal books) ISBN 0-7704-1546-6 pa.: $2.25

+ Pinsent, Gordon.

Based on the television series by Gordon Pinsent, the Sturgess family is seen through the eyes of the young Clement. Ably written for those fans who appreciate such spin-offs. Jean Dodd

5772 C813.
**Wright, Laurali.**
Neighbours: A Novel. Toronto: Macmillan, 1979. 258p. ISBN 0-7705-1791-9 $12.95

Search-for-a-new Alberta-novelist Award.

A chilling story of a psychotic wife and mother living in an otherwise normal neighbourhood. The theme of "my brother's keeper" is rather good, the writing undecorated. Not for the squeamish. Jean Dodd

5773 C813.
**Wright, Richard B.**
Farthing's Fortunes. Scarborough, Ont.: Macmillan-NAL Publishing, 1978, c1976. 415p. (A Signet Book) ISBN 0-7723-0004-6 pa.: $2.50

Clothbound listed *CS* no. 3234.

5774 C813.
**Wyatt, Rachel.**
The Rosedale Hoax. Toronto: House of Anansi Press, 1977. 136p. (Anansi Fiction Series) ISBN 0-88784-061-2 pa.: $4.95

A comedy of modern manners and life styles. A sophisticated, urbane delight with negligible plot but great good humour. Jean Dodd

5775 C813.
**York, Thomas.**
The Musk Ox Passion. Toronto: Doubleday, 1978. 229p. ISBN 0-385-13237-9 $8.95

The bizarre odyssey of Thomas Byrd as he tracks down the musk ox for its downy underhair is related by Byrd himself amidst a cast of zany characters. Humorously improbable, the novel is memorable for its satire of people and events in the Canadian north. Peggy Sinclair

## C813.009 Fiction - History and criticism

5776 C813'.009
**Dooley, David J.**
Moral Vision in the Canadian Novel. Toronto: Clarke, Irwin, 1978. 184p. Bibliographical references and Index. ISBN 0-7720-1218-0 $9.95

1. Canadian fiction (English) – History and criticism.

The author's contention that Canadian novelists merit no special concessions due to their nationality is examined in his discussion of eleven major twentieth-century Canadian authors. An introduction and conclusion neatly sandwich the text. Glenna Stevens

5777 C813'.009
**Harrison, Dick.**
Unnamed Country: The Struggle for a Canadian Prairie Fiction. Edmonton: University of Alberta Press, 1977. 250p. ill. Bibliography: p. 224-242. ISBN 0-88864-019-6 $12.50

1. Canadian fiction (English) – Prairie Provinces – History and criticism. 2. Prairie Provinces in literature.

This work explores nineteenth and twentieth century Prairie fiction as part of the larger Canadian literary scene. Professor Harrison traces the development of particular themes and imagery in five chronological groupings of fiction, although the emphasis is primarily geographical, rather than historical. A compelling study of several writers, notably Laurence and Kroetsch, with a selected bibliography providing guides for further reading. Andrea Trudel

5778 C813'.009
**Moss, John.**
Sex and Violence in the Canadian Novel: The Ancestral Present. Toronto: McClelland and Stewart, c1977. 326p. Bibliography: p. 314-320. Index. ISBN 0-7710-6563-9 pa.: $6.95

1. Sex in literature. 2. Violence in literature. 3. Canadian fiction (English) – 20th century – History and criticism.

Develops and illustrates the thesis that preoccupation with identity has led to the emergence of sex and violence as an organizing principle of the English Canadian novel between 1960 and 1975. A clear and readable analysis by a former academic, but flawed by distortions, unsupported generalizations, and an inaccurate index. Ille-Mai Gerdels

5779 C813'.009
**Moss, John,** ed.
The Canadian Novel. Toronto: NC Press, 1978- v ports. Bibliographical references. ISBN 0-919601-16-5 bd.: $16.95
ISBN 0-919601-04-9 pa.: $8.95

1. Canadian fiction (English) – 20th century – History and criticism.

Contents: vol. 1. *Here and Now.* 1978.

Comprises fourteen varied interpretative and evaluative essays on the novels of Atwood, Davies, Laurence, Munro, Richler and Wiebe. Moss's introduction is too brief and undeveloped, but the selection is good and the book is a useful addition to criticism collections. The first volume of a projected set on the development of the Canadian novel. Ille-Mai Gerdels

## C813.01 Short stories - Collections

5780 C813'.01
**Blaise, Clark,** ed.
Here & Now. Edited by Clark Blaise and John Metcalf. Ottawa: Oberon Press, c1977. 213p. ISBN 0-88750-210-5 bd.: $15
ISBN 0-88750-211-3 pa.: $5.95

1. Short stories, Canadian (English).

Excellent, well-crafted stories, all but two written by Canadians. International in scope and flavour, giving the lie to accusations of parochialism and denigration of CanLit. Jean Dodd

5781 C813'.01
**Blaise, Clark,** ed.
79, Best Canadian Stories. Edited by Clark Blaise and John Metcalf. Ottawa: Oberon Press, 1979. 140p. ISBN 0-88750-314-4 bd.: $15
ISBN 0-88750-315-2 pa.: $6.95

1. Short stories, Canadian (English) – 20th century.

Consists of ten predictably conservative, well-crafted stories with a noticeable autobiographical element. Stand-outs are Mavis Gallant's "With a Capital T" and Elizabeth Spencer's "The Search". One of the better Oberon collections in recent years, with a broad range of subject and style that makes for interesting if unexciting reading. Ille-Mai Gerdels

5782 C813'.01
**Carpenter, David,** ed.
Wild Rose Country: Stories from Alberta. Stories by Rudy Wiebe and others. Ottawa: Oberon Press, c1977. 175p.
ISBN 0-88750-235-0 bd.: $15
ISBN 0-88750-236-9 pa.: $5.95

1. Short stories, Canadian (English) – Alberta.

Thirteen stories with Alberta settings by native Albertans and other Canadians. Wiebe, Kroetsch, McCourt, Kreisel, Livesay and Mitchell are represented. In some of the stories, notably Edward McCourt's and Rudy Wiebe's, the setting is important; in others it is not significant. A good selection. Catharine MacKenzie

5783 C813.01
**Harrison, Dick,** ed.
Best Mounted Police Stories. Drawings by Jorge Frascara. Edmonton: University of Alberta Press, 1978. 258p. ill.
ISBN 0-88864-054-4 pa.: $10

1. Canada. Royal Canadian Mounted Police – Fiction. 2. Short stories, Canadian (English). 3. Short stories, American.

The Royal Canadian Mounted Police are idealized in their role of lawkeepers in this country. In the introduction, contrasts are made between the development of law enforcement in Canada and the United States, especially in opening up the west. Non-violence, devotion to an ideal and the respect of even their enemies were the keynote of their existence. Pat George

5784 C813'.01
**Israel, Charles E.,** ed.
The Newcomers. Toronto: McClelland and Stewart, 1979. 228p. ISBN 0-7710-0158-4 $24.95

1. Canadian fiction (English) – 20th century. 2. Canada – Emigration and immigration – Fiction.

Seven poignant stories by prominent Canadian writers commissioned for a recent television series celebrating our diverse cultural heritage and honouring the struggle of early immigrants to establish their homes in a harsh land. Accuracy of historical detail makes this an excellent educational tool. Amply illustrated by photographs from the film series. Patricia O'Sullivan

5785 C813.01
**Metcalf, John,** ed.
78, Best Canadian Stories. Edited by John Metcalf and Clark Blaise. Ottawa: Oberon Press, 1979. 176p. ISBN 0-88750-277-6 bd.: $15
ISBN 0-88750-278-4 pa.: $6.95

1. Short stories, Canadian (English) – 20th century.

Oberon's eighth annual anthology contains ten stories, only two of which are original. The selection exhibits no unifying principle in purpose or quality, ranging from Barry Grills' and David McDonald's amateurish and trivial contributions to Alice Munro's "The Beggar Maid". A standard choice for the short story collection. Ille-Mai Gerdels

5786 C813'.01
**Ondaatje, Michael,** ed.
Personal Fictions: Stories by Munro, Wiebe, Thomas and Blaise. Toronto: Oxford University Press, 1977. 230p. ports. Bibliographical references. ISBN 0-19-540277-4 pa.: $4.50

1. Short stories, Canadian (English).

Comprises seventeen short stories, most of which provide a thematic exploration of human relationships from a highly subjective point of view. This is a superior selection, but of questionable value, because it lacks critical material and contains only previously anthologized stories. Ille-Mai Gerdels

5787 C813'.01
**Owen, Ivon,** ed.
The Best Modern Canadian Short Stories. Edited by Ivon Owen and Morris Wolfe. Edmonton: Hurtig Publishers, c1978. 318p. ISBN 0-88830-154-5 $12.95

1. Short stories, Canadian (English).

Contains twenty-four contemporary short stories by major Canadian authors. The selection is traditional rather than experimental, and is regionally representative of both settings and writers. A quality collection that develops several unifying themes and exhibits a trend to urban settings. Ille-Mai Gerdels

5788 C813'.01
**Peck, Edward,** ed.
Transitions II: Short Fiction: A Source Book of Canadian Literature. Vancouver: CommCept Publishing, 1978. 291p. ill., ports. ISBN 0-88829-024-1 pa.: $7.65

1. Short stories, Canadian (English).

"Brings together in profile, contour and full colour, the tremendous vitality of the Canadian short story. Intentionally, nearly every geographical possibility appears." -Foreword. Sixteen short stories by Canadian masters of the craft, and their reflections on the genre are contained in this excellent introductory study. Includes biographical sketches and photographs. Recommended. Secondary school and public libraries. Similar in design and format: Peck, E., ed. *Transitions I: Short Plays*, and *Transitions III: Poetry: A Source Book of Canadian Literature.*

5789 C813'.01
**Weaver, Robert Leigh,** comp.
Canadian Short Stories, Third Series. Toronto: Oxford University Press, 1978. 362p. ports. Bibliography: p. 353-362. ISBN 0-19-540291-X pa.: $5.95

1. Short stories, Canadian (English).

"A collection of short fiction first published in the late 1960's and 1970's." The selection is nicely balanced as to themes, tones and styles. Short notes and portraits add to its usefulness. Jean Dodd

5790 C813.01
**Whitaker, Muriel,** ed.
Great Canadian Adventure Stories. Edmonton: Hurtig Publishers, 1979. 224p. ill. ISBN 0-88830-169-3 $12.95

These fifteen traditional and familiar tales of male heroism, set in the Canadian wilderness of the past, successfully explore the psychological dimensions of physical conflicts. Artistic illustrations, a useful introduction, and biographical sketches of the authors illuminate the texts. By recognized writers of the genre, and suitable for readers of all ages. Ille-Mai Gerdels

5791 C813'.01
**Whitaker, Muriel,** ed.
Great Canadian Animal Stories. Illustrated by Vlasta van Kampen. Edmonton: Hurtig Publishers, 1978. 232p. ill. ISBN 0-88830-165-0 $12.95

1. Animals, Legends and stories of.
2. Short stories, Canadian (English).

Sixteen well-chosen animal stories by early and contemporary writers offer a wide spectrum from legend to realism, humour to poignancy. Full-page colour paintings by Vlasta van Kampen illustrate the stories. Biographical notes are included for the authors who range from Charles G. D. Roberts to Fred Bodsworth. Recommended for readers of all ages.

5792 C813'.01
**Wiebe, Rudy,** comp.
Getting Here: Stories. Edmonton: NeWest Press, c1977. 119p. ISBN 0-920316-00-X pa.: $2.95

1. Short stories, Canadian (English) – Alberta.

An anthology of seven stories by Alberta women in all but one of which the protagonist is a woman. There is variety in theme and in the quality of the writing, but the general level of writing is good. Poor production detracts from a readable collection.

5793 C813'.01
**Wolfe, Morris,** ed.
Toronto Short Stories. Edited by Morris Wolfe and Douglas Daymond. Toronto: Doubleday, 1977. 274p. ISBN 0-385-12848-7 bd.: $11.50
1. Short stories, Canadian (English).
An excellent selection of stories, some familiar, some new. Although set in Toronto, they exemplify universal themes. A satisfying work. Jean Dodd

---

**C813.4** Novelists - 19th century - Criticism and interpretation

---

5794 C813'.4
**Beasley, David R.**
The Canadian Don Quixote: The Life and Works of Major John Richardson, Canada's First Novelist. Erin, Ont.: Porcupine's Quill, 1977. 219p. ill., maps, ports. Bibliography: p. 202-204. Index. ISBN 0-88984-020-2 bd.: $12.95 ISBN 0-88984-022-9 pa.: $6.95
1. Richardson, John, 1796-1852. 2. Authors, Canadian (English) – 19th century – Biography.
Presents a scholarly biographical study of the life, times and literary works of Canada's first native-born novelist. The book is strong on research and detail, but weak in delineating its controversial hero, and is marred by a lacklustre style and small print. Too academic to attract a large readership. Ille-Mai Gerdels

5795 C813'.4
**Shields, Carol.**
Susanna Moodie: Voice and Vision. Ottawa: Borealis Press, 1977. 81p. Bibliography: p. 75-81. ISBN 0-919594-46-8 pa.: $8.95
1. Moodie, Susanna, 1803-1885 – Criticism and interpretation.
Shields discusses three major recurring themes which she discerns in Mrs. Moodie's writing: complex personality, sexual reversal, and society, and examines each one in some detail. A cogent and objective analysis designed to place the writer in historical perspective. Lucid and interesting to read. Canadian literature collections in senior secondary school, college and public libraries.

5796 C813'.4
**Tausky, Thomas E.**
Sara Jeannette Duncan: Novelist of Empire. Ottawa: Tecumseh Press, 1979. Bibliography. ISBN 0-919662-55-2 pa.: $3.95
1. Duncan, Sara Jeannette, 1861-1922.
2. Novelists, Canadian (English) – 19th century – Biography.
The writings of Sara Jeannette Duncan bring images of protracted afternoon teas, 'what-not' cabinets, and parlours crowded with over-stuffed furniture. However, there were barbs that although well-concealed, were none-the-less sharp. A curious, but interesting collection. Paula de Ronde

---

**C813.5** Novelists - 20th century - Criticism and interpretation

---

5797 C813'.5
**Grant, Judith Ann Skelton.**
Robertson Davies. Toronto: McClelland and Stewart, c1978. 58p. (Canadian Writers) (New Canadian Library) ISBN 0-7710-3560-8 pa.: $1.95
1. Davies, Robertson, 1913- – Criticism and interpretation.
An excellent introduction to the mind and craftsmanship of one of Canada's major novelists. Concentrating on six novels, Dr. Grant provides a balanced and knowledgeable assessment. Has a useful bibliography. These brief informative monographs of Canadian literary criticism should be in all public and secondary school libraries.

5798 C813'.5
**Morley, Patricia A.**
The Comedians: Hugh Hood and Rudy Wiebe. Toronto: Clarke, Irwin, 1977. 134p. Bibliographical references and Index. ISBN 0-7720-1051-X $9.95
1. Hood, Hugh, 1928- – Criticism and interpretation. 2. Wiebe, Rudy, 1934- – Criticism and interpretation. 3. Comedy.
A recognized literary critic and academic examines the comic structure and Christian vision of both authors as developed in their individual novels. Morley's brief essays are neither original nor profound, and her comparison is reliant on an inadequate methodology, but it is clear and helpful to the student and general reader. Ille-Mai Gerdels

5799 C813'.5
**Morley, Patricia A.**
Morley Callaghan. Toronto: McClelland and Stewart, c1978. 72p. Bibliography: p. 68-72. (Canadian Writers) ISBN 0-7710-6470-5 pa.: $2.95
1. Callaghan, Morley, 1903- – Criticism and interpretation.
"One of a series of handbooks designed to provide the student and general reader with compact and inexpensive introductions to significant figures in the Canadian literary scene". -Title page verso. Individual novels and principal characters are examined in a thematic study of Callaghan's fifty years of writing. Contains a bibliography.

5800 C813'.5
**New, William H.,** ed.
Margaret Laurence. Toronto: McGraw-Hill Ryerson, c1977. 224p. Bibliography: p. 222-224. (Critical Views on Canadian Writers) ISBN 0-07-082521-1 bd.: $9.95
ISBN 0-07-082520-3 pa.: $5.95
1. Laurence, Margaret, 1926- – Criticism and interpretation.
A superficial, cramped collection of articles and reviews by authors, academics and critics that fails to meet some important professional standards of literary criticism. Inconsistent in quality, and marred by repetition, irrelevancy and editorial errors, this selection provides a general introduction, but is unsatisfactory as an in-depth definitive study of Laurence's work and impact. Ille-Mai Gerdels

## C814 Essays

5801 C814.
**Davies, Robertson.**
The Enthusiasms of Robertson Davies. Edited by Judith Skelton Grant. Toronto: McClelland and Stewart, c1979. 320p.
ISBN 0-7710-2565-3 $14.95
Those who yearn for good conversation proceeding from a lively wit must rejoice in the journalism of the well-known novelist, playwright and critic. The collection of essays and reviews is divided into characters, books and the author himself. Catharine MacKenzie

5802 C814.
**Davies, Robertson.**
One Half of Robertson Davies: Provocative Pronouncements on a Wide Range of Topics. Toronto: Macmillan, c1977. 286p.
ISBN 0-7705-1579-7 $10.95
Engaging public speeches filled with wit, wisdom, and charm, consider topics ranging from the humour of Stephen Leacock to the design of haunted houses. Sheila Latham

5803 C814.
**Layton, Irving.**
Taking Sides: The Collected Social and Political Writings of Irving Layton. Edited and introduced by Howard Aster. Oakville, Ont.: Mosaic Press/Valley Editions, c1977. 222p.
ISBN 0-88962-058-X bd.: $12.50
ISBN 0-88962-056-3 pa.: $5.50
A kaleidoscope of early newspaper columns, letters, speeches, and ruminations that range from social and political analysis to a discussion with Eli Mandel regarding Nietzschean philosophy, to the 'state of the art of Canadian poetry'. Recommended for Canadiana collections. Ethel Kellen

5804 C814.
**MacLennan, Hugh.**
The Other Side of Hugh MacLennan: Selected Essays Old and New. Edited by Elspeth Cameron. Toronto: Macmillan, 1978. 301p. ISBN 0-7705-1716-1 $11.95
MacLennan proves his talent as an essayist in this collection of thirty-four of his best works. Arranged chronologically, the essays reflect the author's personal experiences and memories. His whimsical style, unconventional characters and witty expression make for enjoyable reading. Glenna Stevens

5805 C814.
**Richler, Mordecai.**
The Great Comic Book Heroes and Other Essays. Selected and introduced by Robert Fulford. Toronto: McClelland and Stewart, c1978. 194p. (New Canadian Library) ISBN 0-7710-9268-7 pa.: $2.95
Eleven essays originally published in the sixties and early seventies are collected here to help reveal the sensibilities and intellectual make-up of the influential Canadian novelist. Both Richler critics and those interested in critical accounts of the Canadian literary scene, written by an outstanding member of it, will find this assortment useful.
Merike Koger

5806 C815'.0108
**Young, Scott,** comp.
The Best Talk in Town, compiled by Scott Young and Margaret Hogan. Toronto: Clarke, Irwin, 1979. 280p. ill., plates, ports. Index. ISBN 0-7720-1257-1 $14.95

1. Canadian orations (English). 2. Speeches, addresses, etc.

Selected luncheon speeches delivered at the Empire Club of Canada over seventy-five years provide a key to the events and personalities of the period: Stephen Leacock, Stefansson, Billy Bishop, A. Y. Jackson, Nikita Krushchev, David Broadfoot. Compiled by two experienced journalists who have a keen ear for wit and humour, the collection deserves a wide audience.

## C817 Humour

5807 C817.
**Buckler, Ernest.**
Whirligig: Selected Prose and Poetry of Ernest Buckler. Toronto: McClelland and Stewart, c1977. 128p. ISBN 0-7710-1770-7 $7.95

Stephen Leacock Memorial Medal.

Refreshing pieces of satiric wit and humour expose the foibles and pitfalls of everyday life. Sheila Latham

5808 C817.
**Clark, Gregory.**
Ten Cents off Per Dozen: A Gregory Clark Omnibus. Compiled by Anna Ozvoldik. Montreal: Optimum Publishing, c1979. 176p. ill., ports. ISBN 0-88890-116-X $6.95

Presents a cross-section of Clark's tales originally written and published in magazines between 1953 and 1975. The stories celebrate the joy of everyday living, and are characterized by folksiness, sentimentality, simplicity and unsophisticated humour. Pleasing and undemanding reading for teen-agers and adults. Ille-Mai Gerdels

5809 C817.
**Harron, Donald.**
Olde Charlie Farquharson's Testament: From Jennysez to Jobe and After Words. Toronto: Gage Publishing, 1978. 160p. ill.
ISBN 0-7715-9900-5 bd.: $8.95
ISBN 0-7715-9901-3 pa.: $4.95

1. Bible. O.T. – Anecdotes, facetiae, satire, etc.

This lavishly illustrated, Parry Sound version of the Old Testament will delight Charlie's die-hard fans, but others may find the endless puns and word-play tedious. Annemarie Toth

5810 C817.
**Mann, Bill.**
The Retarded Giant: Introducing the Definitive Canadian Joke. Drawings by Aislin. Montreal: Tundra Books, 1977. 96p. ill.
ISBN 0-88776-095-3 pa.: $2.95

1. Canada – Anecdotes, facetiae, satire, etc.

One American's view of Canada is revealed in this collection of jokes and one-liners about Canadian sports, the provinces, the weather, etc. Drawings by the excellent Canadian cartoonist, Aislin, illustrate the work. Annemarie Toth

5811 C817.
**Needham, Richard J.**
The Wit & Wisdom of Richard Needham. Illustrated by Ed Franklin. Edmonton: Hurtig Publishers, c1977. 110p. ill.
ISBN 0-88830-137-5 bd.: $9.95
ISBN 0-88830-138-3 pa.: $3.95

A collection of aphorisms culled from Needham's long-running column in the "Globe and Mail". It is a cynical yet provocative look at subjects ranging from politics to relations between the sexes. Annemarie Toth

5812 C817.
**Russell, Ted.**
Tales from Pigeon Inlet. Selected and edited by Elizabeth Russell Miller. St. John's, Nfld.: Breakwater Books, c1977. 179p. ill.
ISBN 0-919948-51-0 bd.: $10.95
ISBN 0-919948-50-2 pa.: $4.95

1. Newfoundland – Anecdotes, facetiae, satire, etc.

Fashioned from the author's experiences, and enlivened with humour and subtle satire, the distinctive personalities of an imaginary outpost community in Newfoundland in the first half of the twentieth century come to life to charm the reader.

5813 C817.
**Soupcoff, Murray.**
Canada 1984: The Year in Review. Toronto: Lester and Orpen Dennys, 1979.
ISBN 0-919630-09-X $9.95

1. Canadian wit and humor (English).
2. Canada – Civilization – Anecdotes, facetiae, satire, etc.

Orwell's momentous year is fast

approaching, giving Soupcoff the comic opportunity of forecasting what Canada will be like then. The satire is highlighted by Isaac Bickerstaff's numerous satiric cartoons. Annemarie Toth

5814 C817.
**Ward, Norman.**
Her Majesty's Mice. Toronto: McClelland and Stewart, c1977. 159p. ill.
ISBN 0-7710-8824-8 $8.95

The sophisticated reader will welcome Ward's light touch as displayed in this anthology of historical anecdotes and contemporary satire. Some of the material is reprinted from earlier collections. Ward was awarded the Stephen Leacock Memorial Medal for humour for his earlier book, *Mice in the Beer*. Annemarie Toth

## C818 Miscellany

5815 C818.
**Beattie, Jessie L.**
William Arthur Deacon: Memoirs of a Literary Friendship. Hamilton, Ont.: Fleming Press, c1978. 58p. ill., ports.

1. Deacon, William Arthur, 1890-1977 – Correspondence. 2. Beattie, Jessie L., 1896- 3. Authors, Canadian (English) – 20th century – Correspondence.

This book clearly displays the devotion and respect which Jessie Beattie, author of poetry and fiction, held for her literary critic and friend, William Deacon. It consist of excerpts from their letters, supplemented by Beattie's comments. Her flowing style creates a text which can be enjoyed even by the reader who knows little of the people involved. Glenna Stevens

5816 C818.
**Campbell, Wilfred.**
At the Mermaid Inn: Wilfred Campbell, Archibald Lampman, Duncan Campbell Scott in "The Globe" 1892-93. Introduction by Barrie Davies. Toronto: University of Toronto Press, c1979. 353p. Index. (Literature of Canada)
ISBN 0-8020-2299-5 bd.: $25
ISBN 0-8020-6333-0 pa.: $7.50

1. Lampman, Archibald, 1861-1899.
2. Scott, Duncan Campbell, 1862-1947.
3. The Globe (Toronto, Ont.).

A collection of the column, by three Canadian poets which was printed in "The Globe" each week for seventeen months. Subjects are both literary and non-literary, including discussion of political and cultural developments. Access to the many short essays, poems and reviews facilitated by index. Glenna Stevens

5817 C818.
**Clark, Gregory.**
The Best of Greg Clark & Jimmie Frise. Stories by Gregory Clark; illustrated by James Frise. Don Mills, Ont.: William Collins, 1977. 216p. ill. ISBN 0-00-216683-6 $9.95

A collection of the best of Clark's stories illustrated with Frise's famous drawings which appeared in the "Star Weekly" from 1935 to 1939. They not only brightened the thirties but will give present day readers a warm glow of nostalgia. Annemarie Toth

5818 C818.
**Cline, Beverly Fink,** comp.
Louisa Clark's Annual: Life & Literature in British North America by a lady writer residing in the town of Goderich, Canada West. Erin, Ont.: Press Porcépic, c1976. 64p. ill. ISBN 0-88878-133-4 $2.95

The third part of a journal of a fictitious British immigrant to Canada, reflecting the concerns and interests of educated women in the mid-1800's. Cline has thoroughly researched her entries, which include contemporary newspaper articles, poetry and recipes, and has created a character who will both entertain and instruct. Patricia O'Sullivan

5819 C818.
**Gzowski, Peter,** ed.
Peter Gzowski's Spring Tonic. Edmonton: Hurtig Publishers, c1979. ISBN 0-88830-166-9 pa.: $12.95

1. Spring – Canada – Literary collections.
2. Spring – Canada – Miscellanea. 3. Canadian literature (English) – 20th century – Collections.

Optimistic views of past and future springs prevail in most poems, short stories, plays and other contributions by various authors, many of whom are well-known Canadians. An interesting book in which to browse, but of limited value to the serious reader. Glenna Stevens

5820 C818.
**Howarth, Jean.**
Treasure Island: A Collection. Toronto: Dorset Publishing, 1979. 184p. ill.
ISBN 0-88893-012-7 $11.95

These amusing and endearing stories are centred around the fictional island of

Madronna and its inhabitants. The author, originally from Manitoba with a career history of newspaper work and CBC radio, writes as if she were an old resident reporting on the daily goings on in the simple, isolated community. Light reading for the general audience. Merike Koger

5821 C818.

**Johnston, Basil H.**

Moose Meat and Wild Rice. Toronto: McClelland and Stewart, c1978. 188p. ISBN 0-7710-4443-7 $12.95

1. Chippewa Indians – Anecdotes, facetiae, satire, etc.

One catches a glimpse of the Indian sense of humour in this collection of simple short stories about life on the fictional Moose Meat Point Indian Reserve. The focus is on the clash between the cultures of the Ojibway and white man. Johnston is the author of *Ojibway Heritage*, 1976. High school level and up. Annemarie Toth

5822 C818.

**Linder, Norma West.**

Morels and Maple Syrup: A Memoir of Manitoulin Island. Cornwall, Ont.: Vesta Publications, c1977. 160p. ISBN 0-919806-27-9 pa.: $5

In a personal and rather sentimental vein, the author highlights the poignant, happy and fearful moments of childhood in a series of short recollections of her early years with her family on Manitoulin Island. Provides light, nostalgic reading. Patricia O'Sullivan

5823 C818.

**Sherwood, Roland H.**

Atlantic Yesterdays: Unusual Stories of the Famed Atlantic Provinces. Hantsport, N.S.: Lancelot Press, 1978. 92p. ISBN 0-88999-095-6 pa.: $2.95

1. Maritime Provinces – Anecdotes, facetiae, satire, etc.

Fearless women pirates, persuasive preachers and fearsome crooks inhabit this collection of short stories from the Atlantic provinces. History and legend are woven into an entertaining blend of highly readable tales of the colourful past of our Maritime ancestors. Patricia O'Sullivan

5824 C818.

**Simpson, Gregg.**

Luminous Desires: Collected Writings. Edmonton: Derwyddon Press, c1977. 74p. ISBN 0-919960-03-0 pa.: $3.75

Some writings of the Vancouver-based artist and musician including short stories, plays and poems permeated with classical themes and figures from Greek and Roman mythology. For the general reader who delights in wild flights of the imagination and touches of science fiction and fantasy. Merike Koger

5825 C818'.02

**Hamilton, Robert M.,** comp.

The Dictionary of Canadian Quotations and Phrases. Compiled by Robert M. Hamilton and Dorothy Shields. Rev. and enl. ed. Toronto: McClelland and Stewart, 1978. Index. ISBN 0-7710-3844-5 $65

1. Quotations, Canadian (English).
2. Canada – Quotations, maxims, etc.

A revised and greatly expanded volume containing some 10,300 entries arranged by subject. The source of each quotation or phrase is given. A clear type face and well-designed pages make this standard reference a pleasure to use. For all libraries.

## 820 English literature

5826 820'.9

**Campbell, Jane,** ed.

The Practical Vision: Essays in English Literature in Honour of Flora Roy. Edited by Jane Campbell and James Doyle. Waterloo, Ont.: Wilfrid Laurier University Press, 1978. 163p. ISBN 0-88920-066-1 $7.50

1. English literature – History and criticism.

These well-written and scholarly essays cover a wide range of literature from the Junius Manuscripts to Malcolm Lowry, reflecting the broad interests of Dr. Roy. Lack of a thematic approach and index are drawbacks to effective use. Patricia O'Sullivan

5827 821'.7

**Coburn, Kathleen.**

In Pursuit of Coleridge. Toronto: Clarke, Irwin, 1977. 202p. ill., geneal. tables. Index. ISBN 0-7720-1154-0 $12.50

1. Coleridge, Samuel Taylor, 1772-1834 – Manuscripts.

This autobiography of a respected female Canadian academic's research on Coleridge, the poet, is an extremely readable combination of facts and endearing anecdotes, appealing to scholars, students and interested adults alike. The author's deeply-felt Ontario roots and the difficulties encountered by career-minded women earlier in this century are portrayed with honesty and flair. Merike Koger

5828 821'.9'12
**Wiseman, Christopher.**
Beyond the Labyrinth: A Study of Edwin Muir's Poetry. Victoria: Sono Nis Press, 1978. 252p. Bibliography: p. 246-248. Index. ISBN 0-919462-66-9 $10

1. Muir, Edwin, 1887-1959 – Criticism and interpretation.

A critical analysis of Muir as a symbolist poet which recognizes the sophistication of his techniques and challenges the view that his work lacks the style and vigour of his modernistic contemporaries. This scholarly analysis includes a select bibliography of some fifty-six works by and about the poet. Merike Koger

5829 823.
**Lewis, Wyndham.**
Mrs. Dukes' Million. Toronto: Coach House Press, 1977. 365p. ISBN 0-88910-082-9 pa.: $7.50

A talented "Actor-Gang" attempt to dupe an old woman out of her million pound inheritance. A long-lost first novel by this famous Canadian-born British novelist. Peggy Sinclair

5830 823.91
**Murdoch, Derrick.**
The Agatha Christie Mystery. Toronto: Pagurian Press, 1976. 192p. ill., ports. Bibliography: p. 186-187. Index. ISBN 0-88932-034-9 $8.95

1. Christie, Agatha Miller, 1891-1976.

Composed of a highly conjectural biographical first section, unsupported by conventional source material, and a more satisfactory second section that places Christie's works in a historical and critical framework. A comprehensive chronological listing of her books and their stage and film versions is useful. Written for the general reader in a pleasing if unremarkable style. Ille-Mai Gerdels

## C891.79 Ukrainian Canadian literature

5831 891.7'9'32
**Franko, Ivan.**
Fox Mykyta: Ivan Franko's Ukrainian Classic. English version by Bohdan Melnyk. Illustrated by William Kurelek. Montreal: Tundra Books, c1978. 148p. ill. ISBN 0-88776-112-7 $12.95

This first English translation of *Lys Mykyta,* written by one of the greatest Ukrainian authors and published in Ukraine in 1890, is presented in prose rather than the original verse. As the favourite story of generations of Ukrainian children it presents the humorous adventures of a clever fox and other animal characters. Illustrations by the inimitable artist Kurelek provide additional Ukrainian flavour. Andrew Gregorovich

5832 891.8'1'13
**Gabe, Dora.**
Depths: Conversations with the Sea. Translated by John Robert Colombo and Nikola Roussanoff. Toronto: Hounslow Press, c1978. 59p. port. ISBN 0-88882-035-6 pa.: $4.95

Translation of *Glubini.*

Poems written in old age by "the most beloved of Bulgaria's writers." The poet considers the meaning of life and contemplates the approach of death. Text in Bulgarian with English translation on opposite page. Catharine MacKenzie

5833 894'.511
**Faludy, György.**
East and West: Selected Poems of George Faludy. Edited by John Robert Colombo; with a profile of the poet by Barbara Amiel. Toronto: Hounslow Press, c1978. 145p. ports. ISBN 0-88882-025-9 pa.: $4.95

Translations of poems written between 1935 and 1975 reveal a diversity of experience suffered and enjoyed by a Hungarian exile now living in Toronto. Sheila Latham

## 900 History

5834 901.
**Lower, Arthur R. M.**
A Pattern for History. Toronto: McClelland and Stewart, c1978. 381p. Bibliographical references and Index. ISBN 0-7710-5374-6 $16.95

1. History – Philosophy.

In a panoramic sweep of twenty-five hundred years of western civilization, from Judaism to the present, a distinguished Canadian historian searches for trends and patterns to gain a perspective on our present, and our possible future. Readable and thought-provoking. Historians and students of history.

5835 909'.09'644
**Lower, J. Arthur.**
Ocean of Destiny: A Concise History of the North Pacific, 1500-1978. Vancouver: University of British Columbia Press, c1978. 242p. ill., maps, plates, ports. Bibliography: p. 225-233. Index. ISBN 0-7748-0101-8 $16.50

1. North Pacific region – History. 2. Canada – Relations (general) with the North Pacific region.

A good introduction to the political and economic relationships between North American and Asian nations from the time of early European exploration. Although marred by a few inaccuracies this is generally a well-researched volume on a new facet of Canada's role in international relations. Beautifully organized and indexed, with extensive notes. Nikki Lawrence

## 910 Voyages and travels

5836 910'.45
**Anderson, Allan.**
Salt Water, Fresh Water. Toronto: Macmillan, 1979. 391p. ill. ISBN 0-7705-1819-2 $15.95

1. Seafaring life.

Aspects of the sea are chronicled in the oral history tradition of Barry Broadfoot. Anecdotes are organized under such headings as "Hard Work", "Long Hours", "Accidents", "A Nice Boat", and give a highly romanticized view of the men who make their living from the sea. Since neither the contributors nor the locations are identified the stories tend to blend one into another as though one person had led a most unusual life. Barbara Schon

5837 910'.92'4
**Conner, Daniel.**
Master Mariner: Capt. James Cook and the Peoples of the Pacific, by Daniel Conner and Lorraine Miller. Vancouver: Douglas & McIntyre, 1978. Bibliography. Index. ISBN 0-88894-191-9 $16.95

1. Cook, James, 1728-1779.

Captain Cook's final voyage and the Europeans' conception of their contact with the native peoples of the Pacific are emphasized in this narrative account gleaned largely from the ships' journals. This book is handsomely illustrated with maps, photographs of navigational instruments, portraits and reproductions of the sixty-one original engravings done by John Webber during the voyage. Theresa Crosgrey

## 911.7 Historical atlases and historical geography

5838 911.71
**Nicholson, Norman L.**
The Boundaries of the Canadian Confederation. Toronto: Macmillan; Ottawa: Institute of Canadian Studies, Carleton University, 1979. 252p. maps. Bibliography: p. 235-245. Index. (The Carleton Library) ISBN 0-7705-1742-0 pa.: $8.95

1. Canada – Boundaries.

A revised and enlarged edition of the author's *The Boundaries of Canada, Its Provinces and Territories*, published by the Government of Canada in 1954.

A scholarly, well-researched study which analyzes the political, economic and geographic factors involved in the convoluted history and evolution of Canada's provincial, territorial and national boundaries, their ramifications and possible future changes. The clarity of the writing, the organization of the material, and the extensive bibliography recommend this work. Theresa Crosgrey

5839 911'.73
**Gibson, James R.,** ed.
European Settlement and Development in North America: Essays on Geographical Change in Honour and Memory of Andrew Hill Clark. Toronto: University of Toronto Press, c1978. 230p. ill., graphs, maps, ports. Bibliography: p. 224-228. (Research Publications – University of Toronto, Dept. of Geography) ISBN 0-8020-3357-1 pa.: $7.50

1. Clark, Andrew Hill, 1911-1975. 2. United States – Historical geography. 3. Canada – Historical geography. 4. United States – Colonization. 5. Canada – Colonization.

Meticulously researched scholarly essays by prominent Canadian and American historical geographers. College and large public libraries.

## 912 Atlases and maps

5840 912.
**Fullard, Harold,** comp.
Atlas of Canada and the World, compiled by Harold Fullard and B. M. Willet. Milwaukee, Wis.: George Philip Raintree, 1979. 280p. maps. Index. ISBN 0-89810-001-1 standard ed.: $39.95 ISBN 0-89810-002-X deluxe ed. ISBN 0-89810-004-6 library ed.

1. Atlases. 2. Canada – Maps.

Extensive up-to-date coverage of Canada makes this an important acquisition for small Canadian libraries. However, for international coverage, it must be supplemented with a good international atlas such as *Goode's World Atlas*.

5841 912.
**Oxford University Press.**
The New Canadian Oxford Atlas. Prepared by the Cartographic Dept. of the Clarendon Press; advisory editor: Quentin Stanford. Don Mills, Ont.: Oxford University Press, c1977. 172p. graphs, maps. ISBN 0-19-540263-4 pa.: $6.95

1. Atlases, Canadian.

Clear thematic and regional maps are supplemented by statistical tables and graphs illustrating population distribution, resources, climate and economics. Well balanced in its inclusion of other countries, Canadian maps constitute approximately twenty percent of the total. Fully metricated. An attractive, inexpensive purchase for schools, public libraries and individuals.

5842 912'.71
**Matthews, Geoffrey.**
Atlas of Canada in Bold Print. Toronto: Canadian National Institute for the Blind, 1978. 45p. maps. pa.: $8.95

1. Large type books. 2. Canada – Maps.

A bold typeface, heavy lines, understandable symbols and maps in primary colours have been combined effectively in this atlas for visually handicapped students. Maps of Canada's physical, geological, climatic and demographic features are followed by regional economic maps. Statistics for the provinces, and a glossary are included. A basic atlas for general use.

5843 912'.711
**Farley, Albert L.**
Atlas of British Columbia: People, Environment, and Resource Use. Vancouver: University of British Columbia Press, 1979. 136p. ill., graphs, maps. ISBN 0-7748-0092-5 $45

1. British Columbia – Maps. 2. British Columbia – Population – Maps. 3. British Columbia – Maps, Physical. 4. British Columbia – Economic conditions – Maps.

A successor to *British Columbia Atlas of Resources*, 1956.

The maps, illustrations and text of this comprehensive new atlas focus on three major themes: people, environment, and resource use. Succinct explanations face each page of clear, uncluttered maps. A gazetteer and historical and statistical summaries are included. Metric measurements are used. An important reference source for secondary school, college and public libraries.

5844 912'.7127'4
**Weir, Thomas R.**
Atlas of Winnipeg, edited by Thomas R. Weir and Ngok-Wai Lai. Toronto: University of Toronto Press, c1978. 67 leaves, graphs, maps. ISBN 0-8020-5396-3 pa.: $25

1. Winnipeg, Man. – Maps.

From several years of research the well-known geographer has constructed a detailed profile of Winnipeg's development. 151 large-scale coloured maps, graphs, and informative text illustrate physical, historical, political, economic and social concepts. Large format, clear type, spiral binding. Useful for students, educators, urban planners, businessmen, and the general reader.

## 914 Europe

5845 914.6'04'82
**Christopher, Peter.**
Images of Spain. Photographs by Peter Christopher; text by Mordecai Richler. Toronto: McClelland and Stewart, c1977. 191p. ill. ISBN 0-7710-1980-7 $27.50

1. Spain – Description and travel – 1951- – Views.

This handsome photographic study is most creditable in its own right, but it suffers badly from a distinctly jumbled, self-conscious, introductory text and poor organization of notes. Placement of captions at the end of each group of photographs greatly diminishes the effect of the complementary quotations and makes reference awkward. Theresa Crosgrey

5846 914.95'04'7
**MacEwen, Gwendolyn.**
Mermaids and Ikons: A Greek Summer. Toronto: House of Anansi Press, c1978. 110p. ISBN 0-88784-062-0 pa.: $5.95

1. Greece – Description and travel – 1951-
2. Greece – Social life and customs.

A record of the author's very personal reactions and intimate responses to the people, places, and events she encountered during a summer visit to Greece. Presented as a travel diary, it is fragmented and impressionistic, and documents the author's exploration of her own psyche more than her discoveries of Greece. Lucia Herwig

## 915 Asia

5847 915.5
**Beny, Roloff.**
Iran: Elements of Destiny. Designed and photographed by Roloff Beny; editorial direction by Shahrokh Amirarjomand. Toronto: McClelland and Stewart, c1978. 391p. ill., maps. Indexes. ISBN 0-7710-1161-X $50

1. Iran – Description and travel – Views.

A beautifully designed and lavishly illustrated companion volume to the author's *Persia: Bridge of Turquoise.* Colour plates and half tones and line drawings portray various facets of modern Iran. A handsome but expensive adornment for the coffee table.

5848 915'.69'404
**Harpur, Tom.**
The Road to Bethlehem: Two Thousand Years Later. Photographs by Dick Loek. Elgin, Ont.: David C. Cook Publishing, c1977. 95p. ill., map. ISBN 0-89191-098-0 $7.50

1. Christian pilgrims and pilgrimages – Palestine. 2. Palestine – Description and travel.

The author, religion editor of "The Toronto Star", and his wife Mary, walked the one hundred miles from Nazareth to Bethlehem in the footsteps of Joseph and Mary. The juxtaposition of present day reality with Luke's account in the Bible of the trek to Bethlehem, tells of a land which is timeless yet new, stark yet familiar and a part of the imaginative experience of all Christians. Readers of all ages will be fascinated by the pictures which accompany this excellent book. Ann Morrison

## 917.1 Canada - Description and travel

5849 917.1
**Armstrong, Audrey I.**
Sulphur & Molasses: Home Remedies and Other Echoes of the Canadian Past. Don Mills, Ont.: Musson, 1977. 96p. ill. ISBN 0-7737-1013-2 pa.: $5.95

1. Frontier and pioneer life – Canada.
2. Folk-lore – Canada. 3. Canada – Social life and customs.

The author of *Harness in the Parlour* transports readers into family and rural life in great-grandmother's day, when home-concocted remedies and strong linaments were used to treat everything from respiratory ailments to blood poisoning. A fragment of pioneer social history which is worth recording. Amusing anecdotes and appropriate illustrations. Public libraries.

5850 917.1
**Morse, Eric W.**
Fur Trade Canoe Routes of Canada: Then and Now. 2d ed. Toronto: University of Toronto Press, 1979. 136p. ill., maps. Bibliography: p. 111-113. Index. ISBN 0-8020-6384-5 pa.: $5

1. Fur trade – Canada. 2. Trade routes.

First edition listed *CS* no. 3485.

Revisions in this edition are limited to ten pages relating to the Great Dog and Rat Portages and to the Boundary Falls. An index has been added but the bibliography remains unchanged. The smaller paperback format results in slightly smaller illustrations. Minor revisions do not warrant replacement of the earlier edition.

5851 917.1
**Putnam, Donald Fulton.**
Canada: A Regional Analysis, by Donald Fulton Putnam and Robert G. Putnam. Maps by H. E. Mindak. Rev. metric ed. Don Mills, Ont.: J. M. Dent, 1979, c1970. 406p. ill., maps. Bibliographies and Index. ISBN 0-460-90392-6 $14.35

1. Canada – Description and travel.

A slightly enlarged and revised edition of an authoritative Canadian geography. Based upon recent field investigations it incorporates up-to-date information on some of the issues which predominated during the decade. Older publications have been deleted and new ones added to the bibliographies which follow each section. Recommended.

5852 917.1'0022'2

**Anderson, Allan.**

Greetings from Canada: An Album of Unique Canadian Postcards From the Edwardian Era, 1900-1916, by Allan Anderson and Betty Tomlinson. Toronto: Macmillan, c1978. 188p. ill., plates, ports. ISBN 0-7705-1736-6 bd.: $29.95
ISBN 0-7705-1721-8 pa.: $14.95

1. Postal cards – Canada. 2. Canada – Description and travel – 1900-1950 – Views.

A charming visual record of Canada and Canadians in the early twentieth century. Following an excellent introduction, some six hundred black and white and colour postcards representing all parts of Canada and all facets of life are grouped thematically. Social history at its best: informative, vivid, amusing. Delightful browsing for all ages.

5853 917.1'003

**Canada. Permanent Committee on Geographical Names.**

Gazetteer of Canada. Ottawa: Dept. of Energy, Mines and Resources, Surveys and Mapping Branch, 1976-1978. 2v Nova Scotia, 2d ed., 1977. ISBN 0-660-1674-5 pa.: $10 DSS cat. no. M86-14/1977 Yukon Territory, 4th ed., 1976. ISBN 0-660-00393-7 pa.: $2 IC cat. no. N86-21/76

1. Canada – Gazetteers.

Earlier editions of the Nova Scotia and Yukon Territories gazetteers and those for other provinces are listed in *CS* no. 3479.

The number of entries in each of the two new editions of the gazetteers has been substantially increased. Populated places, rivers, lakes, mountains, and other physical features have map locations. A key map and a glossary of generic terms is included. "Each part is kept up to date by cumulative supplements." -Canadiana.

5854 917.1'003

**Hamilton, William B.**

The Macmillan Book of Canadian Place Names. Toronto: Macmillan, c1978. 340p. ill. Bibliography: p. 333-340. ISBN 0-7705-1524-X $20

1. Names, Geographical – Canada.

An informative article on geographical names introduces a selection of twenty-five hundred place names from all Canadian provinces and the Territories. Arranged alphabetically within each province, a succinct note explains the significance of the names which were chosen on the basis of size, historical or human interest. Attractive format. A carefully researched, much-needed reference source.

5855 917.1'04

**MacLennan, Hugh.**

Seven Rivers of Canada: The Mackenzie, the St. Lawrence, the Ottawa, the Red, the Saskatchewan, the Fraser, the St. John. Toronto: Macmillan, 1977. 170p. maps. (Laurentian Library) ISBN 0-7705-1562-2 pa.: $4.95

1. Rivers – Canada. 2. Canada – Description and travel – 1950-

Clothbound listed in *CS* no. 3504. First published 1961.

5856 917.1'04'61

**Martin, Sandra,** ed.

Rupert Brooke in Canada, edited by Sandra Martin and Roger Hall. Toronto: PMA Books, 1978. 154p. ill., ports. ISBN 0-88778-184-5 $15.95

1. Brooke, Rupert, 1887-1915 – Journeys – Canada. 2. Canada – Description and travel – 1900-1950.

A collection of travel articles and letters written during Brooke's two-month visit to Canada in 1913. Originally published in "The Westminster Gazette", the articles provide illuminating impressions and witty views of Canadian cities, landscapes, and people. Sheila Latham

5857 917.1'04'644

**Nägele, Edmund.**

Canada. Introduction by Harry J. Boyle; produced by Ted Smart and David Gibbon. Burlington, Ont.: Locust House Press, 1978. 126p. ill. ISBN 0-920664-00-8 $12.95

1. Canada – Description and travel – 1950- – Views.

An oversize volume of beautiful, well-reproduced colour photographs. The pictures, sharp and clear, provide a good balance between urban and rural subjects, and present some interesting juxtapositions. However, many of the photographs are standards, and although all of Canada is covered, the Maritimes have received disproportionately little coverage. Lucia Herwig.

5858 917.1'04'8644

**Byers, A. R.,** ed.

Canadian Book of the Road. Montreal: Reader's Digest Association; Ottawa: Canadian Automobile Association, 1979. 404p. ill, maps. Index. ISBN 0-88850-080-7 $21.96

1. Automobiles – Road guides – Canada. 2. Canada – Description and travel – 1950- – Guide-books.

This artistically designed guidebook contains 180 detailed and keyed sectional maps surrounded by good colour photographs, line drawings and extensive notes on various aspects of each region. Major cities are dealt with separately. A detailed introduction, 6 indexed general maps, a fold-out symbol chart and an excellent index provide easy access. Theresa Crosgrey

5859 917.1'09'43

**Morse, Randy.**

The Mountains of Canada. Introduction by Andy Russell. Edmonton: Hurtig Publishers, c1978. 144p. ill. Bibliography: p. 143-144. ISBN 0-88830-160-X $29.95

1. Mountains – Canada. 2. Mountaineering – Canada. 3. Canada – Description and travel – 1950- – Views.

Quality photographs of seventy-three of Canada's most spectacular mountains. Morse, an experienced mountaineer, has skillfully combined factual information about each peak with pertinent quotations from literature and comments by climbers. For climbers and arm-chair explorers of scenic grandeur. A pleasingly designed book.

## 917.11 British Columbia

5860 917.11'04'2

**Baltzly, Benjamin.**

Benjamin Baltzly: Photographs & Journal of an Expedition Through British Columbia, 1871. Edited by Andrew Birrell. Toronto: Coach House Press, 1978. 159p. ill., map. Bibliography: p. 24. ISBN 0-88910-043-8 $24.50

1. British Columbia – Description and travel – To 1900. 2. British Columbia – Description and travel – Views.

One in a series of works on early Canadian photographers, this is a pleasing compilation of Baltzly's photographs of the interior of British Columbia in the nineteenth century. The photographs are clearly identified and are followed by excerpts from the photographer's journal which was published in the Montreal "Gazette" in 1872. A valuable volume and a handsome addition to any Canadiana collection. Theresa Crosgrey

5861 917.11'04'4

**Kunelius, Rick.**

Ski Trails in the Canadian Rockies. Banff, Alta.: Summerthought, c1977. 138p. ill., maps. Bibliography: p. 134. Index. ISBN 0-919934-06-4 pa.: $4.95

1. Cross-country skiing – Rocky Mountains, Canadian – Guide-books. 2. Cross-country skiing. 3. Rocky Mountains, Canadian – Description and travel – Guide-books.

The author, a park warden and ski guide, and expert in safety and rescue procedures, devotes the first third of this excellent handbook to a discussion of the purchase and preparation of equipment, safety and survival. What follows is a comprehensive guide to more than seventy trails, graded for difficulty, and supplemented by maps, photographs and checklists. Theresa Crosgrey

5862 917.11'04'4

**McDonald, Jim.**

Hotsprings of Western Canada: A Complete Guide, by Jim McDonald, Donna Pollock and Rob McDermot. Vancouver: Labrador Tea Company, 1978. 162p. diags., maps.

1. Springs – British Columbia. 2. Mineral water – British Columbia. 3. Sulphur springs. 4. British Columbia – Description and travel – Guide-books.

Well-researched and comprehensive geological, historic and scenic descriptions of western Canada's ninety-four hotsprings are presented in a discursive, anecdotal style. Division of the springs into eleven geographic areas, well-supplemented with hand drawn maps keyed to an introductory general map, makes reference clear and straightforward. Emphasis on access makes the guide particularly valuable for the hiker. Theresa Crosgrey

5863 917.11'04'4

**Patton, Brian.**

The Canadian Rockies Trail Guide: A Hiker's Manual to the National Parks, by Brian Patton and Bart Robinson. Rev. ed. Canmore, Alta.: Devil's Head Press, 1978. 266p. ill., maps. Bibliographical references and Index. ISBN 0-9690806-0-3 pa.: $5.95

1. Trails – Rocky Mountains, Canadian – Guide-books. 2. Hiking – Rocky Mountains, Canadian – Guide-books. 3. Rocky Mountains, Canadian – Description and travel – Guide-books.

A revised and largely rewritten version of the 1971 edition, reflecting the expansion and improvement of hiking facilities in the parks. One chapter is devoted to trails in each of the five Rocky Mountain National Parks, and a final one outlines more extended hikes. An attractive, well-organized and illustrated guide for the novice or experienced backpacker.

5864 917.11'04'4

**Wright, Richard.**

Canoe Routes: British Columbia, by Richard Wright and Rochelle Wright. Surrey, B.C.: Antonson Publishing, c1977. 176p. ill. Bibliography: p. 171-173. Index. ISBN 0-919900-20-8 pa.: $5.95

1. Canoes and canoeing – British Columbia. 2. British Columbia – Description and travel – 1950- – Guide-books.

A practical, detailed guide to canoe routes on one hundred rivers and lakes in seven regions of the province. Descriptions of the routes include the length, difficulty, possible hazards and a map. Useful for both the neophyte and the experienced paddler. By the same author *Canoe Routes: Yukon Territory*, 1977.

5865 917.11'3'00222

**Steltzer, Ulli.**

Coast of Many Faces, by Ulli Steltzer and Catherine Kerr. Vancouver: Douglas & McIntyre, 1979. 212p. ill. ISBN 0-88894-232-X $29.95

1. Pacific Coast (Canada) – Description and travel – Views.

More than two hundred black and white photographs provide an objective, episodic study of everyday life in the small, isolated coastal communities of British Columbia. Much of the complementary text consists of the simple, straightforward and often telling commentary of the residents. Popular appeal. Theresa Crosgrey

5866 917.11'33

**McDougall, Duncan.**

Vancouver. Photographs by Duncan McDougall; text by Peter Scholfield. 1st ed. West Vancouver, B.C.: Whitecap Books, c1978. 71p. ill. ISBN 0-92062-001-9 $6.95

1. Vancouver, B.C. – Description – Views.

This is a pictorial essay which highlights Vancouver today. The photographs are arresting and the colours vibrant as one would expect from this well-known Canadian photographer. The accompanying text sets the scene for the photographs giving a brief history of Vancouver and textual comment on the City, the North Shore, Richmond, Burnaby and New Westminster. Light reading, pleasant viewing should make this a popular work for libraries. Margot Hewings.

---

## 917.12 Northern Territories and Prairie Provinces

---

5867 917.1'23

**Wiebe, Rudy.**

Alberta, A Celebration. Photographs by Harry Savage. Edited by Tom Radford. Edmonton: Hurtig Publishers, 1979. 208p. ill. ISBN 0-88830-167-7 $29.95

1. Alberta – Description and travel – Views.

Two renowned Albertans, a creative writer and an artist have combined their talents to produce a narrative and pictorial salute to their province's past and present. Wiebe's fourteen pieces range from history to imaginative fiction; Savage's sensitive photographs focus on the land and the people. A handsome memento of Alberta's Diamond Jubilee. Pleasant, but expensive browsing.

5868 917.123'0222

**Simpkins, Bill.**

Chinook Country: Alberta South. Introduction by Grant MacEwan; foreword by Peter Lougheed. Toronto: Oxford University Press, 1979. 96p. ill. ISBN 0-19-540370-X $12.95

1. Alberta – Description and travel – Views.

Effective photographic composition and an eye for dramatic contrasts are used by the chief photographer for "The Calgary Herald" to illustrate the natural beauty and the diversity of life-styles in southern Alberta. Pleasant armchair exploration of a scenic part of western Canada.

5869 917.123'3'043
**Baird, David M.**
Banff National Park: How Nature Carved Its Splendour. Rev. ed. Edmonton: Hurtig Publishers; Parks Canada, Geological Survey of Canada, c1977. 235p. ill., maps, plates. Index. ISBN 0-88830-132-4 bd.: $9.95 ISBN 0-88830-133-2 pa.: $5.95

1. Banff National Park, Alta. – Guide-books.

This geological introduction to the park is primarily a traveller's guidebook. A general introductory description of the area is followed by a detailed roadlog accompanied by two keyed, fold-out maps which are somewhat awkward to use. Illustrations are varied, and profuse, but much is lost in the largely black and white photographs. Clear access is provided by an excellent cross-referenced index. Theresa Crosgrey

5870 917.123'3'043
**Baird, David M.**
Jasper National Park: Behind the Mountains and Glaciers. Rev. ed. Edmonton: Hurtig Publishers; Parks Canada, Geological Survey of Canada, c1977. 160p. ill., map, plates. Index. ISBN 0-88830-130-8 bd.: $9.95 ISBN 0-88830-131-6 pa.: $5.95

1. Jasper National Park, Alta. – Guide-books.

This is another in the series of geological travel guides to Canada's national parks written by professional geologist Dr. D. M. Baird. Again, a general introduction to the geological history and composition of the area prefaces a detailed roadlog keyed to fold-out maps. Well-illustrated (although more photographs should be in colour) and indexed, it is most useful as a traveller's handbook. Theresa Crosgrey

5871 917.127'4
**Paskievich, John.**
A Place Not Our Own: North End Winnipeg. Foreword by Gregory Grace. Winnipeg: Queenston House, c1978. 80p. ill. ISBN 0-919866-42-5 pa.: $12.95

1. Photography, Artistic. 2. Winnipeg, Man. – Description – Views.

A sympathetic photodocumentary of the people who live in north Winnipeg, the area of the city which is home to the poor and displaced. Although the pictures portray mainly older people, immigrants, Indians and winos engaged in the daily round of living, they express emotions and attitudes that are universal. Lucia Herwig

## 917.13 Ontario

5872 917.13
**Mika, Nick,** comp.
Encyclopedia of Ontario, compiled by Nick Mika and Helma Mika. Belleville, Ont.: Mika Publishing, c1974- v ill. Indexes. ISBN 0-919303-14-5 $25

1. Ontario – Dictionaries and encyclopedias.

Contents: vol. 2. Places in Ontario, Their Name Origins and History: Part I, A – E. 1977. Volume 1 *Historic Sites of Ontario,* was listed in *CS* no. 3604.

This is the first of a three-part work, the second and third parts are in preparation. Five thousand place names of Ontario are arranged alphabetically, with a succinct paragraph providing geographic location, topographical features, and a summary of the settlement history and population growth. Sketch maps, photographs, and an index add to the book's usefulness.

5873 917.13'51'044
**Walker, Susan.**
Exploring Niagara-on-the-Lake and the Niagara Peninsula, by Susan Walker and Dori Herod. Toronto: Greey de Pencier, 1977. 127p. ill., maps. ISBN 0-919872-30-1 pa.: $3.50

1. Niagara-on-the-Lake, Ont. – Description – Guide-books. 2. Niagara Peninsula, Ont. – Description and travel – Guide-books.

The authors, residents of the Niagara area, provide a very readable and comprehensive study of the town. It is introduced by a brief historical sketch and includes a short description of the surrounding area. Detailed, keyed maps, a directory and numerous black and white photographs enhance the descriptive tours of architectural and historic sites, shops, restaurants and the theatres. Theresa Crosgrey

5874 917.13'541
**Filey, Mike.**
Toronto City Life: Old & New. Introduction by David Crombie. Don Mills, Ont.: Nelson, Foster & Scott, 1979. 82p. ill. Bibliography: p. 82. ISBN 0-919324-40-1 bd.: $10.95 ISBN 0-919324-41-X pa.: $6.95

1. Toronto, Ont. – Description – Views.

Another Filey collection of photographs, this time contrasting buildings and locales as they were then and are now. The photographs are accompanied by interesting vignettes of Toronto's past. Lacks an index for ready reference but does afford enjoyable, instructive browsing. Lucia Herwig

5875 917.13'541
**Kilbourn, William.**
Toronto in Words and Pictures, by William Kilbourn and Rudi Christl. Toronto: McClelland and Stewart, c1977. 192p. ill., map. ISBN 0-7710-1022-0 $27.50

1. Toronto, Ont. – Description – Views.

A verbal and visual celebration of Toronto's diversity and dynamism, its physical environment, its buildings, its neighbourhoods, and its peoples. Christl's excellent full-page photographs are interspersed with Kilbourn's literate essays on the city, but narrative and illustrations are not interrelated. A large, well-designed book for leisure browsing.

5876 917.13'84'044
**Kong, Colleen Anderson.**
Ottawa Journal Presents Canada's Capital Inside Out. Ottawa: Waxwing Productions, 1978. 232p. ill., maps. ISBN 0-919988-04-0 pa.: $3.75

1. National Capital Region (Canada) – Description and travel.

Besides the basic guidebook information concerning where to stay, eat, shop and be entertained, this comprehensive look at Ottawa includes a brief historical introduction, directory information, walks and tours, sports and outdoor activities and specialty shopping suggestions. Extremely detailed and well-organized, its maps are useful but illustrations are few and quite smudged. Theresa Crosgrey

## 917.14 Quebec

5877 917.14'27
**Drummond, Michael.**
Montreal and Its Countryside. Photographs by Michael Drummond; introduction by Luc D'Iberville-Moreau. Toronto: Oxford University Press, 1979. 88p. ill. ISBN 0-19-540308-8 $12.95

1. Montreal, Que. – Description – Views. 2. Montreal, Que. (Administrative region) – Description and travel – Views.

Portraits, landscapes and cityscapes create an attractive photographic study of the distinctive look of Montreal and its surrounding countryside which adds so much to the character of the city. The introductory text is adequate but the work suffers from poor organization which makes access awkward. Theresa Crosgrey

## 917.15 New Brunswick

5878 917.15
**Hines, Sherman.**
Atlantic Canada. Foreword by Harry Bruce. Toronto: Clarke, Irwin, c1979. 150p. ill. ISBN 0-7720-1278-4 $24.95

1. Atlantic Provinces – Description and travel – Views.

145 superb colour photographs capture the variety and beauty of Canada's four eastern provinces. Text is limited to identifying captions and an introduction by Harry Bruce. A handsome pictorial essay by an established Nova Scotia photographer. Recommended for arm-chair enjoyment.

5879 917.15
**Trueman, Stuart.**
Tall Tales and True Tales from Down East: Eerie Experiences, Heroic Exploits, Extraordinary Personalities, Ancient Legends and Folklore from New Brunswick and Elsewhere in the Maritimes. Toronto: McClelland and Stewart, 1979. 171p. ISBN 0-7710-8598-2 $12.95

1. New Brunswick – Miscellanea. 2. Maritime Provinces – Miscellanea.

A potpourri of little-known stories from New Brunswick and the other Atlantic provinces beguile readers with accounts of ghosts and ghost ships, sea monsters, smuggling, legendary characters, Indian battles, etc. Entertaining bedside reading.

5880 917.15
**Vroom, Richard.**
Old New Brunswick: A Victorian Portrait. Photographs selected by Richard Vroom; introduction by Arthur Doyle. Toronto: Oxford University Press, 1978. 123p. ill. ISBN 0-19-540293-6 $16.95

1. New Brunswick – Description and travel – 1850-1900 – Views.

This splendid collection of 124 photographs taken in New Brunswick between 1860 and 1918 provides a diverse study of the many aspects of both urban and rural life of the period. Most photographs are accompanied by identification and explanation. The introductory text provides a brief overview of early photography and of the history and geography of New Brunswick in the Victorian era. Theresa Crosgrey

5881 917.15'04'4
**Porteous, John.**
New Brunswick Images. Images Nouveau-Brunswick. Translated by Paula J. O. Read. Fredericton, N.B.: Brunswick Press, 1977. 78p. ill. ISBN 0-88790-094-1 $14.95

1. New Brunswick – Description and travel – 1950- – Views.

Arranged by geographic area, this photographic study offers a general introduction to New Brunswick's character and diversity. The bilingual text accompanying the photographs provides basic description and observation. Successfully creating an overall sense of the province, this work is an ideal guide for the prospective tourist or the young geography student. Theresa Crosgrey

5882 917.15'04'4
**Thompson, Colleen.**
New Brunswick Inside Out: The Only Complete Guide to Canada's Picture Province. Ottawa: Waxwing Productions, c1977. 226p. maps. ISBN 0-919988-02-4 pa.: $3.95

1. New Brunswick – Description and travel – 1950- – Guide-books.

A compact, information-filled guide to each of eight areas of the province offers suggestions for finding accommodation, good food, and for side-trips to some of New Brunswick's scenic areas. A map for each area, and for walking tours, encourages the tourist to explore on his own.

5883 917.15'31
**Majka, Mary.**
Fundy National Park. Illustrated by Joan Gregory and Helen Maffei. Fredericton, N.B.: Brunswick Press, c1977. 94p. ill., maps. ISBN 0-88790-089-5 pa.: $4.75

1. Fundy National Park, N.B.

An interesting combination of historical background, natural history, geology, folklore, and descriptions of recreational possibilities invite the reader to explore and enjoy the park. The attractive book is illustrated with photographs, sketch maps and line drawings. For the tourist or arm-chair traveller.

## 917.16 Nova Scotia

5884 917.16
**Clarke, Wayne.**
Cruising from Nova Scotia: From Yarmouth to Canso, by Wayne Clarke, Judith Penner and George Rogers. Toronto: Greey de Pencier, c1979. 240p. ill., maps. Index. ISBN 0-919872-37-9 $14.95

1. Boats and boating – Nova Scotia – Guide-books. 2. Nova Scotia – Description and travel – 1950- – Guide-books.

Designed to guide the sailor cruising between Yarmouth and Canso. Fun to read, the book covers briefly the history of Nova Scotia. A long chapter, "Anchorages", covers the services available and the chart number for each area. Includes information on weather patterns, birds, animals, fish and fishing, and cooking your catch. There are twenty aerial photographs of specific harbour approaches and sketch maps of areas confusing to navigate. Barbara Schon

5885 917.16'04'2
**Whitelaw, Marjory,** ed.
The Dalhousie Journals. Ottawa: Oberon Press, c1978. 212p. ill., map, plates, port. ISBN 0-88750-290-3 $17.50

1. Dalhousie, George Ramsay, 9th Earl of, 1770-1838. 2. Lieutenant-governors – Nova Scotia – Biography. 3. Nova Scotia – Description and travel – 1800-1850. 4. Nova Scotia – Politics and government – 19th century. 5. Canada – Description and travel – 1800-1850.

Early nineteenth century Nova Scotia observed by the shrewd Scot who was Lieutenant Governor from 1816 to 1820. Dalhousie's journal entries make trenchant comments on education, agriculture, politics and social life; the editor's introduction and notes provide the historical context and clarify terse references. Clear, forceful prose. All libraries.

5886 917.16'23
**Crooker, William S.**
The Oak Island Quest. Hantsport, N.S.: Lancelot Press, 1978. 194p. ill., diagrs., maps. Bibliography: p. 192-194. ISBN 0-88999-078-6 pa.: $4.95

1. Oak Island treasure site, Nova Scotia.

For almost two hundred years a tiny island off the southern coast of Nova Scotia has successfully repulsed efforts to locate its legendary buried treasure. In simple, non-technical language, Crooker reviews some of the theories about the mystery of Oak Island and adds his own speculations. Leisure reading. Schools and public libraries.

5887 917.16'23
**O'Connor, D'Arcy.**
The Money Pit: The Story of Oak Island and the World's Greatest Treasure. Toronto: Longman, c1978. 256p. ill., plates. Bibliography: p. 247-249. Index. ISBN 0-69810-877-9 $11.75

1. Oak Island treasure site, Nova Scotia – History.

The history, personalities, theories and disasters surrounding the baffling and intricate riddle of Oak Island's buried treasure and those who left it are traced in exacting detail in this fast-moving account of a real-life mystery. The narrative is complemented by maps, illustrations of various excavation attempts, photographs and an inclusive index and bibliography. Theresa Crosgrey

5888 917.16'9
**Fitzgerald, Owen.**
Cape Breton. Photographs by Owen Fitzgerald; introduction by Robert J. Morgan. Toronto: Oxford University Press, 1978. 94p. ill. ISBN 0-19-540295-2 $9.95

1. Cape Breton Island, N.S. – Description and travel – Views.

Fitzgerald's eighty-eight photographs have a somewhat 'homey' quality to them, both in subject matter and in quality of reproduction. A native of Cape Breton, he chronicles the daily round of life on his island, in all its diversity, and includes fifteen shots of historic Louisbourg. Lucia Herwig

5889 917.16'9
**Street, David.**
The Cabot Trail. Toronto: Gage Publishing, c1979. 95p. ill. Index. ISBN 0-7715-9450-X bd.: $19.95 ISBN 0-7715-9451-8 pa.: $12.95

1. Cabot Trail, N.S. – Description and travel – Views. 2. Cape Breton Island, N.S. – Description and travel – Views.

A pleasing visual and narrative profile of one of Canada's most beautiful coastal drives. Interviews with sturdy Cape Bretoners who people villages and farms along the Trail have been blended with Street's descriptive notes and superb photographs to capture the essence of the rugged area. For browsing enjoyment.

5890 917.17
**Barrett, Wayne.**
Prince Edward Island. Photographs by Wayne Barrett and Edith Robinson. Toronto: Oxford University Press, 1977. 92p. ill. ISBN 0-19-540276-6 $9.95

1. Prince Edward Island – Description and travel – Views.

Two photographers have assembled eighty-eight colour photographs of Prince Edward Island that portray the varied richness of Canada's province in miniature. Historic Charlottetown, the farming community and the ever-present sea are treated with sensitivity. Some technical problems apparently in the printing of the photographs are a minor irritant in an otherwise lovely collection of photographs. Barbara Schon

## 917.18 Newfoundland

5891 917.18
**Hansen, Ben.**
Newfoundland Portfolio. St. John's, Nfld.: Breakwater Books, c1977. 111p. ill. Index. ISBN 0-919948-40-5 $17.95

1. Newfoundland – Description and travel – Views.

A collection of photographs of Newfoundland presented without comment. Hansen is a competent photographer, if at times somewhat "arty". Most of the photographs present Newfoundland in all its stark ruggedness and beauty with an emphasis on the sea. Of the ninety-six photographs the most pleasing are the sixteen in colour. Barbara Schon

## 917.19 The Yukon and the Arctic

5892 917.19'5
**Buerschaper, P.**
Arctic Journey: Paintings, Sketches, and Reminiscences of a Vanishing World. Toronto: Pagurian Press, c1977. 126p. ill., map. ISBN 0-88932-059-4 $14.95

1. Zoology – Northwest Territories – Franklin. 2. Franklin, N.W.T. – Description and travel.

A short diary of the three weeks which the author, a wildlife artist, spent on Ellesmere and Bathurst Islands, N.W.T., in June, 1976. The birds and animals have been captured in both delicate line drawings and full-colour reproductions. A book for browsing. Lucia Herwig

5893 917.98'04
**The Milepost: The All-the-North Travel Guide.**
Edmonton: Hurtig Publishers, 1978. 498p. ill., maps. Index. ISBN 0-88240-102-5 pa.: $6.95

1. Alaska – Description and travel – Guidebooks. 2. Yukon Territory – Description and travel – Guide-books. 3. British Columbia – Description and travel – Guide-books. 4. Northwest, Canadian – Description and travel – Guide-books.

An essential guide for the traveller to the Canadian Northwest and Alaska, this fully indexed and illustrated manual contains more than seventy maps and provides mile by mile information ranging from the general to the specific. It appears that nothing is omitted from this best-selling annual. Theresa Crosgrey

## 919.8 Polar voyages

5894 919.8
**Bruemmer, Fred.**
Children of the North. Montreal: Optimum Publishing, 1979. 159p. ill. Bibliography: p. 154-157. ISBN 0-88890-095-3 $25

1. Inuit – Arctic regions – Children.
2. Inuit – Arctic regions – Social life and customs.

The outstanding photo-journalist of Canada's North pays fitting tribute to children in the International Year of the Child. He portrays not only Eskimo children but Lapp children as well. Outstanding illustrations, some coloured. For all libraries.

5895 919.8'04
**Rasky, Frank.**
North Pole or Bust. Toronto: McGraw-Hill Ryerson, 1977. 415p. ill., maps, ports. Index. ISBN 0-07-082548-3 $17.95

1. Explorers – Arctic regions. 2. Arctic regions.

A sequel to *The Polar Voyages: Explorers of the North*. Listed in CS no. 3676.

Graphic accounts of the race to the North Pole and the quest for the Northwest Passage which engaged British, American and Scandinavian explorers in the nineteenth and early twentieth centuries. Archival illustrations and excerpts from primary records add credence to the personalized tales of hardship, endurance and courage. Recommended for public and school libraries.

## 920 Biographical reference works

5896 920.
**The Canadian Who's Who.**
Edited by Kieran Simpson. Toronto: University of Toronto Press, 1979. 14th ed. 1089p. ISBN 0-8020-4553-3 $75

1. Canada – Biography.

Thirteenth edition listed in CS no. 3678.

Concise biographical data provided for approximately seven thousand persons selected from a variety of occupational spheres. A list of abbreviations is appended. An essential reference source for all libraries.

5897 920.
**Gould, Ed.**
Ralph Edwards: The Complete Biography of the Crusoe of Lonesome Lake. North Vancouver, B.C.: Hancock House, 1978. 256p. ill. ISBN 0-919654-74-6 $10.95

1. Edwards, Ralph A., d. 1977. 2. Frontier and pioneer life – British Columbia.

Ralph Edwards is the stuff from which heroes are made. His battles against the elements, some humourous, most frightening, as he tried to establish a homestead in the British Columbia wilderness make fascinating reading. As if the battle to survive was not enough, Edwards devoted himself to saving the trumpeter swan from extinction. Highly recommended. Paula de Ronde

5898 920.
**Halpenny, Francess G.,** ed.
Dictionary of Canadian Biography. Toronto: University of Toronto Press, 1966- (in progress). Bibliographies and Indexes. ISBN 0-8020-3351-2 $25

1. Canada – Biography – Dictionaries.

Vol. IV. 1771-1800. c1979. Volumes I, II, III, IX and X listed *CS* no. 3681.

Slightly more than five hundred biographies, ranging in length from six hundred to ten thousand words, a glossary of native peoples, a general bibliography, and a nominal index with cross references to the previously published volumes are contained in this last volume covering the eighteenth century. Two essays provide background reading for some of the major issues of the period.

5899 920.
**MacDonald, Colin S.,** comp.
A Dictionary of Canadian Artists. Ottawa: Canadian Paperback, 1967- (in progress). Bibliographies. ISBN 0-919554-11-3 $9 vol. 1. 3d ed. ISBN 0-919554-04-0 $10 vol. 2. 3d ed. ISBN 0-919554-05-9 $11 vol. 3. 3d rev. ed. ISBN 0-919554-12-1 $13 vol. 4. 2d ed. ISBN 0-919554-13-X $10 vol. 5

1. Artists, Canadian – Dictionaries.

Contents: vol. 1. A-F. 3d ed. 1977. vol. 2. G-Jackson. 3d ed. 1979. vol. 3. Jacobi-Lismer. 3d rev. ed. 1978. vol. 4. Little-Myles. 2d ed. 1978. vol. 5. Nadeau-Perrigard. 1978. Previous editions of volumes 1 to 4 listed *CS* no. 3682.

"Biographical work of living and dead painters, engravers, sculptors, carvers, potters and ceramists." -Publisher's note.

## 920.07 Collective biography

5900 920'.071
**Berton, Pierre.**
The Dionne Years: A Thirties Melodrama. Toronto: McClelland and Stewart; McClelland and Stewart-Bantam, c1977. 232p. ill., maps, ports. Bibliography: p. 221-224. Index. ISBN 0-7710-1215-2 bd.: $12.50 ISBN 0-7704-1540-7 pa.: $2.75

1. Dionne quintuplets.

The birth of identical quintuplets in a small northern Ontario community in 1934 created an unprecedented furor. Berton examines the exploitation of the famous children by commercial interests, the media and governments, and the ensuing rift in the Dionne family. Eyewitness accounts, contemporary records and photographs coupled with a brisk, journalistic style create a sense of immediacy. Popular reading.

5901 920'.07'1
**Newman, Peter C.**
Bronfman Dynasty: The Rothschilds of the New World. Toronto: McClelland and Stewart, 1978. 318p. diagrs., geneal. table, map. Bibliographical references and Index. ISBN 0-7710-6758-5 $17.95

1. Bronfman family. 2. Bronfman, Samuel, 1891-1971. 3. Distilling industries – Canada – Biography. 4. Businessmen – Canada – Biography.

The Editor-in-Chief of Maclean's tells the tale of the building of Canada's most powerful business empire in one generation. Not an authorized version, it depends heavily on reminiscences of those who knew the Bronfmans from the early fish peddling days, the rumrunning during the prohibition era, to the present apex of corporate power. Less detail and more analysis would make it a better book; but nevertheless it belongs in most Canadian collections.

5902 920'.071
**Taylor, Charles.**
Six Journeys: A Canadian Pattern: Brigadier James Sutherland Brown, Bishop William White, James Houston, Herbert Norman, Emily Carr, Scott Symons. Toronto: House of Anansi Press, 1977. 254p. plates, ports. Bibliography: p. 245-254. ISBN 0-88784-057-4 bd.: $14 ISBN 0-88784-056-6 pa.: $7.95

1. Canada – Biography.

The author has selected six Canadians who he believes lived their lives against the Canadian grain, finding support and sustenance for their spirit in other older traditions. Catharine MacKenzie

5903 920.07'1
**Twentieth Century Children's Writers.**
Edited by Daniel L. Kirkpatrick. Preface by Naomi Lewis. Toronto: Macmillan, 1978. 1507p. ISBN 0-312-824-130 $50

1. Children's literature – Bio-bibliography.
2. Children's literature – Biography.

A bio-bibliography of over six hundred English language children's writers. For each a short biographical sketch, a chronological listing of works, a critical essay. Canadian content consists of thirty-one authors and twelve contributors of critical essays. Diane Henderson

5904 920'.071
**Woodcock, George.**
Faces from History: Canadian Profiles & Portraits. Edmonton: Hurtig Publishers, c1978. 254p. ports. Index. ISBN 0-88830-151-0 $29.95

1. Canada – Biography. 2. Canada – Biography – Portraits.

Full-page black and white photographs and pithy biographical sketches of 120 men and women who have made a contribution to Canadian life in the period from the early 1850's to the early 1940's. Clustered around historical and regional themes, the portraits include a variety of personalities from explorers and writers to politicians and businessmen. Interesting browsing.

5905 920'.0716
**Marble, Allan Everett.**
Nova Scotians at Home and Abroad: Including Biographical Sketches of Over Six Hundred Native Born Nova Scotians. Hantsport, N.S.: Lancelot Press, 1977. 431p. graph, map, ports. Bibliography: p. 414-431. ISBN 0-88999-074-3 pa.: $12

1. Nova Scotia – Biography.

Selected according to carefully delineated criteria, more than six hundred Nova Scotians who have achieved success are included in this alphabetically arranged biographical dictionary. Photographs, individual bibliographies, a list of abbreviations and an extensive general bibliography add to the book's usefulness. Of interst to reference libraries in all parts of Canada.

## 921 Biographies of individuals

5906 921.
**Allen, Robert Thomas.**
My Childhood and Yours: Happy Memories of Growing Up. Toronto: Macmillan, 1977. 167p. ISBN 0-7705-1576-2 $9.95

1. Humorists, Canadian – Biography.
2. Children – Anecdotes, facetiae, satire.

A charming, nostalgic recapturing of boyhood in a stable middle-class family in a Toronto neighborhood in the twenties. As season follows season homely memories of places and events, sights and tantalizing smells are evoked. A pleasant escape from the troubled eighties. General recreational reading.

5907 921.
**Baker, William M.**
Timothy Warren Anglin, 1822-96: Irish Catholic Canadian. Toronto: University of Toronto Press, c1977. 336p. ill., facsims., maps, plates, ports. Bibliographical references and Index. ISBN 0-8020-5368-8 $22.50

1. Anglin, Timothy Warren, 1822-1896.
2. Statesmen – Canada – Biography.
3. Canada – Politics and government – 19th century.

A solid, fair-minded study of the influential Catholic journalist-politician and his role in Canadian politics in the second half of the nineteenth century. Based upon extensive research Baker's well-documented biography concentrates on Anglin's public life. For readers who enjoy insights into Canada's political and social history.

5908 921.
**Bearden, Jim.**
Shadd: The Life and Times of Mary Shadd Cary, by Jim Bearden and Linda Jean Butler. Toronto: NC Press, 1977. 233p. ill., ports. Bibliography: p. 250-254. Index.
ISBN 0-919600-73-5 bd.: $13
ISBN 0-919600-74-3 pa.: $5.95

1. Cary, Mary Shadd, 1823-1893. 2. Abolitionists – Canada – Biography.
3. Women, Black – Canada – Biography.
4. Educators – Canada – Biography.

The story of a black woman who fought for women's rights and the abolition of slavery in nineteenth century Canada West. The newspaper she founded in the 1850's served the Underground Railroad, assisting fugitive slaves from the United States. Old photographs, illustrations, letters, etc., complement the lively narrative. Janice Zlatarits

5909 921.
**Beaulieu, Paul,** ed.
Ed Schreyer, A Social Democrat in Power: Selected Speeches, Addresses, and Interviews of Premier Schreyer of Manitoba, 1969-1977. Winnipeg: Queenston House, 1977. 247p. ill., plates, ports.
ISBN 0-919866-23-9 pa.: $2.25

1. Socialism in Manitoba. 2. Manitoba – Politics and government – 1958- 3. Schreyer, Edward, 1935-

A selection of speeches and interviews given during Schreyer's tenure as Premier of Manitoba reveal his political philosophy as a social democrat, and specific stances regarding particular issues. For political science collections in college and public libraries. Ethel Kellen

5910 921.
**Bliss, Michael.**
A Canadian Millionaire: The Life and Business Times of Sir Joseph Flavelle, bart., 1858-1939. Toronto: Macmillan, c1978. 562p. ill., plates, ports. Bibliographical references and Index. ISBN 0-7705-1657-2 $17.95

1. Flavelle, Joseph Wesley, Sir, bart., 1858-1939. 2. Businessmen – Canada – Biography.

City of Toronto Book Award.

The rags-to-riches story of the business genius whose commercial enterprises and philanthropies reached deeply into Canadian life. Excerpts from family and business records and facile prose create Flavelle's several worlds: family, business, church, and public service. A major study enhanced by extensive research and careful documentation. Will interest businessmen, historians and the general reader.

5911 921.
**Bothwell, Robert.**
C. D. Howe, A Biography, by Robert Bothwell and William Kilbourn. Toronto: McClelland and Stewart, 1979. 397p. Index. ISBN 0-7710-4537-9 $19.95

1. Howe, Clarence Decatur, 1886-1960.
2. Statesmen – Canada – Biography.
3. Civil engineers – Canada – Biography.

A commissioned biography of the controversial entrepreneur who used the authority of key cabinet posts to shape Canada's industrial development during the war and post-war years. The briskly written, uncritical portrait is supplemented by copious chapter notes and footnotes and official photographs. Political science collections in senior secondary, college and public libraries.

5912 921.
**Bothwell, Robert.**
Pearson: His Life and World. Toronto: McGraw-Hill Ryerson, c1978. 223p. ill., ports. Bibliography: p. 219-220. Index. (Prime Ministers of Canada) ISBN 0-07-082305-7 $14.95

1. Pearson, Lester B., 1897-1972. 2. Prime ministers – Canada – Biography. 3. Canada – Politics and government – 1963-

A somewhat cursory review of Pearson's life with emphasis on the period 1945 to 1968 in the Ottawa political arena. Little analysis or interpretation; the facade of the affable man in the bow tie is not penetrated. Profusely illustrated popular political biography in capsule form. Junior High to Adult.

5913 921.
**Camp, Dalton.**
Gentlemen, Players and Politicians. Ottawa: Deneau and Greenberg, 1979, c1970. 346p. Index. ISBN 0-88879-013-9 pa.: $7.95

1. Progressive Conservative Party (Canada).
2. Canada – Politics and government – 1935-1957.

Clothbound listed in CS no. 3740.

5914 921.
**Campbell, Maria.**
Halfbreed. Toronto: McClelland and Stewart-Bantam, 1979, c1973. 184p. (Seal Books) ISBN 0-7704-1537-7 pa.: $1.95

1. Métis – The West, Canadian – Biography.

Clothbound listed in CS no. 3741.

5915 921.
**Carpenter, Jock.**
Fifty Dollar Bride: Marie Rose Smith, A Chronicle of Métis Life in the 19th Century. Sidney, B.C,: Gray's Publishing, 1977. 160p. ill., geneal. table, plates, ports. Bibliographical references. ISBN 0-88826-070-9 pa.: $6.95

1. Smith, Marie Rose, 1861-1960. 2. Métis – Canada – Biography.

Although ostensibly a biography of Marie Rose Smith, *Fifty Dollar Bride* is a well-researched portrayal of Métis life in Canada. The indomitable spirit of Marie epitomized the strength of the men and women who were the pioneers of this nation. Carpenter brings history to life in this vivid biography of her grandmother. Paula de Ronde

5916 921.
**Clippingdale, Richard.**
Laurier, His Life and World. Toronto: McGraw-Hill Ryerson, c1979. 224p. ill. Bibliographical references and Index. (Prime Ministers of Canada) ISBN 0-07-082302-2 $17.95

1. Laurier, Wilfrid, Sir, 1841-1919. 2. Prime ministers – Canada – Biography. 3. Canada – Politics and government – 1896-1911.

An associate professor of history has written this brief pictorial biography that analyzes the important aspects of Laurier's career as Prime Minister and emphasizes his interaction with turn-of-the-century Canada. Satisfactorily documented, objectively critical and informative, and useful to the student and general reader. Ille-Mai Gerdels

5917 921.
**Cole, Jean Murray.**
Exile in the Wilderness: The Biography of Chief Factor Archibald McDonald, 1790-1853. Toronto: Burns and MacEachern, 1979. 240p. Bibliography. Index. ISBN 0-88768-084-4 $14.95

1. McDonald, Archibald, 1790-1853.
2. Hudson's Bay Company – Biography.
3. Fur traders – Canada – Biography.
4. The West, Canadian – Biography.

The author, one of McDonald's descendants, has relied heavily on his letters, journals and reports to record his private life and his role in the history of the Red River Settlement and the Pacific Northwest. A readable, thoroughly documented biography that contributes to the literature of the fur trade. Ille-Mai Gerdels

5918 921.
**Coulter, John.**
Prelude to a Marriage: Letters & Diaries of John Coulter & Olive Clare Primrose. Ottawa: Oberon Press, c1979. 145p.
ISBN 0-88750-293-8 bd.: $15
ISBN 0-88750-294-6 pa.: $6.95

1. Coulter, John, 1888- – Correspondence. 2. Coulter, John, 1888- – Biography – Marriage. 3. Primrose, Olive Clare. 4. Dramatists, Canadian (English) – 20th century – Biography.

Fragments of diaries, journals, and letters exchanged between the Irish playwright and a young Canadian during a prolonged pre-marital separation, are skillfully interwoven by narrative. The vicissitudes of financial insecurity, ill-health and emotional stress which marred the deepening relationship are recreated vividly. A poignant and charming cameo of the thirties. Recommended.

5919 921.
**Dempsey, Hugh A.**
Charcoal's World. Saskatoon: Western Producer Prairie Books, c1978. 178p. ill., maps, ports. Bibliography: p. 171-173. Index. ISBN 0-88833-003-0 bd.: $10.95 pa.: $2.25

1. Charcoal (Kainah Indian) – 1856-1896. 2. Kainah Indians – Biography. 3. Indians of North America – Alberta – Biography.

Archives, public records and interviews document the clash between the legendary Blood Indian and the white man in the 1890's. Writing from Charcoal's point of view, insights are given into Indian values and culture. A swift-paced, readable biography supported by contemporary photographs, maps and chapter notes. Students and general readers.

5920 921.
**Dempsey, Lotta.**
No Life for a Lady. Markham, Ont.: PaperJacks, 1977. 207p. ill., plates, ports. ISBN 0-7701-0018-X pa.: $1.95

1. Journalists – Canada – Biography.

Clothbound listed in *CS* no. 3764.

5921 921.
**Desbarats, Peter.**
René: A Canadian in Search of a Country. Newly rev. and updated. Toronto: McClelland and Stewart-Bantam, 1977. 296p. (Seal Books) Index. ISBN 0-7704-1526-1 pa.: $1.95

1. Lévesque, René, 1922- 2. Quebec (Province) – Politics and government – 1960-

Clothbound edition listed *CS* no. 3765.

5922 921.
**Diefenbaker, John G.**
One Canada: Memoirs of the Right Honourable John G. Diefenbaker. Toronto: Macmillan; Scarborough, Ont.: Macmillan-NAL Publishing, 1978, c1975. v ill., ports. Indexes. ISBN 0-7705-1569-X $15.95

1. Prime ministers – Canada – Biography. 2. Canada – Politics and government – 20th century.

Contents: The Tumultuous Years, 1962-1967. c1977. Previous volumes listed in *CS* no. 3772.

Five contentious years in Canadian political history are described by the former Prime Minister who was at the eye of the storm. The viewpoint is not unbiased.

5923 921.
**Diubaldo, Richard.**
Stefansson and the Canadian Arctic. Montreal: McGill-Queen's University Press, c1978. 274p. ill., maps, plates, ports. Bibliography: p. 255-270. Index.
ISBN 0-7735-0324-2 $18.95

1. Stefansson, Vilhjalmur, 1879-1962. 2. Arctic regions – Canadian exploration.

A scholarly and fully documented reassessment of Canada's foremost Arctic explorer and pioneer ethnologist in terms of both his achievement in and contribution to Arctic development. His shortcomings as a temperamental and politically naive administrator, whose inability to deal with governmental bureaucracy and business intricacies brought about his own fall from public favour, are noted. Frieda Ling

5924 921.
**Doyle, James.**
Annie Howells and Achille Fréchette. Toronto: University of Toronto Press, c1979. 131p. ill., plates, ports. Bibliography: p. 121-124. Index. ISBN 0-8020-5450-1 $10

1. Fréchette, Annie Howells, 1844-1938 – Biography. 2. Fréchette, Achille, 1847-1927 – Biography. 3. Authors, Canadian (English) – 19th century – Biography. 4. Translators – Canada – Biography.

In 1877 a prominent American girl, Annie Howells, marries a French-Canadian civil servant. They are both aspiring writers and both have very good political and social connections. Despite this auspicious beginning, James Doyle's biography has an unfinished feeling, no doubt due to the lack of material available on his subjects. A specialized work which could be of interest to serious students of Canadian literature. Paula de Ronde

5925 921.
**Edmonstone, Wayne E.**
Nathan Cohen: The Making of a Critic. Toronto: Lester and Orpen, c1977. 286p. ill., plates, ports. Bibliography: p. 265-268. Index. ISBN 0-919630-94-4 $12.95

1. Cohen, Nathan, 1923-1971. 2. Dramatic criticism – Canada.

This biography of Canada's most important dramatic critic describes Cohen's life from 1923-1971 mainly from Cohen's papers in the National Archives and the published reactions of his critics. Hilary Elliott

5926 921.
**English, John.**
Borden: His Life and World. Toronto: McGraw-Hill Ryerson, 1977. 223p. ill., ports. Bibliography: p. 217-219. Index. (Prime Ministers of Canada) ISBN 0-07-082303-0 $14.95

1. Borden, Robert Laird, Sir, 1854-1937.
2. Prime ministers – Canada – Biography.
3. Canada – Politics and government – 1911-1921.

This political biography of Borden serves as a unifying element underlying a general yet detailed survey of the social, political and economic realities of Canada's first two decades in the twentieth century. Numerous pictures, large print and simplified text make this a good choice for young people's collections. Ethel Kellen

5927 921.
**English, John,** ed.
Mackenzie King: Widening the Debate, edited by John English and J. O. Stubbs. Toronto: Macmillan, c1977. 253p. ISBN 0-7705-1529-0 $19.95

1. King, William Lyon Mackenzie, 1874-1950.
2. Prime ministers – Canada – Biography.
3. Canada – Politics and government – 1911-

Eleven historians and former political associates mark the centennial of Mackenzie King's birth with a collection of essays and reminiscences which examine his achievements in domestic and international politics. There are differing perspectives but the overall attitude is sympathetic. Contains a thirty page bibliography. For students of Canadian politics and history.

5928 921.
**Ferns, S. J.**
Eighty-five Years in Canada, by S. J. Ferns and H. S. Ferns. Winnipeg: Queenston House, c1978. 188p. ill., plates, ports. ISBN 0-919866-38-7 bd.: $10.95
ISBN 0-919866-39-5 pa.: $5.95

1. The West, Canadian – Biography.

The reminiscences of an eighty-five year old Canadian who was a school drop-out at thirteen, are from the perspective of an unskilled and inexperienced youth making his way in times of boom and depression. This unpretentious oral history mirrors working conditions and social mores in Ontario and western Canada prior to World War II. Easy conversational style.

5929 921.
**Firestone, O. J.**
The Other A. Y. Jackson: A Memoir. Toronto: McClelland and Stewart, c1979. 272p. ill. Bibliography: p. 266-270. ISBN 0-7710-3148-3 $18.95

1. Jackson, Alexander Y., 1882-1975.
2. Painters – Canada – Biography. 3. Group of Seven (Canadian Painters) – Biography.

Canada's distinguished and well-loved artist is admirably portrayed in these personal recollections by a friend of many years. Contains a good bibliography. Paula de Ronde

5930 921.
**Flanagan, Thomas.**
Louis 'David' Riel: Prophet of the New World. Toronto: University of Toronto Press, c1979. 216p. Bibliographical references and Index. ISBN 0-8020-5430-7 $15

1. Riel, Louis David, 1844-1885. 2. Red River Rebellion, 1869-1870 – Biography. 3. Riel Rebellion, 1885 – Biography. 4. Métis – The West, Canadian – Biography.

Biography based on new information from Riel's diaries. Discusses his political actions in the context of "millenarianism" and argues that he was not a revolutionary in the modern sense but upon seeing the impending annihilation of the Métis way of life tried to create a new, more perfect order. Refreshingly interesting view of Riel that places his "mental illness" in new perspective. Niki Lawrence

5931 921.
**Freeman, Minnie Aodla.**
Life Among the Qallunaat. Edmonton: Hurtig Publishers, c1978. 217p. ISBN 0-88830-164-2 $9.95

1. Eskimos – Canada – Biography.

A perceptive Inuit woman describes her life in two cultures. Brief, vivid episodes recreate a childhood in the James Bay area, lonely years in the white man's schools and hospitals, and adjustment to urbanized society in southern Ontario. An engagingly candid and sensitive recollection providing a unique insight into Inuit culture. Recommended for school and public libraries.

5932 921.
**French, Alice.**
My Name is Masak. Winnipeg: Peguis Publishers, 1976. 110p. ill., maps. Index. ISBN 0-919566-55-3 bd.: $9
ISBN 0-919566-56-1 pa.: $4

1. Eskimos – Northwest Territories – Biography.

An observant young Eskimo woman describes her childhood in the Western Arctic forty years ago. Recollections of family expeditions to hunt whales and Arctic foxes are juxtaposed with the unfamiliar world of boarding school in Aklavik. A simply written narrative, illustrated with photographs and a sketch map. Junior High level.

5933 921.
**Gilman, Dorothy.**
A New Kind of Country. Toronto: Doubleday, 1978. 125p. ISBN 0-385-13628-5 $6.95

1. Authors, American – 20th century – Biography.

A flimsy journal about self-seeking and self-discovery written by a light-weight American novelist living in a fishing village in Nova Scotia. The book is highly derivative and unoriginal in its philosophical import, but contains some interesting sketches about local life and characters, and provides occasional insight into the human condition. Ille-Mai Gerdels

5934 921.
**Godsell, Patricia,** ed.
Letters & Diaries of Lady Durham. Ottawa: Oberon Press, c1979. 203p. port. Bibliographical references and Index. ISBN 0-88750-323-3 $17.50

1. Durham, Louisa Elizabeth Grey Lambton, Countess of, 1797?-1841. 2. Durham, John George Lambton, 1st Earl of, 1792-1840. 3. Governors general – Canada – Spouses – Biography. 4. Governors general – Canada – Biography. 5. Canada – Politics and government – 1837-1838.

The controversial Durham Report which laid the basis for responsible government in Canada, is viewed through the private journal and letters of quiet Lady Louisa who shared the problems, and the political aftermath, of the 1838 Canadian assignment. Meticulous research, Godsell's careful explanatory notes, and the inclusion of the private secretary's detailed record of the mission, substantiate the account of a devoted wife. An important and very readable new perspective on a milestone in Canadian history.

5935 921.
**Gordon, Walter L.**
A Political Memoir. Toronto: McClelland and Stewart, c1977. 395p. ill., plates, ports. Index. ISBN 0-7710-3440-7 $15.95

1. Canada – Politics and government – 1963-

Six years of political life in the 1960's, as Liberal Party organizer and federal cabinet minister, are the core of these quiet, objective reminiscences. Efforts to curb foreign ownership in Canada alienated colleagues and brought political defeat. An important insight into the rivalries and manoeuvrings in inner government, and a perspective on the Pearson years. Recommended.

5936 921.
**Granatstein, J. L.**
Mackenzie King: His Life and World. Toronto: McGraw-Hill Ryerson, 1977. 202p. ill., ports. Bibliography: p. 197-198. Index. ISBN 0-07-082304-9 $14.95

1. King, William Lyon Mackenzie, 1874-1950.
2. Prime ministers – Canada – Biography.
3. Canada – Politics and government – 1911-

The second volume in the McGraw-Hill Ryerson series on Canadian Prime Ministers compresses thirty eventful years into less than two hundred pages. A popularly-written survey which concludes that King has been underrated by his contemporaries. Numerous carefully selected illustrations evoke Canadian economic and social life in the King era, 1919 to 1948. For school and public libraries.

5937 921.
**Gray, James H.**
The Boy from Winnipeg. Illustrated by Myra Lowenthal. Toronto: Macmillan, 1977, c1970. 204p. ill. (Laurentian Library) ISBN 0-7705-1587-8 pa.: $3.95

1. Journalists – Canada – Biography.

First published 1970. Clothbound listed *CS* no. 3795.

5938 921.
**Gray, James H.**
Troublemaker!: A Personal History. Toronto: Macmillan, c1978. 307p. ill., ports. Index. ISBN 0-7705-1718-8 $14.95

1. Journalists – Canada – Biography.
2. Prairie Provinces – History – 1945-

Author of *The Winter Years.*

Outspoken opposition to editorial policies of the influential "Winnipeg Free Press" and denunciation of foreign exploitation of Alberta's oil resources terminated Gray's promising journalistic career. Social commentary is interwoven with personal reminiscences. A somewhat ironic but useful and readable picture of two important decades in Western Canada, the mid 1930's to the mid 1950's.

5939 921.
**Gray, John Morgan.**
Fun Tomorrow: Learning to be a Publisher and Much Else. Toronto: Macmillan, c1978. 347p. ill., plates, ports. ISBN 0-7705-1710-2 $16.95

1. Macmillan Company of Canada – History.
2. Publishers and publishing – Canada – Biography.

City of Toronto Book Award.

The tale of the author's life from an unlikely, playful beginning which included twice failing his first-year studies at university, to 1946 when he became president of Macmillan of Canada. Especially engrossing is the story of his years as a travelling textbook salesman in the Canadian West during the Depression. Written with wit and charm. For all libraries.

5940 921.
**Hill, Beth.**
The Remarkable World of Frances Barkley, 1769-1845. Sidney, B.C.: Gray's Publishing, 1978. 232p. ill., maps, ports. Bibliography: p. 217-220. Index. ISBN 0-88826-077-6 pa.: $9.95

1. Barkley, Frances, 1769-1845. 2. Voyages to the Pacific coast. 3. British Columbia – Description and travel – To 1900.

The young wife of a sailing vessel captain whose trading expeditions reached around the world, was, in 1786, the first European woman to see British Columbia. Letters, official records and Elizabeth's reminiscences have been interwoven and set in historical context. A carefully researched, engrossing narrative of a woman's ten years at sea. Pleasing design. School, college and public libraries.

5941 921.
**Horwood, Harold.**
Bartlett: The Great Canadian Explorer. Photographs by Bartlett. Toronto: Doubleday, 1977. 194p. ill., maps, plates, ports. Bibliography: p. 186-187. Index. ISBN 0-385-09984-3 $8.95

1. Bartlett, Robert Abram, 1875-1946.
2. Explorers – Canada – Biography.
3. Arctic regions.

Very few people are truly "great" and Bartlett is one of the few. Horwood's book reads like an exciting adventure story as he chronicles the navy voyages of Bartlett, including the journey with Peary in search of the North Pole. A well-researched and much needed account of a man who deserves his place in Canada's navigation history. Paula de Ronde

5942 921.
**Humphreys, David L.**
Joe Clark: A Portrait. Ottawa: Deneau and Greenberg, c1978. 276p. ill., plates, ports. Index. ISBN 0-88879-004-X $9.95

1. Clark, Joe, 1939- 2. Statesmen – Canada – Biography.

A superficial sketch of the former Prime Minister's life from childhood, through university years, his initial ventures into politics, and election to the leadership of the Progressive Conservative Party. Excerpts from Mr. Clark's letters to friends are more interesting and more revealing of the man than the banal narrative. Purchase only if demand is insistent. A more definitive and analytical study is needed.

5943 921.
**Hustak, Allan.**
Peter Lougheed: A Biography. Toronto: McClelland and Stewart, c1979. 251p. ISBN 0-7710-4299-X $14.95

1. Lougheed, Peter, 1928- 2. Prime ministers – Alberta – Biography. 3. Alberta – Politics and government – 1935-

An Edmonton journalist traces Lougheed's career from his boyhood to his rise to a pivotal position in Canadian politics. Interest in a high-profile contemporary politician may compensate for a conscientious but plodding description of the external man. Lacks a table of contents, chapter headings, a bibliography and an index.

5944 921.
**Jaques, Edna.**
Uphill All the Way. Saskatoon: Western Producer Prairie Books, c1977. 244p. ill., plates, ports. ISBN 0-919306-86-1 $10.95

1. Poets, Canadian (English) – 20th century – Biography.

The feisty eighty-five year old whose name is synonymous with simple, homely verse, recalls the vicissitudes of homesteading in Saskatchewan early in the century, and her development as a writer. Small, folksy episodes are recounted in a chatty, colloquial style, and interspersed with the author's poems. An interesting Canadian period piece.

5945 921.
**Johnson, Arthur.**
Margaret Trudeau. Markham, Ont.: PaperJacks, 1977. 210p. ill., plates, ports. ISBN 0-7701-0059-7 pa.: $1.95

1. Trudeau, Margaret, 1948- 2. Prime ministers' wives – Canada – Biography.

The saga of Margaret Trudeau has been done to death by the media, but if one had to have one book about her then Arthur Johnson's work deserves that dubious distinction. Johnson's new angle to this old story is: the press did not kill Margaret as she insists, she committed suicide. Paula de Ronde

5946 921.
**Joudry, Patricia.**
Spirit River to Angels' Roost: Religions I Have Loved and Left. Montreal: Tundra Books, c1977. 196p. ISBN 0-88776-026-0 $8.95

1. Dramatists, Canadian (English) – 20th century – Biography.

With humour and self-mockery playwright Joudry's "spiritual autobiography" charts her course from Roman Catholicism through myriad varieties of mysticism and spiritualism. Her exploits include automatic writing of plays dictated by George Bernard Shaw, founding a new cult, and purported immaculate conception. Annette Wengle

5947 921.
**Kendle, John Edward.**
John Bracken: A Political Biography. Toronto: University of Toronto Press, 1979. 318p. ill., plates. Bibliography: p. 297-303. Index. ISBN 0-8020-5439-0 $17.50

1. Bracken, John, 1883-1969. 2. Progressive Conservative Party (Canada) – History. 3. Prime ministers – Manitoba – Biography. 4. Manitoba – Politics and government – 1922-1948.

Insight into the past and contemporary issue of regional economic disparity and its resultant antagonisms is provided in this biography of the quiet Manitoban. Bracken's political career as Premier of Manitoba, and later as leader of the national Progressive Conservative Party, spanned more than twenty-five years. Well written. Recommended for political science collections. Ethel Kellen

5948 921.
**Knight, Rolf.**
A Man of Our Times: The Life-history of a Japanese-Canadian Fisherman, by Rolf Knight and Maya Koizumi. Vancouver: New Star Books, 1977. 135p. ill., map, ports. Bibliography: p. 134-135. ISBN 0-919888-64-X bd.: $10 ISBN 0-919888-63-1 pa.: $3.95

1. Yoshida, Ryuichi, 1887- 2. Japanese in British Columbia – History. 3. Trade-unions – British Columbia – History. 4. Fishermen – British Columbia – Biography.

A unique portrait of efforts to oppose racism and the exclusion of orientals from trade unions in British Columbia. In 1919 Yoshida participated with other Japanese, in the formation of the labour union which crossed occupational and plant lines and had no racial barriers to membership. Barbara Stewart

5949 921.
**Lamb, James B.**
Press Gang: Post-War Life in the World of Canadian Newspapers. Toronto: Macmillan, 1979. 204p. ISBN 0-7705-1814-1 $12.95

1. Journalists – Canada – Biography.
2. Canadian newspapers (English) – History.

The debilitating effect of ownership by the powerful Thomson chain upon the character of small city and town newspapers permeates these recollections of a newspaperman. Amusing anecdotes about people and events fail to cloak Lamb's growing disillusionment with the realities of a profit-hungry newspaper empire. General interest.

5950 921.
**Le Pan, Douglas.**
Bright Glass of Memory: A Set of Four Memoirs. Toronto: McGraw-Hill Ryerson, c1979. 245p. ISBN 0-07-082945-4 $15.95

1. Authors, Canadian (English) – 20th century – Biography. 2. Diplomats – Canada – Biography.

Four segments of Le Pan's varied career, diplomat, poet, scholar and soldier, are reflected in this beautifully written memoir. Three notable personalities whose lives touched his, General McNaughton, Lord Keynes, and T. S. Eliot, are deftly portrayed; history is re-lived in recollections of the initiation of the Colombo Plan. Incisive, witty observations. General reading.

5951 921.
**Le Sueur, William Dawson.**
William Lyon Mackenzie: A Reinterpretation. Edited and with an introduction by A. B. McKillop. Toronto: Macmillan; Ottawa: Institute of Canadian Studies, Carleton University, 1979. 430p. (The Carleton Library) ISBN 0-7705-1743-9 pa.: $8.95

1. Mackenzie, William Lyon, 1795-1861.
2. Canada – History – 1791-1841.

William Lyon Mackenzie will always be a colourful figure in Canadian history. Le Sueur's biography, although by no means a definitive work, is still a well-balanced and critical look at a man who remains an enigma. One interesting fact is that this manuscript was completed more than seventy years ago! Paula de Ronde

5952 921.
**Legate, David M.**
Stephen Leacock: A Biography. Toronto: Macmillan, 1978, c1970. 298p. ill., plates, ports. Bibliography: p. 283-284. Index. (Laurentian Library) ISBN 0-7705-1666-1 pa.: $5.95

1. Leacock, Stephen, 1869-1944. 2. Humorists, Canadian – Biography.

First published Toronto: Doubleday, 1970. Clothbound listed *CS* no. 3837.

5953 921.
**Lyall, Ernie.**
An Arctic Man: Sixty-five Years in Canada's North. Edmonton: Hurtig Publishers, 1979. 264p. ISBN 0-88830-168-5 $12.95

1. Arctic regions. 2. Canada, Northern – Biography.

A white man who has lived his life in the Canadian Arctic attempts to banish misconceptions created by instant experts about its life and people. His reminiscences are direct, lively and romantic, and are told in the colloquial style of the story-teller. Controversial in its vision of the Eskimo future. Ille-Mai Gerdels

5954 921.
**MacDonald, Andy.**
Don't Slip on the Soap. Don Mills, Ont.: Musson, c1978. 177p. ISBN 0-7737-0037-4 bd.: $12.95 ISBN 0-7737-1021-3 pa.: $7.95

Sequel to *Bread and Molasses*.

Further amusing anecdotes of a large Cape Breton family during the Depression years. Casual, inconsequential entertainment for undemanding readers.

5955 921.
**Macdonald, R. H.**
Grant MacEwan: No Ordinary Man. Saskatoon: Western Producer Prairie Books, c1979. 237p. ill. Index. ISBN 0-88833-029-4 bd.: $16.95 ISBN 0-88833-036-7 pa.: $9.95

1. MacEwan, J. W. G., 1902-1980. 2. Lieutenant-governors – Alberta – Biography. 3. Agriculturalists – Prairie Provinces – Biography. 4. Prairie Provinces – History.

MacEwan's long and multi-faceted career and accomplishments as author, academic, agriculturalist, newspaperman, politician and public servant are recorded in some detail, but there is little analysis of the man or his interaction with major public issues during six decades of active life in the prairie provinces.

5956 921.
**MacEwan, J. W. G.**
Pat Burns, Cattle King. Saskatoon: Western Producer Prairie Books, c1979. 200p. ill., ports. Bibliographical references and Index. ISBN 0-88833-010-3 bd.: $14.95
ISBN 0-88830-035-9 pa.: $7.95

1. Burns, Pat, 1856-1937. 2. Meat industry and trade – Canada. 3. Cattle trade – Canada.
4. Packing-houses – Canada.

The career of the self-made millionaire rancher and meat packer is viewed uncritically in this anecdotal chronicle of his rise from anonymity to business tycoon and senator. Easy, conversational style. Of primary interest to libraries in western Canada.

5957 921.
**MacGregor, James G.**
John Rowand: Czar of the Prairies. Saskatoon: Western Producer Prairie Books, 1978. 240p. Index. ISBN 0-919306-99-3 bd.: $14 ISBN 0-88833-005-7 pa.: $7

1. Rowand, John, 1789-1854. 2. Hudson's Bay Company – History. 3. Fur trade – The West, Canadian – Biography.

Fur trading days in western Canada in the first half of the nineteenth century form the backdrop for a biography of a man who advanced from apprentice with the North West Company to Chief Factor of the Hudson's Bay Company. Archives, letters and journals have been drawn upon to reveal company rivalries and relations with the Indians. An interesting and readable account.

5958 921.
**MacLeod, Wendell.**
Bethune: The Montreal Years: An Informal Portrait, by Wendell MacLeod, Libbie Park and Stanley Ryerson. Toronto: James Lorimer, 1978. 167p. Bibliographical references. ISBN 0-88862-212-0 $12.95

1. Bethune, Norman, 1890-1939. 2. Surgeons – Canada – Biography.

Focusing on the eight years prior to his departure for Spain in 1936, a trio of friends remember the famous surgeon in different environments: medicine, working for universal health care, and left-wing politics. They depict a compassionate man, profoundly disturbed by the prevalence of unemployment, poverty and illness. A revealing tribute. General reading.

5959 921.
**Mardiros, Anthony.**
William Irvine: The Life of a Prairie Radical. Toronto: James Lorimer, 1979. 298p. Bibliography: p. 278-279. Index. ISBN 0-88862-237-6 pa.: $9.95

1. Irvine, William, 1885-1962. 2. Politicians – Canada – Biography. 3. Socialism in Canada.

As a preacher, journalist and founding member of the Ginger Group, the C.C.F. and the N.D.P. Party, Irvine helped sow the seeds of democratic socialism. A sympathetic biography provides a detailed study and analysis of prairie politics, Canadian socialism, and of the social and economic issues facing Parliament in the 1920's and 1930's. Recommended for medium and large public libraries and university collections. Ethel Kellen

5960 921.
**Massey, Raymond.**
A Hundred Different Lives: An Autobiography. Foreward by Christopher Plummer. Toronto: McClelland and Stewart, 1979. 447p. ill., ports. Index. ISBN 0-7710-5856-X $18.95

1. Actors – Canada – Biography.

A sequel to *When I Was Young*.

The distinguished Canadian recalls fifty-two years in the theatre, film, television and radio. Descriptive and non-analytical, the spotlight is on the professional career, the private man remains in the shadows. Coolly detached, impeccably correct, but lacking sparkle. Important as a theatrical memoir. General leisure reading.

5961 921.
**McLeish, John A. B.**
A Canadian for All Seasons: The John E. Robbins Story. Toronto: Lester and Orpen, 1978. 315p. Bibliography: p. 293-298. Index. ISBN 0-919630-79-0 $14.95

1. Robbins, John E., 1903- 2. Diplomats – Canada – Biography.

Many of Canada's prestigious educational and cultural institutions were fostered by an unassuming Canadian whose concern for scholarship, research and a sense of Canadian identity had been the compelling force in his own remarkable career. An interesting but uncritical profile of the respected educator and diplomat. Public and college libraries.

5962 921.
**Morton, W. L.,** ed.
God's Galloping Girl: The Peace River Diaries of Monica Storrs, 1929-1931, edited by W. L. Morton and Vera K. Fast. Preface by R. D. Symons. Vancouver: University of British Columbia Press, 1979. 309p. ill., plates. Bibliographical references and Index. ISBN 0-7748-0110-7 $22

1. Storrs, Monica, 1888-1967. 2. Anglican Church of Canada – Biography. 3. Frontier and pioneer life – Peace River district.
4. Peace River district – History.

Monica Storrs exchanged life in a sheltered, cultured English home for a posting to a frontier Anglican mission in British Columbia's Peace River area in the thirties. In the two years of her twenty-year service recorded in her diaries, the reader is given a clear, honest picture of frontier social conditions from the point of view of a cultivated woman. Paula de Ronde

5963 921.

**Neatby, Leslie H.**

Chronicle of a Pioneer Prairie Family. Saskatoon: Western Producer Prairie Books, 1979. 93p. ill., plates. ISBN 0-88833-022-7 pa.: $5.95

1. Neatby family. 2. Frontier and pioneer life – Saskatchewan. 3. Saskatchewan – Biography.

Life on a Saskatchewan homestead was filled with physical and financial hardship for the large family of a London doctor who migrated to Canada in 1906. Despite material privation the prairie home was rich in affection and encouragement of intellectual excellence. Members of the family who have achieved distinction as academics and authors include Dr. Hilda Neatby, author of *So Little for the Mind*, H. Blair Neatby, and the author, a respected historian. Readable family history for all libraries.

5964 921.

**Nolan, Michael.**

Joe Clark: The Emerging Leader. Photographs by Ted Grant. Don Mills, Ont.: Fitzhenry & Whiteside, 1978. 139p. ill., ports. ISBN 0-88902-436-7 $13.95

1. Clark, Joe, 1939- 2. Politicians – Canada – Biography. 3. Canada – Politics and government – 1963-

A summary profile of Mr. Clark's political career prior to the 1978 election. Replete with photographs, the concentration is upon his election as leader of the Progressive Conservative Party, party organization, and the caucus. Lacks any assessment of his performance as Prime Minister or analysis of his political aims. A political preface.

5965 921.

**O'Leary, Grattan.**

Grattan O'Leary: Recollections of People, Press, and Politics. Foreword by Robert L. Stanfield; introduction and personal postscript by I. Norman Smith Toronto: Macmillan, c1977. 208p. ill., plates, ports. Index. ISBN 0-7705-1523-1 $12.95

1. Statesmen – Canada – Biography.
2. Canada – Politics and government – 1911-

For more than sixty years the articulate journalist, editor and senator participated in the making of Canadian political history. In vigorous prose laced with humour, O'Leary recalls leaders, from Laurier to Trudeau whom he admired and scorned. Politics overshadow private life in these memoirs dictated in his eighty-seventh year. Not a definitive biography.

5966 921.

**Oliver, Peter N.**

G. Howard Ferguson: Ontario Tory. Toronto: Published by University of Toronto Press for the Ontario Historical Studies Series, c1977. 501p. ill., plates, ports. Bibliography: p. 484-486. Index. (Ontario Historical Studies Series) ISBN 0-8020-3346-6 $14.95

1. Ferguson, George Howard, 1870-1946.
2. Prime ministers – Ontario – Biography.
3. Ontario – Politics and government – 1923-1943.

The first in the 'Ontario Historical Studies Series' is a comprehensive, carefully researched study of the shrewd politician who played central roles in Ontario's political life during the first thirty years of this century. Ferguson is revealed in relation to the economic and social issues of the period. Informative reading for everyone interested in politics and history.

5967 921.

**Penfield, Wilder.**

No Man Alone: A Surgeon's Story. Foreword by Lord Adrian. Toronto: Little, Brown, c1977. 398p. ill., ports. Bibliographical references and Index. ISBN 0-316-69839-3 $12.50

1. Montreal Neurological Institute – History.
2. Neurosurgeons – Quebec (Province) – Biography.

A splendid autobiography of the world famous neurosurgeon which reveals his dedication to his profession and his untiring commitment to research. General interest. School and public libraries. Paula de Ronde

5968 921.

**Radwanski, George.**

Trudeau. Toronto: Macmillan; Scarborough, Ont.: Macmillan-NAL Publishing, 1979, c1978. 372p. Bibliography: p. 365-366. Index. ISBN 0-7705-1655-6 bd.: $12.95 ISBN 0-7723-0017-8 pa.: $2.50

1. Trudeau, Pierre Elliott, 1919- 2. Prime ministers – Canada – Biography. 3. Canada – Politics and government – 1963-

The Ottawa editor of "The Financial Times" scrutinizes the enigmatic, controversial figure who is Canada's Prime Minister. Published materials and interviews with Trudeau, his political associates, friends and family examine the early formative years, political philosophy, personal relationships and a decade of government. Radwanski's tolerant analysis provides interesting insights into a complex personality. The quality of the writing and subject interest will have wide appeal.

5969 921.
**Reynolds, Louise.**
Agnes: The Biography of Lady Macdonald. Toronto: Samuel Stevens, c1979. 229p. ill., plates, ports. Bibliography: p. 221-224. Index. ISBN 0-88866-605-5 $14.95

1. Macdonald, Agnes, Baroness Macdonald of Earnscliffe, 1836-1920. 2. Macdonald, John Alexander, Sir, 1815-1891. 3. Prime ministers' wives – Canada – Biography. 4. Prime ministers – Canada – Biography.

The private diary and scrapbooks of the second wife of Canada's first Prime Minister, and their letters, reveal the domestic and political vicissitudes which shadowed their marriage. A carefully researched, well-written biography of an intelligent and spirited political wife which provides a new perspective on Macdonald's family life. Recommended.

5970 921.
**Ritchie, Charles.**
An Appetite for Life: The Education of a Young Artist, 1924-1927. Toronto: Macmillan, c1977. 173p. ISBN 0-7705-1573-8 $10.95

1. Ritchie, Charles, 1906- 2. Diplomats – Canada – Biography.

From the pages of the 1920 diaries steps a sensitive, unsophisticated youth, his aspirations tempered by self doubts. The narrow world of home and college in Halifax and Oxford, the absurdities and the pretensions are observed with cool detachment and wry wit by "the compulsive diarist". A candid and engaging self portrait. Beautifully written. Enthusiastically recommended for young people and adults.

5971 921.
**Ritchie, Charles.**
The Siren Years: A Canadian Diplomat Abroad, 1937-1945. Toronto: Macmillan, 1977, c1974. 216p. Index. (Laurentian Library) ISBN 0-7705-1585-1 pa.: $4.95

1. Diplomats – Canada – Biography.

Clothbound listed in *CS* no. 3889.

5972 921.
**Roger, Gertrude Minor.**
Lady Rancher. North Vancouver, B.C.: Hancock House, c1979. 182p. ill. ISBN 0-88839-038-6 $12.95

1. Ranch life – Saskatchewan. 2. Ranch life – British Columbia. 3. Ranchers – Saskatchewan – Biography. 4. Ranchers – British Columbia – Biography.

Dubbed "That God-damned girl" by a disapproving father-in-law, an eighteen-year old bride learned to pull her weight as a ranch hand, wife and mother, on large ranches in Saskatchewan and British Columbia, in the mid nineteen forties. A readable biography enhanced by some graphic descriptions and an easy, conversational style. Secondary schools and public libraries.

5973 921.
**Rohmer, Richard H.**
E. P. Taylor: The Biography of Edward Plunket Taylor. Toronto: McClelland and Stewart, 1978. 355p. Index. ISBN 0-7710-7709-2 $15.95

1. Taylor, Edward Plunket, 1901- 2. Capitalists and financiers – Canada – Biography.

A chronological, somewhat pedestrian account of the financier's achievements in the corporate world. Admiration for the tycoon's success is pervasive but there is a lack of critical assessment of the public and private man and his enterprises. Stories of Taylor's vast financial empire and horse-racing interests will attract readers.

5974 921.
**Roy, Reginald H.**
For Most Conspicuous Bravery: A Biography of Major-General George R. Pearkes, V.C., Through Two World Wars. Vancouver: University of British Columbia Press, c1977. 388p. ill., maps, plates, ports. Bibliographical references and Index. ISBN 0-7748-0068-2 $15.95

1. Pearkes, George Randolph, 1888- 2. Canada. Army – Biography. 3. Generals – Canada – Biography. 4. Statesmen – Canada – Biography.

A descriptive but not definitive biography of the multi-faceted political and military career of the frequently-decorated Canadian soldier and politician. Diaries, letters, personal files and interviews with Pearkes, cabinet colleagues, civil servants and military personnel have been drawn upon. Interesting for its perspective on twentieth-century issues. General purchase.

5975 921.
**Saunders, Kathleen.**
Robert Borden. Don Mills, Ont.: Fitzhenry & Whiteside, c1978. 63p. ill., ports. Bibliography. (The Canadians)
ISBN 0-88902-232-1 pa.: $1.95

1. Borden, Robert Laird, Sir, 1854-1937.
2. Canada – Politics and government – 1911-1921.

Scientists, politicians, artists, feminists, authors, and explorers are represented in this series of simply written introductions to the lives of famous Canadians. Brief, attractive paperback format. Junior High School level. In the same series and format: English, J. *Arthur Meighen;* Neering, R. *Louis Riel;* Ray, J. *Emily Stowe.*

5976 921.
**Savage, Candace.**
Our Nell: A Scrapbook Biography of Nellie L. McClung. Saskatoon: Western Producer Prairie Books, 1979. 242p. ill. Bibliography: p. 235-242. Index. ISBN 0-88833-027-8 bd.: $17.95 ISBN 0-88833-033-2 pa.: $10.95

1. Feminists – Canada – Biography.
2. McClung, Nellie L., 1873-1951.

The spirited feminist, reformer and writer who challenged the social and political status quo early in the century emerges as a warm, spontaneous personality. Her own writings are skillfully meshed with comments by her contemporaries and newspaper articles, and set in context by a perceptive narrator. A charming portrait of a remarkable woman. Well illustrated and documented.

5977 921.
**Schull, Joseph.**
The Great Scot: A Biography of Donald Gordon. Montreal: McGill-Queen's University Press, c1979. 291p. ill., plates. Bibliographical references and Index.
ISBN 0-7735-0349-8 $24.95

1. Gordon, Donald, 1901-1969 – Biography.
2. Canadian National Railways – Biography.
3. Railroads – Canada – Biography.
4. Bankers – Canada – Biography.

A very readable biography of Donald Gordon who thought he could move mountains, and did. Gordon was a larger-than-life personality who took charge of things, including the Bank of Canada and the Canadian National Railway. A joyous biography to be read more for pleasure than for scholarship. Paula de Ronde

5978 921.
**Scott, Munroe.**
McClure: The China Years of Dr. Bob McClure: A Biography. Don Mills, Ont.: Canec Publishing; Markham, Ont.: Penguin, 1977. 409p. maps, plates, ports.
ISBN 0-919000-12-6 bd.: $14.95 pa.: $3.95

1. McClure, Robert, 1900- 2. Missionaries, Medical – China – Biography.

A half century of political and social upheaval in China molded the career of the dynamic Canadian medical missionary. In peace and in war Dr. McClure circumvented red tape and disregarded personal safety to practise and teach innovative surgery, medicine and rural health care. An absorbing chronicle of an extraordinary Christian.

5979 921.
**Scott, Munroe.**
McClure: Years of Challenge: A Biography. Don Mills, Ont.: Canec Publishing, 1979.
ISBN 0-919000-13-4 $14.95

1. McClure, Robert, 1900- 2. United Church of Canada – Biography. 3. Missionaries, Medical – Biography.

Sequel to *McClure: The China Years of Dr. Bob McClure.*

Following twenty-five years of selfless service to the peoples of China the peripatetic missionary surgeon practised medicine in the Gaza Strip, India, Malaysia and Peru, and served a term as Moderator of the United Church of Canada. Strong biographical interest, adventure, contemporary events and humour are blended in the two volumes. For all libraries.

5980 921.
**Siggins, Maggie.**
Bassett: John Bassett's Forty Years in Politics, Publishing, Business and Sports. Toronto: James Lorimer, 1979. 251p. ill. Index. ISBN 0-88862-284-8 $15.95

1. Bassett, John W. H., 1915- 2. Publishers and publishing – Canada – Biography.
3. Sports team owners – Canada – Biography.

A breezily-written, unauthorized profile of a man who is well-known in many fields. Never shy or introverted, Bassett has left his mark on Canadian sports, politics, business and the media. His flamboyance may grate but in the end a grudging admiration surfaces. Paula de Ronde

5981 921.
**Simcoe, Elizabeth Posthuma.**
Mrs. Simcoe's Diary. Edited by Mary Quayle Innis. Toronto: Macmillan, 1978, c1965. 223p. ill., maps, plates, port. Bibliographical references and Index. (Laurentian Library) ISBN 0-7705-1729-3 pa.: $5.95

1. Simcoe, John Graves, 1752-1806.
2. Lieutenant-governors – Ontario – Biography.

Clothbound listed in *CS* no. 3902.

5982 921.
**Spigelman, Martin S.**
Wilfrid Laurier. Don Mills, Ont.: Fitzhenry & Whiteside, c1978. 62p. ill., facsims., ports. Bibliography: p. 64. (The Canadians) ISBN 0-88902-245-3 pa.: $2.25

1. Laurier, Wilfrid, Sir, 1841-1919. 2. Prime ministers – Canada – Biography. 3. Canada – Politics and government – 1896-1911.

Uniform in length and physical format, each of the brief biographical sketches in this series provides a narrative and pictorial introduction to a noted Canadian. Designed for junior high level, the style is lively and direct. Illustrations are drawn from authoritative sources. In the same series: Careless, J. M. S. *George Brown;* Hacker, Carlotta. *E. Cora Hind.*

5983 921.
**Stacey, C. P.**
A Very Double Life: The Private World of Mackenzie King. Toronto: Macmillan, 1977, c1976. 256p. ill., facsims., plates, ports. Bibliographical references and Index. (Laurentian Library) ISBN 0-7705-1509-6 pa.: $4.50

1. King, William Lyon Mackenzie, 1874-1950.
2. Prime ministers – Canada – Biography.

Clothbound listed in *CS* no. 3912.

5984 921.
**Stewart, Robert.**
Sam Steele: Lion of the Frontier. 1st ed. Toronto: Doubleday, 1979. 303p. ill. Index. ISBN 0-38513-598-X $12.50

1. Steele, Samuel Benfield, Sir, 1849-1919.
2. Canada. Royal Canadian Mounted Police.
3. Police – Canada – Biography.

An original member of the North West Mounted Police, Steele played a decisive role in the policing of the Canadian West in the late nineteenth century. Military service was in the Boer and First Great Wars. A flawless, larger-than-life hero emerges from the admiring chronicle of his exploits. An interesting segment of Canadian history for the general reader.

5985 921.
**Stewart, Roderick.**
The Mind of Norman Bethune. Toronto: Fitzhenry & Whiteside, c1977. 150p. ill., maps, ports. Index. ISBN 0-88902-418-9 bd.: $15.95 ISBN 0-88902-425-1 pa.: $9.95

1. Bethune, Norman, 1890-1939. 2. Surgeons – Canada – Biography.

The individualistic Canadian surgeon who became a contemporary legend through his medical service in Spain and China in the nineteen thirties is revealed through his own writings. Succinct prefatory notes relate excerpts from speeches, medical and political articles and letters to major periods in Bethune's life. Liberally illustrated. Public and secondary school libraries.

5986 921.
**Sturgis, William.**
The Journal of William Sturgis. Edited with an introduction and notes by S. W. Jackman. Victoria: Sono Nis Press, 1978. 136p. ill., map, plates, ports. Index. ISBN 0-919462-54-5 pa.: $5.95

1. Eliza (Ship). 2. Fur trade – Northwest coast of North America. 3. Indians of North America – Northwest coast of North America. 4. Northwest coast of North America – Discovery and exploration.

The value of this work lies in the detailed description of Indian life as it is recorded in William Sturgis' journal. However, it is this same detail that detracts from the readability of the book. Serious history students will find the work useful but for others the going will be rough. Paula de Ronde

5987 921.
**Swainson, Donald.**
Macdonald of Kingston: First Prime Minister. Toronto: Personal Library; Don Mills, Ont.: Thomas Nelson, c1979. 176p. ill. Bibliography: p. 6. Index. (Canada's Heritage in Pictures) ISBN 0-17-600739-3 $10.95

1. Macdonald, John Alexander, Sir, 1815-1891. 2. Prime ministers – Canada – Biography. 3. Canada – Politics and government – 19th century.

Following a eulogistic preface by the late J. G. Diefenbaker the highlights of the career of the colourful nineteenth century statesman are portrayed in pictures and capsule comments. Excerpts from primary materials, excellent archival photographs and political cartoons bring Macdonald to life. Well-researched, effortless visual history for undemanding browsing. Schools and public libraries.

5988 921.
**Teatero, William.**
Mackenzie King: Man of Mission. Toronto: Personal Library publication produced exclusively for Thomas Nelson, 1979. 192p. ill., ports. Bibliographical references and Index. (Canada's Heritage in Pictures)
ISBN 0-17-600740-7 $10.95

1. King, William Lyon Mackenzie, 1874-1950.
2. Prime ministers – Canada – Biography.
3. Canada – Politics and government – 1911-

A pictorial history in which fascinating photographs and a minimum of explanatory text trace the life of Mackenzie King and capture the flavour of his epoch. Particularly recommended for Young Adult collections and for the neighbourhood branch. Ethel Kellen

5989 921.
**Vanderburgh, Rosamond M.**
I Am Nokomis, Too: The Biography of Verna Patronella Johnston. Don Mills, Ont.: General Publishing, c1977. 247p. ill., map. Bibliography: p. 245-247. ISBN 0-7736-0061-2 bd.: $10.95 ISBN 0-7736-1032-4 pa.: $6.95

1. Johnston, Verna Patronella, 1909-
2. Chippewa Indians – Biography.
3. Indians of North America – Ontario.

The life-story of the 1976 "Indian Woman of the Year", as told by an anthropologist friend from various perspectives. In "rebelling" against her own heritage, this courageous woman reaffirmed its past and established its place in the twentieth century. High school and public libraries. Frieda Ling

5990 921.
**Weir, Carolyn.**
The Right Honourable John George Diefenbaker: A Pictorial Tribute. Toronto: Macmillan, 1979. ISBN 0-7705-1850-8 pa.: $9.95

1. Diefenbaker, John G., 1895-1979 – Portraits, caricatures, etc.

Photographs from public and private collections accompanied by brief identifying captions and quotations from Mr. Diefenbaker's speeches and writings, have been grouped chronologically to provide a pictorial review of The Chief's career. The emphasis is upon the warm, human side of the politician in this affectionate memorial compiled by his step-daughter.

5991 921.
**Wilbur, J. R. H.**
H. H. Stevens, 1878-1973. Toronto: University of Toronto Press, c1977. 244p. Bibliographical references and Index. (Canadian Biographical Studies)
ISBN 0-8020-3339-3 $9.50

1. Stevens, Henry Herbert, 1878-1973.
2. Statesmen – Canada – Biography.
3. Canada – Politics and government – 1911-

Critical of the policy of his leader, R. B. Bennett, Stevens, a Conservative Member of Parliament for twenty-four consecutive years, in 1935 broke ranks and formed the ill-fated Reconstructionist Party. The biography gives insight into British Columbia politics and the formation of a minority party. Ethel Kellen

5992 921.
**Wilder, Joseph E.**
Read All About It: Reminiscences of an Immigrant Newsboy. Edited by Fred C. Dawkins and Micheline C. Brodeur. Winnipeg: Peguis Publishers, 1978. 99p. ill., ports. Index. ISBN 0-919566-62-6 bd.: $8.50 ISBN 0-919566-63-4 pa.: $4.50

1. Newsboys – Biography. 2. Winnipeg, Man. – History.

Winnipeg at the beginning of the century, when it was the gateway to opportunity for thousands of immigrants, is recalled from the viewpoint of a young Roumanian Jew. The long journey in steerage and colonist car provide a vividly-sketched preface to the family's struggles for success in the new world. Easy reading. School and public libraries.

5993 921.
**York, Thomas.**
And Sleep in the Woods: The Story of One Man's Spiritual Quest. Toronto: Doubleday, 1978. 221p. ISBN 0-385-13236-0 $8.95

1. Converts – Canada – Biography.
2. Vietnamese Conflict, 1961-1975 – Draft resisters – Arkansas.

An American Draft evader abandons graduate studies for a life of self-imposed hardship in northern New Brunswick and Ontario during the 1960's. While his wife copes with the realities of isolation, privation and subsistence, York immerses himself in reading Greek and emulating the early mystics. A revealing record of an ascetic's quest, leavened by facile prose and sensitivity to nature.

## 929 Genealogy, names, insignia

5994 929'.2'09411
**Franklyn, Mary Eliza,** comp.
The Wearing of the Tartan, compiled by Mary Eliza Franklyn and Isobel MacAulay. Halifax, N.S.: Petheric Press, 1979. 56p. ill. Bibliography: p. 53-54. ISBN 0-919380-30-1 pa.: $2.95

1. Tartans.

A succinct, useful explanation of the etiquette of Highland dress for men, women and children. Compiled with the assistance of Isobel MacAulay, an authority on the subject, the book contains a glossary and some historical background.

5995 929'.371
**Baxter, Angus.**
In Search of Your Roots: A Guide for Canadians Seeking Their Ancestors. Toronto: Macmillan, c1978. 293p. ill. Bibliography: p. 277-291. Index. ISBN 0-7705-1577-0 $17.95

1. Genealogy. 2. Canada – Genealogy.

An experienced genealogist guides the amateur, in clearly explained steps, through a search for his ancestral roots. The principal sources of genealogical information within Canada are described, and suggestions made for pursuing the search in Britain, Europe and other countries. A chatty, well-organized introduction to ancestor hunting. Public and academic libraries.

5996 929'.371
**Jonasson, Eric.**
The Canadian Genealogical Handbook: A Comprehensive Guide to Finding Your Ancestors in Canada. 2d ed., rev. and enl. Winnipeg: Wheatfield Press, 1978. 352p. ill., facsims., maps. Bibliographies. ISBN 0-920374-02-6 pa.: $11

1. Canada – Genealogy – Sources.

First edition listed *CS* no. 3958.

This second edition concentrates on resources available to the family historian in Canada. Provides a comprehensive survey of all major genealogical records including the collections of the Public Archives of Canada and the provincial archives. A useful first book for both beginner and the more experienced genealogist. Brian Land

5997 929'.3716
**Punch, Terrence M.**
Genealogical Research in Nova Scotia. Halifax: Petheric Press, c1978. 132p. ill., maps. Bibliographies and Indexes. ISBN 0-919380-29-8 pa.: $5.50

1. Nova Scotia – Genealogy – Handbooks, manuals, etc.

A compressed, but complete and logically organized guide to searching for one's ancestors. The researcher is directed to primary and secondary sources and to institutions and organizations helpful in providing genealogical information. The straightforward, easy-to-comprehend methodology can be readily adapted to constructing the family tree in other provinces. Public libraries.

5998 929'.3716
**Wright, Esther Clark.**
Planters and Pioneers. Wolfville, N.S.: E. C. Wright, 1978. 300p. ISBN 0-88999-087-5 pa.: $8.95

1. Registers of births, etc. – Nova Scotia. 2. Registers of births, etc. – New Brunswick. 3. Nova Scotia – Genealogy. 4. New Brunswick – Genealogy.

Exhaustive research on the settlers who peopled Nova Scotia in the mid-eighteenth century, prior to the influx of Loyalists, is the basis for an invaluable resource on Maritime genealogy. An alphabetical register of more than three thousand families follows a survey of each of the townships of Nova Scotia, which at that time included the present New Brunswick.

5999 929.8
**Canada. Dept. of the Secretary of State.**
The Arms, Flags and Emblems of Canada. Les armoiries, drapeaux et emblèmes du Canada. Ottawa: Deneau and Greenberg, 1978. 86p. ill. ISBN 0-88879-006-6 pa.: $3.50 DSS cat. no. S2-21/1978

Previous edition listed in *CS* no. 3962 as out-of-print.

A revised and expanded version of the 1967 publication. The flags and floral emblems of each province, regulations for flying the flag, other official Canadian flags are explained and an enlarged glossary of heraldic terms appended. Bilingual text. An authoritative compendium.

## 940 Canada at war

6000 940.3'71
**Read, Daphne,** ed.
The Great War and Canadian Society: An Oral History. Compiled by Gus Richardson and others; introduction by Russell Hann. Toronto: New Hogtown Press, c1978. 223p. ill., ports. Bibliographical references.
ISBN 0-919940-01-3 bd.: $10.95
ISBN 0-919940-02-1 pa.: $4.95

1. European War, 1914-1918 – Personal narratives, Canadian. 2. European War, 1914-1918 – Canada. 3. Canada – Social conditions – 1867-1918.

To support the editor's premise that the Great War was a catalyst which changed the social fabric of Canada, combatants and civilians of the war generation were interviewed. An excellent commentary on oral history, and introductions to the thematically grouped reminiscences lend authenticity. Useful for Canadian history and sociology collections in college, public and school libraries.

6001 940.4
**Goodspeed, D. J.**
The German Wars, 1914-1945. Toronto: Macmillan, 1977. 561p. maps. Bibliographical references and Index. ISBN 0-7705-1570-3 $20

1. European War, 1914-1918 – Causes. 2. European War, 1914-1918 – Influence and results. 3. World War, 1939-1945 – Causes. 4. European War, 1914-1918 – Campaigns. 5. World War, 1939-1945 – Campaigns.

Examining the causes, conduct and outcome of the two world wars of this century, a military historian reviews political and military events between 1871 and 1945. His premise is that the two wars were one prolonged conflict. Readers may question Goodspeed's conclusions but will respect his well-written, informative and carefully documented narrative.

6002 940.4'0971
**Bindon, Kathryn M.**
More than Patriotism: Canada at War, 1914-1918. Preface by Donald Swainson. Toronto: Personal Library, 1979. 192p. ill., map. Bibliography: p. 191. Index. (Canada's Heritage in Pictures) ISBN 0-17-600770-9 $12.95

1. European War, 1914-1918 – Canada.

A capsule summary of Canada's involvement on the Western Front, in which large-print, page-top headings and succinct paragraphs of text provide a coherent chronology for the illustrations. Quotations from speeches, newspapers, and reports of foreign correspondents complement the official photographs and reproductions of posters and documents. An easy pictorial introduction to war history. School and public libraries.

6003 940.4'12'71
**McWilliams, James L.**
The Suicide Battalion, by James L. McWilliams and R. J. Steel. Edmonton: Hurtig Publishers, 1978. 226p. map. Bibliography: p. 222-223. Index.
ISBN 0-88830-152-9 $12.95

1. Canada. Army. 46th Batallion. 2. European War, 1914-1918 – Regimental histories – Canada – 46th Batallion.

From four years' research of official documents, published and unpublished primary and secondary sources, and interviews with survivors, the authors have woven a starkly realistic record of one Canadian battalion's experiences during the First World War. The detailed chronicle of trench warfare is a significant addition to war history. An indictment of war; not pleasant reading.

6004 940.53'15
**Kahn, Leon.**
No Time to Mourn: A True Story of a Jewish Partisan Fighter. By Leon Kahn as told to Marjorie Morris; drawings by Keith Chapman. Vancouver: Laurelton Press, c1978. 212p. ill., plates. pa.: $7.50

1. World War, 1939-1945 – Personal narratives, Jewish. 2. Jews in Poland – Persecutions. 3. Guerrillas – Poland – Biography.

The story of man's inhumanity to man has been depicted many times. With stark simplicity, in words and pictures and in horrific detail, Kahn reveals what it was like to be a Jew in Hitler's Germany. Paula de Ronde

6005 940.53'71
**Douglas, William A. B.**
Out of the Shadows: Canada in the Second World War, by William A. B. Douglas and Brereton Greenhous. Toronto: Oxford University Press, 1977. 288p. ill., maps, ports. Bibliography: p. 279-280. Index.
ISBN 0-19-540257-X $14.95

1. Canada. Armed Forces. 2. World War, 1939-1945 – Canada. 3. World War, 1939-1945 – Campaigns.

Two reputable historians examine Canada's performance in the Second World War against a backdrop of political, economic and social conditions. Activities of the armed forces in various theatres, and issues and crises on the Home Front are objectively assessed. Relevant illustrations complement the lucid narrative of Canada's maturing in the crucible of war. Popular history.

6006 940.54'21

**Swettenham, John.**

Canada's Atlantic War. Illustrated by Fred Gaffen. Toronto: Samuel Stevens, 1979. 154p. ill., maps, ports. Bibliography: p. 149. Index. ISBN 0-88866-604-7 $15.95

1. World War, 1939-1945 – Atlantic Ocean. 2. World War, 1939-1945 – Naval operations, Canadian.

The role played by Canada's Navy in the Battle of the Atlantic during six years of war is described in lively text and illustrated with photographs gleaned from Canadian, British, American and German archives. The Canadian effort is viewed in relation to the total conflict. An authoritative, readable overview for secondary school and public library collections.

6007 940.54'25

**Lindsay, Oliver.**

The Lasting Honour: The Fall of Hong Kong, 1941. Don Mills, Ont.: Thomas Nelson, 1978. 226p. ill., plates. Bibliography: p. 213-215. Index. ISBN 0-241-89946-X $14.95

1. Hong Kong – Siege, 1941.

During two years' service in Hong Kong and a posting to Canadian Defence Headquarters, a British soldier studied the battle areas and researched official military records. Interviews with survivors, letters, and personal accounts support this objective examination of the debacle and its aftermath. Good maps, readable prose, careful documentation. College and public libraries.

6008 940.54'49

**Halliday, Hugh A.**

The Tumbling Sky. Stittsville, Ont.: Canada's Wings, 1978. 324p. ill., maps, plates, ports. Index. ISBN 0-920002-03-X $12.95

1. Air pilots – Canada – Biography. 2. World War, 1939-1945 – Aerial operations, Canadian.

Primary and secondary records have been searched to chronicle the feats of thirty-five Canadian air aces of World War II. The brief, factual accounts are supplemented by lists of Canadian fighter pilots and leading Observers and Radio Operators in both British and Canadian Forces. A useful source of information which is also a record of gallantry.

6009 940.54'59

**Lamb, James B.**

The Corvette Navy: True Stories From Canada's Atlantic War. Toronto: Macmillan; Scarborough, Ont.: Macmillan-NAL Publishing, 1979, c1977. 179p.
ISBN 0-7705-1578-9 bd.: $10.95
ISBN 0-7723-0015-1 pa.: $2.25

1. World War, 1939-1945 – Personal narratives, Canadian. 2. World War, 1939-1945 – Naval operations, Canadian. 3. World War, 1939-1945 – Atlantic Ocean.

The wartime battle to protect the North Atlantic sea lanes to Britain against the marauding German U-boats is described realistically by a former corvette officer. Dangers of convoy escort, the vulnerability of small ships to moods of sea and weather are conveyed vividly. Real-life adventure relieved by laconic humour. Young people and adults.

6010 940.54'59

**Lawrence, Hal.**

A Bloody War: One Man's Memories of the Canadian Navy, 1939-1945. Toronto: Macmillan, c1979. 193p. ill., maps, plates. ISBN 0-7705-1734-X $14.95

1. Canada. Royal Canadian Navy – History. 2. World War, 1939-1945 – Naval operations, Canadian. 3. World War, 1939-1945 – Personal narratives, Canadian.

A well-written, chatty account of a young Canadian seaman's experiences in the Battle of the Atlantic. The dangers and the comradeship, the humour and the hardships are vividly evoked. Maps on end-papers illustrate the patrol and convoy routes, and archival photographs complement the narrative. Engrossing reading.

6011 940.54'72

**Bates, Maxwell.**

A Wilderness of Days: An Artist's Experiences as a Prisoner of War in Germany. Victoria: Sono Nis Press, 1978. 133p. ill. ISBN 0-919462-56-1 bd.: $9.95

1. World War, 1939-1945 – Prisoners and prisons, German. 2. World War, 1939-1945 – Personal narratives, Canadian.

Captured in 1940 when France fell, a Canadian artist survived five years in prison camps and two long, forced marches, one preceding and one concluding the incarceration. Terse, unvarnished prose and stark black and white drawings recreate the reality of physical hardship, hunger and the effects of prolonged captivity. A thoughtful, personal memory of the war. Young people and adults.

6012 940.54'8

**Draper, Alfred.**

Operation Fish: The Fight to Save the Gold of Britain, France and Norway From the Nazis. Don Mills, Ont.: General Publishing, c1979. 377p. ill., maps, plates, ports. Bibliography: p. 369. Index. ISBN 0-7736-0068-X $12.95

1. World War, 1939-1945 – Finance.
2. Gold – History – 20th century.

From government and admiralty papers, official communiqués and eye-witness accounts, a former naval officer reconstructs the stories of danger-fraught trans-Atlantic crossings to Canada at the peak of the submarine war. A tightly written, engrossing story of an extraordinary undertaking. Will have wide appeal.

6013 940.54'81

**Mowat, Farley.**

And No Birds Sang. Toronto: McClelland and Stewart, c1979. 250p. ISBN 0-7710-6618-X $13.95

1. World War, 1939-1945 – Personal narratives, Canadian.

The barbarity and futility of war transformed a swaggering, self-confident junior officer into a seasoned, cynical veteran as his regiment was decimated in Sicily and struggled to survive the carnage of the 1943 Italian campaign. A frank and vividly recreated record of baptism by fire. Spiced with humour. Not vintage Mowat but well worth reading.

6014 940.54'81

**Stanké, Alain.**

So Much to Forget. Agincourt, Ont.: Gage Publishing, 1977. 164p. ISBN 0-7715-9364-3 $7.95

1. World War, 1939-1945 – Personal narratives, Lithuanian.

Translation of *J'aime encore mieux le jus de betterave!*

Five years of war as experienced by a small Lithuanian boy and his family – enemy occupation of their homeland, hunger, deportation and bombings. The brutality and atrocities often incomprehensible to a child are counterbalanced by family affection and the boy's sense of the ridiculous. A simply written, starkly realistic record of the human costs of international conflict. Adolescents and adults.

6015 940.54'86

**Pickersgill, Frank.**

The Making of a Secret Agent: Letters of 1934-1943. Edited with a memoir by George H. Ford. Toronto: McClelland and Stewart, c1978. 279p. ill., map, ports. ISBN 0-7710-7005-5 pa.: $7.95

1. Spies – Canada – Biography. 2. Spies – France – Biography. 3. World War, 1939-1945 – Secret service.

First edition published in 1948 under title *The Pickersgill Letters.*

In letters to family and friends a happy young intellectual comments on student days in Canada and abroad, travels in Europe on the brink of war, and life in occupied France which crystallized for him the meaning of dictatorship. An invaluable perspective on pre-war Europe. Highly recommended for public, college and school libraries.

6016 947.084'2

**Turkow Kaminska, Ruth.**

I Don't Want to Be Brave Anymore. Introduction by Harrison E. Salisbury. Toronto: Lester and Orpen, c1978. 255p. plates, ports. Index. ISBN 0-919630-06-5 $11.95

1. Jews in Russia – Biography. 2. Political prisoners – Russia – Biography.

Ruth Turkow Kaminska spent five years in prison and exile in Siberia because she was a Jewess and wealthy. She survived psychological and physical torture. In her autobiography she asks "what do you expect from a country governed by fear?" Paula de Ronde

6017 956'.5

**Bedoukian, Kerop.**

The Urchin: An Armenian's Escape. Don Mills, Ont.: Longman, c1978. 186p. maps, plates, ports. ISBN 0-7195-3458-5 $14.95

1. Armenian massacres, 1915-1923 – Personal narratives.

The sufferings of an Armenian family from their expulsion in 1915 to the finding of a Canadian home in 1926 are replayed through the memory of an impressionable nine-year-old boy. Unquestioning acceptance of hardship and horror sharpen the poignancy of the immigrant's story. An historical note describes the annihilation of the Armenians by the Turks. Recommended. School and public libraries.

6018 962.4'03

**MacLaren, Roy.**

Canadians on the Nile, 1882-1898: Being the Adventures of the Voyageurs on the Khartoum Relief Expedition and Other Exploits. Vancouver: University of British Columbia Press, c1978. 184p. ill., facsims., map, plates, ports. Bibliography: p. 177-179. Index. ISBN 0-7748-0094-1 $14.95

1. Khartoum Relief Expedition, 1884-1885. 2. Canadians in the Sudan. 3. Sudan – History – 1862-1899.

A lively, well researched account of Canada's two-pronged participation in the Sudan campaigns of the late nineteenth century. One was a daring but ill-conceived attempt to transport British troops up the Nile to relieve Khartoum, the other, the successful building of a desert railway. A new perspective on a little-known episode. Detailed and interesting.

## 970 North America - Discovery and exploration

6019 970'.004'97

**Ashwell, Reg.**

Coast Salish: Their Art, Culture and Legends. North Vancouver, B.C.: Hancock House, c1978. 86p. ill., map, ports. ISBN 0-88839-009-2 pa.: $3.50

1. Salish Indians – Social life and customs. 2. Indians of North America – Northwest coast of North America – Social life and customs.

Ashwell's small publication deals with the history and traditions of the Pacific Northwest Indian tribe, the Coast Salish. He successfully provides an overview of this tribe for the lay reader. The scope of the book includes the tribe's origin, lifestyle, crafts, religion, myths, and cultural decline. Ashwell also discusses the renewal and revival of Coast Salish arts and crafts. The book contains several black and white illustrations and photographs and a section of colour photographs of Coast Salish crafts and art. There is no index. Janice Zlatarits

6020 970'.004'97

**Brand, Johanna.**

The Life and Death of Anna Mae Aquash. Toronto: James Lorimer, 1978. 171p. ill., maps, plates, ports. Bibliography: p. 164-171. ISBN 0-88862-152-3 bd.: $12.95
ISBN 0-88862-153-1 pa.: $6.95

1. Aquash, Anna Mae, 1945-1976. 2. American Indian Movement. 3. Indians of North America – Canada – Biography.

Exposes the FBI's secret and illegal war against civil rights movements in general, and the American Indian Movement in particular, by presenting the officially concealed facts surrounding the murder of a Canadian Indian rights activist on a South Dakota reservation. An objective, well-researched documentary by a journalist concerned with the issue of securing freedom and justice for the powerless. Ille-Mai Gerdels

6021 970'.004'97

**Dumond, Don E.**

The Eskimos and Aleuts. Maps and line drawings by Carol Steichen Dumond. London, Eng.: Thames and Hudson (Oxford University Press), 1977. 180p. ill., maps. Bibliography: p. 161-168. Index. (Ancient Peoples and Places) ISBN 0-500-02089-2 $12.95

1. Eskimos – Antiquities. 2. Aleuts – Antiquities. 3. North America – Antiquities. 4. Arctic regions – Antiquities.

Introductory text for university and community college students on Eskimo and Aleut archaeology. Based on archaeological excavations, it focuses on questions concerning population distribution and intensity. Chronologies discussed include the Northern Archaic, Dorset, Norton and Thule traditions. Well illustrated with detailed site maps and diagrams. Jay Wolofsky

6022 970'.004'97

**Hungry Wolf, Adolf.**

The Blood People: A Division of the Blackfoot Confederacy: An Illustrated Interpretation of the Old Ways. New York: Harper & Row (Fitzhenry & Whiteside), c1977. 370p. ill. Index. ISBN 0-06-450600-2 $14.95

1. Kainah Indians.

This valuable historical record of the social and spiritual practices of this Alberta tribe is complemented by over two hundred beautiful photographs. The author, an adopted Blood Indian, who has embraced their life style, has based his work on personal experience, interviews and archival sources. A lack of coherent organization reduces its value as a reference tool. Impressionistic rather than academic. Nikki Lawrence

6023 970'.004'97
**Mountain Horse, Mike.**
My People the Bloods. Edited and introduced by Hugh A. Dempsey. Calgary: Glenbow-Alberta Institute; Standoff, Alta.: Blood Tribal Council, 1979. 146p. ill., ports. Index. ISBN 0-919224-03-2 $7.95

1. Kainah Indians. 2. Indians of North America – Alberta.

An authoritative portrait of the Blood Indians of southern Alberta in the late nineteenth and early twentieth centuries. Written in the late thirties, but not published, the book stems from memories of Indian elders and the experiences of the author, a Blood, and his family. Daily life, customs and religion are described from the Indian point of view. A significant work.

6024 970'.004'97
**Price, John A.**
Native Studies: American and Canadian Indians. Toronto: McGraw-Hill Ryerson, c1978. 300p. maps. Bibliography: p. 289-299. Indexes. ISBN 0-07-082695-1 pa.: $7.95

1. Indians of North America.

A lucid exposition of the purpose, scope, method, and theoretical framework of modern anthropology with specific reference to the study of North American Indians. Individual discussion on commonly studied concepts includes current issues such as militancy within the urban Indian movement to demonstrate the social relevance of this scientific discipline. Frieda Ling

6025 970'.004'97
**Snow, John.**
These Mountains Are Our Sacred Places: The Story of the Stoney People. Toronto: Samuel Stevens, 1977. 186p. ill., maps, ports. Bibliographical references and Index.
ISBN 0-88866-589-X bd.: $10
ISBN 0-88866-590-3 pa.: $5

1. Assiniboin Indians – History. 2. Indians of North America – Alberta – History.

A well-researched, well-written chronology of the beliefs, lifestyle and values of this tribe, from the period prior to the appearance of the white man, to the present. Particular emphasis is placed on clarifying the understanding of Treaty Seven by the Native Peoples and white men. Kathryn Walker

## 970.41 Native peoples of Canada

6026 970.41'016
**Canada. Indian and Eskimo Affairs Program. Education and Cultural Support Branch.**
About Indians: A Listing of Books. 4th ed. Ottawa: Ministry of Supply and Services, 1977. 382p. ill. Indexes. ISBN 0-662-00714-8 pa.: Free DSS cat. no. R32-30/1977

1. Indians of North America – Bibliography.
2. Indians of South America – Bibliography.

Third edition listed *CS* no. 4015.

"This bibliography is made up of books about the native peoples of North America. Those having Canadian authorship or specific Canadian interest have been indicated by a maple leaf. This edition includes a section of books about Indians which are available in French." -Preface.

## 971 Canada - History

6027 971.
**Berton, Pierre.**
My Country: The Remarkable Past. Toronto: Seal Books, 1979. 340p. ill., plates. Index. ISBN 0-7704-1547-4 pa.: $2.75

1. Canada – History. 2. Canada – Biography.

Clothbound edition listed *CS* no. 4035

6028 971.
**Berton, Pierre.**
The Wild Frontier: More Tales From the Remarkable Past. Maps by Jack McMaster. Toronto: McClelland and Stewart, c1978. 250p. maps, ports. Bibliography: p. 235-239. Index. ISBN 0-7710-1360-4 $14.95

1. Canada – History. 2. Canada – Biography.

Seven unusual individuals gained a niche in Canadian history through their exploits on Canada's frontiers. Less detailed versions of the same tales have been narrated by the author on television. Readers may question some of Berton's character interpretations. Lively popularized history for the uncritical reader.

6029 971.
**Canadian Authors Association.**
Spirit of Canada. Photographs by John de Visser, Murray Sumner, and Richard Vroom. Toronto: Canadian Authors Association, 1977. 96p. ill. pa.: $5.95

1. Canada.

Poetry and prose selections contributed by members of the Canadian Authors Association are combined with excellent black and white photographs to convey the essence of Canada and its peoples. Pleasant, undemanding browsing. Secondary school and public libraries.

6030 971.
**Colombo, John Robert,** ed.
Colombo's Book of Canada. Edmonton: Hurtig Publishers, c1978. 176p. ill., ports. Index. ISBN 0-88830-155-3 bd.: $18.95
ISBN 0-88830-161-8 pa.: $12.95

1. Canada.

A potpourri of fact and fiction, verse, drama and statistics. The FLQ Manifesto and the Canadian Bill of Rights share space with protocol for flying the flag and an interview with Louis Riel. There are useful fragments of information but lack of a general index limits the book's reference value. Interesting for browsing. High school and public libraries.

6031 971.
**Einarsson, Magnus.**
Everyman's Heritage: An Album of Canadian Folk Life. Notre patrimoine: images du peuple canadien. Ottawa: Canadian Centre for Folk Culture Studies, National Museum of Man, 1978. 200p. ill.
ISBN 0-660-00101-2 bd.: $12.50
ISBN 0-660-00124-1 pa.: $8.50

1. Canada – Social life and customs – Pictorial works. 2. Canada – History – Pictorial works.

The richness of Canada's ethnic mosaic is illustrated in two hundred good quality archival photographs. Stemming from a permanent exhibition, "Everyman's Heritage: The Canadian Odyssey", in the National Museum of Man, the photographs are dated, captioned in English and French, and grouped thematically. An interesting pictorial review of the settling of Canada. Browsing for all ages.

6032 971.
**Hamelin, Louis-Edmond.**
Canadian Nordicity: It's Your North Too. Translated by William Barr. Montreal: Harvest House, c1978. 373p. graphs, maps. Bibliography: p. 337-341. Index.
ISBN 0-88772-174-5 pa.: $12.95

1. Canada.

Translation of *Nordicité canadienne.*

Governor General's Literary Award. This recently translated study concentrates on the concept of 'nordicity', or quantitative northerness, in an attempt to analyze and provide a programme for development within the northern context. It offers an interesting viewpoint to those who see the exploitation of resources and expansion of our economy from the traditional southern perspective.
Nikki Lawrence

6033 971.
**Lower, Arthur R. M.**
Colony to Nation: A History of Canada. Maps by T. W. MacLean. 5th ed. Toronto: McClelland and Stewart, c1977. 600p. graphs, maps. Bibliographies and Index.
ISBN 0-7710-5369-X pa.: $11.95

1. Canada – History.

Previous edition listed as out-of-print in CS no. 4051.

6034 971.
**Morton, W. L.**
This Land, These People: An Illustrated History of Canada, by W. L. Morton and L. F. Hannon. Agincourt, Ont.: Gage Publishing, c1977. 248p. ill., ports. Bibliography: p. 236-239. Index. ISBN 0-7715-9332-5 $29.95

1. Canada – History.

The essence of the Canadian experience is succinctly captured in high quality photographs and lucid commentary. A brief and readable overview of Canada's social, political and economic development from the coming of the Norsemen to the present, is augmented by a detailed chronology. The theme is the interaction of geography, history and people. General readers and students.

6035 971.
**Penner, Norman,** ed.
Keeping Canada Together Means Changing Our Thinking. Scarborough, Ont.: Amethyst Publications, c1978. 129p. plates, ports. Bibliographies. ISBN 0-920474-07-1 pa.: $5.95

1. Canada – English-French relations.
2. Quebec (Province) – History – Autonomy and independence movements. 3. Canada – Politics and government.

The issue of Canadian unity, its background, contemporary manifestations, and possible future, is addressed in papers given at York University to a group of senior citizens. There is variety in viewpoint and emphasis, but all contributors probe some facet of Canada's troubled federation. A coherent introduction for the general reader.

6036 971.
**Woodcock, George.**
The Canadians. Don Mills, Ont.: Fitzhenry & Whiteside, 1979. 308p. ill. Index.
ISBN 0-88902-571-1 $19.95

1. Regionalism – Canada. 2. Canada – History. 3. Canada – Civilization.

Based upon his premise that "regionalism, not centralization holds the key to Canadian unity", the west coast scholar examines the distinct geographic, social, political and cultural characteristics in seven regions. A provocative viewpoint which merits examination by thoughtful readers. Profusely illustrated. Public, college and university libraries.

---

**971.002** Canada – History – Miscellany

---

6037 971'.002
**Nicol, Eric.**
Canada, Cancelled Because of Lack of Interest, by Eric Nicol and Peter Whalley. Edmonton: Hurtig Publishers, c1977. 201p. ill., ports. ISBN 0-88830-139-1 $8.95

1. Canada – Civilization – Anecdotes, facetiae, satire, etc.

Satirizes the aspects of Canadian life that in one hundred years will have led to the deconfederation of Canada. Nicol's professional skill and aplomb as a humorist are most evident in his amusing in-jokes, and Whalley's abundant cartoons, though blunt, are funny and appropriate. Of wide, general appeal. Ille-Mai Gerdels

---

**971.004** Canada – History – Ethnic groups

---

6038 971'.004
**Canada. Multiculturalism Directorate.**
The Canadian Family Tree. Rev. and updated ed. Don Mills, Ont.: Corpus Information Services, 1979. 272p. Bibliography: p. 237-238. Index.
ISBN 0-919217-13-3 bd.: $19.95
ISBN 0-919217-14-1 pa.: $12.95

1. Canada – Population – Ethnic groups.

An expanded and revised edition of the 1967 publication, now out-of-print, which was prepared by the Canadian Citizenship Branch, Department of the Secretary of State. An introductory article on the history of Canadian immigration is followed by succinct articles on seventy-eight ethnocultural groups and their contribution to Canadian life. A useful reference.

6039 971'.004'114
**Federation of Francophones Outside Quebec.**
The Heirs of Lord Durham: The Manifesto of a Vanishing People. Translated by Diane Norak. With the support of the Canadian Council of Christians and Jews. Toronto: Burns and MacEachern, 1978- v Bibliography: p. 79. ISBN 0-88768-081-X pa.: $5.95

1. Canadians, French-speaking. 2. French language in Canada.

Contents: vol. 1. The Francophones Outside Quebec Speak Out. c1978. Translation of *Les héritiers de Lord Durham*.

Franco-Canadians are concerned with the alarming rate of assimilation and suggest this results from inadequate provincial language legislation, educational opportunities and regional media. This controversial document, essential reading for an understanding of the implications of language rights, is introduced by Dr. Ramsay's excellent essay placing the current situation in its historical framework. Nikki Lawrence

6040 971'.004'91
**Keywan, Zonia.**
Greater Than Kings: Ukrainian Pioneer Settlement in Canada. Photographs by Martin Coles. Montreal: Harvest House, 1977. 165p. ill., map, ports. Bibliography.
ISBN 0-88772-177-X $14.95

1. Ukrainians in the Prairie Provinces – History. 2. Land settlement – Prairie Provinces – History.

An excellent selection of texts, based on interviews, quotations, and translations, matched by some superb photographs, old and new, make this one of the most interesting books on Ukrainian prairie pioneers in the years 1891-1920. Highly recommended for all libraries. Andrew Gregorovich

6041 971.004'91
**Swyripa, Frances.**
Ukrainian Canadians: A Survey of Their Portrayal in English-language Works. Edmonton: Published for the Canadian Institute of Ukrainian Studies by the University of Alberta Press, 1978. 169p. Bibliography: p. 147-166. Index.
ISBN 0-88864-050-1 bd.: $9.95
ISBN 0-88864-022-6 pa.: $3.95

1. Ukrainians in Canada – Historiography.

A young Saskatchewan-born researcher provides an analysis of literature relating to Ukrainians in Canada published up to 1970, and university theses. Presented chronologically with critical assessments, at times too strongly expressed, this study will be of much interest to general readers, students and researchers. Librarians will find the extensive bibliography valuable. Andrew Gregorovich

6042 971'.004'91791
**Lupul, Manoly R.,** ed.
Ukrainian Canadians, Multiculturalism, and Separatism: An Assessment. Proceedings of the conference sponsored by the Canadian Institute of Ukrainian Studies, University of Alberta, Edmonton, September 9-11, 1977. Edmonton: Published for the Canadian Institute of Ukrainian Studies by the University of Alberta Press, 1978. 177p. (The Alberta Library in Ukrainian-Canadian Studies) ISBN 0-88864-996-7 pa.: $4.95

1. Ukrainians in Canada – Congresses. 2. Canada – Population – Ethnic groups – Congresses. 3. Quebec (Province) – History – Autonomy and independence movements – Congresses.

Eight papers presented at a University of Alberta conference by university professors and people in government, both federal and provincial. The volume touches on subjects of great concern to all Canadians and will be of special interest to larger public libraries and academic libraries. Andrew Gregorovich

6043 971'.004'956
**Broadfoot, Barry.**
Years of Sorrow, Years of Shame: The Story of the Japanese Canadians in World War II. Toronto: Doubleday; Don Mills, Ont.: PaperJacks, 1979, c1977. 370p. ill., map, plates, ports. ISBN 0-385-12550-X bd.: $12.50
ISBN 0-7701-0091-0 pa.: $5.95

1. Japanese in Canada – History. 2. Japanese in British Columbia – History. 3. World War, 1939-1945 – Evacuation of civilians.

Vivid oral history by the author of *Ten Lost Years*. Fails to place the Japanese within the overall Canadian context but is, nonetheless, a moving and interesting account of shameful treatment of citizens. No index, notes or sources given. Nikki Lawrence

6044 971'.004'956
**Japanese Canadian Centennial Project. Committee.**
A Dream of Riches: The Japanese Canadians, 1877-1977. Un rêve de richesses: les Japonais au Canada, 1877-1977. Vancouver: Japanese Canadian Centennial Project, c1978. 190p. ill., ports. Bibliography: p. 189-190. ISBN 0-9690708-0-2 bd.: $17 pa.: $13

1. Japanese in Canada – History. 2. Japanese in Canada – Portraits. 3. Japanese Canadians – Canada – History. 4. Japanese Canadians – Canada – Portraits.

A photographic exhibit assembled in 1977 to commemorate one hundred years of Japanese life in Canada has been distilled into book form. Brief captions, listed in the back of the book, identify the photographs; the narrative is in English, Japanese and French, in parallel columns. A "family-album" type record of one segment of the Canadian mosaic.

6045 971'.004'96
**Thomson, Colin Argyle.**
Blacks in Deep Snow: Black Pioneers in Canada. Don Mills, Ont.: J. M. Dent, c1979. 112p. ill., plates, ports. Index.
ISBN 0-460-90280-6 $8.95

1. Blacks – Canada – History. 2. Blacks – The West, Canadian – History.

In less than one hundred pages the author sketches the history of black immigration to western Canada, profiles two distinguished black pioneers, and briefly introduces five minor personalities. The brief, episodic treatment of an important subject diminishes the book, but the chronology has reference value. A forceful plea for a re-examination of Canada's attitudes toward minorities. Junior high to adult.

6046 971'.004'97
**Dick, Leonard G.**
Broken Spirit. Illustrated by Leonard Stevens. Cobalt, Ont.: Highway Book Shop, c1978. 67p. ill. Bibliography: p. 66-67
ISBN 0-88954-160-4 pa.: $3

1. Indians of North America – Canada – Social conditions.

An alternative perspective on the social

problems facing Native peoples today. The author places the responsibility for change on the Native peoples. They must become part of Canadian society, "for as long as Indian people are treated as 'special' their problems will remain". -Preface. Kathryn Walker

6047 971'.004'97

**Embree, Jesse.**

Let Us Live: The Native People of Canada. Don Mills, Ont.: J. M. Dent, c1977. 64p. ill., maps, ports. Bibliography: p. 64. ISBN 0-460-93588-7 pa.: $3.95

1. Indians of North America – Canada.

A lucid introductory text on the history, cultural contribution, present condition, and future aspirations of Canada's first peoples. The numerous illustrations include drawings of historic scenes, photographs of leaders, folksingers, artists, and aspects of life on reserves. Concludes with biographical sketches of ten Indians, male and female, renowned or little-known, who have made significant contributions to their race. Frieda Ling

6048 971'.004'97

**Jenness, Diamond.**

The Indians of Canada. 7th ed. Toronto: University of Toronto Press; Ottawa: National Museum of Man; Publishing Centre, Supply and Services Canada, 1977. 432p. ill., maps, music, ports. Bibliographical references and Index. ISBN 0-8020-2286-3 $17.50

1. Indians of North America – Canada.

Sixth edition listed CS no. 3990.

"This new edition contains a reprint of the sixth edition omitting only the appendixes and reference to them, and a pocket map unavailable at time of printing. It includes a new foreword to the work and its author by Dr. William E. Taylor, Jr., Director of the National Museum of Man in Ottawa." -Title page verso. An essential reference for libraries which do not have the sixth edition.

6049 971'.004'97

**Price, John A.**

Indians of Canada: Cultural Dynamics. Scarborough, Ont.: Prentice-Hall, 1979. 261p. ill., maps. Bibliography: p. 239-253. Index. ISBN 0-13-456962-8 pa.: $7.95

1. Indians of North America – Canada.

A documented, academic study of the anthropological history and cultural evolution of Canadian Indians and Inuit. This is a clear, structurally and thematically organized text by a York University professor that concludes by relating historical developmental patterns to current Native concerns. Meant for the seriously interested reader and the student of Native studies. Ille-Mai Gerdels

6050 971'.004'97

**Symington, Fraser.**

The First Canadians. Toronto: Natural Science of Canada, c1978. 128p. ill., maps. Index. (Canada's Illustrated Heritage) ISBN 0-919644-13-9 $7.95

1. Indians of North America – Canada.
2. Eskimos – Canada.

An evolutionary history of Canadian Indians reconstructed from archaeological evidence and anthropological theories. Described in culture groups, there are expositions of potlatch, puberty rites, shamanism, the spiritual meaning of masks. Special paragraphs explain tipi-pitching, canoe-building, dog-sleds, cradleboards, games, etc. The short articles are well illustrated. Junior High level. Frieda Ling

6051 971'.004'97

**Updike, Lee R.**

The First People: An Artist's Reconstruction of Five Native Canadian Cultures. Drawings by Lee R. Updike; text by R. D. Symons. Saskatoon: Western Producer Prairie Books, 1978. 141p. ill., map, Index. ISBN 0-919306-95-0 bd.: $14.95
ISBN 0-919306-92-6 pa.: $8.95

1. Indians of North America – Canada.
2. Indians of North America – Canada – Pictorial works.

A graphic account of Canada's first inhabitants ranging from the Eastern Woodland Region, to the Plains, the West Coast, the Subarctic and the Arctic. Illustrated throughout with line sketches. Commissioned by the Metropolitan Educational Association of Toronto in Association with the Ethnohistory Department of the Royal Ontario Museum, the book traces the varied and traditional lifestyles of the five cultures. Jay Wolofsky

6052 971.007

**Hodgetts, A. B.**

Teaching Canada for the '80s, by A. B. Hodgetts and Paul Gallagher. Toronto: Ontario Institute for Studies in Education, c1978. 135p. ISBN 0-7744-0167-2 pa.: $5.95

1. Canada – Study and teaching.

Analyzing the progress made since the appearance of *What Culture? What Heritage?* in 1968, the authors, both former directors of the

Canadian Studies Foundation, conclude that the time has come for "a cooperative and systematic nation-wide effort to improve the quality of studies of Canada in Canadian schools." This volume is their widely acclaimed proposal for such a national syllabus to be taught in the elementary and secondary grades. Ethel Auster

6053 971'.007'11

**Symons, Thomas H. B.**

The Symons Report. Toronto: McClelland and Stewart, c1978. 205p. Bibliographical references. ISBN 0-7710-8380-7 pa.: $1.95

1. Canadian studies. 2. Universities and colleges – Canada – Curricula.

*To Know Ourselves: The Report of the Commission on Canadian Studies* listed CS no. 4082. "An abridged version of volumes 1 and 2 of *To Know Ourselves: The Report of the Royal Commission on Canadian Studies.*" -Title page.

**971.0092** Canada – History – Biographies

6054 971'.00992

**Hubbard, R. H.**

Rideau Hall: An Illustrated History of Government House, Ottawa, From Victorian Times to the Present Day. Forewords by Jules Léger and Georges P. Vanier. Montreal: McGill-Queen's University Press; Ottawa: Government House: Publishing Centre, Supply and Services Canada, 1977. 281p. ill., maps, plans, ports. Bibliographical references and Index. ISBN 0-7735-0310-2 $25

1. Governors general – Canada – Biography. 2. Canada – History. 3. Rideau Hall, Ottawa, Ont. – History.

Hubbard, the chief curator of Canadian Art at the National Gallery of Canada, has produced a detailed account of the home of Canada's Governors General from 1826 to the present. The development of the present Rideau Hall is traced and other official residences are described. Illustrated with photographs, sketches and floor plans. Well researched. Will interest historians, architects and the general reader. Nancy Cohen

**971.03** Canada - History - 1791-1841.

6055 971.03

**Atwood, Margaret.**

Days of the Rebels: 1815/1840. Toronto: Natural Science of Canada, c1977. 128p. ill., facsims., map, ports. Index. (Canada's Illustrated Heritage) ISBN 0-9196-4416-3 $7.95

1. Canada – Civilization – 19th century.

Atwood sets a high standard of writing and understanding of these twenty-five turbulent years in Canada's history. Like others in the series, the narrative is combined with contemporary illustrations. Palatable social history for high school and general adult reading. Similar in format and length, each dealing with a discrete period in Canada's history, from discovery and exploration to the social changes of the 1960's: Horwood, H. *The Colonial Dream, 1497/1760;* Hannon, L. F. *Redcoats and Loyalists, 1760/1840.*

**971.04** Growth of responsible government, 1841-1867.

6056 971.04

**Knight, David B.**

A Capital for Canada: Conflict and Compromise in the Nineteenth Century. Chicago: University of Chicago, Dept. of Geography, 1977. 341p. ill., maps, ports. Bibliography: p. 327-338. (Research Paper – University of Chicago, Department of Geography) ISBN 0-89065-089-6 Processed: $6 (U.S.)

1. Canada – Politics and government – 1841-1867. 2. Canada – Capital – History.

A detailed history and analysis of the patterns of opinion on the contentious question of a central government site in the mid-nineteenth century. Official government papers and contemporary records were scrutinized. A well-documented, chronological account supported by a bibliography of primary and secondary materials. The author's *Choosing Canada's Capital,* which contains the documents upon which this study is based, is complementary. School, college and public libraries.

6057 971.04

**Knight, David B.,** ed.

Choosing Canada's Capital: Jealousy and Friction in the Nineteenth Century. Toronto: McClelland and Stewart; Ottawa: Institute of Canadian Studies, Carleton University, c1977. 228p. maps. Bibliography: p. 226-228. Index. (The Carleton Library)
ISBN 0-7710-9803-0 pa.: $4.95

1. Canada – Capital – History – Sources.

The tensions and jealousies which characterized the search for a capital for the Province of Canada between 1841 and 1859 are revealed in primary documents culled from British, provincial and federal archives. A general introduction and brief chapter introductions set the contentious issue in context. Original maps, a document index and careful research. History buffs and general readers.

## 971.05 Dominion of Canada, 1967-1911.

6058 971.05

**Jones, Mary Fallis.**

The Confederation Generation. Toronto: Royal Ontario Museum, c1978. 112p. ill., map, port. Indexes. ISBN 0-88854-212-7 bd.: $12.50 ISBN 0-88854-220-8 pa.: $5.95

1. Canada – Civilization – 19th century.

Excerpts from contemporary print media and illustrations mainly from from "Canadian Illustrated News" examine the social history of English-speaking urban Canada in the 1870's and 1880's. Satisfactorily researched, well organized and attractively presented by a former teacher, the book is of particular interest to students, and entertaining reading for adult patrons. Ille-Mai Gerdels

6059 971.05'1

**Oppen, William A.,** comp.

The Riel Rebellions: A Cartographic History. Le récit cartographique des affaires Riel. Toronto: University of Toronto Press; Ottawa: Public Archives of Canada; Canadian Govt. Publishing Centre, c1979. 109p. ill., maps. Bibliography: p. 109.
ISBN 0-8020-2333-9 $20

1. Red River Rebellion, 1869-1870 – Maps.
2. Riel Rebellion, 1885 – Maps.

A fresh perspective on the Red River Insurrection of 1869-70 and the Riel Rebellion of 1885, is offered in this study of events as reflected in contemporary maps, plans and charts. The parallel text in English and French establishes the chronology and is a framework for the examination of the adequacy of maps in portraying events. Large libraries.

6060 971.05'4

**Miller, James R.**

Equal Rights: The Jesuits' Estates Act Controversy. Montreal: McGill-Queen's University Press, 1979. 223p. ill., ports. Bibliography: p. 203-213. Index.
ISBN 0-7735-0302-1 $13.95

1. Equal Rights Association for the Province of Ontario. 2. Quebec (Province). Laws, statutes, etc. Act respecting the settlement of the Jesuits' Estates. 3. Jesuit estates.

This is an exemplary history of the interplay between Quebec and Ontario over the compensation of the Jesuits for land lost after the Conquest, the Jesuit Estates Act of 1888, and the subsequent formation of the Equal Rights Association and alienation of the Conservative Party in Quebec. An impressive range and variety of sources. Nikki Lawrence

6061 971.05'5

**Callwood, June.**

The Naughty Nineties, 1890/1900. Toronto: Natural Science of Canada, c1977. 128p. ill., ports. (Canada's Illustrated Heritage) Index.
ISBN 0-919644-21-X $9.95

1. Canada – Civilization – 19th century.

Lively, journalistic narrative coupled with reproductions of contemporary cartoons, photographs, handbills, magazine covers and posters evoke the atmosphere of change and development which characterized the last decade of the nineteenth century. Similar in approach, format and style to others in the series such as: Collins, R. *The Age of Innocence, 1870/1880.* Popularized social history for junior high school to adults.

## 971.06 Twentieth century, 1911-

6062 971.06

**Clery, Val,** ed.

Canada from the Newsstands: A Selection from the Best Canadian Journalism of the Past Thirty Years. Toronto: Macmillan, c1978. 295p. Index. ISBN 0-7705-1720-X bd.: $14.95
ISBN 0-7705-1727-7 pa.: $7.95

1. Canada – History – 1945- 2. Canada – Social conditions.

Consists of twenty-nine predominantly

political Canadian magazine feature articles written by prominent journalists between 1947 and 1977, and compiled by an internationally successful writer and broadcaster. The chronological arrangement, varied journalistic styles, and insights into the Canadian situation will attract the general reader and the student. Ille-Mai Gerdels

6063 971.06
**Hanlon, Michael,** ed.
Page One: A News History of Canada from the Pages of The Toronto Star. Agincourt, Ont.: Gage Publishing, c1978. 140p. ill., maps, ports. ISBN 0-7715-9461-5 pa.: $7.95

1. The Toronto Star. 2. Canada – History – 20th century.

A selection of front pages of the "Toronto Star" recalls almost ninety years of Canadian history. Arranged in chronological order, the front page stories chronicle the major national and international events from 1895 to 1978: wars, labour disputes, Queen Victoria's death, the Halifax explosion, and space exploration. Small print and poorly reproduced pages detract from an interesting browsing book.

6064 971.06'092'2
**McNeil, Bill.**
Voice of the Pioneer. Toronto: Macmillan, c1978. 257p. ill., plates, ports. ISBN 0-7705-1730-7 $14.95

1. Voice of the pioneer (Radio programme). 2. Pioneers – Canada – Interviews. 3. Canada – Biography.

"Pioneers of all sorts – prospectors, scientists, homesteaders, teachers, bush pilots, and many others – tell their fascinating stories here, as they have told them on Canada's best-loved radio program." -Title page. A brief introductory note sets each recollection in a framework of time and place. Photographs are from the Public Archives of Canada.

6065 971.06'23
**Braithwaite, Max.**
The Hungry Thirties, 1930/1940. Toronto: Natural Science of Canada, c1977. 127p. ill., ports. Index. (Canada's Illustrated Heritage)

1. Canada – Civilization – 20th century.

Graphics from newspapers, periodicals, posters, photographs and advertisements are combined with a fast-paced journalistic style to evoke the mood of the decade. Unemployment, dust-bowl farming, politics, fashion and entertainment are vividly sketched. The inside covers carry an illustrated chronology of the major events of each year. Pictorial social history for general browsing. In the same series and format: Craig, J. *The Years of Agony: 1910-1920;* Craig, J. *The Crazy Twenties: 1920-1930;* Ross, A. *The Booming Fifties: 1950-1960.*

6066 971.06'4
**Drache, Daniel,** ed.
Debates and Controversies: Essays From This Magazine. Toronto: McClelland and Stewart, c1979. 205p. ISBN 0-7710-2882-2 pa.: $6.95

1. Canada – Politics and government – 1963- 2. Canada – Economic conditions – 1945- 3. Canada – Civilization – 20th century.

Critical issues confronting Canada in the last quarter of the twentieth century are analysed in a series of essays selected from "This Magazine". Canada's economic dependence on other countries, its cultural institutions, Quebec nationalism and labour, are scrutinized from the Leftist point of view. Not easy reading.

6067 971.06'4
**Harbron, John D.**
Canada Without Quebec. Don Mills, Ont.: Musson, 1977. 164p. maps. Bibliography: p. 157-159. Index. ISBN 0-7737-0033-1 bd.: $10.95 ISBN 0-7737-1016-7 pa.: $6.95

1. Canada – Politics and government – 1963- 2. Quebec (Province) – Politics and government – 1960- 3. Quebec (Province) – History – Autonomy and independence movements.

An international affairs journalist argues for the secession of Quebec. He illustrates Bolton's thesis that American history is a struggle for escape from European colonialism to the establishment of autonomous states, by drawing parallels with Mexico's development. Although marred by anti-Marxist bias this work expands our insular approach to the national unity question. Nikki Lawrence

6068 971.06'43
**Stursberg, Peter.**
Lester Pearson and the Dream of Unity. Toronto: Doubleday, 1978. 456p. plates, ports. Index. ISBN 0-385-13478-9 $17.95

1. Pearson, Lester B., 1897-1972. 2. Canada – Politics and government – 1963-

Segments of edited interviews with more than sixty leading Canadian politicians provide the commentary on major events and problems during the Pearson regime.

Interesting for browsing but does not constitute a coherent analysis of national political issues between 1963 and 1968. A second volume will focus on Pearson the diplomat and statesman.

6069 971.06'44

**Berkowitz, S. D.,** ed.

Canada's Third Option, edited by S. D. Berkowitz and Robert K. Logan. Toronto: Macmillan, c1978. 282p. ISBN 0-7705-1589-4 pa.: $8.95

1. Nationalism – Canada. 2. Canada – Politics and government – 1963- 3. Canada – Economic conditions. 4. Canada – Social conditions.

The option espoused in this work, exploring the constitutional, cultural and socio-economic facets of the unity dilemma, is the revision of the British North America Act for a radically altered constitution and a fundamental change in our social arrangements, e.g. national bilingualism. Essays by well-known "activist intellectuals" stimulate the expansion of our thinking beyond the traditional federalist-separatist polarities. Nikki Lawrence

6070 971.06'44

**Burke, Stanley.**

Swamp Song, by Stanley Burke and Roy Peterson. Vancouver: Douglas & McIntyre, 1978. ISBN 0-88894-212-5 $5.95

1. Canada – Politics and government – 1963- – Anecdotes, facetiae, satire, etc.

An experienced political journalist and a successful cartoonist update their *Chronicles of the Swamp* with this fourth illustrated fable about the absurdities of Canada's political history. A satire of topical interest and general appeal for adults and older teen-agers, but too coy and contrived for the discriminating, sophisticated reader. Ille-Mai Gerdels

6071 971.06'44

**Drouin, Marie Josée.**

Canada Has a Future. Prepared for the Hudson Institute of Canada by Marie Josée Drouin and B. Bruce-Briggs. Preface by Herman Kahn. Toronto: McClelland and Stewart, 1978. 285p. graphs. Index. ISBN 0-7710-2892-X $12.95

1. Twentieth century – Forecasts.

A neo-conservative analysis of the economic, political and social directions Canada can take in the next twenty years, by members of the policy research Hudson Institute. The work claims to be a study based on a quickly sketched methodology, however, the personal viewpoint predominates in tone and example. No bibliography. Minimal notes. Nikki Lawrence

6072 971.06'44

**Geddes, Gary,** ed.

Divided We Stand. Toronto: Peter Martin, 1977. 216p. ISBN 0-88778-174-8 bd.: $15 ISBN 0-88778-175-6 pa.: $7.95

1. Nationalism – Canada. 2. Nationalism – Quebec (Province).

A collection of poems, short stories, essays and speeches reflecting the economic, cultural and political turmoil of the seventies. Highly personal comments by those Canadians involved in shaping and reflecting our perceptions of this decade, Lévesque, Atwood, Watkins, focusing on the relationship between Quebec and the remainder of Canada. Uneven content but interesting perspectives. Nikki Lawrence

6073 971.06'44

**Menzies, Heather.**

The Railroad's Not Enough: Canada Now. Toronto: Clarke, Irwin, 1978. 318p. ill. Index. ISBN 0-7720-1226-1 $11.95

1. Canadians – Interviews. 2. Public opinion – Canada. 3. Nationalism – Canada – Public opinion.

A free-lance writer traversed the country seeking to crystallize the meaning of Canada and its future, in interviews with ordinary Canadians. Capsule introductions of the individuals and the retention of the local idiom create a convincing sense of time and personality, but no pervasive concern about national unity is disclosed. Interesting, but not conclusive. Popular appeal.

6074 971.06'44

**Porter, Anna,** ed.

Farewell to the Seventies. Edited by Anna Porter and Marjorie Harris. Don Mills, Ont.: Thomas Nelson, c1979. 255p. ill. Index. ISBN 0-17-600772-5 $14.95

1. Canada – Civilization – 1945-

A disorganized collection of more than two hundred contributions on Canada in the seventies by well-known Canadians writing on their areas of expertise. This is a superficial, journalistic review, short on thought and analysis, unbalanced in content, and marked by occasional inanities. Meant for a wide, general audience. Ille-Mai Gerdels

6075 971.06'44
**Westell, Anthony.**
The New Society. Toronto: McClelland and Stewart, c1977. 237p. Bibliography: p. 223-226. Index. ISBN 0-7710-8946-5 bd.: $8.95

1. Internationalism. 2. Canada – Politics and government – 1963- 3. Canada – Economic conditions – 1965- 4. Canada – Economic policy.

Analyzes the flaws of Canada's political, economic and social structures and presents a blueprint for revamping them to create a collective society along supranational lines. The clear, informed writing reflects Westell's extensive journalistic and academic experience. An ambitious, provocative work designed to stimulate discussion and controversy. Ille-Mai Gerdels

## 971.1 British Columbia

6076 971.1
**Norris, John,** ed.
Personality and History in British Columbia: Essays in Honour of Margaret Ormsby, edited by John Norris and Margaret Prang. Vancouver: J. J. Douglas, 1977. 171p. ISBN 0-88894-04-75 bd.: $12.50

1. British Columbia – History.

These essays by former students honour the retired head of the Department of History at University of British Columbia. Subjects vary from the character of the British Columbia frontier to John Sullivan Deas, the black entrepreneur of British Columbia salmon canning. Included is an essay on Dr. Ormsby and a bibliography of her writings. Published originally as a special issue of "B.C. Studies", Winter 1976-1977.

6077 971.1
**Pethick, Derek.**
British Columbia Disasters. Langley, B.C.: Stagecoach, 1978. 220p. ill., ports. Bibliography: p. 213-220. ISBN 0-88983-023-1 $10.95

1. Disasters – British Columbia. 2. British Columbia – History.

Fifteen disasters, including epidemics, floods, shipwrecks, and an avalanche, in the period from 1862 to 1948, are described. For each one a bibliography of published and unpublished sources is provided. Mediocre writing, lack of an index, and inadequate identification of quotations may limit interest. Popular reading.

6078 971.1'004
**Amstatter, Andrew.**
Tomslake: A History of Sudeten Germans in Canada. Saanichton, B.C.: Hancock House, 1978. 183p. Bibliography: p. 181-183. Index. ISBN 0-88839-002-5 $9.95

1. Germans in British Columbia – History. 2. Germans in Czechoslovakia – History.

Germany's seizure of the Sudetenland in 1938 precipitated the flight of thousands of Germans opposed to Nazi ideology. Urban refugees, lacking agricultural skills, struggled to farm unproductive land in northeastern British Columbia. In simple anecdotal reminiscences the reality of one ethnic group's pioneering experiences in Canada is effectively recorded. College and public libraries.

6079 971.1'004
**Fisher, Robin.**
Contact and Conflict: Indian-European Relations in British Columbia, 1774-1890. Vancouver: University of British Columbia Press, 1977. 250p. ill., map, plates, port. Bibliography: p. 213-239. Index. ISBN 0-77480-065-8 $21

1. Indians of North America – British Columbia – History. 2. Acculturation.

John A. MacDonald Prize.

Based on the premise that the fur trade prior to 1858 did not critically disrupt native culture but that later rapid settlement, culminating in the government's attack on native tradition in the 1890's caused their decline. Detailed bibliography of primary and secondary sources and extensive footnotes complement this valuable and scholarly reference tool. Nikki Lawrence

6080 971.1'004
**Kilian, Crawford.**
Go Do Some Great Thing: The Black Pioneers of British Columbia. Vancouver: Douglas & McIntyre, c1978. 188p. ill., plates, ports. Bibliography: p. 173-181. Index. ISBN 0-88894-180-3 $12.95

1. Blacks – British Columbia – History. 2. Blacks – British Columbia – Biography.

From the gold rush days of 1858, black citizens have played an important role in British Columbia life. This is a journalist's lively and anecdotal account of black history, based mainly on information provided in James W. Pilton's M.A. thesis (UBC 1951).

6081 971.1'004
**Leonoff, Cyril Edel.**
Pioneers, Pedlars, and Prayer Shawls: The Jewish Communities in British Columbia and the Yukon. Victoria: Sono Nis Press, 1978. 255p. ill., ports. Bibliographical references and Index. ISBN 0-919462-74-X $15

1. Jews in British Columbia – History.
2. Jews in the Yukon Territory – History.

More than one hundred years of Jewish life in British Columbia and the Yukon are presented pictorially by the archivist of the Jewish Historical Society of British Columbia. Grouped regionally and thematically, more than two hundred photographs are linked to time periods and events by brief descriptive paragraphs. Chapter notes and a glossary are included. Introductory in nature.

6082 971.1'004
**Woodcock, George.**
Peoples of the Coast: The Indians of the Pacific Northwest. Edmonton: Hurtig Publishers, c1977. 223p. ill., maps, ports. Bibliography: p. 215-218. Index. ISBN 0-88830-136-7 $17.95

1. Indians of North America – Northwest coast of North America.

Secondary sources and his own observations are the basis for this examination of the culture of coastal Indians from prehistoric times to the twentieth century. Illustrations are pleasingly combined with a well-written narrative. For the interested layman.

6083 971.1'00992
**Cameron, Donald.**
Seasons in the Rain: An Expatriate's Notes on British Columbia. Toronto: McClelland and Stewart, c1978. 208p. ISBN 0-7710-1847-9 pa.: $6.95

1. British Columbia – Biography.

Deftly drawn profiles of a disparate group of personalities, musicians, sailors, union officials, artists, are woven together to form a perceptive and warmly human pastiche of the British Columbia the expatriate Cameron has known. Shorter versions of most of the readable, crisply written pieces appeared in "Weekend Magazine" between 1974 and 1976. Bedside reading.

6084 971.1'02
**Akrigg, G. P. V.**
British Columbia Chronicle, 1847-1871: Gold & Colonists, by G. P. V. Akrigg and Helen B. Akrigg. Vancouver: Discovery Press, 1977. 439p. ill., maps, plates, ports. Bibliography: p. 411-420. Index. ISBN 0-919624-03-0 $17.50

1. British Columbia – History – To 1871.

A sequel to *British Columbia Chronicle, 1778-1846* listed in *CS* no. 4157.

"This present chronicle addresses itself to the fascinating task of recording British Columbia's history during the twenty-five years that elapsed between the boundary treaty of 1846 and the entry of the Crown Colony of British Columbia into the Dominion of Canada in 1871." -Prologue.

6085 971.1'03
**Broadfoot, Barry.**
The Pioneer Years, 1895-1914: Memories of Settlers Who Opened the West. Markham, Ont.: PaperJacks, 1978, c1976. 403p. ill., plates, ports. ISBN 0-7701-0060-0 pa.: $5.95

1. The West, Canadian – History. 2. The West, Canadian – Biography.

Clothbound listed in *CS* no. 3554.

6086 971.1'03
**Knight, Rolf.**
Stump Ranch Chronicles and Other Narratives. Vancouver: New Star Books, 1977. 144p. ill., ports. Bibliography: p. 142-144. ISBN 0-919888-74-7 bd.: $9.95 ISBN 0-919888-73-9 pa.: $3.95

1. Arntzen, Arnt, 1890- 2. Koeppen, Ebe, 1907- 3. Frontier and pioneer life – The West, Canadian. 4. Labor and laboring classes – The West, Canadian – Biography.

The rigours of twentieth century pioneer life in the British Columbia interior are revealed in taped interviews and diary excerpts. Two sturdy European immigrants who wrested a subsistence living by homesteading and labour in logging, mining and construction camps describe their struggles wryly but without rancor. Personalized social history. Of general interest.

6087 971.1'1'04
**Owen, Margaret.**
So We Bought the Town: A Los Angeles Family's Flight from the City into a Jade Treasure Trove. Vancouver: Mitchell Press, 1977. 191p. ill., maps, plates. ISBN 0-88836-022-3 pa.: $7.50

1. Owen family. 2. Country life – British Columbia, Northern.

A Los Angeles family, weary of city living, found a satisfactory alternative in northern British Columbia. The years in the wilderness, highlighted by the discovery of an important jade deposit, are described with artless good humour. Interest in the story compensates for poor writing surfeited with colloquialisms. Leisure entertainment for "back to the simpler life" enthusiasts.

6088 971.1'33
**Kloppenborg, Anne,** ed.
Vancouver's First Century: A City Album 1860-1960. Vancouver: J. J. Douglas, c1977. 151p. ill., plan, ports. ISBN 0-88894-146-3 $19.95

1. Vancouver, B.C. – History.

An affectionate tribute to Vancouver's first one hundred years has been compiled by the editors of "Urban Reader". Early photographs, meticulously restored, are combined with extracts from memoirs, journals, contemporary newspaper commentaries and capsule summaries of each decade. A visually attractive city history.

## 971.2 Prairie provinces

6089 971.2
**Artibise, Alan F.**
Western Canada Since 1870: A Select Bibliography and Guide. Vancouver: University of British Columbia Press, c1978. 294p. ill. Indexes. ISBN 0-7748-0090-9 bd.: $17.50 ISBN 0-7748-0091-7 pa.: $6.75

1. The West, Canadian – Bibliography.
2. The West, Canadian – History – Bibliography.

More than thirty-six hundred books, pamphlets, periodical articles and unpublished theses relating to the four western provinces, have been selected from the social sciences. The material is logically organized, adequately indexed and its use explained. An important research source on the social history of Western Canada for secondary schools, universities and public libraries.

6090 971.2
**Palmer, Howard,** ed.
The Settlement of the West. Calgary: University of Calgary: Comprint Publishing, c1977. 271p. graphs, maps. Bibliographical references. pa.: $6

1. Land settlement – Prairie Provinces – Congresses. 2. Prairie Provinces – History – Congresses. 3. Prairie Provinces – Emigration and immigration – Congresses.

Various aspects of prairie settlement are examined by a group of historians, geographers, political scientists, sociologists, economists and an English professor. Howard Palmer's cogent preface sets the framework for the eleven papers on this decisive period in western Canadian development. Well-documented, readable essays. College and public libraries.

6091 971.2'004
**Getty, Ian A. L.,** ed.
One Century Later: Western Canadian Reserve Indians Since Treaty 7: Western Canadian Studies Conference. Edited by Ian A. L. Getty and Donald B. Smith. Vancouver: University of British Columbia Press, c1978. 153p. ill., map, plates, ports. Bibliography: p. 139-144. Filmography: p. 145-149.
ISBN 0-7748-0103-4 bd.: $16.50
ISBN 0-7748-0105-0 pa.: $6.95

1. Indians of North America – The West, Canadian – Congresses. 2. Indians of North America – The West, Canadian – Government relations - Congresses.

A compilation of scholarly papers presented at the conference on political, social and cultural issues facing Native peoples. Both historic and current problems are represented: education, art, government relations, Native organizations, the fur trade and Treaty Seven (1877). Each paper contains extensive footnotes. Kathryn Walker

6092 971.2'004
**Kostash, Myrna.**
All of Baba's Children. Edmonton: Hurtig Publishers, c1977. 414p. Bibliographical references. ISBN 0-88830-144-8 $12.95

1. Ukrainians in Western Canada – History.

A well known journalist writes passionately from a feminist and radical viewpoint about the Ukrainian community in her small Alberta town and her own alienation from her Ukrainian heritage. Although neither scholarly nor a history this book is useful because it vividly describes some of the Ukrainian experience in Canada since the arrival of baba (grandmother) at the turn of the century. Andrew Gregorovich

6093 971.2'004
**Piniuta, Harry.**
Land of Pain, Land of Promise: First Person Accounts by Ukrainian Pioneers, 1891-1914. Saskatoon: Western Producer Prairie Books, 1978. 225p. ill., ports. Bibliography: p. 209-216. Index. ISBN 0-88833-002-2 $11

1. Ukrainians in Western Canada. 2. Ukrainians in Western Canada – History.

There is no better introduction to the struggles, hardship and heartbreak of prairie pioneers than this selection of fifteen personal accounts. They provide an excellent insight into a universal human experience told vividly but unpretentiously. A popular and interesting book which will appeal to all readers. Andrew Gregorovich

6094 971.2'02
**Cavell, Edward.**
Journeys to the Far West. Toronto: James Lorimer, 1979. 176p. map. Bibliography: p. ix. ISBN 0-88862-270-8 $22.95

1. Canada, Western – History. 2. Canada, Western – Description and travel – Views.

From the diaries, journals and photographic records kept by explorers, surveyors, gold seekers and gentlemen adventurers who travelled the Canadian West in the latter half of the nineteenth century has been fashioned a vivid collage. Archival photographs and excerpts from contemporary accounts, grouped geographically, recreate the spirit of the period. College, public and school libraries.

6095 971.2'02
**Thompson, John.**
The Harvests of War: The Prairie West, 1914-1918. Toronto: McClelland and Stewart, c1978. 207p. ill., graph. (The Canadian Social History Series) Bibliographical references and Index. ISBN 0-7710-8560-5 pa.: $6.95

1. European War, 1914-1918 – Prairie Provinces. 2. Prairie Provinces – History – 1905-1945. 3. Prairie Provinces – Social conditions.

A thoughtful study of the economic, political and social stresses brought by war to peoples of the Canadian prairies. Based solidly upon examination of contemporary records and manuscripts in national, provincial and university archives, Thompson offers a well-written social history. Of interest to students, historians and the general reader. College, public and university libraries.

## 971.23 Alberta

6096 971.23
**Brooks, Bill.**
Alberta. Text and photographs by Bill Brooks; edited by John Robert Colombo. Willowdale, Ont.: Hounslow Press, c1978. 92p. ill., port. ISBN 0-88882-020-8 $11.95

1. Alberta – Description and travel – 1950- – Views.

A collection of eighty full-colour plates illustrating the variety and natural beauty of Alberta, by the author of *The Colour of Canada*. The text is limited to one-line captions identifying the photographs. Pleasant browsing.

6097 971.23
**Cashman, Tony.**
A Picture History of Alberta. Edmonton: Hurtig Publishers, c1979. 212p. ill. ISBN 0-88830-157-X $15.95

1. Alberta – History – Pictorial works.

One hundred years of the province's history are mirrored in more than four hundred black and white archival photographs. Brief, chatty comments introduce the topically arranged visuals, and captions identify individual reproductions. A few Paul Kane reproductions are included. No index. A visually attractive, pictorial history. Schools and public libraries.

6098 971.23
**Fryer, Harold.**
Alberta: The Pioneer Years. Langley, B.C.: Stagecoach, 1977. 192p. ill., map, ports. Bibliography: p. 192. ISBN 0-88983-012-6 bd.: $15.95 9-88983-014-2 pa.: $8.95

1. Frontier and pioneer life – Alberta.
2. Alberta – History. 3. Alberta – Biography.

Colourful personalities and events from Alberta's pioneer past are recalled in thirty-nine brief, easy-to-read stories. Photographs from federal and provincial archives and libraries enhance the narrative. Casual reading in secondary school and public libraries.

6099 971.23
**MacGregor, James G.**
A History of Alberta. Edmonton: Hurtig Publishers, c1977. 335p. ill., maps, ports. Index. ISBN 0-88830-063-8 bd. ISBN 0-88830-140-5 pa.: $6.95

1. Alberta – History.

First edition listed CS no. 4189.

A reprint of the first edition published in 1972. Three items have been added to "the historical highlights" to bring the chronology to 1976, but the text, illustrations and maps remain unchanged. Libraries which own the 1972 edition may not wish to purchase this one.

6100 971.23

**Russell, Andy.**

Men of the Saddle: Cowboys of the Foothills, by Andy Russell and Ted Grant. Scarborough, Ont.: Van Nostrand Reinhold, 1978. ISBN 0-442-29878-1 bd.: $19.95 ISBN 0-442-29880-3 pa.: $9.95

1. Cowboys – Alberta. 2. Ranch life – Alberta.

An award-winning photographer and a knowledgeable writer have melded their talents to document realistically the everyday life of the western cowboy through the cycle of the seasons. Russell's anecdotal account of ranching in the west is enhanced by almost one hundred excellent visual studies, a number of them in colour. An attractive and informative study. Public and secondary school libraries.

6101 971.23'004

**Dempsey, Hugh A.**

Indian Tribes of Alberta. Calgary: Glenbow-Alberta Institute, 1978. 88p. ill., map, ports. Bibliography: p. 87-88. ISBN 0-919224-00-8 pa.: $3

1. Indians of North America – Alberta.

A detailed description, in an intriguing narrative style, of the life and habits of ten Indian tribes including the Blackfoot, the Blood and the Woodland Cree. The discussion is based on a combination of archaeological evidence recovered from campsites and hunting areas and ethnohistorical accounts, and is enhanced by a large number of illustrations. Young people and adults. Jay Wolofsky

6102 971.23'004

**Potrebenko, Helen.**

No Streets of Gold: A Social History of Ukrainians in Alberta. Vancouver: New Star Books, 1977. 311p. ill., maps. Bibliography: p. 304-311. ISBN 0-919888-70-4 bd.: $13.50 ISBN 0-919888-69-0 pa.: $5.95

1. Ukrainians in Alberta – History.

Most useful for its account of the harsh experiences of the author and her Ukrainian immigrant family, plus some information on the leftist Ukrainian community. But forcing the facts into her Marxist viewpoint, the factual inaccuracies and the heavy reliance on communist newspaper sources for biographies limits its value. Andrew Gregorovich

6103 971.23'3

**Foran, Maxwell.**

Calgary: An Illustrated History. Photographs assembled by Edward Cavell; cartography Geoffrey J. Matthews. Toronto: James Lorimer; Ottawa: National Museum of Man, National Museums of Canada, 1978. 192p. ill., maps, ports. Bibliography: p. 185-188. Index. (The History of Canadian Cities) ISBN 0-88862-224-4 $19.95

1. Calgary, Alta. – History.

Calgary's commercial, political and social development from 1875 to 1965 is reviewed in this well-documented, comprehensive survey. Archival photographs, maps and tables are combined with lucid text to convey the flavour and dynamism of a burgeoning urban centre. General readers and students of urban affairs will find it interesting and informative.

## 971.24 Saskatchewan

6104 971.24

**Bocking, D. H.**

Saskatchewan, A Pictorial History to 1945. D. H. Bocking for the Saskatchewan Archives Board. Saskatoon: Western Producer Prairie Books, 1979. 209p. Index. ISBN 0-88833-017-0 bd.: $29.95 ISBN 0-88833-042-1 pa.: $18.95

1. Saskatchewan – History – Pictorial works.

Historical illustrative materials, cartoons, photographs, broadsheets and drawings have been combined with excerpts from diaries, letters and reminiscences to depict Saskatchewan from 1883 to 1945. A companion volume, a comprehensive, analytical history of the province will be prepared by Dr. John Archer. This visual summary, marking the Saskatchewan Diamond Jubilee is recommended for general reading.

6105 971.24

**Regehr, T. D.**

Remembering Saskatchewan: A History of Rural Saskatchewan. Saskatoon: University of Saskatchewan, Extension Division, c1979. 74p. ill., maps. Bibliographical references: p. 70-73. ISBN 0-88880-076-2 $5

1. Frontier and pioneer life – Saskatchewan.
2. Saskatchewan – History.

A succinct examination of the factors which have shaped the development of society in rural Saskatchewan. Regehr's premise is that geographical features, climate, and isolation have affected the way in which people live. There are chapter notes, archival illustrations, but no index in this attractive social history. College, public and secondary school libraries.

## 971.27 Manitoba

6106 971.27
**Burke, Marguerite V.**
The Ukrainian Canadians. Scarborough, Ont.: Van Nostrand Reinhold, 1977. 64p. ill., maps. Bibliography: p. 64. (Multicultural Canada Series) ISBN 0-442-29863-3 pa.: $3.95

1. Ukrainians in Manitoba – Juvenile literature.

An attractively designed, well illustrated fictional account of three generations of a Ukrainian family in Manitoba which describes their settlement, struggles and success. Provides an especially good introduction to Ukrainian Canadian folk art, traditions and culture for eleven to fourteen year olds which adults also will enjoy reading.
Recommended. Andrew Gregorovich

6107 971.27'01
**MacEwan, J. W. G.**
Cornerstone Colony: Selkirk's Contribution to the Canadian West. Saskatoon: Western Producer Prairie Books, 1977. 228p. ill., maps, plates, port. Bibliography: p. 227-228. Index. ISBN 0-919306-80-2 $12.50

1. Selkirk, Thomas Douglas, 5th Earl of, 1771-1820. 2. Red River Settlement, Man.

The first twenty-five troubled years of the agricultural settlement established by Lord Selkirk on the Red River in 1811 are traced in this general, uncritical account. A more definitive work is John Gray's 1963 publication, *Lord Selkirk of Red River* (CS no. 3796).

6108 971.27'4
**Artibise, Alan F.**
Winnipeg: An Illustrated History. Toronto: James Lorimer; Ottawa: National Museums of Man, National Museums of Canada, 1977. 224p. ill., maps, ports. Bibliography: p. 216-219. Index. (The History of Canadian Cities) ISBN 0-88862-150-7 bd.: $12.95 ISBN 0-88862-151-5 pa.: $8.95

1. Winnipeg, Man. – History.

Three major phases of the city's economic, social and political history, from 1874 to 1970, are clearly described and illustrated with excellent photographs, maps and statistical tables. The introduction outlines the early period from 1812 to 1874. A well-conceived, comprehensive and visually interesting profile for both information seekers and browsers.

6109 971.27'4
**Bellan, Ruben C.**
Winnipeg, First Century: An Economic History. Winnipeg: Queenston House, c1978. 270p. ill., map, plates. Bibliographical references and Index. ISBN 0-919866-34-4 bd.: $12.95 ISBN 0-919866-35-2 pa.: $5.95

1. Winnipeg, Man. – History. 2. Winnipeg, Man. – Economic conditions.

An economist at the University of Manitoba chronicles the economic history of Winnipeg from the early 1879's to the mid 1970's, and analyses the impact which periods of expansion, recession, and two world wars have had upon it. Black and white archival photographs support the text. Geography and history collections in college, public and senior secondary school libraries.

## 971.3 Ontario

6110 971.3
**Hall, Roger.**
A Picture History of Ontario, by Roger Hall and Gordon Dodds. Edmonton: Hurtig Publishers, 1978. 224p. ill., maps. Bibliography: p. 221. Index. ISBN 0-88830-163-4 $15.95

1. Ontario – History.

Two archivists remedy Ontario history's long submergence in the national scene in this chronologically and thematically arranged collection. Excellent parallelling text contains discussion of major political and social changes from 1790 to 1970. Valuable photographs of working and social life at the turn of this century. Nikki Lawrence

6111 971.3'0016
**Aitken, Barbara B.,** comp.
Local Histories of Ontario Municipalities, 1951-1977: A Bibliography: With Representative Trans-Canada Locations of Copies. Toronto: Ontario Library Association, 1978. 120p. Bibliography: p. 117-118. ISBN 0-88969-012-X pa.: $9

1. Ontario – History – Bibliography.
2. Ontario – History, Local – Bibliography.

Previous edition listed CS no. 4207.

Some seventeen hundred local histories produced since 1950 are included in this new edition. A list of major historical societies in Ontario and their serial publications and major church archives are included in the appendices. A comprehensive and useful reference work.

6112 971.3'0016
**Morley, William F. E.**
Ontario and the Canadian North. Toronto: University of Toronto Press, c1978. 322p. ill., maps. Indexes. (Canadian Local Histories to 1950: v. 3) ISBN 0-8020-2281-2 $25

1. Union catalogs – Canada. 2. Ontario – History – Bibliography – Union lists. 3. Canada, Northern – History – Bibliography – Union lists.

Volume 1 listed in *CS* no. 4067.

The third and final volume of this series contains more than one thousand titles published before 1950. The first part is devoted to local histories of Ontario, the second, largely to those of the Yukon and the Northwest Territories. Bibliographical and descriptive information on each work is given, and a geographical as well as a general index provided. A thorough and invaluable addition to Canadian bibliographical tools.

6113 971.3'02
**Robeson, Virginia R.,** ed.
Upper Canada in the 1830's. Toronto: Ontario Institute for Studies in Education, 1977. 112p. ill., maps, ports. Bibliographical references. (Documents in Canadian History) (Curriculum Series) ISBN 0-7744-0143-5 pa.: $5.25

1. Ontario – History – 1791-1841 – Sources.

Designed to stimulate interest in the predominant issues and personalities of the era, reproductions of selected primary materials have been assembled. Problems of migration, land grants, industry, religion and education can be examined in contemporary letters, diaries, speeches, maps and reports. A useful student reference for secondary school and public libraries. In the same series: *Lower Canada in the 1830's*, and *New France 1713-1760*.

6114 971.3'03
**Brown, Ron.**
Ghost Towns of Ontario. Langley, B.C.: Stagecoach, 1978- v ill., maps, ports. Bibliography: p. 194-197. Index. ISBN 0-88983-018-5 bd.: $11.95 ISBN 0-88983-020-7 pa.: $5.95

1. Cities and towns, Ruined, extinct, etc. – Ontario. 2. Ontario – History.

Contents: vol. 1. Southern Ontario. 1978.

Histories of the settlement and subsequent desertion of over one hundred communities. Well researched, enthusiastically written handbook of local history with an extensive bibliography and an index that effectively accommodates changes. Cluttered appearance detracts from its aesthetics; however it is a valuable and indispensable reference tool. Nikki Lawrence

6115 971.3'03
**Schull, Joseph.**
Ontario Since 1867. Toronto: McClelland and Stewart, c1978. 400p. ill., ports. Bibliography: p. 382-384. Index. (Ontario Historical Studies Series) ISBN 0-7710-7990-7 $15.95

1. Ontario – History – 1867-

The first one-volume history of the province published in fifty years is comprehensive but not definitive. Using secondary sources, Schull traces Ontario's political, economic, social and cultural development to 1961. A well-written narrative with notes, photographs and a good index. Popular history for students and general reading.

6116 971.3'03
**Wilson, Barbara M.,** ed.
Ontario and the First World War, 1914-1918: A Collection of Documents. Toronto: Champlain Society for the Government of Ontario; University of Toronto Press, 1977. 201p. ill., plates. Bibliography: p. 185-192. Index. (Ontario Series of the Champlain Society) ISBN 0-8020-2255-3 $15

1. European War, 1914-1918 – Ontario – Sources. 2. Ontario – History – 1867-1918 – Sources. 3. Ontario – Social conditions – Sources.

Documents illustrating aspects of life at home emphasizing the social changes wrought through increased industrialization. A 119 page introduction thematically arranged into chapters such as 'Women' and 'Universities' effectively places the papers within their historical framework. Another excellent collection by the Champlain Society. Nikki Lawrence

6117 971.3'5'02

**McBurney, Margaret.**

Homesteads: Early Buildings and Families from Kingston to Toronto, by Margaret McBurney and Mary Byers. Toronto: University of Toronto Press, 1979. Bibliography. Index. ISBN 0-8020-2357-6 $15

1. Historic buildings – Ontario. 2. Pioneers – Ontario. 3. Dwellings – Ontario. 4. Ontario – History – 1791-1841.

The architectural and social history of pre-Confederation homes, churches, mills and inns have been traced through contemporary public records, diaries, local histories and personal recollections. An unusually informative introduction sets the regionally arranged accounts in context. Illustrated with Hugh Robertson's fine photographs and line maps. Interesting vignettes of nineteenth century Ontario. Recommended.

6118 971.3'54

**Byers, Mary.**

Rural Roots: Pre-Confederation Buildings of the York Region of Ontario, by Mary Byers, Jan Kennedy, and others. Photographs by Hugh Robertson. Toronto: University of Toronto Press, 1977, c1976. 248p. ill., maps. Bibliography: p. 236-238. Index.
ISBN 0-8020-2230-8 bd.: $15
ISBN 0-8020-6287-3 pa.: $6.50

1. Historic buildings – Ontario – York (Regional Municipality). 2. York, Ont. (Regional Municipality) – History.

Legends and local history add interest to this well-documented study of the early architecture of York County. The book is the result of a Junior League project to record all buildings erected before 1855. 130 houses and churches have been described. The black and white photographs are by Hugh Robertson. Maps indicate locations. Nancy Cohen

6119 971.3'541

**Armstrong, Christopher.**

The Revenge of the Methodist Bicycle Company: Sunday Streetcars and Municipal Reform in Toronto, 1888-1897, by Christopher Armstrong and H. V. Nelles. Toronto: Peter Martin, c1977. 214p. ill., ports. Bibliographical references and Index.
ISBN 0-88778-168-3 $12.95

1. Street-railroads – Ontario – Toronto – History. 2. Sunday legislation – Ontario – Toronto – History. 3. Toronto, Ont. – Politics and government.

City of Toronto Book Award.

Well-written analysis of the conflict between evangelical leaders in late Victorian Toronto and the financially powerful owners of the Toronto Railway Company. The issue was municipal corruption and reform and the fear of increased secularization of the new industrial working class. Entertaining as well as edifying local history. Nikki Lawrence

6120 971.3'541

**Arthur, Eric R.**

From Front Street to Queen's Park: The Story of the Ontario Parliament Buildings. Contains a chapter on the Ontario collection by Fern Bayer. Toronto: McClelland and Stewart, 1979. 160p. ill. Bibliography: p. 156. Index. ISBN 0-7710-0010-3 $22.50

1. Parliament Buildings (Ontario) – History.

City of Toronto Book Award.

Earlier sites are briefly discussed by the architect who wrote *No Mean City* but here he concentrates on the turmoil surrounding the competition for the design of the present buildings and descriptions of the ironwork and wood and stone carvings that grace them. Over two hundred photographs reveal the richness of artistic detail. Suitable for high school students. Nikki Lawrence

6121 971.3'541

**Berchem, F. R.**

The Yonge Street Story, 1793-1860: An Account From Letters, Diaries, and Newspapers. Toronto: McGraw-Hill Ryerson, c1977. 192p. ill., maps, ports. Bibliography: p. 184-189. Index. ISBN 0-07-082567-X $11.95

1. Toronto, Ont. – Streets – Yonge Street – History. 2. Ontario – History – To 1867.

Traces the growth of one of Ontario's "military streets or roads" that was created by Simcoe to link the bases at Toronto and Penetanguishene. Good popular history describing the settlement of this major route, the Mackenzie Rebellion, and the daily life and times of its inhabitants. Lovingly illustrated with line drawings by the author. Nikki Lawrence

6122 971.3'541

**Dendy, William.**

Lost Toronto. Toronto: Oxford University Press, 1978. 206p. ill., plan. Bibliographical references and Index. ISBN 0-19-540294-4 $19.50

1. Historic buildings – Ontario – Toronto.
2. Toronto, Ont. – Buildings.

City of Toronto Book Award.

The former archival historian with the Toronto Historical Board graphically illustrates the large segment of Toronto's architectural heritage which has been lost in the destruction of important nineteenth and early twentieth century buildings. Archival and contemporary photographs enhance the narrative. An authoritative work for urban planners and those interested in preserving the significant past. Nancy Cohen

6123 971.3'541

**Martyn, Lucy Booth.**

Toronto: 100 Years of Grandeur: The Inside Stories of Toronto's Great Homes and the People Who Lived There. Toronto: Pagurian Press, c1978. 240p. ill., ports. Bibliography: p. 227-235. Index. ISBN 0-88932-071-3 $14.95

1. Historic buildings – Ontario – Toronto. 2. Toronto, Ont. – Buildings. 3. Toronto, Ont. – Biography. 4. Toronto, Ont. – History.

An archivist, formerly at the University of Toronto, presents a detailed description of the architecture of some of Toronto's grandest homes, and thereby an aspect of Toronto history and a glimpse of the lives of some grand Torontonians. Nancy Cohen

6124 971.3'541

**Roberts, William.**

Houses of Old Toronto. Paintings by William Roberts; text by Mary Anne Roberts. Toronto: Pagurian Press, c1977. 96p. ill. Bibliography: p. 95-96. ISBN 0-88932-063-2 $19.95

1. Historic buildings – Ontario – Toronto. 2. Toronto, Ont. – Buildings.

Twenty watercolours and line drawings portray Roberts' favourite early public buildings and homes in the Yonge, Parliament and Dundas street area. Mary Anne Roberts has contributed an informative historical sketch for each building. Well researched. Nancy Cohen

6125 971.3'541

**Utting, Gerald.**

Toronto the Good: An Album of Colonial Hogtown. Vancouver: Bodima Books, 1978. 140p. ill. ISBN 0-88875-001-3 pa.: $7.95

1. Historic buildings – Ontario – Toronto. 2. Toronto, Ont. – Buildings.

Historical photographs of public and commercial buildings, universities, churches and homes, many of which have since been demolished, are prefaced with a brief explanatory text recreating the spirit of the past. The author decries the indiscriminate destruction of a city's architectural history. No bibliography or index. Of special interest to Torontonians.

6126 971.3'57

**Theberge, C. B.**

The Trent-Severn Waterway: A Traveller's Companion, by C. B. Theberge and Elaine Theberge. Toronto: Samuel Stevens, 1978. 171p. ill., port., maps. Bibliography: p. 150-157. ISBN 0-88866-592-X bd.: $14.95 ISBN 0-88866-591-1 pa.: $8.95

1. Trent-Severn Waterway, Ont. – History.

The unique 240 mile waterway which links Lake Ontario with Georgian Bay is depicted in a framework of historical beginnings and contemporary importance. Interesting facts about communities in the Trent-Severn corridor, maps, archival photographs, and reproductions of early paintings, complete the picture. An excellent guide to an inviting recreational area. Schools and public libraries.

## 971.4 Quebec

6127 971.4'02

**Miquelon, Dale,** ed.

Society and Conquest: The Debate on the Bourgeoisie and Social Change in French Canada, 1700-1850. Toronto: Copp Clark, c1977. 219p. Bibliography: p. 216-219. (Issues in Canadian History) ISBN 0-7730-3132-4 pa.: $5.95

1. Canadians, French-speaking – Social conditions. 2. Canada – History – 1763-1791. 3. Quebec (Province) – History – 1791-1841.

Sixteen judiciously selected essays written by eminent historians over a period of years, represent a range of historical interpretation of a controversial issue, the impact of the Conquest on French Canadian society and economy. An important source of authoritative opinion on a sensitive issue. Colleges and public libraries.

6128 971.4'04

**Bernard, André.**

What Does Quebec Want? Toronto: James Lorimer, 1978. 160p. diagrs., graph, map. Bibliography: p. 159-160. ISBN 0-88862-139-6 bd.: $13 ISBN 0-88862-138-8 pa.: $5.95

1. Quebec (Province) – Politics and government – 1960- 2. Quebec (Province) – History – Autonomy and independence movements.

A senior political scientist at the University of Montreal explains that there is a high degree of consensus in Quebec's French-speaking community on what Quebec wants: survival of the French language and culture, economic improvement and greater control over the Quebec economy. Of the political alternatives available for implementing the needed changes, the author believes the Parti québecois is the most convincing. All libraries.

6129 971.4'04
**Fullerton, Douglas H.**
The Dangerous Delusion: Quebec's Independence Obsession. Toronto: McClelland and Stewart, c1978. 240p. ill. ISBN 0-7710-3217-X $14.95

1. Quebec (Province) – Officials and employees – Biography. 2. Quebec (Province) – Politics and government – 1960- 3. Quebec (Province) – History – Autonomy and independence movements.

A native of Quebec, closely associated with its political leaders for fifteen years, Fullerton analyzes the political and social discontent which culminated in the 1976 Parti québecois victory. Empathy with the Québecois does not temper his distrust of the péquistes, nor moderate his denunciation of the economic implications of separatism. A federalist perspective. General purchase.

6130 971.4'04
**Vallières, Pierre.**
The Assassination of Pierre Laporte. Translated by Ralph Wells. Toronto: James Lorimer, 1977. 192p. ill. ISBN 0-88862-137-X bd.: $13 ISBN 0-88862-136-1 pa.: $5.95

1. Laporte, Pierre, 1921-1970. 2. Quebec (Province) – History – October crisis, 1970.

Translation of *"L'éxécution" de Pierre Laporte.*

While raising some pertinent, disturbing questions regarding federal actions, this is basically an unverified, opinionated version of the "October Crisis" and the subsequent assassination of Mr. Laporte. It is valuable because of the insight it provides into the political perception of strident FLQ members and segments of the Quebec populace. Recommended for inclusion in all adult collections. Ethel Kellen

6131 971.4'17
**MacKay, Donald.**
Anticosti: The Untamed Island. Toronto: McGraw-Hill Ryerson, 1979. 160p. ill., maps. Bibliography: p. 156-157. Index. ISBN 0-07-082933-0 $12.95

1. Anticosti Island – History.

Dominating the shipping routes in the Gulf of St. Lawrence lies the reef-encircled island explored by Jacques Cartier and Louis Jolliet. In three hundred years of changing fortunes Anticosti has been a French fiefdom, a logging centre, a graveyard of ships and a fisherman's paradise. An interesting, well-illustrated, journalistic account for popular reading.

6132 971.4'212
**Mitchell, Elaine Allan.**
Fort Timiskaming and the Fur Trade. Toronto: University of Toronto Press, c1977. 306p. ill., map, plates, ports. Bibliography: p. 279-285. Index. ISBN 0-8020-2234-0 $17.50

1. Hudson's Bay Company – History. 2. Fur trade – Quebec (Province) – Témiscaminque – History. 3. Fort Témiscaminque, Que. – History. 4. Témiscaminque, Que. – History.

Traces the impact of the fur trade on Northern Ontario from the first French posts in the 1670's until the absorption of Hudson's Bay Company land by Canada in 1870. An excellent picture of the country and life based on newly discovered materials in the papers of Col. Angus Cameron Nairne. Valuable biographical appendix. Nikki Lawrence

## 971.5 New Brunswick

6133 971.5
**Hocking, Anthony.**
New Brunswick. Toronto: McGraw-Hill Ryerson, 1978. 64p. ill., maps. Index. (Canada Series) ISBN 0-07-082686-2 $8.95

1. New Brunswick.

General, concise articles on the salient features of the province's history, geography, government, economic conditions, culture and recreation. Few maps but many photographs. Sturdily bound. Similar pictorial overviews of Canada and each of the provinces provide basic introductory information for students and the general reader. By the same author: *Prince Edward Island; The Yukon and Northwest Territories.*

6134 971.5'03
**Forbes, Ernest R.**
The Maritime Rights Movement, 1919-1927: A Study in Canadian Regionalism. Montreal: McGill-Queen's University Press, c1979. 246p. map. Bibliography: p. 229-237. Index. ISBN 0-7735-0321-8 bd.: $21.95 ISBN 0-7735-0330-7 pa.: $8.95

1. Regionalism – Maritime Provinces.
2. Maritime Provinces – History – 1918-1945.

The first spontaneous regional protest in Canada transcended provincial boundaries, political, economic and social affiliations. From thorough research of primary and secondary materials the author analyses the causes, the manifestations, and the federal government action which defused the movement. A well-organized, carefully documented and timely study of regional disenchantment. Academic and larger public libraries.

## 971.6 Nova Scotia

6135 971.6
**Elliott, Shirley.**
Nova Scotia Book of Days: A Calendar of the Province's History. Halifax: Nova Scotia Communications & Information Centre, 1979. 128p. ill. Index. ISBN 0-88871-013-5 bd.: $10 ISBN 0-88871-012-7 pa.: $6

1. Nova Scotia – History.

Patterned on Chambers' *Book of Days*, this calendar prepared by Nova Scotia's Legislative Librarian, relates the day by day history of the province. Well chosen historical illustrations of excellent quality enhance the record. A fine choice for all collections of Nova Scotia history.

6136 971.6
**Pryke, Kenneth G.**
Nova Scotia and Confederation, 1864-74. Toronto: University of Toronto Press, 1979. 240p. map. Index. (Canadian Studies in History and Government) ISBN 0-8020-5389-0 $17.50

1. Canada – Politics and government – 1841-1867. 2. Canada – History – Confederation, 1867.

Historians and political scientists will welcome this careful study of Nova Scotia's political history between 1864 and 1874 by a University of Windsor history professor. Chapter notes buttress the text. University and large public libraries.

6137 971.6'22
**Metson, Graham,** ed.
The Halifax Explosion: December 6, 1917. Includes the complete text of *The Halifax Disaster* by Archibald MacMechan. Toronto: McGraw-Hill Ryerson, 1978. 173p. ill., facsims., map, ports. ISBN 0-07-082797-4 bd.: $14.95 ISBN 0-07-082798-2 pa.: $8.95

1. Halifax, N.S. – Explosion, 1917.

MacMechan's hitherto unpublished eyewitness report is supplemented by primary documents relating to the catastrophe and its aftermath, interviews, photographs and a sketch map of Halifax in 1917. This official, objective record represents an important addition to the contemporary literature on a major Canadian disaster. Recommended for college, public and school libraries.

6138 971.6'22
**Monnon, Mary Ann.**
Miracles and Mysteries: The Halifax Explosion, December 6, 1917. Hantsport, N.S.: Lancelot Press, 1977. 144p. ill. Bibliography: p. 142-144. ISBN 0-88999-071-9 pa.: $3.95

1. Halifax, N.S. – Explosion, 1917.

Memories of survivors and published secondary sources have been drawn upon, but optimum use has not been made of them. A chatty, somewhat disjointed tale marred by the mediocrity of the writing. Purchase if additional material needed on this memorable disaster.

6139 971.6'9'01
**McLennan, John S.**
Louisbourg from Its Foundation to Its Fall, 1713-1758. 4th ed. Halifax, N.S.: Book Room, 1979. 328p. ill., plates. Bibliographical references and Index. pa.: $10.95

1. Louisbourg, N.S. – History.

A reissue, in quality paperback, of an important scholarly work which has been out-of-print for several years. The vicissitudes of the French fortress on Cape Breton are traced from its beginnings to 1758, ten years before its destruction. Careful footnoting and excerpts from early letters, journals, memoirs, ships' logs and documents lend authority to this detailed text. All libraries.

## 971.8 Newfoundland

6140 971.8
**Brown, Cassie.**
Standing into Danger: A Dramatic Story of Shipwreck and Rescue. Toronto: Doubleday, 1979. 391p. ill., maps. ISBN 0-385-13681-1 $14.95

1. Shipwrecks – Newfoundland. 2. World War, 1939-1945 – Naval operations, American.

Taped interviews with survivors and rescuers, letters and official documents have been used to reconstruct the wartime sea disaster in which two American ships and more than two hundred crewmen were lost off Newfoundland's south coast in the winter of 1942. The ensuing naval inquiry forms an important part of the story. An involving account. General interest.

6141 971.8'004
**Rowe, Frederick W.**
Extinction: The Beothuks of Newfoundland. Toronto: McGraw-Hill Ryerson, c1977. 162p. ill., maps, ports. Bibliography: p. 158-162. Index. ISBN 0-07-082351-0 $10.95

1. Beothuk Indians.

A well-researched book for both a general and an advanced audience, in which the author identifies the facts and long-accepted myths concerning the history of the Beothuks. Gaps in evidence and contradictory information are discussed to relate the difficulties in recreating the origin, culture and extinction of these people. Kathryn Walker

6142 971.8'004
**Such, Peter.**
Vanished Peoples: The Archaic Dorset & Beothuk People of Newfoundland. Toronto: NC Press, 1978. 94p. ill., diagrs., facsims., maps, plates, ports. Bibliography: p. 89. Index. ISBN 0-919600-84-0 bd.: $12.95 ISBN 0-919600-83-2 pa.: $5.95

1. Beothuk Indians. 2. Eskimos – Newfoundland.

A few inaccuracies notwithstanding, the author, piecing together archaeological, ethnological, and historical records, presents a fascinating theory on the possible link of the Beothuks to the great migration from Central Asia 30,000 years ago, and suggests Canadian archaeology as the key to unanswered puzzles regarding the New World and its native peoples. For secondary school students and the general reader. Frieda Ling

6143 971.8'01
**Moyles, Robert G.**
"Complaints Is Many and Various, but the Odd Divil Likes it": Nineteenth Century Views of Newfoundland. Toronto: PMA Books, 1977. 187p. ill., map, plates, ports. Bibliography: p. 176-185. ISBN 0-88778-160-8 pa.: $4.95

1. Newfoundland – Social life and customs. 2. Newfoundland – Description and travel – 1800-1850. 3. Newfoundland – Description and travel – 1850-1900.

Clothbound listed *CS* no. 4275.

6144 971.8'04
**Murray, Hilda Chaulk.**
More than Fifty Percent: Women's Life in a Newfoundland Outport 1900-1950. St. John's, Nfld.: Breakwater Books, 1979. 160p. ill. Bibliography. ISBN 0-919948-74-X bd.: $14.95 ISBN 0-919948-75-8 pa.: $9.95

1. Women – Newfoundland.

Interviews with twenty-three citizens of the fishing village of Elliston on Trinity Bay indicate that the role of women in a Newfoundland outport differed greatly from that of women on mainland North America. Based on a Master's thesis.

## 971.9 The Canadian North

6145 971.9'002
**Cooke, Alan.**
The Exploration of Northern Canada: 500 to 1920, A Chronology, by Alan Cooke and Clive Holland. Toronto: Arctic History Press, c1978. 549p. maps. Bibliography: p. 447-505. Index. ISBN 0-7710-2265-4 $50

1. Canada, Northern – Discovery and exploration – Chronology. 2. Canada, Northern – Exploring expeditions – Chronology.

A meticulously researched reference work detailing northern events and expeditions from their beginning in the Irish legend of St. Brendan until the advent of air travel in the 1920's. This beautiful volume, by two curators at the Scott Polar Research Institute, also contains an index of names, historical maps, and an extensive bibliography of primary sources. Nikki Lawrence

6146 971.9'01

**McGhee, Robert.**

Canadian Arctic Prehistory. Toronto: Van Nostrand Reinhold, 1978. 128p. ill., maps. Index. (Canadian Prehistory Series) ISBN 0-442-29813-7 pa.: $6.95

1. Eskimos – Canada – Antiquities. 2. Canada, Northern – Antiquities.

A fascinating reconstruction, from archaeological discoveries of prehistoric migratory life in the Canadian Arctic from the end of the Ice Age, through various evolutionary stages to the full flowering of the Inuit culture. Attractively illustrated and simply but beautifully told. For the general reader. Frieda Ling

6147 971.9'1'02

**Green, Lewis.**

The Gold Hustlers. Anchorage, Alaska: Alaska Northwest Publishing, c1977. 339p. ill., facsims., map, ports. Bibliography: p. 323-329. Index. ISBN 0-88240-088-6 pa.: $7.95

1. Treadgold, A. N. C., 1863-1951. 2. Klondike gold fields. 3. Mining engineers – Yukon Territory – Biography. 4. Yukon Territory – Biography.

Following the rush of gold panners to the Klondike in the late 1890's, came the promoters and stock manipulators who battled for control of vast tracts of still productive land. Green, a geologist, has constructed a detailed and interesting history of "the other gold rush", the seventy years of placer mining in the Yukon, and the men who dominated it.

6148 971.9'1'02

**Moyles, Robert G.,** ed.

From Duck Lake to Dawson City: The Diary of Eben McAdam's Journey to the Klondike, 1898-1899. Saskatoon: Western Producer Prairie Books, c1977. 135p. ill., maps, plates, ports. Bibliography: p. 135. Index. ISBN 0-919306-88-8 $9.95

1. McAdam, Ebenezer, 1859-1927. 2. Klondike gold fields. 3. Yukon Territory – Description and travel – To 1900.

The glitter of gold in the Klondike lured McAdam and four companions from Montreal on a fourteen-month over-land journey to the Yukon in the spring of 1898. Lean and unembellished, the daily journal provides a graphic account of everyday life on the rivers and trails, the hardships, dangers, and monotony. A worthwhile addition to gold rush lore. Secondary schools and public libraries.

6149 971.9'1'02

**North, Dick.**

The Lost Patrol. Anchorage, Alaska: Alaska Northwest Publishing, c1978. 138p. ill., graph, maps, ports. Bibliography: p. 136-138. ISBN 0-88240-106-8 pa.: $4.95

1. Fitzgerald, Francis J., 1869-1911. 2. Canada. Royal North West Mounted Police. 3. Northwest, Canadian – History.

From the patrol leader's diaries, official records, letters and dispatches, the author has reconstructed the tragedy of a routine RCMP patrol in the Northwest Territories in 1910 during which four officers lost their lives. An interesting account of the policing of the Arctic at the beginning of the century. Schools and public libraries.

6150 971.9'1'02

**Paterson, Thomas W.**

Ghost Towns of the Yukon. Langley, B.C.: Stagecoach, 1977. 148p. ill., maps, ports. Bibliography: p. 144. Index. ISBN 0-88983-009-6 pa.: $5.95

1. Cities and towns, Ruined, extinct, etc. – Yukon Territory. 2. Klondike gold fields. 3. Yukon Territory – History.

Deserted as the gold dust fever abated, some thirty once bustling centres on the major waterways are described as they were and as they are today. The resurgent interest in gold may entice a new generation of gold seekers. Leisure reading for school and public libraries.

6151 971.9'1'02

**Sinclair, James M.**

Mission: Klondike. Vancouver: Mitchell Press, 1978. 266p. ill., maps, plates, ports. Bibliography: p. 259-261. Index. ISBN 0-88836-024-X pa.

1. Sinclair, John A., d. 1905. 2. Klondike gold fields. 3. Missionaries – Yukon Territory – Biography.

The diaries of his father, a Presbyterian missionary, and other contemporary letters, records, and articles from newspapers and periodicals have been woven into a general history of the Yukon during the Klondike Gold Rush. Photographs, taken by the clergyman during his two and one half years in the north, provide an excellent pictorial record of life in the goldfields at the end of the century. General interest.

6152 971.9'3

**Smith, James K.**

The Mackenzie River, Yesterday's Fur Frontier, Tomorrow's Energy Battleground. Agincourt, Ont.: Gage Publishing, c1977. 259p. map. Bibliography: p. 249-252. Index. ISBN 0-7715-9980-3 $12.95

1. Mackenzie River, N.W.T.

A readable review of the role which the Mackenzie River watershed has played in Canadian history, and its potential importance in the struggle for energy sufficiency in the future. A map illustrates the drainage basin of the river, the location of the Athabasca tar sands, and existing and proposed pipelines. The timeliness of the topic and the easy conversational style recommend it to the non-specialist.

## 973 Canadian/American physiographic regions and features

6153 974.799

**Donaldson, Gordon.**

Niagara! The Eternal Circus. Toronto: Doubleday, 1979. 217p. ill. Bibliography: p. 261-264. Index. ISBN 0-385-12309-4 $11.50

1. Niagara River region – New York and Ontario – History.

The many facets of the great waterfall, its history, engineering, electric power potential, its legends, attraction for tourists, and as a perennial mecca for dare-devil feats, are blended into a smooth and witty narrative. Donaldson, a journalist and free-lance writer, has done exhaustive research and provides historical photographs, maps on end-papers, and an index. Of wide general interest.

6154 977'.03

**King, B. A.**

The Faces of the Great Lakes. Photographs by B. A. King; text by Jonathan Ela; introduction by Sigurd Olson. Rexdale, Ont.: John Wiley, c1977. 190p. ill., maps. ISBN 0-87156-196-4 $24.50

1. Great Lakes region – Description and travel. 2. Great Lakes.

The geology, physical characteristics, and the impact of history and industrial development upon the lakes are outlined in a lucid narrative. King's superb photographs, which follow the text, are grouped geographically, each group preceded by a map. No index or bibliography. A large, attractively designed book for informative browsing. College, public and school libraries.

6155 978'.0022

**Woodall, Ronald.**

Taken by the Wind: Vanishing Architecture of the West, by Ronald Woodall and T. H. Watkins. Don Mills, Ont.: Gage Publishing, 1977. 200p. ill. Index. ISBN 0-7736-0058-2 $29.95

1. The West – Description and travel – Views. 2. Architecture – The West. 3. The West – History. 4. Frontier and pioneer life – The West. 5. The West, Canadian – Description and travel – Views. 6. Architecture – The West, Canadian. 7. The West, Canadian – History. 8. Frontier and pioneer life – The West, Canadian.

The colour photographs of ghost towns, farms, ranches, mines, schools, churches, cemeteries and railway stations have captured the essence of frontier life. The superficial text adds little to a fascinating pictorial study. Nancy Cohen

# Part Two
# Canadian
# Periodicals

ABBREVIATIONS FOR PERIODICAL INDEXES

| | |
|---|---|
| API | Alternative Press Index |
| CELI | Canadian Essay and Literature Index |
| CGP | Canadian Government Publications |
| CLPL | Index to Canadian Legal Periodical Literature |
| CPI | Canadian Periodical Index |
| HA | Historical Abstracts |
| MLAB | Modern Language Association Bibliography |
| PAIS | Public Affairs Information Service. Bulletin |

**Antiques & Art.** 1974. bi-m. $12.95, single issue $1.50. Left Bank Publications Ltd. P.O. Box 97103, Richmond, B.C. V6Y 2A2. ISSN 0700-5571 Bk. rev.: 2-5.

The Canadian magazine for fine art collectors and investors, is a handsomely designed magazine with attractive eye-catching covers and with well-written, in-depth articles, as well as news items, auction news, market information, book reviews and a calendar of events on a variety of subjects, including antiques, collectables, art and furniture. Sherrill Cheda

**The Asianadian:** An Asian Canadian Magazine. 1978. q. $4, institutions $6, single issue $1.25. Asianadian Resource Workshop, Box 1256, Station Q, Toronto, Ont. M4T 2P4. ISSN 0705-8861 Bk. rev.: 2-5.

A well-illustrated, clean copy, "little magazine" with well-researched feature articles, reviews, poetry, interviews, international news and community news of interest to Asians in Canada and to non-Asians who would like an inside perspective not found in the mass media. A thematic approach is used. Recent subjects have been history, women, work, political movements and children. Sherrill Cheda

**Atlantis.** 1975. s.a. $7, institutions $12. Acadia University, c/o Dept. of History, Wolfville, N.S. B0P 1X0. ISSN 0702-7818 Bk. rev.: 10-20. Indexed: CELI

An inter-disciplinary women's studies journal devoted to critical and creative writing in English and French on the topic of women. It includes research and theoretical articles, which are scholarly but not dry, reviews of books, films, photographs, graphic work and poetry, in a variety of disciplines (literature, history, sociology, psychology, art). Especially useful for community colleges and university libraries. Sherrill Cheda

**Brick: A Journal of Reviews.** 1977. 3/yr. $5.50, single issues $2. Brick, Ilderton, Ont., P.O. Box 219, N0M 2A0. ISSN 0382-8565 Bk. rev.: 30-50.

A journal of reviews which concentrates on Canadian writers and publishers with specific attention to small press publications, not necessarily only the recent ones. Attractively illustrated, it reviews books, plays, magazines. A recent issue was devoted to James Reaney. Sherrill Cheda

**CLIC's Legal Materials Letter.** 1977. 11/yr. $10. Canadian Law Information Council, 2010 Tower B, Place de Ville, 112 Kent St., Ottawa, Ont. K1P 5P2. ISSN 0704-0393. Bk. rev.: 10-20.

Designed specifically for the non-lawyer who needs information on current Canadian legal materials, this newsletter provides book reviews, notes of recent publications, notes on articles of interest, tips in using legal materials. The only bibliographic guide for Canadian legal materials of interest to the public. Gail Dykstra

**Canada Quilts.** 1973. 5/yr. $6, single issues $1.25. Conroy Publications, 360 Stewart Drive, Sudbury, Ont. P3E 2R8. ISSN 0381-7369. Bk. rev.: 5-10.

A specialty magazine for Canadian quilters with at least seven patterns per issue, notice of shows, exhibits and contests, plus feature "how-to" articles, and biographies, book reviews and puzzles. All instructions are graphically illustrated and there are photographs of finished quilts and designs. Excellent for those interested in crafts, design, fashion, sewing and pattern making. Sherrill Cheda

**Canadian Genealogist.** 1979. q. $15. Generation Press, 172 King Henry's Boulevard, Agincourt, Ont. M1T 2V6. ISSN 0707-3232. Bk. rev.: 5-10.

This quarterly contains "news and notes for genealogists", articles on family history, biographical sketches, book reviews and "What's in a Name", the latter being a reader-participation section for questions. The attractive layout, with photographs and maps to supplement the articles, helps to make this an enjoyable publication for the historian or genealogist. Glenna Stevens

**Canadian Lawyer.** 1977. bi-m. $10, foreign $12. H.P. Publications, 44 Charles St. W., Toronto, Ont. M4Y 1R8. ISSN 0703-2129. Indexed: CLPL.

Glossy, designed for lawyers' waiting rooms but containing interesting articles, notes on recent developments in Canadian law, interviews with, and profiles of, lawyers of recognized stature in Canada, humorous asides and occasional cartoons. Useful for the general reader interested in the law. Gail Dykstra

**Canadian Musician.** 1979. bi-m. $10. Norris Publications, 2453 Yonge St., Suite 3, Toronto, Ont. M4P 2E8. ISSN 0708-9635.

Aimed primarily at amateur and professional performers, *Canadian Musician* is technically oriented; the reader should have a solid understanding of music. Regular columns by noted instrumental specialists. Don Sedgwick

**Canadian Poetry.** 1977. s.a. $8. The Editors, Canadian Poetry, University of Western Ontario, Dept. of English, London, Ont. N6A 3K7. ISSN 0704-5646. Bk. rev.: 2-5.

Each issue is divided into three sections – studies, documents, and reviews. Material may be either contemporary or archival; articles are attractively presented and substantially footnoted. Due to its academic nature, this publication is more suited to the student of Canadian poetry than to the reader with only a casual interest in this genre. Glenna Stevens

**Canadian Women's Studies: Les cahiers de la femme.** 1978. q. $10, institutions $15. Centennial College Women's Studies, 651 Warden Ave., Scarborough, Ont. M1L 3Z6. ISSN 0706-8204. Bk. rev.: 5-10.

A creative new bilingual quarterly for women, which includes interviews, poetry, book reviews, articles, art, biographies, etc. by leading Canadian women writers on all aspects of women's lives. Issues are centred around a theme: the arts, health, work, and the journal has a mixture of short and long articles. Of particular interest to community colleges, universities, medium-sized and large public libraries. Sherrill Cheda

**The Children's Book News.** 1978. q. $5, adults, $1 children. Children's Book Centre, 229 College St., 5th Floor, Toronto, Ont. M5T 1R4. ISSN 0705-0038. Bk. rev.: 5-10.

Formerly: *Children's Book Newsletter*. A newsletter publication containing brief book reviews, reports on events and information about children's authors. Most issues include a list of bookstores across Canada which stock the books recommended in *The Children's Book News*, and/or a list of new books. Pleasant, light reading for those interested in the world of children's literature. Glenna Stevens

**The Compass:** A Provincial Review. 1977. 3/yr. $8, institutions $10. The Compass, Box 632, Sub Station 11, University of Alberta, Edmonton, Alta. T6G 2E0. ISSN 0703-5470. Bk. rev.: 2-5.

A publication of essays, commentaries, short stories, poetry and reviews. Range of appeal is broad; those interested in browsing as well as those with a background in English literature will find the scope and diversity of the content enjoyable. Glenna Stevens

**Cross Country.** 1975. 3/yr. $9, institutions $12, single issues $2.50. Cross Country, 5572 Clark St., Montreal, Que. H2T 2V4. ISSN 0318-6075. Bk. rev.: 2-5. Indexed: CELI.

Includes a wide range of contemporary American and Canadian poetry and critical articles in an attempt to establish an audience for Canadian writing in the United States. For collections specializing in poetry and literature. Sherrill Cheda

**Development Directions.** 1978. 9/yr. free. Canadian International Development Agency, 200 Promenade du Portage, Hull, Que. K1A 0G4. ISSN 0705-064X. Bk. rev.: 2-5.

Incorporating *Cooperation Canada* and *Contact*. A newsmagazine on international development, it includes news briefs on agricultural efforts and situations in Third World countries, reports, articles and book reviews. Layout, photography and readability make this publication suitable for the public library. Glenna Stevens

**Diver Magazine:** The Canadian Underwater Authority. 1978. 8/yr. $10. Seagraphic Publications Ltd., Boater's Village, 1601 Granville St., Vancouver, B.C. V6Z 2B3. ISSN 0706-5132.

Continues: *Diver and Underwater Adventure* (1977-1978). A full colour, well-illustrated magazine for divers which includes news, recipes, equipment evaluations, an events calendar and a directory of suppliers and clubs, feature articles on diving, underwater photography, archaeology and travel. Sherrill Cheda

**Early Canadian Life.** 1976. m. $9, single issue .95¢. Early Canadian Life, 591 Argus Road, Oakville, Ont. L6J 3J4. ISSN 0700-8104. Bk. rev.: 5-10.

Canada's national heritage newspaper is a newsprint monthly publication devoted to Canada's history. It includes feature articles on history, personal reminiscences and genealogy, as well as archival photographs, book reviews, news and recipes. Sherrill Cheda

**Essays on Canadian Writing.** 1976. q. $9, institutions $18, single issue $3. Essays on Canadian Writing, York University, 356 Stong College, Downsview, Ont. M3J 1P3. ISSN 0313-0300. Indexed: CELI, CPI, MLAB. Bk. rev.: 20-30.

A scholarly journal of criticism, this publication contains essays about Canadian authors and their works. Issues are of substantial length (175-200 pages each); contents vary from several comprehensive articles to numerous shorter ones. Contributions may include academic criticism, reports of interviews and the occasional annotated bibliography. Glenna Stevens

**Fuse: The Cultural Media and News Magazine.** 1976. bi-m. $9, institutions $18, single issue $1.95. Arton's Publishing, 31 Dupont St., Toronto, Ont. M5R 1V3. ISSN 0226-8086.

Formerly: *Centrefold: The Artists' News Magazine.* A visually attractive, up to date Canadian cultural news magazine with criticism of the new arts and technologies and reporting on social issues and civil rights. It includes reviews of books, television, video, records, exhibitions and fashion as well as feature articles on writers, media, economics, art, political issues and education. Excellent for urban high schools, colleges, universities and large public libraries. Sherrill Cheda

**Germination.** 1976. q. $3, single issue .75¢. River Hebert, N.S. P.O. Box 40, B0L 1G0. ISSN 0704-6286. Bk. rev.: 2-5.

A literary "little magazine" which publishes poetry with emphasis on work by previously unpublished poets. It also includes a review section which reviews books of published poets. Should appeal to collectors specializing in Canadian poetry or small presses. Sherrill Cheda

**The Island Magazine.** 1976. s.a. $4, institutions $5. Heritage Foundation, Box 922, Charlottetown, P.E.I. C1A 7L9. ISSN 0384-8175. Bk. rev.: 2-5.

Features the history and folklore of Prince Edward Island and is attractively designed and illustrated with photographs. Each issue contains feature articles, genealogy and book reviews. Excellent for Canadian history collections. Sherrill Cheda

**A Journal of Our Time.** 1977. irreg. $4.50. Traditional Studies Press, Box 984, Adelaide St. P.O., Toronto, Ont. M5C 2K4. ISSN 0381-6524.

Contains short essays and poems on topics concerning life and its meaning; illustrations accompany the text. Pleasant reading for those interested in browsing; thought-provoking for those with a strong curiosity about the complexities of life. Glenna Stevens

**The Journal of the Canadian Library Science Society. La revue de la Société Bibliothéconomie Canadienne:** An Annual Review and a Selection of the Best Writing from the Canadian Library Publications. 1977. a. $12, students $9. Parabola Systems, 55 Water Street, Suite 200, Vancouver, B.C. V6B 1A2. ISSN 0778-2274.

Reprints of selected articles which have appeared in Canadian library periodical literature are grouped under the name of the periodical from which they have been excerpted. The selections are prefaced with a review article commenting on the issues which have been predominant in the library community during the preceding year.

**Labour. Le Travailleur.** 1976. a. $6. Dalhousie University, Department of History, Halifax, N.S. B3H 4H8. ISSN 0700-3862. Bk. rev.: 5-10. Indexed: API, HA.

A scholarly, interdisciplinary, bilingual journal of Canadian labour studies dealing with both contemporary and historic materials. Each issue contains approximately ten feature articles and a similar number of in depth book reviews by outstanding authorities in the field. Of interest to universities, colleges and large public libraries. Sherrill Cheda

**Log House.** 1979. a. $5. The Canadian Log House, P.O. Box 1205, Prince George, B.C. V2L 4V5. ISSN 0708-6458.

Formerly: *Canadian Log House.* A colourfully illustrated annual with articles by people who have built their own log houses, illustrations for log house construction, log house costing, regional log house building, crossword puzzles, and everything you ever wanted to know about log house construction. Sherrill Cheda

**Music Magazine.** 1978. bi-m. $8. Music Magazine, 56, The Esplanade, Suite 202, Toronto, Ont. M5E 1A7. ISSN 0705-4009.

An attractive journal focusing on Canadian and international personalities in the music field. Interviews, feature articles, book and record reviews and a regular column by the award-winning composer Michael Colgrass. Recommended for all public libraries. Don Sedgwick

**Parliamentary Government.** 1979. q. $5. Institute for Research on Public Policy, 60 Queen Street, 12th Floor, Ottawa, Ont. K1P 5Y7. ISSN 0709-4582.

Distributed free of charge to members of the House of Commons, Senate and provincial and territorial assemblies, it covers topics on which both citizens and parliamentarians should be informed: e.g., What parliamentary committees can and cannot do. Bilingual. Highly recommended for academic and public libraries.

**Perception: A Canadian Journal of Social Comment.** 1977. bi-m. $10, single issue $1.75. Canadian Council on Social Development, 55 Parkdale, Box 3505, Station D, Ottawa, Ont. K1Y 4G1. ISSN 0740-5263. Bk. rev.: 2-5. Indexed: CPI, PAIS.

Formerly: *Canadian Welfare* and *Digeste Social*. A Canadian journal of social comment, it features in-depth articles by well-known writers around a theme (families, native peoples, media) as well as reports on housing, taxation and social issues with correspondents from all regions in Canada, and book reviews of interest to public, high school, college and university libraries. Sherrill Cheda

**Periodics.** 1977. 2/yr. $10. Paul de Barros and Daphne Marlatt, Box 69375, Postal Station K, Vancouver, B.C. V6K 4W6. ISSN 0701-2748. Bk. rev.: 2-5.

Each issue of *Periodics* is a collection of contemporary material: stories, essays, letters, poems. Contributions are short, and generally directed to an audience formally studying literature rather than one reading it simply for enjoyment. Glenna Stevens

**Polyphony:** The Bulletin of the Multicultural History Society of Ontario. 1977, s.a. $5. Multicultural History Society of Ontario, 43 Queen's Park Crescent East, Toronto, Ont. M5S 2C3. ISSN 0704-7002.

A publication produced to record the multi-ethnic history of Ontario, gathers materials both from printed sources and informal interviews. Numerous photographs supplement the substantial text. Of most interest to archivists and historians, but also of interest to the general public and to immigrants. Glenna Stevens

**Racar: Revue d'art canadienne. Canadian Art Review.** 1974. 2/yr. $8, single issue $4.50. Racar, P.O. Box 4148, Station E, Ottawa, Ont. K1S 5B2. ISSN 0315-9906. Bk. rev.: 2-5.

A scholarly international and historical review with articles and book reviews by leading scholars who examine the art and architecture of Canada and other countries. Geared toward academics, museum and gallery personnel and art amateurs. Sherrill Cheda

**Report.** 1977. 11/yr. $10, single issue $1.25. Report, 1280, rue St.-Marc, Suite 208, Montreal, Que. H3H 2G1. ISSN 0708-9864. Bk. rev.: 2-5. Indexed: CPI.

A popular public affairs review concentrating on Canadian politics, economics and social policy, with news, commentary, articles, analysis and book reviews, well illustrated with photographs. Of interest to all public school and college libraries. Sherrill Cheda

**Studies in Canadian Literature.** 1976. bi-a. $6, institutions $8, single issue $3.25. University of New Brunswick, Dept. of English, Fredericton, N.B. E3B 5A5. ISSN 0380-6995. Bk. rev.: 2-5. Indexed: CPI.

A scholarly and critical journal devoted to the study of Canadian literature, both English and French of all periods. Of special interest to college and university libraries. Sherrill Cheda

**Upstream:** A Canadian Women's Publication. 1976. m. $6, institutions $15. Feminist Publications of Ottawa, 424B Queen St., Ottawa, Ont. K1R 5A8. ISSN 0700-9992. Bk. rev.: 2-5.

A Canadian women's publication, it is a monthly national news magazine which contains news stories, feature articles, interviews, columns on law, international news and arts, reviews of books, films and plays. Of interest to all libraries in Canada. Sherrill Cheda

**Wilderness Arts and Recreation.** 1977. bi-m. $5, Big Bear Wilderness Services Ltd., Edson, Alta. P.O. Box 2640, T0E 0P0. ISSN 0705-3150.

A bi-monthly digest of interest to those who enjoy the outdoors, camping, tripping and back packing. The winter 1980 issue included articles on woodfires, the wolf willow, parachute shelters, campfires, important plants to know and ice fishing. Sherrill Cheda

# Part Three
# Index

# Part Four Publishers' Directory

Academic Press Canada Limited
55 Barber Greene Rd.
Don Mills, Ont.
M3C 2A1

Acorn Books Ltd.
1509 Campus Tower
1145-87 Ave.
Edmonton, Alta.
T6G 0Y1

Addiction Research Foundation
33 Russell St.
Toronto, Ont.
M5S 2S1

Addison-Wesley (Canada) Ltd.
P.O. Box 580
36 Prince Andrew Place
Don Mills, Ont.
M3C 2T8

The Advisory Council on the Status of Women
151 Sparks Street
P.O. Box 1541, Station B
Ottawa, Ont.
K1P 5R5

Alaska Northwest Publishing
Order from Hurtig Publishers

Albatross Publishing House
P.O. Box 33766
Postal Station D
Vancouver, B.C.
V6J 4L6

Alcuin Society
P.O. Box 94108
Richmond, B.C.
V6Y 2A2

All About Us/Nous Autres Canada Inc.
P.O. Box 1985
Ottawa, Ont.
K1P 5R5

Thomas Allen & Son Ltd.
250 Steelcase Road East
Markham, Ont.
L3R 2S3

Amethyst Publications Limited, see Consolidated Amethyst Communications Ltd.

Ampersand Publishing Services Inc.
R.R. 1
Caledon, Ont.
L0N 1C0

Anansi, see House of Anansi

Anchor Press
Order from Doubleday

Anglican Book Centre
600 Jarvis St.
Toronto, Ont.
M4Y 2J6

Anson-Cartwright Editions
229 College St.
Toronto, Ont.
M5T 1R4

Antonson Publishing Ltd.
12165 97th Ave.
Surrey, B.C.
V3V 2C8

Arctic History Press
c/o McClelland and Stewart
25 Hollinger Rd.
Toronto, Ont.
M4B 3G2

Arctic Institute of North America
University Library Tower
2920 24 Ave. N.W.
Calgary, Alta.
T2N 1N4

Art Gallery of Ontario
Publications Department
Grange Park
317 Dundas St. West
Toronto, Ont.
M5T 1G4

Association for Media and Technology in Education in Canada
Order from Teachers' Library and Resource Centre

Association of Canadian Televison and Radio Artists (ACTRA)
105 Carlton St.
Toronto, Ont.
M5B 1M2

Association of Universities and Colleges of Canada
151 Slater St.
Ottawa, Ont.
K1P 5N1

Atlantic Provinces Economic Council
One Sackville Place
Halifax, N.S.
B3J 1K1

Aviation Publishers
P.O. Box 1361
Station B
Ottawa, Ont.
K1P 5R4

Avondale Press
P.O. Box 451
Willowdale, Ont.
M2N 5T1

Aya Press
P.O. Box 303
Station A
Toronto, Ont.
M5W 1C2

Baker Book House
Order from G.R. Welch Company Ltd.

Ballantine Books of Canada
5390 Ambler Drive
Mississauga, Ont.
L4W 1Y7

Ballantrae Foundation
P.O. Drawer 1420
Calgary, Alta.
T2P 2L6

Bantam Books of Canada Ltd.
60 St. Clair Ave. E.
Suite 601
Toronto, Ont.
M4T 1N5

Beatty & Church
103 Church St.
Suite 208
Toronto, Ont.
M5C 2G3

Bell Books Ltd.
612 Herald Building
206-7th Ave. S.W.
Calgary, Alta.
T2P 0W7

Best of Bridge Publishing Ltd.
2729 Wolfe St. South West
Calgary, Alta.
T2T 3R8

Between the Lines
97 Victoria St. North
Kitchener, Ont.
N2H 5C1

Bibliographical Society of Canada
32 Lowther Ave.
Toronto, Ont.
M5R 1C6

Black Moss Press
Order from Firefly Books Ltd.

Black Rose Books Ltd.
Order from University of Toronto Press

Blackfish Press
1851 Moore Ave.
Burnaby, B.C.
V8B 4N4

Boag Foundation Ltd.
576 Keith Road
West Vancouver, B.C.
V7T 1L7

Book Centre, Inc.
1140 Beaulac St.
Montreal, Que.
H4R 1R8

The Book Press Ltd.
P.O. Box 461
Adelaide Post Office
Toronto, Ont.
M5C 2J5

Book Room, see Halifax Book Room

Book Society of Canada Limited
4386 Sheppard Ave. E.
P.O. Box 200
Agincourt, Ont.
M1S 3B6

Boreal Institute for Northern Studies
University of Alberta
CW 401
Bio Science Building
Edmonton, Alta.
T6G 2E9

Borealis Press Ltd.
9 Ashburn Dr.
Ottawa, Ont.
K2E 6N4

Boston Mills Press
R.R. #1
Cheltenham, Ont.
L0P 1C0

Breakwater Books Ltd.
277 Duckworth St.
St. John's, Nfld.
A1C 1G9

Breezy Creeks Press
P.O. Box 104
Aurora, Ont.
L4G 3H1

Brick/Nairn
P.O. Box 219
Ilderton, Ont.
N0M 2A0

Brunswick Press
Phoenix Square
Fredericton, N.B.
E3B 5A2

B.R. Buszek
Cranberrie Cottage
R.R. 1
Granville Ferry, N.S.
B0S 1K0

Bureau of Municipal Research
2 Toronto St.
Suite 306
Toronto, Ont.
M5C 2B6

Burns & MacEachern Limited
Order from Macmillan Company of Canada Limited

Butterworth and Co. (Canada) Ltd.
2265 Midland Ave.
Scarborough, Ont.
M1P 4S1

Bybooks,
P.O. Box 4085
Station E
Ottawa, Ont.
K1S 5B1

CBC Learning Systems
CBC Merchandising
Box 500
Terminal A
Toronto, Ont.
M5W 1E6

C.D. Howe Research Institute
2064 Sun Life Building
Montreal, Que.
H3B 2X7

Calliope Press
P.O. Box 466
Station T
Toronto, Ont.
M6B 4C2

Cambridge University Press
510 North Ave.
New Rochelle, N.Y.
10801

Camden House Publishing
Camden East, Ont.
K0K 1J0

Canada. Dept. of Consumer and Corporate Affairs
Order from Supply and Services Canada

Canada. Department of External Affairs
Order from Supply and Services Canada

Canada Law Book Ltd.
80 Cowdray Ct.
Agincourt, Ont.
M1S 1S5

Canada West Publishing
P.O. Box 995
Summerland, B.C.
V0H 1Z0

Canada's Wings
P.O. Box 393
Stittsville, Ont.
K0A 3G0

Canadian Arctic Resources Committee
46 Elgin St.
Room 11
Ottawa, Ont.
K1P 5K6

Canadian Association for Adult Education
29 Prince Arthur Ave.
Toronto, Ont.
M5R 1B2

Canadian Association for Health, Physical Education and Recreation
333 River Rd.
10th Floor
Vanier City, Ont.
K1L 8B9

Canadian Association for the Mentally Retarded
Kinsmen Bldg.
4700 Keele St.
Downsview, Ont.
M3J 1P3

Canadian Association for Publishing in Philosophy
c/o Philosophy Department
University of Toronto
Toronto, Ont.
M5S 1A1

Canadian Association in Support of the Native Peoples
251 Laurier Ave. W.
Suite 904
Ottawa, Ont.
K1P 5J6

Canadian Authors Association
Order from Methuen Publications

Canadian Bar Association
130 Albert St.
Ottawa, Ont.
K1P 5G4

Canadian Broadcasting Corporation
P.O. Box 500
Station A
Toronto, Ont.
M5W 1E6

Canadian Century Publishers
P.O. Box 129
Lancaster, Ont.
K0C 1N0

Canadian Chamber of Commerce
1080 Beaver Hall Hill
Suite 710
Montreal, Que.
H2Z 1T2

Canada Council of Churches
40 St. Clair Ave. E.
Toronto, Ont.
M4T 1M9

Canadian Council on Children and Youth
323 Chapel St.
Ottawa, Ont.
K1N 7Z2

Canadian Council on Social Development
55 Parkdale Ave.
P.O. Box 3505
Postal Station C
Ottawa, Ont.
K1Y 1E5

Canadian Council on Urban and Regional Research
251 Laurier West
Ottawa, Ont.
K1P 5J6

Canadian Crafts Council
46 Elgin St.
Suite 16
Ottawa, Ont.
K1P 5K6

Canadian Dimension
P.O. Box 1413
Winnipeg, Man.
R3C 2Z1

Canadian Economic Policy Committee
1155 Metcalfe Ave.
Montreal, Que.
H3B 2V5

Canadian Education Association
252 Bloor St. W.
Suite S850
Toronto, Ont.
M5S 1V5

Canadian Environmental Law Research Foundation
1 Spadina Cres.
Suite 303
Toronto, Ont.
M5S 2J5

Canadian Federation of Film Societies
P.O. Box 484
Station A
Toronto, Ont.
M5W 1E4

Canadian Film Institute
303 Richmond Rd.
Ottawa, Ont.
K1Z 6X3

Canadian Government Publishing Centre,
see Supply and Services Canada

Canadian Hospital Association
410 Laurier Ave. W.
Ottawa, Ont.
K1R 7T6

Canadian Institute of Chartered Accountants
250 Bloor St. East
Toronto, Ont.
M4W 1G5

Canadian Institute of International Affairs
15 King's College Circle
Toronto, Ont.
M5S 2V9

Canadian Jewish Congress
1590 Ave. Doctor Penfield
Montreal, Que.
H3G 1C5

Canadian Law Information Council
Suite 2010, Tower B
Place de Ville
112 Kent St.
Ottawa, Ont.
K1P 5P2

Canadian Library Association
151 Sparks St.
Ottawa, Ont.
K1P 5E3

Canadian Manufacturers' Association
1 Yonge St.
14th Floor
Toronto, Ont.
M5E 1J9

Canadian Medical Association
P.O. Box 8650
Ottawa, Ont.
K1G 0G8

Canadian Mental Health Association
2160 Yonge St.
Toronto, Ont.
M4S 2Z3

Canadian Museums Association
331 Cooper St.
Suite 400
Ottawa, Ont.
K2P 0G5

Canadian National Institute for the Blind
1929 Bayview Ave.
Toronto, Ont.
M4G 3E8

Canadian Newspaper Services International
96 Eglinton Ave. E.
Suite 304
Toronto, Ont.
M4P 1C5

Canadian Paperback Publishing
370 Queen Mary St.
Ottawa, Ont.
K1K 1W7

Canadian Pharmaceutical Association
175 College St.
Toronto, Ont.
M5T 1P8

Canadian Plains Research Centre
University of Regina
Regina, Sask.
S4S 0A2

Canadian Rehabilitation Council for the Disabled
1 Yonge St.
Suite 2110
Toronto, Ont.
M5E 1E8

Canadian Securities Institute
P.O. Box 225
Commerce Court South
Toronto, Ont.
M5L 1E8

Canadian Stage and Arts Publications Ltd.
52 Avenue Road
2nd Floor
Toronto, Ont.
M5R 2G3

Canadian Tax Foundation
100 University Ave.
Toronto, Ont.
M5J 1V6

Canadian Teachers' Federation
110 Argyle St.
Ottawa, Ont.
K2P 1B4

Canadian Theatre Review Publications
York University
4700 Keele St.
Downsview, Ont.
M3J 1P3

Canadian Toy Testing Council
P.O. Box 6014
Station J
Ottawa, Ont.
K2A 1T1

Canadian Volleyball Association
333 River Rd.
Ottawa, Ont.
K1L 8B9

Canadian Yachting Association
333 River Rd.
Ottawa, Ont.
K1L 8B9

Canadiana House
P.O. Box 306
Station F
Toronto, Ont.
M4Y 2L7

Canec Publishing and Supply House
47 Coldwater Road
Don Mills, Ont.
M3B 1Y9

CANLIT
P.O. Box 6274
Station C
Victoria, B.C.
V8P 5L5

CAPAC, see Composers, Authors and Publishers Association.

Cardwell House Inc.
270 Union St. W.
Fergus, Ont.
N1M 1V4

Carleton University
Institute of Canadian Studies
Colonel By Drive
Ottawa, Ont.
K1S 5B6

Carswell Company Ltd.
2330 Midland Ave.
Agincourt, Ont.
M1S 1P7

Catalyst
315 Blantyre Ave.
Scarborough, Ont.
M1N 2S6

Centennial Publications
600 Shaftesbury Blvd.
Winnipeg, Man.
R3P 0M4

Central Mortgage and Housing Corporation
La Salle Academy
373 Sussex St.
Ottawa, Ont.
K1A 0P7

Charlton International Publishing Inc.
299 Queen St. W.
Toronto, Ont.
M5V 1Z9

Charters Publishing Co.
P.O. Box 400
Brampton, Ont.
L6V 2L3

Chimo Publishing
1162 Klarecroft Way
Oakville, Ont.
L6H 3A2

Clarke, Irwin & Company Limited
Clarwin House
791 St. Clair Ave. W.
Toronto, Ont.
M6C 1B8

Clock House Publications
P.O. Box 103
R.R. 1
Peterborough, Ont.
K9J 6Y5

Cloudburst Press Ltd.
Order from Douglas & McIntyre Ltd.

Coach House Press
401 Huron St. (rear)
Toronto, Ont.
M5S 2G5

Coles Publishing Co. Ltd.
Order from H.B. Fenn & Co. Ltd.

Collier Macmillan Canada Ltd.
539 Collier-Macmillan Dr.
Cambridge, Ont.
N1R 5W9

William Collins Sons & Co. Canada Ltd.
100 Lesmill Rd.
Don Mills, Ont.
M3B 2T5

CommCept Publishing
470 Granville St.
Suite 524
Vancouver, B.C.
V6C 1H7

Community Planning Press
c/o CPAC Bookshop
49 Canterbury St.
St. John, N.B.
E2L 2C6

Composers, Authors and Publishers
Association of Canada Ltd.
1240 Bay St.
Toronto, Ont.
M5R 2C2

Comprint Publishing Company
Box 4642
Postal Station C
Calgary, Alta.

Conrad Press
Conrad Grebel College
Waterloo, Ont.
N2L 3G6

Conservation Council of Ontario
45 Charles St. E.
Toronto, Ont.
M4Y 1S2

Consolidated Amethyst
Communications Inc.,
Unit 6,
60 Barbados Blvd.
Scarborough, Ont.
M1J 1K9

Consumers Association of Canada
Room 801
251 Laurier Avenue W.
Ottawa, Ont.
K1P 5Z7

Cooperative Press Associates
Order from Ontario Federation of Labour

Copp Clark Limited
517 Wellington St. W.
Toronto, Ont.
M5W 1G1

Corpus Information Services Ltd.
1450 Don Mills Rd.
Don Mills, Ont.
M3B 2X7

Coteau Books
Thunder Creek Pub. Co-operative Ltd.
P.O. Box 239
Substation 1
Moose Jaw, Sask.
S6H 5V0

Council of Ontario Universities
130 St. George St.
Suite 8039
Toronto, Ont.
M5S 2T4

Cromlech Press
McMaster University
P.O. Box 1023
Hamilton, Ont.
L8S 4L6

Croom Helm Ltd.
2 - 10 St. John's Rd.
London, England
S.W. 11

Cross Country Press
5572 Clark St.
Montreal, Que.
H2T 2V4

CTR Publications, see Canadian Theatre Review Publications

DPG Publishing Co., see Dumont Press

Daniel Books of Toronto
Box 488,
Adelaide St. Post Office
Toronto, Ont.
M5C 2J6

Dalhousie University
School of Library Service
Halifax, N.S.
B3H 4H8

Peter Davies
London, England
Order from William Collins Sons & Co.
Canada Ltd.

Richard De Boo Limited
70 Richmond St. E.
Toronto, Ont.
M5C 2M8

Dell International of Canada Ltd.
c/o Howell Warehouses Ltd.
514 Carlingview Dr.
Rexdale, Ont.
M9W 5R3

Deneau and Greenberg Publishers
Suite 205,
305 Metcalfe St.
Ottawa, Ont.
K2P 1S1

J.M. Dent and Sons (Canada) Ltd.
100 Scarsdale Rd.
Don Mills, Ont.
M3B 2R8

Derwyddon Press
Lodge North
P.O. Box 7694
Station A
Edmonton, Alta.
T5J 2X8

Detselic Enterprises
6147 Dalmarnock Cres. N.W.
Calgary, Alta.
T3A 1H3

Devil's Head Press Ltd.
P.O. Box 125
Canmore, Alta.
T0L 0M0

Discovery Press
P.O. Box 46295
Station G
Vancouver, B.C.
V6R 4G6

Dodd, Mead & Company (Canada) Ltd.
25 Hollinger Rd.
Toronto, Ont.
M4B 3G2

Dorset Publishing Inc.
Order from Beatty & Church

Doubleday Canada Limited
105 Bond St.
Toronto, Ont.
M5B 1Y3

J.J. Douglas, see Douglas & McIntyre Ltd.

Douglas, David & Charles
c/o Serv-West Distribution Ltd.
1875 Welch St.
North Vancouver, B.C.
V7P 1B7

Douglas & McIntyre Ltd.
1615 Venables St.
Vancouver, B.C.
V5L 2H1

Duke University
6697 College Sta.
Durham, N.C.
27708

Dumont Press
97 Victoria St. N.
Kitchener, Ont.
N2H 5C1

Dundurn Press Limited
P.O. Box 245
Postal Station F
Toronto, Ont.
M4Y 2L5

Eden Press Women's Publications
245 Victoria Ave.
Suite 12
Montreal, Que.
H3Z 2M6

Eden Watts Corporation
P.O. Box 6277
Station F
Hamilton, Ont.
L9C 5S3

Les Editions Heritage
300, ave Arran
Saint-Lambert, Que.
J4R 1K5

Editions L'Etincelle
2031 rue Saint-Dennis
Montreal, Que.
H2X 3K8

Energy Probe
43 Queen's Park Cres. E.
Toronto, Ont.
M5S 2C3

H.B. Fenn and Company Ltd.
2421 Drew Rd.
Mississauga, Ont.
L5S 1A1

Fforbez Publications Ltd.
2133 Quebec St.
Vancouver, B.C.
V5T 2Z9

Fiddlehead Poetry Books
c/o English Dept.
University of New Brunswick
P.O. Box 4400
Fredericton, N.B.
E3B 5A3

Film Publications of Canada
175 Bloor Street E.
Toronto, Ont.
M4W 3G4

Financial Post Books
481 University Ave.
Toronto, Ont.
M5W 1A7

Fineglow Plays
P.O. Box 41
Postal Station P
Toronto, Ont.
M5R 2S6

Firefly Books Ltd.
2 Essex Ave.
Unit 5
Thornhill, Ont.
L3T 3Y7

Fitzhenry & Whiteside Ltd.
150 Lesmill Rd.
Don Mills, Ont.
M3B 2T5

Fleming Press
93 Paradise Rd. N.
Hamilton, Ont.
L8S 3S9

Formac Publishing Limited
P.O. Box 1688
284 Main St.
Antigonish, N.S.

Fortress Publications
P.O. Box 241
Unit B
221 Barton St. E.
Stoney Creek, Ont.
L8G 3X9

The Fraser Institute
Order from Macmillan Company
of Canada Ltd.

Frontier Books
P.O. Box 1228,
Station A
Surrey, B.C.
V3S 2B3

Gage Educational Publishing
164 Commander Blvd.
Agincourt, Ont.
M1S 3C7

Gage Publishing Limited
164 Commander Blvd.
Agincourt, Ont.
M1S 3C7

Gale Research Co.
Book Tower
Detroit, Mich.
48226

Gall Publications
1293 Gerrard St. E.
Toronto, Ont.
M4L 1Y8

Garnet Publishing Co.
P.O. Box 2071
Vancouver, B.C.
V6H 3S3

General Publishing Co. Limited
30 Lesmill Rd.
Don Mills, Ont.
M3B 2T6

Ginn and Company
3771 Victoria Park Ave.
Scarborough, Ont.
M1W 2P9

GLC Publishers Limited
115 Nugget Ave.
Agincourt, Ont.
M1S 3B1

Glenbow-Alberta Institute
Glenbow Museum
9th Ave. & 1st St., S.E.
Calgary, Alta.
T2G 0P3

Good Medicine Books
P.O. Box 844
Invermere, B.C.
V0A 1K0

Gray's Publishing Limited
P.O. Box 2160
Sidney, B.C.
V8L 3S6

Green Bushell
34 Ross St.
Toronto, Ont.
M5T 1Z9

Green Tree Publishing Company Ltd.
1137 Queen St. E.
Toronto, Ont.
M4M 1K9

Greey de Pencier Publications Ltd.
Order from Thomas Nelson & Sons (Canada)

Griffin House Publishers
461 King St. W.
Toronto, Ont.
M5V 1K7

Guidance Centre, Faculty of Education, University of Toronto, see University of Toronto Guidance Centre

Habitex (published by Les Edition de l'Homme)
Order from Collier Macmillan Canada Ltd.

Halifax Book Room
The Book Room Limited
P.O. Box 272
1664-1666 Granville St.
Halifax, N.S.
B3J 2N7

Hancock House Publishers Ltd.
10 Orwell St.
North Vancouver, B.C.
V7J 3K1

Harbour Publishing
Box 119
Madeira Park, B.C.
V0N 2H0

Harper & Row
Order from Fitzhenry & Whiteside

Harvest House Ltd. Publishers
4795 St. Catherine St. W.
Montreal, Que.
H3Z 2B9

D.C. Heath Canada Ltd.
100 Adelaide St. W.
Suite 1600
Toronto, Ont.
M5H 1S9

Heritage House Publishing Co. Ltd.
5543-129th St.
Surrey, B.C.
V3W 4H4

Historical and Scientific Society of Manitoba
212 - 190 Rupert Ave.
Winnipeg, Man.
R3B 0N2

The Highway Book Shop
Cobalt, Ont.
P0J 1C0

Hodder & Stroughton Ltd.
55 Nugget Ave., Unit J
Agincourt, Ont.
M1S 3L1

Holt, Rinehart and Winston of Canada Ltd.
55 Horner Ave.
Toronto, Ont.
M8Z 4X6

Houghton, Mifflin Canada Ltd.
150 Steelcase Rd. W.
Markham, Ont.
L3R 1B2

Hounslow Press
124 Parkview Ave.
Willowdale, Ont.
M2N 3Y5

House of Anansi Press Limited
Order from University of Toronto Press

House of Grant (Canada) Ltd.
Order from J.M. Dent and Sons (Canada) Ltd.

Hurtig Publishers
10560-105th St.
Edmonton, Alta.
T5H 2W7

Hyperion Press
300 Wales Avenue
Winnipeg, Man.
R2M 3S9

Information Access, see Micromedia Limited

Institute for Research on Public Policy
P.O. Box 9300,
Station A
Toronto, Ont.
M5W 2C7

Institute of Public Administration of Canada
897 Bay St.
Toronto, Ont.
M5S 1Z7

Intermedia Press
P.O. Box 3294
Vancouver, B.C.
V6B 3X9

Inter-ski Services
Order from Rand McNally & Co.

International Self-counsel Press Ltd.
306 West 25th St.
North Vancouver, B.C.
V7N 2G1
International Self-counsel Press Ltd.
Eastern distribution:
Toronto Star Syndicate
21 Royalcrest Rd.
Unit 8
Rexdale, Ont.
M9V 2L6

Inuit-Tapirisat of Canada
176 Gloucester St.
3rd Floor
Ottawa, Ont.
K2P 0A6

Irwin-Dorsey Ltd.
265 Guelph St.
Georgetown, Ont.
L7G 4B3

Japanese Canadian Centennial Project
P.O. Box 69747
Station K
Vancouver, B.C.
V5K 4Y7

Jesperson Press
17 Calver Ave.
St. John's, Nfld.
A1C 2X1

KCB Publications Inc.
19 Daly Ave.
Ottawa, Ont.
K1N 6E1

Kenlaw Communications Inc.
73 Seneca St.
Ottawa, Ont.
K1S 4X6

The Killaly Press
764 Dalkeith Ave.
London, Ont.
N5X 1R8

Labrador Tea Company
Order from Gordon Soules Book Publishers

Ladysmith Press
73B Second Ave.
Ottawa, Ont.
K1S 2H4

Johanna Lamberger
3555 Côte des Neiges, #317
Montreal, Que.
H3H 1V2

Lancelot Press Limited
P.O. Box 425
Hantsport, N.S.
B0P 1P0

Laurelton Press
1194 Wolfe Ave.
Vancouver, B.C.
V6H 1V5

Legal Services Commission of British Columbia
744 W. Hastings
Vancouver, B.C.
V6C 1A5

Lester and Orpen Dennys Ltd.
Order from Macmillan Company of Canada

Little, Brown & Co. (Canada) Ltd.
25 Hollinger Rd.
Toronto, Ont.
M4B 3G2

Locust House Press
513 Locust St.
Burlington, Ont.
L7S 1V3

Log House Publishing Co. Ltd.
P.O. Box 1205
Prince George, B.C.
V2L 4V3

Longman Canada limited, see Academic Press Canada Limited

James Lorimer & Co.
Order from Clarke, Irwin & Co. Ltd.

Lyndeview Publications Ltd.
328 Lyndeview Dr.
Whitby, Ont.
L1N 3A3

McClelland and Stewart Ltd.
25 Hollinger Rd.
Toronto, Ont.
M4B 3G2

Macdonald-Raintree, Canada
2130 King St. E.
Suite A
Hamilton, Ont.
L8K 5W7

McGill-Queen's University Press
Purvis Hall
1020 Pine Ave. W.
Montreal, Que.
H3A 1A2

McGraw-Hill Ryerson Ltd.
330 Progress Ave.
Scarborough, Ont.
M1P 2Z5

Maclean Hunter Ltd.
Attn: M. Smee
5th Floor
481 University Ave.
Toronto, Ont.
M5W 1A7

McMaster University Library Press
McMaster University
Mills Memorial Library
Hamilton, Ont.
L8S 4L6

Macmillan Company of Canada Ltd.
70 Bond St.
Toronto, Ont.
M5B 1X3

Ruth McPherson
5 Welland St. North
Thorold, Ont.
L2V 2B8

Management and Fund Raising Centre
123 Edward St.
Suite 301
Toronto, Ont.
M5G 1E2

Manitoba Historical Society, see Historical and Scientific Society of Manitoba

Manitoba Métis Federation Press
300-275 Portage Ave.
Winnipeg, Man.
R3B 2B3

Manitoba Museum of Man and Nature
190 Rupert Ave.
Winnipeg, Man.
R3B 0N2

Manna Publishing
585 St. Christophe
St. Jean, Que.
J3B 1J7

Memorial University of Newfoundland
Institute of Social & Economic Research
Elizabeth Ave.
St. John's, Nfld.
A1C 5S7

Merrit Publishing Company Limited
200-443 University Ave.
Toronto, Ont.
M5G 1T8

Methuen Publications
2330 Midland Ave.
Agincourt, Ont.
M1S 1P7

Metropolitan Toronto Library Board
789 Yonge St.
Toronto, Ont.
M4W 2G8

Micromedia Limited
144 Front St. West
Toronto, Ont.
M5S 1G2

Mika Publishing Company
P.O. Box 536
200 Stanley St.
Belleville, Ont.
K8N 5B2

Ministry of Government Services
Publications Centre
3B7 Macdonald Block
Queen's Park
Toronto, Ont.
M7A 1N8

Ministry of State for Urban Affairs
Order from Supply and Services Canada

Mitchell Press Ltd.
P.O. Box 6000
Vancouver, B.C.
V6B 4B9

Modern Canadian Library, Inc.
335 Bay St.
Suite 1106
Toronto, Ont.
M5H 2R3

William Morrow & Co. Inc.
Order from Gage Publishing Limited

Mosaic Press/Valley Editions
P.O. Box 1032
Oakville, Ont.
L6J 5E9

Mount Allison University
Ralph Pickard Bell Library
Sackville, N.B.
E0A 3C0

Museum Restoration Service
P.O. Box 390
Bloomfield, Ont.
K0K 1G0

Musson Book Company
30 Lesmill Rd.
Don Mills, Ont.
M3B 2T6

National Council of Women of Canada
270 MacLaren St.
Ottawa, Ont.
K2P 0M3

The National Gallery of Canada
419 Bank St.
Ottawa, Ont.
K1A 0M8

National Institute on Mental Retardation
Kinsmen Bldg.
York University Campus
4700 Keele St.
Downsview, Ont.
M5G 1T8

National Library of Canada
395 Wellington St.
Ottawa, Ont.
K1A 0N4

National Museum of Man, see National Museums of Canada

National Museums of Canada
Publishing Division
300 Laurier Ave. W.
Ottawa, Ont.
K1A 0M5

National Postal Museum
Confederation Heights
Ottawa, Ont.
K1A 0B1

National Profile Ltd.
P.O. Box 1085
Postal Station B
Rexdale, Ont.
M9V 2B3

Natural Science of Canada Limited
254 Bartley Drive
Toronto, Ont.
M4A 1G1

NC Press Ltd.
24 Ryerson Ave.
P.O. Box 4010,
Station A
Toronto, Ont.
M5W 1H8

Thomas Nelson & Sons (Canada) Ltd.
81 Curlew Drive
Don Mills, Ont.
M3A 2R1

Nelson, Foster and Scott Ltd.
30 Lesmill Rd.
Don Mills, Ont.
M3B 2T6

New American Library of Canada Ltd.
81 Mack Ave.
Scarborough, Ont.
M1L 1M8

New Delta
Order from Véhicule Press

New Hogtown Press
12 Hart House Circle
University of Toronto
Toronto, Ont.
M5S 1A1

New Press
30 Lesmill Rd.
Don Mills, Ont.
M3B 2T6

NeWest Press, The Western Publishers
11441-84th St.
Edmonton, Alta.
T5B 3B5

New Star Books
2504 York Ave.
Vancouver, B.C.
V6K 1E3

Nimbus Publishing Limited
P.O. Box 1590
Halifax, N.S.
B3J 2Y3

Northern Miner Press Ltd.
Publications Division
7 Labatt Ave.
Toronto, Ont.
M5A 3P2

Nova Scotia Museum
1747 Summer St.
Halifax, N.S.
B3H 3A6

Nova Scotia. Communications and
Information Centre
1597 Hollis St.
P.O. Box 637
Halifax, N.S.
B3J 2T3

November House
Order from Douglas & McIntyre Ltd.

Oberon Press
401a Inn of the Provinces
Ottawa, Ont.
K1R 7S8

October Publications. Editions D'Octobre
P.O. Box 3104
Station D
Willowdale, Ont.
M2R 3G5

Ontario Association of Art Galleries
Visual Arts Ontario
8 York Street
Toronto, Ont.
M5J 1R2

Ontario. Multicultural Development Branch
77 Bloor St. W.
5th Floor
Toronto, Ont.
M5S 1M2

Ontario Educational Communications Authority (TV Ontario)
2180 Yonge St.
Toronto, Ont.
M4S 1B7

Ontario Federation of Labour
15 Gervais Dr.
Suite 202
Don Mills, Ont.
M3C 1Y8

Ontario Genealogical Society
P.O. Box 66
Postal Station Q
Toronto, Ont.
M4T 2L7

Ontario Historical Society
1466 Bathurst St.
Toronto, Ont.
M5R 3J3

Ontario Institute for Studies in Education
Publications Division
252 Bloor St. W.
Toronto, Ont.
M5S 1V6

Ontario Library Association
73 Richmond Street W.
Suite 402
Toronto, Ont.
M5H 1Z4

Ontario Publications Centre
880 Bay St.
5th Floor
Toronto, Ont.
M7A 1N8

Ontario Secondary School Teachers' Federation
60 Mobile Dr.
Toronto, Ont.
M4A 2P3

Optimum Publishing Co. Ltd.
Montreal Star
Information Services Division
245 James St. W.
Montreal, Que.
H2Y 1M6

Oolichan Books
P.O. Box 10
Lantzville, B.C.
V0R 2H0

Otter Press
P.O. Box 747
Waterloo, Ont.
N2J 4C2

Oxford University Press
70 Wynford Dr.
Don Mills, Ont.
M3C 1J9

The Paget Press
Order from LPGE Small Press Distribution

Paideia Press
P.O. Box 1450
St. Catharines, Ont.
L2R 7J8

Pagurian Press Limited
Order from Macmillan of Canada

P. & O. Business Publications
R.R. #1
Ashburn, Ont.
L0B 1A0

PaperJacks Ltd.
330 Steelcase Rd.
Markham, Ont.
L3R 2M1

Paulist/Newman Press
455 King St. W.
Toronto, Ont.
M5V 1K7
Order from Trinity Press

Peguis Publishers Limited
462 Hargrave St.
Winnipeg, Man.
R3A 0X5

Pendragon House Ltd.
2525 Dunwin Dr.
Mississauga, Ont.
L5L 1T2

Penguin Books Canada Limited
2801 John St.
Markham, Ont.
L3R 1B4

Pennsylvania State University Press
215 Wagner Bldg.
University Park, Pa.
16802

Penstock Publications Ltd.
P.O. Box 365
Oakville, Ont.
L6L 5M5

Penumbra Press
P.O. Box 340
Moonbeam, Ont.
P0L 1V0

Personal Library, Publishers
Order from John Wiley and Sons

Peter Martin Associates Ltd., see PMA Books

Petheric Press Ltd.
1663 Market St.
P.O. Box 8171
Halifax, N.S.
B3K 5L9

Pharos Press
1255 Victoria Ave.
Victoria, B.C.
V8S 4P3

The Pikadilly Press
8 Argyle St.
London, Ont.
N6H 1Y3

Pitman Publishing
517 Wellington St. W.
Toronto, Ont.
M5V 1G1

Playwrights Canada
8 York St.
6th Floor
Toronto, Ont.
M5J 1R2

Playwrights Co-op, see Playwrights Canada

Playwrights Press, see Playwrights Canada

PMA Books (formerly Peter Martin
Associates)
280 Bloor St. W.
Suite 305
Toronto, Ont.
M5S 1W1

Pollution Probe
University of Toronto
43 Queen's Park Cres.
Toronto, Ont.
M5S 2C3

Porcépic, see Press Porcépic

The Porcupine's Quill, Inc.
Order from Mosaic Press/Valley Editions

Potlach Publications Limited
Order from Eden Watts Corporation

The Prairie Publishing Company
P.O. Box 264
Postal Station C
Winnipeg, Man.
R3M 3S7

Prentice-Hall of Canada Ltd.
1870 Birchmount Rd.
Scarborough, Ont.
M1P 2J7

Press Gang Publishers
603 Powell St.
Vancouver, B.C.
V6A 1H2

Press Porcépic Ltd.
Order from Macmillan of Canada

Print N' Press
14 Budd Ave.
St. Stephen, N.B.
E3L 1E9

Progress Books
3rd Floor
71 Bathurst St.
Toronto, Ont.
M5V 2P6

Public Archives of Canada
395 Wellington St.
Ottawa, Ont.
K1A 0N3

Publishing Centre, Supply and Service
Canada, see Canadian Government
Publishing Centre

Pulp Press
Order from Beatty & Church

Pythagorean Press
P.O. Box 127
Station A
Toronto, Ont.
M4C 5W7

Queen City Publishing Ltd.
P.O. Box 369
Station Z
Toronto, Ont.
M5N 2Z5

Queen's University
Industrial Relations Centre
Kingston, Ont.
K7L 3N6

Queenston House Publishing Co. Ltd.
102 Queenston St.
Winnipeg, Man.
R3N 0W5

Quick Canadian Facts
P.O. Box 99
Station M
Toronto, Ont.
M6S 4T2

Railfare Enterprises Ltd.
P.O. Box 33
West Hill, Ont.
M1E 4R4

Ragwood Press
Heritage Foundation
P.O. Box 922
Charlottetown, P.E.I.
C1A 7L9

George Philip Raintree, Inc.
Order from Macdonald-Raintree, Canada

Rand McNally & Co.
P.O. Box 7600
Chicago, Ill.
60680

Random House of Canada Limited
5390 Ambler Dr.
Mississauga, Ont.
L4W 1Y7

W.F. Rannie, Publisher
P.O. Box 700
51 Central Ave.
Beamsville, Ont.
L0R 1B0

Reader's Digest Association (Canada) Ltd.
215 Redfern Ave.
Montreal, Que.
H3Z 2V9

Real Estate Press
P.O. Box 222
7 Drysdale Cres.
Willowdale, Ont.
M2N 5S8

Red Rock Publishing Co. Limited
77 Mowat Ave.
Suite 207
Toronto, Ont.
M6K 3E2

Dave Reid
Reid's Art Materials
5847 Victoria Drive
Vancouver, B.C.
V5P 3W5

Renewable Energy in Canada
415 Parkside Drive
Toronto, Ont.
M6R 2Z7

George Rickard Studio
755 North Mile Road
London, Ont.
N6H 2X7

Royal Life Saving Society of Canada
550 Church St.
Toronto, Ont.
M4Y 2E1

Royal Ontario Museum
Publications Department
100 Queen's Park
Toronto, Ont.
M5S 2C6

The Royal Society of Canada
344 Wellington St.
Ottawa, Ont.
K1A 0N4

Saannes Publications Ltd., see Gall Publications

St. Francis Xavier University Press
St. Francis Xavier University
Antigonish, N.S.
B2G 1C0

Saltaire Publishing Ltd.
9536 Ardmore Dr.
P.O. Box 2003
Sidney, B.C.
V8L 3S3

Samuel-Stevens Publishers Limited
554 Spadina Cres.
Toronto, Ont.
M5S 2J9

Sand Hill Books
Laughing Horse Gallery
64 King St. S.
P.O. Box 352
St. Jacobs, Ont.
N0B 2N0

Saunders of Toronto Ltd.
250 Steelcase Rd.
Markham, Ont.
L3R 2S3

Seal Books, see McClelland and Stewart-Bantam

Self-counsel Press, see International Self-counsel Press

Andrew Sharp Publications
5 Dufresne Court
Don Mills, Ont.
M3C 1B8

Simon & Pierre Publishing Company Ltd.
Order from Macmillan Company of Canada Ltd.

Simon & Schuster
Order trade books from Musson
Order pocketbooks from PaperJacks

Social Science Research Council of Canada
151 Slater St.
Suite 415
Ottawa, Ont.
K1P 5H3

Society for Art Publications
Artscanada
3 Church St.
Toronto, Ont.
M5E 1M2

Soft Press
28 Woodgate Dr.
Toronto, Ont.
M6N 4W3

Sono Nis Press
1745 Blanshard St.
Victoria, B.C.
V8W 2J8

Sotheby Parke Bernet (Canada) Ltd.
170 Bloor St. W.
Suite 412
Toronto, Ont.
M5S 1T9

Gordon Soules Book Publishers
525-355 Burrard St.
Vancouver, B.C.
V6C 2G8

Special Libraries Association, Toronto Chapter
c/o Ruth Smith
Toronto-Dominion Bank, Library
Dept. of Economic Research
P.O. Box 1
Toronto Dominion Centre
Toronto, Ont.
M5K 1A2

Sportbook Ltd.
P.O. Box 302
Agincourt, Ont.
M1S 3T0

Square Deal Publications
Order from Macmillan Company, Canada

Stagecoach Publishing Co.
P.O. Box 3399
Langley, B.C.
V3A 4R7

Standards Council of Canada
350 Sparks St.
Suite 1205
Ottawa, Ont.
K1R 7S8

Steel Rail Publishing
P.O. Box 6813
Station A
Toronto, Ont.
M5W 1X6

Stone and Cox
2nd Floor
100 Simcoe St.
Toronto, Ont.
M5H 3G2

Strayer Publications Ltd.
P.O. Box 1710
Calgary, Alta.
T2P 2L7

Summerthought Ltd.
P.O. Box 1420
Banff, Alta.
T0L 0C0

Supply and Services Canada
Canadian Government Publishing Centre
Marketing Division
Hull, Que.
K1A 0S9

Talonbooks Ltd.
Order from University of Toronto Press

Tantalus Research Limited
P.O. Box 34248
2405 Pine St.
Vancouver, B.C.
V6J 4N8

Task Force on Canadian Unity, see Ministry of Supply and Services

Teachers' Library and Resource Centre
Winnipeg School Division, No. 1
436 William Ave.
Winnipeg, Man.
R3A 0J4

Tecumseh Press Ltd.
8 Mohawk Cres.
Ottawa, Ont.
K2H 7G6

Texchuck Enterprises Ltd.
P.O. Box 7244
Saskatoon, Sask.
S7K 4J2

Theatrebooks
659 Yonge St.
Toronto, Ont.
M4Y 1Z9

Thistledown Press
668 East Place
Saskatoon, Sask.
S7J 2Z5

Thunder Creek Publishing
1188 Duffield Cres.
Moose Jaw, Sask.
S6H 5M4

Totem Books
100 Lesmill Rd.
Don Mills, Ont.
M3B 2T5

Tree Frog Press Limited
10717 – 106 Ave.
Edmonton, Alta.
T5H 3Y9

Trident Press Ltd.
P.O. Box 3629
Station B
842 Main St.
Winnipeg, Man.
R2W 3R4

Trinity Press
960 Gateway
Burlington, Ont.
L7L 5K7

Tundra Books, Inc.
Order from William Collins & Sons & Co. Canada, Ltd.

Turnstone Press
University of Manitoba
St. John's College
Winnipeg, Man.
R3T 2M5

Tutor Press, see Energy probe

Twayne Publishers
Order from G.K. Hall & Co.

Ucrainica Research Institute
85 Christie Street
Toronto, Ont.
M6G 3B1

Ukrainian Free Academy of Sciences
202 – 456 Main St.
Winnipeg, Man.
R3B 1B6

Ukrainian Women's Association
154 East 10th Ave.
Vancouver, B.C.
V5T 1Z4

United Church Observer
85 St. Clair Ave. E.
Toronto, Ont.
M4T 1M8

United Church Publishing House
47 Coldwater Rd.
Don Mills, Ont.
M3B 1Y9

University of Alberta Press
Room 450
Athabasca Hall
Edmonton, Alta.
T6G 2E8

University of British Columbia Press
303 – 6344 Memorial Rd.
Vancouver, B.C.
V6T 1W5

University of Chicago
Department of Geography
5828 South University Ave.
Chicago, Ill.
60637

University of Chicago Press
11030 Langley Ave.
Chicago, Ill.
60626

University of Guelph
Guelph, Ont.
N1G 2W1

University of Ottawa Press
63 Hastey Ave.
Ottawa, Ont.
K1N 6N5

University of Saskatchewan
News and Publications
Room 20
Education Bldg.
Saskatoon, Sask.
S7N 0W0

University of Toronto
Centre of Criminology
130 St. George St.
Room 8001
Toronto, Ont.
M5S 1A1

University of Toronto
Faculty of Library Science
Library Science Alumni Association
Order from University of Toronto Press

University of Toronto
Guidance Centre
Faculty of Education
1000 Yonge St.
Suite 304
Toronto, Ont.
M4W 2K8

University of Toronto Press
5201 Dufferin St.
Downsview, Ont.
M3H 5T8

University of Victoria
Order from GLC Publishers Ltd.

University of Victoria
Social Sciences Research Centre
University of Victoria Bookstore
P.O. Box 2200
Victoria, B.C.
V8W 3A8

University of Western Ontario
Faculty of Education
1137 Western Road
London, Ont.
N6G 1G7

University of Western Ontario
McIntosh Art Gallery
London, Ont.
N6A 3K7

Valley Editions/Mosaic Press, see Mosaic Press/Valley Editions

Vancouver Art Gallery
1145 W. Georgia
Vancouver, B.C.
V6E 3H2

Van Nostrand Reinhold Ltd.
1410 Birchmount Rd.
Scarborough, Ont.
M1P 2E7

Véhicule Press
P.O. Box 125,
Station La Cité
Montreal, Que.
H2X 3M0

Vesta Publications Limited
P.O. Box 1641
Cornwall, Ont.
K6H 5V6

The Vine Press
21 Gwendolen Ave.
London, England
SW15 6ET

Virgo Press
Order from Beatty & Church

Waterloo Music Co.
3 Regina St. N.
Waterloo, Ont.
N2J 4A5

Watson & Dwyer Publishing Ltd.
166 Roslyn Road
Winnipeg, Man.
R3L 0G8

R.J. Watts & Associates Ltd.
4010 Bayridge Cres.
West Vancouver, B.C.
V7V 3K4

Waxwing Productions Ltd.
139 Scarborough Rd.
Toronto, Ont.
M4E 3M4

Wedge Publishing Foundation
229 College St.
4th Floor
Postal Station 13
Toronto, Ont.
M5T 1R4

G.R. Welch Company Limited
960 Gateway
Burlington, Ont.
L7L 5K7

Western Extension College Educational Publishers
Central Avenue North
Box 110
Saskatoon, Sask.
S7K 3K1

Western Producer Prairie Books
2310 Millar Ave.
P.O. Box 2500
Saskatoon, Sask.
S7K 2C4
Order from University of Toronto Press
(Ontario and the East)

Wheatfield Press
Box 205
St. James Postal Station
Winnipeg, Man.
R3J 3R4

Whitecap Books
2229 Jefferson Ave.
West Vancouver, B.C.
V7V 2A9

John Wiley and Sons Canada Ltd.
22 Worcester Rd.
Rexdale, Ont.
M9W 1L1

Wilfrid Laurier University Press
Wilfrid Laurier University
Alumni Hall
Waterloo, Ont.
N2L 3C5

The H.W. Wilson Co.
950 University Ave.
Bronx, N.Y.
10452

The Winnipeg Art Gallery
300 Memorial Blvd.
Winnipeg, Man.
R3C 1V1

Women's Educational Press
Order from University of Toronto Press

Women's Press, see Women's Educational Press

Women's Writing Collective
331 Wellesley St. E.
Toronto, Ont.
M4X 1H2

World Literacy of Canada
692 Coxwell Ave.
Toronto, Ont.
M4C 3B6

E.C. Wright
P.O. Box 710
Wolfville, N.S.
B0P 1X0

Wright Communications
P.O. Box 44
Station A
Mississauga, Ont.
L5A 2Y9

The Writer's Union of Canada
24 Ryerson Ave.
Toronto, Ont.
M5S 1M5

Yonge Street Press
W. Sheldon
645 Yonge St.
Toronto, Ont.
M4Y 1Z9

York Publishing & Printing Co.
c/o G.M. Cowan
21 Tichester Rd.
Suite 603
Toronto, Ont.
M5P 1P3

York University
4700 Keele St.
Downsview, Ont.
M3J 1P3

York University
Osgoode Hall Law School
4700 Keele St.
Downsview, Ont.
M3J 1P3

Yorkminster Publishing Ltd.
57 Yorkminster Rd.
Willowdale, Ont.
M2P 1M4

www.ingramcontent.com/pod-product-compliance
Lightning Source LLC
Chambersburg PA
CBHW081331090726
47907CB00011B/2443

* 9 7 8 1 4 8 7 5 7 7 0 7 0 *